THE BOOKS

OF THE

CHRONICLES.

THEOLOGICALLY AND HOMILETICALLY EXPOUNDED

BY

DR. OTTO ZÖCKLER, D.D.,

PROFESSOR OF THEOLOGY IN THE UNIVERSITY OF GREIFSWALD, PRUSSIA.

TRANSLATED, ENLARGED, AND EDITED

BY

JAMES G. MURPHY, LL. D.,

PROFESSOR IN THE GENERAL ASSEMBLY'S AND THE QUEEN'S COLLEGE AT BELFAST.

Wipf & Stock
PUBLISHERS
Eugene, Oregon

Wipf and Stock Publishers
199 W 8th Ave, Suite 3
Eugene, OR 97401

The Books of the Chronicles
an Exegetical and Doctrinal Commentary
By Zöckler, Otto J.
ISBN 13: 978-1-55635-404-5
ISBN 10: 1-55635-404-5
Publication date 4/4/2007
Previously published by Charles Scribner, 1877

PREFACE TO VOL. VII. OF THE OLD TESTAMENT.

THIS volume completes the Commentary on the Historical Books of the Old Testament, written during the period of the reconstruction of the theocracy after the return from exile. It contains:

1. THE FIRST AND SECOND BOOK OF CHRONICLES, by Dr. OTTO ZÖCKLER, Professor in the Prussian University of Greifswald (1874), translated and edited by Professor JAMES G. MURPHY, LL.D., of Belfast, who is already well known to the American public by his Commentaries on Genesis, Exodus, and the Psalms. Professor Murphy has departed from the method of the other volumes by giving a literal translation of the text instead of the authorized version with emendations in brackets.

2. EZRA, by Dr. FR. U. SCHULTZ, Professor in the University of Breslau (1876), translated and edited by Dr. CHARLES A. BRIGGS, Professor of Hebrew and the Cognate Languages in the Union Theological Seminary, New York, who prepared in part the Commentary on the Psalms for this work.

3. NEHEMIAH, by Dr. HOWARD CROSBY, Chancellor of the University of New York. Dr. Crosby had finished his work in manuscript before the German Commentary of Dr. Schultz appeared (1876), but he has added a translation of the Homiletical sections from Schultz.

4. ESTHER, by Dr. SCHULTZ, translated and edited by Dr. JAMES STRONG, Professor of Exegetical Theology in Drew Theological Seminary, Madison, N. J. Dr. STRONG has translated the frequent Latin citations, added the Textual and Grammatical notes, enlarged the list of exegetical helps, and furnished an excursus on the Apocryphal additions to Esther, and another on the liturgical use of the book among the Jews.

The remaining three of the twenty-four volumes of this Commentary are in the hands of the printer, and will be published at short intervals.

PHILIP SCHAFF.

BIBLE HOUSE, NEW YORK, December, 1876.

PREFACE.

THE matter and the whole form of the books of Chronicles afford a sufficient warrant for allowing the homiletic and even the theological part of the exposition to fall more into the background here than elsewhere in this Bible-work. In the following work also, on account of the numerous parallels with the books of Samuel and Kings, an almost exclusive predominance of the historical element might easily be permitted. For with regard to theological and homiletic comment, the corresponding portions of these books have already received a fruitful and valuable treatment in the able works of Bähr and Erdmann, so that reference to them might in every instance have been sufficient. And where anything peculiar to Chronicles was to be explained, it almost always referred to portions like the genealogical lists in 1 Chron. ii.–ix., the various supplements to the history of war, and the highly characteristic episodes on the history of worship, which belonged rather to the outer surface, the rind and shell of the theocratic and evangelical system, than to its spiritual ground and essence, and therefore needed rather to be explained historically, than to be considered or applied dogmatically or practically. The homiletic remarks might, therefore, in this volume be omitted as a distinct section, and a group of sections might be thrown together as a basis for the development of theological or evangelical and ethical principles. But besides, it appeared necessary in Chronicles to dwell more frequently on difficulties of a chronological kind, and on apologetic problems connected therewith, on account of which it was requisite, besides and along with those evangelical reflections, to introduce several *excursus*, some of considerable length, as that on Ophir after 2 Chron. viii., and that on the chronology of the kings during the time of the separate kingdom after 2 Chron. xxxii.

Of recent literary helps, some that appeared in the course of printing could not be fully employed; for example, the second edition of the commentary of Thenius on the books of Kings (in the *Kurzgefasstes exegetisches Handbuch zum Alten Testament*, Leipzig, S. Hirzel), and the treatise of H. Brande, *Die Königsreihen von Juda und Israel nach den biblischen Berichten und den Keilinschriften* (Leipzig, Al. Edelmann),—a praiseworthy attempt to remove the chronological differences between the statements of the books of Kings and Chronicles on the one hand, and those of the Assyrian monuments on the other, in which some at least of the discrepancies between the biblical and Assyro-Babylonian computation of time brought forward by Assyriologists, especially by Schrader, have met with an interesting, if not quite satisfactory explanation. And of the simultaneously-appearing third revised edition of C. F. Keil's *Lehrbuch der historisch-kritischen Einleitung in die kanonischen Schriften des Alten Testaments*, (Frankfurt a. M., Heyder und Zimmer) obviously no use could be made.

With regard to the question, How the very numerous proper names, especially of persons, in the text of Chronicles were to be treated in their transference into German, the author was presented with a problem not quite easy to solve. Perfect consistency could only be attained either by a close adherence to the text of Luther, or by the thorough restoration of a spelling adapted as strictly as possible to the Hebrew sound; in which latter case, however, names such as Jehova, and the household words Noah, Isaak, Israel, Saul, Salomo, Hiskia, etc., must have given way to the more correct forms Jahve, Noach, Jitschak, Jisrael, Schaul, Schelomo, Jechizkijahu. As this would not have corresponded with the rule elsewhere adopted in our Bible-work, we have taken a middle course. All the well-known current forms of the Lutheran Bible that have been as it were canonized by a usage of several centuries in the tradition of evangelical Germany, especially the divine name Jehova and all names of prominent men of God (patriarchs, prophets, kings, etc.), and of important holy places, we have left wholly unaltered, only with the addition, once for all, of the more exact orthography in parentheses (usually on the first occurrence of the name in question). All less current names, because they belong to less important persons and places, and especially if they occur only once, are immediately and directly expressed in the way more agreeable to the Hebrew sounds; and only when there is a very great deviation from the received orthography in the Lutheran text is this difference noted by the insertion of a parenthesis. For this intermediate course between the customary and the modern mode of writing, we are glad to be able to refer among others to the late Oehler as warrant, who, in p. 146 of the lately published first part of his posthumous *Theologie des Alten Testaments* (Tübingen, Heckenhauer), expresses his agreement in principle with the rule here laid down, when he declares that such forms as Jehova, Jordan, etc., are less correct than "Jahve, Jarden," etc., yet not to be supplanted by these more correct forms, and proceeds accordingly throughout the text of his work.

DR. O. ZÖCKLER.

GREIFSWALD, *October* 1873.

[Translating into English, we shall use the English mode of spelling the ordinary names.
J. G. M.]

THE BOOKS OF CHRONICLES.

INTRODUCTION.

§ 1. ON THE IMPORT OF CHRONICLES AS A HISTORICAL WORK, AND ON ITS RELATION TO THE BOOKS OF SAMUEL AND KINGS.

THE last book of the Old Testament canon forms a comprehensive history, which recapitulates the progress of the people of God from Paradise to the close of the Babylonish captivity in a peculiar point of view, partly extracting, partly repeating, and partly supplementing the contents of the earlier canonical books of history, with the exception of the books of Ezra, Nehemiah, and Esther, which are later in point of contents than our book.

1. The *first* or *genealogical* portion of the work especially *extracts or summarily recapitulates* the earlier historical books. It embraces the first nine chapters, according to the present division, and contains the genealogies of the patriarchs, the twelve tribes, and the inhabitants of Jerusalem, till the beginning of the kingdom (occasionally even beyond it), in order to exhibit the genealogical connection of David, as well as the Levites and priests of his time, with the antediluvian patriarchs of the human race. Only here and there, particularly with respect to the statements concerning the tribes of Judah, Simeon, and Levi, this form is changed into that of a completion or enlargement of the former record by peculiar genealogical or historical additions. As a mere repetition of the statements contained in the earlier books, appear several genealogical notices of the first chapter; for example, those relating to the races of the table of nations and the princes of Edom (Gen. x. 36).

2. The second or strictly historical portion of the work partly repeats and partly completes, sometimes with a great fulness of details, the historical books after Moses and Joshua, especially the books of Samuel and Kings. It extends from 1 Chron. x. to the end of 2 Chron., and mainly presents a history of the kings of Judah from David to Zedekiah, or rather to the edict of Cyrus at the close of the Babylonish captivity. A process of abbreviating, of only summarily recapitulating, and even of wholly passing over a great deal of historical material, now takes place, inasmuch as the writer ignores the facts relating to the private life of David and Solomon, especially when they are unfavourable to their moral character, and in the time after Solomon intentionally turns away his eye from the fortunes of the northern kingdom, and confines himself almost exclusively to the Jewish history of this period. Yet for the whole time from David to the exile he appears more as a supplementer than as a concise repeater of the authors of the books of Samuel and Kings, inasmuch as the intrinsic importance of the addition made by him almost always exceeds that of the passages omitted, and both the omission and the addition appear to have in view certain fixed tendencies, especially the endeavour to glorify the theocratic order of the priests and Levites. If we take into account this particular tendency, as well as the altered circumstances in which he wrote, we arrive at the following points as characteristic of his work, compared with his older predecessors, especially the authors of the books of Samuel and Kings.

a. The books of Samuel and Kings having originated (been reduced to their present form) during the Babylonish exile, are a proper Israelitish national work, treating the history of both kingdoms, Israel and Judah, with equal attention. On the contrary, the Chronist appears as a specially Jewish (Judaising) writer, who belonged to the time after the exile, possibly even of the post-Persian dominion (Hellenic), and from his late age lay too remote from the events of the once existing kingdom of Israel; and, moreover, from his rigid theocratic position, took so little interest in the fortunes of the northern kingdom, that he excluded them altogether from his regard, and produced merely a Jewish chronicle.

b. The standpoint of those older Israelitish national historians is that of the prophet, while the younger Jewish Chronist occupies that of the priest and the Levite. Whereas the former, in accordance with the total depression, the apparently almost hopeless destruction, of the Mosaic temple worship in the exile, take a predominantly spiritual direction, averse to the external side of the theocratic worship, the latter, writing after the exile, at the time of the restored national sanctuary, exhibits a more lively interest in the external institutions and modes of worship, as well as in the order of priests and Levites appointed to take charge of it. From this sacerdotal ecclesiastical direction there follows a third important point of difference.

c. The moral causes of the national misfortune that broke in upon the people, especially their constantly-repeated lapse into idolatry, with which those older historians were most anxiously engaged, are cast into the shade, and often studiously ignored, by the Chronist, so that in the picture presented by him there appears a much smaller number of the gloomy shadows and dark spots of religious apostasy, and consequent national humiliation by heavy divine judgments. While the former obviously follow the tendency "to hold up to them a warning picture, in the tragic history of the Hebrew nation, of the danger of the relapse of a not yet elevated people among heathen nations, and in the narrative of the successive sins of their fathers to give a theodicy to the race already bewildered with respect to the promises and the faithfulness of Jehovah, and show them that their national misfortunes are to be ascribed to their own guilt; on the other hand, for the author of Chronicles, who lived after the exile, from which time the people, purified by affliction, adhered with stern obstinacy to their national God, and who no longer distinguishes accurately between the different kinds of ancient superstition (appears indeed to identify the impure Jehovah-worship of the northern kingdom with complete idolatry), accounts of the earlier superstition must have been of less consequence, because they presented to him less didactic matter and historical interest than to the authors of the older historical work" (Movers).

d. With this is connected the tone of panegyric usual with our author, frequently deviating from the unvarnished manner of the older historians, his apologetic endeavour to make the heroes of the foretime and their deeds to stand forth in the most glorious light, by giving prominence to the more externally than internally significant and ethically important moments, and especially by statistical data concerning the greatness of the temporal and spiritual state of the kings, the magnitude of the festivals celebrated by them, etc.

e. Finally, with regard to the outward form of representation, the younger work contrasts very strongly with the older. As well by its less pure Hebrew style, presenting so many traces of a late age, as by its often striking monotony, want of independence and poverty of ideas, its dry annalistic method of statement continued through long sections, and its inclination to direct copying and mere transcribing of the old books of Kings, it falls very far behind the classical originality, the fresh and genial historiographic skill of the other.

To bring these differences between the literary peculiarity of the two parallel elaborations of the history of the people of God till the exile under a single formula, we may with Keil distinguish the older books of Kings as the fruit of the *prophetic* form of history, and Chronicles as the product of the *hagiographic* mode. Our work, indeed, belongs more closely to that special development of hagiographic historiography, which, in contrast with the *popular* method of the books of Ruth and Esther (and with the *prophetic* mode of the historic sections of Daniel), may be termed the *sacerdoto-Levitical*, and in which the preference for annalistic statement (appearing also in the books of Ezra and Nehemiah, the continuations of Chronicles) must be accounted eminently characteristic. Keil[1] justly denies that any one of these special moments, whether popularity, the sacerdoto-Levitical, or *the annalistic* character, should be applied to the collective historical works of the hagiographic part of the canon. "Common to the collective hagiographic books of history, and characteristic of them, is simply the retreat or the absence of the prophetic view of the course of history according to the divine plan of salvation unfolding itself in the events, instead of which appear individual points of view that show themselves in the prosecution of parenetic, didactic ends, and have a definite influence on the selection and treatment of the facts."

[1] *Bibl. Comment. on Chron., Ezr., Neh., and Esth.*, Introd. p. viii.

§ 2. NAME OF CHRONICLES. RELATION TO THE BOOKS OF EZRA AND NEHEMIAH.

Of the two most widely accepted designations of our historical work, the one pointing to its annalistic character, the other to the relation of supplement or completion which it bears to the older books of Kings, the former rests on the Hebrew phrase דִּבְרֵי הַיָּמִים. This phrase, before which, according to 1 Kings xiv. 19, 29, xv. 7, 23, the word סֵפֶר (or, according to Esth. vi. 1, סֵפֶר זִכְרֹנוֹת) is to be supplied, means "events of the day, course of events" (*res gestæ dierum*), and thus presents our work as a "Book of current events," as a "Chronicle:" which name, not as a literal, but a correct rendering of דִּבְרֵי הַיָּמִים, has been made current by Jerome for the Latin, and by Luther for the German Church.[1] So far as this denomination in the quoted passages of the Old Testament refers to divers other historical works, in particular to those old Israelitish royal annals often quoted by our Chronist, the "books of the Chronicles of the Kings of Israel and Judah" (as in Esth. ii. 23, vi. 1, x. 2, the Medo-Persian royal annals, the "book of the Chronicles of the Kings of Media and Persia"), it appears to be a rather indefinite designation, by which our work should be distinguished quite generally as belonging to the class of annalistic works covering a long space of time. Whether this name proceeds from the author himself, or owes its origin to a later (certainly very old, and at all events pre-Masoretic) tradition, at any rate, the denomination brought into currency by the Sept. Παραλειπόμενα (*liber* Paralipomenōn) is more significant for the characteristic position and import of the work as a historical book, especially for its relation to the earlier historical books of the canon. For this name, which is to be explained, not with Movers, by *supplementa*, relics from other historical works, but, in accordance with the patristic tradition in Pseudo-Athanasius (*Synopsis Scr. S.*, in *Athanasii Opp.* ii. p. 83: παραλειφθέντα πολλὰ ἐν ταῖς βασιλείαις περιέχεται ἐν τούτοις), in Jerome (*Ep. ad Paulin:* . . . "*prætermissæ in Regum libris historiæ*"[2]) and Isidore of Seville (*Origen*, lib. vi. c. 1, p. 45: "*Paralipomenon græce dicitur, quod prætermissorum vel reliquorum nos dicere possumus,*" etc.), by "omitted, overlooked in the other historical works," sets forth in a striking manner the position taken by our author as the supplementer of the prophetical historians, and has therefore the advantage over the Hebrew denomination of greater definiteness, although it appears neither quite free from misapprehension nor adapted to the collective characteristics of our history.

Our work, moreover, forms, according to its original plan, as well as the oldest tradition, only one "book of annals" or supplements, for not only the old numeration of the books of the Old Testament in Josephus (*c. Ap.* i. 8), Origen (in Euseb. *H. Eccl.* vi. 25), and Jerome (*Prolog. galeat.*), according to which the canon consists of twenty-two books, but also the later computation made by Jerome and in the Talmud (*Baba bathra*, fol. 14), extending to twenty-four books, recognises only one book of Chronicles; and that the Masora regarded it as a single work is evident from the remark at the close of its text, that 1 Chron. xxvii. 25 forms the middle of the whole. The present general division (even in the recent Hebrew editions) into two books, springs from the Alexandrine translators and Jerome their follower, and may have been occasioned on their part by the existence of some great section or interval at the point of division, 1 Chron. xxix. 29 f., in the majority of older Hebrew MSS. This bipartition of the work (which even Melito of Sardis knew, Euseb. *H. Eccl.* iv. 26, as his list of the holy scriptures includes Παραλειπομένων δύο) cannot be regarded as unsuitable, since, apart from the almost equal length of the two parts, the end of the reign of David, on which the writer dwells with greater fulness than on that of any other king, presented a most fitting point of pause and division.

The identity of the close of the second book, ch. xxxvi. 22 f., with the beginning of the book of Ezra, especially as the passage presents no truly satisfactory close for our work, raises the expectation that some connection exists between it and the latter book. In favour of this is farther the close affinity of the style of each, the mode of quoting the law common to both,

[1] Jerome's *Prolog. galeat.: Dibre hajamim*, i.e. *verba dierum, quod significantius* chronicon totius divinæ historiæ *possumus appellare, qui liber apud nos Paralipomenon primus et secundus inscribitur.*

[2] The whole passage (*Opp. ed. Vallars.* t. i. p. 279) runs thus: *Paralipomenon liber*, i.e. *instrumenti veteris epitome, tantus et talis est, ut absque illo, si quis scientiam scripturarum sibi voluerit arrogare, se ipsum irrideat; per singula quippe nomina juncturasque verborum et prætermissæ in Regum libris tanguntur historiæ et innumerabiles explicantur evangelii quæstiones.*

as well as the decided preference of both for genealogical registers, statistical lists, and minute descriptions of acts of religion, in which also the same formulæ are not seldom used (see Remark). As no small part of these idioms belong also to the book of Nehemiah, the hypothesis is natural, that the three books, even if proceeding from different authors, have been subjected to a common revision by a later writer. This hypothesis is more probable than both the other attempts to solve the problem, namely, that either Chronicles and Ezra (Movers), or Chronicles, Ezra, and Nehemiah (Zunz, Ew., Berth., Dillm., Davidson, etc.), originally formed a single work proceeding from one author. For in such unity of origin of the three works, their separation before the close of the canon into three or (in case of Ezra and Nehemiah having originally formed one work) into two books remains purely inexplicable. The author of such separation would have had no rational ground for retaining 2 Chron. xxxvi. 22, 23 at the same time as the close of the first and the opening of the second part. The double place of these verses leads much rather to a common redactor of the two writings than to an identity of author. The majority also of the already-mentioned common idioms, and other qualities, are sufficiently explained by the hypothesis, that the present very homogeneous form of the two, or at most three pieces, arises partly from having proceeded from the same circle of sacerdotal and Levitical views, endeavours, and learned researches, and partly from having gone through the hands of the same redactor. And even if one author of the two or three works must be affirmed, there can be as little doubt of the fact, that he conceived Chronicles as an independent and separate work, as of the independence and original distinctness of the books of Ezra and Nehemiah, which are clearly separated from one another in the Hebrew text by the new superscription, Neh. i. 1. Comp. § 3. [There seems to be no reason why one author may not continue the work of another on the same plan and in a similar style.—J. G. M.]

Remark.—On the numerous verbal points of contact noticed by Pareau, *Institutio interpr. V. T.* p. 419,[1] between Chronicles and Ezra, applying also in great part to the book of Nehemiah, see Movers, *Krit. Untersuchungen*, p. 17 f.; Hävernick, *Einl.* ii. 1, 269 ff., and especially Bertheau, *Kurzgef. exeg. Handb.*, Einleit. p. xix. f. The latter recounts: *a.* a number of like grammatical inflections and constructions, namely, 1. The short way of subordinating relative clauses by placing them after a construct state (1 Chron. xxix. 3; 2 Chron. xxxi. 19; Ezra i. 5; Neh. viii. 10); 2. The use of the infinitive with ל to express must or shall (1 Chron. v. 1, ix. 25, xiii. 4, xv. 2, etc.; 2 Chron. ii. 8, viii. 13, xi. 22, etc.; Ezra iv. 3, x. 12; Neh. viii. 13); 3. The extremely frequent use of the prep. ל, partly before the object as *nota accusativi*, partly after an accus. in continuation (1 Chron. xxviii. 1; 2 Chron. xxvi. 14, xxviii. 15, xxxiii. 8; Neh. ix. 32), especially before כֹּל, to include all in enumerations (1 Chron. xiii. 1; 2 Chron. v. 12; Ezra i. 5, vii. 28; Neh. xi. 2), after the prep. עַד, where in former usage the word subordinate to this followed immediately (1 Chron. xxviii. 7, 20; 2 Chron. xiv. 12, xvi. 12, 14, xvii. 12, etc.; Ezra iii. 13, ix. 4, 6, x. 14) before the adverbial infin. הַרְבֵּה (2 Chron. xi. 12, xvi. 8; Neh. v. 18); 4. The abundant use of prepositions in general, for example, in such phrases as עַד נֶגֶד, Neh. iii. 26; בְּפִתְאֹם, 2 Chron. xxix. 36; בְּיוֹמָם, Neh. ix. 19; 5. The placing of the article before a verb for the *pron. relat.* (1 Chron. xxvi. 28, xxix. 8, 17; 2 Chron. xxix. 36, xxxiv. 32; Ezra viii. 25, x. 14, 17; Neh. ix. 33). Moreover, Bertheau himself is obliged to acknowledge with regard to these constructions, that "they occur occasionally also in other books of the Old Testament, especially the later." That they may be laid to the account of the idiom of one single author of the books compared, will be the less evident, because some of these constructions, as the quoted passages show, occur not more than once in any one of these writings, and therefore by no means belong to the prominent characteristics of their style.

b. On the contrary, single phrases quoted by him, or standing constructions of certain words, point somewhat more definitely to identity of authorship. Thus the construction עַמֵּי הָאֲרָצוֹת, 2 Chron. xiii. 9; Ezra iii. 3, ix. 1, 2, 11; Neh. ix. 30, x. 29 (comp. also מַלְכֵי הָאֲרָצוֹת, Ezra ix. 7; יֹשְׁבֵי הָאֲרָ׳, 2 Chron. xv. 5; גּוֹיֵי הָאֲרָ׳, 2 Chron. xxxii. 13, 17, etc.), הֵכִין לֵב, 1 Chron. xxix. 18; 2 Chron. xii. 14, xix. 3, xx. 33, xxx. 19; Ezra vii. 10; הֵכִין in

[1] *Quod peculiare est in dictione utriusque libri Chronicorum, id etiam in dictione libri, qui Ezræ tribuitur auctori ejusque nomen præ se fert, animadvertitur, quatenus lingua Hebraica conscriptus est.*

several other constructions; הִתְנַדֵּב, "to offer freely at the temple," 1 Chron. xxix. 5, 6, 9, 14, 17; 2 Chron. xvii. 16; Ezra i. 6, ii. 68, iii. 5 ff.; Neh. xi. 2; בִּזָּה, 2 Chron. xiv. 13, xxviii. 14; Ezra ix. 7; Neh. iii. 36; קִבֵּל, 1 Chron. xii. 18, xxi. 11; 2 Chron. xxix. 16; Ezra viii. 30; מְלֶאכֶת בֵּית יְהוָה (or מ' ב' אֱלֹהִים), 1 Chron. xxiii. 4, xxvi. 30; Ezra iii. 6, vi. 22; Neh. x. 34, xi. 22, etc. Yet all these phrases occur not exclusively in our books, but occasionally elsewhere (הִתְנַדֵּב, for example, in Judg. v. 2, 9; הָאֲרָצוֹת in several constructions also, 2 Kings xviii. 35, and often in Ezek.; בִּזָּה also in Esther and Daniel; קִבֵּל there also, and in Prov. and Job, etc.). Actual idioms of the books of Chron., Ezra, and Neh., from which their derivation from one author may seem to follow, are properly only such phrases as עַל עָמְדָם, 2 Chron. xxx. 16, xxxv. 10; Neh. viii. 7, ix. 3, xiii. 11; חֶדְוָה, 1 Chron. xvi. 27; Neh. viii. 10; Ezra vi. 16; כְּפוֹר, "basin," 1 Chron. xxviii. 17; Ezra i. 10, viii. 27; עַד לְמֵרָחוֹק, 2 Chron. xxvi. 15; Ezra iii. 13 (comp. the other constructions with עַד לְ in 2 Chron. xvi. 14, xxvi. 8, xxxvi. 16, etc.); מִתְוַדִּים in the plur., 2 Chron. xxx. 22; Neh. ix. 3; comp. Ezra x. 1; פְּלֻגָּה, of divisions of the Levites, 2 Chron. xxxv. 5; Ezra vi. 18. To this may be added such phrases and formulæ resting on the priestly and legal ideas and facts of these books, as כַּמִּשְׁפָּט, 1 Chron. xxiii. 31; 2 Chron. xxxv. 13, xxx. 16; Ezra iii. 4; Neh. viii. 18 (this phrase is peculiar to our books, while the synonymous כַּכָּתוּב בַּתּוֹרָה occurs often in the older writings); הוֹדוּ וְהַלְלוּ לַיהוָה, 1 Chron. xvi. 4, xxiii. 30, xxv. 3, etc.; Ezra iii. 11; likewise the liturgical form לְהוֹדוֹת וּלְהַלֵּל, and "for He is good, for His grace endureth for ever," 1 Chron. xvi. 34, 41; 2 Chron. v. 13; Ezra iii. 11; not less the standing phrases in describing festivals, בְּשִׂמְחָה (1 Chron. xii. 40, xxix. 9, 17; 2 Chron. xv. 15, xx. 27, xxix. 30, 36, xxxi. 23, 26; Ezra iii. 12) and עַל־יְדֵי דָוִיד (1 Chron. xxv. 2, 6; 2 Chron. xxiii. 18, xxix. 27; Ezra iii. 10); lastly, the official names of certain temple ministers and sacred musicians found only in our books, especially נְתִינִים, הַמְשֹׁרְרִים and מְצִלְתַּיִם. If we add to these common properties, extending even to literal agreement in expression, the preference in these three writings for genealogies and lists of officers and the like (comp. 1 Chron. i.–ix.; Ezra iii., vii. 1–5, viii., x. 20 ff.; Neh. vii. 6 ff., x. 1 ff., xi., xii.), as well as the great prominence of the temple musicians and porters as an institution mentioned with peculiar interest (1 Chron. vi. 16 ff., ix. 14 ff., xv. 16 ff., xvi. 4 ff., xxiii. 5, xxv. 1 ff., xxvi. 12 ff.; 2 Chron. v. 12 ff., viii. 14 ff., xxiii. 13 ff., xxxi. 11 ff., xxxiv. 12 f., xxxv. 15; Ezra ii. 42, 70, iii. 10 f., vii. 7, x. 24; Neh. vii. 1, 45, x. 29, xi. 17 ff., xii. 24 ff., xiii. 5), there grows up a certain probability for the presumption of one author for the three writings in question. But this presumption cannot be regarded as "altogether established" and "fully demonstrated" (Bertheau, p. xx.). The great majority of the coincidences adduced are sufficiently explained by supposing a plurality of authors, nearly of the same date, inspired by a like Levitico-sacerdotal interest and impulse, drawing from the like sources, of whom the last, in order to produce a uniform edition of these similar historical works, submitted his two predecessors to a common revision. Comp. on the other hand, Keil (*Comment.* p. 15 ff.), who, however, certainly derives at least two of the works in question, Chronicles and Ezra, from one author; and, on the other hand, Bleek, *Einleit. ins A. T.* (2d edit. § 171, p. 404), who, coming nearer the truth, claims distinct authors for the three books, but regards the author of Chronicles as the last writer and the redactor of the books of Ezra and Nehemiah. The question not immediately affecting our problem, whether the books of Ezra and Nehemiah are to be regarded as forming originally one work, or as independent productions of different authors, will have to be incidentally treated in the following investigation concerning the author of our book and the time of its composition.

[The arguments from the above phenomena for a redaction of these books are not convincing. An author writing in the language of the people, especially in the East, will use and repeat the current phrases of his day. The rise of new habits, objects, and acts will demand new words and constructions for their expression. These two circumstances are nearly sufficient to account for all the diversities and identities that have been noted, without having recourse to the hypothesis of one author or one redactor. A familiarity with the previous authors of the Old Testament will probably balance the account.—J. G. M.]

§ 3. AUTHOR, AND TIME OF COMPOSITION.

As Chronicles at its close mentions the edict of Cyrus permitting the return of the Jews from the Babylonish exile (2 Chron. xxxvi. 22 f.), and in 1 Chron. iii. 19–24 it traces the descendants of Zerubbabel through six generations (see the exposition of the passage and Remark at the end of the section), it cannot have been composed, or at least put in its present form, before the time of Zerubbabel, or for a considerable time after Ezra. With an average of thirty years for each of the generations after Zerubbabel, the last, consisting of the seven sons of Elioenai, must be supposed to flourish after the year 350 B.C. The last decade of the Persian monarchy, if not the beginning of the Grecian period, is, moreover, indicated by several other circumstances, among which are the following:—

a. The computation employed in 1 Chron. xxix. 7 (in the history of David) by Dariks, אֲדַרְכֹּנִים, a Persian gold coin, occurring also in the books of Ezra and Nehemiah,—that, whether first stamped under Darius Hystaspis or not, refers the time of the composition of the work to the Persian sway over the Jews, or even some time after it;[1]

b. The name בִּירָה, castle, likewise indicating the Persian period, designates the temple as a magnificent building (1 Chron. xxix. 1, 19),—a term only occurring elsewhere in the books of Esther and Nehemiah, which there designates either the palace of the Persian monarch (Esth. i. 2, 5, ii. 3, 8; Neh. i. 1), or the castle near the temple of Jerusalem, the later Βᾶρις (Neh. ii. 8, vii. 2);

c. The orthography and Chaldaizing style betraying a pretty late age (comp. Remark on § 2);

d. The position of the work in the canon as the last of the Hagiographa, and thus after the books of Ezra and Nehemiah, to which it would scarcely have been subjoined by the collectors, if any certain knowledge of its composition before or even contemporary with them had existed in Jewish tradition;

e. The circumstance that the books of Ezra and Nehemiah, for which, on account of the already adduced verbal and other coincidences with our books, an almost identical date of composition must be asserted, must have been already written a considerable time after their heroes and traditional authors, as the proper memoirs of Ezra and Nehemiah were used as sources in them,—the age of these men (Neh. xii. 26, 47) is represented as already in the distant past; and, moreover, lists of the chiefs of the Levites (Neh. xii. 23) and of the high priests (Neh. xii. 10 ff.) are given therein, that extend down to Jaddua, the holder of the high priest's office in the time of Alexander the Great. That this Jaddua, according to Josephus (*Antiq.* xi. 8), high priest during the last years of the Persian Empire, as well as under Alexander, was a contemporary of the author of the book of Nehemiah, appears in fact very probable, according to the twelfth chapter of the book. Yet Ewald and Bertheau have gone too far, when they infer, from the manner in which both in Ezra and Nehemiah Cyrus and his successors are constantly mentioned as *Persian* kings (Ezra i. 1, iv. 5; comp. iv. 7, vi. 1, etc.), that the Grecian monarchy had already commenced. The author might consider it suitable to give prominence to the Persian nationality of these kings, in contrast with the former kings of Judah. And all else that, after Spinoza, has been urged by de Wette, Berthold, Gramberg, and others (recently again by Nöldecke, *Die alttestamentl. Literat.*, 1868, p. 63 f.), for the origin of the book under the Macedonic or the Seleucidic government, amounts only to hypercritical conjectures (comp. Keil, *Apolog. Versuch*, p. 17 ff.; Hävernick, *Einl.* ii. 274 ff.).

If our book appears from the above considerations, especially those adduced under *c–e*, to belong to a time falling after Ezra and Nehemiah, it is impossible for Ezra himself to be the author. The Talmud, indeed, regarded him as the common originator of the book called after him and of Chronicles (*Baba bathr.* fol. 15, 1: *Esra scripsit librum suum et genealogiam in libro Chronicorum usque ad se*), in which it was followed by most Rabbins, some Fathers, as Theo-

[1] That the composition must have taken place during the Persian rule, and before Alexander the Great, can scarcely be inferred from the mention of this coin (against Movers). For as Bleek justly remarks, p. 398: "It may well be imagined, and is in itself quite natural, that a silver or gold coin, once introduced into the country and extensively circulated, will continue in currency long after the dynasty that coined it has ceased to rule."

doret, and later theologians, as Carpzov, Heidegger, Pareau, Starke, Lange, Eichhorn (*Einl.* iii. 597 ff.), Hävernick, Welte, Keil (*Apolog. Versuch*, p. 144 ff., *Einl.* p. 497; comp. *Comment.* p. 14), and Jul. Fürst (*Gesch. der bibl. Lit.* ii. 210, 537 ff.), and others. But he can no more have written the book of Chronicles than the book of Ezra itself. Both belong notoriously to a later age; and in view of their manifold internal and external connection, the hypothesis of Movers, that a writer living some centuries after Ezra wrote both works as a continuous whole, though afterwards separated (Mov. *Krit. Unters.* p. 14 ff.), would commend itself, were it not necessary to take into account the relation of the book of Nehemiah to both, and to admit some sort of connection among the three books. To show that this consists in being derived from the same author has been attempted by Zunz (*Gottesdienstl. Vorträge der Juden*, Berlin 1832, p. 18 ff.), Ewald (*Gesch. des v. Isr.* i. p. 264, 2d edit.), Bertheau (*Kurzgef. exeg. Handb.*, Einl. p. 15), Graf (*Die geschichtl. Bücher des A. T.* p. 114 ff.), Dillmann (in Herzog's *Real-Encycl.*, Art. "Chronik"), Davidson (*Introd. to the Old Test.* ii. p. 115 sq.). They have regarded the books of Chronicles, Ezra, and Nehemiah as three constituent parts of a single historical work, composed in the end of the Persian or the opening of the Grecian period. But against this are the following considerations:—

1. The identity of Ezra i. 1–3 with 2 Chron. xxxvi. 22 f., which is more easily understood if we regard it as the work of a redactor who wished to show the second of the two originally separate works to be a kind of continuation of the first, than if we suppose that the narrative originally proceeded from 2 Chron. xxxvi. 23 to Ezra i. 4, and then, after rending the two books asunder, the opening words of the second concerning the edict of Cyrus were repeated at the close of the first. Comp. Keil, *Comm.* p. 14 f.: "For such a separation with an addition there seems to be no ground, especially as the edict of Cyrus must be repeated. The introduction of this edict with the words, 'And in the first year of Cyrus, king of Persia, that the word of the Lord by the mouth of Jeremiah might be fulfilled, etc.,' is so closely connected with the close of the description of the destruction of Jerusalem and the carrying away of Judah to Babylon, 'and they were servants to him (King Nebuchadnezzar) and his sons until the reign of the Persians, *to fulfil* the word of the Lord by the mouth of Jeremiah . . . to fulfil seventy years,' ver. 20 f., that the edict of Cyrus cannot be separated from the foregoing; much rather must the same author, who wrote vers. 20, 21, and represented the seventy years of exile as the fulfilment of Jeremiah's prophecy, have also mentioned the edict of Cyrus, and connected it with this prophecy. This connection of the edict with that prophecy furnishes an incontrovertible proof that the verses containing the edict form an integral part of Chronicles." On the whole, the supposition of a supplementary separation of a history originally forming one whole is attended with serious difficulties; and neither the apparently somewhat abrupt close of Chronicles, as it now stands (with וְיָעַל, "And let him go up"), nor the circumstance that the opening words of Ezra, though verbally coinciding in general with the closing words of Chronicles, yet differ from them in some particulars (namely, for בְּפִי of 2 Chron. xxxvi. 22, מִפִּי, and for יְהוָה אֱלֹהָיו עִמּוֹ of 2 Chron. xxxvi. 23, יְהִי אֱל' ע'), can be satisfactorily reconciled with the hypothesis of separation, both phenomena agreeing better with the supposition, that the conforming hand of a later redactor had established a coincidence in the main between two passages that were originally somewhat different.

2. The plan, also, of the books of Ezra and Nehemiah, clearly aiming at the presentation of contemporary or very recent history, speaks against the hypothesis of their original immediate connection with the book of Chronicles. Whatever there is in the plan of this work, or in the position of the writer, with respect to the sources used by him resembling the historiographic method of the other two books, is easily explained by supposing the authors to be guided in general by the same views, and to write in the same, or nearly the same times.

3. And as neither these merely subordinate resemblances of plan and form, nor the already mentioned verbal and orthographical coincidences, suffice to disprove the independent character of the three works, neither can the circumstance, that the author of the apocryphal third book of Ezra, from the way in which he strings together 2 Chron. xxxvi. 21 and Ezra i. 1, seems not to have been acquainted with the separation of Chronicles from Ezra, nor the phenomenon parallel to this circumstance, that the Talmud, the Masora, and the ancient Christian Church count the books of Ezra and Nehemiah generally as one book. At the ground of this latter phenomenon obviously lies the Jewish endeavour not to let the number

of the books of the Old Testament exceed that of the twenty-two letters of the Hebrew alphabet (Origen in Euseb. *H. Eccl.* vi. 25; Jerome, *Prol. gal.;* Talmud, *Baba bathr.*, in Buxtorf, *Tiberias*, c. xi. p. 108 sqq.),—an endeavour from which the oldest Church Fathers, in their lists of the canonical Scriptures of the Old Testament, were not free, and of which the circumstance that two of the oldest MSS. of the Septuagint, the cod. Alexandrinus and the Friderico-Augustanus, separate the book of Nehemiah by no interval from that of Ezra (comp. Tischendorf's *Vetus Testamentum juxta* LXX. *Interpretes*, edit. iv. 1869, *T. I.* p. 611), must be regarded as a later effect.

If, according to all this, the connection of these three books is not to be viewed as a unity, forbidding their original independent existence, and if, notwithstanding all traces of an almost contemporary origin, no common author needs to be assumed for them, nothing is more natural than to regard one of the two or three supposed authors as the originator of that redactional conformation on which the present affinity and mutual relation of the three books, so far as it betrays the hand of a literary reviser, depends. And in all probability this redactor was the author of Chronicles, as a compilation presupposing the existence of the other two, and adapting itself to them. The already extant works concerning Ezra and Nehemiah, proceeding perhaps from the younger contemporaries of these men, may have served as the occasion and impulse to this writer to present the previous history of God's people in a like spirit of Levitical, priestly pragmatism, and in a similar annalistic method, and so to project his review of the progress of the kingdom of God from Adam to the end of the exile, running parallel with the earlier historical books, which he partly supplements and partly abstracts. That he prefixed the closing verses of this work as an introduction to its sequel the book of Ezra, to mark externally the connection of the two works, must be considered more probable from the above remarks, than the reverse hypothesis of Bleek, that "he brought over the first verses of that work (Ezra) as the close of this latter." Comp. throughout Bleek, *Einl.* § 171, p. 404 f., with whose representation of the origin of our three works we only differ on this subordinate point, while we must regard it otherwise as the most satisfactory solution of the present question.

Concerning the person of this author of Chronicles and final redactor of Ezra and Nehemiah, who belonged to the last years of the Persian dynasty, only this can be established, that he must have belonged to the Levites of the second temple, and in particular to the singers or song-masters, in whom he takes a special interest, as the constant putting of them forward (as also the porters) along with priests and Levites in many parts of his work shows; see above, § 2, Remark, p. 6. When Keil (*Comment.* p. 17 ff.) urges against this hypothesis the fact, that "in all places where he speaks of musicians and porters we also find the priests mentioned," sufficient attention is not paid to the fact, that this express mention of such inferior officers as singers and musicians, along with the priests and other officials of the temple, implies a special interest in them on the part of the author. Certainly the porter is often mentioned in the same places; but the interest of the narrator in the musicians and their doings (into which he often enters minutely, while he only mentions the porters by the way) plainly outweighs everything else. And nothing is obviously deducted from the authority and credibility of our writer, if we think of him as an Asaph of the later sanctuary, though his identification with Ezra the priest becomes thereby impossible.

Remark.—The difficult passage 1 Chron. iii. 19–24, the full elucidation of which we must reserve for the commentary itself, names from Hananiah, the son of Zerubbabel, five other generations, represented by Shechaniah, Shemaiah, Neariah, Elioenai, and Hodaiah, the last of which generations, Hodaiah with his six brothers, which appears to be nearly contemporary with the author of our work, can scarcely, even if we reckon a generation at 30 years, have flourished before 350 or 340 B.C. To this date points also another note contained in ver. 22. The Hattush here mentioned as great-grandson of Zerubbabel, is perhaps the same Hattush mentioned, Ezra viii. 2, as a descendant of David, and as brought under Ezra from Babylon to Judea. Now, as in vers. 22 and 23 the grandsons of Neariah, a younger brother of this Hattush, are mentioned, we shall thus be carried down beyond the year 400, as the earliest possible time of the drawing up of this genealogy; and the omission of some intervening members after Hattush would carry it down considerably later. These chronological combinations taken from 1 Chron. iii. 19 ff. may not appear absolutely certain and indisputable, as the Hattush of Ezra might possibly be different from that of our passage (comp. Keil, *Einl.*

p. 496), and as, especially in ver. 21, where all connection of the בְּנֵי רְפָיָה with the foregoing is wanting, the suspicion (uttered by Vitringa, Heidegger, Carpzov, etc.) of corruption, or the supposition that a fragment of some other genealogy has crept into the text (Hävern., Movers, Keil, etc.), appears sufficiently plausible. Notwithstanding this uncertainty and partial obscurity of the passage, the opinion expressed is probable enough; and the more so, the more clearly the other considerations (under *c–e*) above mentioned point to a still later time than that of Ezra and Nehemiah.

[The data presented by the books of Ezra, Nehemiah, and Chronicles, prove, at most, that a touching hand was applied to them after the lifetime of Ezra and Nehemiah, simply adding a few names to a list or pedigree. But this comes far short of proving that these works were not produced by Ezra and Nehemiah, the authors to whom they are usually assigned. To give even plausibility to this negative conclusion, it is necessary to apply our modern notions or habits of composition to the men of ancient times, before printing was invented, or the rules of literature determined. There is great risk of mistake in taking this important step, as the modern man of letters is liable to carry up into those primitive days his own subjective views, and make a world of ancient literature after the fashion of the nineteenth century. To infer, for instance, that a work was not composed till the last person now named in it had lived and flourished, may seem legitimate. Yet it is not necessarily true even of modern works, as names and facts may be added by an editor or continuator. Still less can it be affirmed of ancient works antecedent to printing, especially when they are of national importance, and under the care of men competent and authorized to make such trifling additions as are supposed by some to discredit the authorship of Ezra and Nehemiah.—J. G. M.]

§ 4. MATTER, PLAN, AND OBJECT OF THE WORK.

In regard to matter, Chronicles falls, as already stated, into two main divisions—a shorter genealogical, i. 1–9, and a longer historical one. If we take into account the several groups of genealogical and historical material that exist within these main parts, the following detailed scheme of contents results:—

I. Genealogical tables or registers, with brief historical data, 1 Chron. i.–ix.
- *a.* Genealogies of the patriarchs from Adam to Israel and Edom, with the descendants of the latter till the era of kings, i.
- *b.* The sons of Israel and the generations of Judah till David, with David's posterity till Elioenai and his seven sons, ii.–iv. 23.
- *c.* The generations of Simeon, and the transjordanic tribes of Reuben, Gad, and half-Manasseh, till the deportation of the latter by the Assyrians, iv. 24–v. 26.
- *d.* The generations of the Levites, with a statement of their cities in the different tribes, v. 27–vi.
- *e.* The generations of the remaining tribes, except Dan and Zebulun, and in particular, of the Benjamite house of Saul, vii., viii.
- *f.* The inhabitants of Jerusalem till the period of kings, with the genealogy of Saul repeated, forming the transition to the history of David, ix.

II. History of the kings in Jerusalem from David to the exile.

1. David, x.–xxix.
   - *a.* Introduction; the fall of the house of Saul, x.
   - *b.* David's elevation to the throne; arrangement of his residence at Jerusalem; wars and enumeration of the people, xi.–xxi.

     [Removal from Hebron to Jerusalem, xi. 1–9; the heroes and worthies of David, xi. 10–xii.; preparation for removing the ark to Jerusalem, xiii.; David's house-building, family, and wars with the Philistines, xiv.; the solemn conveyance of the ark, xv., xvi.; David's purpose to build a temple to the Lord, xvii.; his wars, xviii.–xx.; the numbering of the people, with the plague; determination of the place for the future temple, xxi.]

c. David's arrangements concerning the temple; other spiritual and temporal regulations; last will and death, xxii.–xxix.

[Provisions for the temple, xxii.; division of the Levites and priests, and order of their service, xxiii.–xxvi.; division of the war officers, and order of the service, xxvii.; last directions concerning the transfer of the government to Solomon, and end of David, xxviii., xxix.]

2. Solomon, 2 Chron. i.–ix.
   a. His solemn sacrifice at Gibeon, and his riches, i.
   b. The building and consecration of the temple, ii.–vii.
   c. Solomon's building of cities, and serfs; religious ordinances; navigation to Ophir; intercourse with the queen of Sheba; glory; length of reign, and end, viii., ix.
3. The kings of Judah, from Rehoboam to Zedekiah, x.–xxxvi.
   a. Rehoboam; the prophet Shemaiah, x.–xii.
   b. Abijah, xiii.
   c. Asa; the prophets Azariah son of Obed, and Hanani, xiv.–xvi.
   d. Jehoshaphat; the prophets Micah son of Imlah, Jehu son of Hanani, etc., xvii.–xx.
   e. Joram; letter of the prophet Elijah, xxi.
   f. Ahaziah, xxii. 1–9.
   g. Athaliah, xxii. 10–xxiii.
   h. Joash; the prophet Zechariah, son of Jehoiada, xxiv.
   i. Amaziah, xxv.
   k. Uzziah, xxvi.
   l. Jotham, xxvii.
   m. Ahaz; the prophet Oded, xxviii.
   n. Hezekiah; the prophet Isaiah, xxix.–xxxii.
   o. Manasseh and Amon, xxxiii.
   p. Josiah; the prophetess Huldah, xxxiv., xxxv.
   q. Jehoahaz, Jehoiakim, Jehoiachin, Zedekiah; close, xxxvi.

From this survey of contents, the following points appear characteristic for the standpoint and plan of our historian:—

1. The taking up of the kingdom of David as a moment in the history of the tribe and state of Judah, with the corresponding retreat of the genealogy and history of the northern tribes (of which Dan and Zebulun are not even mentioned; Issachar, Naphtali, Asher, and half-Manasseh are only briefly noticed), and especially of the reigns of Saul and Ishbosheth, at the same time with the total omission of Jeroboam and his successors, which determines that of the prophets of the northern kingdom, and thus the action of Elijah, Elisha, etc.

2. The prominence given to the tribe of Levi, its ordinances and divisions, offices and functions,—a moment appearing with characteristic force as well in the genealogical portion (1 Chron. v. 27–vi. 66) as in the history of David (1 Chron. xxiii.–xxvi.), of Solomon and his temple-consecration (2 Chron. v. ff.), of Rehoboam, Asa, Joash, Hezekiah, and Josiah.

3. The preference for reporting genealogical series, which goes so far, that one list of this kind is unnecessarily repeated (that of the house of Saul, 1 Chron. viii. 29 ff.; comp. with ix. 35 ff.); and in the history of David, a register of his heroes, worthies, and offices, is inserted several times in apparently improper places (thus 1 Chron. xii., the list of the heroes adhering to him during his persecution by Saul, that of his worthies who raised him to the throne in Hebron, and xxvii., the summary of his forces, princes, and officers, for which a more suitable place would have been xviii. 12 ff.).

4. The visible inclination to dwell on the glorious periods of the theocracy and the theocratic worship, and by depicting such bright seasons, and treating as briefly as possible the contrary times of darkness and superstition, to display conspicuously the full blessing of preserving pure the national religion of Jehovah and the legitimate temple-service: on which account, such reigns as those of David, Solomon, Asa, Jehoshaphat, Joash, Hezekiah, and Josiah, are depicted with peculiar delight; while the last days of Solomon, the rule of Ahaziah and Athaliah, and that of the last kings before the exile, are despatched with comparative brevity, or entirely omitted, like the whole history of the kingdom of Ephraim.

The above-mentioned moments appear still more clearly as favourite points of history and fundamental peculiarities of our historian, if we compare the course of his historical representation with that of the parallel historical books, especially the books of Samuel and Kings. Characteristic for the time before the kings is his endeavour, by suitable abbreviations of the genealogical sections of Genesis, to give the clearest possible view of the descent of the house of David from the antediluvian patriarchs; comp. 1 Chron. i. 1–4 as an abridgment of Gen. v.; 1 Chron. i. 5–23 as a corresponding abbreviation of Gen. x.; 1 Chron. i. 24–27 as contracted from Gen. xi. 10–26; 1 Chron. i. 29–33 as recapitulated from Gen. xxv. 1–15; 1 Chron. i. 35–54 as recapitulated from Gen. xxxvi. 10–43; 1 Chron. ii. 1–5 as a summary of the list of Jacob's sons (especially those of Perez) in Gen. xlvi. 8–12; also 1 Chron. ii. 10–12 (list of the descendants of Ram to Jesse) with Ruth iv. 19–22; and in particular, the list of the Levitical cities, 1 Chron. vi. 39–66, with Josh. xxi. 10–39. There is throughout, as these parallels show, an endeavour aiming at the exaltation of the Davidic sovereignty as the brightest point of the history of God's people before the exile, by which the author has been guided in the genealogical preface to his history. For the history of David are equally significant, both that which is omitted of the books of Samuel, and that which is added as a supplement. He has here omitted most of the facts concerning the relation of David to Saul and his house (in particular the reign of Ishbosheth, 2 Sam. i.–iv. 9); nearly all the events of David's private life, especially those less favourable to his call, as the scene with Michal (2 Sam. vi. 20–23); the adultery with Bathsheba (2 Sam. xi., xii.); the dishonour of Tamar by Amnon; Amnon's death by Absalom, and Absalom's rebellion, with its consequences (2 Sam. xiii.–xix.); the revolt of Sheba (2 Sam. xx.); the delivery of some descendants of Saul to the Gibeonites for execution (2 Sam. xxi. 1–14); David's thanksgiving song and last words (2 Sam. xxii., xxiii. 1–7); Adonijah's attempt at usurpation, and the thereby hastened anointing of Solomon (1 Kings i.); lastly, David's last will regarding Joab, the sons of Barzillai, and Shimei (1 Kings ii. 1–9). On the contrary, he has supplemented the account of the older historians by his list of the brave men from all tribes who joined David during the persecution of Saul, and the warriors who made him king in Hebron (1 Chron. xii.), by his account of the part taken by the Levites in the conveyance of the ark (1 Chron. xv., xvi.), his long descriptions of David's preparations for the building of the temple (xxii.), his no less full statistical description of the priests and Levites, and the military and civil officers under David (xxiii.–xxvii.), and his account of the arrangements made by David shortly before his death in a great assembly of the people (xxviii., xxix.). It is not less characteristic, that the author has omitted in Solomon's history a number of facts which refer to the private life of this king, and are partly unfavourable to his character, as the punishment of Joab, Shimei, and Adonijah (1 Kings ii. 13–46), the marriage with Pharaoh's daughter (1 Kings iii. 1–3), the wise judgment of the king, and the full picture of his glory and wisdom (1 Kings iii. 16–v. 1), his palace (1 Kings vii. 1–12), his polygamy and idolatry, with the consequences following as a divine judgment (1 Kings xi. 1–40), while he reports all that relates to the building and consecration of the temple, the building of cities, bond-service, trade with Ophir, etc., at equal, if not greater length, than in the books of Kings. Lastly, in the period from Solomon to the exile, he significantly omits the whole history of the ten tribes, their kings and prophets, with the sole exception of the friendly or hostile relations in which they stood to the kingdom of Judah (to which belongs also the letter of Elijah given in 2 Chron. xxi. 12 ff.). On the contrary, regarding the kingdom of Judah in this period, a whole series of supplementary accounts are given, especially such as serve to glorify the theocratically-disposed sovereigns of this kingdom, but others also that exhibit along with these bright places darker shadows of the apostasy and the resulting national misfortune; as accounts of Rehoboam's cities of defence, reception of the Levites driven from the northern kingdom, and family connections (2 Chron. xi. 5–24); of Abijah's war with Jeroboam, his wives and children (xiii. 3–21); of Asa's victory over the Kushite Zerah, and the action of the prophets Azariah and Hanani under this king (xiv. 3–15, xv. 1–15, xvi. 7–10); of Jehoshaphat's internal and external administration, and his great victory over the allied Ammonites, Moabites, and others (xvii.–xx.); of Joram's fratricide, idolatrous reign, and punishment (xxi. 2–4, 11–19); of Joash's final fall into idolatry after the death of Jehoiada (xxiv. 15–22); of Amaziah's increase of his army and idolatry (xxv. 5–10, 14–16); of Uzziah's successful war with the Philistines and Arabians, his fortifications and his troops (xxvi. 6–15); of Jotham's fortifications and victory over the Ammonites (xxvii. 4–6); of the theocratic reforms of Hezekiah, his Passover, and the abundance of his treasures (xxix. 3–31, xxxii. 27–30); of Manasseh's removal to Babylon, repentance, and return from captivity (xxxiii. 11–17); of Josiah's Passover, and the part taken in it by the priests and Levites (xxxv. 2–19).

The author has no very fixed principle in making his abbreviations and additions; otherwise, notwithstanding his theocratic tendencies, he would have imparted some traces of David's family history, and along with the building of the temple and the cities, would have noticed that of Solomon's palace (1 Kings vii. 1–12); he would perhaps have been silent on the idolatry of Joash and Amaziah, as well as of Solomon, and have dwelt longer on the bright point of the Jewish monarchy in the reign of Josiah; and if it concerned him to bring out the dark shadow of apostasy with the light spots of this later period, he might have given a fuller account of the idolatrous reign of Ahaz, and of the misgovernment of the last kings, Jehoiakim, Jehoiachin, Zedekiah, etc. The inconsistency indicated by a dim perception of his design, and a want of thorough pragmatism, rests undoubtedly on the nature of his sources, the disproportion in the matter of which must have produced a similar defect in himself, and prevented him from exhibiting a uniform whole resulting from a single casting. On the whole, however, the correctness of our remarks on the prevailing tendency of the author is not prejudiced by these anomalies. It is indubitable, from his priestly-Levitical standpoint, that he wished in general to relate the theocratic civil and religious history of the Jews from David with a chief regard to their bright periods, and a recognition of their times of apostasy being invariably attended with divine judgments, and to hold up to his contemporaries a mirror encouraging them to fear God, and warning them against unfaithfulness to the Lord. Otherwise than the author of the books of Kings, who relates the events more objectively in their natural order, "our author places the facts and occurrences in connection with the conduct of the prince and the people toward the Lord, and endeavours so to illustrate the historical facts, that they teach how God rewards the faithful with peace and blessing, and visits the revolt from His covenant with penal judgments. The narrative thus acquires a parenetic character that often rises to the rhetorical manner. This parenetico-rhetorical stamp of his work meets us not only in the many speeches of the agents, but also in many historical delineations (for example, in Joram, 2 Chron. xxi.; in Ahaz, xxviii.; in Manasseh, xxxiii.; and in Zedekiah, xxxvi. 12–21). From this parenetic tendency, and the reflective mode of viewing history, is explained the greater part of his deviations from the parallel accounts in Samuel and Kings, as well the omission of collateral circumstances as the pictorial descriptions of religious regulations and festivals, the manifest object of which is to awaken in the mind of the reader delight and joy in the attractive services of the Lord, and to confirm the heart in fidelity to the Lord and His law" (Keil, *Comment.* p. 11). On account of this property, directed with special preference to the worship and the officers of worship, this history has been designated as specially Levitical,—a designation which is only suitable and free from misconception, when we bear in mind that it is not the Levites as such, but as the ministers of the lawful theocratic worship, the source of all salvation and blessing for the people of God, to whom the author devotes his special attention. "The Chronist wishes, not to glorify the Levites and the Levitical worship, but rather to lead the proof, from the history of the kingdom in Israel, that faithfulness to the covenant which the Lord has made with Israel brings happiness and blessing; neglect of it, misery and perdition. But Israel shows fidelity in walking after the standard of the law given by Moses, when he worships Jehovah the God of his fathers in His sanctuary, as He has appointed in the ordinances of worship. The author lays stress on the Levitical worship only so far as the faithfulness of Israel shows itself in its careful observance" (Keil, *Comm.* p. 8).

Remark.—The forty or more parallel sections which the part of Chronicles, common with the books of Samuel and Kings, presents, now in longer, now in shorter form, and now in corresponding, now in deviating sequence, are exhibited in the following table (from Keil, *Einl.* p. 479; comp. Davidson, *Introd.* p. 81 sq., and Tübingen *Theolog. Quartalschr.* 1831, p. 209 ff.):—

1 Chron.	x. 1–12,	1 Sam.	xxxi.
,,	xi. 1–9,	2 Sam.	v. 1–3, 6–10.
,,	xi. 10–47,	,,	xxiii. 8–39.
,,	xiii. 1–14,	,,	vi. 1–11.
,,	xiv. 1–7, 8–17,	,,	v. 11–16, 17–25.

1 Chron. xv., xvi.,	2 Sam. vi. 12–23.
,, xvii.,	,, vii.
,, xviii.,	,, viii.
,, xix.,	,, x.
,, xx. 1–3,	,, xi. 1, xii. 26–31.
,, xx. 4–8,	,, xxi. 18–22.
,, xxi.,	,, xxiv.
2 Chron. i. 2–13,	1 Kings iii. 4–15.
,, i. 14–17,	,, x. 26–29.
,, ii.,	,, v. 15–23.
,, iii. 1–v. 1,	,, vi., vii. 13–51.
,, v. 2–vii. 10,	,, viii.
,, vii. 11–22,	,, ix. 1–9.
,, viii.,	,, ix. 10–28.
,, ix. 1–12, 13–28,	,, x. 1–13, 14–29.
,, ix. 29–31,	,, xi. 41–43.
,, x. 1–xi. 4,	,, xii. 1–24.
,, xii. 2, 3, 9–16,	,, xiv. 21–31.
,, xiii. 1, 2, 22, 23,	,, xv. 1, 2, 6–8.
,, xiv. 1, 2, xv. 16–19,	,, xv. 11–16.
,, xvi. 1–6, 11–14,	,, xv. 17–24.
,, xviii. 2–34,	,, xxii. 2–35.
,, xx. 31–xxi. 1,	,, xxii. 41–51.
,, xxi. 5–10, 20,	2 Kings viii. 17–24.
,, xxii. 1–6, 7–9,	,, viii. 25–29, ix. 16–28, x. 12–14.
,, xxii. 10–xxiii. 21,	,, xi.
,, xxiv. 1–14, 23–27,	,, xii. 1–17, 18–22.
,, xxv. 1–4, 11, 17–28,	,, xiv. 1–14, 17–20.
,, xxvi. 1–4, 21–23,	,, xiv. 21, 22, xv. 2–7.
,, xxvii. 1–3, 7–9,	,, xv. 33–36, 38.
,, xxviii. 1–4, 26, 27,	,, xvi. 2–4, 19, 20.
,, xxix. 1, 2,	,, xviii. 2, 3.
,, xxxii. 1–21,	,, xviii. 13–xix. 37.
,, xxxii. 24, 25, 32, 33,	,, xx. 1, 2, 20, 21.
,, xxxiii. 1–10, 20–25,	,, xxi. 1–9, 18–24.
,, xxxiv. 1, 2, 8–32,	,, xxii., xxiii. 1–3.
,, xxxv. 1, 18–24, 26, 27, xxxvi. 1–4,	,, xxiii. 21–23, 28, 29–34.
,, xxxvi. 5, 6, 8–12,	,, xxiii. 36, 37, xxiv. 1, 5, 6, 8–19.
,, xxxvi. 22, 23,	Ezra i. 1, 2.

The value of this table of parallel passages consists in this, that it not only exhibits the mutual relation of the sections, showing now an extension, now an abridgment, on the part of our author, but also indicates where deviations in the order of the several events take place. For in the order of his materials the Chronist by no means agrees throughout with the books of Samuel and Kings; as he, in 1 Chron. xi. 10–47, takes a list of David's heroes from 2 Sam. xxiii. 8–39, and attaches it to events which are parallel with 2 Sam. v., and the account in 2 Sam. v. he does not reproduce *continuo*, but takes beforehand the section 2 Sam. vi. 1–11 (see 1 Chron. xiii. 1–14), as he farther places the history of David's numbering of the people, and of the plague, 2 Sam. xxiv., not quite at the end of the section belonging to David, but subjoins to it accounts of David's provision for the building of the temple, as well as his spiritual and temporal officers (1 Chron. xxii.–xxix.); as he also, in Solomon's history, takes beforehand the small section concerning Solomon's treasures and troops, 1 Kings x. 26–29, and places it beside that which is related in 1 Kings iii.–v., and so on. That which appears arbitrary in these deviations, vanishes when we reflect that our author followed not so much the books of Samuel and Kings in their existing state, as certain old sources partly lying at their foundation, and partly deviating from them; and thus the nature of his sources had an effect on determining the arrangement and sequence of his materials.

[To this very thoughtful and interesting section it may be added, that the author of Chronicles confines his attention to David, and the kingdom founded on the promise made to him in 2 Sam. vii. Hence he excludes from direct consideration the kingdom of the ten tribes, which gradually fell into idolatry, and had long ceased to exist at the time in which he wrote. The facts do not warrant us in limiting his theme or his aim more than this, and therefore prevent us from charging him with any inconsistency which an imaginary limit of a narrower kind might create. The temple and its ordinances of worship become a prominent matter of fact in the kingdom of God, and its ministers and services claim a corresponding place in the history of this kingdom, without any motive in the writer more special than zeal for the glory of the true and living God.—J. G. M.]

§ 5. SOURCES OF THE CHRONIST.

From a closer examination of the contents of the several sections, it appears an indubitable fact that the peculiar stamp of our history depends on the nature of certain sources used by the author, which must have been in great part different from the historical books contained in the canon, and must have included many other accounts in addition to these.

I. Of the genealogical tables and registers, and the geographical terms in the first or genealogical part (1 Chron. i.–ix.), only the introductory data referring to the patriarchs and the posterity of Edom, which are contained in 1 Chron. i.–ii. 2, appear to be wholly and without exception taken from Genesis (see the special proof above, § 4, p. 11). A derivation of these data from any other source than Genesis is improbable, for this reason, that they follow very exactly the order of this book (extracting and recapitulating from Gen. v., x., xi., xxv., xxxvi., and xxxv. 22 ff.), and they do not present a single supplementary notice. A quite different impression is made by a comparison of the following genealogies and historical notices with the corresponding data of the Pentateuch, the book of Joshua, and the other historical books. These matters occur in those older books neither as continuous series of names, nor as genealogical lists interwoven with shorter or longer historical data (as, for example, ch. iv. 22 f., iv. 39–43, v. 10–19). So far as they occur in them, they appear in quite a different connection, seldom forming longer series running through many generations; not leaving the impression of genealogical registers, or dry lists of names with occasional historical statements, but rather as integral moments of pragmatic narrative; while, in our book, they bear throughout the character of a genealogical register. In many deviations also, which are found in the number of generations, the genealogical materials of our book appear independent of the older histories; such as in the diverse spelling of many names, which may rest partly on mere errors of writing (which might easily creep in, especially in lists of names; compare the collection of notorious errors of this kind in Movers' *Krit. Unters.* p. 66 ff., and see beneath, in our exeg. explanations, *passim*), but in no small part owe their origin to a different tradition; as so many differences regarding geographical data (for example, regarding the names of the Levitical cities, 1 Chron. vi. 39–66, compared with Josh. xxi. 10–39) must be referred to diverse old traditions, and, therefore, to peculiar sources. And such must be those of his sources that had in great measure prepared the way for his collecting and arranging propensity, in so far as they themselves contained longer genealogical series, composed in like manner, and interwoven with like historical data, and so were not pragmatically-fashioned historical works from which he must have artificially constructed his lists. He himself testifies in some places, that what he presents in genealogies and other lists of names is not the fruit of his arranging and editing care, but is derived from sources of a genealogical kind. For at the tribe of Gad, 1 Chron. v. 17, he refers to a list of the families of this tribe that was prepared in the time of Jotham, king of Judah, and Jeroboam II. of Israel; at Issachar, 1 Chron. vii. 2, he refers to a census of this tribe made in the time of David; and it is said, ix. 1, that a census of "all Israel," that is, of the whole northern kingdom, had been made. And as in the second or historical portion reference is several times (xxiii. 3, 27, xxvi. 31, xxvii. 24) made to a census in the reign of David, and as the book of Nehemiah, which so nearly resembles our work in contents, mentions a list of the heads of the Levitical houses prepared in the time of the high priest Johanan (xii. 23), and a register found by Nehemiah of the families that returned with Zerubbabel from the exile (vii. 5; comp. also Ezra ii. 59, 62), it appears not only highly probable, but absolutely certain, that there were ample and authentic genealogical sources from which our author took his lists. And it certainly appears from 1 Chron. xxiv. and ix. 1 (comp. Neh. xii. 23) as if a part at least of these sources had been a constituent part of a greater historical work, namely, that old chronicle of the kingdom which is entitled, 1 Chron. xxvii. 24, *Dibre hajjamim* (the book of the chronicles of King David), and, ix. 1, as "the book of the kings of Israel." In particular, the short lists in 1 Chron. v. and vii. of the ten tribes according to their families and houses, may be extracts from the genealogical and statistical part of these old annals of the kingdom; while the lists of a purely chronological kind, which refer to celebrated families or to single persons, of public or of eminent private character, may have come rather from the old family archives, to which our author, or other collectors before him, had found access. It is at all events natural to suppose that the endeavours of the times of Zerubbabel and Ezra to enter into relation with the time before the exile, and to make the most diligent use of the connection with it, prepared the way for his hunting up and making use of these genealogical registers. "In the endeavour of the new community to restore the old relations, the divisions of the tribes, being connected with the whole remnant of the old community, must have acquired a new importance, and Chronicles is itself a proof of the attention that was paid to them. Its author gladly admits lists into his work, because he himself in this respect moves in the direction prevalent in his time. In short, from various sides comes to us the certainty, that the author of Chronicles was able to draw older lists of the divisions of the tribes and their number from other sources perhaps, but also, according to his own showing, from historical works in which the results of the registration and numeration of the families were collected. And his lists themselves point to a derivation from historical works; for they contain brief historical accounts standing in the closest connection with the recited names, and in them occurs the remark that something has continued "unto this day" (1 Chron. iv. 41, 43, v. 26),—a remark which, it is evident, cannot proceed from him who was charged with making out the lists, and is not added by the author of Chronicles, because it refers not to his time, but to the date of the work used by him, and is taken thence along with the other data" (Bertheau, p. xxxi. f.). Even an approximately exact determination of the date of these lists can scarcely be given, because often an old list may have been carried on some steps, either by our author or by some earlier investigators or collectors before him, so that its original closing point can no longer be clearly ascertained. Meanwhile, the fact that there were older or younger genealogical sources on which he rested in ch. ii.–ix., is by no means disturbed or rendered doubtful by the partial uncertainty of their age, or the impossibility of sharply separating them from one another.

II. A still more ample array of ancient sources and accounts must have been accessible to our author for his second or historical part; for at the death of almost every king he refers to writings in which his acts and the events of his reign are recorded; only in Joram, Ahaziah, Athaliah, and in the later kings Jehoahaz, Jehoiachin, and Zedekiah, are these references to older sources wanting. He cites in all the following sources:—

1. In David, the "words" (*dibre*) of Samuel the seer, of Nathan the prophet, and Gad the seer ("spier"), 1 Chron. xxix. 29; 2. In Solomon, the "words" of Nathan the prophet, the prophecy (נְבוּאָה) of Ahijah of Shilo, and the "visions" (חֲזוֹת) of Iddi the seer against Jeroboam the son of Nebat, 2 Chron. ix. 29; 3. In Rehoboam, the "words" of Shemaiah the prophet and of Iddo the seer, xii. 15; 4. in Abijah, the "Midrash" of Iddo the prophet, xiii. 22; 5. In Asa, the book of the kings of Judah and Israel, xvi. 11; 6. In Jehoshaphat, the "words" of Jehu the son of Hanani, which were inserted in the book of the kings of Israel, xx. 34; 7. In Joash, the "Midrash" of the book of the kings, xxiv. 27; 8. In Amaziah, the book of the kings of Judah and Israel, xxv. 26; 9. In Uzziah, a "writing" (כְּתָב) of Isaiah the prophet, xxvi. 22; 10. In Jotham, the book of the kings of Israel and Judah, xxvii. 7; 11. In Ahaz, the book of the kings of Judah and Israel, xxviii. 26; 12. In Hezekiah, the "vision" (חָזוֹן) of Isaiah the prophet, in the book of the kings of Judah and Israel, xxxii. 32; 13. In Manasseh, the "words" of the kings of Israel, as well as the words of Chosai, xxxiii. 18, 19; 14. In Josiah, the book of the kings of Israel and Judah, xxxv. 27; 15. In Jehoiakim, the same work, xxxvi. 8.

That this list of sources admits, nay demands, a considerable number of reductions, appears indubitable, if we reflect that the thrice quoted "book of the kings of Judah and Israel" can hardly have been different from the as often quoted "book of the kings of Israel and Judah," and also bear in mind the obvious identity of the "book of the kings of Israel" mentioned in No. 6, and the "words of the kings of Israel" quoted in No. 13, with that Israelito-Jewish book of Kings. For the name "Israel" in the latter two references can only be the collective designation of the whole people (as it deals, in both cases, with accounts of the kingdom of Judah, and not of the northern kingdom); and the phrase "book," or "words,"—that is, events, history of the kings of Israel,—appears to be merely an abbreviation of the more complete title. According to this well-ascertained assumption, which is shared by almost all recent writers (Movers, Ewald, Bertheau, Dillm., Keil, Graf, and Fürst, *Gesch. der bibl. Liter.* ii. p. 214), the sources here quoted of a properly historical (not prophetical) character reduce themselves to one chief work—a great annalistic history of the kingdom of all Israel. It remains doubtful whether the book used by the author for the reign of Joash, which he calls the "Midrash" of the book of Kings, was identical with this great work, or different from it. For the identity, Keil had formerly maintained (*Einl.* 1 Aufl. p. 494) that the history of Joash agrees as exactly with 2 Kings as the history of those kings for which the book of the kings of Israel and Judah is quoted; but he has recently acknowledged the objections raised to this by Bertheau to be on the whole plausible, or at all events difficult to refute. Accordingly, it would be hazardous to hold the phrase מִדְרַשׁ סֵפֶר as at once equivalent to the simple סֵפֶר, even if we wished to take מִדְרָשׁ, after 2 Chron. xiii. 22, in the sense of essay, treatise (so Ewald, *Gesch. Isr.* i. 295), and not rather, as appears more obvious, and creates no tautology with סֵפֶר, in that of exposition, commentary (Gesen., Thenius, Fürst, etc.). And the assumption appears not far-fetched, that "the connection in which the apostasy of the king, the prophecy of Zechariah, and the victory of a small number of Syrians over the numerous host of the Jews stand in Chronicles, was set forth prominently in a Midrash or exposition of the book of the kings of Israel and Judah" (Bertheau, p. xxxiii.). The weight of these grounds for assuming the diversity of the "Midrash" of the book of the kings quoted 2 Chron. xxiv. 27 from that book itself, cannot be mistaken. Yet it still remains uncertain whether we are to regard it as an explanatory work referring to the whole book of Kings, that might be used even elsewhere without express mention by our author, or as consisting of elucidations or digressive additions referring merely to the reign of Joash and its relations. The first view is that of Fürst (in p. q.), who, on the ground of Talmudic usage, explains the term Midrash by "enlargement of the history from oral or written tradition," and transfers this process of legendary enlargement of the old book of Kings, or embellishment of it with historical "Midrash," to the first Persian period, without being able, however, to adduce definite grounds for this course.

It is difficult, also, to decide the question concerning the relation of the book of the kings of Israel and Judah, so often quoted by our author, to the works often adduced in the canonical books of Kings, which are there separately designated as "the book of the chronicles (*dibre hajjamim*) of the kings of Israel," and the book of the chronicles of the kings of Judah. In contents, these annalistic sources of the canonical book of Kings must be identical with the chief written source of our Chronist, as the mostly verbal agreement of the accounts concerning the same transaction in that, as in this, shows. But what was to the author of the book of Kings two distinct works, one referring to the north and one to the south kingdom, this the Chronist must have had before him in the shape of one single work; for he quotes it under the name of the book of the kings of Israel for several of the southern kings, and for such even after the downfall of the northern kingdom as Manasseh, Josiah, and Jehoiakim. It is now a question, however, whether this single source of the Chronist was a later elaboration or combination of the *dibre hajjamim*, or old annals, quoted separately by the author of the book of kings of Israel and Judah, which were no longer extant, or was to be held as nothing else than our present book of Kings, so that the wavering manifold way of designating it was to be set down merely to the account of the defect of our author in diplomatic accuracy. Against the latter assumption (still not unfavourably discussed by Keil, p. 20 of his *Comment.*) speaks decidedly, *a*, the circumstance that the Chronist often refers to the book of the Kings, etc., as a source presenting full details, whereas the canonical books of Kings present not at all a fuller, but quite a briefer statement (comp. for example, his account of Jotham 2 Chron. xxvii. with 2 Kings xv. 32–38); *b*, the circumstance that the Chronist presents a mass of accounts for which we look in vain in the books of Kings; and *c*, the statement contained in 2 Chron. xxxiii. 18 concerning Manasseh, that his prayer to God, and the words of the seers that spake to him, are written in the words of the kings of Israel, by which our canonical book of Kings, with its very meagre account of Manasseh, cannot possibly be meant. Equally impossible is, however, also the supposition of the identity of the annalistic sources of the Chronist with the double *ditre hajjamim* of the books of Kings (Keil, Bleek, Davidson, etc.); for these are uniformly quoted as two different works, the one referring to Israel, the other to Judah. On the other hand, the Chronist never uses the name *dibre hajjamim* for his source; for it could only be in 1 Chron. xxvii. 24 that he referred to it under this name, which, however, cannot be called probable, and if it were the case, would of itself prove nothing. In short, the apprehension of the "book of the kings of Israel and Judah" as a later combination of the *dibre hajjamim* mentioned in the books of Kings (Ewald, Bertheau, Dillm., Graf, Nöldecke, etc.) remains alone probable. Scarcely anything more definite can be ascertained concerning the form and date of these two annalistic sources, of which the older, twofold in form, forms the basis of the books of Kings; the younger, parallel to this, that of Chronicles. Only so much appears, that they bore not a political-official, but rather a prophetical character,—that is, they were not at once identical with the official records of the acts and events of the several reigns made by the royal chancellors or historiographers (מַזְכִּירִים) (as Jahn, Movers, Stähelin, and others thought), but *annalistic representations of the history of the kingdom derived from these official records*, composed by *prophetic writers*, and, therefore, conceived in a prophetic spirit, and like our books of Kings and Chronicles, founded upon them, breathing a prophetic pragmatism. Farther, with respect to the date of these old annalistic histories of the kingdom, this at least appears certain, that the older works used by the author of the books of Kings were composed before the fall of the two kingdoms, as the oft-recurring formula "unto this day" presumes clearly the existence of the kingdom in question, and that the new elaboration of those old annals used as the chief source of the Chronist must have originated at least before the exile, because this also sometimes presents the phrase under circumstances that forbid the dating of the collection after the exile (see 2 Chron. v. 9, viii. 8, x. 19, xxi. 10, and therewith comp. 1 Kings viii. 8, ix. 13, 21, xii. 19, 2 Kings ii. 22, viii. 22, x. 27, xiv. 7, xvi. 6). Comp. Keil, *Comment.* p. 21 ff., who justly infers the composition of the sources in question before the exile from the double circumstance—"that, on the one hand, the references to these annals in both kingdoms continue not to the last kings, but (so at least in the book of Kings, 2 Kings xv. 31, xxxiv. 5) close for the kingdom of Israel with Pekah, for that of Judah with Jehoiakim; on the other hand, in several events the formula 'unto this day' occurs, which, because it mostly refers not to the time of the exile, but to the times of the still existing kingdom, cannot proceed from the authors of our canonical books of Kings and Chronicles, but is taken over from the sources used, and in these can only then be rightly conceived, if they were written a more or less brief time after the events." How completely arbitrary are, therefore, such dates as those of Nöldecke (*Die Alttestamentl. Literat.* p. 59), namely, that the *dibre hajjamim*, or "old lost chronicles of the kings of Israel and Judah," were first composed about 550 B.C., during the exile, and the head source of the Chronist thence derived (the book of the kings of Israel and Judah), like the parallel canonical books of Kings, were of still later origin,—this needs no special proof. And again, that the latest times before the exile might very well be the date of the prophetic annals serving the Chronist as chief source, must be evident enough, when we think of the efforts of a king like Josiah, and the learned literary labour of a prophet like Jeremiah. Against Bähr's opinion (*Die Bücher der K.* vol. vii. of the *Bibelw.* p. ix. ff.), that for the activity of an annalistic collector such as is now under consideration, the time shortly before the fall of the kingdom, the time of complete disorder, seems to be the least adapted, Keil appears to be justified in mentioning the prophet Jeremiah, who belongs precisely to this time, and must have been particularly occupied with the older sacred writings. And like the writings of this prophet, an annalistic historical work such as that in question might very well escape the destructive catastrophes of the time of Nebuchadnezzar, and by some means come into the hands of its later extractors and redactors (namely, the author of the canonical book of Kings, who, according to Bähr, p. viii., wrote still during the exile and in Babylon, and then our author after the exile).

Further, with regard to the prophetical writings above enumerated under Nos. 1, 2, 3, 6, 9, 12, and 14, it is a question whether we are to see in these independent historical works, or mere constituent parts of the before-mentioned "book of the kings of Israel and Judah." Against the independence affirmed by most older writers, and recently by Bleek, Davidson, Fürst, Keil, etc., and for the hypothesis that they were merely sections of the great annalistic book of Kings, named after certain contemporary prophets, Ewald, Berth., Dillm., Nöldecke, and even Bähr in p. q., mainly urged the circumstance, that of two of these prophetic writings, the *dibre* of Jehu (No. 6) and the "vision" of Isaiah (No. 12), it is expressly said by the Chronist that they were in the book of the kings of Israel and Judah, or what amounts to the same thing, were inserted in it (No. 6). But, 1. What is said of these two writings can scarcely be transferred at once to all other writings of this kind; the notice referring to their incorporation into the greater historical work, or their belonging to it, must have been repeated oftener than once or twice, if serious doubt of their independence were to be justified. 2. The "Midrash" of the prophet Iddo mentioned 2 Chron. xiii. 22 (No. 4), even because it is called a *Midrash*, cannot possibly be regarded as a separate section or integral part of the great book of Kings; rather might it have been a separate part of the after-mentioned (xxiv. 27) "Midrash of the book of Kings," but would still even then be considered distinct from that older historical work. 3. The statement made regarding Isaiah, 2 Chron. xxvi. 22, that he "wrote (כָּתַב) the acts of Uzziah, first and last," may certainly refer to a historical book composed by him, and incorporated at once into the great book of Kings, and so be understood in the sense of that hypothesis; but by the prophecy (נְבוּאַת) of Ahijah of Shilo, and the visions (חֲזוֹת) of Iddi against Jeroboam (2 Chron. ix. 29, No. 2), it is highly improbable that we are to understand historical works. These writings, as well as the incidentally-mentioned vision of Isaiah (2 Chron. xxxii. 32), appear to have been rather books of prophecy, with occasional historical notices; writings which, from their predominant character, were little fitted for incorporation in a great historical work, and of which, therefore, if such incorporation took place, it needed to be expressly mentioned (as in the vision of Isaiah above). 4. And where these writings of prophets are introduced with the term *dibre*, "words," as in Samuel, Nathan, and Gad (No. 1), in Nathan (No. 2), in Shemaiah and Iddo (No. 3), in Jehu (No. 6), and in Chozai (No. 10), it is at least as natural, after the analogy of the superscriptions in Amos i. 1, Jer. i. 1, etc., to think of books of prophets as of historical notices; and it is at all events significant, that only of one of these prophetic works, the *dibre* of Jehu son of Hanani, is its insertion in the book of the kings of Israel expressly mentioned, whereas of the remainder nothing of the kind is stated. 5. The *dibre* Chozai (דִּבְרֵי חוֹזָי), indeed, 2 Chron. xxxiii. 19, are named along with "the words of the kings of Israel" (as in ver. 18) as historical sources for the reign of Manasseh, and thus plainly distinguished from the book of Kings, and by no means represented as part of it. Whether these *dibre* Chozai were actually the writing of an otherwise unknown prophet, Chozai or Chazai (possibly an abbreviation of חֲזָיָה; comp. Fürst, ii. 216), or the phrase be rather identical with דִּבְרֵי הַחֹזִים in the previous verse, so that an error in writing is to be assumed, and the original reading, according to the λόγοι τῶν ὁρώντων of the Sept., restored,—in any case, here is an independent prophetic book, distinct from the old book of Kings, which is not very favourable to the hypothesis that all these various writings belong to that historical work. 6. And the somewhat obscure and ambiguous phrase לְהִתְיַחֵשׂ after the form of quotation, "Are they not written in the words of Shemaiah the prophet and of Iddo the seer" (2 Chron. xii. 15; see above, No. 3), can afford no proof of the dependence of the two works to which it refers. For whether we interpret this enigmatical phrase by "on genealogy," or, supplying דָּוִד or בֵּית דָּוִיד, by "on the genealogy of the house of David,"[1] in no case does it appear an addition from which the dependence of the "words of Iddo the

[1] The latter assumption is rendered probable by the rendering of the Targumist: "in the genealogy of the house of David." It has, at all events, far more for it than the unmeaning καὶ πράξεις αὐτοῦ of the Sept. (which Movers, p. 179, labours in vain to reduce to a various reading of the original), or the no less unintelligible *et diligenter exposita* of the Vulg. Comp. also Fürst in p. q., p. 215, and in his Hebrew Lexicon under התיחש.

seer," that is, their belonging to a greater work of another kind, must be concluded; for not the place where those words of Iddo are to be found (Ew., Berth., etc.), but rather the end they are to serve,—their purpose, namely, to be a genealogy,—appears to have been intended by the preposition לְ. 7. Further, from the circumstance that "reference is made for the whole history of David, Solomon, Rehoboam, Jehoshaphat (as well as Uzziah) to prophetic writings, and likewise for the whole history of Asa, Amaziah, Jotham, Ahaz, and Josiah to the book of the kings of Israel and Judah" (Berth. p. xxxvi.), no argument can be drawn for the assumption of one connected historical work of which those prophetic writings were only separate facts. From that circumstance, it merely follows "that in some kings the prophetic writings, in others the history of the kingdom, contained everything important on their life and reign, and that the history of the kingdom presented also accounts concerning the action of the prophets in the kingdom, as the prophetic writings concerning the affairs of the kings" (Keil, p. 23). What grounds determined the Chronist to refer for the one king to the royal annals, and for the other to the prophetic writings, it is impossible to conjecture, and it would be equally impossible to ascertain, in the case of the dependence of both kinds of writing (so if the question were about only two ways of quoting one and the same greater work). 8. Lastly, if (by Bähr, in p. q., p. viii. ff.) the verbal agreement of certain sections declared by our Chronist to be taken from the writings of particular prophets, as Nathan, Shemaiah and Iddo, Isaiah and Chozai, with the sections of the books of Kings that are quoted as taken from the old royal annals of Israel or of Judah, is urged to make it probable "that the book of the kings of Judah consisted of the historical writings of several prophets or seers," this line of argument cannot be admitted as cogent. For Chronicles exhibits in the reigns of Solomon, Rehoboam, Abijah, Uzziah, and Manasseh, along with some things verbally agreeing with the books of Kings, whole series of accounts exclusively its own, for which the prophetic writings in question must have formed the source. And that a partly verbal accordance of their accounts with those of the old book of Kings takes place, only proves that this work was composed by the use of still older prophetic writings, to which a very high value belonged as contemporary records, but not that those prophetic writings formed integral parts of the book of Kings. It may be that the words of Nathan the prophet were taken in great part into his work by the later compiler of those *dibre hajjamim* from which the author of the canonical book of Kings mainly drew, and likewise the words (*res gestæ*, note-books) of Gad, Shemaiah, Iddo, etc. But must the independent existence of these old prophetic sources forthwith cease? Might not these prophetic books, also, like the *dibre hajjamim* or the "history of the kings of Israel and Judah" derived from them, if not collectively, yet in great part, have been preserved through the storms of the exile, to serve the collectors after the exile as sources and helps for their annalistic compilations? Where so many and so variously named sources are adduced, as in our author, it is most natural to suppose him actually to have access to a very rich field of original materials. The contrary supposition, which refers the constant change in his citations partly to unnecessary parade of literary knowledge and unmeaning fondness for a piebald multiplicity of terms, partly to inaccuracy or negligence, encounters far greater difficulties, and makes such a variety of hypothetical helps necessary, that it cannot be regarded as moving on the soil of sound historical investigation.

Moreover, it must be, and is confessed by the opponents of our hypothesis, for example by Bertheau, p. xxxviii., that our author, besides the sources actually cited, may have used an indefinite number of such works as he did not find it necessary to adduce. Thus, for his list of David's heroes (1 Chron. xi. 10–47), David's worthies in Hebron (xii.), the military and civil officers of this king (xxvii.), the families and divisions of the Levites, priests, singers, etc. (xxiii.–xxvi.), he certainly used old documents, which, however, he does not think it necessary expressly to adduce, perhaps because it was understood of itself that they were of an official kind, and therefore trustworthy (comp. for example, 2 Chron. xxxiv. 4, where the author makes Josiah mention at the feast of the Passover a כְּתָב of David and a מִכְתָּב of Solomon concerning the services of the Levites and priests, or the temple liturgy,—documents, without doubt, which he himself had used in those sections of his first book [xxiii.–xxvi.]), or which he did not cite, "because he had taken them wholly into his work" (Keil), so that there was no place for a reference to them for further details. That our canonical books of Samuel and Kings belong to these rich sources used by our author is still possible; for the frequent verbal coincidence of his accounts with those of these books, may in some cases rest on the direct use, as well as on the copying, of a common ancient source; and it would not be impossible that by the words of Samuel the seer (דִּבְרֵי שְׁמוּאֵל הָרֹאֶה) cited in 1 Chron. xxix. 29 our books of Samuel were meant. Yet the pretty numerous material as well as formal and verbal variations, which the parallel texts present almost everywhere, form a weighty counterpoise against this supposition; and what Movers, p. 95 ff., de Wette (*Einl.* § 192*a*), Ewald (*Gesch.* i. 238), Bleek (*Einl.* § 167, p. 400), and recently Graf (*Die geschichtl. Bücher*, p. 114 ff.) have adduced in its favour, appears, from the replies produced by Hävernick, Bertheau, and especially by Keil (*Einl.* § 144, 2), to be, if not quite refuted, yet shaken in such a degree, that far the greater probability lies on the side of those who exclude our books of Samuel and Kings from the sources used by the Chronist.

§ 6. CREDIBILITY OF THE CHRONIST.

The question of the credibility of our author would be simply answered by the remarks already made on his historical sources, and would admit of no unfavourable answer, if throughout and in every respect a faithful use of his sources may be presumed. That this praise can only be conceded to him in a limited sense, has been recently asserted, after the example of K. H. Graf (in p. q. p. 114 ff.), again by several critics, as Ed. Riehm (*Stud. und Krit.* 1868, ii. p. 376 ff.), H. Schultz (*Alttestamentl. Theol.* ii. p. 274 f.), H. Holtzmann (in Bunsen's *Bibelwerk*, vol. iv. part 2, p. 12 ff.), and even Bertheau (*Jahrb. f. deutsche Theol.* 1866, p. 159 f.). The latter had formerly defended the substantial credibility of the author, as one employing good old sources, and using them with sedulous care, against the blunt attacks of de Wette and Gramberg (who made the Chronist merely copy the books of Samuel and Kings, but in all places deviating from them, distorting them in an arbitrary manner, misinterpreting, embellishing, or supplementing by invented additions[1]), and thus almost without reserve accepted that which J. G. Dahler (*De libr. Paralip. auctoritate atque fide hist.*, Argentor. 1819), Movers (*Krit. Untersuch.*, etc.), Keil (*Apol. Versuch* and *Einl. ins A. T.*), Hävernick (*Einl.* 1839), Ewald, and others had brought forward on behalf of the Chronist.[2] On the contrary, he is now (*Jahrbücher f. d. Theol.* in p. q., in a review of Graf's work, and in art. "Chronik" in Schenkel's *Bibel-Lex.*) gone over to the modified reproduction of the de Wette-Gramberg view attempted by Graf, at least so far as to confess that he had not formerly estimated highly enough, nor duly considered, the proper action of the author of Chronicles; he had taken him for a more trustworthy and objective extractor from his sources than he really was. Th. Nöldecke has gone still farther, in his treatise on *Die Alttestamentl. Literat.* (1868, p. 59 ff.). By such sentences as, "All great wars mentioned only in Chronicles must be very suspicious," "his narrative is therefore very defective," "he proceeds very negligently, and often contradicts himself," and so on, he has almost wholly returned to the position of Gramberg, and has thereby incurred the severe censure even of F. Hitzig. The latter not long ago (in a conversation on Nöldecke's paper concerning the inscription of Mesha, king of Moab, in the Heidelberg *Jahrb. der Literat.* 1870, p. 437) expressed his surprise to hear Mr. Nöldecke assert that "the account 2 Chron. xx. is a strange story, only a transformation of 2 Kings iii., with the removal of difficulties, and the addition of a great deal of edifying matter." He further remarks: "This is the strangest thing that has occurred to the writer since Volkmar wished to see the Apostle Paul in the false prophet of the Apocalypse. Has Mr N ever thought of the origin of the valley of Jehoshaphat in Joel iv. 2? Has he

[1] De Wette, *Beitr. zur Einl. ins A. T.* i., Halle 1806, and *Lehrb. der hist.-krit. Einl.*, etc., 1817, 6th ed. 1845; C. P. W. Gramberg, *Die Chron. nach ihrem geschichtl. Charakter und ihrer Glaubwürdigkeit neu geprüft*, Halle 1823. Comp. also Gesenius, *Gesch. der Hebr. Sprache und Schrift*, 1815, § 12, p. 37 ff., and *Komment. zu Jes.*, 1821, i. 268 ff.

[2] *Kurzgef. exeg. Handb.*, Einl. p. xliii.: "That the author of Chronicles ever intentionally distorted the sense or made false statements does not appear from the comparison of the sections parallel with Samuel and Kings. The parallel sections rather warrant the assumption, that even where he imparts accounts and statements that are not found in the other books of the O. T., he adhered most closely to his sources," etc. Quite similar to this is the language of Dillmann in the art. "Chronik" in Herzog's *Real-Encycl.* p. 693.

read Movers on Chronicles? And is he always so bright, that he should stain the hypotheses of others? *Quis tulerit Gracchos?*" etc.

We cannot but see in this venomous onslaught of the Heidelberg theologian a chastisement on the whole deserved; for even in the more moderate and more carefully supported views of Graf there is expressed, in our opinion, a great deal of hypercritical arrogance and vehement prejudice against our author. Accordingly he appears as a biassed historian going to work in an unconscionable manner, idealizing, embellishing, and often capriciously transforming on a narrow Levitical principle, moved by the desire to write the history of the Jews, so that it shall be an impressive admonition to keep the commandments of God, especially to observe the ordinances of worship, and at the same time a solemn warning against apostasy from God. Instead of adhering closely to that which is found in his sources, he stamps on his work (which is a history of the Church more than of the people or kingdom) throughout his Levitical-priestly tendency, along with the characteristic spirit of his late age; he writes the history so as the variously-distorting and colouring mirror of the fourth century B.C. reflects it, and on behalf of the tastes and requirements of his contemporaries, seizes glaring colours, institutes striking contrasts, and handles the original material capriciously after his manner (comp. Berth. in the *Jahrbüchern für deutsche Theol.* in p. q.). Thus he makes use of the books of Samuel and Kings as if not the only, yet the principal sources, leaves out what appears to have no interest for his time and tendency, and alters their reports in various places as he requires, by means of enlarging insertions, various changes of meaning, and recastings, so that the number of passages borrowed by him from these books appears much smaller than it really is. Such is, above all, his whole history of David (1 Chron. x.–xxix.), a work formed by the manifold transformation of the corresponding account in the books of Samuel; only the lists of names inserted therein, especially those in ch. xxiii.–xxvii., are derived from special sources,—by no means, however, more respectable nor earlier than the exile; and the words of Samuel the seer, of Nathan the prophet, and of Gad the seer, mentioned 1 Chron. xxix. 29, are not special prophetic writings of a high age, but mere sections of our canonical books of Samuel. Thus it cannot be determined how far those sources are only freely and inaccurately used by him; and this applies as well to the sources of the history of David as to the genealogical sources used by him in the time before David (in 1 Chron. i.–ix.). Farther, our Chronist's representation of the history of Solomon (2 Chron. i.–ix.) is merely elaborated on the basis of 2 Kings i.–xi., with the omission of Solomon's secular doings, his palace building, and idolatry; only in viii. 36 gleams forth a peculiar source different from 1 Kings ix. 17–19, which is used by him. Such sources also, differing from the text of the book of Kings, are used in the sections on Rehoboam (2 Chron. xi. 5–xii. 18–23), Abijah, Asa, Jehoshaphat, Ahaziah, Joash, Uzziah, Jotham, and Hezekiah. Throughout the Chronist has made use of these sources, which are all to be referred to the "book of the kings of Israel and Judah" lying at the root of the canonical books of Kings, in accordance with his object. This transforming bias of the Chronist appears most surprising in the narrative of the fall of Athaliah by the co-operation of the priests and Levites (xxiii.); as also in the embellished accounts of the successful wars of Abijah against the northern kingdom (xiii.), in which, at the most, the statement of the three cities conquered by him (ver. 19) rests on old written sources; and likewise in the account of Solomon's ascending the throne (1 Chron. xxviii. 29), the deviations of which from 1 Kings i. are due to the inventive turn of the Chronist, and not to any written or oral traditions whatever; as well as in the accounts concerning the divisions of the priests, Levites, and singers in David's preparation for the temple, and in the building and consecration of it by Solomon, wherein it is evidently the design of the writer to represent the relations of these religious officials as already existing at the time of the founding of the temple.

The πρῶτον ψεῦδος of Graf's accusations and suspicions of the historical character of our work consists in the totally unfounded presupposition, that the author made use of the canonical books of Samuel and Kings almost alone, as sources, and that his deviations from them are to be ascribed to the caprice of the redactor. We have already shown it to be extremely probable that our author made no use whatever of these books (§ 5). The number of passages in which there is a verbal coincidence of his accounts with those of the older historical books is comparatively small, and even these may without much difficulty be regarded as flowing from a common source, so that the assumption that they belong to the sources of our author appears by no means necessary. But even if it were proved, both that he drew from the historical books of the canon, and that he made a free use of them with an occasional departure from them, his credit as a trustworthy historian in all essential matters would suffer no more than it would from a similar use of his other materials.

1. For his parenetic tendency permitted him, if he did not interfere with the objective historical fact, in numerous cases to transform the old accounts to suit his peculiar Levitical-ecclesiastical pragmatism, to which, in respect of the times of our author, as full a privilege must be conceded as to the theocratico-prophetic pragmatism of the older historians (comp. the examples to be adduced under No. 4). And that the non-subjective mode of our historian, compared with the more objective fashion of the books of Kings, led to no distortions, falsifications, or arbitrary transformations of facts, is manifest from the circumstance already noticed, that he has not kept back all that was at his command on behalf of his pragmatic tendency, and has often omitted matters of consequence for his point of view, so that he may be justly charged with a certain degree of inconsistency (comp. § 4).

2. A quite harmless and allowable class of alterations, that our author makes in his materials, refers to the genealogical lists, especially those of the first part, where he in part arranges anew and groups in certain proportions the lists of names taken from the Pentateuch, not so much to aid the memory as to exhibit the numerical law and symbolic import of these parts of sacred history. Thus he not only in ch. i. keeps apart the ten patriarchs from Adam to Noah and the ten from Noah to Shem, but derives, certainly without defining or marking this by giving express prominence to the number, 70 nations from Noah, 70 families from Abraham, and 70 descendants from Judah (i. 28, ii. 25), refers the eight sons of Jesse to the sacred number seven, and leaves out, partly from a religious and symbolic consideration, the tribe of Dan repeatedly in his enumeration of the tribes (see on vii. 12). It is obvious that by none of these idealizing changes of the genealogical matter that come to hand is a proper distortion of the historical relations effected, and still less by so many other less intentional alterations, such as the transpositions and reductions in the series of names in Genesis; for example, iv. 1 ff.

3. Another class of alterations, which proceed as little from caprice or culpable negligence, belongs to the linguistic department. It consists in the exchange of many phrases and turns belonging to the old Hebrew for the corresponding phrases of the later language, and has in most cases no deeper ground than such orthographic changes as the *scriptio plena* instead of the *defectiva*, and the reverse—the introduction of later, Aramaizing forms instead of the older ones. To this belong the change of older formations, as מַמְלָכָה, תְּחִנָּה, עוֹלָם, etc., into the later מַלְכוּת, תַּחֲנוּן, עֵילוֹם; the change of the construction by omission of the *infin. absol.* with the verb *finit.*, or by the use of the preposition אֶל or of ה *loc.* in verbs of motion, as בּוֹא, הָלַךְ, עָלָה; the avoiding or paraphrasing of certain pregnant constructions of the older language, and the like (comp. the collection of numerous examples of all these in Movers, p. 200 ff.; and after him, in Hävernick and Keil, *Einl.* § 142, p. 482 ff.). These deviations from the old forms of the sources are of the less importance, as they are carried to a very small extent, and the character of the original may almost always be clearly distinguished from that of the chronicle.

4. Of scarcely more importance are those changes occasioned by the religious and dogmatic views of the author, which, without touching the facts, bring out new aspects of the religious side of the history. For example, in the account of David's numbering of the people, where the author (1 Chron. xxi. 1) refers that which in the older account (2 Sam. xxi. 1) is represented as the direct effect of the divine wrath to the subordinate activity of Satan, and where he represents God's "being entreated" at the end of the older account (2 Sam. xxiv. 25) in a more concrete and pictorial manner as an "answering from heaven by fire upon the altar of burnt-offering" (comp. also 2 Chron. vi. 1 with 1 Kings viii. 54 f.); or as in such pragmatic reflective additions as 2 Chron. vii. 11 ("all that he wished to do in the house of Jehovah and in his own house was successful," for which the older parallel 1 Kings ix. 1 has only "what he wished to do," etc.); likewise 2 Chron. viii. 11 (the ground on which Solomon built a separate house for Pharaoh's daughter; comp. 1 Kings ix. 24); 2 Chron. xxii. 7 (giving prominence to the divine dispensation occasioning the death of king Ahaziah; comp. 2 Kings

viii. 29); 2 Chron. xviii. 31 ("And Jehovah helped him, and God drove them from him;" comp. the account omitting all such remarks, 1 Kings xxii. 32 f.); also 1 Chron. x. 13 f. (remark on Saul's deserved death; comp. 1 Sam. xxxi. 12), and xi. 3 (reference to Samuel's prophetic announcement of the coronation of David at Hebron; comp. 2 Sam. v. 3).

5. A further class of deviations from the older parallel accounts involves a number of actually erroneous statements, that are mostly to be ascribed to old corruptions of the text either found in the sources of the Chronist or introduced into his work by the fault of negligent transcribers, and therefore cannot affect the character and credibility of the author. The only nearly certain example of an error on his part, arising apparently from geographical ignorance, is the explanation of the Tarshish ships of the Red Sea as being designed to trade to Tarshish (2 Chron. ix. 21 and xx. 36). This appears, according to 1 Kings x. 22, xxii. 49, to be a real misinterpretation, which can be removed no more by an identification of Tarshish with Ophir than by the supposition that our author was acquainted with a place of the name of Tarshish (thus, an eastern Tartessus) in Ophir or its neighbourhood (comp. Bähr on 1 Kings x. 22, and the exeg. expl. given on 2 Chron. ix. 21). If we except this one passage, all else of an erroneous nature in his text is most probably to be reduced to errors in copying, that either existed in his sources or were introduced into his text. Under this head come especially the numbers which deviate from those in the books of Samuel and Kings, on account of which it has been thought necessary (by de Wette, Gramberg, etc.) to impute to him arbitrary exaggeration of the greatness of Israel before the exile, of his armies, population, treasures, offerings, etc., without considering that the older historical books often exhibit notorious corruptions of the text in numbers (for example, the 30,000 chariots of the Philistines in 1 Sam. xiii. 5, or the 70 men and 50,000 men of Bethshemesh in 1 Sam. vi. 19; comp. more examples of this kind in Wellhausen, *Der Text der Bücher Samuelis*, etc., pp. 20, 66, 81, 133, 219, etc.), and that in some cases Chronicles gives the smaller and more credible number; for example, 2 Chron. ix. 25, where it mentions 4,000 stalls for Solomon's horses, which is certainly more correct than the parallel text 1 Kings v. 6, where the number of these horses and stalls amounted to 40,000 (comp. Bähr's crit. note on the p., p. 26). As notorious instances of textual corruption in numbers not due to the author, are to be noted 1 Chron. xxi. 5, where the 1,100,000 men in Israel rests on a simple clerical error for 800,000; 2 Chron. xvi. 1, where, instead of the 36th, the 16th year of Asa is to be read (as in the previous verse instead of the 35th the 15th); 2 Chron. xx. 2, where the 42 years of King Ahaziah's age, instead of the 22 of 2 Kings viii. 26, appear to have arisen from the exchange of מ and כ. That the use of the letters for numbers is very ancient, and was adopted long before the Masoretic recension, is proved by the circumstance that the Sept. exhibits in its text a great deal of the errors in numbers arising from the exchange of letters, and indeed not merely in Chronicles, but in various other books; for example, in Ezra ii. 69, where it reproduces the error of 61,000, instead of 41,000, Darics from the Hebrew text (comp. Neh. vii. 70–72), and often also in the books of Samuel, etc. Along with these numerical errors resting on the corruption of the text, there are a great many cases in which the Chronist himself or his source before him shows decided differences in his numbers from the other canonical books; and these are by no means at once to be ascribed to the boastful and exaggerating bias of the author. Rather, as Keil (*Komm.* p. 30) justly points out, are we to bear in mind, with regard to these different numbers, *a.* "That they are generally round numbers determined only to thousands, depend therefore not on actual numbering but on loose estimates of contemporaries, and assert nothing more than that the size of the army and the number of the slain or the captives was rated very high;" and *b.* "That in the quantity of gold and silver collected by David for the building of the temple,—100,000 shekels or hundredweight (כִּכָּרִים) of gold and 1,000,000 hundredweight of silver, 1 Chron. xxii. 13,—the actual amount cannot be ascertained, because we know not the weight of the shekel of that day,"—a circumstance that must be taken into account in many other differences, as the exegesis of the several passages will show.

6. Actual deviations from the older historical works, but still none that can be charged to our author as wilful distortions or falsifications, are contained in many of the speeches ascribed to David, Abijah, Asa, and other kings, or even to private persons, especially prophets; for example, the speeches of David given in 1 Chron. xiii. 2 f., xv. 12 f., xxviii. 2–10, xxix. 1 ff., 10 ff., which have little or no parallel in the books of Samuel; that of Abijah, 2 Chron.

xiii. 4–12; of Asa, 2 Chron. xiv. 11; of Azariah son of Oded, 2 Chron. xv. 1–7; of Hezekiah, 2 Chron. xxxii. 7 f., etc. That the greater number of those speeches, if not all, were contained in the sources of our author, may be concluded with sufficient certainty from the one circumstance, that three speeches of Solomon which he communicates (2 Chron. i. 8–10, vi. 4–11, 12–42) occur in almost the same words in the book of Kings, whence his fidelity and care in the reproduction of such pieces are manifest. Here the speeches of different persons distinguish themselves in a characteristic manner by their line of thought, their figures and turns; the peculiar speech and style of the Chronist is stamped upon them only in a comparatively small degree. This is very striking in three of David's speeches, namely, in the longer addresses relating to the future building of the temple by Solomon (1 Chron. xxii. 7–16, xxviii. 2–22, xxix. 1–5). Here the author appears, as the manifold conformity of that which is put in the mouth of David with his peculiarities in thought, speech, etc., shows, to have acted pretty freely, and without resting on sources to have attempted an ideal reproduction of the thoughts moving the soul of the aged king and uttered by him. But the prayer of David annexed to the last of these addresses, 1 Chron. xxix. 10–19, proves itself to be derived from ancient sources by its manifold coincidence with the Psalms of David (see on vers. 11 and 15), especially ver. 18, with which it agrees in the characteristic accumulation of predicates of God. And all the other speeches in question show similar traces of old original peculiarities foreign or remote from the Chronist's manner of thought, speech and style; for example, that of Abijah, 2 Chron. xiii. 4–12, that, among other accordances with our author, exhibits in the phrases אֲנָשִׁים רֵקִים and בְּנֵי בְלִיַּעַל clear marks of their connection with the usage of the time of David and Solomon; that of Hezekiah, 2 Chron. xxxii. 7 f., in which the phrase זְרוֹעַ בָּשָׂר reminds us of his intercourse with the prophet Isaiah (Isa. xxxi. 3); lastly, the shorter or longer utterances handed down by various prophets, which generally contain much that is original, especially that of Azariah son of Oded addressed to King Asa, 2 Chron. xv. 1–7, which, by its remarkable coincidence with parts of the *Oratio eschatologica* of Christ, as Matt. xxiv. 6 f., Luke xii. 19, proves itself to be an old independent creation of the genuine prophetic stamp (comp. C. P. Caspari, *Der syrisch-ephraim. Krieg*, Christiania 1849, p. 55 ff.). Thus it is essentially the same with the speeches given by our historian as with those in the other historical books, from the Pentateuch and Judges down to the Acts of the Apostles and the Gospel of John. The original and subjective proper to the late reporter appears in them connected as matter and form, as seed and shell, without any sharp distinction of the reporter's addition from the original text. But a certain formative influence of the original type proper to the old source appears in the diction and style of the younger writer. And as the glass transmits no light without imparting its peculiar hue, or the instrument conveys no tone without its own individual modification, so the physiognomy of the speeches in our book exhibits that mutual influence of the proper individuality of the author and of the materials that have come down to him from the past, that interchange of subjectivity and objectivity, which displays itself in a similar way in the speeches of Judges and Kings (especially the prophetical; comp. Delitzsch, *Komm. zu Jesaja*, Einl. p. xiv. f.), and also in the New Testament, in the speeches of Christ in John, and of Peter, Stephen, and Paul in the Acts of the Apostles.

7. The last class of deviations chargeable to the subjectivity of the Chronist relates to the descriptions of religious festivals, particularly in the history of David (1 Chron. xv., xvi.), Solomon (2 Chron. v.–vii.), Hezekiah (xxix.–xxxi.), and Josiah (xxxv.), where the same circumstantial description of certain acts of worship, especially of the playing and singing of the Levites and priests, constantly recurs, and always in essentially the same rhetorical dress, and with the same phrases and liturgical formulæ (comp. § 2 above). It may seem at first sight that the author in such descriptions dates back the liturgical usages and ceremonies of his own age, and transfers not only his Levitical and priestly mode of thought, but the religious customs and performances of his time, uncritically to the worship of the reigns of David, Solomon, Hezekiah, etc. But the suspicions in this direction expressed by de Wette, Gramberg, and recently by Graf, Nöldecke, Holtzmann, and others, rest on a twofold misconception—(1) That the sacrificial worship, according to the rules of Leviticus, or the introduction of music and singing of psalms, dates from the exile; and (2) that our author, whenever he treats of the occurrence of such usages, writes wholly without ancient

sources, and so lays himself open to the charge of arbitrary falsifications of history in favour of his own views and times. On the contrary, the essentials of the form of worship undoubtedly go back to the times of Moses, or at all events, long before the exile; and the modification which our author makes in his accounts of the festivals consists only in individual touches and details, whereby he endeavours to trace out for himself and his readers a clear picture of the actual events. That he herein allowed himself a certain drawing together of far-separated times and customs, a presentation of earlier usages in the light of the current times,—in short, a modernizing process in minor particulars,—does not on the whole mar the credibility of his narrative. It may be that in 1 Chron. xvi. 8–36, in describing the solemn conveyance of the ark to Jerusalem, he lets a psalm be introduced by Asaph and his brethren which David had not literally composed for this solemnity, but which was an ideal reproduction of the psalm then sung, but springing from a later time; that he allowed himself here the same sort of substitution as if a modern historian were to set back Luther's "Ein feste burg," etc., from the year 1530, or from the time of the Augsburg Diet, to which its origin was really due, till the year 1521, or the time of the Diet of Worms. In like manner, what is said (1 Chron. xxviii. 11–19) of the several materials and vessels of the future temple which David reckoned up and handed over to Solomon may involve a proleptic idealizing and altering of the transaction, which forms a deviation not only from the far simpler and shorter account in the book of Kings, but from that which lay before the author regarding the last acts of the reign of David. And so it may be with several other details of religious action in the statements of our author; for example, his notice of the temple gates and porticos under David (1 Chron. xxvi. 16–18), of the reform of Hezekiah (2 Chron. xxix. ff.), etc. On the whole, these freer combinations of historical events, corresponding with the priestly Levitical pragmatism and parenetic tendency of the author, derogate nothing from the credibility of his narrative. It remains, therefore, highly probable, that much if not most of these modifications of the history before the exile had its root in the sources before the author, particularly in the "book of the kings of Israel and Judah," the harmony of which, with his views and predilections, must neither be exaggerated nor underrated (comp. Del. in p. q., p. xvi.).

On the whole, a marked subjective colouring of his narrative in the direction of the priestly-Levitical standpoint may be ascribed to our author; he may be charged with having less aptitude for quiet, strictly objective conception and presentation of his materials than his predecessors, the authors of the books of Samuel and Kings, and with putting forward his didactic-moralizing bent often too strongly, and not always free from a legal externality of thought and intuition. But it appears unwarranted to reproach him with a want of love for the truth or an uncritical levity in dealing with facts, or to charge him with wilful invention or falsification of history; for the solid foundation of old original tradition gleams forth at every step of his narrative, and conveys, even where he goes farthest from the parallel text of the books of Kings, and brings in the most important supplements to their report, the impression of the highest trustworthiness: for example, in the accounts of Rehoboam's building of forts and his domestic concerns (2 Chron. xi. 5 ff., 18 ff.); in the statements concerning the three cities conquered by Abijah, and concerning his family (xiii. 19–21); in the history of Jehoshaphat, so full of concrete details of the most trustworthy kind (xvii.–xx.); in the surprisingly exact yet obviously authentic statements concerning Amaziah's troops hired from Israel, and the plundering raid in which they engaged after they were discharged (xxv. 5 ff.); in the history of Manasseh, for the details of which he certainly, not without grounds, refers to older sources, as the book of the kings of Israel and the words of Chozai (xxxiii.), etc. The Levitical-priestly and legal external stamp of his history may be regarded as a characteristic mean between the prophetic pragmatism of the older historians, as the authors of the books of Samuel and Kings, and the pharisaic pragmatism of the writers after the canon, as the author of the 2 Maccabees, or Josephus.[1] Yet he stands incomparably nearer to his prophetic predecessors of the time of or immediately before the exile, than to these Epigoni of all Old Testament history; and not a trace is to be discovered in him, either

[1] Comp. H. Schultz, *Alttestamentl. Theol.* ii. p. 274 f., and Oehler's remark on this passage (*Allg. liter. Anzeig.* 1870, Nov., p. 340): "The way in which here (in Chron.) the doctrine of retribution comes forth, forms the transition to the pharisaic rejection of it, as the comparison of the second book of Maccabees exhibits also in this point the partition between Judaism in the canon and after it."

of the spiritless externality or fanatical rigorism of the doctrine of retribution as it appears in such apocryphal books as Judith, 2 Maccabees, etc., or of the Rome-favouring, and therefore anti-national and untheocratic, pragmatism of the Pharisee Josephus.

Remark.—With respect to the text of Chronicles, Jerome perceived that the greatest critical care must be taken, especially on account of the many names which are presented in it, and have been variously corrupted and distorted in the Sept. and the Itala: "*Ita et in Græcis et Latinis codicibus hic nominum liber vitiosus est, ut non tam Hebræa quam barbara quædam et Sarmatica nomina congesta arbitrandum sit.*" Thus he speaks in his *Præf. in lib. Paralip. juxta Sept. interp.* (Opp. t. x. p. 432, edit. Vall.); and he relates there that he employed a learned Jew of Tiberias, and with him compared the text, "*a vertice ut aiunt usque ad extremum unguem.*" In the relative fidelity and accuracy that otherwise notoriously exists in this part of the Alexandrine version (and the Itala, which agrees with it word for word),[1] this observation, which he was compelled to extend on further examination to the numerical data of Chronicles, and to many other details, is certainly remarkable. In a still higher degree must he have been surprised, on a more extended knowledge of languages and an exacter method of critical investigation, by the state of the text of another old version of our book, the Syriac version or Peshito (with its omissions of whole series of names, its various gaps and interpolations, its transpositions and occasional arbitrary deviations from the original).[2] The acknowledgment of no small uncertainty of the original Hebrew text itself is forced upon us in view of this serious corruption of the oldest versions, in which the later of necessity participate; for example, the Arabic version derived from the Peshito, likewise the comparatively young Targum originating scarcely before the seventh century (published, with a Lat. vers., by M. F. Beck, *Augustæ Vindel.* 1680, and with greater critical care by Dav. Wilkins, *Amstelædam.* 1715, 4); and hence arises for expositors the equally important and difficult problem of a frequent correction of the Masoretic text, to be cautiously executed and wisely limited, according to those versions, as well as the parallel passages in the older books of the canon. This necessity of an occasional amendment in numbers and names, imposed by the peculiarity of the text of Chronicles, was acknowledged by J. Alb. Bengel; for on 2 Chron. xxviii. 1 (comp. xxix. 1) he adds the marginal note, *Hic videtur lectio Græca, quæ viginti quinque annos Achazo tribuit, præferenda Hebræo.* "Errors may have more easily crept into the books of Chronicles, because they were not publicly read as the books of Moses," etc. (Contributions to Bengel's exposition, and his remarks on the *Gnomon N. T.* from manuscript notes, published by Dr. Osk. Wächter, Leips. 1865, p. 18.) To this well-grounded conjecture regarding the very numerous textual errors of our book Bertheau also points (*Komm.* p. xlvii.): "It appears as if the same careful regard was not paid to the text by the Jews in older times, to which we owe the faithful transmission of that form of the text of most other books of the Bible that came into general acceptance about the time of Christ; comp. for example, 1 Chron. xvii. 18, 21; 2 Chron. ii. 9, x. 14, 16, xx. 25, xxvi. 5." That, moreover, the endeavour to refer the deviations of the Chronist from the other historical books of the Old Testament to mere corruptions of the text may be carried too far, and has been carried too far perhaps by Movers (p. 50 ff.), at all events by Laur. Reinke in his *Beiträgen zur Erkl. des Alten T.*, Abhandl. I., has been justly pointed out by Davidson, *Introd.* ii. p. 114 sq.

[The only error here traced to the Chronist, and supposed to arise from his ignorance of ancient geography, is the statement that ships of Tarshish (1 Kings x. 22, xxii. 49) were ships trading to Tarshish (2 Chron. ix. 21, xx. 36). It may turn out, however, that the error

[1] Movers (p. 93) calls the translation of Chronicles in the Sept. "a careful, skilfully-performed, and strictly literal version;" he praises it as "one of the best efforts of these translators," and as "by far surpassing that of the books of Samuel and Kings proceeding from another author." On the close adherence of the old Itala to the text of the Sept., comp. Röntsch, *Itala und Vulgata* (Marb. 1869); Fr. Kaulen, *Geschichte der Vulgata* (Mainz 1868), p. 137 ff.; and Ernst Ranke, *Par Palimpsestorum Wirceburgensium*, etc., Vindob. 1871.

[2] As examples of omission of long series of names, comp. 1 Chron. ii. 45, 47–49, iv. 7 ff.; also of leaving out other long sections, 1 Chron. xxvi. 13–27, 2 Chron. iv. 11–17, xxix. 10–19; of interpolations, 1 Chron. xii. 1, 17–19, xvi. 3, 42; of transpositions, 1 Chron. xii. 15, 2 Chron. xxviii. 23–25; of deviations from the text or very free translations, 1 Chron. ii. 52, iv. 12–18, iv. 33–39, 2 Chron. xxii. 19, etc. Comp. Bertheau, p. xlviii.; and for the like peculiarities of the Arabic version derived from it, Roediger, *de orig. et indole Arab. librorum V. T. historic. interpretationis*, Hal. 1829, p. 104.

lies with the modern critic rather than with the ancient chronicler. It is recorded that Pharaoh Neko (617–601 B.C.) employed Phœnician mariners to sail from the Arabian Gulf round Africa, and return by the Pillars of Hercules (Herod. iv. 42),—a voyage which was accomplished *in three years.* Herodotus accepts the fact, though he discredits the statement, that in sailing round Africa they had the sun on the right,—a statement which goes to prove the veracity of the reporters. And until it is proved that the Phœnicians were not acquainted with this way of reaching Tarshish by hugging the shore of Africa, and bartering as they went along for ivory and other African commodities, the geographical error has not been brought home to this ancient and otherwise accredited writer. (See further on the passages in the *Comm.*) We merely add to what has been here so ably and thoughtfully said on the general question of credibility, that the supposed bias or leaning of the writer of Chronicles is due not to any real narrowness or onesidedness, but to the necessity of having some distinct and important end in going over the same ground as the former historical works. This end is that which justifies the production of another history of the past times. The chronicler, we have no doubt, had the Pentateuch and the former prophets before him, containing the history of the dealings of God with man from the beginning, to the fall of the kingdom of Judah by the capture of the city of David and the burning of the temple of Solomon. He could have no reason for going over any part of this ground, unless he had some new aspect of the history to signalize, and some new lesson to convey to the people of God on returning from the captivity. This new thing is the distinct and exclusive history of the kingdom of David, with its peculiar arrangements for the worship of the temple, in which the orders of priests and Levites were established, and the masters of song took a prominent part. This is to be the system of things until it has given birth to a new economy or development of the kingdom of God on earth. And the new lesson, which is indeed an old lesson, is the uniform dependence of national prosperity and progress on intelligent and voluntary walking with God in all His ordinances and commandments. Chronicles therefore stands to the older history as Deuteronomy to the preceding four books of Moses, or as John to the synoptical Gospels. It would have no warrant for its place in the canon, if it did not show an object distinct from that of the older history; and instead of ascribing its peculiar characteristic to the idiosyncrasy of the author, it behoves us to discern in it the special purpose for which it was appended to the previous record. We do not expand this hint at present, but leave it to the consideration of the reader. With regard, moreover, to the psalm committed by David to Asaph, 1 Chron. xvi. 7, for thanking the Lord, see on the passage.—J. G. M.]

§ 7. LITERATURE.

Neither the exegetical nor the critical literature of this book is very rich; indeed, there is scarcely one portion of the Old Testament that has found fewer labourers either in the one respect or the other. The older Jewish commentators shrank from the many difficulties which the genealogies of the first chapters presented. Yet a tolerably full commentary on our book has been ascribed to Rashi (R. Solomon Isaaki, † 1105), which, however, according to J. Weisse in *Kerem Chemed* (Prague 1841; comp. Fürst, *Bibl. Jud.* ii. 85), cannot proceed from this celebrated Rabbinical scholar of the Middle Ages. Other Rabbinical commentaries are those of Joseph ben David Aben Jechija (comp. the edit. of D. Wilkins, *Paraphrasis Chaldaica in ii. lib. Chron. auctore R. Josepho*, Amstel. 1715), and of Isaac ben R. Sol. Jabez; comp. Carpzov. *Introd. in Vet. T.* p. 298; also R. Simon's *Hist. Critique du V. Test.*, Par. 1680, p. 30.

Of the Church Fathers, Jerome (only in a cursory and meagre way in his *Quæstiones Hebr. in Chron.*, Opp. t. iii. 851 sq.), Theodoret, and Procopius of Gaza have commented on Chronicles; comp. *Theodoreti* ἐρωτήσεις εἰς β. α΄κ. β΄ Παραλειπ., Opp. edit. Schulze, t. i. p. 554 ff., and *Procopii Gaz. scholia in libb. Reg. et in Paralip.*, edit. Jo. Meursius., Lugd. Bat. 1620, 4.—A "Latin commentary on Chronicles of the 9th century" has been published by Abr. Rahmer, Thorn 1866.

Modern expositors since the Reformation.—None of the Reformers have treated Chronicles exegetically, not even Brenz, by whom there are commentaries on the collective historical books of the Old Testament. The expository writings of the sixteenth and seventeenth centuries are mostly collected in M. Pole, *Synopsis criticorum*, etc., Lond. 1669 ff.—Special prominence is merited by *Lud. Lavateri Comment. in Paralip.*, Heidelb. 1599, on account of the very careful treatment of the genealogical lists. Comp. also Victorin Strigel, *Comm. in libb. Sam.*, *Reg.*, *et Paralip.*, Lips. 1591; Erasm. Sarcerius, *Comm. in lib. Chron.*, Basil. 1560; and the Catholic commentaries of Nic. Serrarius (*Comm. in lib. Reg. et Paralip.*, Lugd. Bat. 1618), Casp. Sanctius (*in Paralip. ll. ii.*, Antw. 1624, Lugd. 1632), Jac. Bonfrère (*Comm. in libr. Reg. et Paralip.*, Tornac. 1643). Likewise M. Fr. Beck, *Paraphr. Chaldaica ii. libr. Chron.*, Aug. Vindel. 1680, 83.

Of the eighteenth century: Aug. Calmet's *Commentaire litéral sur tous les livres de l'anc. et nouv. Test.*, Par. 1707 ff.—Jo. Clerici, *Comment. in Hagiogr.*, Amstel. 1731.—Joh. H. Michaelis, *Uberiores adnot. in Hagiographos V. T. libros*, Hal. 1720, vol. iii. (the first book of Chronicles treated by J. H. Michaelis, the second by J. J. Rambach).—H. B. Stark, *Notæ selectæ in Pent.*, *Jos.*, *Jud.*, *Sam.*, *Reg.*, *Chron.*, *Esr.*, *et Neh.*, Lips. 1714.—Chr. Starke's *Synopsis*, part iii. 2d edit., Leipz. 1756.—J. D. Michaelis, *Uebers. des Alt. Test. in Anmerkungen für Ungelehrte*, part xii., 1785.

Of the nineteenth century: J. B. D. Maurer, *Comm. gram. crit. in V. T.* vol. i., Lips. 1835.—E. Bertheau, *Die Bücher der Chronik erklärt* (fifteenth issue of the *Kurzgef. exeget. Handbuch zum A. T.*), Leipz., Brockhaus, 1865.—C. F. Keil, *Bibl. Komm. über die nachexilischen Geschichtsbücher: Chron.*, *Ezr.*, *und Esth.* (part v. of the *Bibl. Komment. über das A. T.*), Leipz., Dörffl., and Franke, 1870 [translated in Clark's Foreign Theological Library].—B. Neteler, *Die Bücher der biblischen Chronik, übersetzt und erklärt*, Münster, Coppenrath, 1872 (second issue by this publisher of the General Commentary on the Holy Scriptures of the Old Testament on Catholic Principles).

Introductory critical monographs:—*a.* Of destructive tendency: De Wette, *Beiträge zur Einleitung ins A. T.*, part i., Leipz. 1806 (comp. above, § 6).—C. P. W. Gramberg, *Die Chronik nach ihrem geschichtlichen Charakter und ihrer Glaubwürdigkeit geprüft*, Halle 1823.—K. H. Graf, *Die geschichtlichen Bücher des A. T.*, two historico-critical discussions, Leipz. 1866, p. 114 ff.

b. Of apologetic tendency: J. G. Dahler, *De libr. Paralip. auctoritate et fide historica*, Argentor. 1819.—E. F. Keil, *Apol. Versuch über die Bücher der Chronik und über die Integrität des Buches Esra*, Berl. 18[illegible]3.—F. C. Movers, *Kritische Untersuchungen über die bibl. Chronik*, Bonn 1834.—M. Stuart, *Critical History and Defence of the O. Test. Canon* (concerning especially the Pentateuch, the writings of the prophets, and of Solomon, Esther, and Chronicles), Andover, U. S., 1845.—Bertheau, Art. "Chronik" in Schenkel's *Bibellexicon*, vol. i. p. 528 ff. (also in his critique of Graf's monogr. in the *Jahrb. für deutsche Theol.* 1866, p. 158 ff.).

Exegetical and critical monographs on particular passages: B. Kennicott, *Comparatio capitis undecimi libri 1 Chron. cum. cap. quinto libri 2 Samuelis*, in *Diss. super ratione textus Hebraici V. T.*, *ex Angl. Lat. vertit G. A. Teller*, Lips. 1756.—Jul. Wellhausen, *De gentibus et familiis Judæis, quæ 1 Chron. ii.-iv. enumerantur*, Göttingen 1870.—Seb. Schmid, *De literis Eliæ ad Joramum*, Argentor. 1717 (on 2 Chron. xxi. 12–15).—C. P. Caspari, *Der syrisch-ephraimitische Krieg unter Jotham und Ahas*, Christiania 1849 (especially on 2 Chron. xxvii., xxviii.).—K. H. Graf, *Die Gefangenschaft und Bekehrung Manasse's* 2 Chron. xxxiii., *Theol. Stud. u. Krit.* 1859, part iii. p. 467 ff.—Against him: E. Gerlach, *Die Gefangenschaft and Bekehrung Manasse's ebendas.*, 1861, part iii. p. 503 ff., and L. Reinke, *Die Geschichte des Königs Manasse und die darin liegende angebliche Schwierigkeit* (in vol. viii. of his *Beiträge zur Erklärung des A. T.*, 1872, p. 115 ff.).—Comp. also Eberh. Schrader, *Die Keilinschriften und das Alte Test.*, Giessen 1872, pp. 238-243; which excellent work, like the papers on this subject by the same author in the *Zeitschrift der Deutschen morgenländ. Gesellschaft*, and in the *Theol. Stud. u. Krit.* (1869, 70, 71), contains rich monographic contributions to the exposition as well of the other historical books of the Old Testament as especially of Chronicles.

THE BOOKS OF CHRONICLES.

FIRST BOOK.

§ 1. GENEALOGICAL TABLES OR PEDIGREES, WITH SHORT HISTORICAL STATEMENTS INTERSPERSED.—Ch. i.–ix.

a. Genealogies of the Patriarchs from Adam to Isaac's Sons Israel and Edom, with the Posterity of the Latter till the Times of the Kings, Ch. i.

1–3 Adam, Sheth, Enosh. Kenan, Mahalalel, Jered. Henoch, Methushelah,
4, 5 Lamech. Noah, Shem, Ham, and Japheth. The sons of Japheth: Gomer,
6 and Magog, and Madai, and Javan, and Tubal, and Meshech, and Tiras. And
7 the sons of Gomer: Ashkenaz, and Riphath,[1] and Togarmah. And the sons of
8 Javan: Elisha, and Tarshishah, Kittim, and Rodanim.[2] The sons of Ham:
9 Cush and Mizraim, Put and Kanaan. And the sons of Kush: Seba, and
Havilah, and Sabta, and Rama, and Sabtecha. And the sons of Rama: Sheba
10 and Dedan. And Kush begat Nimrod; he began to be a hero on the earth.
11 And Mizraim begat the Ludim,[3] and the Anamim, and the Lehabim, and the
12 Naphtuhim. And the Pathrusim, and the Kasluhim, of whom came the
13 Pelishtim, and the Kaphtorim. And Kanaan begat Zidon, his first-born, and
14, 15 Heth. And the Jebusite, and the Amorite, and the Girgashite. And the
16 Hivite, and the Arkite, and the Sinite. And the Arvadite, and the Zemarite,
17 and the Hamathite. The sons of Shem: Elam, and Asshur, and Arpakshad,
18 and Lud, and Aram, and Uz, and Hul, and Gether, and Meshech.[4] And
19 Arpakshad begat Shelah, and Shelah begat Heber. And to Heber were
born two sons; the name of the one was Peleg [division]; for in his days was
20 the earth divided; and his brother's name was Joktan. And Joktan begat
21 Almodad, and Sheleph, and Hazarmaveth, and Jerah. And Hadoram, and
22, 23 Uzal, and Diklah. And Ebal, and Abimael, and Sheba. And Ophir, and
Havilah, and Jobab. All these are sons of Joktan.
24–27 Shem, Arpakshad, Shelah. Eber, Peleg, Reu. Serug, Nahor, Terah. Abram;
28, 29 that is, Abraham. The sons of Abraham: Isaac and Ishmael. These are their
generations: Ishmael's first-born was Nebaioth; then Kedar, and Adbeel, and
30, 31 Mibsam. Mishma, and Dumah, Massa, Hadad, and Tema. Jetur, Naphish,
32 and Kedemah: these are sons of Ishmael. And the sons of Keturah, Abra-
ham's concubine: she bare Zimran, and Jokshan, and Medan, and Midian,
33 and Ishbak, and Shuah; and Jokshan's sons: Sheba and Dedan. And the
sons of Midian: Ephah, and Epher, and Henoch, and Abida, and Eldaah: all
34 these are the sons of Keturah. And Abraham begat Isaac; the sons of Isaac:
35 Esau and Israel. The sons of Esau: Eliphaz, Reuel, and Jeush, and Jalam,
36 and Korah. The sons of Eliphaz; Teman, and Omar, Zephi, and Gatam,
37 Kenaz, and Timnah, and Amalek. The sons of Reuel; Nahath, Zerah,
38 Shammah, and Mizzah. And the sons of Seir: Lotan, and Shobal, and

39 Zibon, and Anah, and Dishan, and Ezer, and Dishan. And the sons of
40 Lotan: Hori and Homam; and Lotan's sister was Timnah. The sons of
Shobal: Aljan,[5] and Manahath, and Ebal, Shephi,[6] and Onam; and the sons
41 of Zibon: Ajah and Anah. The sons of Anah: Dishon; and the sons of
42 Dishon: Hamran,[7] and Eshban, and Ithran, and Keran. The sons of Ezer:
Bilhan, and Zaavan, and Jaakan; the sons of Dishan: Uz and Aran.
43 And these are the kings that reigned in the land of Edom before the sons of
Israel had kings: Bela, son of Beor; and the name of his city was Dinhabah.
44, 45 And Bela died, and Jobab, son of Zera of Bozrah, reigned in his stead. And
Jobab died, and Husham, of the land of the Temanites, reigned in his stead.
46 And Husham died, and Hadad, son of Bedad, who smote Midian in the land
47 of Moab, reigned in his stead; and the name of his city was Ajuth.[8] And
48 Hadad died, and Samlah of Masrekah reigned in his stead. And Samlah
49 died, and Shaul of Rehoboth by the river reigned in his stead. And Shaul
50 died, and Baal-hanan, son of Hakbor, reigned in his stead. And Baal-hanan
died, and Hadad[9] reigned in his stead; and the name of his city was Pahi;
and the name of his wife was Mehetabel, daughter of Matred, daughter of
51 Mezahab. And Hadad died; and the dukes of Edom were: the duke of
52 Timnah, duke of Aljah,[10] duke of Jetheth. Duke of Oholibamah, duke of
53 Elah, duke of Pinon. Duke of Kenaz, duke of Teman, duke of Mibzar.
54 Duke of Magdiel, duke of Hiram: these are the dukes of Edom.

[1] דִּיפַת is certainly an error of the pen for רִיפַת, Gen. x. 3, which is found here in many MSS. and editions, as well as in the Sept. and the Vulg.

[2] רוֹדָנִים appears to be an error of the pen or an arbitrary amendment for דֹּדָנִים, Gen. x. 4, which many MSS. and older editions present here also. But comp. the exposition.

[3] So (לוּדִים) the *Keri* in our passage, which, however, may rest on a confirmation with Gen. x. 13. The *Kethib* has לוּדִיִּים, a long plural form, which is to לוּדִים as in English Lydian would be to Lydan, or as in Hebrew כֻּשִׁיִּים, Am. ix 12, to כּוּשִׁים, 2 Chron. xxi. 6.

[4] On מֶשֶׁךְ instead of מַשׁ, Gen. x. 23, see the Commentary.

[5] Instead of Aljan (עַלְיָן) many MSS. have Alvan (עַלְוָן), in accordance with Gen. xxxvi. 23.

[6] For שְׁפִי some MSS. have שְׁפוֹ, as in Gen. xxxvi. 23. So in ver. 36, where the name צְפִי is in a number of MSS. changed into צְפוֹ, as in Gen. xxxvi. 11.

[7] For חַמְרָן a considerable number of MSS. have חֶמְדָּן, as in Gen. xxxvi. 26.

[8] For the *Kethib* עָיוּת the *Keri* has עֲוִית, as in Gen. xxxvi. 35.

[9] For הֲדַד some MSS. read הֲדַר, which is the usual reading in Gen. xxxvi. 39, while there also several MSS. present הדד. Hadad's city פָּעִי, which, in the same parallel, is פָּעוּ, some good codices here also change into פָּעוּ.

[10] For עַלְיָה the *Keri* gives עַלְוָה, according to Gen. xxxvi. 40.

EXEGETICAL.

PRELIMINARY REMARK.—The whole of these patriarchal forefathers of the house of David down to Israel and Edom, sons of Isaac, appear to be divided into two nearly equal parts, to the second of which is added an appendix on the descendants of Edom till the times of David. The first part, vers. 1–23, enumerates the 10 antediluvian patriarchs from Adam to Noah, the 3 sons of Noah, and the 70 nations descending from them (on this number 70, see the Remark under ver. 23). In the second part, vers. 24–42, are given the 10 generations from Shem to Abraham, the sons of Abraham by Hagar, Keturah, and Sarah, and the stocks derived from them, which again amount to 70 (see under ver. 42). The appendix, vers. 43–54, mentions the kings of the Edomites before David, that are also given in Gen. xxxvi., as well as the 11 there named dukes of Edom. In all these genealogical and ethnological statements the author adheres closely to the matter, and where he does not merely abbreviate, as several times in the second part, and partly also in the appendix, even to the words of Genesis, of which ch. v. and x. (the table of nations) serve him till ver. 23, and ch. ii., xxv., xxxvi. till the end as sources and models. He reports in the briefest manner concerning the patriarchs before Noah, and concerning Noah himself, and his sons (vers.

1–4), of whom he merely gives the names, 13 in number, without even remarking that the first 10 of these names denote successive generations and the last 3 brothers. He might certainly presuppose in his readers sufficient knowledge of the relations of these holy and venerable names from the earliest foretime. He knew that to them as well as to himself belonged "the faculty to perceive in all these names the indications and foundations of a rich ancient history" (Berth.). And it was scarcely otherwise with the names of the following series, reaching further into the more known history, which he also brings together in a brief and bare report. Even where we are unable to perceive the historical importance of the prominent names, and the grounds on which they must have been of interest to every pious Israelite, the fact of such importance is to be presumed in every case, and for every single name. Comp. Ewald, *Gesch. d. Volkes Israel*, 2d edit. i. 479: "These dry names from a hoary antiquity, when we know how to awaken them from their sleep, do not remain so dead and stiff, but announce and revive the most important traditions of the ancient nations and families, like the petrifactions and mountain strata of the earth, which, rightly questioned, tell the history of long vanished ages."[1]

§ I. *The Patriarchs before Noah, the three Sons of Noah, and the* (70) *Nations descending from them:* vers. 1–23.

1. *From Adam to Noah's Sons:* vers. 1–4.—On the stringing together of the bare names, without any explanation, see Preliminary Remark. The names are all taken from Gen. v.: the rich contents of this oldest genealogy of primeval history is here reduced to the shortest possible form of an abstract. For the conjectural etymology of the several names (Adam = man; Sheth = substitute; Enosh = weak, frail man; Kenan = gain or gainful, etc.), see vol. i. p. 121 f. of the *Bibelwerk*.—The order of the names of the three sons of Noah is Shem, Ham, and Japheth; as always in Genesis also, though Ham (Gen. ix. 24) was the youngest of the three. Comp. our Introductory Remarks on the prophet Daniel (*Bibelwerk*, part xiii. p. 11), where it is made probable that this order, like that of the names Noah, Daniel, and Joab (in Ezekiel), depends on euphonic principles (so Delitzsch, *Komm. über die Genes.*, 4th edit. 1872, p. 233).

2. *From Noah's Sons to Abraham; the Table of Nations:* vers. 5–23.—This abstract from the Mosaic table of nations Gen. x. has abridged this larger genealogical ethnographic account to the present narrow limits, chiefly by omitting the opening and closing notes, and passing over the remarks on the kingdom of Nimrod at Babel, and the spread of the Shemites and Hamites in their countries (vers. 5, 9–12, 18–20). Here, again, there is that abbreviating and condensing process which is characteristic of the author. For the ethnological and geographical import of the several names, comp. the commentary on Genesis by the editor (vol. i. p. 171 of the *Bibelwerk*), and the monographs on the table of nations there cited.

a. The Japhethites: vers. 5–7.—The names of the descendants of Japheth, 14 in number (7 sons and 7 grandsons), open the series in Gen. x. of stems and nations to be enumerated, perhaps because they represented the strongest and most widely-spread body (Japheth = "enlarging," Gen. ix. 27), scarcely because he passed for the first-born of Noah; for Shem, who is always placed before Japheth, even when only the two are named together, is to be regarded as such; see especially the decisive passages, Gen. ix. 23, 26 (against Starke, Bertheau, etc.). [These texts are not decisive; and Shem was born in the 503d year of Noah, Gen. xi. 11, and therefore two years at least after Japheth, Gen. v. 32.—J. G. M.]—The view recently again maintained with ingenuity and learning by J. G. Müller (*Die Semiten in ihrem Verhältniss zu Chamiten und Japhetiten*, Gotha 1872), that the so-called Shemites are nothing but Japhethites or Indogermans Hamitized in language, is in any case at variance with the Biblical genealogy of the sons of Noah, whether Shem or Japheth be the first-born.—Ver. 6. *Riphath.* This form, rejected by the Masoretes in favour of the probably erroneous (resting on an old clerical error) דִּיפַת, has not only the weight of so old witnesses as the Sept. and Vulg. for it (see the Crit. Note on ver. 6), but also the circumstance that plausible ethnographic explanations can be adduced for Riphath, but not for Diphath; comp. the name Ῥιφαταῖοι = Παφλαγόν in Joseph. *Antiq.* i. 6, and the ὄρη Ῥίπαια, on the ground of which Knobel has attempted to show in Riphath the ancestor of the Kelts (against which the Paphlagonian cities Tibia and Tobata [Bochart, *Geogr. Sacra*, p. 198 seq.], produced by the ancients in defence of the reading דִּיפַת, cannot, from their smallness and insignificance, be taken into account).—Ver. 7. *Tarshishah* (תַּרְשִׁישָׁה), a later form for תַּרְשִׁישׁ, which is usual in Gen. (x. 4) and elsewhere in the O. T. (also 2 Chron. ix. 21, xx. 36), the *ah* of motion having in this form melted into one word with the name itself. "With this are to be compared the modern Greek names, obtained by the wearing away of the proposition εἰς and the article, Stalimene = Lemnos, Stambul = (Konstantino)polis, Satines = Athenæ, Stanko = Kos," etc. (Berth.). —*Rodanim,* רוֹדָנִים; many transcribers and older editors wish to change this into the דֹּדָנִים of Gen. x. 4, although even there some old authorities (Sam., Sept., Jerome, *Quæst. in Gen.*) read רוֹדָנִים. The decision is difficult, because, on the one hand, Knobel's reference of Dodanim to the Dardani is verbally doubtful; on the other hand, the Rhodians (= Rodanim) appear too unimportant a part of the Hellenic race to be put on the same footing with Æolians (= Elishah), Etruscans (= Tarshish), and Cyprians or Karians (= Kittim). And yet the placing of Kittim and Rodanim together, and the consideration that the sea trade of the Rhodians might have become very important for such oriental nations as the Phœnicians and the Hebrews, appear to speak more for the reading of our book than for the original (comp. Berth.).

[1] Comp. also Wellhausen, *De gentibus et fam. Judæis*, etc., p. 4, where, with respect to the genealogical lists in the beginning of Chronicles, it is well remarked: *Quo fit, ut cœmeterii quasi speciem nobis præbeant hæc capita cipporum pleni: fuit ætas, cui breves suffecere tituli ad resuscitandam sepultorum memoriam;—interjectis sæculis, nedum millenniis, leguntur tituli, sed quo referantur, quid sibi velint, nescitur.*

And if Dodanim were to pass for the original form, and yet the application to the Dardani be untenable, the reference to Dodona would be internally still less probable than that to the Rhodians.

b. The Hamites: vers. 8–16.—Of these are named 4 sons, 24 grandsons, and 2 great-grandsons, being 30 descendants in all. Nimrod, ver. 10, does not count among the grandsons, as he appears only as a famous individual (hero), not as a head or founder of a people (patriarch). His introduction, therefore, is different from that of those previously named, not by וּבְנֵי (see vers. 5–9; and comp. Gen. x. 2–7), but by יָלַד, as Gen. x. 8, which verse is literally transcribed by the Chronist. By the formula: "he began to be a hero on the earth," the nature and import of Nimrod are briefly and pithily expressed, so that a repetition of the further statements of Genesis concerning him (x. 9–12) is not necessary. Comp. as a parallel from the New Testament: *ὅς καὶ παρέδωκεν αὐτόν* (or *ὁ καὶ παραδοὺς αὐτόν*), with which the evangelists are wont to characterize Judas Iscariot.—On לוּדִיִּים, ver. 11, see Critical Note.

c. The Shemites, particularly the non-Hebrews: vers. 17–23.—Of them are named in all 23 members, namely (as the parallel passage Gen. x. 23 more exactly shows), 5 sons, 5 grandsons, and 16 other descendants. That in ver. 17 the names Uz, Hul, Gether, Meshech, which properly denote grandsons of Shem by Aram, are appended at once to the 5 sons of Shem (so that they appear to be his sons, and thus the number of his sons would be 9, and that of his grandsons only 1), is a circumstance sufficiently explained, as the similar case in ver. 4 of Noah's sons: the author presumed the relation of the 4 as sons to Aram to be sufficiently known, and therefore thought it unnecessary to repeat the words וּבְנֵי אֲרָם before עוּץ from Gen. x. 23. Less probable is the supposition that the words in question fell out by a mistake of the copyist, or that the Chronist, deviating from the Pentateuch, really took the nations Uz, Hul, Gether, and Meshech to be sons, not grandsons, of Shem (as Knobel, *Völkertafel*, p. 252).—Moreover, almost all manuscripts give the last name in ver. 17 מֶשֶׁךְ; only a few conform to the reading in Genesis (מַשׁ), for which also the Sept. there presents Μοσόχ = מֶשֶׁךְ; and so might the Chronist have read in the text of Genesis. It is also in favour of Meshech being the original name, that Mash as a national name is quite unknown, while Meshech occurs as the name of a Shemite or Arabic tribe along with Kedar in Ps. cxx. 5.—Ver. 22. *Ebal,* עֵיבָל, is called in the parallel Gen. x. 28 rather Obal, עוֹבָל; yet the Sept. seems to have read עֵיבָל, for it gives the name as Εὐάλ. Comp. the similar but reverse case of Homam (=Hemam) under ver. 39.—The 14 descendants of Japheth, 30 of Ham, and 26 of Shem, amount to 70 nations descended from Noah. This number the author intended to bring out; for with him, or before him, other Jewish expositors might have discovered the symbolic number 70 in the Mosaic table of nations (it may, in fact, be gathered from it; comp. J. Fürst, *Gesch. der bibl. Liter. und des jüdisch-hellenischen Schriftthums*, i. p. 119); and this number of the nations of the globe, occasionally enlarged to 72, plays otherwise an important part in the Jewish circle of thought. This is shown by its frequent mention in the Talmud, and its occurrence in the Gnostic writings and the Pseudo-Clementine (*Recogn.* ii. 42). To this belong also such biblical passages as Num. xi. 16 and Luke x. 1 ff.; for the 70 elders appointed by Moses in the wilderness (with the 70 members of the Jewish Sanhedrin on this model), as well as the 70 disciples chosen by Jesus, appear to be due to a symbolic reference to the 70 nations of the globe (comp. Godet, *Commentaire sur l'évangile de Luc*, 1870, ii. p. 21). And there is actually a deeper sense in the view, that the total number of the nations of the earth is = the sacred ideal number 70 (7 × 10, the humanly complete, elevated and multiplied by the power of the Divine Spirit; comp. my *Theol. naturalis*, i. p. 716). And why should we not have as good a right, in the popular phraseology of Hebrew antiquity, to speak of the "70 nations of the world," as of the 4 winds, the 4 quarters of heaven, the 12 signs of the zodiac, without uttering anything untrue or against nature, though such expressions may have no exact scientific basis? There seems then to be no reason to hesitate, from a dogmatic-apologetic point of view, to acknowledge that the number 70 was intended by the author to apply to the descendants of Noah. The only thing that can be said against it is, the absence of an express intimation, such as Matthew gives at the close of his genealogy of Jesus, in the form of a recapitulation of the several groups of numbers (i. 17). Yet the pedigree by Luke (iii. 23–38) wants also such a recapitulation, though its symbolic construction out of 77 = 7 × 11 members is no less certain than that of Matthew. If Keil objects to our view, which is that of almost all recent expositors, that the number 70 is only obtained by making, "in the sons of Shem, the personal names Arpakshad, Shelah, Heber, Peleg, and Joktan to be names of nations, contrary to the view of Genesis, in which the five names denote persons, the ancestors of the nations descending from Heber through Peleg and Joktan," this refutes nothing. For the number 70 is obtained throughout, and not merely in the case of Arpakshad, etc., by the addition of all names, those of the patriarchs, who only became nations in their sons, as well as these sons themselves, and their descendants. In other words, it is quite reasonable, and corresponds entirely with the spirit and method of the genealogizing ethnography of the Hebrews, to regard all higher or lower members of old pedigrees as *in abstracto* equivalent factors and representatives of definite co-ordinate races in the subsequent history, though this view may be *in concreto* impracticable. Comp., moreover, the evangelical-ethical principles under ch. ix.

§ II. *The Patriarchs from Shem to Abraham, and the Descendants of the latter through Ishmael, Keturah, Edom* (*70 stems in all*): vers. 24–42.

1. *From Shem to Abraham:* vers. 24–27.—The 10 members of this line are exactly coincident with Gen. xi. 10–32, though with the omission of

all historical details. And the Chronist follows the genealogical account of the Masoretic text, which represents Abraham himself as the tenth of the line, not that of the Sept., which inserts a Kenan (Καϊνᾶν) between Arpakshad and Shelah, thus following a tradition that regarded Terah, the father of Abraham, as the tenth from Shem. Bertheau (in the annual report of the "Deutsche Morgenl. Gesellschaft," 1845–46) has attempted to make it probable that this tradition was the older, and that the name קֵינָן stood originally in the text of Genesis.—Ver. 27. Abram, perhaps for the sake of brevity, and to avoid all needless accumulation of names, afterwards (from Gen. xvii. 5) Abraham, in which the author, in his brief manner, notices the change of name, is alone named as a son of Terah, Nahor and Haran and their posterity being omitted.

2. *Abraham's Sons and their Descendants:* vers. 28–34.—They fall, like those of Noah and Terah, into three stocks or branches under Ishmael, Keturah, and Isaac. The Chronist places the former groups first, because, like the genealogists in the primeval history, he wished first to enumerate the remote stocks, and then to take up the people of God. The same process from without to within placed the genealogy of the Japhethites and Hamites before the Shemites, and determines, further, that of Isaac's posterity the Edomite branch is first treated, and then the Israelite.

a. Ishmael and his Twelve Sons: vers. 29–31.—The twelve names agree exactly with the list in Gen. xxv. 12–16, with respect to the order as well as the words. And the introductory אֵלֶּה תֹּלְדוֹת, ver. 29, the predicate בְּכוֹר, "the first-born" before Ishmael (comp. Gen. xxv. 13), and the closing formula, "These are the sons of Ishmael" (ver. 31; comp. Gen. xxv. 16), show how closely the author adheres to the Mosaic record. The designation of Ishmael as the "first-born" is only to be explained by this faithful adherence to the original, not by the wish of the author to justify his placing the Ishmaelites before the descendants of Israel (as Bertheau seems to think); for this position needed no justification, because it necessarily followed from the genealogical method of our author (see on ver. 28). [In our author's version of ver. 29, "the first-born" is made to refer to Nebaioth, and not to Ishmael, as above. This seems to be correct.—J. G. M.]

b. The Descendants of Keturah: vers. 32, 33.—The six sons and seven grandsons of Abraham by Keturah are not given literally as in Gen. xxv. 1–4. On the contrary, the Chronist has left out three great-grandsons there named—Asshurim, Letushim, and Leummim, descendants of Dedan—whether intentionally, on account of the plural form of the names, or because he did not find them in his copy of Genesis, must remain undetermined. That Medan and Midian, ver. 32, are only different pronunciations of the same name (comp. Gen. xxxvii. 28, 36), the number of the sons of Keturah was originally and properly five, and the total number of her descendants only twelve, is an arbitrary conjecture of Bertheau, while pushing too far the endeavour to find certain symbolic numbers everywhere.

c. The Two Sons of Isaac, Esau, and Israel, and the Descendants of the former: vers. 34–42.—*And Abraham begat Isaac.* This notice, leading back to the statement in ver. 28, appears occasioned by Gen. xxv. 19, where the same words (only with הוֹלִיד for וַיּוֹלֶד) occur immediately after the enumeration of the sons of Keturah. This reference to Abraham was not in itself necessary here; but comp. also the reference to Shem above in ver. 24.—Ver. 25. Esau's sons, enumerated exactly after Gen. xxxvi. 4, 5 (though without naming their mothers, the three wives of Esau), as in general the author henceforth reports very closely from Gen. xxxvi., following which also he annexes the Seirites or aborigines of Idumæa to the proper Edomites, and treats both as belonging to one and the same family of nations.—Ver. 36. *Sons of Eliphaz.* These, five in number, are given exactly as in Gen. xxxvi. 11; for the name of the third, Zephi, is only a by-form of Zepho, as in ver. 40 a Shephi appears in place of the Shepho, Gen. xxxvi. 23; comp. the Crit. Remark. But if the names Timnah and Amalek are annexed, apparently as sons of Eliphaz, this is probably a similar breviloquence to that in vers. 4 and 17; the author presumes it sufficiently known to his readers, that Timnah, Amalek's mother, was not a son, but rather a concubine of Eliphaz (another wife besides Adah, the mother of those five sons first named); comp. Gen. xxxvi. 12. So have the Sept. (in the cod. Alex.) and numerous older Jewish and Christian expositors solved the difficulty, and of the moderns, J. H. Michaelis, Starke, Keil, etc.; whereas Bertheau, having regard to vers. 39 and 51, where actually a separate stem and then a stem-prince Timnah are counted, prefers to assume that "the Chronist, interpreting the genealogical language, and perceiving in the family names the stem-relations that lie at their root, has explained the statements of Genesis concerning Timnah, so that by them the connection of two stems Timnah and Amalek with the other stems of Eliphaz shall be indicated, and they are accordingly counted in the same line with these stems as sons of Eliphaz." This assumption seems to us too artificial, and ascribes to the Chronist a higher degree of bold independence and wilfulness in his operations than is admissible or consistent with his evident piety and conscientiousness in recording the facts of primeval history that were handed down to him.—Ver. 37. *Sons of Reuel.* These are entered four in number, exactly as in Gen. xxxvi. 13. There are thus in all 10 grandsons (6 sons of Eliphaz and 4 of Reuel) who are assigned by our author to Esau, and who, with the three sons of Jeush, Jalam, and Korah (sons of Oholibamah), form the 13 family or stem chiefs (φύλαρχοι, Sept. Gen. xxxvi. 15) of the Edomites. Against Bertheau, who would here make out a 12 from the 13 families, by reducing Amalek, ver. 36, to a secondary place, comp. Keil, p. 36: "Neither Chronicles nor Genesis knows 12 tribes of Edom, but both books give 13 grandsons (rather descendants) of Esau; and these 13 grandsons are, by the report of Genesis, the 13 phylarchs of Edom which are distributed among the 3 wives of Esau, so that the 13 families may be reduced to 3 stems. And in Genesis, Amalek is not placed in a looser connection with the remaining tribes, but on the contrary, is not only, ver. 12, counted with the sons of Adah, perhaps because Timnah stood to Adah, the wife of Esau, in the same relation as Hagar to Sarah, but also in ver. 16 is reckoned to the dukes of the sons of Eliphaz. Thus Genesis counts not 5, but 6 stems of Eliphaz; and Chronicles has not fully effaced the number 12, as Bertheau further asserts, but the 13 sons and grandsons of Esau, who became phylarchs, are fully entered, and only their designation as אַלּוּפֵי בְנֵי עֵשָׂו left out, because unnecessary for the genealogy of the descendants of Esau."—Vers. 38-42. The 7 sons of Seir and their descendants, or the (mingled since Esau's invasion with his descendants) Seirite or Horite aborigines of Idumæa according to their tribes. These aborigines of the mountains of Edom, though not of Abrahamic descent, yet, from their gradually formed connection and intermingling with the descendants of Esau, are so reckoned as if they belonged to the Edomite family of nations. And this occurs not only here in Chronicles, where they are introduced as בְּנֵי שֵׂעִיר, but also in Gen. xxx. 20-30, where they are called חֹרִי, "dwellers in caves, Troglodytes." Comp. also on these Horites, our exp. of the book of Job, vol. x. of the *Bibelw.* p. 238.—The names of the seven sons of Seir, that is, the seven Seirite chiefs, agree exactly with Genesis; and likewise their descendants, in number 18 men and 1 woman, Timnah, ver. 39. Only Oholibamah, a second Seiritess named in Gen. xxxvi. 25, has been passed over by the Chronist, according to his wont in general to reckon only male members in his genealogical lists. On the deviations of some forms from the text of Genesis, as Homam, ver. 39, for Hemam; Aljan, ver. 40, for Alwan, etc., see Crit. Note.—The total names enumerated from Abraham amount to about 70, whether the two Timnahs, the mother of Amalek, ver. 36, and the sister of Lotan, ver. 39, or the Edomite and the Seirite Timnah be included, in which case there are exactly 70, or both or one of them be excluded from the number, and so then be only 68 or 69. Bertheau (whom Kamphausen, in Bunsen's *Bibelw.*, follows), counting in the former way, finds 12 descendants of Esau, 13 of Keturah, 2 of Isaac, 16 of Esau, and 27 of Seir, and so obtains the number 70; Keil, in the latter way, regards the Seirite Timnah as only mentioned by the way, and therefore excluded, and consequently reckons only 26 descendants of Seir, and in all, only 69 descendants of Abraham. Though the latter be right in many of his objections to Bertheau's mode of reckoning (for instance, its exclusion of Ishmael, and inclusion of Esau and Israel), yet he certainly goes too far when he utterly denies the design of the Chronist to follow up his list of 70 descendants of Noah with the same number of those of Abraham. This design, though not carried out with mathematical exactness, and therefore not expressly mentioned here (any more than in ver. 5 ff.), appears in fact to have had a distinct influence on the selection and arrangement of his genealogical lists. The incidental agreement of the number in vers. 29-42 with that in vers. 5-23 shows this, just as the decade of the patriarchs between Noah and Abraham, in its agreement with that of the patriarchs before Noah (comp. vers. 24-27 with vers. 1-4), points to design.

APPENDIX.—*The Edomite Kings and Chiefs till the beginning of Kingdom of Israel:* vers. 43-54.

1. *The Kings:* vers. 43-51*a*.—A nearly literal repetition from Gen. xxxvi. 31-39; only the words וַיִּמְלֹךְ בֶּאֱדֹם (ver. 43) before בֶּלַע, and in ver. 51 after בַּעַל חָנָן, the words בֶּן־עַכְבּוֹר are left out, which, however, many MSS. here also supply. On the variants in Ajuth, ver. 46, and in Hadad and Pai, ver. 50, see Crit. Notes.—Ver. 51. *And Hadad died.* This statement (וַיָּמָת הֲדָד) is wanting in the parallel texts of Genesis, where, after entering Hadad (or rather Hadar) as the last king, the formula וְאֵלֶּה שְׁמוֹת serves to introduce the then following list of the phylarchs and their seats. By the sentence "and Hadad died," along with the following, "and there were" (וַיִּהְיוּ), this list of phylarchs is here brought into a far closer connection with the foregoing register of kings than in Genesis,—into a connection, indeed, which at first sight looks as if the Chronist intended to represent the dukes as successors of the kingdom terminated by Hadad's death, and so report a transition from the monarchic to the aristocratic form of government in Edom. This supposition, however, which Bertheau, Kamph., and others defend, is not absolutely necessary; the ו *consec.* in וַיִּהְיוּ "may express merely the order of thought; that is, may connect the mention of the dukes only in thought with the enumeration of the kings, or intimate that besides the kings there were also dukes, who could govern the nation and country" (Keil). The latter supposition is the more probable, as the following list is owing to a statistical and chronographic rather than a genealogical tendency, as will presently be shown.

2. *The Dukes:* vers. 51-54.—This list agrees in the order and form of the 11 names given exactly (on the variant Aljah for Alwah, ver. 51, see Crit. Note) with Gen. xxxvi. 40-43. Yet it has received from the Chronist another superscription and subscription, of which the former runs thus: "and there were the dukes of Edom" (אַלּוּפֵי אֱדוֹם instead of א' עֵשָׂו, Gen. xxxvi. 40, the name of the people and land taking the place of the *n. propr.* of the patriarch), and the latter: "these are the dukes of Edom" (for which that of Genesis is more circumstantial: "These are the dukes of Edom according to their habitations in the land of their possessions: this is Esau, the father of Edom"). And the list treats not so much of the enumeration of certain persons as of that of the seats of certain (perhaps hereditary) dukes of the nation or phylarchs, according to which they are briefly named, "the duke of Timnah," etc. The list has thus a geographical, not a genealogical import; it is a list of neighbouring principalities of Edom, not of Edomite princes. The number eleven of these principalities forms an approximative parallel with the number twelve of the tribes of Israel; it agrees also nearly with the number of the descendants of Esau above named (ver. 36 ff.); but it could only by violent means and arbitrary hypotheses be made to agree with this number, or reduced to the number twelve (comp. the remarks against Berth. on ver. 37).

b. The Sons of Israel, and the Generations of Judah down to David, with David's Descendants to Elioenai and his Seven Sons.—Ch. ii.–iv. 23.

1. *The Twelve Sons of Israel and the Descendants of Judah:* ch. ii. 1–41 (*with an Appendix relating chiefly to the Posterity of Caleb:* vers. 42–55).

Ch. ii. 1. These are the sons of Israel: Reuben, Simeon (Shimon), Levi, and Judah,
2 Issachar, and Zebulun. Dan, Joseph and Benjamin, Naphtali, Gad, and
3 Assher. The sons of Judah: Er, and Onan, and Shelah; three were born to
him of the daughter of Shuah, the Canaanitess; but Er, the first-born of
4 Judah, was evil in the eyes of the Lord, and He slew him. And Thamar his
daughter-in-law bare him Perez and Zerah: all the sons of Judah were five.
5, 6 The sons of Perez: Hezron and Hamul. And the sons of Zerah: Zimri, and
7 Ethan, and Heman, Calcol, and Dara:[1] five of them in all. And the sons
of Carmi: Achar, the troubler of Israel, who transgressed in the accursed
8 thing. And the sons of Ethan: Azariah.
9 And the sons of Hezron, that were born to him: Jerahmeel, and Ram, and
10 Celubai. And Ram begat Amminadab; and Amminadab begat Nahshon,
11 prince of the sons of Judah. And Nahshon begat Salma, and Salma begat
12, 13 Boaz. And Boaz begat Obed, and Obed begat Jesse. And Jesse begat his
14 first-born Eliab, and Abinadab the second, and Shima the third. Nathanael
15, 16 the fourth, Raddai the fifth. Ozem the sixth, David the seventh. And their
sisters, Zeruiah and Abigail: and the sons of Zeruiah: Abishai, and Joab, and
17 Asahel, three. And Abigail bare Amasa; and the father of Amasa was Jether
the Ishmaelite.
18 And Caleb, son of Hezron, begat with Azubah his wife,[2] and with Jerioth;
19 and these are her sons: Jesher, and Shobab, and Ardon. And Azubah died;
20 and Caleb took to him Ephrath, and she bare him Hur. And Hur begat
21 Uri, and Uri begat Bezalel. And afterwards Hezron went in to the daughter
of Machir, father of Gilead; and he took her when he was sixty years old,
22 and she bare him Segub. And Segub begat Jair, who had twenty and three
23 cities in the land of Gilead. And Geshur and Aram took the towns of Jair
from them, with Kenath and her daughters, sixty cities. All these are sons
24 of Jair, the father of Gilead. And after the death of Hezron, in Caleb-
ephrathah, Abiah, Hezron's wife, bare him Ashur (Ashchur), father of Tekoah.
25 And the sons of Jerahmeel, the first-born of Hezron, were Ram, the first-
26 born, and Bunah, and Oren, and Azem of Ahijah. And Jarahmeel had another
27 wife, and her name was Atarah; she was the mother of Onam. And the
sons of Ram, the first-born of Jerahmeel, were Maaz, and Jamin, and Eker.
28 And the sons of Onam were Shammai and Jada; and the sons of Shammai:
29 Nadab and Abishur. And the name of Abishur's wife was Abihail,[3] and she
30 bare him Ahban and Molid. And the sons of Nadab: Seled and Appaim;
31 and Seled died childless. And the sons of Appaim: Ishi; and the sons of
32 Ishi: Sheshan; and the sons of Sheshan: Ahlai. And the sons of Jada,
33 brother of Shammai: Jether and Jonathan; and Jether died childless. And
the sons of Jonathan: Peleth and Zaza. These were the sons of Jerahmeel.
34 And Sheshan had no sons, but only daughters. And Sheshan had an
35 Egyptian servant, whose name was Jarha. And Sheshan gave his daughter to
36 Jarha his servant to wife; and she bare him Attai. And Attai begat Nathan,
37 and Nathan begat Zabad. And Zabad begat Ephlal, and Ephlal begat Obed.
38, 39 And Obed begat Jehu, and Jehu begat Azariah. And Azariah begat Helez,
40 and Helez begat Elasah. And Elasah begat Sismai, and Sismai begat Shal-
41 lum. And Shallum begat Jekamiah, and Jekamiah begat Elishama.

Appendix: Three Series of Descendants of Caleb: vers. 42–55.

42 And the sons of Caleb, brother of Jerahmeel, were Mesha, his first-born;
he was the father of Ziph; and the sons of Mareshah, the father of Hebron.[4]

43, 44 And the sons of Hebron: Korah, and Tappuah, and Rekem, and Shema. And
45 Shema begat Raham, father of Jorkeam;[5] and Rekem begat Shammai. And
the son of Shammai was Maon; and Maon was father of Bethzur.
46 And Ephah, Caleb's concubine, bare Haran, and Moza, and Gazez; and
47 Haran begat Gazez. And the sons of Jehdai: Regem, and Jotham, and Geshan,
48 and Pelet, and Ephah, and Shaaph. Caleb's concubine Maacha bare[6] Sheber
49 and Tirhanah. And she bare Shaaph the father of Madmannah, Sheva,
father of Machbenah, and father of Gibeah; and Caleb's daughter was Achsah.
50 These were the sons of Caleb the son[7] of Hur, first-born of Ephrathah:
51 Shobal, father of Kiriath-jearim. Salma, father of Bethlehem, Hareph, father
52 of Bethgader. And Shobal, father of Kiriath-jearim, had sons: Haroeh,
53 and the half of Menuhoth.[8] And the families of Kiriath-jearim were the
Ithrite, and the Puthite, and the Shumathite, and the Mishraite. From
54 these came the Zorathite and the Eshtaolite. The sons of Salma: Bethlehem,
and the Netophathite, Ataroth of the house of Joab, and half of the Mena-
55 hathite, the Zorite. And the families of the scribes dwelling at Jabez were
the Tirathites, Shimathites, Suchathites: these are the Kenites that came
from Hammath, father of the house of Rechab.

[1] For דָּרַע many MSS., as well as the Syr. and the Chald., give הַּרְדַּע, as in 1 Kings v. 11.

[2] אִשָּׁה (for which אִשְׁתּוֹ was to be expected) is wanting in two MSS., according to de Rossi, *Var. Lect.*—The Pesh. and Vulg. appear to have read אִשְׁתּוֹ אֵת for אִשָּׁה וְאֵת.

[3] Instead of אֲבִיהַיִל, a number of MSS. and printed editions have אֲבִיחַיִל. The same vacillation is also found in 2 Chron. xi. 18, in the like-named wife of Rehoboam.

[4] Instead of מָרֵשָׁה might possibly (after the proposal of Keil) be read מֵישָׁע, and instead of אֲבִי חֶבְרוֹן rather the *nom. composit.* אֲבִי־חֶבְרוֹן. Comp. the Exeg. Expl.

[5] For יָרְקְעָם the Sept. exhibits 'Ιεκλάν; and so for the following רֶקֶם.

[6] Instead of the unexpected masc. ילד, some MSS. present the fem. יָלְדָה.

[7] Instead of בֶּן־חוּר, the Sept. appears to have read בְּנֵי־חוּר, which is perhaps the original form. Comp. Exeg. Expl.

[8] On the probably corrupt words הראה חצי המנחות, see Exeg.

EXEGETICAL.

Preliminary Remark.—The author here begins to enroll his detailed genealogies of the tribes of Israel, extending to the end of ch. viii. After premising a list of the 12 sons of Jacob as the general basis of the whole, vers. 1, 2, he begins with the enumeration of the generations and families of the tribe of Judah, which he then pursues in ch. iii. and iv. 1–23, and completes in several parts. No order, regulated by definite historical, geographical, or any systematic principles, lies at the base of this enumeration; he seems rather to have combined into a whole, as far as possible, the more or less fragmentary genealogies of certain branches and families of the house of Judah as they came down to him from antiquity; but this whole is very defective in the unity and homogeneity of its several parts. For of the five immediate descendants of Judah, that founded the tribe of Judah by a numerous posterity, his three sons Shelah, Perez, and Zerah, and his two grandsons Hezron and Hamul, only Zerah (ii. 6–8), Hezron (ii. 9–iii.), and Shelah (iv. 21–23) have their genealogies given with any fulness; Hamul is entirely passed over, and Perez is only followed out in the line of Hezron. This line (under which the Chronist sums up all that was known of the descendants of Caleb and of the Jephunnite Calebites) is treated with special care and fulness: to it belongs the whole series of the descendants of David till the times after the captivity (ch. iii.), and at least the more considerable part of the genealogical fragments in ch. iv. 1–23, which serve as a supplement to ch. ii. 9–55, and of which it is often doubtful which of the members previously named they continue or supplement.

1. *The Twelve Sons of Israel:* vers. 1, 2.—These are given in an order deviating from Gen. xxxv. 23 ff., so that the 6 sons of Leah stand first, then the son of Rachel's maid, Dan; after that the 2 sons of Rachel, Joseph and Benjamin; and lastly, the 3 remaining sons of the maids (Naphtali, Bilhah's son; Gad and Asher, Zilpah's sons). This separation of Dan from his full brother Naphtali is surprising, and can hardly be satisfactorily explained. For if we suppose that Rachel (see Gen. xxx. 3 ff.) regarded Dan, born of her maid Bilhah, as in a sense her own son, and so he is named before Joseph and Benjamin, yet still it is a question, why not also Naphtali, who was likewise born before her own sons. The procedure of the Chronist in regard to Dan is in several respects enigmatical; comp. on ch. vii. 12. [It is probable that Naphtali was born about the same time with Gad, and is therefore classified with him.—J. G. M.]

2. *The Descendants of Judah:* vers. 3-41.—*a.* The 5 sons of Judah, the 2 sons of Perez, and the descendants of Zerah: vers. 3-8.—Vers. 3, 4. *The sons of Judah*, etc. The five sons of Judah, three legitimate, born of the daughter of Shuah

the Canaanite, Er, Onan, and Shelah, and two born in incest of Tamar, his daughter-in-law, Perez and Zerah, are given in accordance with Gen. xxxviii., and in the same order (comp. also Gen. xlvi. 12). The author recalls this his source by taking over word for word the remark on Er in Gen. xxxviii. 7: "But Er the first-born of Judah was evil in the eyes of the Lord, and He slew him."—Ver. 5. *The sons of Perez*, etc. (Hezron, perhaps the "blooming, fair;" Hamul, the "forgiven," or the "tender, weak;" comp. *Bibelw.* i. p. 432). These occur in two registers of the Pentateuch, the list of the children of Israel who went down to Egypt with Jacob, Gen. xlvi. 12, and in that of the families of Judah in the Mosaic age, Num. xxvi. 21.—Vers. 6–8. *And the sons of Zerah.* Five such are named: Zimri, Ethan, Heman, Calcol, and Dara. On the first of these names, which might possibly be wrongly written (זִמְרִי for זַבְדִּי, Josh. vii. 1), see under ver. 7. The four following names, especially if we read for the last, Darda, with a great number of old witnesses (see Crit. Note), agree surprisingly with the four men compared with Solomon in 1 Kings v. 11: Ethan the Ezrahite, and Heman, and Calcol, and Darda, the the sons of Mahol. The assumption of an identity of these four wise men with the four younger sons of Zerah is very natural; it has been already asserted by Grotius, Clericus, Lightfoot (*Chronol. V. T.* p. 24), Hiller (*Onom. Sacr.*), and others, and recently by Movers (p. 237) and Bertheau, who insisted on the circumstance, that in 1 Kings v. 11 contemporaries of Solomon were not intended (no more than in Ezra xiv. 14, xviii. 20, contemporaries of Daniel); further, on the probable identity of Zerah with Ezrah the father of Ethan mentioned in 1 Kings v. 11 (אֶזְרָח=זֶרַח); and lastly, on the statement of the Rabbinical book *Seder Olam*, which says (p. 52, ed. Meyer) of the sons of Zerah named in our passage: "These were prophets who prophesied in Egypt," and thus appears to confirm expressly their being of the class of Hakamim. But the argument raised of late, especially by Hengstenberg (*Beiträge zur Einl.* ii. 61 f., and on Ps. lxxxviii.), Keil (*Apol. Vers.* p. 164 ff.; comp. *Comment.* p. 39 ff.), as well as Bähr (on 1 Kings v. 11, *Bibelw.* vii. p. 30), against the identity of these persons, seems to be more weighty and decisive. For, 1. The variant "Darda" for "Dara" in our passage, however old, appears clearly to have arisen from the endeavour to harmonize; 2. To this endeavour the notice in the *Seder Olam* owes its origin; 3. That at least near contemporaries of Solomon are named in 1 Kings v. follows from the manifest and undeniable identity of Ethan the Ezrahite with the so-named composer of Ps. lxxxix., and from the very probable identity of Heman with "Heman the Ezrahite," the composer of Ps. lxxxviii.; 4. If the Ethan and Heman of 1 Kings v. 11 be identical with the composers of these Psalms, they are also probably to be regarded as Levites of the family of the sons of Korah (see the superscr. of these Psalms), who are in 1 Chron. xv., xvii., and xix. called masters of song, and belong not to the family of Judah, and might at the most have found admission into it as adoptive sons of Zerah (Hengstenberg, *Beiträge zur Einl. ins A. T.* ii. 71),—an assumption, however, which is too artificial; 5. The express designation of Calcol and Darda in Kings as "sons of Mahol" makes it difficult to assume their identity with the sons of Zerah, as the latter must be regarded not as immediate sons, but later descendants of Zerah; 6. Of the pre-eminent wisdom of the sons of Zerah, neither the canonical Old Testament nor the apocryphal literature has anything to report; even such passages as Jer. xlix. 7, Baruch iii. 22 ff. are silent on the subject. The assumption of the identity of these with the names in 1 Kings v. can only be maintained on the presupposition that וּבְנֵי in our passage means not strictly sons, but later descendants of Zerah (so recently Keil, in *Comment.* p. 41). But this expedient has its difficulty, and by no means suffices to destroy the force of most of the arguments here adduced against the identity. We must therefore take the surprising coincidence of the names to be accidental, or assume with Movers (*Chron.* p. 237) that we have in the present passage the peculiar genealogical combination of a later author. For the conjecture of Ewald, that Heman and Ethan, "the two great singers of the tribe of Judah, were taken by the Levitical music schools into their company and family, and therefore were afterwards (in the superscriptions of Ps. lxxxviii. and lxxxix.) reckoned to the tribe of Levi" (*Gesch. d. V. Isr.* iii. 1, p. 84), is no less artificial than that of Hengstenberg. [But of these considerations, Nos. 1 and 2 contain a mere subjective assumption. No. 3 assumes, without necessity, that the Ethan of 1 Kings v. and the composer of Ps. lxxxix. are one, since two Ethans may descend from the one patriarch. No. 4 assumes that the composers of Ps. lxxxviii. and lxxxix. were Levites, whereas the epithet Ezrahite appears to be added expressly to distinguish them from the Levites of those names. No. 5 assumes that Mahol is a proper name, which remains to be proved. No. 6 assumes that the wisdom of Zerah's sons is not probable, because it is not elsewhere mentioned. This argument of itself has little if any weight. On the other hand, one motive to insert these sons of Zerah in the list was probably their occurrence in 1 Kings v., and the Chronist, according to his wont, is silent on their wisdom, for the sake of brevity, as it was elsewhere recorded.—J. G. M.]—Ver. 7. *And the sons of Carmi: Achar;* that is, Achar was descended from Carmi. Comp. the oft-recurring use of the plural בְּנֵי, where only one descendant is named (vers. 8, 30, 31, 42, and Gen. xlvi. 23). By Achar, as the addition, "the troubler of Israel" (עָכָר, properly "the troubled"), shows, is meant the Achan of the book of Joshua (vii. 1 ff., xxii. 20), whose name must have been known to the author of this book in the by-form Achar, as he puts the valley of Achor in etymological connection with it (vii. 26, xv. 7). The link that connects Carmi, the father or ancestor of this Achar, with Zerah is wanting; but from Josh. vii. 1, where he is called a son of Zabdi, the son of Zerah, it is highly probable that he springs from Zimri, the first named of the sons of Zerah, whether Zimri in our passage be an error of the pen for Zabdi, or the reverse, or Zabdi be a son of Zimri, and thus several links of the series from Zerah to Achar have been omitted. On Carmi, comp. also ch. iv. 1 and Num. xxvi. 6, where a family of Reuben bears the name.—Ver. 8. *And the sons of Ethan: Azariah.* This Ethanite Azariah is not otherwise known: no probable reason can be assumed why he only of the sons of Ethan is mentioned.

b. The Descendants of Hezron: vers. 9–41.—*α.* His three sons, ver. 9.—*And the sons of Hezron that were born to him.* The passive נוֹלַד stands "for the indefinite active, so that the following accusatives with אֶת depend on the virtual notion of the active 'one bare him;' comp. Gen. iv. 18, xxi. 5, xlvi. 20, and the sing. נוֹלַד in a similar position, 1 Chron. iii. 4, xxvi. 6" (Berth.). The name Ram is, in the New Testament genealogies of Jesus, Matt. i. 3, 4, Luke iii. 33, Aram; comp. רָם, Job xxxii. 2, with אֲרָם, Gen. xxii. 21. The name כְּלוּבָי is undoubtedly a by-form of כָּלֵב, ver. 18, or, as this name is written in iv. 11, of כְּלוּב: it is an *adject. gentil.*, that stands to its stem כְּלוּב, as צוֹפַי, 1 Chron. vi. 11, to צוֹף, vi. 20 (Ewald, *Lehrb.* § 164, *c*), or as in Greek Μανιχαῖος (the *n. pr.* of the well-known Persian sectary) to Μάνης. Accordingly, the celebrated forefather of Bezaleel had of old three names—Caleb, Celub, the Celuban. Comp. underneath on ver. 18 ff. and on ver. 40. The three here named, Jerahmeel, Ram, and Celubai, appear to have been actual sons or immediate descendants of Hezron, whereas the sons of Hezron afterwards appended,—Segub, ver. 21, and Ashur, ver. 24,—as they are co-ordinated with his later descendants, may possibly be sons in a wider sense. At all events, they did not belong to the aforesaid founders of the three celebrated lines of Hezronites, which are analyzed in the following passage, though in an order different from the present enumeration, the family of Ram being placed first, and that of Jerahmeel transferred to the end (comp. on ver. 18).

β. The family of Ram, as first of the three Hezronite lines. His precedence is explained by the circumstance that the house of David sprang from him. The posterity of Ram is therefore carried down to David in seven members. The six members to Jesse, the father of David, are found also in the book of Ruth iv. 19–21; comp. the genealogies in Matt. i. and Luke iii.—Ver. 10. *Nahshon, prince of the sons of Judah.* This distinguishing epithet, which is wanting in Ruth, points to Num. i. 7, ii. 3, vii. 12, where Nahshon is named as the prince of Judah at the exodus. As this date, according to the most probable interpretation of the number 430, Exod. xii. 40, is to be placed fully four centuries after the time of Judah, several members must have fallen out between Hezron, the grandson of Judah, and Nahshon, as well as between Nahshon and Jesse, as the series Salma, Boaz, Obed, and Jesse is not sufficient to fill up the interval of 400 years between Moses and David. [If the 430 years count from the call of Abraham, which has not yet been disproved, the exodus was only 210 years after the descent of Judah into Egypt, instead of four centuries.—J. G. M.]—Ver. 11. *Salma.* Instead of שַׂלְמָא, the book of Ruth has, iv. 20, שַׂלְמָה, but in the following verse שַׂלְמוֹן, which has passed into the New Testament (Luke iii. 32, Σαλμών, and so Matt. i. 4, 5, where Luther has Salma).—Vers. 13–15. The seven sons of Jesse. According to 1 Sam. xvii. 12 (comp. ch. xvi. 6 ff.), Jesse had 8 sons,—a difference which is most easily explained by the supposition that one of the eight died without posterity, and therefore was not included by later genealogists.—*His first-born Eliab.* So is the eldest called in the books of Samuel; on the contrary, in 1 Chron. xxvii. 18 the form Elihu appears to have come into the place of Eliab. The Peshito has in our passage 8 instead of 7 sons of Jesse, of whom it calls the seventh Elihu, the eighth David; the first 6 agree with the Masoretic text.—*And Shima the third.* The name שִׁמְעָא, occurring thus in 1 Chron. xx. 7, is in 2 Sam. xiii. 3 and xxi. 22 in the Keri שִׁמְעָה; on the contrary, in the Kethib of the latter passage שִׁמְעִי, and in Samuel (xvi. 6, xvii. 13) twice שַׁמָּה. The latter is merely an abbreviated form of שִׁמְעָה.—The names of the next three brothers occur nowhere else.—Vers. 16, 17. *And their sisters, Zeruiah and Abigail.* Both sisters obtained great celebrity through their heroic sons,—Zeruiah, as the mother of Abishai, Joab, and Asahel (1 Sam. xxvi. 6, 2 Sam. ii. 18, iii. 39, vi. 16, etc.), who are always named after their mother, never after their less celebrated father; Abigail, as mother of the commander Amasa, who was involved in Absalom's rebellion (2 Sam. xvii. 25, xix. 14, xx. 10), whom she bare to Jether the Ishmaelite. This יֶתֶר is called 2 Sam. xvii. 25 יִתְרָא, with the epithet הַיִּשְׂרְאֵלִי, for which, according at least to our passage, the correct form is הַיִּשְׁמְעֵאלִי; for the Israelitish descent of the man would have needed no distinct notice. Abigail herself appears, besides, according to 2 Sam. xvii. 25, as a daughter of Nahash and sister of Zeruiah, and therefore not a full, but only a half sister of David.

γ. The family of Caleb, as second of the three Hezronite lines: vers. 18–24.—The question, how this first list of his descendants is related to the second in vers. 42–49, Wellhausen (p. 13 seq.) has endeavoured to answer by regarding the Caleb in ver. 42 as corresponding to the Celubai in ver. 9, designating the order in which the special genealogies of the three Hezronite lines occurred, by the names Ram (ver. 10 ff.), Jerahmeel (ver. 25 ff.), and Caleb (ver. 42 ff.), and considering the genealogy of Caleb (vers. 18–24) as a later insertion, whereby the Chronist has disfigured the original and normal development of his genealogy of the Hezronites. He holds that, indeed, this insertion itself is again a conglomerate of genealogical fragments of various origin, as appears most clearly from the reference of vers. 21–23 to Hezron himself, the father of Caleb.[1] Indeed, even vers. 10–17 are probably an interpolation, whereby the Chronist has endeavoured to extend the pedigree of the Hezronites originally beginning with Jerahmeel ("the first-born of Hez-

[1] "... *Quæ ver.* 18 *sqq. leguntur, ex variis fontibus hausta a Chronicographo demum ei Chesronæorum catalogo interposita sunt, qui quasi fundamentum est totius structuræ hujus genealogiæ*" (*l.c.* p. 13).—Comp. p. 16: "... *farrago sunt omnia* (vers. 18–24), *ex meris congesta fragmentis.*"

ron," ver. 25), on the basis of the book of Ruth, the Ram of which (Ruth iv. 19) appears to him as a son of Hezron and a brother of Jerahmeel and Caleb, whereas he is in truth, according to ver. 25, a son of Jerahmeel and grandson of Hezron. Accordingly, the old genealogical table before the Chronist had only two lines of Hezronites (Jerahmeelites and Calebites), and his supplementing action had extended this register, so that he first added a Ram son of Hezron, with his posterity (vers. 10–17), different from Ram son of Jerahmeel, and then a second Caleb (vers. 18–24), with many other descendants than those of the younger brother Jerahmeel, ver. 42 ff. It cannot be denied that many reasons appear to recommend this bold hypothesis. It explains in a satisfactory way the circumstance that the first-born Jerahmeel, whose genealogy we should expect first, appears after those of his two younger brothers, and also the surprising duplication of the names Ram and Caleb. But the hypothesis comes short of absolute certainty in many points which require to be adduced for confirmation. And especially it still remains doubtful which of the different old traditions concerning the descendants of the old prince of Judah, Caleb the companion of Joshua, whether that in ver. 18 ff., or that in ver. 42 ff., or that in iv. 11, 15 ff., is to be pronounced the oldest and most trustworthy, and whether we are entitled to reject for one of them all the others at once as totally untrustworthy, and containing no element of historical truth. If it were to be assumed that originally there were two persons of this name, a Caleb son of Hezron (ii., iv. 11 ff.) and a Caleb son of Jephunneh (iv. 15 ff.), this duplication would warn us to be so much the more cautious in the reception or rejection of this or that one of the various traditions that are attached to these honourable names: the still greater complexity of the collective genealogies of Caleb would all the more favour the conjecture that each of the series referred to him must be accounted in the one or the other way as authentic, as containing in itself elements of the genuine posterity of Caleb.—Ver. 18. *Begat with Azubah his wife.* הוֹלִיד אֶת, either "begat with" (as elsewhere הוֹלִיד מִן, ch. viii. 8, 9) or "caused to bring forth" (comp. Isa. lxvi. 9). The following words, אִשָּׁה וְאֶת־יְרִיעוֹת, appear to be corrupt. If we translate (with D. Kimchi, Piscat., Osiand., and others), "with Azubah, a wife, and with Jerioth," two things are strange: the indefinite designation of Azubah as a wife, אִשָּׁה (for which we should expect "his wife," אִשְׁתּוֹ), and the circumstance that of the second wife no son is named. If we regard (with Hiller, J. D. Mich.) וְאֵת as explicative, with Azubah a wife, that is, Jerioth, we establish a mode of expression which is without a parallel in our book. It is impossible to render "And Caleb begat Azubah and Jerioth" (B. Striegel). We must either hold אִשָּׁה, which is, moreover, wanting in two MSS. (see Crit. Note), with Berth. and Kamph., as a marginal note that has crept into the text, designed to prevent the translation "begat Azubah," or adopt the reading of the Pesh. and the Vulg., אִשְׁתּוֹ אֶת, which gives the sense, "begat with Azubah his wife Jerioth, and these are her (Jerioth's) sons." The latter appears the most satisfactory (comp. Keil). The names of her three sons occur nowhere else in the Old Testament.—Ver. 19. *And Azubah died, and Caleb took to him Ephrath*, namely, to wife. To this second wife of Caleb, whose name in ver. 50 (comp. iv. 4) is Ephrathah, belongs Hur, who is also mentioned Exod. xxxi. 2 as the grandfather of Bezalel. By this we are scarcely to understand that Ephrathah was properly a local name equivalent to Bethlehem (Gen. xxxvi. 16, 19; Micah v. 1), so that Hur would be designated a descendant of Caleb, born at Bethlehem, or originating thence (an assumption to which Bertheau seems inclined).—On ver. 20, comp. Exod. xxxi. 2, xxxv. 30.—Ver. 21. *Afterwards Hezron went in to the daughter of Machir.* "Afterwards," וְאַחַר, that is, after the birth of those three sons mentioned ver. 9, whose mother is not named. The whole notice, extending to ver. 24, of Hezron's descendants, born in his old age of the daughter of Machir the Gileadite, and of a son Ashur, born after his death of a third wife Abiah (ver. 24), is undoubtedly surprising, and unsuitable to the present place: the series of Hezron's sons and their descendants is thereby violently interrupted, and the above-mentioned interpolation theory of Wellhausen has in this case a very strong support. If we hold the present order to be original, we must assume, with Keil, that the here mentioned descendants of Hezron "were somehow more closely connected with the family of Caleb than with that of either Ram or Jerahmeel." On Machir the first-born of Manasseh, to whom Moses gave the land of Gilead, comp. Gen. l. 23; Num. xxxii. 40; Deut. iii. 15. As he is here and ver. 23 called "father of Gilead,' so is it said Num. xxvi. 29 that he begat Gilead. Comp. Num. xxvii. 1, from which it follows that, by this paternal relation of Machir to Gilead, more must be meant than the bare notion of a descent of the Israelitish population of Gilead from Machir, and that there must have been a definite person, Gilead, son of Machir and grandfather of Zelophehad. By the designation father of Gilead, the present Machir is distinguished from later persons of the same name; comp. 2 Sam. ix. 4, xvii. 27.—Ver. 22. *And Segub begat Jair.* This Jair, the grandson of Hezron through Segub, belonged on the mother's side to the tribe of Manasseh, and occurs therefore elsewhere, as Num. xxxii. 41, Deut. iii. 14, as a Manassite. His family, after the conquest of Og king of Bashan under Moses, received the territory of Argob, and gave to the conquered cities which Moses handed over to him the name Havvoth-Jair (חַוֹּת יָאִיר), "tent-villages of Jair," or "life of Jair" (comp. Num. xxxii. 41; Deut. iii. 14; Josh. xiii. 30; 1 Kings iv. 13), with which designation the name "Judah on Jordan," Josh. xix. 34 (that is, the colony of Jews in Gilead east of the Jordan), is most probably identical; comp. v. Raumer, *Palæst.* 4th edit. p. 233; Hengstenb. *Gesch. des Reichs Gottes im A. T.* ii. p. 258; Hoffm. *Blicke in die früheste Gesch. des gelobten Landes*, i. (1870) p. 114.—Ver. 23. *And Geshur and Aram*, the Geshurites and Aramæans, which is scarcely a hendiadys for "the Aramæans of Geshur," but rather points to an alliance of the Geshurites with the neighbouring Aramæans. For Geshur (2 Sam. iii. 3, xiii. 37, xv. 8) was a region in Aram or Syria, lying on the north-west border of Bashan near Hermon and the eastern bank of the Jordan, that in David's time (comp. on ch. iii. 2) had a king of its own, and formed at that time an independent kingdom, not subject to Israel,—in the opinion of Hitzig (*Gesch. d. Volks Israel*, i. p. 28 ff.), an Amorite kingdom of Arian (?) origin, though Moses in the distribution of the country had assigned it to Manasseh (Josh. xiii. 13; comp. xii. 5).—*With Kenath and her daughters, sixty cities.* So should the "אֶת־קְנָת וגו be most probably taken, as a farther district, besides the villages of Jair, which the Geshurites and Aramæans took, and not as an explanatory apposition to these (comp. Berth.). For the preceding statement, that the villages of Jair amounted to twenty-three (ver. 22), is much too definite to allow it to be supposed that the now named sixty daughter towns of Kenath form an inexact repetition of the same designation. Much rather the difference of the two districts: "the villages of Jair" and the "daughters of Kenath," appears in the clearest manner from Num. xxxii. 41, 42, according to which, of the two Manassites Jair and Nobah, the former conquered the "Havvoth Jair," the latter the "Benoth Kenath." Only in their sum total were these places sixty in number, and only to this sum total does the present שִׁשִּׁים עִיר apply. Whether, therefore, the group of towns designated by "Kenath" (now Kanwat, on the western slope of Jebel Hauran) and her daughters numbered exactly thirty-seven towns (as Keil thinks), remains uncertain; and the number sixty may very probably be a round number (comp. also Deut. iii. 12–14; Josh. xiii. 30). On the time when the Geshurites and Aramæans took the sixty towns, nothing can be ascertained from our passage. Certain it is that the later Judge of Israel, Jair (Judg. x. 4), possessed again at least thirty of these towns under the name of Havvoth-Jair, which must have survived to still later times. *All these are sons of Jair*, not the sixty towns, but the afore-mentioned Segub and Jair and their descendants and correlatives. It may be conjectured that the genealogical source used by the Chronist was originally more full, so that כָּל אֵלֶּה referred not merely to these two names.—Ver. 24. *And after the death of Hezron in Caleb-ephrathah.* This place, which does not elsewhere occur, might possibly be the same as Ephrathah or Bethlehem-ephrathah (see on ver. 19); the name of Caleb's second wife Ephrath might be somehow connected with this her place of abode and death. "In 1 Sam. xxx. 14 a part of the south of Judah is called 'Negeb Caleb,' because it belonged to the family of Caleb; in analogy with which the town or place, in which Caleb and his wife Ephrath dwelt, might be called 'Caleb of Ephrathah,' if Ephrath had brought it as a dowry to him, as in Josh. xv. 18 f." (Keil). Or from the Negeb Caleb, as the southern part of Caleb's territory, 1 Sam. xxx. 14, "possibly the northern part might be distinguished by the more definite name 'Caleb of Ephrathah,' that is, of Bethlehem" (Berth.). None of these interpretations of this obscure phrase is perfectly satisfactory; and there is therefore much plausibility in the emendation of Wellhausen, founded on a various reading presented by the Sept. (ἦλθε Χαλὲβ εἰς Ἐφραθά = בָּא כָלֵב אֶפְרָתָה), "And after Hezron's death Caleb went to Ephrath, the wife of his father Hezron." Here for בְּ is read בָּא; for אֵשֶׁת, וְאֵשֶׁת; and for אֲבִיָּה, אָבִיו—a change which is certainly somewhat radical; but the resulting sense is not improbable (comp. Gen. xxxv. 22). As the text stands, here is a third wife of Hezron, called Abiah (comp. vers. 9 and 21), who bears to him "Ashur, father of Tekoa" (comp. iv. 5–7), as a *fil. postumus* after his death. This Ashur (whom Wellhausen is disposed to change into an אִישׁ־חוּר, and to identify with Hur, Caleb's son by Ephrath, ver. 19) is called father of Tekoa, as lord and chieftain of the town Tekoa, the home of the prophet Amos, two hours south of Bethlehem (comp. Josh. xv. 59), where this place still exists under the name Tekua (comp. Robinson's *Pal.* ii. p. 406).

δ. The family of Jerahmeel, the third line of Hezron: vers. 25–41.—*Of Jerahmeel* (he whom God pities, whom He loves = θεόφιλος) *the first-born of Hezron:* ver. 9. As there was a negeb Caleb (ver. 24) and a negeb of the Kenites, so there was a negeb of the Jerahmeelites, 1 Sam. xxvii. 10; comp. xxx. 29. This is a proof of the strength and power of this line springing from the oldest Hezronites.—*Ram the first-born.* Wellhausen, perhaps without ground, takes this Ram to be originally identical with the Ram of ver. 10, the founder of the Ramite family, from which David sprang; comp. on iv. 21.—*And Bunah, and Oren, and Ozem of Ahijah.* The last of these names, אֲחִיָּה, should not apparently designate a fifth son of Jerahmeel, because in that case the ו should not be wanting. It appears rather to be the name of the mother of the four sons, and a מֵ before אֲחִיָּה appears to have fallen out before the ם of the foregoing וָאֹצֶם (comp. viii. 9). This conjecture, thrown out by Jun., Tremell., Clericus, J. H. Mich., J. Lange, and approved by all the moderns, appears the more probable, as in the following verse mention is made of a second wife of Jerahmeel, and the Syr. and the Sept. in our verse have reckoned only four sons, the latter rendering אֲחִיָּה by ἀδελφὸς αὐτοῦ.—Ver. 26. *Atarah; she was the mother of Onam*, whose family is traced out vers. 28–33. The name עֲטָרָה appears to signify "crown," a name not unsuitable for a female, Prov. xxxi. 10. Yet it might signify "wall, fort," as the sing. of עֲטָרוֹת, the city (comp. Num. xxxii. 3, 34 f.; Josh. xvi. 5, 7, xviii. 13; and Wellhausen, p. 25).—Vers. 28–30. Onam's family continues itself in pairs of sons to Abishur and Nadab, his grandsons, and to their sons. On the name "Abihail," comp. Crit. Note.—Ver. 31. *And the sons of Sheshan* (descendants; see on ver. 7), *Ahlai.* This Ahlai must have been a daughter, not a son, of Sheshan, great-grandson of Nadab, ver. 29; for (ver. 34) Sheshan had no sons, but only daughters: Ahlai was therefore his heiress; but whether the same daughter who (ver. 35) married the Egyptian Jarha must remain uncertain. The remark of Hiller (*Onom. S.* p. 736), therefore, on Sheshan: *Quicquid habuit liberorum, s. nepotum, sustulit ex unica filia Achlai*, is not quite correct.—Ver. 33. *These were the sons of Jerahmeel.* This subscription (going back to ver. 25) includes 23 descendants of Jerahmeel. It deserves notice, that 23 descendants of Jerahmeel, with the preceding descendants of Judah (from ver. 3), make up the sum of 70 members of the house of Judah, namely, sons of Judah, 5 ; of Perez, 2 ; of Zerah, 5 ; Carmi, Achar, and Azariah, 3 ; Ram and his descendants (including the 2 daughters of Jesse, and Jether father of Amasa), 21 ; Caleb and his descendants, 10 ; and Jerahmeel and his descendants, 24. This new number 70 of the ancestors of the Jews, made out by Bertheau, loses weight and certainty, because it includes several females, against all genealogical rule reckons the father and mother of Amasa as two members, and excludes the 13 descendants of Sheshan, which sprang from the Egyptian servant Jarha (vers. 34–41), treating them as a mere offshoot (comp. Keil, p. 46). And would not the Chronist, if he had actually wished to represent the posterity of Judah, after the manner of that of his father Israel, Gen. xlvi. 26 f., as 70 souls, have overturned this reckoning again by his later additions, and especially the supplements given in iv. 1–23, and altogether effaced the impression made thereby? Wellhausen's interpolation theory, even if only approximately true, by no means agrees with this assumption of a tendency in the writer to symbolic numbers in his enumerations in vers. 3–33. —Vers. 34–41. The family of Jarha, the Egyptian servant. This Jarha occurs nowhere else ; he may have served Sheshan during the sojourn of Israel in Egypt ; for the latter branched off from Judah in the ninth generation, and belonged thus to the time before Moses. Most of the old expositors, perhaps rightly, presume that Jarha, only after he was made a free man and a proselyte by Sheshan (comp. Ex. xxii. 20, xxiii. 9), married his daughter ; comp. the law concerning intermarriage between Israelites and Egyptians, Deut. xxiii. 8 ; also David's Egyptian servant, 1 Sam. xxx. 13 ff. Of the 13 here named descendants of Jarha, none occur elsewhere in the history of the Old Testament. Their names, indeed, recur several times, some of them, for example, in ch. iii., among the descendants of David ; but it is not in the remotest degree probable that any of these belong to the list of the descendants of Jarha.

Appendix to the Genealogy of the House of Judah: Three Series of Descendants of Caleb, with Names chiefly of Geographical Import: vers. 42–55.

a. The first series : Mesha's posterity : vers. 42–45.—*And the sons of Caleb, brother of Jerahmeel.* This introduction leaves no doubt that the same Caleb is meant as in ver. 18, and that this is an appendix to his genealogy already communicated. *Mesha his first-born ; he was the father of Ziph.* Though almost all the following names : Ziph, Mareshah, Hebron, appear to be local names, yet Mesha (מֵישָׁע) sounds decidedly like a personal name ; comp. the Moabitish king of this name, who has recently become celebrated by his monument of victory (2 Kings iii. 4). As, on the other hand, Ziph (זִיף) appears to be the town adjacent to Hebron which is mentioned Josh. xv. 55, the same that gave its name to the wilderness of Ziph known to us from the history of David, 1 Sam. xxiii. 14 ff., xxv. 2, and which Robinson has recognised (ii. 417 ff.) in certain ruins on a hill south-east of Hebron, nothing is more natural than to perceive in Mesha the father of Ziph a lord or chieftain, or even the founder, of the town of Ziph (comp. on ver. 24). By Ziph might also be meant the place mentioned Josh. xv. 24, pretty far from Hebron in the plain (Shephelah) situated not far from Marash, the ancient Mareshah (so thinks Keil against Bertheau).—*And the sons of Mareshah the father of Hebron.* Mareshah is scarcely the name of that town mentioned Josh. xv. 44 and 2 Chron. xi. 8 along with Ziph, which occurs in the times of the Maccabees and the Romans under the name of Marissa, and is preserved in the ruins of Marash in the Shephelah, half an hour south of Beit-jibrin (v. Raum. *Palæst.* 3d edit. p. 192 ; Robinson, ii. 693 ; Tobler, *Dritte Wanderung*, pp. 129, 142). The expression "father of Hebron" makes the reference to this town very improbable ; for at no time is any dependence of the ancient Hebron (Num. xiii. 23) on that very remote Mareshah recorded. We must rather, as the reading of the Masoretic text now runs, regard Mareshah as the proper name of some old tribe chief, and hold the Hebron signalized among his sons as most probably a person or tribe distinct from the well-known city Hebron (comp. v. 28 and Ex. vi. 18, where חֶבְרוֹן is likewise a personal name). So, justly perhaps, Wellhausen and Keil, who is, moreover, disposed to consider the text corrupt, and proposes the following emendation (see Crit. Note) : "and the sons of Mesha were Abi-Hebron." This conjecture is supported by the analogy of such compounds as Abidan, Abiezer, Abinadab ; the simple Hebron in ver. 43 might very well be an abbreviated form of Abihebron (comp. En-tappuah, Josh. xvii. 7, with the shorter Tappuah, Josh. xvi. 8). [It is simpler and easier to regard Hebron as a person, named, if you will, after a former Hebron.—J. G. M.]—Ver. 43. *And the sons of Hebron : Korah, and Tappuah, and Rekem, and Shema.* These four names also must rather be names of persons or tribes than of towns. For Korah and Shema occur only as personal names ; Rekem once indeed as the name of a city, Josh. xviii. 27, but belonging to Benjamin, and several times as a personal name : in Num. xxxi. 8 as the name of a Midianite prince ; and 1 Chron. vii. 18 as the name of a descendant of Manasseh. Only Tappuah ("apple") recurs merely as the name of a city (Josh. xii. 17, xv. 34, xvi. 8 ; comp. xvii. 7), which, however, proves nothing for the case in point, and by no means establishes a reference to this or that so-called city.—Ver. 44. *And Shema begat Raham, father of Jorkeam.* For יָרְקְעָם, which occurs nowhere else, the Sept. exhibits Ἰεκλάν ; whence Bertheau concludes that it was originally יָקְדְעָם, as in Josh. xv. 56. But this name "Jokdeam" the Sept. renders by Ἰεκδαάμ, and here it reads twice in succession Ἰεκλάν. It exhibits the same also for רֶקֶם, and thereby obscures the original relation of the genealogical data in our passage ; some of the four sons of Hebron (ver. 43), first Shema and then the penultimate Rekem, have their genealogy traced. With Shammai the son of this Rekem comp. the so named persons above ver. 28 and below iv. 17, and also the celebrated leader of the Pharisees of this name, the antagonist of Hillel in the time of Jesus (Joseph. *Antiq.* xiv. 9. 4).—Ver. 45. *And Maon was father of Beth-Zur.* Both Maon and Bethzur are cities in the hill country of Judea; comp. for the former, which is now called Main, and is pointed out as a castle in ruins, with cisterns, etc., on a hill in Carmel south of Hebron, Josh. xv. 55; 1 Sam. xxiii. 24 f., xxv. 2; Robinson, ii. 421; for the latter, the site of which is to be sought north of Hebron on the road to Jerusalem, Josh. xv. 58; 2 Chron. xi. 7; v. Raumer, *Pal.* p. 163. There is no decisive reason for excluding a reference to these places. Maon the son of Shammai may be regarded as the founder of the city so called (comp. Judg. x. 12, where Maon is the name of a non-Israelitish tribe, along with Amalek and the Zidonians); Bethzur may then have been founded as a colony from Maon, a genetic relation, which is here expressed in a manner not quite usual by "father of Bethzur" (for above in vers. 24, 42, and below in vers. 50, 51, it is not descent of a colony from its mother city, but government of cities by their princes or lords, that is designated in this manner).

b. The second series: posterity of Ephah and Maachah, the two concubines of Caleb: vers. 46-49.—*And Ephah, Caleb's concubine.* The name עֵיפָה, occurring elsewhere (ver. 47 and i. 33) as a man's name, seems here, where it designates a secondary wife of Caleb, to point to a non-Israelitish origin of its possessor, whether she be regarded as a person or a race. Of the latter opinion is Wellhausen, p. 12, who takes this non-Israelitish *gens* mingling with the Calebites to belong to Midian; and on the contrary, the second concubine of Caleb, designated as Maachah, ver. 48, to be a *gens* belonging to Canaan. Of the three sons of Ephah, Haran and Gazez are not otherwise known. The middle name Moza occurs Josh. xviii. 26 as the name of a city of Benjamin; but this can scarcely be connected with the son of Caleb and Ephah. That Gazez (Sept. Γεζουέ) is first named as a third son, and then as a grandson of Caleb, may be explained in two ways,—either so that the statement: "and Haran begat Gazez" (which is omitted in the Sept.), be taken as a more exact addition to the foregoing mention of Gazez, or that there were really two descendants of Caleb of the same name, a son and a grandson (uncle and nephew; comp. ch. iii. 10). The former is the more probable assumption. —Ver. 47. *And the sons of Jehdai.* It is not clear how this Jehdai (יֶהְדָּי) is genealogically connected with the foregoing. Hiller in the *Onom. S.* conjectures without ground that he was one and the same person with Moza, ver. 46; Jehdai might as well be a second concubine of Caleb. Of the six sons of Jehdai also, of whose names only some (Jotham; comp. Shaaph, ver. 49) occur elsewhere, we know nothing more.—Ver. 48. *And Caleb's concubine Maachah bare Sheber and Tirhanah.* Though this name מַעֲכָה occurs often (comp. iii. 2, vii. 16, viii. 29, xi. 43; also the *nom. gentilic.* הַמַּעֲכָתִי, 2 Kings xxv. 23; 1 Chron. iv. 19), yet nothing certain can be conjectured concerning its present bearer; that she was a Canaanitess is a mere conjecture of Wellhausen. The two sons of Maachah occur nowhere else. The masc. יָלַד (for which some MSS. have יָלְדָה; see Crit. Note) may arise from the writer thinking of the father, whom he does not name.—Ver. 49. *And she bare* (besides the two already mentioned) *Shaaph, the father of Madmannah.* This city of Judah, mentioned Josh. xv. 31, may be preserved in the present Miniay or Miniah south of Gaza. Its "father" Shaaph, clearly different from him who is so named ver. 47, may be regarded as its prince or founder (comp. on ver. 42): even so Sheva (on which name comp. 2 Sam. xx. 25, Keri) in reference to Machbenah, and the unnamed father in reference to Gibeah. Machbenah, belonging no doubt to Judah, is no further known. Joshua also, xv. 57, names a Gibeah in the mountains of Judah, whether the same with the village Jeba mentioned by Robinson and Tobler, on a hill in Wady Mussur, remains a question; comp. Keil on Josh. xv.—*And Caleb's daughter was Achsa.* This closing notice puts it beyond doubt that the Caleb hitherto (from ver. 46) spoken of is the same as Caleb the son of Jephunneh and father of Achsa (whom he promised and gave to the conqueror of Debir as a reward, Josh. xv. 16 ff.; Judg. i. 12). This is Caleb son of Jephunneh, the contemporary of Moses and Joshua; and therefore it seems difficult to identify him at once with the brother of Jerahmeel and son of Hezron mentioned in vers. 18 and 42 (comp. on ver. 18). For this Hezronite, a great-grandson of Judah through Perez, appears to have been older than Moses and Joshua; but our passage, as also ch. iv. 15, refers clearly to that contemporary of Joshua who is mentioned in the books of Joshua and Judges. That this younger Caleb is a descendant of the Hezronite is highly probable, because in the descendants of one and the same stock it is easy for the collateral genealogies to intermingle, as they have done here and in iv. 15 ff. (comp. besides, the remarks on ch. iv. 11, 13, 15). If we assume accordingly two Calebs, an older, the Hezronite, of whom we read vers. 9 (under the name Celubai), 18, 42-45, and then again vers. 50-55, and a younger, whose genealogy is given in our verses (46-49) and in ch. iv. 15 ff., we do not go so far as some older expositors (even Starke), who assume with a double Caleb a double Achsa, a daughter of the Hezronite Caleb (supposed to be here mentioned), and a daughter of the Jephunnite Caleb (Josh. xv.; Judg. i.). As little do we approve of Movers' conjecture (*Chron.* p. 83), that the words, "and Caleb's daughter was Achsa," are a spurious interpolation of a later hand. But Keil's conjecture, also, that the expression "daughter" denotes here "grand-daughter, descendant," that it is the Achsah of Josh. xv. 16 that is here spoken of, but as a later descendant of the old Hezronite Caleb, and not a daughter of the Jephunnite, we cannot accept, as it obviously does violence to the term "daughter." Finally, we reject also Bertheau's attempt to admit only one Caleb, and to refer the diversity in the accounts of him here and before to the inexact manner of the genealogical terms that express also geographical relations; as well as Ewald's opinion, that Caleb in vers. 42-49 is the Caleb of the book of Joshua; the Caleb in vers. 9, 18–20, and 50–55, on the contrary, is a quite different person, whose real name was Celubai. (On the somewhat different, and at all events more probable hypothesis of Wellhausen, see above on ver. 18.)

c. The third series: posterity of Hur, son of Caleb: vers. 50–55.—As Hur is doubtless the grandfather of Bezaleel mentioned ver. 19, we have here again a line going back to Caleb the Hezronite.—*These were the sons of Caleb.* This introductory sentence, the generality of which does not suit the following statement, giving a genealogy of only one son of Caleb, appears to indicate that the whole section is taken from an originally different connection.—*The son of Hur, first-born of Ephrathah* (comp. ver. 19): *Shobal.* As, after Shobal in the following verse, Salma and Hareph are also named as sons of Hur, it appears more correct to read for בֶּן־חוּר, with the Sept., the plur. בְּנֵי־חוּר. In the Masoretic pointing, indeed, the names Salma and Hareph follow Shobal, father of Kiriath-jearim, without close connection by וְ; and בֶּן־חוּר appears in some measure as a superscription. Whether Shobal be the same with the brother of Hur and son of Judah mentioned ch. iv. 1, must remain doubtful. The town of Kiriath-jearim, of which he is here called the father, that is, founder or chief, is that old Gibeonite town which is otherwise called Kiriath-baal or Baalah (comp. Josh. ix. 17, xv. 9, 60), and lay in the north-west corner of Judah, on the border of Benjamin, probably the present Kureyet el Enab (wine town), on the road from Jerusalem to Jaffa (Robinson, ii. 588 ff.; Keil on Josh. ix. 17).—Ver. 51. *Salma, father of Beth-lehem.* The coincidence of name with the Beth-lehemite ancestor of David of the house of Ram mentioned ver. 17 is perhaps only accidental; comp. on ver. 54.—*Hareph, father of Beth-gader*, of the same place, which in Josh. xii. 13 is Geder, and in Josh. xv. 36 Gederah; comp. ch. xii. 4, xxvii. 28. Keil thinks rather of Gedor (גְּדוֹר), Josh. xv. 58, 1 Chron. iv. 4, xii. 7, but with less ground. The name Hareph does not occur elsewhere, though חָרִיף, Neh. vii. 24, x. 20 (comp. הַחֲרוּפִי, 1 Chron. xii. 5), may be only a variation of the same name.—Ver. 52. *Haroeh and the half of Menuhoth.* These words, unintelligible to the old translators: הָרֹאֶה חֲצִי הַמְּנֻחוֹת, for which the Sept. gives three proper names: 'Αραὰ καὶ Αἰσὶ καὶ 'Αμμανὶθ, and the Vulg. the unmeaning words: *qui videbat dimidium requietionum*, are obviously corrupt. Let us read after ch. iv. 2, where a Reaiah son of Shobal occurs, for רְאָיָה הָרֹאֶה (for to regard the former as a mere by-form of רְאָיָה, as many old expositors do, is inadmissible), and for חֲצִי הַמְּנֻחוֹת according to ver. 54: וַחֲצִי הַמָּנַחְתִּי or וַחֲצִי הַמָּנַחַת. The text thus amended (according to Bertheau's conjecture) gives Reaiah and Hazi-hammanahath, that is, half of the Manahathite, as sons of Shobal, two Jewish families, of which the latter may be part of the inhabitants of the town Manahath, ch. viii. 6. The situation of this place is determined by ver. 54, where Zorah is mentioned as a neighbouring town, to be near the border of Judah, towards Dan. Reaiah seems from ch. iv. 2 not to have continued as a local name, but to have been the ancestor of the citizens of Zora; so that his former seat is also to be sought in the north-west of Judah.—Ver. 53. *And the families of Kiriath-jearim were the Ithrite*, etc. These families of Kiriath-jearim are annexed to the already named sons of Shobal as other sons, descendants of the same ancestor. The four families are adduced in the fundamental text as singulars: the Ithrite, the Puthite, etc. The three last named occur nowhere else; on the contrary, to the family of the Ithrites, ch. xi. 40 (2 Sam. xxiii. 38), belonged Ira and Gareb, two of David's heroes.—*From these came the Zorathite and the Eshtaolite.* Zorah, the home of Samson (Judg. xiii. 2, xvi. 31), now Sura, between Jerusalem and Jabneh; Eshtaol, a town on the border of Judah and Dan, near Zorah (comp. Judg. xvi. 31, xviii. 11), probably the present Um Eshteijeh. —Ver. 54. *The sons of Salma: Bethlehem* (the family of Bethlehem; comp. ver. 51) *and the Netophathite.* The town Netophah must, as follows from the reference of its inhabitants to Salma, be sought close by Bethlehem; comp. ch. ix. 16; 2 Sam. xxiii. 28 f.; 2 Kings xxv. 23; Ezra ii. 22; Neh. vii. 26, whence appears the comparative celebrity of this town, whose site has not yet been discovered.—*Ataroth of the house of Joab.* This is certainly the name of a town, which is to be interpreted, not "crowns," but rather "walls, forts," of the house of Joab; comp. on ver. 26. The site is as uncertain as that of the following Hazi-hammanahath (half Manahath); comp. ch. viii. 6. On the contrary, הַצָּרְעִי at the close points certainly to the known border city Zorah mentioned in the foregoing verse; for צָרְעִי is only formally different from צָרְעָתִי, being derived from the masc. of צָרְעָה, which may have been used along with the feminine as the name of the town, although this cannot be proved. The Zorites of our verse must have formed a second element of the inhabitants of Zorah, along with the Zorathites of the previous verse descended from Shobal.—Ver. 55. *And the families of the scribes dwelling at Jabez.* This Jewish town of Jabez (יַעְבֵּץ), whose name recurs ch. iv. 9 f. as that of a descendant of Judah, is quite unknown in site, but must apparently be sought, like all the places mentioned from ver. 53, in the north of Judah, on the borders of Benjamin or Dan. Of the families of scribes in Jabez, however, three are mentioned: the Tirathites, Shimathites, and Suchathites. These three names the Vulg. has applied appellatively to the functions of these three classes of learned men, translating: *canentes et resonantes et in tabernaculis commorantes.* It is possible that the Jewish doctors consulted by Jerome in the translation of our book (perhaps the rabbi from Tiberias, with whom he collated the text from beginning to end; comp. Introd. § 6, Rem.) had presented an etymological basis for this interpretation, in seeking to refer—1. תִּרְעָתִים to תְּרָעָה, "jubilee song, trumpet sound;" 2. שִׁמְעָתִים to שִׁמְעָה, "report, echo" (or perhaps to שְׁמָעָה, Aram. שְׁמַעְתָּא, *traditio legis*; comp.

Wellhausen, p 30); 3. שׁוּכָתִים to שׁוּכָה = סֻכָּה, "hut, booth;" comp. Lev. xxiii. 34 ff. If the etymology here were correct, and it commends itself at all events more than the partly deviating one which Bertheau (by reference of the first term to the Chald. תְּרַע, door, and thus making תִּרְעָתִים a synonym of שֹׁעֲרִים, porters) has attempted, the functions assigned to the three classes of Sopherim, and giving origin to their names, would belong to divine worship, and resemble those of the Levites. And this seems to agree very well with the closing remark: *these are the Kenites, that came from Hammath, father of the house of Rechab*, as a certain connection or spiritual relationship may be shown, as well of the Kenites as of the Rechabites, with the Levites, if we think on the one hand of Jethro, father-in-law of Moses, the priest of the Midian-Kenites in the region of Sinai (Ex. ii. 15, iii. 1; comp. Judg. i. 16, iv. 11, 17), and of his influence on the legislative and religious activity of Moses (Ex. xviii.); on the other hand, of the priestly fidelity of the family of the Rechabites, as Jer. xxxv. (comp. 2 Kings x. 15) describes them, of their constant "standing before the Lord," and, moreover, of the ancient tradition still surviving among the nominal descendants of the Rechabites in Yemen, that the house of Rechab descended from Hobab or Keni (Judg. i. 16), the father-in-law of Moses (comp. A. Murray, *Comment. de Kinæis*, Hamb. 1718; Nägelsbach on Jer. xxxv., vol. xv. p. 254 of *Bibelwerk*). On a fair examination of these circumstances, it appears highly probable that the certainly foreign (1 Sam. xv. 6) yet highly honoured Kenites, in like manner as the Gibeonites, ministered of old in the sanctuary of Israel, and that the Rechabites of the times of the Kings and a ter the exile (Neh. iii. 14) were descendants of these old Kenite temple ministers, who, by adherence to one part of their ancient wont and use, kept themselves distinct from the great mass of the people. The naming of Hammath also, as "father of the house of Rechab," agrees very well with this hypothesis; for if Jonathan the Rechabite that met with Jehu king of Israel, and was honoured by him (2 Kings x. 15, 23), was a son of Rechab, so may Hammath have been father or forefather of this Rechab, and so ancestor of the whole family. Though all this rises little above the range of the hypothetical, and though in particular the question remains dark and unanswerable, why this Kenite family of Sopherim from Jabez is directly attached to Salma the father of Bethlehem, and through him to Hur the son of Caleb (whether on account of some intermarriage having taken place between a Kenite and an heiress of the house of Salma?), yet it is on the whole probable that those three names are really designations of three classes of ministers in the sanctuary, and not proper names of families, as the Sept. (Ἀργαθιείμ, Σαμαθιείμ, Σωκαθιείμ) held, and a majority of recent expositors still hold. Besides, Wellhausen's attempt to refer that which is stated, both in our verse concerning the Kenites or Rechabites of Jabez, and generally from ver. 50 on concerning the posterity of Hur and their settlements in the north of Judah to the time after the exile, and so ascribe these statements to bias and fancy, and to admit only the foregoing genealogy, vers. 42–49, which assigns to the Calebites settlements in the south of Judah around Hebron, as historically reliable, that is, referring to the time before the exile,—this whole attempt (pp. 29–33) falls short of satisfactory proof. There is no ground for holding that which is reported of the Calebites as inhabitants of Kiriath-jearim, Bethlehem, Netophah, Zorah, etc., to be a collection of later traditions than the foregoing accounts of Calebite families in Tappuah, Maon, Bethzur, etc. Neither do we know the geographical position of the several places mentioned in the two sections (vers. 42-49 and 50-55) so well, as to be able to assert that the former refers only to the south, the latter only to the north, of Judah. Respecting Jabez, for example, the seat of the Kenites, it is by no means determined that it is to be sought in the neighbourhood of Bethlehem and Kiriath-jearim (comp. above). In short, it is advisable to avoid such violent attempts to solve the problem here presented as the assumption of a genealogy of Calebites before and after the exile, and to approve the more cautious remark of Bertheau: "We can easily imagine the motive which led the Chronist to communicate this verse, though we are unable completely to perceive its contents."

[The term כְּלוּבָי, ver. 9, seems to be, if not a patronymic, at least a virtual plural, and may well indicate more than one Caleb. The name was famous and frequent in the tribe of Judah. The first of the name appears in vers. 18-24. He is designated "the son of Hezron," though Ram is not, evidently to distinguish him from others of the name. He may have been born 50 or 58 years after Jacob came down to Egypt, as his father was born shortly before that event. He has by his wife Azubah three sons, or perhaps grandsons; and after her death he marries Ephrath, and by her has a well-known son Hur, who was the contemporary of Moses, Ex. xvii. 10. The episode about his father Hezron marrying again when sixty years old, is brought in partly from the concurrence in the foregoing paragraph of the two names Caleb and Ephrath, which are combined in the name of the place where he died, and partly from the high antiquarian interest which it possesses. Hezron was born before Jacob went down to Egypt, and therefore most probably died within 110 years from that date. He died, not in Egypt, but in Caleb-Ephrathah. This implies the presence and power of Caleb in the region of Hebron as a sheik giving name to a place in his estate. In this quarter Abraham, Isaac, and Jacob had resided and acquired some property in land, Gen. xxiii. Caleb of the line of Judah held possession of this estate during the early period of Israel's residence in Egypt, when they were still a free and honoured people. And there his father died in a town called after the united names of himself and his wife. After the Israelites, however, were reduced to slavery by the Pharaoh that knew not Joseph, the occupation of this region by the descendants of Judah was rendered precarious or entirely interrupted. In this paragraph, then, we have a most unexpected and interesting glimpse of what was taking place in the time of the first Caleb; and in this view of the passage we see that it occupies its right place.

A second Caleb is presented to us in vers. 42–49. He is distinct from the former in everything but the name: 1. In the mode in which he is introduced, namely, in an appendix after the three sons of Hezron have been brought forward in order; 2. In his sons and wives, which are all quite different from those of his namesake; 3. In his time, as he is the father of Achsah, and therefore lived in and after the 40 years of the wilderness, two or three generations later than the former Caleb; 4. In his place, as a careful examination of the two paragraphs will show; 5. In his designation as "the brother of Jerahmeel," while the former is called "the son of Hezron;" for this phrase cannot mean the son of the Jerahmeel already mentioned, as this would be a superfluous addition, and would not square with the time of this Caleb. Some will conceive that the term "brother" is here used in a wide sense to denote a kinsman of Jerahmeel, a member of the family. But it is more simple to consider Jerahmeel here to be a descendant of the former Jerahmeel, not otherwise mentioned, just as Celub in ch. iv. 11 is said to be a brother of Shuah, who is not previously mentioned. This appendix is thus in its right place, as it signalizes an important member of the Jerahmeelite clan, 1 Sam. xxvii. 10, Caleb the son of Jephunneh.

A third Caleb comes before us in a second appendix: vers. 50–55. He is clearly different from each of the others, as he is "the son of Hur, the first-born of Ephrathah," and therefore not a Jerahmeelite like the second, but the grandson of the first.

There is nothing to hinder us taking this view of the whole passage, and it might be supported at much greater length. It deals fairly with the author, as it presumes him to observe order, and endeavours not to import confusion into his narrative by a preconceived theory. We submit it to the judgment of the reader.—J. G. M.]

2. *The Descendants of David to Elioenai and his Seven Sons:* ch. iii.

CH. III. 1. And these were the sons of David, that were born to him in Hebron:
the first-born Amnon, of Ahinoam the Jezreelitess; the second Daniel, of
2 Abigail the Carmelitess. The third Absalom,[1] the son of Maachah, daughter
3 of Talmai king of Geshur; the fourth Adonijah, son of Haggith. The fifth
4 Shephatiah of Abital; the sixth Ithream, by Eglah his wife. Six were born
unto him in Hebron, and he reigned there seven years and six months; and
5 he reigned thirty and three years in Jerusalem. And these were born to him
in Jerusalem: Shima, and Shobab, and Nathan, and Solomon, four, of Bath-
6, 7 shua daughter of Ammiel. And Ibhar, and Elishama,[2] and Eliphelet. And
8 Nogah, and Nepheg, and Japhia. And Elishama, and Eliada, and Eliphelet, nine.
9 All the sons of David, except the sons of the concubines, and Tamar their sister.
10 And the son of Solomon: Rehoboam, Abiah his son, Asa his son, Jehosha-
11, 12 phat his son. Joram his son, Ahaziah his son, Joash his son. Amaziah his
13 son, Azariah his son, Jotham his son. Ahaz his son, Hezekiah his son,
14, 15 Manasseh his son. Amon his son, Josiah his son. And the sons of Josiah:
the first-born Johanan, the second Jehoiakim, the third Zedekiah, the fourth
16 Shallum. And the sons of Jehoiakim: Jechoniah his son, Zedekiah his son.
17, 18 And the sons of Jechoniah the captive: Shealtiel his son. And Malchiram,
19 and Pedaiah, and Shenazzar, Jecamiah, Hoshama, and Nedabiah. And the
sons of Pedaiah: Zerubbabel and Shimei; and the son[3] of Zerubbabel:
20 Meshullam and Hananiah, and Shelomith their sister. And Hashubah, and
21 Ohel, and Berechiah, and Hasadiah, Jushabhesed, five. And the son[4] of
Hananiah: Pelatiah and Jesaiah; the sons[5] of Rephaiah, the sons of Arnan,
22 the sons of Obadiah, the sons of Shechaniah. And the sons of Shechaniah:
Shemaiah; and the sons of Shemaiah: Hattush, and Igal, and Bariah, and
23 Neariah, and Shaphat, six. And the son of Neariah: Elioenai, and Hezekiah,
24 and Azrikam, three. And the sons of Elioenai: Hodaiah,[6] and Eliashib, and
Pelaiah, and Akkub, and Johanan, and Delaiah, and Anani, seven.

[1] For לְאַבְשָׁלוֹם many MSS. and most old prints read אַבְשָׁלוֹם. Comp. Exeg. Expl.

[2] וֶאֱלִישָׁמָע in this first place is perhaps an error of the transcriber for וֶאֱלִישׁוּעַ, which appears not only in the two parallel passages xiv. 5 and 2 Sam. v. 15 (after וְיִבְחָר), but also in *cod. Vat.* of the Sept., as it gives Ἐλισά.

[3] For וּבֶן before זְרֻבָּבֶל some MSS., as well as the old translators, read וּבְנֵי, an unnecessary amendment (comp. Exeg. Remark on ii. 7).

[4] The same variation as in ver. 19 (see Note 2).

[5] For בְּנֵי, "sons of," the Sept. reads from this to the end of the verse בְּנוֹ, "his son," so that from Hananiah to Shechaniah it yields a series of seven successive generations. So also R. Benjamin in R. Azariah de Rossi in *Meor Aenajim* (comp. Zunz, *Gottesdienstliche Vorträge der Juden*, p. 31).

[6] *Keri:* הוֹדַוְיָהוּ (for which, according to the Hebrew law of sounds, we should expect הוֹדַוְיָהוּ). The *Kethib* הודויהו cannot be so pronounced, and appears to arise from a confusion of the forms *Hodavjahu* and *Hodijahu*.

EXEGETICAL.

Preliminary Remark.—After the family of Ram, the middle son of Hezron was carried down, ii. 10–17, only to Jesse the father of David, and the genealogies of Caleb and Jerahmeel were interposed, ii. 18–55, the line of Ramites, starting from David, is resumed and traced from David to the time after the captivity. This is given in three paragraphs, of which the first registers all the sons of David except those born of concubines, vers. 1–9; the second, the series of kings of the house of David from Solomon to Jechoniah and Zedekiah, vers. 10–16; and the third, the descendants of Jechoniah to the seven sons of Elioenai, vers. 17–24. The names in the second of these paragraphs mostly recur, those in the third, at least partly, in the genealogy of Jesus in Matthew (whereas Luke iii. 23 ff. presents a totally different series of names from David to Shealtiel, and again from Zerubbabel to Joseph).

1. *The Sons of David:* vers. 1–9. *a.* The six sons born in Hebron: vers. 1–4.—These six senior sons of David are, with one exception, enumerated literally as in 2 Sam. iii. 2–5.—*The first-born Amnon, of Ahinoam the Jezreelitess;* literally, "to Ahinoam." The לְ before אחינעם designates the wife to whom the son belonged. Comp. on this Ahinoam, 1 Sam. xxv. 43, xxvii. 3, and on Amnon, who is also called Aminon (2 Sam. xiii. 20), 2 Sam. xiii.—*The second Daniel, of Abigail the Carmelitess.* Instead of שֵׁנִי, properly "a second," stands in the parallel 2 Sam. iii. 3 מִשְׁנֵהוּ, "his second," with which הַמִּשְׁנֶה, 1 Chron. v. 12, is to be compared. A more important difference from 2 Sam. iii. 3 is כִּלְאָב, quite another name, which stands there for דָּנִיֵּאל. This other designation of the second son of David may be explained by the supposition of a real double name, as in Uzziah Azariah (comp. on 2 Chron. xxvi. 1), Jehoiakim Eliakim, Mattaniah Zedekiah (comp. also on ver. 15). The variant Δαλουία (perhaps = דְּלָיָה) presented by the Sept. in 2 Sam. iii. 3 may be an error of transcription for Δανιήλ (or inversely "Daniel," a later variation for the original Delaiah); but the name Cilab is still unexplained. On Abigail, the widow of Nabal the Carmelite (not to be confounded with Abigail the sister of David, ii. 16), comp. 1 Sam. xxv. 3 ff.—Ver. 2. *The third Absalom.* For אַבְשָׁלוֹם is also found אֲבִישָׁלוֹם, 1 Kings xv. 2, 10. The לְ before אַבְשָׁלוֹם might, in another connection, serve to lay emphasis on the name ("the well-known Absalom;" comp. Isa. xxxii. 1). Here, however, in a mere list of names, it scarcely has this import, but seems rather to have come into the text through an oversight, in consequence of the foregoing לְאָב in לַאֲבִיגַיִל. Other attempts to explain this לְ (which is wanting in some copies; see Note) are quite worthless, and deserve to be noted only as *curiosa;* for example, Kimchi's proposal to take לְ for לֹא, thereby designating him as properly not an Absalom, a father's peace, but a rebel, or Hiller's supposition (*Onom. S.* p. 733) that לְאַבְשָׁלוֹם is a fuller form for the simpler and more usual אַבְשָׁלוֹם, etc. On Geshur, comp. above ii. 23; on Adonijah, son of Haggith, comp. 1 Kings i. and ii.—Ver. 3. *By Eglah his wife,* לְעֶגְלָה אִשְׁתּוֹ; quite similar to 2 Sam. iii. 5, לְעֶגְלָה אֵשֶׁת דָּוִד. This addition "his wife," or "wife of David," appears to be inserted merely to make a full-toned conclusion of the series, and scarcely to distinguish Eglah as the most eminent wife of David, as some Rabbis and recently Thenius on 2 Sam. iii. 5 think, who take Eglah only for another name of Michal, 1 Sam. xviii. 20, or even substitute מִיכַל as the original reading for עֶגְלָה (so Thenius).—Ver. 4. For the historical notices in this verse comp. 2 Sam. ii. 11, v. 5. The statement in 2 Sam. ii. 10 (from which Ishbosheth appears to have reigned only two years in Mahanaim) conflicts only apparently with the seven years of the residence of David in Hebron; on which see Hengstenb. *Gesch. d. Reiches Gottes unter dem A. B.* ii. 2, p. 114 f.

b. The thirteen sons of David born in Jerusalem: vers. 5–9. These sons of David (of whom four are by Bathsheba) are again mentioned xiv. 7–11, in the history of David. Less complete is the list in the parallel passage 2 Sam. v. 14–16, by the omission of the last two.—Ver. 5. The four sons of Bathsheba, or, as she is here called, *Bathshua.* The two names, occurring beside one another, receive their explanation from the intervening form בַּת־שֶׁוַע; as this, however, is obviously weakened from בַּת־שֶׁבַע (as בַּת־שׁוּעַ again is a weakening of בַּת־שֶׁוַע), the latter form appears to be the oldest and most original. Two other peculiarities of the names contained in our verse are—1. שִׁמְעָא as the name of the first of Bathsheba's four sons, for which stands in xiv. 4 and 2 Sam. v. 14 שַׁמּוּעַ; 2. Ammiel (עַמִּיאֵל) as the name of the father of Bathsheba, for which in 2 Sam. xi. 3 is the form Eliam (אֱלִיעָם), containing the two elements of the name transposed. It is uncertain which of these two forms is correct and original.—Vers. 6–8. Here follow the nine sons born at Jerusalem of other wives. *And Ibhar, and Elishama, and Eliphelet.* As the two parallel passages xiv. 5 and 2 Sam. v. 15 agree in presenting after Ibhar an Elishua, אֱלִישׁוּעַ, Elishama in our passage appears clearly an error of transcription, especially as this name occurs again in ver. 8. The following name Eliphelet (אֱלִיפֶלֶט) is found also in xiv. 5, although in the somewhat abbreviated form אֶלְפֶּלֶט; on the contrary, it is wanting in 2 Sam. v. 15, where only one Eliphelet, the last of the series, is mentioned. It is uncertain whether this want be original, and the double position is the result of some error of the Chronist or his voucher (as Berth. thinks). That David should have repeated the same name in the sons of his different wives is of itself not incredible.—Ver. 7. *And Nogah, and Nepheg, and Japhia.* The name נגה, omitted by an oversight in 2 Sam. v. 15, is certainly original, though nothing be known concerning this Nogah, perhaps because he died early and childless. "The view of Movers, p. 229, that this name was not originally in the text, and came in by a false writing of the following נפג, has arisen from an undue preference for the text of the books of Samuel" (Berth.).—Ver. 8. *And Elishama* (comp. on ver. 6), *and Eliada, and Eliphelet, nine.* For אלידע appears xiv. 7 בעלידע, scarcely correct; for the other parallel 2 Sam. v. 16 and the Sept. and Syr. versions in xiv. 7 have אלידע (Sept. *cod. Vat.* Ἐλιαδί—*cod. Alex.*, indeed, Βαλλιαδί).—Ver. 9. *All the sons of David, except the sons of the concubines.* These sons of David by concubines or slaves are also unnamed elsewhere; but their existence appears from 2 Sam. v. 13, xii. 11, xv. 16, xvi. 22.—*And Tamar their sister*, not the only one, but the sister known from the history (2 Sam. xiii. 1 ff.).

2. *The Kings of the House of David from Solomon to the Exile:* vers. 10–16.—As far as Josiah, they are enumerated, without naming any non-reigning descendants, as a simple line of sovereigns, embracing in it fifteen members (with the omission of the usurper Athaliah as an idolater and a foreigner) by the addition of a בנו, "his son," to each. At variance with this course, four sons of Josiah are then named, not perhaps in him, the great reformer, "to introduce a pause in the long line of David's descendants" (Berth.), but "because with Josiah the regular succession ceased" (Keil).—*The first-born Johanan, the second Jehoiakim, the third Zedekiah, the fourth Shallum.* To Josiah succeeded, 2 Kings xxiii. 30, 2 Chron. xxxvi. 1, his son Jehoahaz as king. This Jehoahaz is called in Jer. xxii. 11 properly Shallum; he was thus, as the present list shows, the youngest, or at all events one of the youngest, among them; not to be identified with the first-born Johanan, as many older writers (Seb. Schmidt, Starke, etc.), and of the moderns, for example, Hitzig (*Begriff der Kritik*, etc., p. 182 ff., and *Gesch. d. Volks Isr.* p. 246), do. For, 1. The statement of Jeremiah, that Shallum became king in his father's stead, is quite positive and unhesitating. 2. From comparing 2 Kings xxiii. 31, 36, with 2 Chron. xxxvi. 2, 5, it appears that Jehoahaz was two years younger than Jehoiakim, and therefore not the first-born. 3. The preferring of a younger son before an older to the throne is not surprising, if we consider the analogous case of Solomon, who, though one of the youngest of the sons of David (the youngest of the four sons of Bathsheba), succeeded to the throne. 4. The double name Jehoahaz Shallum is not more surprising than Jehoahaz Johanan would be; the mutually exchanging names are in both cases, if not quite alike in meaning, yet expressive of similar ideas (יהואחז, "whom Jehovah holds," and שלום, "who is requited (of God)," and so יהוחנן); comp. the numerous cases of double naming, of which some examples are quoted on ver. 1, also *Simonis Onom.* p. 20. The only inaccuracy that can be imputed to the Chronist in the present statements is, that he names Shallum in the last place, and so appears to favour the opinion that he was the youngest of the four brothers, whereas Zedekiah was much younger than he; indeed, as a comparison of 2 Kings xxiii. 31 with xxiv. 18 shows, at least 13 or 14 years younger (for Shallum was 23 years old when he ascended the throne, while Zedekiah, who ascended the throne 11 years later, was then only 21 years of age). How this inaccuracy in the order is to be explained, Keil shows very well, p. 55 f.: "In our genealogy Zedekiah is placed after Jehoiakim and before Shallum, because, on the one hand, Jehoiakim and Zedekiah held the throne a longer time, each for eleven years; on the other hand, Zedekiah and Shallum were the sons of Hamutal (2 Kings xxiii. 31, xxiv. 18), Jehoiakim the son of Zebidah (2 Kings xxiii. 36). With respect to age, they should have succeeded thus: Johanan, Jehoiakim, Shallum, and Zedekiah; and in regard to their reign, Shallum should have stood before Jehoiakim. But in both cases those born of the same mother Hamutal would have been separated. To avoid this, Shallum appears to have been reckoned beside his brother Zedekiah in the fourth place." Regarded thus, the passage loses its obscurity, which Nägelsbach has still imputed to it (on Jer. xxii. 11), without going quite so far as Hitzig, who here lays a whole series of errors to the charge of the Chronist. Comp. against the imputations of the latter, Movers, p. 157 f.: "The two names (Johanan and Jehoahaz) are to be distinguished exactly as Jehoiakim and Jehoiachin; had the Chronist named Jehoahaz along with Shallum, or, as Hitzig thinks right, called him the first-born, the error would certainly have been undeniable. Further misled by the passage of Jeremiah, he has taken Shallum for another son of Josiah, the fourth, and different from Jehoahaz. Shallum Jehoahaz is certainly named the fourth in ver. 15, incorrectly indeed, for he was the third; but the Chronist could not mistake the passage of Jeremiah, for it clearly says: 'who (Shallum) reigned instead of Josiah his father.' How should an error in the Jewish line of kings occur in a Jewish historian!"—Ver. 16. *And the sons of Jehoiakim: Jechoniah his son, Zedekiah his son.* Instead of יכניה = יכון יהו (whom God establishes), the son of Jehoiakim in 2 Chron. xxxvi. 9, as in 2 Kings xxiv. 8 ff., bears the equivalent name Jehoiachin (יהויכין; comp. יויכין, Ezek. i. 2), whereas he is called, Jer. xxiv. 1, xxvii. 20, xxviii. 4, and Esth. ii. 6, יכניה, quite as here and Jer. xxii. 24, 28, xxxvii. 1, Conjahu (כניהו, an abbreviation of יכניה, יכניהו). The Zedekiah here named can only be regarded as a son of Jechoniah, and so a grandson of Jehoiakim and great-grandson of Josiah; for the בנו added to his name uniformly designates in the previous genealogical line the son of the aforesaid: and the circumstance, that this son of Jechoniah is named here apart from his other sons, may find its explanation in this, that this Zedekiah, perhaps the first-born, did not go into captivity with his father and brethren, but died beforehand as a royal prince in Jerusalem. He is therefore not to be confounded with the Zedekiah who was mentioned in the foregoing

verse as a third son of Josiah, and, 2 Kings xxiv. 17 ff., 2 Chron. xxxvi. 11, became successor of Jechoniah on the throne; he is a grand-nephew of king Zedekiah, who before his accession was called Mattaniah, and whose subsequent name, as well in Chronicles (2 Chron. xxxvi. 10) as in Kings (2 Kings xxiv. 17 ff.), is uniformly written צִדְקִיָּהוּ (not, as here, צִדְקִיָּה). This last variety of name is merely graphical, though in the present case, where the double name (Mattaniah Zedekiah) serves as a mark of the king, it may have a further import. Against the assumption of some ancients (even of Starke), that the Zedekiah of our verse is the same as king Zedekiah, who is quoted (ver. 15) as a son of Jehoiachin, because he was his successor on the throne, comp. the just remarks of Calov. in the *Biblia illustrata*. With respect to 2 Chron. xxxvi. 10, where Zedekiah the successor of Jehoiachin appears to be erroneously termed his brother, which in reality is only inexactness, or a wider sense of the word אָח (= relative in general), see on the passage.

3. *The Descendants of Jechoniah to the Seven Sons of Elioenai*: vers. 17–24.—*And the sons of Jechoniah the captive.* It is certainly possible to translate the words וּבְנֵי יְכָנְיָה אַסִּר with the Sept., Vulg., Kimchi, Jun., etc., and even Keil: "And the sons of Jechoniah were Assir." But the appellative meaning of אַסִּר, "the captive," adopted by Luther, Starke, Berth., Kamph., is decidedly preferable. For, 1. As one of the sons of Jechoniah, the early deceased Zedekiah, has been already named, we expect here a remark of Jechoniah indicating that he as captive or in captivity begat the sons now to be named. 2. An Assir, as connecting link between Jechoniah and Shealtiel, nowhere occurs, neither in Matt. i. 12 nor in the *Seder Olam Sutta* (comp. Herzfeld, *Gesch. d. V. Israel*, i. 379). 3. The absence of בְּנוֹ after אַסִּר, while it stands after שְׁאַלְתִּיאֵל, makes it impossible to see in Assir a link between Jechoniah and Shealtiel. 4. Neither can Assir be regarded as a brother of Shealtiel, because the copula could not then be wanting between the two names, and because the singular בְּנוֹ after שְׁאַלְתִּיאֵל is inexplicable, if two sons of Jechoniah were named. 5. The combination proposed by Keil (p. 57), that Assir, the only son of Jechoniah besides the early deceased Zedekiah, left only a daughter, by whom he became the father-in-law of Neri, a descendant of David of the line of Nathan, and by this son-in-law, again (Luke iii. 27), the father, or strictly the grandfather, of Shealtiel, of Malchiram, Pedaiah, and the other sons named ver. 18, fails through its excessive artificiality, and through this, that it takes בְּנוֹ at the close of our verse, notwithstanding the constant use of the Chronist in the foregoing genealogy, in the sense of his grandson. 6. The single objection that can be made to the appellative meaning of אַסִּר, that it wants the article, loses much of its force from the abrupt and merely allusive manner of our genealogist. 7. The Masoretic accentuation points out אַסִּר as an appellative addition to יְכָנְיָה, a circumstance not to be overlooked in the present case, as it proves our interpretation to be supported by no less respectable and ancient authorities than the opposite one.—Ver. 18. *And Malchiram, and Pedaiah*, etc. These six other sons of the captive Jechoniah, Kimchi, Tremell., Piscat., Hiller, Burmann, and recently Hitzig on Hag. i. 1, 12, regard not as brothers, but as sons of Shealtiel, because Zerubbabel elsewhere appears (Hag. i. 1; Ezra iii. 2, v. 2; Matt. i. 12) as son, or at all events direct successor, perhaps grandson, of Shealtiel, whereas here he would appear to be his nephew, if his father Pedaiah (ver. 19) had actually to pass for a brother of Shealtiel. Against this hypothesis is—1. The copula before מַלְכִּירָם, which makes it impossible to regard the six named in our verse otherwise than as brothers of Shealtiel. 2. The paternal relation of Pedaiah to Zerubbabel, as attested ver. 19, may be easily reconciled with the elsewhere attested filial relation of Zerubbabel to Shealtiel, by the assumption of intermarriage or adoption; in other words, the Chronist's making Zerubbabel to be son of Pedaiah and nephew of Shealtiel may well be taken for a more exact statement than that of the other reporters (Hag., Ezra, and Matt.). Besides, the five sons of Jechoniah named along with Shealtiel and Pedaiah are otherwise unknown. Only of Pedaiah are further descendants known in the following verses.—Ver. 19. *And the sons of Pedaiah: Zerubbabel and Shimei.* The latter is not elsewhere named: concerning the former, of whose identity with the celebrated prince and leader of the first band of returning captives, 536 B.C., there can be no well-founded doubt (although Hottinger, S. J. Baumgarten, Starke, and the ancients incline to assume two or even three different Zerubbabels), comp. on the previous verse.—*And the son of Zerubbabel: Meshullam and Hananiah.* On the somewhat surprising sing. וּבֶן, on account of the plural number of sons, and the variant וּבְנֵי, see Crit. Note. Bertheau, moreover, justly remarks: "In the names of the sons of Zerubbabel appear to be reflected the hopes of the Israelites at the time of the return from Babylon, in Meshullam (friend of God), comp. Isa. xlii. 19, Hananiah (grace of God), Berechiah, Hasadiah, Jushab-Chesed (mercy will return)."—*And Shelomith their sister.* She is perhaps named after the first two sons, because she sprang from the same mother. Her name divides the collective family of Zerubbabel into two groups, the former of two, the latter of five sons. Possibly the second group contains exclusively or chiefly younger sons of Zerubbabel born after the return from the exile.—Ver. 21. *And the son of Hananiah: Pelatiah and Jeshaiah.* The two grandsons of Zerubbabel are otherwise unknown, but must have belonged to the contemporaries of Ezra, about 450 B.C.—*The sons of Rephaiah, the sons of Arnan, the sons of Obadiah, the sons of Shechaniah.* In what relation these four families stand to Pelatiah and Jeshaiah, the sons of Hananiah, is not clear, as the express statement that their heads, Rephaiah, etc., were sons of Hananiah, and brothers of those two, is wanting; and the various readings of the old translators (Sept., Vulg., Syr.), that give, instead of the plur. בְּנֵי, always the sing. with the suff. בְּנוֹ, thereby

originating a continuous line of descent, with seven members from Hananiah to Shechaniah, have little claim to credibility. For, 1. The line of David's descent would, if ver. 21 actually reckoned seven successive generations, seem to be continued far into the 3d century B.C. (for in vers. 22–24 four generations more are added),—much further than a rational estimate of the age of our author, who must have lived at the latest about 330 B.C., will admit (comp. Einl. p. 3). 2. The assumption of an addition to the series, arising from a younger writer than the Chronist, is extremely doubtful. 3. The Hattush of ver. 22 appears to be the same with the descendant of David bearing the same name mentioned Ezra viii. 2, a younger contemporary of Ezra, which is quite possible, and even probable, if this Hattush be the fourth in descent from Zerubbabel, but, on the contrary, impossible if he be the ninth. 4. The brief mode of enumerating with the mere בְּנוֹ, appending the son only to the father without mention of other descendants, does not agree with the verses around from ver. 18, in which a more copious enumeration, almost in every number giving a plurality of children, is presented. If it appear, on the whole, most probable that the sons of Rephaiah, etc., are designations of contemporary families of the house of David, not successive generations, it still remains doubtful how these families are connected with the last-named descendant of Zerubbabel. On this there are, in the main, two opinions among recent expositors: *a.* Ew., Berth., Kamph., etc., take Rephaiah, Arnan, Obadiah, and Shechaniah, as well as the two before named, Pelatiah and Jeshaiah, to be sons of Hananiah, and assume that, on account of the great celebrity and wide extension of their families, these last four sons are named, "not as individuals, but as families" (for which cases like ch. i. 41, ii. 42, iv. 15, xxiv. 26, etc., afford examples).

b. Movers, Herzfeld, Hävernick, Keil see in these four families, generations "whose descent the Chronist could not or would not more precisely define, and therefore merely enumerates one after another" (Herzf.), and are inclined to regard the whole series from בְּנֵי רְפָיָה to the end of the chapter as "a genealogical fragment, perhaps inserted afterwards into the text of Chronicles" (Keil), and accept where possible the assumption defined by the ancients, as Heidegger, Vitringa, Carpzov, etc., of a corruption of the present Masoretic text, perhaps a gap before בְּנֵי רְפָיָה (so likewise Keil). We may reserve the choice between these two views; for while the assumption of a corruption of the text seems to be natural enough, and to be rendered even probable by the change of בְּנֵי into בנו in the Sept., yet, on the other hand, we scruple to ascribe to the Chronist an uncertain or defective knowledge concerning the families of the house of David after Zerubbabel, as it is to be presumed that he would be especially well informed on matters so near his own time.—Ver. 22. *And the sons of Shechaniah: Shemaiah.* The plur. בְּנֵי, as in i. 41, ii. 42, etc. On Hattush son of Shemaiah, then named in the first place, see on previous verse, and Introd. § 3, Rem. The closing notice, that six sons of Shemaiah are named in all, is strange, because only five of them are named; and it is quite unfeasible, with J. H. Mich., Starke, and others (as in Gen. xlvi. 15), to assume that the father is included. We can scarcely escape the assumption, that one of the six names has fallen out of the text by an old error of transcription; but we can hardly regard the sixth name *Sesa* (*Sessa*), presented by the Vulg. in the *Edit. Sixt.* of 1590, as anything else than a poor emendation arising from the number שִׁשָּׁה, since no other text presents this name.—Ver. 23. *And the son of Neariah: Elioenai.* With the latter name, which is here written without ה (אֶלְיוֹעֵינַי), but elsewhere in full אֶלְיְהוֹעֵינַי (my eyes unto Jehovah), comp. Ezra viii. 4, and, with respect to the sentence which contains its etymology, Ps. xxv. 15.—Ver. 24. *And the sons of Elioenai: Hodaiah*, etc. With the name הוֹדַיְוָהוּ (or perhaps הוֹדוּיָהוּ, "praise Jehovah, praise God") compare the shorter form הוֹדַוְיָה, v. 24, ix. 7, Ezra ii. 40, and הוֹדְוָה, Neh. vii. 43; see also Crit. Note.

The seven sons of Elioenai here named, if we are to suppose a direct genealogical connection of the families enumerated from ver. 21*b* with the before-named descendants of Zerubbabel (if, consequently, the assumption of Movers, Herzfeld, and Keil, that vers. 21*b*–24 form an unconnected interpolation, is to be rejected), would be the seventh generation inclusive from Zerubbabel, and, if the length of a generation be fixed at 30 years, would have to be placed near the middle of the 4th century B.C., as, for example, Bertheau (p. 35) reckons the years 386–356 B.C., Ewald (*Gesch. d. V. Isr.* 2d edit. i. 229) the time after 350, as the period of the existence of the seven sons of Elioenai, who are supposed to be contemporary with the author of Chronicles. The assumption that we are here dealing with direct descendants of Zerubbabel is liable to serious doubt. For, besides the loose connection of בְּנֵי רְפָיָה and the following families in ver. 21, it appears to favour the fragment hypothesis, that "in the genealogy of Jesus, Matt. i., not a single name of the descendants of Zerubbabel agrees with the names in this register," and that at least seven members must be supposed to be overleaped at once by Matthew or his genealogical voucher (so Clericus, and recently Keil). In reply to this, it may be assumed certainly, that those descendants of Zerubbabel whose pedigree is traced by the Chronist to his own time need not necessarily have been the direct ancestors of Joseph (or Mary), but that the line of Abiud, Eliakim, etc., leading to Jesus in Matthew, might have sprung from another of the seven sons of Zerubbabel. Besides, Matthew must have made very great omissions in the interval of 500 years between Zerubbabel and Joseph, as he reckons only twelve members for this period (comp. the edit. of the *Bibelw.* on Matt. p. 8 f.): an omission of six or seven successive members would be nothing inconceivable in his mode of proceeding. And if the genealogy of Hananiah, communicated at length by the Chronist, in particular the family of Elioenai with his seven sons, were deemed worthy of special notice on account of their celebrity, high reputation, and eminent services on behalf of the theocracy, this would not prove that the New Testament pedigree of Jesus must necessarily have mentioned these famous descendants of Zerubbabel as belonging to the ancestors of our Lord. For lowliness and obscurity, not splendour and fame, should be the characteristic of the pedigree of Jesus after the exile. If the line of the ancestors of Jesus, reaching from David to the exile, according to Matthew's arrangement, contains crowned heads, and thus forms a lofty range of royal names, it corresponds to the plan of the apostolic genealogists, that the third line from the exile to Joseph and Mary should include in it chiefly undistinguished names, and thus form a descending line which ends in the carpenter Joseph (see Lange, p. 6). Nothing decisive can thus be inferred from a comparison of the New Testament genealogies of the Messiah with our passage for the relation of the names therein contained to the posterity of Zerubbabel, or for the question whether those named in vers. 21*b*–24 are to be regarded as descendants or as remoter connections of this prince.

3. *Supplements to the Genealogy of the House of Judah* (*leading to the Genealogical Survey of the Twelve Tribes of Israel*): ch. iv. 1–23.

CH. IV. 1. The sons of Judah: Perez, Hezron, and Carmi, and Hur, and Shobal.
2 And Reaiah son of Shobal begat Jahath; and Jahath begat Ahumai and
Lahad: these are the families of the Zorathite.
3 And these were[1] of the father of Etam: Jezreel, and Ishma, and Idbash;
4 and the name of their sister was Hazelelponi. And Penuel the father of Gedor,
and Ezer the father of Hushah: these are the sons of Hur the first-born of
Ephrathah, the father of Bethlehem.
5, 6 And Ashur the father of Tekoah had two wives, Helah and Naarah. And
Naarah bare him Ahuzzam, and Hepher, and Temeni, and the Ahashtari:
7 these were the sons of Naarah. And the sons of Helah: Zereth, Izhar,[2] and
Ethnan.
8 And Koz begat Anub and Zobebah, and the families of Aharhel the son
9 of Harum. And Jabez was honoured above his brethren; and his mother
10 called his name Jabez, saying, Because I bare him with sorrow. And Jabez
called on the God of Israel, saying, If thou wilt bless me indeed, and enlarge
my border, and thy hand be with me, and thou deal without evil, that it
grieve me not! And God brought that which he had asked.
11 And Celub the brother of Shuhah begat Mehir; he was the father of Esh-
12 ton. And Eshton begat Beth-rapha, and Paseah, and Tehinnah the father of
the city Nahash: these are the men of Rechah.
13 And the sons of Kenaz: Othniel and Seraiah; and the sons of Othniel:
14 Hathath. And Meonothai begat Ophrah: and Seraiah begat Joab father of
the valley of the carpenters; for they were carpenters.
15 And the sons of Caleb son of Jephunneh: Iru, Elah, and Naam; and the
sons of Elah and Kenaz.
16 And the sons of Jehalelel: Ziph and Ziphah, Tiria and Asarel.
17 And the son[3] of Ezrah: Jether, and Mered, and Epher, and Jalon; and she
conceived [and bare][4] Miriam, and Schammai, and Ishbah father of Eshtemoa.
18 And his wife, the Jewess, bare Jered the father of Gedor, and Heber the father
of Socho, and Jekuthiel the father of Zanoah: and these are the sons of Bithiah
daughter of Pharaoh, whom Mered took.[5]
19 And the sons of the wife of Hodiah, the sister of Naham: the father of
Keilah the Garmite, and Eshtemoa[6] the Maachathite.
20 And the sons of Shimon: Amnon and Rinnah, Benhanan and Tulon;[7] and
the sons of Ishi: Zoheth and Benzoheth.[8]
21 The sons of Shelah son of Judah: Er the father of Lechah, and Ladah the
father of Mareshah; and the families of the house of byssus work, of the house
22 of Ashbea. And Jokim, and the men of Cozeba, and Joash, and Saraph, who
23 ruled over Moab, and Jashubi-lehem[9]: and these are ancient things. These are
the potters and the dwellers in Netaim and Gederah; with the king, in his
service, they dwelt there.

[1] For וְאֵלֶּה אֲבִי עֵיטָם, which gives no tolerable sense, read with some MSS. וְאֵלֶּה בְּנֵי אֲבִי עֵיטָם, or with the Sept., Vulg., and some other MSS. וְאֵלֶּה בְּנֵי עֵיטָם.

[2] So (יִצְחָר) in the *Kethib*. The *Keri* וְצֹחַר is designed to gain a name better known (comp. Gen. xxiii. 8, xlvi. 10).

[3] For וּבֶן some MSS. have וּבְנֵי, which is perhaps to be preferred, as in vers. 13, 16, 19, 20.

[4] For וַתַּהַר, "and she conceived," the Sept., following perhaps another reading, give *καὶ ἐγέννησεν* 'Ιεθέρ (Vulg.: *genuitque Mariam*). For מִרְיָם they exhibit Μαιών (*cod. Vat.* Μαρών).

[5] This closing sentence וְאֵלֶּה . . . מָרֶד stands here probably in the wrong place, and is tc be placed after וְיָלוֹן, ver. 17; see Exeg. Expos.

[6] Before אֶשְׁתְּמֹעַ (which the Sept. here renders by 'Ισθημωή, whereas in ver. 17 it has 'Εσθεμών [*cod. Vat.* 'Εσθαιμών]) וַאֲבִי seems to have fallen out, as the parallel אֲבִי קְעִילָה indicates.

[7] *Kethib:* תּוּלוֹן; *Keri:* תִּילוֹן.

[8] Before בֶּן־זוֹחֵת, which (not as, for example, בֶּן־חָנָן immediately before) is not a *nom. propr.*, but denotes "son of Zoheth," the name of this son seems to have fallen out.

[9] Jerome (perhaps on the ground of a somewhat different text, but more probably only following the arbitrary interpretation of an old Jewish Midrash) renders the words from וְיוֹקִים: *et qui stare fecit solem, virique mendacii et securus et incendens, qui principes fuerunt in Moab, et qui reversi sunt in Lachem.*

EXEGETICAL.

Preliminary Remark. — This section, unusually rich in obscurities and difficulties, is characterized on the one hand as a supplement to the pedigree of Judah already communicated, embracing numerous fragments of old genealogies; on the other hand, as a transition and introduction to the genealogical and chorographical survey of the twelve tribes except Judah, contained in iv. 24–vii. In common with the latter group of genealogies, it makes frequent reference to the places in the territory of each tribe, and inserts brief historical or archæological notices, which are of considerable value on account of the antiquity of the events recorded (vers. 9, 10, 14, 21–23). We are reminded of the former notices of the families of Judah in ch. ii., not only by the superscription connecting the introductory verse of this chapter, with its enumeration of some of the most eminent descendants of Judah (ver. 1), but also by the abundance of the details communicated concerning many more or less celebrated Jewish families (at all events a proof that the tribe of Judah passed with the author for the most important of all, and that the most special notices concerning it lay before him); as well as by the loose order of the several fragments, in which a similar neglect of the formation of longer lines of generations standing in direct succession to one another betrays itself, as in those supplementary reports concerning various descendants of Caleb at the close of ch. ii., and perhaps in the closing verses of ch. iii. Nowhere is this fragmentary character of the genealogical notes of our author so striking as in the present section, which presents no less than ten or twelve isolated fragments of lines or genealogical notices, having no visible connection with that which precedes or follows. The whole, in fact, looks almost like a gathering of genealogical pebbles, rolled together from various quarters, and consisting of older and younger parts, that are kept together only by their common connection with the tribe of Judah. That anything here communicated refers to the state of things after the exile, is assumed by Bertheau (p. 36), perhaps without sufficient ground. Yet it cannot be positively asserted that the author (who in ch. iii. traced the house of David down to his own late times) here describes only ancient relations, and purposely has not overstepped the limits of the exile.

1. *The Superscription:* ver. 1.—*The sons of Judah: Perez, Hezron, and Carmi, and Hur, and Shobal.* These five are called "sons" of Judah, as appears from ii. 3 ff., only in a wider sense; for Perez only was an actual son of Judah (ii. 5); Hezron was his grandson; Carmi, as the probable grandson of Zerah (ii. 7), was his great-grandson; Hur the son of Caleb, son of Hezron, was his great-great-grandson (ii. 18, 19); and Shobal son of Hur was his grandson's great-grandson (ii. 50). The putting together of these five descendants is highly peculiar, and cannot be satisfactorily explained in its historical grounds. Several of the families founded by them certainly became chief families in the tribe of Judah, but not all; in particular, the prominence of Carmi between names so celebrated as Hezron and Hur is so truly strange, as to justify the suspicion that this name is not genuine, and to favour the hypothesis of Wellhausen (p. 20), that for כַּרְמִי is to be read כְּלֻבַי, Celubai=Caleb (see ii. 9). If this were the original reading, we should obtain a series of directly succeeding descendants of Judah (comp. ii. 3, 9, 18 f., 50), and so far as our verse is a superscription for the following, it would merely indicate descendants of Hezron, who is also named in ch. ii. as the ancestor of a widely-spread stock of Jewish families. This indication, however, would by no means correspond with the following verses. For only by uncertain conjecture do we think to find in vers. 5–7 descendants of Hur, in vers. 11–15 descendants of Caleb, in vers. 16–23 other Hezronites of different lines (comp. on the respective passages). On the whole, the several groups of our section are strung together without much connection; and that they form no continuous line of descent (by which the line started in ver. 1, if the proposed emendation be accepted, would be carried forward) is at all events clear and beyond a doubt. The matter, therefore, must rest with the remark of Bertheau: "Why in our passage precisely these five 'sons' of Judah are enumerated, while in Gen. xlvi. 1 and 1 Chron. ii. other names occur in a different order, is a question we should only be able to answer if we could state the point

of time in the history and development of the tribe of Judah to which our series refers, and were in a position to trace further from other sources the relations of the families of Judah here exhibited. As matters stand, we must be contented with the general remark, that the families designated by our five names were without doubt the prominent families in the time of the author of our series, and are therefore enumerated as sons of Judah. It is surprising, certainly, that in the following pedigree, vers. 2–20, this arrangement almost entirely disappears, and that in vers. 21–23 Shelah, sixth 'son' of Judah, is introduced by way of appendix."

2. *The Zorathites*, a line of descent from Shobal: ver. 2.—*And Reaiah son of Shobal* (the son who is probably latent under הָרֹאֶה, ii. 52, on which see) *begat Jahath.* יַחַת is no further mentioned as a descendant of Judah through Shobal, but occurs often as a Levite name; comp. vi. 5, 28, xxiii. 10 ff., xxiv. 22, 2 Chron. xxxiv. 12.—His sons also, Ahumai and Lahad, occur nowhere else. On the contrary, the closing notice, "these are the families of the Zorathite," refers us to well-known ground, in so far as a descent of the inhabitants of Zorah from Shobal (the ancestor of Kiriath-jearim, the mother city of Zorah and Eshtaol) is manifest from ii. 50–53. The present verse therefore stands plainly in the relation of a supplement to that passage.

3. *A Line of Descent from Hur:* vers. 3, 4.—*And these were of the father of Etam.* So is it to be amended instead of the unmeaning "and these were Abi Etam" of the Masoretic text, or with the Sept. and Vulg.: "And these were the children of Etam." עֵיטָם, whether it be an element of a personal name אֲבִי עֵיטָם, or itself denote an old patriarch or family, points at all events to the inhabitants of an old Jewish mountain city not far from Bethlehem and Tekoa (2 Chron. xi. 6), which occurs in the history of Samson (Judg. xv. 8). Jezreel also, the first-named son of Etam, occurs Josh. xv. 56 as a mountain city of Judah; comp. the *nom. gentil.* "the Jezreelitess" referring to this city, and applied to Ahinoam the wife of David, iii. 1. On the contrary, Ishma, Idbash, and their sister Hazelelponi are mentioned only here. Whether the name of the last is the name of a family or of an individual (comp. Ew. § 273*e*) remains doubtful.—Ver. 4. *And Penuel the father of Gedor.* Penuel (פְּנוּאֵל) is here the name of a patriarch of Jewish descent, but in viii. 25 of a Benjamite. With the city Penuel or Peniel, east of the Jordan and south of Jabbok (Gen. xxxii. 31 f., Judg. viii. 8, 17, 1 Kings xii. 25), the name here has no connection. On the contrary, that of his son Gedor occurs also as a name of a town in the tribe of Judah (Josh. xv. 58; comp. 1 Chron. iv. 39, xiii. 7), and this town, preserved as a ruin in the present Jedur (Robins. ii. 592), is to be referred to the son of Penuel as its father or founder. We meet, indeed, in ver. 18 with a certain Jered as "father of Gedor," whence we may conclude that the posterity of both formed the population of this Gedor.—*And Ezer the father of Hushah.* עֵזֶר ("help") occurs elsewhere as a man's name (vii. 21, xii. 9), but not in the genealogies of the house of Judah. The site of the town Hushah founded by this Ezer is unknown; but the *nom. gentil.* חֻשָׁתִי occurs several times, namely, in the Davidic hero Sibbechai, 1 Chron. xi. 28, xx. 4, 2 Sam. xxiii. 27.—*These are the sons of Hur the first-born of Ephrathath, the father of Bethlehem.* Comp. ii. 19, and on Hur's relation to Bethlehem ii. 51, where more precisely than here Salma the son of Hur is called "father of Bethlehem." "The circumstance, moreover, that in our verses (3 and 4) other names and persons are enumerated as descendants of Hur than in ii. 50–55, betokens no difference; for there is no ground for the assumption that in the latter passage all his descendants are given" (Keil). Our passage is thus, like ver. 2, supplementary to ii. 50–55, so far as it repeats and confirms some of the names and affinities there mentioned, and adds other new ones.

4. *Ashur the father of Tekoa and his descendants:* vers. 5–7. According to ii. 24, this Ashur was a posthumous son of Caleb [? Hezron] by Abiah. That he was properly a son of Caleb, and no other than Hur (חוּר = אַשְׁחוּר, that is, אִישׁ חוּר, Ew. § 273*b*), is a hypothesis of Wellhausen, grounded on several rather forced emendations of the text (p. 14 sq.; comp. above on the p.)—Ver. 6. *And Naarah bare him Ahuzzam*, a son mentioned nowhere else. Why Naarah's sons are enumerated first, while Helah was named ver. 5 as the first, and Naarah the second, wife of Ashur, remains uncertain. Hepher the second son of Naarah is at all events different from the Gileadite of this name mentioned xi. 36 and Num. xxvi. 32 f., but might possibly be the patriarch or founder of the district Hepher, 1 Kings iv. 10, in the south of Judah, not far from Tappuah, where a Canaanitish king resided in early times (Josh. xii. 17).—*Temeni* (תֵּימְנִי) or Temani (Southern), the third son, will designate a neighbouring family of the tribe of Judah. *Ahashtari*, that is, the family of those from Ahashtar, is wholly unknown.—Ver. 7. *And the sons of Helah: Zereth, Izhar, and Ethnan.* These names occur only here. The צֹחַר of the *Keri*, instead of the *Kethib* יִצְחָר, occurs as the name of a son of Simeon, Gen. xlvi. 10, and of a Canaanitish king, Gen. xxiii. 8; but these names have obviously nothing to do with the son of Ashur and Helah.

5. *Koz and his descendants*, among whom is Jabez: vers. 8–10. This section wants all genealogical connection with the families already mentioned.—*And Koz begat Anub.* A Koz (with the art. הַקּוֹץ) occurs afterwards, xxiv. 10, as a Levite, and also in Ezra ii. 61 and Neh. iii. 4, in which latter passage, moreover, the Levitical descent is not expressed, so that possibly a Jew descended from this Koz might be meant. In what relation our Koz stands to those before named, whether he belonged to the sons of Ashur (as Glassius, Tremell., Piscator, Starke, etc., think), is quite uncertain. The name of his son עָנוּב appears, moreover, to be identical with that of the town עֲנָב, Josh. xi. 21, xv. 50 (a place not far from Debir in the south of Judah); for the Sept.

(*cod. Alex.*) renders it by Ἀνώβ. If this identification be correct, עָנוּב, "the grape," would be the product of קוֹץ, a "thorn," and the present genealogical notice thus present an allegorical sense, reminding us of the fable of Jotham (Judg. ix.), and of Matt. vii. 16 (comp. Hiller, *Hierophyt.* i. p. 464).—*Zobebah and the families of Aharhêl the son of Harum.* These are quite unknown.—Ver. 9. *And Jabez was honoured above his brethren.* Jabez here is probably the name of another descendant of Koz; for the וַיְהִי connects the notice of him closely with that which precedes. The town Jabez, the inhabitants of which are mentioned ii. 55, may perhaps have been founded by him; from which might be surmised a connection of himself and of those named, ver. 8, with Shobal the son of Hur (ii. 50). But all this is very uncertain.—*I bare him with sorrow.* This maternal utterance, discovering the fundamental meaning of the name יַעְבֵּץ = "son of sorrow" (comp. the root עָצַב, the second and third radicals of which are here transposed), reminds us of similar exclamations of mothers in the patriarchal age, as Gen. iv. 25, xix. 37 f., xxix. 32–35, xxxiii. 20. In like manner, the statement that Jabez was "honoured above his brethren," reminds us of Gen. xxxiv. 19 (Hamor the son of Shechem). And by the vow of this Jabez to the "God of Israel" (comp. Gen. xxviii. 20, xxxiii. 20) recorded in ver. 10, as well as by the new explanation of the name, which is contained in the terms of this vow (a second reference of יַעְבֵּץ to the root עצב, but with a new turn, לְבִלְתִּי עָצְבִּי, "that thou grieve me not"), we are carried back to the scenes of Genesis (comp. Gen. xvii. 17 ff., xviii. 12, xxi. 6, xxvi. 8, etc.), so that we have here an undoubted primeval historical record. Even the rhetorical clothing of the vow, a mere antecedent clause, with אִם wanting a consequent, but with clear emphasizing of the עָצְבִּי coming in at the end as the point of the whole, reminds us of the ancient style of the Pentateuch; comp. Gen. xxviii. 20 ff.; Num. xxi. 2, etc.—*And God brought that which he had asked.* This statement, occupying the place of consequent to the aposiopesis אִם־בָּרֵךְ תְּבָרְכֵנִי, serves to explain the above notice that Jabez was honoured above his brethren, and exhibit him as the lord of a wide domain, and the possessor of the divine blessing. Observe, moreover, the name אֱלֹהִים used here (as in v. 20, 25, 26) instead of יְהוָֹה, which occurs elsewhere in these genealogical sections (for example, ii. 3, v. 41, etc.).

6. *The Men of Rechah:* vers. 11, 12.—*And Celub the brother of Shuhah begat Mehir.* This Celub (כְּלוּב) bears indeed the same name as the famous hero Caleb or Celubai (ii. 9), but is distinguished by the addition "the brother of Shuhah" from his more illustrious namesake, and cannot possibly have passed with our genealogist for the same person (as Wellhausen, p. 20, thinks). The choice of the form כְּלוּב, which stands to כָּלֵב as עָנוּב, ver. 8, to עָנָב, while the famous Caleb the son of Jephunneh, ver. 15, is designated by his usual name, shows that in the view of the writer the owners of the two names are to be kept apart. It is doubtful whether שׁוּחָה be a man's or a woman's name; its identification with חוּשָׁה, ver. 4, is not admitted (against Starke and other old writers). Mehir the son, and Eshton the grandson, of Celub occur nowhere else.—Ver. 12. *And Eshton begat Beth-rapha,* that is, perhaps, the house or family of Rapha, who is otherwise unknown; for neither the Benjamite Rapha (viii. 2) nor the offspring of Rapha (xx. 4–8) can apply here. And the two following descendants of Eshton remain at least uncertain. Paseah might possibly be the ancestor of the "sons of Paseah" introduced among the Nethinim (Ezra ii. 49; Neh. vii. 51); Tehinnah occurs not elsewhere, though perhaps the city Nahash, of which he is the father or founder, may be connected with Nahash the father of Abigail, the step-sister of David (see ii. 16; 2 Sam. xvii. 25).—*These are the men of Rechah,* the inhabitants perhaps of the town Rechah, a place not elsewhere named.

7. *The Descendants of Kenaz:* vers. 13, 14.—*And the sons of Kenaz: Othniel and Seraiah.* That Kenaz (קְנַז), the "father" of Othniel the judge (Judg. i. 13 ff., iii. 9), sprang from Hezron the grandson of Judah, appears to follow from this, that Caleb the son of Jephunneh is several times designated a Kenizzite (קְנִזִּי), and so placed in a certain genealogical relation to Kenaz. It is to be observed, indeed, that Kenaz, if really father or grandfather, and not a more remote ancestor of Othniel, would have been younger than Caleb or a contemporary of nearly the same age. Caleb and Othniel are usually called "brothers," on account of their common relation to Kenaz (Josh. xv. 17; Judg. i. 13); and, indeed, in the latter place Othniel is called the "younger brother" of Caleb (we must therefore translate, with Bachmann, the son of Kenaz, younger brother of Caleb, with which, however, Josh. xv. 17 would conflict; see Keil, p. 63). Hence appears the possibility that both the companion of Joshua, Caleb the son of Jephunneh (who was eighty-five years old at the conquest of Canaan, Josh. xiv. 10 f.), and Othniel the judge, at least a generation younger (the conqueror of Cushan-rishathaim), stood in a common relation to an otherwise unknown patriarch Kenaz. Of what nature this relation was, whether it was that Caleb, by means of his father Jephunneh, was a grandson of Kenaz (as appears to have been the case, Num. xxxii. 12), and that Othniel, either through Jephunneh or some other, was likewise his grandson, or perhaps great-grandson, must remain uncertain. Possibly Kenaz is merely the name of a race external to Israel, belonging in fact to Edom, Gen. xxxvi. 11, 1 Chron. i. 36, 53, to which Caleb became somehow related in the march through the wilderness, and from which also Othniel was descended. Knobel (on Gen. xxxvi. 11, p. 281) conceives the relationship thus: "The 'Kenizzite' is perhaps a surname of Caleb, originating from some Kenizzites having passed into his family during the journey of Moses. After Jephunneh's death, one of them appears to have married Caleb's mother, and had by her Othniel. His name being afterwards for-

gotten, he was designated by the name of his tribe."—Seraiah, Othniel's brother, occurs only here; we meet with a later Jew of this name, who returned with Zerubbabel, Ezra ii. 2.—*And the sons of Othniel: Hathath.* On the phrase וּבְנֵי before only one name, see ii. 7. Yet the plural might here possibly refer also to Meonothai as brother of Hathath (ver. 14), if a וּמְעוֹנֹתַי had fallen out at the end of our verse, or if the genealogist had presupposed that Meonothai was brother to Hathath, and therefore hastened at once to the statement of his descendants. Othniel's sons occur nowhere else. The name Meonothai might also be connected with the town Maon (Josh. xv. 55), or with the Meunim (Ezra ii. 50; Neh. vii. 52).—Ver. 14. *And Meonothai begat Ophrah.* We can scarcely think of Ophrah as the Benjamite town of this name (Josh. xviii. 23; 1 Sam. xiii. 17), or even of the home of Gideon in the tribe of Manasseh (Judg. vi. 11).—*And Seraiah begat Joab father of the valley of the carpenters.* This occurs here as a place founded by Joab son of Seraiah (ver. 13), called the "Valley of the carpenters or the craftsmen" (חֲרָשִׁים), and in Neh. xi. 35; and, indeed, as a place not far from Jerusalem, on the north side. Whether it had received its name after the exile, and whether Joab, the founder of the colony, is to pass for one of those Joabs in Zerubbabel's time who are mentioned Ezra ii. 6, Neh. vii. 11 (to which hypothesis Berth. seems inclined), must remain doubtful.

8. *The Descendants of Caleb the Son of Jephunneh:* ver. 15.—That this Jephunnite Caleb is probably the same with him whose genealogy is given ch. ii. 46-49 (and therefore with the Caleb of Num., Josh., and Judg.), and different from the Hezronite Celubai or Caleb (ii. 9, 18, 42 ff., 50 ff., perhaps his ancestor [rather descendant]), has been fully shown on ii. 49.—*Iru, Elah, and Naam.* These three sons of Caleb occur nowhere else; for the second, Elah, must have been combined with the Edomite prince of the same name mentioned i. 52, as Kenaz might be identical with the Kenaz named there, ver. 53. This Calebite Kenaz cannot be the same as the father of Othniel (ver. 13); rather as grandson or great-grandson, he bore the same name as his ancestor. Why "the sons of Elah" are set down between this Kenaz and Naam in the series of the sons of Caleb we can no longer explain. It is inadmissible, at all events, to translate, with a number of older expositors (including Starke): "and the sons of Elah were (also) Kenaz," as if ו before קְנַז could be anything but the copula. As the words run, Kenaz is appended to the aforementioned descendants of Caleb, of whom the sons of Elah take the fourth place, as the fifth and last; only if a name were fallen out before וּקְנַז (as Keil supposes) could Kenaz be regarded as belonging to the sons of Elah.

9. *Jehalelel's Sons:* ver. 16.—*Ziph and Ziphah, Tiriah and Asarel.* Only the first of these is known, and, indeed, as the supposed father of one of those towns in Judah which are named in Josh. xv. 24, 55. Even of Jehalelel we know nothing more. A quite arbitrary hypothesis of some older scholars makes out of him rather a woman, the supposed second wife of Kenaz, ver 13, whose first wife was (?) Jephunneh.

10. *Ezrah's Posterity:* vers. 17, 18.—*And the sons of Ezrah: Jether, and Mered, and Epher, and Jalon; and she conceived,* etc. If the sing. וּבֶן is to be retained, we may compare such cases as iii. 19, 21, 23, etc.; but see Crit. Note. The here-named Ezrah occurs nowhere else; he belongs, at all events, to a grey antiquity, as the father of old Jewish towns like Eshtemoa, Socho, Zanoah, etc. It is not clear how he is connected with the foregoing or following families of Judah. Of his four sons, the last, Jalon, occurs only here even in name; the names Jether and Epher occur elsewhere, but in other families (Jether, ii. 32, comp. 53; and Epher, xi. 33 and v. 24); further notices of them are wanting. On the contrary, the closing sentence of ver. 18 shows, with respect to Mered, that probably all the names from ver. 17*b* ("and she conceived," etc.) denote descendants of this man by two wives, a "Jewess" and a "daughter of Pharaoh." And as the words וַתַּהַר וגו׳, standing as they now do after the name of the fourth son of Ezrah, and wanting a feminine subject, yield no rational sense, the removal (proposed by Bertheau, and adopted by Kamph., Keil, and others) of that closing sentence: "and these are the sons of Bithiah daughter of Pharaoh, whom Mered took," to our passage after וְיָלוֹן, commends itself as a very suitable amendment; comp. the Crit. Note. וַתַּהַר is then to be taken as a synonym of וַתֵּלֶד (which is given by the Sept. and the Vulg.), and the names Miriam (מִרְיָם, for which, perhaps, מָרוֹם, as in Sept. *cod. Vat.* or the like, is to be read, as we expect to find a man's name in the first place), Shammai, and Ishbah then denote the sons born to Mered by Pharaoh's daughter; whereupon in ver. 18 the names of those descended from the Jewess are added. We obtain here, accordingly, two lines descending from Mered—one Egyptian, from which (and in particular from Ishbah the third son of Pharaoh's daughter) the inhabitants of the town Eshtemoa (Sept. Ἐσθεμών or Ἐσθαιμών), on the mountains of Judah, the present Samua, south of Hebron, drew their origin (comp. Josh. xv. 15, xxi. 14, and ver. 19), and one Jewish, from which three towns of Judah are derived:—1. Gedor, comp. on ver. 4; 2. Socho, perhaps the present Suweikeh, in the lowland south west of Jerusalem, comp. Josh. xv. 35, 1 Sam. xvii. 1, etc.; 3. Zanoah, perhaps the present Sanuah, in the lowland near Zorah, comp. Josh. xv. 34 (though the other Zanoah on the mountains of Judah, Josh. xv. 36, the site of which we do not know, might be meant). Of the names of the three "fathers" or founders of these towns, Jekuthiel (יְקוּתִיאֵל, probably "fear of God") occurs nowhere else; while Jered (comp. Gen. v. 15) and חֶבֶר occur elsewhere, the latter pretty often (Gen. xlvi. 17; Num. xxvi. 45; Judg. iv. 11, 17; 1 Chron. viii. 17).—*And these are the sons of Bithiah,* etc. These words, in the position which we have assigned to them, are not a subscription for the preceding, but rather an introduction to the following words וַתַּהַר וגו׳. We know nothing more of this daughter of Pharaoh. בַּת־פַּרְעֹה may be merely a general phrase for

מִצְרִית, an Egyptian; so thinks Hitzig, *Gesch. d. V. Isr.* p. 64, who, indeed, without right, might thus degrade the Pharaoh's daughter of the Exodus, the foster-mother of Moses, into a common Egyptian. No less arbitrary is the opposite conjecture of the older Rabbins, and recently of Fürst (*Gesch. d. bibl. Liter.* i. 319), that this same king's daughter Thermuthis, the protectress of Moses, is here meant. The name Miriam, at the head of the descendants of this Egyptian, seems to have given rise to this identification with Thermuthis (comp. Wagenseil, *Sota*, p. 271). The opinion of Osiander, Hiller, J. H. Michaelis, Starke, etc., that we are not to think of an Egyptian here, as Bithiah is a Hebrew name, and Pharaoh the name of a Jew, is also arbitrary, and directly against the phrase בַּת־פַּרְעֹה (comp. 2 Chron. viii. 11; 1 Kings ix. 24).

11. *The Sons of the Wife of Hodiah:* ver. 19. —*And the sons of the wife of Hodiah, the sister of Naham.* Hodiah (הוֹדִיָּה), as the present *St. constr.* אֵשֶׁת, and its occurrence as the name of several Levites after the exile, in the book of Nehemiah (Neh. viii. 7, ix. 5, x. 11), show, is not a woman's, but a man's name. We know neither the name of Hodiah's wife nor her relation to the foregoing; for that נַחַם, whose sister she is said to be, is the same as נַעַם, Caleb's son, ver. 15, no one will seriously assert.—*The father of Keilah the Garmite, and Eshtemoa* (or perhaps "the father of Eshtemoa;" see Crit. Note) *the Maachathite.* The two designations, "the Garmite" and "the Maachathite," are to us equally obscure and unintelligible; the latter may, perhaps, contain an allusion to Maachah the third wife of Caleb, ii. 48. The situation of Keilah (קְעִילָה), a town in the lowland of Judah (Josh. xv. 44), has not yet been ascertained. On Eshtemoa, see ver. 17.

12. *Descendants of Shimon and Ishi:* ver. 20. —*And the sons of Shimon: Amnon,* etc. We know not otherwise either Shimon or his four sons, and therefore cannot indicate his place in the genealogy of Judah. That he was a Hezronite, like all the foregoing, is a mere conjecture of Wellhausen (p. 20).—*And the sons of Ishi: Zoheth and Benzoheth.* The name Ishi was also borne by a Jerahmeelite (ii. 31), the son of Appaim, and by a Simeonite, iv. 42. Neither can be meant here, especially as a son Zoheth, not there mentioned, and an anonymous grandson of this Zoheth, are added as descendants.

13. *Descendants of Shelah, third son of Judah:* vers. 21–23.—*The sons of Shelah son of Judah.* On this third son of Judah by the Canaanitess Bathshua, see ii. 3; Gen. xxxviii. 5. The absence of the copula ו before בְּנֵי שֵׁלָה (as before בְּנֵי יְהוּדָה, ver. 1) marks the beginning of a new genealogical series; and, indeed, a series that is of the more importance, because the posterity of Shelah is entirely omitted in ch. ii.—*Er the father of Lechah, and Ladah the father of Mareshah.* This Er is not to be confounded with Shelah's brother, the first-born of Judah (as Bertheau thinks); rather is this a similar case of uncle and nephew having the same name, as in Ram, for example, ii. 9; comp. ver. 25. We know no more of the town Lechah (לֵכָה) founded by this younger Er; but Mareshah, founded by his brother Ladah, is no doubt the present Marash in the Shephelah; see on ch. ii. 42.—*And the families of the house of byssus work, of the house of Ashbea.* This house of byssus work (cotton factory) may have been situated in Egypt, or possibly in Palestine. We know as little of its situation as of the "house of Ashbea" (בֵּית אַשְׁבֵּעַ, rendered by Jerome: *domus juramenti*). For the cultivation of cotton (בּוּץ, here defectively בֻּץ) also in Syria and Palestine, comp. Ezek. xxvii. 16; Pausan. v. 5. 2; Pococke, *Morgenl.* ii. 88; Robinson, ii. 612, 628, iii. 432.—Ver. 22. *And Jokim, and the men of Cozeba,* etc. The strange rendering of these and the following words in the Vulg. (see Crit. Note) seems to have been occasioned by an old Rabbinical combination of the words אֲשֶׁר בָּעֲלוּ לְמוֹאָב with the narrative of the book of Ruth; the יוֹקִים = *qui stare fecit solem* are accordingly Elimelech, the *viri mendacii* his sons Mahlon and Chilion, who removed with him to Moab, and married daughters of this land; and in ישבי לחם is indicated their return to Bethlehem, etc. Our passage in reality states a total or partial conquest of Moab, effected in ancient times by several descendants of Shelah, whose names are not otherwise known to us. יוֹקִים appears contracted from יוֹיָקִים. The men of כֹּזֵבָה might be the inhabitants of כְּזִיב, Gen. xxxviii. 5 (=אַכְזִיב, Josh. xv. 44), the birthplace of Shelah, in the lowland of Judah. An altogether strange and now inexplicable name occurs at the end, יָשֻׁבִי לֶחֶם, "which the punctuators would scarcely have so pronounced, if the pronunciation had not been so handed down to them" (Berth.).—*And these are ancient things,* that is, not merely "before the exile, in the period of the kings," as Bertheau thinks (p. 46), who endeavours to convert this notice into an indirect support of his hypothesis, that in vers. 7–20 the generations and families of Judah after the exile are reported, while vers. 21–23 form an appendix referring to the period of kings, but certainly without warrant; the words merely bespeak a high age, belonging to the grey foretime, for the traditions concerning Jokim, the men of Cozeba, etc. (comp. Wellhausen, p. 23, n. 1).—Ver. 23. *These are the potters and the dwellers in Netaim and Gederah.* הֵמָּה, "these," appear to refer to the whole descendants of Shelah (with the natural exception of those "byssus workers," ver. 21, that could not well be at the same time potters), and not merely those named in ver. 22 (as Berth.); for this verse has its closing notice in וְהַדְּבָרִים עַתִּיקִים. It is not known where Netaim (נְטָעִים, "plantings") was; perhaps it means royal gardens near Jerusalem, or near those pleasure gardens of Solomon in the Wady Urtus at Bethlehem (see on Song i. 1, vol. xiii. p. 29 of *Bibelw.*); comp. also Uzziah's

gardens, 2 Chron. xxvi. 10. Gederah (גְּדֵרָה, "fence") is perhaps the town mentioned Josh. xv. 36 in the lowland of Judah (the present village Gedera, about an hour south-west of Jabneh; see Keil on 1 Chron. xii. 4).—*With the king, in his service, they dwelt there.* To what king this alludes is uncertain; probably no single king (as Uzziah, or David, or Solomon) is meant: but the phrase applies to the kings of the house of David in general, who, from the beginning, inherited extensive private domains, where not merely cattle-breeding, tillage, and gardening were pursued, but also handicrafts, as the pottery here mentioned, the cotton-weaving, ver. 21, and perhaps carpentry, ver. 14.[1]

It has been already remarked that Bertheau's assumption, that vers. 1-20 of our chapter "presented a description of the generations and families of the tribe of Judah which were living soon after the exile (the time of Zerubbabel, Ezra, and Nehemiah)," but vers. 21-23 formed an appendix relating to earlier times, was not well founded, and finds no sufficient support in the assertion, "and these are ancient things." Comp. the full refutation which Keil (p. 66 ff., note 2) has given to this hypothesis. Neither is the concomitant assumption tenable, that there are exactly twelve families of the house of Judah in vers. 1-29, and of Judah, too, after the exile, in the days of Zerubbabel; for the families mentioned are not arranged according to the sons and grandsons of Judah in ver. 1, but are strung together loosely, and without any mark of connection. Instead of twelve, also, a smaller number of families may be brought out by another mode of reckoning; as, for example, Ewald, in a far more arbitrary way indeed than Bertheau, has found twelve families in the whole of our section, including Shelah and his descendants in vers. 21-23 (*Gesch.* i. p. 471). Both appear to be merely accidental—the number twelve of the families named, according to Bertheau's reckoning, and the circumstance that many of the persons and places in our section recur in Ezra and Nehemiah. To the latter circumstance, strongly urged by Bertheau, Keil has justly opposed the no less undeniable fact, that most of the places already occur in Joshua, and very many of the persons in Samuel and Kings, and that, with respect to the geographical coincidences with Ezra and Nehemiah, the historical contents of these books, that were almost exclusively enacted on the soil of Judah, and among Israelites of Jewish extraction, should in great part be taken into account in explanation of this. Comp. also what has been urged above in the Preliminary Remark, p. 53.

[1] Moreover, the engineer of the "Palestine Exploration Fund," Captain Warren, has recently discovered remains of the pottery of these royal factories in Jerusalem. See *Our Work in Palestine*, London 1873, p. 149.

c. The Families of Simeon, and the Transjordanic Tribes of Reuben, Gad, and half-Manasseh (till the Deportation of the latter by the Assyrians).—Ch. iv. 24–v. 26.

1. *The Families of Simeon:* ch. iv. 24–43.

Ch. iv. 24. The sons of Simeon were Nemuel, and Jamin, Jarib, Zerah, Shaul.
25, 26 Shallum his son, Mibsam his son, Mishma his son. And the sons of Mishma:
27 Hamuel his son, Zaccur his son, Shimi his son. And Shimi had sixteen sons
and six daughters; but his brethren had not many sons: and all their family
did not multiply, like the sons of Judah.
28, 29 And they dwelt at Beer-sheba, and Moladah, and Hazar-shual. And at
30 Bilhah, and at Ezem, and at Tolad. And at Bethuel, and at Hormah, and at
31 Ziklag. And at Beth-marcaboth, and at Hazar-susim, and at Beth-biri, and
32 at Shaaraim: these were their towns until the reign of David. And their
33 villages, Etam, and Ain, Rimmon, and Tochen, and Ashan, five towns. And
all their villages that were round these towns unto Baal. This was their
habitation, and they had their own genealogy.
34, 35 And Meshobab, and Jamlech, and Joshah the son of Amaziah. And Joel,
36 and Jehu the son of Josibiah, the son of Seraiah, the son of Asiel. And
Elioenai, and Jaakobah, and Jeshohaiah, and Asaiah, and Adiel, and Jesimiel,
37 and Benaiah. And Ziza the son of Shiphi, the son of Allon, the son of Jedaiah,
38 the son of Shimri, the son of Shemaiah. These are they that entered by name
39 princes in their families; and their father-houses spread greatly. And they
went to the entrance of Gedor,[1] to the east of the valley, to seek pasture
40 for their flocks. And they found fat and good pasture, and the land was
wide on all sides, and quiet, and peaceful; for they were of Ham who dwelt
41 there before. And these written by name came in the days of Hezekiah
king of Judah, and smote their tents, and the Meunites[2] that were found
there, and destroyed them unto this day, and dwelt in their stead; for there
42 was pasture there for their flocks. And of them, of the sons of Simeon, five
hundred men went to mount Seir; and Pelatiah, and Neariah, and Rephaiah,

43 and Uzziel, the sons of Ishi, were at their head. And they smote the
remnant that had escaped of Amalek, and dwelt there unto this day.

[1] The Sept gives here Γεράρ, whence גְּדֹר might possibly be an error of transcription for גְּרָר.

[2] So (הַמְּעוּנִים) the *Keri*, whereas the *Kethib* gives הַמְּעִינִים, and the Sept. accordingly Μιναίους.

EXEGETICAL.

Preliminary Remark.—This account of the tribe of Simeon includes in it a genealogical, a geographical, and a historical section. The first (vers. 24–27) gives the five sons of Simeon, and traces the posterity of the last, Shaul, through a series of generations; the second (vers. 28–33) recounts their dwelling-places till the time of David; the third (vers. 34–43) contains two migrations or conquests of Simeonite families, one in the time of Hezekiah into a region previously inhabited by Hamites, another without a date to Mount Seir, into a district previously Amalekite. These accounts partake of the same fragmentary character as the sections referring to the following tribes. Comp. moreover, K. H. Graf, *Der Stamm Simeon, a contribution to the History of Israel*, Meissen 1866, and, with respect to the geography, the great work of the Englishmen E. H. Palmer and T. Drake, *The Desert of the Exodus*, etc., Cambridge 1871, one of the most valuable publications of the "Palestine Exploration Fund," with specially valuable contributions to the geography of the south of Palestine. With the conclusion of these inquirers, that the south border of Palestine, in particular of the tribe of Simeon, must be extended much farther than is usually supposed, agrees also Consul Wetzstein, *Ueber Kadesh und Palästina's Südgrenze* (Excursus III. in Delitzsch's *Comment on Gen.*, 4th edit.).

1. *The Five Sons of Simeon, and the Descendants of Shaul*: vers. 25–27.—*Nemuel, and Jamin, Jarib, Zerah, Shaul.* The list in Num. xxvi. 12–14 also names five sons of Simeon, and quite the same as here, except Jarib, who is there Jakin (יָכִין), of which it appears to be a corruption. On the contrary, in the older parallels, Gen. xlvi. 10, Ex. vi. 15, six sons of Simeon are enumerated, among whom an Ohad stands in the third place, who is wanting here and in Numbers, perhaps because his posterity had died out so soon as to form no distinct family; and in the first place a Jemuel, who corresponds to the Nemuel of our passage, and in the last a Zohar, instead of the Zerah here before the last. It is plain that we have here equivalent names, as צֹחַר, *candor*, is not very remote from זֶרַח, *ortus solis* (comp. Mal. iii. 20; Luke i. 78), and also נְמוּאֵל (with whom Hitzig on Prov. xxx. 31, perhaps too boldly, identifies the conjectural king Lemuel of Massa) appears only a by-form of יְמוּאֵל, day of God. It is uncertain whether we are to regard the forms given in Genesis and Exodus at once as original. It is at least plain, from the agreement of Num. xxvi. 12–14 with our passage, that the Chronist has not adopted an arbitrary form of the names, as Gramberg assumes.—Ver. 25. *Shallum his son*, etc. Only of Shaul, the last (perhaps the youngest) of the sons of Simeon, whose mother is called a Canaanitess in the parallel accounts of Genesis and Exodus, are further descendants reported in six succeeding generations, Shallum, Mibsam, Mishma, Hamuel, Zaccur, and Shimi. By the words, "and the sons of Mishma," at the beginning of ver. 27, these six generations are divided into two groups, of which, however, the second, only lineal, without any collateral descendants; comp. the plur. וּבְנֵי in like cases, as i. 41, ii. 31, iii. 16, 22, etc.—Ver. 27. *And Shimi had sixteen sons and six daughters.* This father of a very large and flourishing family is brought into prominence, like Elioenai, iii. 24; comp. the descendants of Jacob, Jesse, David, Job, and Ps. cxxvii. 3, cxxviii. 3.—*But his brethren* (the remaining Simeonites, not merely Shimi's immediate brothers) *had not many sons.* This is the reason that their whole "family did not multiply like that of Judah." With this agrees the comparatively small number of the Simeonites in the census under Moses (Num. i.–iv.), and the way in which this smaller tribe was included in the stronger tribe of Judah in the division of the land, Josh. xix. 1.

2. *The original Dwelling-Places of the Simeonites in the Southern Part of the Land of Judah*: vers. 28–33; comp. Josh. xix. 2–8.—With the names of the Simeonite dwelling-places reported in this old parallel, those here named agree in the main, and in particular with respect to the separation into two groups, one of thirteen, the other of five towns. Only the second group consists there of only four towns (see on ver. 32), and in the first group, notwithstanding the statement that thirteen towns are reported, ver. 6, fourteen are actually named; between Beer-sheba and Moladah a Sheba is inserted, a name (שֶׁבַע) which appears to be a repetition of the second component of בְּאֵר שֶׁבַע, occasioned by negligence in copying, but possibly also = שְׁמַע, a town named, Josh. xv. 26, before Moladah (of the latter opinion is, for example, Keil, on Josh. xix. 2 and our passage). There are several unessential differences of form or orthography between our passage and Josh. xix., as in the latter בָּלָה for בִּלְהָה, ver. 29, אֶלְתּוֹלַד for תּוֹלָד, בְּתוּל for בְּתוּאֵל, חֲצַר סוּסָה for חֲצַר סוּסִים, בֵּית לְבָאוֹת (house of lions) for בֵּית בִּרְאִי, and שָׁרוּחֶן (pleasant harbour) for שַׁעֲרַיִם (two gates). It cannot be shown which of these forms is the more original: some of the deviations may rest on mere errors of transcription, as might so easily happen in places that scarcely ever occur again. Moreover, the book of Joshua (xv. 26–32) repeats the most of them as belonging to the towns of the south of Judah, and certainly with some variations of form (for example, בַּעֲלָה for Bilhah, כְּסִיל for Bethul, שִׁלְחִים for Shaaraim, Madmannah for Beth-marcaboth, Sansannah for Hazar-susim). Most of these places are still undiscovered; Beer-sheba survives

in Bir-es-Seba; Moladah probably in the ruins Tel Milh, south of Hebron, on the road to Aila;[1] Hormah, the older name of which was Shephath, in the ruin Sepata, two and a half hours south of Khalasa; Ziklag in Kasluj, east of this Sepata; and Shaaraim in Tell Sheriah, between Beer-sheba and Gaza.—*These were their towns until the reign of David, and their villages.* With almost all recent expositors, וְחַצְרֵיהֶם is certainly to be attached to ver. 31, for the parallel, Josh. xix. 6, speaks of "towns and their villages," and all that are named in ver. 32 are expressly named "towns." Moreover, the separation of וחצריהם from the foregoing, occasioned by the date "until the reign of David," is already very old; for the old translators agree with the Masoretic text in transferring the word to the following verse. The reason why the date "until the reign of David" was inserted here, and not in ver. 33 (where it would be less surprising), appears to be this, that the changes occurring from the time of David in the habitations of the Simeonites, consisting in their partial removal by the Jews (comp. ver. 34 ff.), applied only to the thirteen towns already named, whereas the five towns, with their villages to be named in the following verse, remained still an undiminished possession of the Simeonites. So, justly, Keil, following Rashi and Kimchi, and partly against Bertheau, who assumes as the object of the subscription merely an allusion to Ziklag (comp. 1 Sam. xxvii. 6), or perhaps to others of the forementioned towns, as belonging from the time of David no longer to the tribe of Simeon, whereas such a limitation of the sense is foreign to the words; and, moreover, Ziklag was severed from Simeon by the Philistines before the reign of David (1 Sam. xxvii. 6).—Ver. 32. *Etam, and Ain, Rimmon, and Tochen, and Ashen, five towns.* After the thirteen towns, the parallel, Josh. xix. 7, gives a second group, not a pentapolis, but only a tetrapolis, with the omission of Tochen, and the change of Etam (עֵיטָם) into Ether (עֶתֶר). It is hard to say where the original is to be sought. We are scarcely entitled, with Movers (p. 73) and Bertheau, to charge both texts with inaccuracy, and to affirm that the series of these towns originally ran thus: תֹּכֶן, עֶתֶר, עֵין רִמּוֹן, עָשָׁן, so that by an oversight two cities were made out of one En-rimmon (which occurs in Neh. xi. 29), and by another oversight Tochen fell out of the text of Joshua, and by a third the name עֶתֶר, which is proved to be original by the subsequent mention of such a town in Josh. xv. 43, has in Chronicles been supplanted by the better known עֵיטָם. Against this conjecture Keil has justly urged: 1. The רִמּוֹן and עַיִן are counted as separate cities not merely in Josh. xix. 7, but also in Josh. xv. 32, and the union of the two names into an En-rimmon in Nehemiah may be explained simply from the contiguity of the two places (of which Rimmon is discovered in "Rum er Rummanin," four hours north of Beer-sheba, and Ain appears to have been the name of an old well lying near it), or possibly by a coalescence of the two at a later period; 2. Etam, if it actually came into the text by exchange with the original Ether, should have been, not at the head of the list, but the last but one (where עֶתֶר stands in Josh. xix. 7); and 3. There were notoriously two Etams, one in the mountains of Judah south of Bethlehem, 2 Chron. xi. 6, and one in the Negeb of Judah on the border of Simeon, which occurs in the history of Samson, Judg. xv. 8, 11, and must be the place here meant, where a locality near Ain and Rimmon is intended. This leaves nothing unsolved but the difference of the number, being only four in Joshua, and five here. The hypothesis of Keil, that תֹּכֶן is only another name for עֶתֶר, is not well grounded.—Ver. 33. *And all their villages that were round these towns unto Baal.* The parallel, Josh. xix. 8, is more full: "and all the villages that were round these towns, unto Baalath-beer, Ramath-negeb." Hence בַּעַל appears to be an abbreviation of the fuller name בַּעֲלַת בְּאֵר, and the group of villages extending to this Baalath-beer (or Bealoth, as it is called Josh. xv. 24) bore the name Ramath-negeb or Ramah of the south, with which Ramoth-negeb, 1 Sam. xxx. 27, is manifestly identical. "An attempt has been recently made to determine the situation of this place, in doing which it is to be observed that Baal or Baalath-beer is not to be counted among the towns of Simeon; for it is only said that the villages of the last-named towns extend to Baal, that is, in the direction and perhaps very near to Baal, so that we are warranted in seeking our Baal in a region somewhat more remote from the towns, if it had otherwise a peculiar character and adaptation to denote the direction in which the territory of Simeon extended. Now Walkott found near Ramet el Khulil, about an hour north of Hebron, a second Ramah, called Ramet el Amleh, and also two heights with old sites. A whole group of places on hills, which can be observed at one glance, and present a grand and peculiar aspect, is here found: there is no doubt that the Ramoth-negeb, 1 Sam. xxx. 27, is to be sought here. As there is a remarkable well in Ramet el Khulil, the conjecture arises that here is a Baalath-beer, a well-town; and a confirmation of this conjecture presents itself in the designation of this place by the addition Ramoth-negeb." So Bertheau, after Roediger (review of Robinson's *Bibl. Sacra*, Halle'sche Literaturztg. 1843, No. 111); whereas Keil on Josh. xix. 8 is inclined to seek Baalath-beer and Ramoth-negeb in a more southerly situation than Ramet el Khulil, which is not far from Hebron; and the best chartographers of the day (Menke in ch. iii. of his *Bible Atlas*, Gotha 1868) place the localities in question south-west of the Dead Sea, on the caravan road leading to Hebron.—*This was their habitation, and they had their own genealogy,* that is, their own register of families as a separate independent tribe, though they dwelt in the territory of Judah, and were much less in number and extent than this contiguous tribe. On the substantively used infin. הִתְיַחֵשׂ, genealogy (properly, entrance in the register), comp. Introd. § 5.

3. *History of the Two Migrations or Conquests of the Simeonites:* vers. 34–43.—*a.* First expedition, in the time of Hezekiah: vers. 34–41.—*And Meshobab, and Jamlech, and Joshah,* etc. These thirteen princes of the tribe of Simeon are

[1] So also Palmer and Drake, p. 303.

only made prominent because they were the leaders of the present expedition, not because the former genealogical series (vers. 24–26) was continued by them. For although of some of them (Joshah, Jehu, and Ziza) the descent for several generations is given, yet the connection of these small genealogical lines with that earlier series is wanting. With the remarkable form יַעֲקֹבָה, "to Jacob" (reckoned to him), comp. the analogous form יְשַׂרְאֵלָה, 1 Chron. xxv. 14, and other examples in Ewald, *Lehrb.* p. 670, n. 1, 7th edit. —Ver. 38. *These are they that entered by name princes in their families* (not: "these were famous, celebrated princes," as Luther). A phrase essentially the same occurs in ver. 41; comp. also xii. 31; Num. i. 17; Ezra viii. 25. "Princes of families" are, moreover, not heads of families, but "heads of the houses into which the families were divided" (Keil).—*And their father-houses spread greatly,* unfolded and branched out into a great multitude. On בֵּית־אָבוֹת, plural of the compound בֵּית־אָב, comp. Ewald, § 270, p. 657, where the same plural is cited from 2 Chron. xxxv. 5, Num. i. 2, 18, 20, vii. 2, etc., and the similar בֵּית בָּמוֹת, high houses, from 1 Kings xii. 31, 2 Kings xvii. 29, 32.—*And they went to the entrance of Gedor* (scarcely "to the west of Gedor," as Keil, for this would have required the addition of הַשֶּׁמֶשׁ to לִמְבוֹא), *to the east of the valley.* What valley is uncertain, as the definite article only points to some known valley near Gedor, a place that cannot itself be determined; but the identification of this הַגַּיְא with the valley of the Dead Sea is a very precarious conjecture of Ewald and Bertheau, for the valley of the Dead Sea with its southern continuation bears in the O. T. the standing name of הָעֲרָבָה. Equally uncertain is the conjecture of the same inquirers, and of Kamph., Graf, Mühlau (also of Menke in ch. iii. of his *Bible Atlas*), that גְּדֹר is an error of transcription for גְּרָר (Γεράρ in Sept.; see Crit. Note). A place so far west as Gerar (now Kirbet el Gerar) on the river Gerar can scarcely have been used to mark the border of the Simeonite pasture lands; and the mode of expression is not fitted to indicate the west and east bounding points of the region occupied by the Simeonites (comp. also on ver. 41). On the other hand, to identify Gedor with the town גְּדוֹר named in Josh. xv. 58, situated on the mountains of Judah, has its difficulties. For it must also be presumed that the Meunim named in ver. 41 were the inhabitants of the adjacent hill-town Maon, Josh. xv. 55; and the region of this hill-town of Judah cannot be that intended here, as the latter is described, ver. 40, as on all sides (literally "on both sides;" יָדַיִם, as in Gen. xxxiv. 21) open, and therefore clearly as a plain.—Ver. 40. *For they were of Ham who dwelt there before.* For the phrase, comp. Judg. xviii. 7, 28. These men of Ham, whom the Simeonites found as inhabitants, peaceable and harmless inhabitants of the country in question, and subdued, may have been Egyptians, Cushites, or Canaanites; most probably they belonged to the last branch of the Hamites, as the region in question is contiguous to Palestine. Hitzig ("The Kingdom of Massa" in Zeller's *Theolog. Jahrbüchern*, 1844, p. 269 ff., and on *Prov.* p. 312) gratuitously supposes the Amalekites to be designated by "the men of Ham" (likewise Hoffmann, *Blicke in die früheste Geschichte des heiligen Landes*, p. 73): for the history of the second expedition of the Simeonites refers to the Amalekites, vers. 42, 43, and it is a question whether the Amalekites were Hamites (Knobel on Gen. x. 13, 23, and comp. above on i. 36 f.); and the circumstance that these Hamites were nomades does not compel us to think of Amalekites (Ludim, Hyksos?), since many Canaanitish tribes lived as nomades; for example, those of Laish, Judg. xviii.—Ver. 41. *Came in the days of Hezekiah.* Here is a quite definite chronological date, that shows still more positively than the reference to the reign of David in ver. 31, the high age and the certainty of these notices.—*And smote their* (the Hamites') *tents, and the Meunites that were found there.* The smiting refers first to the tents or dwellings of the Hamites, and then to the Meunites found there, who are therefore foreigners who had come to dwell among the Hamites. מְעוּנִים (for which the *Kethib* has מְעִינִים and the Sept. Μιναῖοι) are here, as in 2 Chron. xxvi. 7 (comp. xx. 1), probably inhabitants of the town Maon near Petra, east of the Wady Musa (Robinson, iii. 127). Their being involved in the fate of the Hamites implies that the scene of the present event lay to the east, though it cannot be further defined. Against the reading proposed by some old expositors (Luther, Starke), וְאֶת־הַמְּעֹנִים, "and the fixed habitations," in contrast with the forementioned tents, see Bochart, *Geogr. Sacra*, p. 138.—*And destroyed them unto this day, and dwelt in their stead.* וַיַּחֲרִימֻם, *ad internecionem usque eos exciderunt* (J. H. Mich.), *deleverunt* (Vulg.). Comp. הֶחֱרִים, ban, extirpate, in 2 Chron. xx. 23, xxxii. 14, 2 Kings xix. 11, Isa. xxxvii. 11. The term "unto this day" points to the time of composition, not by the Chronist, but by the old historical sources at least before the exile employed by him.

b. Second expedition of the Simeonites against Mount Seir: vers. 42, 43.—*And of them, of the sons of Simeon, five hundred men went to Mount Seir.* Nothing more precise is stated regarding the time of this expedition; it may have been before or after that in the time of Hezekiah. And the statement, "of them, of the sons of Simeon," is quite general, and sets no limit either to the Simeonites named vers. 34–37 or to those before enumerated, vers. 24–27. Keil, who exchanges the Ishi of our verse with Shimi, ver. 27, is arbitrary in thinking only of the latter; and no less so is Bertheau, who refers the words to the part of the Simeonites described ver. 34 ff. Of the surmise, that the event of our verse is somehow connected with that referred, vers. 34–41, to the time of Hezekiah, and is to be regarded as in some measure a continuation of it (Ew., Berth., Kamph.), there is not the slightest hint in the text, even if the valley of the present expedition to Mount Seir could be situated in the same direction from the tribe of Simeon as that of the former; see on vers. 39, 40.—Ver. 43. *And they smote the remnant that had escaped of*

Amalek, that is, those Amalekites who escaped annihilation in the victories of Saul and David over this hereditary foe of the Israelites (who were formerly settled, Judg. v. 14, xii. 15, comp. Num. xiii. 29, chiefly in Paran or half-Manasseh east of Jordan; comp. Hitzig, *Gesch. d. V. Isr.* pp. 26, 104); comp. 1 Sam. xiv. 48, xv. 7; 2 Sam. viii. 12. These who thus escaped had retired into the Idumean mountains, and there intermingled partly with the Edomites (comp. i. 36 f.). Here they were now sought out and extirpated by the Simeonites under the sons of Ishi, while the conquerors occupied their seats. From a comparison of the present passage with Mic. i. 15, ii. 8–10, Isa. xxi. 11, xxviii. 12, etc., which appear to indicate an advance of the Israelites who believed in Jehovah far into the south and south-east in the times of Hezekiah and Isaiah, Hitzig (*Das Königreich Massa*) has, with the concurrence of Bunsen, Bertheau, etc., developed his hypothesis of the founding of an Israelitish kingdom of Massa east or south-east of Seir (not far from Dumah; comp. Gen. xxv. 44; 1 Chron. i. 30) by the colony of Simeonites here mentioned, and has assigned to it as kings, Agur and Lemuel, the authors of the two appendices to the book of Proverbs. Comp. our substantially concurring judgment concerning this hypothesis on Prov. xxx. 1 ff., vol. xii. p. 208 of the *Bibelw.* The objections urged against this hypothesis by Graf (*Der Stamm Simeon*, p. 12 ff.) and Mühlau (*De prov. Aguri*, etc., *orig.* p. 24 f.) certainly point out much that is not and cannot be proved in it, but are not sufficient to show that it is a mere fancy picture. At all events, the traditions, that in accordance with our passage part of the tribe of Simeon penetrated far into Arabia and founded there an Israelitish colony, are as widespread as they are ancient. Arabian legends even make the tribe of Simeon found the city and the temple of Mecca. See Hoffmann, *Blicke*, etc., p. 124.

2. *The Tribes of Reuben, Gad, and half-Manasseh:* ch. v.

α. *The Tribe of Reuben:* vers. 1–10.

CH. V. 1. And the sons of Reuben, the first-born of Israel,—for he was the first-born;
but, because he defiled his father's bed, his birthright was given to the sons of
2 Joseph the son of Israel, though he was not to be registered as first-born. For
Judah was mighty among his brethren, and of him was the prince; and Joseph
3 had the birthright.—The sons of Reuben, the first-born of Israel: Hanoch and
4 Pallu, Hezron and Carmi. The sons of Joel: Shemaiah his son, Gog his son,
5, 6 Shimi his son. Micah his son, Reaiah his son, Baal his son. Beerah his son,
whom Tilgath-pilneser king of Asshur carried away; he was prince among the
Reubenites.
7 And his brethren by their families, in the register after their generations:
8 the chief Jeiel, and Zechariah. And Bela the son of Azaz, the son of Shema,
9 the son of Joel; he dwelt in Aroer, even unto Nebo and Baal-meon. And eastward he dwelt unto the entrance into the wilderness from the river Euphrates;
10 for their cattle multiplied in the land of Gilead. And in the days of Saul they
made war with the Hagarites, and they fell by their hand; and they dwelt in
their tents on all the east side of Gilead.

β. *The Tribe of Gad:* vers. 11–17.

11 And the sons of Gad dwelt over against them, in the land of Bashan, unto
12 Salcah. Joel the chief, and Shapham the second, and Janai and Shaphat[1] in
13 Bashan. And their brethren by their father-houses: Michael, and Meshullam,
14 and Sheba, and Jorai, and Jachan, and Zia, and Eber, seven. These are the
sons of Abihail the son of Huri, the son of Jaroah, the son of Gilead, the son
15 of Michael, the son of Jeshishai, the son of Jahdo, the son of Buz. Ahi the
16 son of Abdiel, the son of Guni, chief of their father-houses. And they dwelt in
Gilead in Bashan, and in her daughters, and in all the suburbs of Sharon[2] unto
17 their outgoings. All of them were registered in the days of Jotham king of
Judah, and in the days of Jeroboam king of Israel.

γ. *War of the Tribes of Reuben, Gad, and half-Manasseh with Arab Nations:* vers. 18–22.

18 And the sons of Reuben, and Gad, and the half-tribe of Manasseh, of valiant
men bearing shield and sword, and drawing the bow, and skilful in war, were
19 forty and four thousand and seven hundred and sixty going forth to war. And
20 they made war with the Hagarites, and Jetur, and Naphish, and Nodab. And
they were helped against them, and the Hagarites were delivered into their
hand, and all that were with them; for they cried to God in the battle, and He

21 was entreated of them, because they trusted in Him. And they took their
cattle; their camels fifty thousand, and sheep two hundred and fifty thousand,
22 and asses two thousand, and souls of men a hundred thousand. For many fell
slain, because the war was of God; and they dwelt in their stead until the
captivity.

δ. *The half-Tribe of Manasseh:* vers. 23, 24.

23 And the sons of the half-tribe of Manasseh dwelt in the land, from Bashan
24 unto Baal-hermon and Senir and Mount Hermon; these were many. And
these were the heads of their father-houses, even Epher, and Ishi, and Eliel,
and Azriel, and Jeremiah, and Hodaviah, and Jahdiel, valiant heroes, famous
men, heads of father-houses.

ε. *Carrying of the Three East-Jordanic Tribes into Exile:* vers. 25, 26.

25 And they were untrue to the God of their fathers, and lusted after the gods
26 of the people of the land, whom the Lord destroyed before them. And the God
of Israel stirred up the spirit of Pul king of Asshur, and the spirit of Tilgath-
pilneser king of Asshur, and he carried them away, the Reubenites, and the
Gadites, and the half-tribe of Manasseh, and brought them to Halah and Habor,
and the mountain and the river Gozan, unto this day.

[1] For וְשָׁפָט the Sept. read שֹׁפֵט or סֹפֵר; for it gives the words וְיַעְנַי וְשָׁפָט בַּבָּשָׁן by: καὶ Γανὶν ὁ γραμματεύς ἐν Βασάν.

[2] For שָׂרוֹן the *cod. Vat.* of the Sept. has Γεριάμ (possibly from an original שִׂרְיוֹן; comp. Exeg. Note).

EXEGETICAL.

Preliminary Remark.—The three east-jordanic tribes are closely connected by our genealogist on account of their common fate, not only by being here placed together, although by this arrangement the eastern half of Manasseh are severed from their western kindred, but also by the insertion of two historic episodes referring to the common doings and fortunes of the three. The first of these pieces is inserted between Gad and half-Manasseh; the second is transferred to the end, because it describes the catastrophe by which the three tribes lost their independence. "An endeavour after an equable distribution of the historical matter" (Berth.) may lie at the ground of this; for even to the genealogical account of the Reubenites a short war notice, ver. 10, is appended. But the notable thing is, that the more copious and important of these historical notices refer to the common acts and the common fall of the three (it is not observed that the tribe of Gad, in connection with whose generations the war report, vers. 18–22, is given, played a specially prominent part in it), by which our section is distinguished as one compact group from the genealogical series of our chapter.

1. *The Tribe of Reuben:* vers. 1–10.—The introductory vers. 1, 2 treat of the birthright of Reuben in its relation to that of Joseph.—*For he was the first-born; but because,* etc. These words to the close of ver. 2 form a parenthesis, which, reminding us in its opening words of Gen. xlix. 4, set forth the ground on which the birthright of Joseph is mentioned along with that of Reuben.—*Though he was not to be registered as first-born,* literally, "though not to register (לְ before הִתְיַחֵשׂ, to denote that which *should* take place; see Ew. § 237, *c*) for the first birth," that is, in the rank of the first-born. The subject here is perhaps not Reuben (Sept., Vulg.), but Joseph, as Kimchi and other Rabbinical expositors justly observe; for the statement of the following verse refers to Joseph as the chief person spoken of here.—Ver. 2. *For Judah was mighty among his brethren.* גָּבַר, was strong, mighty, in numbers and influence; comp. Gen. xlix. 8 ff.; Judg. i. 1, and ch. ii.–iv.—*And of him was the prince* (namely, David, xxviii. 4; 1 Sam. xiii. 14, xxv. 30), or, "and of him should be one of the princes" (Kamph.). This concealed reference to the Davidic kingdom that sprang from Judah reminds us in its form of Mic. v. 1 (comp. מִמֶּנּוּ here with מִמְּךָ there, and לְנָגִיד with לִהְיוֹת מוֹשֵׁל there).—*And Joseph had the birthright.* To him were allowed two territories (according to the right of first birth, Deut. xxi. 15–17), one for Ephraim and one for Manasseh.—Ver. 3. *Hanoch and Pallu, Hezron and Carmi.* So are the four sons of Reuben named Gen. xlvi. 9, Ex. vi. 14; comp. Num. xxvi. 5–7.—Vers. 4–6. The descendants of Joel, as a single line of Reubenites, which is carried through several generations. From which of the four sons this line descended, the author of the present list knew, and perhaps even the Chronist, who incorporated it into his work; but the knowledge is lost to after times.—*Shemaiah his son, Gog his son,* etc. The first בְּנוֹ after שְׁמַעְיָה the Sept. has read as a *nom. propr.*, and therefore inserted between Shemaiah and Gog another descendant of Joel, Βαναιά, whereby his whole descendants are increased from seven to eight, though scarcely in accordance with the original text. The seven names occur also elsewhere, but only here in reference to the descendants of Reuben.—Ver. 6. *Beerah his son, whom Tilgath-pilneser carried away.* The Chronist always writes תִּלְּגַת פִּלְנְאֶסֶר, whereas in 2 Kings the

only form of writing is תִּגְלַת פִּלְאֶסֶר (comp. the similar difference between "Nebuchadrezzar" of Jeremiah and Ezekiel and "Nebuchadnezzar" of the other books; see on Dan. i. 1). Whether G. Oppert's interpretation of the name = תִּגְלַת־ פִּלְאֶ־סַחַר, "prayer to the son of the Zodiac," the Assyrian Hercules, be correct, or the certainly preferable one of Schrader (*Tuklat-habal-asar*, "trust in the son of the house of grace," or, "he who trusts in the house of grace," that is, in the god Adar; comp. Schrader, *Die Keilinschriften und das Alte T.*, 1872, pp. 134 f., 237), the form used in the books of Kings appears the more original.—*He was a prince among the Reubenites*, that is, Beerah. He was prince of a family of Reubenites, not of the whole tribe; for the לְ (לָרְאוּבֵנִי) indicates a looser sort of connection than the relation of prince to the whole tribe, to be expressed by the *stat. constr.* The adjective form, "the Reubenite," denotes here, as in ver. 26 and xxvi. 32, generally those belonging to the tribe of Reuben; comp. ver. 18, גָּדִי, and iv. 2, הַצָּרְעָתִי, and similar forms in Chronicles.

—Vers. 7–9. *The brothers of Beerah*, that is, the families among the descendants of Joel most nearly related to his family.—*And his brethren by their families* (before לְמִשְׁפְּחֹתָיו supply אִישׁ, every one by his family; comp. Num. ii. 34, xi. 10), *in the register after their generations* (or order of birth): *the chief Jeiel*, etc. הָרֹאשׁ, the head, the first, the chief of the family. Comp. ver. 12 and ix. 17, where, however, this epithet stands after the name of the person in question, while in xii. 3, xxiii. 8, as here, it stands before. —Ver. 8. *And Bela the son of Azaz, the son of Shema, the son of Joel;* scarcely any other than the Joel of ver. 4. From him sprang Bela in the third generation, a clear proof that he belonged only in the wider sense to the brethren of Beerah, who descended from him in the seventh generation, and that he was at all events considerably older than the latter; see on ver. 10.—*He dwelt in Aroer, even unto Nebo and Baal-meon.* Aroer, now a ruin, Arrayr on the river Arnon (comp. Josh. xii. 2, xiii. 9, 16); Nebo, a place on Mount Nebo, in the range of Abarim, over against Jericho (Num. xxxii. 38, xxxiii. 47); Baal-meon, perhaps the ruins Myun, two miles south of Heshbon (comp. Num. xxxii. 38, where it is also found along with Nebo).—Ver. 9. *And eastward he dwelt, unto the entrance into the wilderness from the river Euphrates*, that is, to the line where the great wilderness begins, that extends from the Euphrates to the east border of Peræa, or Gilead as it is called in this verse; for Gilead (Gen. xxxi. 21, xxxvii. 25; Josh. xiii. 11, xvii. 1; Judg. v. 17, etc.) is the general term usual in the Old Testament for the territory of Israel east of the Jordan; comp. on ver. 16.—Ver. 10. *And in the days of Saul* (the first king of Israel) *they made war with the Hagarites* (or Hagarenes; comp. Ps. lxxxiii. 7), the same North Arabian tribe that appears, vers. 19, 20, as the adversary of the east-jordanic Israelites, perhaps the 'Αγραῖοι of Strabo, xiii. p. 767, occurring, according to Schrader, in the form *Hagaranu* (or Ha-ar-gi-'i) several times in the Assyro-Babylonian cuneate inscriptions. —*And they fell by their hand*, or, even into their hands, of which the consequence was, that the victors dwelt in the tents of the vanquished (that is, occupied their country, Gen. ix. 27), "on all the east side of Gilead," that is, on the whole east border of the land of Gilead and beyond it (with עַל־כָּל־פְּנֵי comp. עַל פְּנֵי, "close before," Gen. xvi. 12). Who are these conquerors? Are they the Reubenites in general, or only those of the family of Bela? Against the latter alternative, which is defended by Keil, appears to be the circumstance that in vers. 8, 9 Bela is spoken of in the singular. But this singular begins even in ver. 9*b* to pass into the plural (מִקְנֵיהֶם), and the mighty outspreading of the Belaites mentioned there seems intended to prepare for the notice of their war with their Hagarene neighbours. Moreover, the statement in ver. 8, that Bela was great-grandson of Joel, while Beerah was his descendant in the seventh generation, corresponds with the fact that this conquest of the Hagarites preceded the deportation of the Reubenites under Beerah by Tilgath-pilneser, ver. 6, some centuries. After the removal of a considerable portion of the Reubenites, so wide an outspreading of another Reubenite family as is here related would scarcely have taken place. We must therefore refer what is recorded from ver. 7 of the family of the brothers of Beerah, and especially of that of Bela, to a much earlier time than that which is related in ver. 6, because the narrative issues in the present notice of a war in the time of Saul; and there is no good ground why we should isolate this war notice, and regard it as an unconnected appendix to the genealogy of Reuben (against Berth. and others, and also against Hoffmann, *Das gelobte Land in den Zeiten des getheilten Reichs*, etc. 1871, p. 27).

2. *The Tribe of Gad:* vers. 11–17.—*And the sons of Gad dwelt over against them in the land of Bashan*, that is, over against the Reubenites dwelling beside the Dead Sea in the mountain range of Abarim or Moab, and also beyond the Jordan in middle Gilead, which formed the southern part of the former kingdom of Og king of Bashan (Num. xxi. 33; Deut. iii. 11). The extension of this tract inhabited by the Gadites to the east is shown to be considerable by the addition "unto Salchah" (as in Josh. xiii. 11). For Salchah, now Sulkhad, lies on the southern slope of Jebel Hauran, six or seven hours east of Bozra, and therefore about thirty hours in a direct line east from Jordan.—Ver. 12. *Joel the chief, and Shapham the second, and Janai and Shaphat in Bashan*, that is, dwelling, the יָשְׁבוּ of the previous verse completing the sense here. It is uncertain how these four Gadite heads of families are genealogically connected with the immediate descendants of Gad named in Gen. xlvi. 16. The omission of those seven sons of Gad enumerated in Genesis (Ziphion, Haggi, Shuni, Ezbon, Eri, Arodi, Areli) is surprising, and raises the suspicion of a gap in the text. On the variant reading of the Sept. for וְשָׁפָט, see Crit. Note. As שָׁפָט occurs elsewhere as a proper name, for example, iii. 22, its retention here is the less doubtful.—Ver. 13. *And their brethren by their father-houses*, that is, by the families at whose head they stood, and which were named after them.

For the plur. בֵּית אֲבוֹתֵיהֶם, comp. on iv. 38. Luther has erroneously taken the phrase for a singular, and therefore translated, "and their brethren of the house of their fathers," etc. The term "brethren" stands naturally in as wide a sense as in ver. 7. A statement of the country where they dwelt does not follow the names of these seven brothers of the four Gadite heads of families already named. But their pedigree is first given, vers. 14, 15, through eight generations, terminating in a not otherwise known Buz, who has perhaps as little to do with his namesake the son of Nahor, Gen. xxii. 21, as with the progenitor of Elihu, Job xxxii. 2.—Ver. 15. *Ahi, the son of Abdiel, the son of Guni, chief of their father-houses.* This Ahi we may suppose to have lived at the beginning of the eighth century B.C., under Jeroboam II. of Israel, or half a century later, under Jotham of Judah, as ver. 17 shows.—Ver. 16. *And they dwelt in Gilead, in Bashan, and in her daughters, and in all the suburbs of Sharon unto their outgoings.* The first of these designations of place is the widest and most general: it embraces both "Bashan and her daughters" and "the suburbs of Sharon;" see on ver. 9. The suffix in בִּבְנֹתֶיהָ refers to both countries, the more extensive Gilead and the narrower Bashan forming merely the northern part of Gilead; and the "suburbs" or pastures (מִגְרְשִׁים, as in Num. xxxv. 2 ff.; Josh. xxi. 11 ff.; Ezek. xlviii. 15) of Sharon are no doubt to be sought in Gilead, as nothing is known of a dwelling or a grazing of any Gadites on the well-known plain of Sharon, west of Jordan, between Cæsarea and Joppa (Song ii. 1; Isa. xxxiii. 9, xxxv. 2, lxv. 10); and the "outgoings" of the suburbs of Sharon are not necessarily outgoings or boundaries on the sea, as Keil, referring to Josh. xvii. 9, will have it; comp. on the contrary, Num. xxxiv. 4, 5. Kamph. is right, who at the same time mentions a plausible conjecture of the early expositors, that Shirion should be read for Sharon. But we see no reason why there should not be a Sharon east of the Jordan. Comp. Smith's *Bibl. Dict.*, Art. "Sharon." —Ver. 17. *All of them were registered in the days of Jotham*, etc. "All of them" refers to the collective families of the Gadites from ver. 11, not merely to those mentioned ver. 13 ff. Of the two kings of the eighth century under whose reign the registration took place, that of the rightful kingdom of Judah is, contrary to the order of time, named first. We meet with no other notices of these two registrations of the tribe of Gad, of which that undertaken by Jeroboam II. of Israel (825–784), at all events, coincides with the restoration of the old boundaries of the northern kingdom mentioned 2 Kings xiv. 25 ff. A temporary subjection of the tribe of Gad by Jotham of Judah (759–743), or perhaps by his predecessor, the powerful Uzziah (811–759), as a prelude to the second registration here mentioned, is easily conceivable, because after Jeroboam's death a long weakening of the northern kingdom by internal strife and anarchy ensued, from which it recovered under Pekah's reign of twenty years (759–739). Comp. Keil, p. 77, where, however, Pekah's reign, probably by an error of the press, is stated to be of only ten years' duration.

3. *War of the Tribes of Reuben, Gad, and half-Manasseh with Arab Tribes:* vers. 18–22.—On the reason why this account is inserted here after the families of Gad, see Preliminary Remark.—*Of valiant men*, literally, of sons of valour (מִן בְּנֵי חַיִל; comp. גִּבּוֹרֵי חַיִל, ver. 24). These and the following descriptions of the military prowess of these tribes are confirmed by 1 Chron. xii. 8, 21, at least with regard to Gad and half-Manasseh. With לְמוּדֵי מִלְחָמָה, comp. the partic. *Pual* מְלֻמְּדֵי, Song iii. 8 and ch. xxv. 7. The number 44,760, which certainly rests on an exact numeration, nearly agrees with that given in Josh. iv. 13, but not with the added numbers yielding a far greater sum in Num. i. 21, 25, xxvi. 7, 18. The difference is explained by this, that the statements in Numbers refer to the time when the whole tribes of Reuben, Gad, and half-Manasseh were armed for war under Moses, and in a wandering state, and each of these tribes, at least of the first two, numbered more than 40,000 men fit for war, whereas the present statement, like that in Josh. iv. 13, refers to the time after they were settled beyond the Jordan, when the number of troops available for external service was naturally much smaller; comp. on xxi. 5.—Ver. 19. *And they made war with the Hagarites.* The same tribe of northern Arabs with which Reuben alone, ver. 10, had been at war. The present common fight of all the tribes beyond the Jordan with this tribe is perhaps to be dated later than that of Reuben; comp. ver. 22.—*And Jetur, and Naphish, and Nodab.* The first two tribes (of which יְטוּר has given name to the district of Ituræa) occurred in i. 31 and in Gen. xxv. 15 as descendants of Ishmael. Nodab, also a Beduin tribe, occurs nowhere else. The name appears to signify "noble, princely," and might possibly be the source of the Nabatæans (Arab. *nabt*); for to identify this at once with נְבָיוֹת, Gen. xxv. 13, Isa. lx. 7, as is usually done, has its difficulties; comp. Chwolsohn, *Die Sabier*, i. 698; Quatremère, *Les Nabatéens*, Par. 1835; Muhlau, *De prov. Aguri et Lemuelis orig. et indole*, p. 28 f.—Ver. 20. *And they were helped against them.* וַיֵּעָזְרוּ, namely, of God; comp. 2 Chron. xxvi. 15; Ps. xxviii. 7.—*And all that were with them*, namely, the Ituræans, etc., the confederates of the Hagarites.—*And he was entreated of them.* וְנַעְתּוֹר is not an unusual form of the *perf. Niphal* (for וְנֶעְתַּר, Isa. xix. 22), but, what alone suits for continued narrative, as here, *infin. abs. Niph.*, with a perfect meaning; comp. נַחְתּוֹם, Esth. viii. 8; נַהֲפוֹךְ, Esth. ix. 1.—Ver. 21. *Camels, fifty thousand.* Luther, Starke, and even Kamph., in Bunsen's *Bibelwerk*, incorrectly (not observing the plur. חֲמִשִּׁים), "five thousand." The enormous numbers, that are explained by the great riches in herds of the north Arabians, remind us of the like statements regarding the rich booty in the war with Midian, Num. xxxi. 11, 32 ff.—Ver. 22. *For many fell slain.* The greatness of the defeat which the foe sustained accounts for the extremely great value of the booty taken from them. On the further explanatory sentence, "for the war was of God," comp.

2 Chron. xxv. 20; 1 Sam. xvii. 47.—*And they dwelt in their stead*, in the seats of the conquered tribes; unhindered, they made use of their abodes and pastures, "until the captivity," until the deportation decreed by Tilgath-pilneser, ver. 6.

4. *The half-Tribe of Manasseh:* vers. 23, 24.—*From Bashan unto Baal-hermon and Senir and Mount Hermon.* As Bashan is the district inhabited by Gad bordering on the south, ver. 12, it denotes here the south border, while Baal-hermon (Judg. iii. 3, or "Baal-Gad under Hermon," Josh. xii. 7, xiii. 5), Senir (later, by the Arabs, Sunir; according to Ezek. xxvii. 8, the name of a part of the Hermon range; according to Deut. iii. 9, an Amorite name for the whole of Hermon), and Mount Hermon (or Antilibanus, now Jebel esh Sheik) designate the north border. On account of this wide extent from south to north, and also in breadth, it is said of those belonging to this half-tribe, "these were many;" comp. Num. xxvi. 34, where the number of military age in this whole tribe is said to be 52,700.—Ver. 24. *And these were the heads of their father-houses, even Epher.* The ו before עֵפֶר may be rendered "even"; but it is surprising, and raises the suspicion that perhaps a name has fallen out. None of these heads of families of East Manasseh is otherwise known, so that we know nothing of the deeds for which they were called "valiant heroes, famous men."

5. *Carrying away into Exile of the three east-Jordanic Tribes:* vers. 25, 26.—*And they were untrue*, etc., namely, the three eastern tribes named in the following verse, and not merely the Manassites. For the terms, as for the fact, comp. 2 Kings xvii. 7 ff.—*The people of the land, whom the Lord had destroyed before them*, are the Amorites and the subjects of Og of Bashan.—Ver. 26. *And the God of Israel stirred up the spirit of Pul.* וַיָּעַר, as 2 Chron. xxi. 16 (comp. xxxi. 26; Ezra i. 1, 5). L. Lavater justly remarks: *in mentem illis dedit, movit eos, ut expeditionem facerent contra illos.* Pul is, moreover, named as the beginner of the oppressions coming from Assyria (comp. 2 Kings xv. 19 f.); the removal itself is completed by Tiglath-pileser, as the sing. וַיַּגְלֵם, referring only to him, shows. Besides, the Assyriologists, especially Rawlinson, Schrader (p. 124 ff.), declare Pul to be the same with Tiglath-pileser, and his name a mere mutilation of the latter name, because the Assyrian inscriptions nowhere exhibit any such thing as a ruler Pul almost contemporary with Tiglath-pileser.—*Carried them away, the Reubenites*, etc. The suffix in וַיַּגְלֵם is more precisely defined by the following accusatives לָראוּבֵנִי וגו', introduced by ל (according to later usage); comp. Ew. § 277*e*.—*And brought them to Halah and Habor, and the mountain and the river Gozan, unto this day.* חֲלַח, perhaps = כֶּלַח, Gen. x. 11, at all events = Καλαχήνη, a region described by Strabo and Ptolemy: "On the east side of the Tigris, near Adiabene, north of Nineveh, on the borders of Armenia." Not far from this Halah (the name of which occurs on the Assyrian monuments in the form *Kal-hu;* comp. Schrader, *Die Keilenschriften und d. A. T.* p. 20 f.) is to be sought חָבוֹר, perhaps a district in North Assyria, after which both the mountain Χαβώρας (Ptolem. vi. 1), near the Median border, and a river flowing into the Tigris (*Khabur Chasanicæ*, now Khabur), are named. We are not here to think of the Mesopotamian river Chaboras, rising at Nisibis, and falling into the Euphrates near Circesium, as its Hebrew name is כְּבָר, Ezek. i. 1. The river Gozan, also, is scarcely to be sought in Mesopotamia (where there is certainly a district Γαυζανῖτις, the present Kaushan, bordering on that river Chebar, and where also Schrader, p. 161, has pointed out a place *Guzana*, near Nisibis—*Nasibina*—in an Assyrian inscription), but perhaps in the border land of Assyria and Media, where the Median city Γαυζανία, mentioned by Ptol. vi. 2, lay, and where also a river Ozan (in full, Kizil-Ozan, the red Ozan) is found, the Mardos of the old Greeks, rising south-east of the lake Urumiah, forming the boundary of Assyria and Media, and falling into the Caspian Sea. As all these places point to the north of Assyria and to Media, so the term before the last, "the mountain," appears to mean the Median highlands; and, indeed, הָרָא seems to be the Aramaic form for the Hebrew הָר, mountain, the popular designation in that region of the Median highlands (al Jebal among the Arabs); comp. also 2 Kings xvii. 6, where, in place of הָרָא, the "cities of Media" (עָרֵי מָדַי) are named. Keil on our passage and on 2 Kings xvii. 6, Bähr on the latter, Ew. (*Gesch.* iii. p. 318), M. Niebuhr (*Gesch. Assurs und Babels*), Wichelhaus (*Das Exil der* 10 *Stämme*, in the *Deutschen Morgenl. Zeitschr.* v. 467 ff.), Kamph. on our passage, etc., are here right; while Thenius, Berth., Hitz. think, without sufficient grounds, of parts of Mesopotamia, near the Euphrates. Moreover, not merely the Chronist, but the sources used by him, appear to have assumed as the place to which Tiglath-pileser removed the tribes beyond the Jordan, the same region in the north of Assyria to which, 2 Kings xvii. 6, some decennia afterwards, Shalmaneser transplanted the remaining tribes of the northern kingdom. Whether this statement be historically correct, or involve the confounding of two different events (as Berth. will have it), must remain undecided. From 2 Kings xv. 29, where the country to which Tiglath-pileser brought the 2½ tribes is simply called Asshur, the inaccuracy of the present statements cannot be proved.

d. The Family of the Levites, with a Statement of their Seats in the different Tribes.—Ch. v. 27–vi. 66.

1. *The Family of Aaron, or the High-priestly Line to the Exile:* ch. v. 27–41.

Ch. v. 27, 28. The sons of Levi: Gershon, Kohath, and Merari. And the sons of
29 Kohath: Amram, Izhar, and Hebron, and Uzziel. And the sons of Amram:

Aaron, and Moses, and Miriam. And the sons of Aaron: Nadab and Abihu,
30 Eleazar and Ithamar. Eleazar begat Phinehas, and Phinehas begat Abishua.
31, 32 And Abishua begat Bukki, and Bukki begat Uzzi. And Uzzi begat Zerahiah,
33 and Zerahiah begat **Meraioth**. Meraioth begat Amariah, and Amariah begat
34, 35 Ahitub. And Ahitub begat Zadok, and Zadok begat Ahimaaz. And Ahi-
36 maaz begat Azariah, and Azariah begat Johanan. And Johanan begat
Azariah, he that served as priest in the house that Solomon built in Jeru-
37, 38 salem. And Azariah begat Amariah, and Amariah begat Ahitub. And
39 Ahitub begat Zadok, and Zadok begat Shallum. And Shallum begat Hilkial
40 and Hilkiah begat Azariah. And Azariah begat Seraiah, and Seraiah begat
41 Jehozadak. And Jehozadak went away, when the LORD carried away Judah
and Jerusalem by the hand of Nebuchadnezzar.

2. *The Descendants of Gershom, Kohath, and Merari, in a Double Series:* ch. vi. 1–15

CH. VI. 1, 2. The sons of Levi: Gershom, Kohath, and Merari. And these are the
3 names of the sons of Gershom: Libni and Shimi. And the sons of Kohath:
4 Amram and Izhar, and Hebron and Uzziel. The sons of Merari: Mahli and
5 Mushi. And these are the families after their fathers.
6 To Gershom: Libni his son, Jahath his son, Zimmah his son. Joah his
son, Iddo his son, Zerah his son, Jeatherai his son.
7 The sons of Kohath: Amminadab his son, Korah his son, Assir his son.
8, 9 Elkanah his son, and Ebiasaph his son, and Assir his son. Tahath his son,
10 Uriel his son, Uzziah his son, and Shaul his son. And the sons of Elkanah:
11 Amasai and Ahimoth. Elkanah his son,[1] Elkanah of Zoph his son, and Nahath
12, 13 his son. Eliab his son, Jeroham his son, Elkanah his son. And the sons of
Samuel: the first-born[2] Vashni, and Abiah.
14 The sons of Merari: Mahli, Libni his son, Shimi his son, Uzzah his son.
15 Shima his son, Haggiah his son, Asaiah his son.

3. *The Ancestors of the Levitical Songmasters Heman, Asaph, and Ethan:* vers. 16–34.

16 And these are they whom David set over the singing in the house of the
17 LORD, after the resting of the ark. And they ministered before the dwelling
of the tent of meeting with singing, until Solomon built the house of the Lord
18 in Jerusalem, and they attended in their order to their service. And these
are they who attended, and their sons: of the sons of Kohath: Heman the
19 singer, the son of Joel, the son of Samuel. The son of Elkanah, the son of
20 Jeroham, the son of Eliel, the son of Toah. The son of Zuph,[3] the son of
21 Elkanah, the son of Mahath, the son of Amasai. The son of Elkanah, the
22 son of Joel, the son of Azariah, the son of Zephaniah. The son of Tahath,
23 the son of Assir, the son of Ebiasaph, the son of Korah. The son of Izhar,
the son of Kohath, the son of Levi, the son of Israel.
24 And his brother Asaph, who stood on his right hand, Asaph the son of
25 Berechiah, the son of Shima. The son of Michael, the son of Baaseiah, the
26 son of Malchiah. The son of Ethni, the son of Zerah, the son of Adaiah.
27, 28 The son of Ethan, the son of Zimmah, the son of Shimi. The son of Jahath,
the son of Gershom, the son of Levi.
29 And the sons of Merari, their brethren on the left hand: Ethan the son of
30 Kishi, the son of Abdi, the son of Malluch. The son of Hashabiah, the son
31 of Amaziah, the son of Hilkiah. The son of Amzi, the son of Bani, the son of
32 Shamer. The son of Mahli, the son of Mushi, the son of Merari, the son of Levi.
33 And their brethren the Levites, given for all service of the tabernacle of
34 the house of God. And Aaron and his sons offered on the altar of burnt-
offering, and on the altar of incense, for all the work of the holy of holies,
and to atone for Israel, in all that Moses, the servant of God, had com-
manded.

4. *The Series of High Priests from Eleazar to Ahimaaz (in the time of Solomon):* vers. 35–38.

35 And these are the sons of Aaron: Eleazar his son, Phinehas his son,

36, 37 Abishua his son. Bukki his son, Uzzi his son, Zerahiah his son. Meraioth
38 his son, Amariah his son, Ahitub his son. Zadok his son, Ahimaaz his son.

5. *The Towns of the Levites:* vers. 39–66.

39 And these are their dwellings, by their districts, in their border, of the
sons of Aaron: of the family of the Kohathites, for to them was the lot.
40 And they gave them Hebron, in the land of Judah, and its suburbs round
41 about it. And the field of the city and its villages they gave to Caleb the
42 son of Jephunneh. And to the sons of Aaron they gave the free towns,[4]
Hebron and Libnah and its suburbs, and Jattir and Eshtemoa and its suburbs.
43, 44 And Hilen[5] and its suburbs, Debir and its suburbs. And Ashan and its
45 suburbs, and Bethshemesh and its suburbs. And out of the tribe of Benjamin:
Geba and its suburbs, and Allemeth and its suburbs, and Anathoth and its
suburbs; all their cities were thirteen cities in their families.
46 And to the sons of Kohath that remained of the family of the tribe, were
47 from the half-tribe, the half of Manasseh, by lot, ten cities. And to the sons
of Gershom for their families, of the tribe of Issachar, and of the tribe of
Asher, and of the tribe of Naphtali, and of the tribe of Manasseh, in Bashan,
48 thirteen cities. To the sons of Merari for their families, of the tribe of
Reuben, and of the tribe of Gad, and of the tribe of Zebulun, by lot twelve
cities.
49 And the sons of Israel gave to the Levites the cities and their suburbs.
50 And they gave by lot out of the tribe of the sons of Judah, and the tribe of
the sons of Simeon, and the tribe of the sons of Benjamin, these cities which
they called by names.
51 And of the families of the sons of Kohath, some had the cities of their
52 border out of the tribe of Ephraim. And they gave them the free towns,
Shechem and its suburbs in Mount Ephraim, and Gezer and its suburbs.
53, 54 And Jokmeam and its suburbs, and Beth-horon and its suburbs. And
55 Aijalon and its suburbs, and Gathrimmon and its suburbs. And out of the
half-tribe of Manasseh, Aner and its suburbs, and Bilam and its suburbs,
to the family of the remaining sons of Kohath.
56 To the sons of Gershom, out of the family of the half-tribe of Manasseh,
57 Golan in Bashan and its suburbs, and Ashtaroth and its suburbs. And out
of the tribe of Issachar, Kedesh and its suburbs, Daberath and its suburbs.
58, 59 And Ramoth and its suburbs, and Anem and its suburbs. And out of the
60 tribe of Asher, Mashal and its suburbs, and Abdon and its suburbs. And
61 Hukok and its suburbs, and Rehob and its suburbs. And out of the tribe of
Naphtali, Kedesh in Galilee and its suburbs, and Hammon and its suburbs,
and Kiriathaim and its suburbs.
62 To the sons of Merari that remained, out of the tribe of Zebulun, Rim-
63 mono and its suburbs, Tabor and its suburbs. And beyond Jordan by
Jericho, east of Jordan, out of the tribe of Reuben, Bezer in the wilderness
64 and its suburbs, and Jahzah and its suburbs. And Kedemoth and its
65 suburbs, and Mephaath and its suburbs. And out of the tribe of Gad,
66 Ramoth in Gilead and its suburbs, and Mahanaim and its suburbs. And
Heshbon and its suburbs, and Jazer and its suburbs.

[1] The *Kethib* is אֶלְקָנָה בְּנוֹ; the *Keri* puts בְּנֵי for בְּנוֹ, and places אֶלְקָנָה (with *Athnach*) as a separate superscription. The text is, at all events, corrupt (see Exeg. Expl.), whether the first אֶלְקָנָה is to be erased, and בְּנֵי to be read, or the second אלקנה removed, and the sing. בְּנוֹ to be retained.

[2] After הַבְּכוֹר, the name יוֹאֵל must have fallen out, as the comparison of 1 Sam. viii. 2 shows (comp. also ver. 18).

[3] The *Kethib* has בֶּן־צִיף; the *Keri*, more correctly, בֶּן־צוּף.

[4] For אֶת־עָרֵי הַמִּקְלָט, some old prints, after the *Bibl. Veneta Rabb.* 1525, have אֶת־עָרֵי יְהוּדָה הַמִּ׳. The MSS. (see de Rossi, *Var. Lect.*) do not show this addition, which appears to have come into the text from the margin.

[5] For חִילֵן (in Josh. xxi. 16, חֹלֹן), the more accurate MSS. have, according to *R. Norzi* and *Ed. Neapolit.*, חִילֹן.

EXEGETICAL.

Preliminary Remark. — Of the five subdivisions into which this section falls, the first (v. 27-41) is a list of the high priests from Aaron to the exile, which appears to be taken from a peculiar older source, partly because one portion of the high priests is enumerated again (vi. 35-38) under a different genealogical form (instead of הוֹלִיד before the name, בְּנוֹ comes after it), partly because Gershon (v. 27) appears instead of "Gershom," which is used throughout ch. vi. But the four divisions also in ch. vi. bear a more or less fragmentary character ; only the genealogies of the three Davidic songmasters Heman, Asaph, and Ethan (vers. 16-34), appear to be complete in themselves, and without defect. In the register of the three Levitical families Gershom, Kohath, and Merari (vers. 1-15), many names are obviously wanting, and some parts, especially in the series of the Kohathites, vers. 7-13, appear to have come down in a state of some confusion. The list of the Levitical cities, vers. 39-66, presents great corruptions of the text in considerable number, with many inaccuracies, and a notorious perversion of the original order (see on vers. 49, 50), as a cursory comparison of it with that drawn from other sources in the book of Joshua, xxi., will show. And lastly, the short list of the high priests appears clearly to be a fragment from its breaking off with Ahimaaz ; is, moreover, closely connected with the preceding remarks in vers. 33, 34, on the ministry of the Aaronites in the temple, and might be fitly formed with these two verses into a special section referring to the ἀρχιερατικὸν γένος of the house of Levi and its functions. Comp. moreover, H. Graf, *Zur Gesch. d. St. Levi*, in A. Merx's *Archiv. f. Wissenschaftliche Erforschung des A. T.* vol. i. 1870 (hypercritical on the content of our chapter, and throughout).

1. *The Family of Aaron, or the High-priestly Line to the Exile:* v. 27-41. *a.* Aaron's descent from Levi: vers. 27-29.—*Gershon, Kohath, and Merari.* So run the names of the three sons of Aaron in the Pentateuch, Gen. xlvi. 11, Ex. vi. 18. The form גֵּרְשׁוֹן is there constant, while for קְהָת is occasionally קֳהָת.—Ver. 28. The names of the four sons of Kohath (the father of the chief Levitical line) are literally the same in Ex. vi. 18. Likewise the names of the three children of Amram, and those of the four sons of Aaron, ver. 29, agree literally with Ex. vi. 20, 23 ; comp. Num. iii. 2-4, and in 1 Chron. xxiv. 2, the account of the premature death of Nadab and Abihu by a divine judgment, reminding us of Lev. x. 1 ff.—*b.* The descendants and successors of Eleazar (Num. xx. 28; Josh. xiv. 1) in the office of high priest: vers. 30-41. Only this series of high priests from Eleazar is given here, as in vi. 35 ff., not that from Ithamar, as the former only is strictly legitimate. That the line from Ithamar, to which Eli belonged (1 Sam. ii. 30),—whose son was Phinehas, and grandson, Ahitub (1 Sam. iv. 11, xiv. 3), further, Ahitub's son Ahijah or Ahimelech (comp. 1 Sam. xiv. 3 with xxii. 9 ff.), lastly, this Ahimelech's son Abiathar (from whom Solomon took the high-priesthood to give it to Zadok, 1 Sam. xxii. 20 ; 1 Kings ii. 26-35),—was not unknown to our author, is shown by his account in 1 Chron. xxiv. 3 ff. But the line of Eleazar only must have passed with him as really legitimate ; for here, and in vi. 35 ff., he ignores the line of Ithamar running parallel with it for several generations (from Uzzi, ver. 31, the contemporary of Eli, to Zadok, the contemporary and rival of Abiathar, ver. 34). On the relation existing between those collateral lines in the times of Saul and David we find nothing certain, either in our books or in those of Samuel or Kings. So much appears certain, however, from various intimations in the latter books, that the statement of Josephus (*Antiq. Jud.* viii. 1. 3; comp. ch. v. 12), that the descendants of Eleazar kept quiet, and lived as private persons during the supremacy of Eli, Phinehas, Ahitub, and Ahimelech, is incorrect, and rests on mere conjecture. Rather, from 1 Kings iii. 4 ff. (comp. 1 Chron. xvi. 39), Zadok appears to have presided at Gibeon, contemporary with Abiathar (the constant companion of David, 1 Sam. xxii. 20-23) at Jerusalem over the service of the sanctuary ; and even before David, there seems to have been a certain co-existence of different sanctuaries with different high priests in different places,—an assumption that is at least better supported than the conjecture proposed by Thenius on 2 Sam. viii. 17, that, in David's time, the two high priests of the collateral houses might have held office in alternate years.—Ver. 35. *And Ahimaaz begat Azariah.* As Ahimaaz (ver. 38) is son of Zadok, he belongs to the reign of Solomon, within which also his son Azariah may have been high priest. Without doubt, the notice standing in ver. 36, beside a younger Azariah (grandson of the other), "he that served as priest (כִּהֵן, Ex. xl. 13; Lev. xvi. 32) in the house that Solomon built in Jerusalem," only suits the present Azariah, the grandson of Zadok. For in 1 Kings iv. 2, also, Azariah the son (more exactly grandson) of Zadok is named as priestly prince under Solomon ; his grandson of the same name in ver. 36 cannot have lived before the time of Rehoboam, or even Asa or Jehoshaphat. We must therefore assume, with Bertheau, that the words quoted from ver. 36*b* originally stood after the name עֲזַרְיָה, ver. 35*a*,—an assumption which, from the second occurrence of the same name shortly after, and from the notorious occurrence of such erroneous transpositions in our section (see on ver. 49 f.), involves no difficulty, and at least commends itself more than the attempt of Keil to identify the Azariah of ver. 36 with the high priest of this name under king Uzziah (who, 2 Chron. xxvi. 17, boldly resisted the attempt of this king to burn incense in the sanctuary).[1] The name Azariah appears to have often recurred in the family of the high priest in the time of the kings ; for as our series contains this name no less than three times (vers. 35, 36, 40), we know from other accounts several other high priests of the name before the exile ; thus, besides the one in Uzziah's time, another in the time of Hezekiah, 2 Chron. xxi. 10, who cannot possibly be identi-

[1] It is only an insipid rabbinical conceit, which Keil should not have reproduced, of Rashi and Kimchi to apply the words, ver 36*b*, "he that served as priest in the house that Solomon built," to the bold stand of the Azariah, under Uzziah, against this king recorded in 2 Chron. xxvi. 17. But no less untenable is Neteler's assertion (*Chron.* pp. 58, 240), that Azariah was the son of Jehoiada, the husband of Jehoshabath, and effecter of that revolution which raised Joash to the throne (2 Kings xi.; 2 Chron. xxiii. 1 ff.); see on 2 Chron. xxiii. 8.

cal with those here mentioned. For the one named in ver. 40 as the son of Hilkiah (2 Kings xxii.) may have lived under Josiah, nearly a century after Hezekiah; of all the three Azariahs of our section, therefore, only the first (ver. 35) can coincide with one of the elsewhere mentioned high priests of this name, and this can have been no other than that contemporary of Solomon named in 1 Kings iv. 2.[1]—Ver. 37. *And Azariah begat Amariah.* This is the Amariah mentioned, 2 Chron. xix. 11, in the history of Jehoshaphat. Here Oehler, Art. "Hoherpriester" in Herzog's *Real-Encycl.* vi. 205, is certainly right, though opposed by Keil; in the sixty-one years between Solomon's death and Jehoshaphat's accession, the four high priests named between Zadok and Amariah may very well have followed in succession.—Ver. 38. *And Ahitub begat Zadok.* In the neighbourhood of this second Ahitub, whom we must place at the beginning or middle of the ninth century B.C., we miss the Jehoiada who dethroned Athaliah, and governed some time for the young king Joash (who was perhaps, however, not properly high priest, but only "chief of the priesthood of his time," that is, a very influential priest; see on 2 Chron. xxiii. 8). Even so somewhat later in the vicinity of Shallum is wanting the Uriah, known from 2 Kings xvi. 10 ff., who was high priest under king Ahaz. The list from vers. 37-40, or for the last period of the kings (ninth, eighth, and seventh centuries), appears very defective and concise, like the New Testament genealogies of Jesus (Matt. i. 8-10; Luke iii. 28-31), which make the longest leaps in this very epoch. The number of the links omitted in our list between the high priests for the time of Solomon (ver. 36) and Seraiah must be at least seven; for with the ten generations of high priests enumerated vers. 36-40, correspond seventeen generations of the house of David, from Solomon to Zedekiah (comp. iii. 10-27); and there is no reason why the line of priests should have a less rapid succession of generations than that of kings. —Ver. 41. *And Jehozadak went away,* to captivity in Babylon. הָלַךְ stands here for the usual more definite הָלַךְ בַּגּוֹלָה, Jer. xlix. 3. The carrying away of this Jehozadak must have taken place before the destruction of Jerusalem (perhaps 599); for at the destruction of Jerusalem (588), not he, but his aged father Seraiah, grandson of Hilkiah, was high priest, as appears from the account in 2 Kings xxv. 18, 21, of his capture by Nebuchadnezzar and execution at Riblah. Jehozadak, in exile, became father of that Joshua who returned 536 B.C. with Zerubbabel at the head of the exiles, Ezra iii. 2, v 2, Hag. i. 1.

With the series here given of the high priests from Aaron to the exile, agrees that in Ezra vii. 1-5, which is more summary, and makes even greater omissions. If we compare the sixteen names there given, from Seraiah to Aaron, with twenty-two of our list, the shorter list of Ezra appears to be an abbreviated extract of the present longer one. But the author of the latter cannot have aimed at absolute completeness. The הוֹלִיד used by him to denote the descent is quite as much a mere phrase of indefinite and elastic meaning as the בֵּן of Ezra. Moreover, the argument of Gramberg, p. 55, from the repeated occurrence of the same names in our list, for the assumption of an arbitrary process of compiling by the Chronist, has been long refuted by Movers, Keil, and others. On the extra-biblical traditions concerning the series of high priests before the exile, in Josephus, in the *Seder Olam,* etc., comp. Lightfoot, *Ministerium templi, Opp.* t. i. p. 682 sqq.; Selden, *De successione in pontif.* l. i.; and Reland, *Antiq.* ii. c. 2. So far as these accounts supplement the statements of our text, they are almost devoid of any historical authority. [The line from Aaron is not said to be a list of actual high priests. External influence seems to have often determined who should be the actual high priest.—J. G. M.]

2. *The Descendants of Gershom, Kohath, and Merari:* vi. 1-15.—These are first given alone with their sons (vers. 1-4); then follow further genealogical statements regarding the descendants of the most important of these sons, who became the ancestors of the three chief families of the Levites. That in the Kohathite family the line of Amram, the father of Aaron, is not given again, as in v. 27 ff., is explained by this, that the families of the Levites, not that of the high priest, are here to be registered. For the form "Gershom," comp. on v. 27. The two sons each of Gershom and Merari, and the four sons of Kohath, bear the same names as in the Pentateuch, Ex. vi. 16-19, Num. iii. 17-20, xxvi. 57 ff.—Ver. 4*b*. *And these are the families of Levi, after their fathers.* This formula, found by the author in his source, seems rather to be the superscription for the following special genealogy of the Levites, than the subscription to what precedes; but comp. Ex. vi. 19, where the same words serve clearly as the subscription to the list of the sons and grandsons of Levi.—Vers. 5, 6. *Descendants of Gershom.—To Gershom: Libni his son,* etc. The לְ before גֵּרְשׁוֹם serves for introduction, and therefore stands in another sense than in Ezra ii. 6, 16, where it is *nota genitivi;* comp. rather Ps. xvi. 3; Isa. xxxii. 1.—Jeatherai, the last in this eight-link chain of the descendants of Gershom, may have lived in the times of Saul and David, but is not otherwise known. That some of the names in this series, Jahath, Zimmah, and Zerah, occur also among the ancestors of Asaph, who springs from the line of Shimi (vers. 24-28), does not warrant the identification of the two series, nor (as Bertheau affirms) the assumption that "these are inserted, not because they lead to Jeatherai, but because they belong to the ancestors of Asaph." As if the recurrence of the same names in different lines were not usual in our genealogical sections!—Vers. 7-13. *Descendants of Kohath.* Three series of names, each beginning with a new בְּנֵי or וּבְנֵי (vers. 7, 10, 13), without exhibiting their genealogical connection. The very beginning: "The sons of Kohath: Amminadab his son," involves a surprising deviation both from ver. 3 and from Ex. vi. 18 ff., where no Amminadab occurs among the sons of Kohath. As the latter parallels, as ver. 23, agree in naming

[1] With Keil's and Bähr's attempt (*Bibelw.* part vii. p. 25 ff.) to regard the "Azariah son of Zadok" of this passage, not as priest or high priest, but as the first of the great civil functionaries of Solomon, we cannot agree, because הַכֹּהֵן is thereby taken in too abnormal a sense. Comp. Gesen.-Dietrich on the word כֹּהֵן.

an Izhar as the link between Kohath and Korah, with Keil and the majority of older expositors, Amminadab is to be regarded as a by-name of Izhar; for to regard Amminadab, with Bertheau, as a descendant of Izhar, and suppose an omission of the latter by some oversight, is less probable. Why should not the name Amminadab, otherwise occurring among the descendants of Judah as father of Nahshon and father-in-law of Aaron (Ex. vi. 23; Num. vi. 23; Ruth i. 19; comp. 1 Chron. ii. 10), by some no longer discoverable cause, serve as a by-name to Izhar, the second son Kohath?—*Korah his son, Assir his son, Elkanah his son, and Ebiasaph his son.* If we compare the series in vers. 18–23 of the ancestors of Heman, which presents so many points of contact with the present, that it may and must be used for the elucidation of several of its obscurities, it appears that Ebiasaph also (the father of that second Assir who is named ver. 8) is a son of Korah, and a brother of that first Assir; and in fact Assir, Elkanah, and Ebiasaph appear in Ex. vi. 24 as sons of Korah. Thus these three, notwithstanding the inexact phraseology of our list, which seems to exhibit them as father, son, and grandson, are rather to be taken for brothers. That Ebiasaph, the third of these Korahites, had a son Assir, and this a son Tahath, is recorded also in the genealogy of Heman, ver. 22. On the contrary, the names of the three following members, Uriel, Uzziah, and Shaul, vary from the parallel names Zephaniah, Azariah, and Joel, in the line of Heman, ver. 21; whence it would appear natural to assume a double name (favoured by the known identity of the king's name, Uzziah-Azariah) for these three members; but this is liable to grave doubts.—Ver. 10. *And the sons of Elkanah: Amasai and Ahimoth.* Among the ancestors of Heman also, ver. 20, an Amasai is named as son of an Elkanah. It is natural to identify that Elkanah with the present, to take him for a son of Joel, son of Azariah, and so supply the severed connection between Shaul, ver. 9, and Elkanah. The present Elkanah might also, indeed, be the son of Korah mentioned ver. 8, and brother of Ebiasaph. It is impossible, however, to decide absolutely.—Ver. 11. *Elkanah his son, Elkanah of Zoph his son,* or "Elkanah Zophai." As the text is here notoriously corrupt, and an Elkanah, be it the first or the second, is redundant (see Crit. Note), it should perhaps be emended, with Bertheau, "Elkanah his son, Zophai his son," etc. In this case, a desirable agreement with ver. 20 is gained, where Elkanah appears, not indeed as son, but as grandson of Amasai (through a certain Mahath omitted in our text), and where, further, Zuph is named as son of this Elkanah, a name that is obviously identical with Zophai (comp. Kelubai, ii. 9, with Kelub, iv. 11).—Ver. 12. *Eliab his son, Jeroham his son, Elkanah his son.* As "Nahath," the father of Eliab, bears a name that is closely allied in etymology to Toah, the son of Zuph (or Zophai), in the series of the ancestors of Heman, ver. 19, and so may pass for a by-form of this name, אֱלִיאָב also appears to be a collateral form of אֱלִיאֵל, ver. 19; but Jeroham and Elkanah coincide exactly with the two there named predecessors (or rather descendants) of Eliab. Hence the two parallel series actually agree out and out, from Zuph to the last Elkanah. So much the more certainly is a שְׁמוּאֵל בְּנוֹ (comp. ver. 18), forming the transition to ver. 13, to be supposed omitted at the end of our verse, or the assumption at least to be made that the author (as follows at once from ver. 13) meant by the last Elkanah no other than the father of Samuel.—Ver. 13. *And the sons of Samuel: the first-born Vashni, and Abiah.* That here the name of Joel, who was actually the first-born of Samuel, and is named, ver. 18, as his proper scion, has fallen out, appears indubitable from 1 Sam. viii. 2; comp. Crit. Note. On the whole, the present genealogy of Kohath coincides with that of the ancestors of Heman in vers. 18–23, though the text of our list appears the more defective, inaccurate, and partly corrupt.—Vers. 14, 15. *Descendants of Merari*, of the line of Mahli, from whom six generations of direct descendants are given. Against Bertheau's attempt to identify the names Mahli, Libni, Shimi, Uzzah, Shema, Haggiah, Asaiah with those of the ancestors of Ethan in vers. 29–32 (Mushi, Mahli, Shamer, Bani, Amzi, Hilkiah, Amaziah), in order to represent the three series of our section as mere parallels to the three series of the following section, see the remarks of Keil (p. 89). The latter justly asserts, in reference to ver. 4*a*: "The vers. 14 and 15 furnish a list of the family of Mahli, whereas the ancestors of Ethan, vers. 29–32, belong to the family of Mushi. Accordingly, our series cannot be designed to introduce Ethan or Ethan's ancestors. This hypothesis is altogether a castle in the air."

3. *The Ancestors of the Levitical Songmasters Heman, Asaph, and Ethan:* vers. 16–34.—*And these are they whom David set over the singing in the house of the Lord;* comp. xv. 17 ff. and 2 Chron. xxxix. 27.—עַל־יְדֵי־שִׁיר, properly: "to the hands of song," that is, for the singing, for the purpose of leading and executing it.—*After the resting of the ark;* from the time when the ark (אֲרוֹן הַבְּרִית = אָרוֹן), instead of its previous wandering, had a permanent abode on Mount Zion, 2 Sam. vi. 2, 17.—Ver. 17. *And they ministered before the dwelling of the tent of meeting with singing.* "Before the dwelling;" for in the court, before the holy tent, or before the temple, took place the public worship, consisting of sacrifice and singing. The genitive, "of the tent of meeting" (institution), is explicative of the dwelling, that is, the dwelling of God among His people. This means, in the first place, the tent of institution or meeting (אֹהֶל־מוֹעֵד), which David erected on Zion, as the immediate predecessor of the stone temple (2 Sam. vi. 17 ff.; 1 Chron. xxi. 28 ff.; 2 Chron. i. 3), and along with which the old Mosaic tent of meeting continued a long time in Gibeon, with a separate service (1 Chron. i. 29; 2 Chron. i. 3; 1 Kings iii. 4). That this Davidic tent on Zion is intended in the first place, is shown partly by the following reference to the building of Solomon's temple, and partly by the circumstance that the following genealogy takes its start from the three songmasters of David.—*And they attended in their order to their service.* "In their order" (בְּמִשְׁפָּטָם), that is, according to the order prescribed by David,—so, namely, that (ver. 18 ff.)

Heman the Kohathite, as chief leader of the whole choir, should stand in the middle, Asaph the Gershonite, with his choir, on his right, and Ethan the Merarite on his left, in conducting the sacred singing of the temple (comp. xvi. 37 ff., xxiv. 1; 2 Chron. xxx. 16).—Ver. 18. *And these* (the following) *are they who attended, and their sons*, with the choirs formed of their sons and their families. The names of their sons, see in xxv. 2–4. Here it is intended to trace, not so much the descendants of these songmasters from David's time down, as rather their ancestors up to Levi.—*Of the sons of Kohath: Heman the singer.* He stands before the rest, and is distinguished from them by the mere predicate, "the singer" (הַמְשׁוֹרֵר; Sept. ὁ ψαλτῳδός), because the chief leading of the temple singing belonged to him. He appears here as the grandson of Samuel, which is chronologically and genealogically admissible, and is needlessly questioned by Hitzig (*Gesch. d. Isr.* p. 125 f.), who denies that Samuel belonged to the house of Levi. On the series of Kohathites now following to ver. 23, consisting of twenty-two generations, and its relation to that in vers. 7–13, see above.—Ver. 23. *The son of Levi, the son of Israel.* Only here is this ascent beyond Levi to the patriarch of all Israel; comp. Luke iii. 38: τοῦ Ἀδὰμ τοῦ Θεοῦ.—Vers. 24–28. The ancestors of Asaph the Gershonite.—*And his brother Asaph.* "Brother," obviously in a wider sense, as relative and fellow-officer in the sacred service. On the relation of his genealogy, including fifteen members to the earlier series of Gershonites, see on vers. 5, 6.—Vers. 29–32. The ancestors of Ethan the Merarite.—*And the sons of Merari, their brethren on the left*, forming the choir standing on the left. For the name Jeduthun (יְדוּתוּן, "praiseman"), otherwise occurring for Ethan, perhaps an honorary surname, comp. xvi. 41, xxv. 1; 2 Chron. xxxv. 15; Neh. xi. 17. The series of Ethan's ancestors must be greatly abbreviated, as it contains only twelve names up to Merari.—Ver. 32. *The son of Mahli, the son of Mushi, the son of Merari.* If Mahli and Mushi, ver. 4, be named together as sons of Merari (as also Lev. iii. 20), this does not contradict our passage, as Mahli is plainly enough designated, not as son, but as grandson of Merari, therefore as nephew or perhaps grand-nephew of Mushi the younger son of Merari. On the diversity of the whole series, vers. 29–32, from that in vers. 14, 15, see on these verses.—Ver. 33 f. *And their brethren the Levites, given for all service*, etc. "Their brethren the Levites" are other Levites beside the singers already mentioned. A general notice of the ministry of the Levites not belonging to the families of the singers thus closes our section, as the like notice of the liturgical functions of the singers themselves (vers. 16, 17) opened it. נְתוּנִים, "given to all service," that is, given to Aaron and his descendants, to the priestly family appointed for service in the performance of worship; comp. Num. iii. 9, viii. 16–19, xviii. 6; also Samuel's consecration or dedication to the temple service, 1 Sam. i. 11, 28, and the *oblati* of monkery in the middle ages, for example, Bernard, etc.—Ver. 34. *And Aaron and his sons offered.* There are three functions of the priestly portion of the Levites:—1. Sacrifice (on the altars of burnt-offering and incense), Num. xviii. 1–7; 2. Ministration in the holy of holies, 1 Chron. xxviii. 13; 3. Propitiation or expiation for Israel, Lev. xvi. 32.—*In all that Moses, the servant of God, had commanded.* For this honourable designation of Moses, comp. Num. xii. 7; Deut. xxxiv. 5; Josh. i. 1, 13; Heb. iii. 2 ff.

4. *The Series of High Priests from Eleazar to Ahimaaz:* vers. 35–38.—This section is closely connected with the two preceding verses; for it states who were "the sons of Aaron" named, ver. 34, as the conductors of the priestly service in the temple. This series (which agrees essentially with v. 30–34; comp. Ezra vii. 1–5) is brought down only to Ahimaaz, the contemporary of Solomon (comp. 2 Sam. xv. 27), because in the whole section, from ver. 16, a "source is used in which the prominent families of Levi in the time of David (and Solomon) were described, and along with the genealogies of Heman, Asaph, and Ethan, that of Ahimaaz also stood, which the author of Chronicles was induced to insert for the sake of completeness and confirmation of the former series" (Bertheau). This series of high priests, breaking off with the time of Solomon, does not form a specially suitable transition to the following list of the Levitical cities (against Keil), although by its introductory words (especially by the suffix in מוֹשְׁבוֹתָם, ver. 38, that points to וְאֵלֶּה בְּנֵי אַהֲרֹן, ver. 35) it appears closely connected with the foregoing section.

5. *The Cities of the Levites:* vers. 39–66.—*And these are their dwellings, by their districts in their border*—the border which was then assigned to the several Levitical families. The superscription may have stood in the document which the Chronist here follows; it is wanting in the list of the dwellings of the Levites, Josh. xxi., which runs in the main parallel to this, but deviates in form and in many details. For טִירָה (from טוּר, *circumdare*), in early times, village of nomades, of tents (Gen. xxv. 16; Num. xxi. 10), here district, circuit of dwellings, comp. Ps. lxix. 26.—*Of the sons of Aaron, of the family of the Kohathites; for to them was the lot.* These words form the special superscription to vers. 40–45. After הַגּוֹרָל, perhaps רִאשֹׁנָה has fallen out; comp. Josh. xxi. 10. At all events, the first lot is here in question.—Vers. 40, 41 agree almost literally with Josh. xxi. 11, 12, only Hebron has there its old name Kiriath Arba; and for "in the land of Judah," stands "on the mountains of Judah."—*And its suburbs round about it.* מִגְרָשִׁים is the standing phrase for the pastures (Kamph.) or commons belonging to the cities, as distinguished from the field שָׂדֶה, or arable land, ver. 41. For the historical contents of ver. 41, comp. also Josh. xiv. 14, xv. 13.—Ver. 42. *And to the sons of Aaron they gave the free towns Hebron and Libnah.* As Hebron only was a free town (עִיר מִקְלַט הָרֹצֵחַ, place of refuge for the manslayer), the plural appears at least inexact. The parallel, Josh. xxi. 13, has the correct form עִיר. The same occurs with respect to Shechem, ver. 52.—*And Jattir, and Eshtemoa, and its suburbs.* After יַתִּיר, the standing addition

וְאֶת־מִגְרָשֶׁיהָ, which is found in Josh. xxi. 13 as always.—Ver. 43. *And Hilen and its suburbs.* Instead of חִילֵן, Josh. xxi. 15 has the more correct חֹלֹן (comp. Josh. xv. 51).—Ver. 44. *And Ashan and its suburbs.* The name עָשָׁן in this place appears more correct than עַיִן in Josh. xxi. 16. Immediately after this Ashan the name of Juttah must have fallen out, as appears from Josh. xxi.; as in ver. 45 the name of Gibeon before Geba. This twofold omission is indirectly confirmed by the closing notice in ver. 45: "all their cities were thirteen cities in their families;" for at present, the list referring to the tribes of Judah, Simeon, and Benjamin, vers. 42-45, contains only eleven cities. Besides, the third of the Levitical cities in Benjamin is called, Josh. xxi. 18, not Allemeth (עָלֶמֶת), but Almon (עַלְמוֹן). It is impossible to decide which is the original form.—Vers. 46-48 give summarily only the number, not the names, of the cities of the remaining Levites of the families of Kohath, Gershom, and Merari (parallel to vers. 5-7 in Josh. xxi.); the enumeration by name follows ver. 51 ff.—*Of the family of the tribe, from the half-tribe.* Between these words of ver. 46 (הַמַּטֶּה and הַמַּחֲצִית) there is an obvious gap; according to Josh. xxi. 5, the words "Ephraim, and of the tribe of Dan and" have here fallen out.—Ver. 47. *And of the tribe of Manasseh in Bashan.* More exactly, Josh. xxi. 6, "and of the half-tribe of Manasseh in Bashan," though we may do without the missing חֲצִי. Vers. 49, 50 disturb the progress of the enumeration, which, after the summary statements of the foregoing three verses, raises the expectation of a specification of the cities of the other Kohathites in a way so surprising, that their original occupation of another place, and that before ver. 39*b* ("of the sons of Aaron," etc.), admits of no doubt; comp. Josh. xxi., where they stand in vers. 8, 9 as superscription of the list of cities assigned to the priests. As they are there annexed to the summary statement, vers. 5-7, which forms here vers. 46-48, a mechanically proceeding compiler takes them over with these at once, and the Chronist, who followed this compiler, neglects to repair his negligence. —*These cities which they called by names.* The plurals שֵׁמוֹת and יִקְרְאוּ are suitable explanations, instead of the corresponding singulars in Josh. xxi. 9, as the subject, "the sons of Israel," is easily supplied to the verb from ver. 48, and several names of cities are given. The masc. אֶתְהֶם, instead of אֶתְהֶן, may be only an oversight (Berth., Keil).—Vers. 51-55. *The cities of the remaining Kohathites;* comp. Josh. xxi. 20-26. *And of the families of the sons of Kohath.*—Instead of וּמִמִּשְׁפְּחוֹת, is perhaps to be read וּלְמִשְׁפְּחוֹת, "and with respect to the families," etc.—Ver. 52. For the pl. "free towns," comp. on ver. 42.—Ver. 53. *And Jokmeam.* Josh. xxi. 22 gives for this יָקְמְעָם an otherwise unknown קִבְצַיִם; but the Sept. confirms the former reading by its Ἰεκμαάν.—Ver. 54. *And Aijalon and its suburbs, and Gath-rimmon and its suburbs.* In Josh. xxi. 23, 24, these two Levitical cities, with two others here omitted, Eltekeh and Gibbethon, belong to the tribe of Dan. According to this, before these words a whole verse has fallen out: "and of the tribe of Dan, Eltekeh and its suburbs, Gibbethon and its suburbs." That the mention of the tribe of Dan is here for the second time avoided (comp. ver. 46), can scarcely be called accidental; comp. on vii. 12. —Ver. 55. *Aner and its suburbs, and Bilam and its suburbs.* Josh. xxi. 25 calls the two Levitical cities in West Manasseh rather Tanach and Gath-rimmon; but these names appear to be errors of transcription originating in the foregoing verse. In this case, our text should be the more correct, only that בִּלְעָם (Josh. xvii. 11) should perhaps be changed into יִבְלְעָם.—*To the family of the remaining sons of Kohath.* These words, formally annexed to "they gave," etc., ver. 52*a*, form a kind of subscription, in which, perhaps, the singular "family" should be changed into the plural; comp. לְמִשְׁפְּחוֹת, Josh. xxi. 26.—Vers. 56-61. *The cities of the Gershonites;* comp. Josh. xxi. 27-33.—*Golan in Bashan.* That Golan is one of the six cities of refuge, like Hebron, Shechem, etc., is not mentioned; this again is one of the omissions in which our text abounds. For the name Ashtaroth, Josh. xxi. 27 substitutes Beeshterah (בְּעֶשְׁתְּרָה), perhaps compounded of בֵּית־עַשְׁתְּרָה. This city (Deut. i. 4, Josh. xiii. 12, once the seat of king Og) was perhaps formerly called Ashteroth-karnaim, Gen. xiv. 5, now Tell Ashteroth, some hours north-west of Edrei.—Ver. 57. *Kedesh and its suburbs.* For קֶדֶשׁ, Josh. xxi. 28 has more correctly קִשְׁיוֹן, as in ver. 58 the reading יַרְמוּת, Josh. xxi. 29, is perhaps more correct than רָאמוֹת, and עֵין גַּנִּים than עָנֵם.—Ver. 59. *Mashal* (מָשָׁל) is contracted for מִשְׁאָל, Josh. xix. 26. On the contrary, חוּקֹק, ver. 60, appears to be wrongly transcribed for חֶלְקָה, which Joshua has in our passage and xix. 25 (חֻקֹּק in Naphtali, Josh. xix. 24, cannot be here intended).—Ver. 61. *Kedesh in Galilee.* Of this city, also, it is not noted that it belonged to the six free towns, Josh. xxi. 32. On its site, west of the lake Merom, where Kedes now lies, see Rob. iii. 682, Raumer, *Palæst.* p. 116.—The following Hammon corresponds to Hammoth-dor, Josh. xxi. 32, and to Hammath, Josh. xix. 35, which three forms appear all to point to hot springs in the vicinity of the place. In Joseph. *Antiq.* xviii. 2. 3, the name is Ἀμμαοῦς. For Kiriathaim, Josh. xxi. 32 has the contracted form Kartan (קַרְתָּן), that stands to the present full form as דֹּתָן, 2 Kings vi. 13, to דֹּתַיְנָה, Gen. xxxvii. 17.—Vers. 62-66. *The cities of the Merarites;* comp. Josh. xxi. 34-37.—*To the sons of Merari that remained,* namely, the Levites, as the fuller form הַלְוִיִּם הַנּוֹתָרִים, Josh. xxi. 34, shows, which may mean, "those of the Levites still to be mentioned."—*Rimmono and its suburbs, Tabor and its suburbs.* Here the names of two other cities of Zebulun have fallen out, Jokneam and Kartah. But even the two here named have other names there, where, for רִמּוֹנוֹ, the probably less correct דִּמְנָה appears (comp. the repeated mention of a city רִמּוֹן in Zebulun, Josh. xix. 13), and where, in place of our תָּבוֹר, stands the name נַהֲלָל, which is certainly identical with Nahalol, Judg. i. 30, and is perhaps found in the present Nalul, south-west of Nazareth. It is hard to say how our תָּבוֹר came into the text instead of the undoubtedly original נהלל; possibly the author meant, instead of the city, only the region where it lay—Mount Tabor (Movers); possibly the name of the city fell out, and of the determination of its site, that was perhaps included in the words עַל גְּבוּל כִּסְלֹת תָּבוֹר, only the last word remains (Berth.); or possibly the place bore two quite different names.—Vers. 63, 64 are wanting in some editions of the books of Joshua, where they are xix. 36, 37. But the most and best MSS. contain them, and there is no decisive reason for their condemnation as spurious; see the particulars in Fay on the passage.—*And beyond Jordan by Jericho, east of Jordan.* This determination of place (which is often found in like terms, Num. xxii. 1, xxvi. 3, xxxiv. 15; comp. on 2 Chron. viii. 3) is wanting in the book of Joshua, which in other respects agrees with our verse, only that it omits not to mark Bezer as a free town.—Ver. 65. *And out of the tribe of Gad, Ramoth in Gilead.* Here also is wanting the mention of its being a city of refuge; comp. Josh. xxi. 36, where also the name is written, not as here, רָאמוֹת, but רָמוֹת, as of the two places mentioned in the following verse, the latter is there not Jaazer but Jazer; comp. Num. xxi. 32. The situation of these towns is wholly unknown.

Moreover, let us compare, with respect to the Levitical cities in general, the not unimportant remark of Hengstenberg, *Gesch. d. Reichs Gottes unter dem A. B.* ii. 1, p. 259: "the number of the cities in all amounted to forty-eight. At first sight, for a comparatively small tribe, this appears to be too great. But this appearance vanishes, when we consider that in these cities, not the Levites alone, but, along with them, craftsmen and others from the other tribes dwelt, who made often the greater part of the population; comp. Lev. xxv. 33; 1 Chron. vi. 40, 41 (Caleb as inhabitant of the lands of Hebron), etc." There is weight also in his remark, p. 260, on the many differences between our list and Josh. xxi.; these "are most easily explained by the fact that some of the cities assigned to the Levites were at the time (when the land was divided among the twelve tribes) in possession of the Canaanites, and as the hope of their immediate conquest failed, were first recovered from them by others, in whose possession they remained, on account of the inconvenience of the change." In many cases this assumption may be correct, and serve to explain the double names, as Ashan and Ain, Allemeth and Almon, Kedesh and Kishion, Anem and En-gannim, Tabor and Nahalal, etc. (See on vers. 44, 45, 57, 58, 62.) But that, besides numerous corruptions of the text, errors in transcription, and omissions of names, sentences, and clauses, took place not merely in our text, but also in that of Joshua, must have been abundantly evident from our exegetical and critical remarks.

e. The Families of the Remaining Tribes (except Dan and Zebulun), and in particular of the Benjamite House of Saul.—Ch. vii. viii.

1. *The Families of Issachar, Benjamin, Naphtali, West Manasseh, Ephraim, and Asher:* ch. vii.

α. The Tribe of Issachar: vers. 1–5.

CH. VII. 1. And the sons[1] of Issachar: Tola and Puah, Jashub[2] and Shimron, four.
2 And the sons of Tola: Uzzi, and Rephaiah, and Jeriel, and Jahmai, and
Jibsam, and Samuel, heads of their father-houses to Tola, valiant heroes in
their generations; their number in the days of David was twenty and two
3 thousand and six hundred. And the sons of Uzzi: Izrahiah; and the sons of
4 Izrahiah: Michael, and Obadiah, and Joel, Ishiah, five heads in all. And with
them, by their generations, by their father-houses, troops of the host of war,
5 thirty and six thousand; for they had many wives and sons. And their
brethren of all the families of Issachar, valiant heroes, eighty and seven
thousand was their register for all.

β. The Tribe of Benjamin: vers. 6–11.

6, 7 Benjamin: Bela, and Becher, and Jediael, three. And the sons of Bela:
Ezbon, and Uzzi, and Uzziel, and Jerimoth, and Iri, five, heads of father-
houses, valiant heroes; and their register was twenty and two thousand and
8 thirty and four. And the sons of Becher: Zemirah, and Joash, and Eliezer,
and Elioenai, and Omri, and Jerimoth, and Abiah, and Anathoth, and Alemeth:
9 all these were the sons of Becher. And their register by their generations,
heads of their father-houses, valiant heroes, twenty thousand and two hundred.

10 And the sons of Jediael: Bilhan; and the sons of Bilhan: Jeush,[3] and
Benjamin, and Ehud, and Chenaanah, and Zethan, and Tarshish, and Ahishahar.
11 All these were sons of Jediael, by the heads of the fathers, valiant heroes,
seventeen thousand and two hundred going out in the host for war.

γ. *Another Tribe, and the Tribe of Naphtali:* vers. 12, 13.

12, 13 And Shuppim and Huppim, sons of Ir: Hushim, sons of another. The
sons of Naphtali: Jahziel, and Guni, and Jezer, and Shallum, sons of Bilhah.

δ. *Half-Tribe of Manasseh (west of Jordan):* vers. 14–19.

14 The sons of Manasseh: Ashriel,[4] whom his concubine, the Aramitess, bare;
15 she bare Machir, the father of Gilead. And Machir took a wife for Huppim
and Shuppim, and the name of his sister was Maachah, and the name of the
16 second was Zelophehad; and Zelophehad had daughters. And Maachah,
wife of Machir, bare a son, and she called his name Peresh; and the name of
17 his brother was Sheresh; and his sons were Ulam and Rekem. And the sons
of Ulam: Bedan: these are the sons of Gilead, the son of Machir, the son of
18 Manasseh. And his sister Hammolecheth bare Ishod, and Abiezer, and
19 Mahlah. And the sons of Shemidah: Ahian, and Shechem, and Likhi, and
Aniam.

ε. *The Tribe of Ephraim:* vers. 20–29.

20 And the sons of Ephraim: Shuthelah, and Bered his son, and Tahath his
21 son, and Eladah his son, and Tahath his son. And Zabad his son, and
Shuthelah his son; and Ezer and Elad; and the men of Gath that were born
in the land slew them, because they came down to take away their cattle.
22 And Ephraim their father mourned many days, and his brethren came to
23 comfort him. And he went in to his wife, and she conceived and bare a son,
24 and he called his name Beriah, because it went evil with his house. And his
daughter was Sherah, and she built Beth-horon, the nether and the upper, and
25 Uzzen-sherah. And Rephah his son, and Resheph and Telah his son, and
26, 27 Tahan his son. Ladan his son, Ammihud his son, Elishama his son. Non
28 his son, Joshua his son. And their possession and their habitations were
Bethel and her daughters, and eastward Naaran, and westward Gezer and
her daughters, and Shechem and her daughters unto Ajjah[5] and her daughters.
29 And on the side of the sons of Manasseh, Bethshean and her daughters,
Taanach and her daughters, Megiddo and her daughters, Dor and her
daughters; in these dwelt the sons of Joseph the son of Israel.

ζ. *The Tribe of Asher:* vers. 30–40.

30 The sons of Asher: Imnah, and Ishuah, and Ishui, and Beriah, and Serah
31 their sister. And the sons of Beriah: Heber and Malchiel; he is the father
32 of Birzavith.[6] And Heber begat Japhlet, and Shomer, and Hotham, and
33 Shua their sister. And the sons of Japhlet Pasach, and Bimhal, and
34 Ashvath: these are the sons of Japhlet. And the sons of Shemer: Ahi, and
35 Rohgah, and Hubbah,[7] and Aram. And the son of Helem his brother:
36 Zophah, and Imna, and Shelesh, and Amal. The sons of Zophah: Suah, and
37 Harnepher, and Shual, and Beri, and Imrah, Bezer, and Hod, and Shamma,
38 and Shilshah, and Ithran, and Beera. And the sons of Jether: Jephunneh,
39 and Pispah, and Ara. And the sons of Ulla: Arah, and Hanniel, and Riziah.
40 All these were the sons of Asher, heads of father-houses, choice, valiant heroes,
heads of the princes: and their register for the service in war was twenty and
six thousand.

[1] For וְלִבְנֵי read וּבְנֵי, as the Sept. *cod. Alex.* reads καὶ οὗτοι υἱοὶ Ἰσσάχαρ (*cod. Vat.* has καὶ τοῖς υἱοῖς Ἰσσ.).

[2] So the *Keri:* the *Kethib* has יֹשָׁיב.

[3] יְעִישׁ in the *Kethib*.

[4] אַשְׂרִיאֵל appears to be a gloss introduced into the text by the double writing of the following consonants, אשר יל.

[5] So (עַיָּה) all the best MSS. and prints. The עַזָּה of some other MSS. and editions is an error of the pen or the press introduced into the text by the influence of the Sept., Vulg., and Targ.; comp. de Rossi, *Var. lect. ad h. l.*

[6] So the *Keri*: it is doubtful how the *Kethib* ברזות is to be pronounced (בִּרְזוֹת? with Gesen., who supposes it to be a woman's name).

[7] For יְחֻבָּה is to be read, with the *Keri*, וְחֻבָּה.

EXEGETICAL.

1. *The Tribe of Issachar:* vers. 1–5.—*And the sons of Issachar.* That וְלִבְנֵי is an error of the pen for וּבְנֵי (comp. ver. 20, v. 11, etc.), occasioned by the many לִבְנֵי in the previous section (vi. 42, 46, 47, etc.), is probable in itself, and is confirmed by the Sept. *cod. Alex.* (see Crit. Note). To regard the לְ as introductory, "as for the sons of Issachar," is impossible, because the names of the four sons immediately follow. On the constant *Keri* (יִשָּׂכָר, "obtained by hire") referring to the name יִשָּׂשכָר, and on its probable pronunciation, comp. the expositors on Gen. xxx. 16, and Dietrich's *Gesenius.*—*Tola and Puah, Jashub and Shimron.* So run the names also in Num. xxvi. 23 ff., while in Gen. xlvi. 15 the second and third vary (פֻּוָּה for פּוּאָה, and יוֹב for יָשׁוּב).—Ver. 2. *Uzzi and Rephaiah*, etc. These sons of Tola occur nowhere else They are here designated "heads of their father-houses to Tola" their parent; this addition לְתוֹלָע serves to define לְבֵית אֲבוֹתָם more exactly; but it is somewhat strange, which raises the suspicion of corruption.—*Valiant heroes in their generations,* after their births, that is, as they are registered. Before לְתֹלְדוֹתָם a הִתְיַחְשָׂם appears to have fallen out; comp. ver. 9. Less probable is the connection of לְתֹלְדוֹתָם with the following מִסְפָּרָם, against the accentuation, which Keil proposes, "after their births their number was," etc Moreover, the number 22,600 for the men of Issachar fit for service in David's time should rest on the known census made by Joab under this king (ch. xxi.; 2 Sam. xxiv.), and therefore, like the following numbers, vers. 4, 5, 7, 11, etc., should be credible and accurate.—Ver. 3. *Five heads in all,* namely, Izrahiah the father with his four sons.—Ver. 4. *And with them,* namely, the five heads of families mentioned ver. 3 (עַל in וַעֲלֵיהֶם, "with, along with"). The number 36,000 for this family alone is at first sight surprising; but the following remark: "for they (those five heads) had many wives and sons," is sufficient to explain and justify it, pointing to an unwonted fruitfulness of this family, and making it conceivable that the grandson of Izrahiah should have nearly twice as many descendants (36,000) as the patriarch Tola (22,600).—Ver. 5. *And their brethren . . . eighty and seven thousand was their register,* literally, their register with respect to all (לַכֹּל). In this sum total of all the tribes of Issachar in the time of David are included—1. The 22,600 descendants of Tola; 2. The 36,000 of Izrahiah; and 3. "Their brethren," 28,400 of the other families of the tribe not mentioned by name. The credibility of these numbers is shown by the circumstance that in the two enumerations under Moses the men of Issachar fit for service were respectively 54,400 (Num. i. 29) and 64,300 (Num. xxvi. 25). The comparatively slow increase (about 23,000) during the centuries from Moses to David is due to the desolating troubles in the time of the judges.

2. *The Tribe of Benjamin:* vers. 6–11.—*Benjamin: Bela, and Becher, and Jediael, three.* A בְּנֵי or וּבְנֵי appears to have fallen out before בִּנְיָמִן. If only three sons of Benjamin are here enumerated, this seems to contradict Gen. xlvi. 21, where ten sons of Benjamin are named; also Num. xxvi. 38, where at least five are named; and 1 Chron. viii. 1 f., where at all events five are enumerated, though some of them are different from those in Numbers. The relation of these four different registers may be thus exhibited:—

Gen. xlvi.	Num. xxvi.	1 Chr. viii.	1 Chr. vii.
Bela.	Bela.	Bela.	Bela.
Becher.			Becher.
Ashbel.	Ashbel.	Ashbel.	
Gera.			
Naaman.			
Ehi.	Ahiram.	Ahrah (אַחְרַח).	
Kosh.			
Muppim.	Shephuphan.		
Huppim.	Hupham.		
Ard.			
		Nochah (נוֹחָה).	
		Raphah (רָפָא).	
			Jediael.

From this comparison, it appears that—1. Jediael occurs only here, and may be corrupted from the Ashbel of the other three lists, or a synonymous by-form of it. If this conjecture of most old expositors (with which the derivation of אשבל from אֶשְׁבַּעַל [Wellhausen, *Text d. B. Sam.* p. 31] would not agree) were well grounded, our text would give three sons of Benjamin agreeing with Genesis, and pass over in silence the remaining seven. 2. Becher the second son of Benjamin, is, to our surprise, wanting in Num. and 1 Chron. viii., although a family of nine sons, growing into 20,200 men, are given underneath (vers. 8, 9). His omission in those lists in Num. xxvi. may arise from this, that he did not attain to great numbers in the time of Moses, but only in the days of David and Solomon, whose enumerations lie at the basis of the data here. 3. Some of the differences in the other names prove to be mere variations of pronunciation or structure; thus Ehi, Ahiram, and Ahrah are one and the same; also Muppim (מֻפִּים, probably written by mistake for שְׁפִּים; see on ver. 12) and Shephupham, Huppim and Hupham. 4. Two of the ten names in Gen. xlvi., as the partly more correct genealogy in Num. xxvi. 38–40 shows, are not sons, but grandsons of Benjamin, Naaman and Ard, who were sons of Bela. 5. The two names in Gen xlvi. that have no parallel, Gera and Rosh, appear to have died childless, or to have not been blessed with a numerous offspring, to whose existence the later genealogists were not led to make any further reference.—Ver. 7. *And the sons of Bela . . . five*, etc. Their names do not agree with the names of the sons of Bela given in viii. 3 and in Num. xxvi. 40; the difference will rest on this, that a part of these heads of father-houses of the family of Bela, or perhaps all of them, were later descendants of their ancestors, and therefore sons in a wider sense.—*Valiant heroes.* גִּבּוֹרֵי חֲיָלִים here and in ver. 10 for the otherwise usual and more concrete גִּבּוֹרֵי חַיִל (vers. 2, 9, etc.).—Ver. 8. *And the sons of Becher*, etc. Of the names of these nine sons of Becher, the last two, Anathoth and Alemeth, occur otherwise as cities of Benjamin; Alemeth (in the varied form עָלֶמֶת), vi. 45, and Anathoth there and Isa. x. 30, Jer. i. 1, both as Levitical cities.—Ver. 9. *Heads of their father-houses, valiant heroes.* רָאשֵׁי בֵּית אֲבוֹתָם is in explanatory apposition with לְתֹלְדוֹתָם, and גִּבּוֹרֵי חַיִל with the former. The heads of houses are, at the same time, designated as heroes of war. See a similar construction in Ezra iii. 12. —Ver. 10. *And the sons of Bilhan: Jeush, and Benjamin, and Ehud*, etc. Of these grandsons of Jediael, the first is called in the *Kethib* "Jeish" (see Crit. Note); the second bears the name of the patriarch, his ancestor; the third is a namesake of Ehud the judge (Judg. iii. 15), who was of the family of Gera, and scarcely identical with the present one (Gen. xlvi. 21). Chenaanah, כְּנַעֲנָה, may incline us to think (with Berth.) of a Canaanitish family incorporated with the Benjamites. The names Tarshish, otherwise denoting a precious stone, and Ahishahar, brother of the morning blush, point to the glory and fame of their bearers, and may be surnames, which afterward became personal names.—Ver. 11. *All these were sons*, descendants, *of Jediael, by the heads of the fathers* registered. רָאשֵׁי הָאָבוֹת stands briefly for רָאשֵׁי בֵּית אָבוֹת. The לְ before רָאשֵׁי seems to be redundant; it is also wanting in the Sept., and is perhaps to be erased, though it may be dependent on a הִתְיַחְשָׂם (ver. 9) to be supplied in thought, and in this case to be retained. The 17,200 men of Jediael's family fit for war, with the 20,200 men of Becher's and 22,034 of Bela's, make up 59,434 warriors or heads of houses in Benjamin when David made his census, about 14,000 more than in the days of Moses, when all the families of Benjamin presented in the field 45,600 men (Num. xxvi. 41). In weighing the grounds for this not very rapid increase during a period of three or four centuries, it is proper to take into account the catastrophe of the first period of the judges, whereby the whole tribe of Benjamin was reduced to 600 men (Judg. xx. 47). The number of 280,000 Benjamite warriors given, 2 Chron. xiv. 7, for the time of Asa is explained in this way, that there, not heads of houses, but individuals fit for military service, are included.

3. *Another* (unnamed) *Tribe, and the Tribe of Naphtali*: vers. 12, 13.—*And Shuppim and Huppim, sons of Ir.* This first half of the verse contains pretty certainly a supplement to the genealogy of Benjamin; for the names Shuppim and Huppim coincide with those of two by the sons of Benjamin, as they are called Gen. xlvi. 21 (the word מֻפִּים there appears, as has been said, corrupted from שְׁפִּים); and that these two Benjamites, whose more correct forms are preserved in Num. xxvi. 39, appear here as בְּנֵי עִיר, is easily reconciled with other statements, for עִיר is most probably identical with עִירִי the son of Bela, ver. 7; hence those who are called, Gen. xlvi. and Num. xxvi., sons of Bela, appear here more correctly as his grandsons. Thus our verse contains so far nothing difficult or enigmatical. —*Hushim, sons of another*, or "sons of Aher" (אַחֵר). It is possible that these words also refer to a Benjamite family, for the name חֻשִׁם, in the varying form חוּשִׁים or חֻשִׁים, is found, viii. 8, 11, among the Benjamites as the son of a Shaharaim, who might lie hid under the אַחֵר of our passage (so thinks Davidson, *Introd.* ii. 51, who proposes the middle form שַׁחַר as common ground for אַחֵר and שַׁחֲרַיִם). But it is more probable that חֻשִׁם denotes the only son of Dan mentioned Gen. xlvi. 23, who is himself indicated by the mysterious אחר. For—1. Both in Gen. xlvi. and Num. xxvi. Dan immediately follows Benjamin, and he stands in the first passage, as here, between Benjamin and Naphtali. 2. The name שׁוּחָם, which Num. xxvi. 42 gives for the only son of Dan, is different only in form from the חֻשִׁם of our passage and the חֻשִׁים of Genesis; we may suppose a חוּשָׁם or שְׁחוּחָם (comp. שְׁפוּפָם, Num. xxvi. 39) as common ground-form for both. 3. Decisive for the reference of ver. 12*b* to the tribe of Dan is the בְּנֵי בִלְהָה at the close of ver. 13, a note referring obviously, Gen. xlvi. 25, to Dan and Naphtali, the two sons of Bilhah. The avoiding to name Dan, and concealing him under the indefinite אַחֵר (comp. Ezra ii. 31), recall the former surprising omissions of this tribe in vi. 46–54, and appear to rest like these on a peculiar dislike of our author to record particulars concerning a tribe that had early separated itself from the theocratic community by the establishment of a foreign worship; comp. Judg. xvii. xviii. That the name Dan occurs three times in our book (ii. 2, xii. 35, xxvii. 22) certainly appears to stand against this

hypothesis proposed by Bertheau, and approved by other moderns, as Kamph., Böhmer (*Zur Lehre vom Antichrist, Jahrb. f. deutsche Theol.* 1859, p. 449), and to favour either the view of Ewald, who supposes an accidental omission of the name of Dan and of some other words by a corruption of the text, or that of Keil, who, with the ancients, finds in the words "Hushim, sons of Aher," only a Benjamite family (named viii. 8, 11). But that here again a corruption of the text accidentally affects the name of Dan, whom we expect to meet between Benjamin and Naphtali, is scarcely credible; and against the addition of the words in question to the foregoing series of Benjamites is the absence of the copula ו before חֻשִׁם. There is therefore considerable probability in the assumption of Berth., that the omission of Dan is as little accidental here as in the list of the twelve tribes in Rev. vii. 5–8, and that it has a theocratic, judicial import, as it points to the fall of Dan into idolatry. From the Rabbinical tradition concerning Judg. xviii. 30, where the name of Moses is supposed to be intentionally changed into Manasseh, that it might not occur in the history of the Danite sanctuary, nothing can be drawn in support of this assumption, as this is only an insipid conceit in explanation of the *Keri* מנשה (against Berth.). It is also to be borne in mind that another tribe, that of Zebulun, is wholly passed over in our series, the omission of which may well be called accidental (as, for example, that of the tribes Asher and Gad in the list of tribe-princes, xxvii. 16–24). Comp. the evangelical-ethical principles, No. 2.—*The sons of Naphtali: Jahziel, and Guni, and Jazer, and Shallum.* The parallel lists, Gen. xlvi. 24, Num. xxvi. 48 f., give these names, only the first is there Jahzeel (יַחְצְאֵל) and the last Shillem (שִׁלֵּם). For the addition, "sons of Bilhah," see on ver. 12.

4. *The half-Tribe of Manasseh* (west of Jordan): vers. 14–19.—*The sons of Manasseh: Ashriel, whom his concubine the Aramitess bare.* That here it is treated of the western half of Manasseh is understood of itself after the former communications concerning East Manasseh, v. 23 f. Of the six families of West Manasseh named in Num. xxvi. 30, 34, and Josh. xvii. 2, only two are mentioned here, Ashriel and Shemida (ver. 19). But Ashriel, from the more exact accounts in Num. xxvi. 31, is not a son, but a grandson, of Manasseh, by his father Gilead. Now, as the following sentence referring to the Aramæan concubine of Manasseh, "she bare Machir the father of Gilead," seems designed to explain how Ashriel could be called a son of Manasseh and his concubine, it seems necessary to assume that he sprang from her in the fourth degree as the son of Gilead and grandson of Machir. But this assumption is as doubtful as the Masoretic expedient, which separates the words אֲשֶׁר יָלְדָה by an *Athnach* under the latter from the following פִּילַגְשׁוֹ וגו', and requires the supplement of some unmentioned wife to the "whom she bare." The sagacious hypothesis of Movers (assented to by Berth. and Kamph.) here commends itself, that the name Ashriel, as a gloss arising from writing twice the consonants immediately following אשר יל, is to be erased, and so the sense is to be gained: "the sons of Manasseh, whom his Aramæan concubine bare: she bare Machir," etc. Comp. the Sept. on Gen. xlvi. 26: ἐγένοντο δὲ υἱοὶ Μανασσῆ, οὓς ἔτεκεν αὐτῷ ἡ παλλακὴ ἡ Σύρα.—Ver. 15. *And Machir took a wife for Huppim and Shuppim,* etc. The whole verse is so obscure, that the assumption either of interpolation or of the omission of some words seems unavoidable. Bertheau proceeds in the former way, rejects the words לְחֻפִּים וּלְשֻׁפִּים as a gloss from ver. 12, and by means of some other changes, especially the insertion of ver. 18*a*, arrives at the sense: "and Machir took a wife, whose name was Maachah, and the name of his sister was Hammolecheth; and the name of his brother (the second) was Zelophehad." Somewhat less violent is the emendation attempted by Movers (p. 89), which limits itself to the change of אֲחֹתוֹ before מעכה into הָאַחַת, and yields the sense: "and Machir took a wife from Huppim and from Shuppim (לְ standing for מִן, and pointing to a marriage of Machir with two wives out of the families of Huppim and Shuppim, ver. 12); the name of the first was Maachah, and the name of the second Zelophehad." Keil conjectures an omission of some words, among these the name of Ashriel, the first son of Gilead, but at the same time the intrusion of senseless interpolations in ver. 15*a*; while, on the contrary, he regards as critically impregnable the words of the second half verse: "and the name of the second is Zelophehad; and Zelophehad had daughters (only)." Several gaps are also supposed in the emendations of older writers, as in that of J. H. Michaelis, who endeavours to squeeze out the sense: "and Machir took to wife (the sister of) Huppim and Shuppim, and the name of his sister (namely of Huppim) was Maachah, and the name of the second (here named son of Manasseh) was Zelophehad." From the unsatisfactory character of all these attempts, it is plain that a correct interpretation of the verse must be given up. So much only is clear from the second gloss, whether it be preserved intact or in some way corrupted, that therein Zelophehad was called the brother or near relative of Machir, and was the same who, Num. xxvii. 1, xxxvi. 1 ff., Josh. xvii. 3, was called the father of a great number of daughters.—Ver. 17. The sons of Maachah here mentioned, Peresh and Sheresh, as also the sons of the latter, Ulam and Rekem, occur only here.—Ver. 17. *And the sons of Ulam: Bedan.* The Masoretic text names a judge Bedan, 1 Sam. xii. 11, where, however, perhaps בָּרָק is to be read.—*These are the sons of Gilead, the son of Machir.* Bertheau, perhaps rightly, proposes here the change (favoured by ver. 41 and by ii. 21): "These are the sons of the father of Gilead, of Machir the son of Manasseh."—Ver. 18. *And his sister Hammolecheth bare Ishod.* The Vulg. explains this not elsewhere occurring name appellatively: *Regina* (as Kimchi, queen of a part of Gilead). Rightly?—The first of her sons, Ishod, "man of fame, of glory," is otherwise unknown; on the contrary, the second appears to be identical with the Abiezer named Josh. xvii. 2, the chief of one of the families of Manasseh. If this were so, he would have to pass for the ancestor of Gideon, Judg. vi. 11, 15. But

Abiezer in Joshua, or Jezer (אִיעֶזֶר) as it is in Num. xxvi. 30, appears as first son of Manasseh after Machir, not as the mere sister's son of this Machir, as here; for which reason the identity is doubtful. Whether the following name מַחְלָה denotes a brother of these two, or a sister (comp. Mahlah, the daughter of Zelophehad, Num. xxvi. 33, xxvii. 1), is doubtful.—Ver. 19. *And the sons of Shemidah.* A son of Manasseh, Josh. xvi. 2, or, more exactly, of Gilead, Num. xxvi. 32. The names of his four sons, except Shechem, שֶׁכֶם, who appears, Josh. xvii. 2, as an immediate son of Manasseh, but, Num. xxvi. 32, as a son of Gilead, occur nowhere else; for Bertheau's attempts to connect Likhi with Helek, Num. xxvi. 30, and Aniam (אֲנִיעָם) with נֹעָה, one of the daughters of Zelophehad, Num. xxvi. 33, Josh. xvii. 3, are arbitrary.

5. *The Tribe of Ephraim:* vers. 20–29.—*Shuthelah, and Bered his son,* etc. Shuthelah appears also, Num. xxvi. 25, as founder of a chief family of Ephraim. This family is here traced through six generations to a second Shuthelah, ver. 21, to whom are then added Ezer and Elad, two brothers of the older Shuthelah, and therefore sons or near descendants of Ephraim.—*And the men of Gath, that were born in the land, slew them,* namely, Ezer and Elad. The Avim (Avites), driven by the Philistines from their seats between Hazerim and Gaza, Deut. ii. 23, are said to be born in the land, in contrast with the intruders. Hence Ew., Berth., Kamph. will have these Avim to be here meant, whereas Keil thinks rather of the Philistines, whose settlement in south-west Palestine, in the district of Gath, was attested even in the time of Abraham, or even of the Canaanites, but not the Avites, of whom there is no tradition that they had spread to Gath. At any rate, reference is here made to a very old event, as Ephraim, the son of Jacob, still lived and begat other children. This can scarely have taken place before the descent into Egypt, as Ephraim was born in Egypt, Gen. xlvi. 20 (against Ewald). We must suppose it to have occurred during the sojourn in Egypt, and to have been a warlike expedition from the land of Goshen, that may have fallen in the interval from Gen. l. 13–23. The verb יָרַד is not absolutely against this assumption, which was advocated by older expositors (Rossi, Kimchi, L. Lavater, Grot., Calov., etc.), and accepted by more recent ones, as Fürst (*Gesch. d. bibl. Lit.* i. 318). When the Ephraimite host marched from the wilderness of Shur or Paran, we may very well regard this as a descent upon the district of Gath (without directly identifying Ephraim with Paran, as Hitzig does, *Gesch. Isr.* p. 48).—Ver. 22. *And Ephraim, their father, mourned many days.* Bertheau will, without ground, take these words figuratively, and apply them to the whole tribe of Ephraim; the going in of Ephraim to his wife, mentioned ver. 23, can only be taken literally; and as there is no indication that a younger Ephraim is meant (as Keil), it is plainly recorded of the old patriarch Ephraim that he begat a son, Beriah, after those two sons were slain by the Gathites. Ewald perhaps goes too far, when he makes the sons Rephah and Resheph, ver. 25, be born to Ephraim in this latter period. Rather is the interwoven historical notice of the raid of Ezer and Elad against Gath and its results to be regarded as closed with ver. 23, and the following passage from ver. 24 to be taken as the continuation of the genealogy of Ephraim.—*And he called his name Beriah, because it went evil with his house,* "because there had been calamity (בְּרָעָה) in his house." This etymology of the name בְּרִיעָה, reminding us of the well-known derivations of Genesis (especially Gen. v. 9, 29, 30), speaks for the undoubted antiquity of the present account. For the relation of this Ephraimite to his namesake of Benjamin, see on viii. 13 f.—Ver. 24. *And his daughter was Sherah,* namely, Ephraim's daughter (ver. 20), not Beriah's, who is only mentioned by the way. The places Nether and Upper Beth-horon built, that is, fortified, by this Sherah, probably a powerful heiress, correspond (Robinson, iii. 273 ff.) to the present Beit Ur et-Tachta and Beit Ur el-Foka, on the road from Jerusalem to Joppa. They lay at the south border of the tribe of Ephraim, on a strip of land stretching out between the tribes of Benjamin and Dan. Uzzen-Sherah must be sought in their immediate neighbourhood. The name (אֻזֵּן = אֹזֶן, ear) points to a like projection or skirt as its site.—Vers. 25–27. *Joshua's forefathers.*—*And Rephah his son, and Resheph.* These two can scarcely pass for actual sons of Ephraim; comp. Num. xxvi. 35 f. It is uncertain to which of the families of Ephraim there mentioned they belonged.—*And Telah his son,* that is, Rephah's son, who is the chief person, while Resheph is only mentioned by the way. The Tahan named as the son of this Telah appears different from the Tahan named Num. xxvi. 25 as son of Ephraim, but might belong to his posterity.—Ver. 26. *Ladan his son,* etc. The name לַעְדָּן occurs, xxiii. 7 f., xxvi. 21, also as the name of a Levitical family, but only here as an Ephraimite. Elishama, the son of Ammihud, meets us, Num. vii. 48, x. 22, as prince of the tribe of Ephraim in the time of Moses. His grandson was Joshua the son of Non, or Nun, as it is constantly spelled in the Pentateuch and Joshua. [This episode corresponds in antiquarian interest with the notices concerning Caleb in ch. ii. The simplest exposition of the passage is obtained by making a pause after "Shuthelah his son," and another after "Rephah his son." Ezer and Elad are then the second and third sons of Ephraim. This younger but greater son of Joseph became heir to the portion of ground which Jacob had taken from the Amorite in the region of Shechem, Gen. xlviii. 22. Hence, in the early period of Israel's sojourn in Egypt, we find Ephraim in this quarter asserting his claim and taking possession of this domain. The presence, or perhaps the aggression, of his family provoked the Philistines, and in a warlike encounter these two sons of Ephraim were slain by the men of Gath. After this another son was born to Ephraim, of whom Sherah, the builder or fortifier of towns, and Rephah were most probably the daughter and son, though they are generally regarded as the immediate children of Ephraim. Then we have a fifth son of Ephraim, Resheph, through whom Joshua is the eighth in descent from Ephraim. After the exploits of Sherah, it is probable that the tribe lost its hold on this region, and the bondage in Egypt com-

menced. We learn from this curious passage that there were nine generations in the line of Joshua during the sojourn in Egypt.—J. G. M.]—Vers. 28, 29 attach as a geographical notice of the dwelling-places of the Ephraimites, ver. 28, and West Manassites, ver. 29, to their genealogies, as the account of the Levitical cities, vi. 39 ff., to the preceding genealogy of Levi, or as the like geographical notice of the dwelling-places of the Simeonites, iv. 28 ff., to the preceding genealogy. —*Bethel and her daughters*, that is, the surrounding hamlets belonging to Bethel. Bethel, now Beitin, on the borders of Benjamin and Ephraim (Josh. xvi. 2, xviii. 15), was originally assigned to the former tribe (Josh. xviii. 22), but afterwards belonged to the kingdom of the ten tribes, and therefore to Ephraim. Our genealogist regards only this later relation.—*Naaran* bears in Josh. xvi. 7 the name נַעֲרָתָה, lengthened by ה local, and seems to be identical with Neara, north of Jericho (comp. Joseph. *Antiq.* xvii. 13. 1).—*Gezer* (Josh. xvi. 3) lay between Bethhoron and the sea, in the south-west corner of Ephraim, while the next named, Shechem and Ajjah, lay on the north-west. For the uncertainty of the reading עַזָּה, see Crit. Note. The only here occurring עַיָּה lay not far from Shechem (Neapolis, Nablous), perhaps in the region of Michmethah (Josh. xvi. 6, xvii. 7).—Ver. 29. *And on the side of the sons of Manasseh*, on their border, and in their possession. עַל יְדֵי, as in vi. 16. The four cities now named, Bethshean, Taanach, Megiddo, and Dor, lie properly (like Ibleam joined with them, Josh. xvii. 11) outside the territory of Manasseh, in that of the tribes of Issachar and Asher bordering it on the north. They were, however, to be assigned to Manasseh as remote dwelling-places towards the north, and serve here to mark the north border of the whole territory of "the sons of Joseph," as the Ephraimite cities named, ver. 28, determined their south border.

6. *The Tribe of Asher:* vers. 30–40.—*The sons of Asher: Imnah, and Ishuah, and Ishui, and Beriah.* So Gen. xlvi. 17, whereas, Num xxvi. 44 ff., Ishui is omitted. Beriah's sons Heber and Malchiel occur also in Gen. xlvi. and Num. xxvi., but the last, Birzajith, only here (perhaps a woman's name, see Crit. Note; but perhaps also = בְּאֵר זַיִת, "well of the olive," and so a local name).—Vers. 32–34. Heber's descendants for three generations. The name Shomer (שׁוֹמֵר), ver. 32, recurs, ver. 34, in the form שֶׁמֶר (*in pausa* שָׁמֶר), without warranting a difference between the two. For the name Ahi (אֲחִי) in ver. 34 (which is not to be taken appellatively, "brother," as the following ו shows), comp. v. 15, where a Gadite is so called.—Vers. 35–38. Descendants of Helem, as it appears, the son of Heber, and brother of Shemer, who was called Hotham in the third place after Japhlet and Shomer, ver. 32. One of the two names, either חוֹתָם or חֵלֶם, seems to have arisen from a slip of the pen, but which is uncertain. So it is with Ithran, the last but one of the eleven sons of Zophah, ver. 37, who reappears in the following verse under the name of Jether, and perhaps also with Ulla, ver. 39, which may be = Beera, the last son of Zophah, on the supposition of a very gross error of the pen.—Ver. 40. *All these were the sons of Asher*, etc. This collective notice is like that in ver. 11; the plur. חֲיָלִים, as in ver. 5.—*Heads of the princes* (Vulg. *duces ducum*), that is, captains of the greater divisions of the army, at the head of which stood the נְשִׂיאִים, *elati, magnates, optimates.*—*And their register for the service in war*, that is, not that of the whole tribe of Asher, but only that of the family of Heber, as the most powerful and flourishing. The limitation to this one family explains how the present list of warriors (it is expressly designated as such, in contrast with registers including the whole inhabitants of the country; comp. ix. 22) yields only 26,000 men of war, whereas for the whole tribe of Asher, the numbers 41,500 and 53,400 are given in Num. i. 41, xxvi. 47.

2. *Again the Families of Benjamin, especially the House of Saul:* ch. viii.

1. *The Families of Benjamin:* vers. 1–28.

CH. VIII. 1. And Benjamin begat Bela his first-born, Ashbel the second, and Ahrah
2, 3 the third. Nohah the fourth, and Rapha the fifth. And the sons of Bela
4 were Addar, and Gera, and Abihad. And Abishua, and Naaman, and Ahoah.
5 And Gera, and Shephuphan, and Huram.
6 And these are the sons of Ehud (these are the heads of the fathers to the
7 inhabitants of Geba, and they removed them to Manahath. Even Naaman,
and Ahiah, and Gera, he removed them): and he begat Uzza and Ahihud.
8 And Shaharaim begat, in the field of Moab, after he had sent them away,
9 Hushim and Baarah, his wives. And he begat of Hodesh his wife: Jobab, and
10 Zibiah, and Mesha, and Malcam. And Jeuz, and Shobiah, and Mirma: these
11 were his sons, heads of fathers. And of Hushim he begat Ahitub and
12 Elpaal. And the sons of Elpaal: Eber, and Misham, and Shemer; he built
Ono and Lod, and her daughters.
13 And Beriah and Shema (these were the heads of fathers for the inhabi-
14 tants of Aijalon; these put to flight the inhabitants of Gath). And Ahio,[1]
15, 16 Shashak, and Jeremoth. And Zebadiah, and Arad, and Eder. And Michael,
and Ishpah, and Joha, sons of Beriah.

17, 18 And Zebadiah, and Meshullam, and Hizki, and Heber. And Ishmerai,
and Izliah, and Jobab, sons of Elpaal.
19, 20 And Jakim, and Zichri, and Zabdi. And Elienai, and Zillethai, and Eliel.
21 And Adaiah, and Beraiah, and Shimrath, sons of Shimi.
22, 23 And Ishpan, and Eber, and Eliel. And Abdon, and Zichri, and Hanan.
24, 25 And Hananiah, and Elam, and Antothijah. And Iphdeiah, and Penuel, sons
of Shashak.
26, 27 And Shamsherai, and Sheharjah, and Athaliah. And Jaareshiah, and
28 Elijah, and Zichri, sons of Jeroham. These were heads of fathers in their
generations, chiefs; these dwelt in Jerusalem.

2. *The House of Saul:* vers. 29–40.

29 And at Gibeon dwelt Abi-gibeon; and his wife's name was Maachah.
30 And his first-born son was Abdon, and Zur, and Kish, and Baal, and Nadab.
31, 32 And Gedor, and Ahio, and Zecher. And Mikloth begat Shimah; and these
also, beside their brethren, dwelt in Jerusalem with their brethren.
33 And Ner begat Kish, and Kish begat Saul, and Saul begat Jonathan, and
34 Malchi-shua, and Abinadab, and Esh-baal. And the son of Jonathan was
35 Merib-baal; and Merib-baal begat Micah. And the sons of Micah: Pithon,
36 and Melech, and Tarea, and Ahaz. And Ahaz begat Jehoaddah; and Jehoad-
37 dah begat Alemeth, and Azmaveth, and Zimri; and Zimri begat Moza. And
38 Moza begat Binah: Rapha his son, Elasah his son, Azel his son. And Azel
had six sons; and these are their names: Azrikam, Bocheru,[2] and Ishmael, and
39 Sheariah, and Obadiah, and Hanan; all these were the sons of Azel. And
the sons of Eshek his brother: Ulam his first-born, Jeush the second, and
40 Eliphelet the third. And the sons of Ulam were valiant heroes, archers, and
had many sons and sons' sons, a hundred and fifty; all these were of the sons
of Benjamin.

[1] Instead of a proper name אַחְיוֹ, the Sept. read אָחִיו, as they render ὁ ἀδελφὸς αὐτοῦ. The conjecture of Bertheau, that the appellative is the original sense, and that the name Elpaal, which from ver. 18 we expect here, has fallen out before this אחיו, so that the text was originally וְאֶלְפַּעַל אָחִיו וְשָׁשָׁק, is very plausible. See Exposition

[2] For בֹּכְרוּ (with the closing *u* of proper names, comp. גַּשְׁמוּ, Neh. vi. 6) the Sept. (πρωτότοκος αὐτοῦ) and some Hebrew MSS. read בְּכוֹרוֹ, incorrectly however, as six sons of Azel are announced.

EXEGETICAL.

Preliminary Remark.—This full supplement to the shorter genealogy of Benjamin in vii. 6–11 appears in its whole plan and form to have been taken from another document, when we regard the frequent occurrence of הוֹלִיד, the collection of many families in vers. 6–28, without expressing their relation with the nearest immediate descendants of Benjamin; and lastly, the termination of the whole genealogy, in a register of the house of Saul, reaching down nearly to the exile (or perhaps quite beyond it, as Bertheau will have it). The latter phenomena remind us of ch. iii. and iv. in relation to ch. ii., and show that the Chronist had before him genealogical accounts of the tribe of Benjamin, and the royal house descending from it, of the same extent and exactness as of Judah and the royal house of David.

1. *Families of Benjamin:* vers. 1–28.—*a. Sons of Benjamin and Bela:* vers. 1–5.—For the relation of the five sons of Benjamin here mentioned to those of the parallel list, see on vii. 6. Keil is perhaps right in supposing that only those sons are mentioned here who founded families of Benjamin. That Ahrah = Ahiram, Num. xxvi. 38, and also = Ehi, Gen. xlvi. 21, appears certain. It is possible that the not otherwise occurring names Nohah and Rapha correspond to the Shephupham and Hupham of the parallel list, Num. xxvi., or at least denote descendants of these two sons of Benjamin.—Ver. 3 ff. *And the sons of Bela were Addar, and Gera,* etc. The suspicion that the list of the sons of Bela contains several errors of transcription, is raised by the recurrence of the name Gera. אַדָּר also appears to be a transcriptive error for אַרְדְּ, Gen. xlvi. 21, שְׁפוּפָן for שְׁפוּפָם, and חוּרָם possibly for חוּפָם, Num. xxvi. 39. At any rate, several are found among these six sons of Bela, that appear in Gen. xli. 21 and Num. xxvi. 38 f. among the sons of Benjamin; in particular, the first of the two Geras is like the Gera there; and Naaman there appears again here. Only Abihud, Abishua, and Ahrah occur exclusively here as sons of Benjamin.

b. Sons of Ehud: vers. 6, 7.—*And these are the sons of Ehud.* As Ehud (אֵחוּד, union, from אחד) is radically different from Ehud (אֵהוּד, mild, from אהד, to be mild), the well-known judge Ehud, the son of Gera, Judg. iii. 15, has nothing to do with the person here named.—*These are the heads of the fathers to the inhabitants of Geba.* These words, with the following notice of the removal to Manahath, are a parenthesis; the names of the sons of Ehud, Uzzah and Ahihud, follow at the close of ver. 7. For Geba, that is, "Geba of Benjamin," now Jeba, a Levitical city, comp. vi. 45; 1 Sam. xiii. 3, 16. The place is the same as "Gibeah of Benjamin," 1 Sam. xii. 2, 15, xiv. 2, 16 (comp. Knobel on Isa. x. 29). For Manahath, a place of uncertain situation, of which the inhabitants were partly from Judah, see on ch. ii. 52 (Hazi-hammenuhoth). The subject to וַיַּגְלוּם is the three men named in ver 7, of whom, as the sing. הוּא shows, the last must have been the proper originator of the removal. Whether this Gera was the first or the second of the sons of Bela so named, is as uncertain as the other details of this old historical event.

c. Descendants of Shaharaim: vers. 8-12.—*And Shaharaim begat in the field of Moab,* etc. This Shaharaim, and his connection with the genealogy of Benjamin, are quite unknown. That he was the same as Ahishahar, vii. 10, or Shechariah, ver. 26, or that he lies hid under אחר (= שַׁחַר), —all these are uncertain conjectures. Neither do we know the ground of his coming to the field of Moab, or of his tarrying there.—*After he had sent them away,* (namely) *Hushim and Baarah, his wives.* מִן שִׁלְחוֹ, literally, "from his sending;" שִׁלְחוֹ, *inf. Piel,* retaining the *i* and rejecting the *Dag. f.* (Ew. § 238, *d*). The suff. in אוֹתָם may, though masc., refer only to the two wives whose names are appended (comp. Ew. § 309, *c*). The construction is thus more loose and negligent than in vers. 6, 7, since to the prefixing of the verb is added an *enallage generis.* Moreover, the first of the two names has not a feminine form (חוּשִׁים), and is only known as such by the following נָשָׁיו.—Ver. 9. *And he begat of Hodesh his wife,* namely, his third, after the dismissal of the two above named; perhaps a Moabitess, as the names of some of her sons have a Moabitish sound, particularly מֵישָׁא (comp. the king of Moab, מֵישַׁע, 2 Kings iii.), מַלְכָּם (name of the idol of Ammon and Moab, Jer. xlix. 1, 3), etc. For הוֹלִיד מִן, comp. on ii. 18.—Vers. 11, 12. Here follow the descendants of Shaharaim by Hushim, and these are certainly, in contrast with those Moabites, genuine Israelitish and cisjordanic, as the reference of the places Ono and Lod, west of the tribe of Benjamin, to one of them (probably to Elpaal, to whom the הוּא appears to apply) shows. Ono, without doubt adjacent to Lod, occurs also in Ezra ii. 33, Neh. vii. 37, xi. 35, as a place in West Benjamin (properly by situation in Dan), and Lod is certainly Lydda, afterwards Diospolis, now Ludd or Lidd, north of Ramleh, near the road from Jaffa to Jerusalem. In vers. 17, 18 follows a further series of sons of an Elpaal, whose identity with the present one is uncertain.

d. Benjamite Heads of Families of Aijalon, ver. 13, *and of Jerusalem* (see ver. 28): vers. 13-28.—*And Beriah and Shema,* etc. There is no visible genealogical connection of these and the next following with the foregoing names. On the contrary, a partly genealogical connection seems to exist between the five heads of families in vers. 13 and 14 and the following names in vers. 15-27. For in vers. 15, 16 are "sons of Beriah" enumerated, in vers. 22-25 "sons of Shashak" (see ver. 14); and if we may connect "the sons of Shimi" in vers. 19-21 with Shema, ver. 13 (because שֶׁמַע and שִׁמְעִי look like two forms of the same name), and discover in "the sons of Jeroham," vers. 26, 27 (by assuming an error of the pen), descendants of Jeremoth, ver. 14, it will be still more natural to combine "the sons of Elpaal," vers. 17, 18, with the fifth of the heads of families in ver. 13 f., and suppose "Ahio," ver. 14 = Elpaal, read אָחִיו, with the Sept., instead of אַחְיוֹ, and supply אֶלְפַּעַל before it (according to Bertheau's proposed emendations; see Crit. Note). Many doubts, however, remain in force against this hypothesis, especially the circumstance that both ver. 13 and ver. 15 (where the descendants of Beriah, the first of the five heads of families, are enumerated) begin with a mere ו instead of a more distinct formula of introduction (such as in ver. 6, 'וְאֵלֶּה וגו).—*These were the heads of fathers for the inhabitants of Aijalon . . . Gath.* A historical notice *in parenthesi,* like that in vers. 6, 7. Aijalon, now Jalo, lay west of Gibeon, in the earlier district of Dan, where also Ono and Lod as Benjamite colonies were situated (comp. on ver. 12); see Josh. x. 12, xix. 42. Because Beriah and Shema are here named as conquerors of the inhabitants of Gath, Bertheau thinks we may infer an identity of the present fact with that mentioned vii. 21 ff., that the Benjamite family Beriah, after the defeat there recorded (in which Ezer and Elad fell), came to the help of Ephraim against the Gathites, overcame and chastised them, in gratitude for which they were admitted by the Ephraimites into their community, whence Beriah is there represented as a late-born son of Ephraim. That this is a mere fancy is manifest from the impossibility of understanding the account of Ephraim and his sons in vii. 21 ff. otherwise than literally (see on the passage). Besides, the name Beriah is by no means so rare that the identity of these persons and events can be inferred from it alone (comp. for example, Asher's son Beriah, vii. 30). And why might not Gath, in the long period of conflict between Israel and the Philistines, have been the object of repeated attacks by Israel?—Vers. 15, 16. *And Zebadiah, and Arad, and Eder,* etc. Of these six sons of Beriah nothing further is known, though their names almost all occur elsewhere: Zebadiah, ver. 17, among Elpaal's sons, and also xii. 7, Ezra viii. 8, x. 20; Michael still oftener, etc.—Vers. 17, 18. *And Zebadiah, and Meshullam, and Hizki,* etc. Of these seven sons of Elpaal, Bertheau will identify three, Meshullam, Heber, and Ishmerai, with the three sons of Elpaal in ver. 12, Misham, Eber, and Shemer, to make the identity of the Elpaal in both places probable. But this assumption is the more uncertain, the more doubtful it is whether that earlier Elpaal family that dwelt in Ono and Lydd can, by a supposed migration, be connected with the present family in Jerusalem (see ver. 28).—Ver. 19 ff. On Shimi, Shashak, and Jeroham, and their probable identity with Shema, Shashak, and Jeremoth, vers. 13, 14, see above. Of the sons of these three heads of families given as far as ver. 27, nothing is known elsewhere, although their names mostly recur.—Ver. 28. *These were heads of fathers in their generations, chiefs.* The repetition of רָאשִׁים serves scarcely (as the Vulg., *principes inquam*, and some older expositors will have it) to lay stress on the idea of heads, which would be here quite unmeaning. The sense rather appears to be, "that the persons named in the genealogical lists are cited as heads (of houses); and this appears to be noted, that those cited as sons of such and such persons may not be taken for individual members of houses" (Keil).—*These dwelt in Jerusalem,* not merely the heads, but their families, who cannot be supposed to be separate from them.

2. *The House of Saul:* vers. 29–40 (comp. ch. ix. 35–44, where this section, with the exception of vers. 39, 40, recurs).—*a.* Saul's Ancestors: vers. 29–32.—*And at Gibeon dwelt Abi-gibeon; and his wife's name was Maachah.* The plur. יָשְׁבוּ refers also to the sons of Abi-gibeon, to be named in the following verse. Gibeon is now el Jib, two and a half hours north-west of Jerusalem; comp. Rob. ii. 351. The here appellatively-named Abi-gibeon, that is, father (founder) of Gibeon (comp. the like remarks in ii. 42 ff.), bears in ix. 35 the name Jeiel or Jeuel (יְעוּאֵל; *Kethib* יְעוּאֵל). His descent from Benjamin is not given, and he occurs only here; and so it is with Maachah his wife, whose name, however, is of frequent occurrence (comp. on ii. 48).—Ver. 30. *And his first-born son was Abdon,* etc. Instead of the eight sons of Abi-gibeon here named, ch. ix. 36 f. enumerates ten; and, in fact, the names of two seem to have fallen out of our passage, namely Ner (between Baal and Nadab) and Mikloth (at the end of the series, ver 31), for their descendants are given in the following verses. It is doubtful whether the names בַּעַל and נָדָב at the close of our verse are to be combined into one, בַּעַלְנָדָב (as Wellh., *Text d. B. Sam.* p. 31, will have it). In chap. ix. 37 we find Zechariah in place of the present זָכֶר.—Ver. 32. *And Mikloth begat Shimah.* In ix. 38 he is called Shimam.—*And these also,* namely Shimah and his family, *beside their brethren, dwelt in Jerusalem with their brethren.* "These also" perhaps points only to Mikloth's family as likewise dwelling in Jerusalem. The "brethren" of these descendants of Shimah are the remaining Benjamites, in the first phrase ("beside their brethren") perhaps those dwelling outside of Jerusalem to the west and north, and in the second ("with their brethren") those settled in Jerusalem itself.

b. The Family of Ner, and the House of Saul: vers. 33–45.—*And Ner begat Kish, and Kish begat Saul.* As in 1 Sam. ix. 1, xiv. 51, the father of Kish is called Abiel, Ner is an earlier ancestor, perhaps the father or grandfather of the Abiel. Possibly, indeed, there was originally in the text, "And Ner begat Abner (comp. 1 Sam. xiv. 51), and Kish begat Saul;" for it is scarcely conceivable that the celebrated general Abner, the uncle of Saul, should be originally wanting in this genealogy (comp. Berth. and Kamph.).—*And Saul begat Jonathan . . . and Eshbaal.* Instead of these four sons of Saul, 1 Sam. xiv. 49 names only three—Jonathan, Ishui, and Malchishua. But Ishui is, as appears from 1 Sam. xxxi. 2 and 1 Chron. x. 1, only another name for Abinadab; and thus the three, who are the three that fell with Saul, quite agree with the first three of those here named. But Eshbaal is no other than Ishbosheth, the well-known rival of David, 2 Sam. ii. 8 ff. The change of the second element of this name (בַּעַל) into בֹּשֶׁת, "shame, idol," expressing abhorrence and contempt, may be compared with Jerubbaal, Judg. vi. 32, changed into Jerubbesheth (יְרֻבֶּשֶׁת), 2 Sam. xi. 21, or with the name of the son of Ishbosheth, who is here called Meribbaal (so, with a slight difference in orthography, מְרִי־בַעַל, ix. 40), but in 2 Sam. iv. 4, xxi. 7, Mephibosheth (or perhaps מְרִיבֹשֶׁת, as at least Berth. thinks; but comp. Wellh., *Der Text d. B. Sam.* p. 31).—Ver. 35. The sons of Micah, the son of the lame Meribbaal, are four in number, the same as in ix. 41, 42, only that the last but one is called Tahrea (תַּחְרֵעַ) instead of Tarea (תַּאְרֵעַ).—Ver. 36. *And Ahaz begat Jehoaddah.* The descendants of this Ahaz are traced through ten generations. For יְהוֹעַדָּה (יוֹעַדָּה) stands in ix. 42 יַעְרָה, by a mistake of ר for ד. Of the two following names, Alemeth occurs (with a slight variation) in ix. 45 as a Benjamite place, and Azmaveth twice, xi. 33 and xii. 3, as a Benjamite person.—Ver. 37. Instead of Rapha (רָפָא), the parallel ix. 43 has the longer and more original form Rephaiah (רְפָיָה).—Ver. 38. For the name Bocheru, the second of the sons of Azel, comp. Crit. Note.—Ver. 40. *And the sons of Ulam were valiant heroes, archers.* For the expression, comp. v. 18. For the thing, namely, the warlike prowess of the tribe of Benjamin, comp. Judg. xx. 16, Gen. xlix. 27.—*And had many sons and sons' sons, a hundred and fifty.* For מַרְבִּים, properly "multiplying" sons, comp. vii. 4, Lev. xi. 42. As grandsons of Ulam and grand-nephews of Azel (who was the thirteenth in descent from Saul), the hundred and fifty here mentioned were the fifteenth generation from Saul. If we reckon for every generation a maximum average of thirty years, the resulting sum of 450 years from the time of Saul (1095–1055) would terminate in the middle or second half of the 7th century B.C., and therefore in the time before the exile. Against Bertheau's attempt to assign the sons and grandsons of Ulam to the time after the exile, Keil justly remarks on the whole: "This reckoning is too high. Sixty years cannot be allowed for Saul and Jonathan, as Jonathan fell in the year 1055, and his son Meribbaal was then only five years old, and therefore born in 1060. In the following generations also not more than twenty-five years on an average (?) can be allowed. Accordingly, the grandsons of Ulam's sons, who were the twelfth generation from Micah (son of Meribbaal), may have come into the world about 730 B.C., have grown into the host of 150 grandsons of Ulam about 760-700. But even if thirty years be reckoned for each generation, the last-named generation of 150 grandsons and great-grandsons of Ulam would have lived in the period from 660-600, and therefore before the exile, at least before the first great deportation of the people under Jehoiachin, 599 B.C." Moreover, the traces of a representation of the relations of the tribe of Benjamin after the exile which he has endeavoured to show in our chapter,—for example, the occurrence of several names of places and persons of our section in the history of the times of Ezra and Nehemiah, the connection of the Benjamites in the land of Moab mentioned vers. 8-10 with the "princes in Moab" (פחת מואב) named in Ezra ii. 6, viii. 4, x. 30, Neh. iii. 11, vii. 11, the form בֹּכְרוּ corresponding with נִשְׁמוֹ, the near agreement of the number 150 with the numbers of some families in Ezra and Nehemiah (comp. Ezra ii. 18-30, viii. 3 ff.), etc.,—would only render it probable that the present genealogical account extends beyond the exile, if we were entitled to suppose that a number of links had fallen out in the series of generations from Saul to Ulam and his grandsons. The possibility of such assumption is as undeniable as it is precarious to take it for granted without any sufficient ground.—*All these were of the sons of Benjamin.* "All these" goes back to ver. 1, and includes the whole of the names in our section.

f. The Inhabitants of Jerusalem till the Times of the Kings, with a Repetition of the Genealogy of Saul.—Ch. ix.

1. *The Inhabitants of Jerusalem:* vers. 1–34.

CH. IX. 1. And all Israel was registered; and, behold, they are written in the book
of the kings of Israel; and Judah[1] was carried away to Babel for his trans-
2 gression. And the former inhabitants, that were in their possession in
3 their cities, were Israel, the priests, the Levites, and the Nethinim. And in
Jerusalem dwelt, of the sons of Judah, and of the sons of Benjamin, and of
the sons of Ephraim and Manasseh.
4 Uthai the son of Ammihud, the son of Omri, the son of Imri, the son of
5 Bani,[2] of the sons of Perez the son of Judah. And of the Shilonites:[3] Asaiah
6 the first-born, and his sons. And of the sons of Zerah: Jeuel and their
brethren, six hundred and ninety.
7 And of the sons of Benjamin: Sallu the son of Meshullam, the son of
8 Hodaviah, the son of Hassenuah. And Ibneiah the son of Jeroham, and
Elah the son of Uzzi, the son of Michri, and Meshullam the son of Shephatiah,
9 the son of Reuel, the son of Ibnijah. And their brethren in their generations,
nine hundred and fifty and six; all these men were chiefs of their father-
houses.
10, 11 And of the priests: Jedaiah, and Jehoiarib, and Jachin. And Azariah
the son of Hilkiah, the son of Meshullam, the son of Zadok, the son of
12 Meraioth, the son of Ahitub, a prince of the house of God. And Adaiah the
son of Jeroham, the son of Pashhur, the son of Malchijah, the son of Maasai,
the son of Adiel, the son of Jahzerah, the son of Meshullam, the son of
13 Meshillemith, the son of Immer. And their brethren, heads of the father-
houses, a thousand and seven hundred and sixty, able men for the work[4] of
the service in the house of God.
14 And of the Levites: Shemaiah the son of Hashub, the son of Azrikam,
15 the son of Hashabiah, of the sons of Merari. And Bakbakkar, Heresh, and
Galal, and Mattaniah the son of Micah, the son of Zicri, the son of Asaph.
16 And Obadiah the son of Shemaiah, the son of Galal, the son of Jeduthun,
and Berechiah the son of Asa, the son of Elkanah, who dwelt in the villages
17 of the Netophathites.—And the porters: Shallum, and Akkub, and Talmon,
18 and Ahiman, and their brethren; Shallum the head. And hitherto he was in
the king's gate eastward; these are the porters for the camps of the sons of
19 Levi.—And Shallum the son of Kore, the son of Ebiasaph, the son of Korah,
and his brethren, for the house of his father, the Korhites, were over the work
of the service of the keepers of the thresholds of the tents; and their fathers
20 in the camp of the Lord were keepers of the entry. And Phinehas the son
21 of Eleazar was formerly prince over them; the LORD with him. Zechariah[5]

22 the son of Meshelemiah was porter at the door of the tent of meeting. All
these that were chosen to be porters at the thresholds were two hundred
and twelve; they were registered in their villages: David and Samuel the
23 seer had ordained them in their trust. And they and their sons were over
24 the gates of the house of the LORD, at the house of the tent, by wards. To
25 the four winds were the porters, to the east, west, north, and south. And
their brethren in their villages were to come in seven days from time to time
26 with them. For they were in trust, the four head keepers of the gates, these
Levites, and were[6] over the chambers and treasuries of the house of God.
27 And they lodged around the house of God; for on them was the charge, and
28 they had to open every morning. And some of them were over the vessels
29 of service, for they brought them in and out by tale. And some of them
were appointed over the vessels, even over all the holy vessels, and over the
30 flour, and the wine, and the oil, and the frankincense, and the spices. And
of the sons of the priests some were compounders of the ointment of the spices.
31 And Mattithiah of the Levites, who was the first-born of Shallum the Korhite,
32 was in trust over the baking in pans. And of the Kohathites their brethren,
33 some were over the shew-bread, to prepare it every Sabbath. And these the
singers, heads of the fathers for the Levites, were free[7] in the chambers; for
they were over them in the service day and night.
34 These are the heads of the fathers for the Levites, heads in their generations; these dwelt in Jerusalem.

2. *Register of Saul's Family repeated:* vers. 35–44.

35 And in Gibeon dwelt the father of Gibeon, Jeiel;[8] and his wife's name was
36 Maachah. And his first-born son Abdon, and Zur, and Kish, and Baal, and
37, 38 Ner, and Nadab. And Gedor, and Ahio, and Zechariah, and Mikloth. And
Mikloth begat Shimam; and they also, beside their brethren, dwelt in Jerusalem with their brethren.
39 And Ner begat Kish, and Kish begat Saul, and Saul begat Jonathan, and
40 Malchi-shua, and Abinadab, and Eshbaal. And the son of Jonathan was
41 Merib-baal: and Merib-baal begat Micah. And the sons of Micah: Pithon,
42 and Melech, and Tahrea. And Ahaz begat Jarah; and Jarah begat Alemeth,
43 and Azmaveth, and Zimri; and Zimri begat Moza. And Moza begat Bina,
44 and Rephaiah his son, Elasah his son, Azel his son. And Azel had six sons;
and these are their names: Azrikam, Bocheru, and Ishmael, and Sheariah, and
Obadiah, and Hanan; these were the sons of Azel.

[1] The Sept., the Vulg., and Luther attach וִיהוּדָה to the foregoing words (τῶν βασιλέων Ἰσραὴλ καὶ Ἰούδα), with an arbitrary interpretation of the following הָגְלוּ וגו׳ (μετὰ τῶν ἀποικισθέντων εἰς Βαβυλῶνα,—*translatique sunt in Babyl.*).

[2] For the *Kethib* בֶּן־בְּנִימִן־בְּנִי is doubtless to be read the *Keri* בֶּן־בָּנִי מִן־בְּנֵי (comp. the name בָּנִי in vi. 31, among the Merarites).

[3] For הַשִּׁלֹנִי, since שִׁילֹה (שִׁלוֹן) is a city of Ephraim, must apparently have been read, according to Gen. xxvi. 20, הַשֵּׁלָנִי (the Shelanites, descendants of Shelah, third son of Judah). The incorrect pointing הַשִּׁילֹנִי appears to have arisen from the *scriptio plena:* הַשֵּׁילָנִי. Comp. Neh. xi. 5, where, instead of הַשִּׁילֹנִי, we should also perhaps point הַשֵּׁלָנִי.

[4] Before מְלֶאכֶת a ל (in consequence of the ל at the end of חֵיל) seems to have fallen out. Comp. εἰς ἐργασίας of the Sept., and ch. vii. 2, xii. 25 (also F. Böttcher, *Neue exeg. krit. Aehrenlese*, iii. 223).

[5] Before זְכַרְיָה a ו seems to have fallen out.

[6] For וְהֵם הַלְוִיִּם וְהָיוּ the original text seems to have been וּמִן הַלְוִיִּם הָיוּ; comp. ver. 14.

[7] *Kethib:* פְּטִירִים. *Keri:* פְּטוּרִים.

[8] So the *Keri*. The *Kethib* is יְעוּאֵל.

EXEGETICAL.

Preliminary Remark.—Of the two unequal sections into which our chapter falls, the second, vers. 35–44, coincides almost literally with viii. 29–38, and so presents only a repetition of the register of Saul and his house there given, preliminary to the narrative of the fall of his dynasty following in ch. x. The first section, vers. 1–34, presents in its first half, containing a list of the heads of families dwelling in Jerusalem, vers. 4–17, several points of contrast with a similar list in Neh. xi. 3–19. The plan of both lists is at all events the same; and if, with Bertheau, of the three chiefs of Judah, vers. 4–6, we put Uthai beside Athaiah (Neh. xi. 4), and Asaiah beside Maaseiah (ver. 5) (so that only the third name, Jeuel, has nothing corresponding to it in Nehemiah); if we consider the recurrence of the Benjamite chiefs Sallu and Hodaviah in Neh. xi. 7–9 (where, certainly, the remaining names are wanting); if we compare the six chiefs of the priestly divisions with those corresponding in number and mostly in name in the list of Nehemiah, and find *here* (vers. 10–13) the series: Jedaiah, Jehoiarib, Jachin, Azariah, Adaiah, Masai, *there* the series: Jedaiah, Joiarib, Jachin, Seraiah, Adaiah, Amashai; if we observe among the chief of the Levites two, Shemaiah and Mattaniah, verbally identical, and a third, Obadiah (= Abda in Nehemiah), approximately so; if, lastly, we perceive at least two of the four chiefs of the porters, Shallum and Akkub, common to both lists,—a pretty general agreement even in names appears to prevail between the two registers. It seems natural, also, either with Zunz (*Gottesdienstl. Vorträge der Juden*, p. 31; also Herzfeld, *Gesch.* p. 298) to conceive our list modelled after that of Nehemiah, or both drawn from one source, and in like manner referring to the inhabitants of Jerusalem after the exile, as Movers (p. 234), Berth., Kamph., etc., do. But if both lists are based upon one common document, relating to the times of Ezra and Nehemiah, and arising from them, we should expect a more complete agreement with regard to all the names. The accordance of the names in only half of the whole number given, and the resemblance in place (giving first the sons of Judah, then the sons of Benjamin, then the priests, and then the Levites and porters), are sufficiently explained by supposing a general continuity of the inhabitants of Jerusalem before and after the exile, and laying the diversities of the two lists to the account of the altering, disturbing, and partly destroying effects of the exile, and the similarities to that of the endeavour of those returning with Zerubbabel and Ezra to restore as far as possible the former state of things. The following exegetical treatment of the passage will prove that, with this presupposition, the assumption of the origin of our present list before the exile, in contrast with the obvious reference of Nehemiah's list to the times after the exile, has nothing of moment against it, and is even demanded by ver. 2 and other indications.

1. Vers. 1–3. *Transition from the Genealogical Registers of the Twelve Tribes to the Enumeration of the Inhabitants of Jerusalem.—And all Israel was registered; and, behold, they are written in the book of the kings of Israel; and Judah was carried away.* By the Masoretic accentuation, which plainly separates וִיהוּדָה from the foregoing words, and makes it the subject of a new sentence (comp. Crit. Note), the first sentence appears to treat of Israel in the narrow sense, that is, of the northern kingdom, and its kings in particular (so Berth., Kamph., etc.). But the phrase "all Israel" makes it more natural here to think of the people of the south as well as of the north; and it is also in favour of this, that the expression: "the book of the kings of Israel," is in 2 Chron. xx. 34 manifestly of like import with "the book of the kings of Judah and Israel," or "Israel and Judah," as well as that the universal sense of the term "Israel" is found at the beginning of the second verse. Keil therefore justly remarks: "The antithesis of Israel and Judah is analogous to that of Judah and Jerusalem;" that is, Israel denotes the whole covenant people, Judah a part. To understand the name Israel of the whole people is also demanded by the position of our verse at the end of the genealogies of all the tribes of Israel, and not merely of the ten northern tribes. That ver. 1 effects the transition from the genealogies to the following enumeration of the inhabitants of Jerusalem, and so forms properly the close of the genealogies in ch. ii.–viii., is so obvious, that Bertheau has not been able to bring forward a single tenable ground for his counter assertion, that "the verse forms obviously a new beginning." For the affirmation, that "we perceive in it a brief introduction to the historical accounts of the tribe of Judah, or of the Israelites after the exile," can furnish no ground for this, because it not only contradicts the assertion that Israel is to be understood of the northern kingdom, but cannot be reconciled with the letter of the verse (that begins with the connective וְ). The same exegete justly declares against the further assertion of Berth., that ver. 1 cannot be written by our historian himself, but must have been taken literally from his source,—an assertion which is devoid of all solid ground.—*For their transgression:* so ch. v. 25 f., 41.—Ver. 2. *And the former inhabitants, that were in their possession in their cities.* Movers, Berth., and Kamph., who find in the following list the inhabitants of Jerusalem after the exile, in the time of Nehemiah, will understand by these "former inhabitants" those citizens of Jerusalem who dwelt there in the time of Zerubbabel and his immediate successors, before Jerusalem was newly peopled from the surrounding districts. It is much more natural, with almost all old expositors, and with Keil, to refer הָרִאשֹׁנִים here to the inhabitants of Jerusalem before the exile; for, in that case, "the inhabitants in their possession in their cities" are in no way opposed as former inhabitants of Jerusalem to the later, but both appear so placed side by side that this opposition is excluded. The parallel Neh. v. 15, quoted by Bertheau, where the governors from Zerubbabel to Ezra are opposed as הַפַּחוֹת הָרִאשֹׁנִים to Nehemiah as the later פֶּחָה, proves indeed the possibility of understanding the predicate הראשונים in the sense of "before the exile," but not the necessity. And from the dwelling "in their cities" (comp. Ezra ii. 70; Neh. vii. 23, xi. 1 f.) nothing can be concluded in favour of this interpretation.—*Were Israel, the priests, the Levites, and the Nethinim.* "Israel"

denotes here obviously the lay element of the citizens, that which is otherwise designated by עָם beside כֹּהֵן (Isa. xxiv. 2; Hos. iv. 9). For the notion and name of the Nethinim, properly the "bestowed," that is, the temple ministers, comp. Num. viii. 19; Josh. ix. 27; 1 Sam. i. 11; Ezra ii. 43, viii. 17, 20, and elsewhere.—Ver. 3. *And in Jerusalem dwelt of the sons of Judah*, etc. These words are not a superscription of the list of those dwelling in Jerusalem in contrast with those living in other cities (as Berth., etc.). The list rather begins with these words, so that thus the verse serves to introduce the contents of the greater part of our chapter (to ver. 34), and corresponds to ver. 35. This close connection of our verse with the following special enumeration of the families of Jerusalem (ver. 4 ff.), and the mention of "the sons of Ephraim and Manasseh" as fellow-citizens with them in Jerusalem (comp. 2 Chron. xxxiv. 9), are against referring the present list to the time after the exile. The book of Nehemiah (xi. 3) announces its list corresponding to ours in quite another way, so that there no doubt at all remains of its exclusive reference to conditions and relations after the exile. Moreover, the circumstance that the following list contains no names of Ephraimites and Manassites in Jerusalem, is simply explained by this, that of the former only a very few families dwelt in Jerusalem, while the Jews and Benjamites formed the bulk of its population. On the evangelical and theocratic import of the association of Ephraim and Manasseh with Judah, Benjamin, and Levi in the citizenship of Jerusalem, comp. below, evangelical and ethical principles, No. 1.

2. Vers. 4-17. *Special Enumeration of the Inhabitants of Jerusalem, and first, of the Heads of Families of Judah and Benjamin, of the Priests and Levites*: vers. 4-6.—Three heads of families out of the three chief branches of Judah, those of Perez, Shelah, and Zerah (comp. ii. 3, 4).—*Uthai, the son of Ammihud . . . of the sons of Perez.* The name Uthai might be etymologically equivalent to that of the Athaiah (עֲתָיָה) mentioned Neh. xi. 4 as a head of a family of the sons of Perez; for עוּתַי=עוּתְיָה, "whom Jehovah helps," might, if we regard the somewhat obscure root עתה as a by-form of עוּת, have the same meaning as עֲתָיָה. But to the still diverse form is to be added the quite different series of ancestors that connect Athaiah with Perez (Uzziah, Zechariah, Amariah, Shephatiah, Mahalalel, instead of the present Ammihud, Omri, Imri, Bani). It seems therefore very doubtful whether Uthai be the same with Athaiah. For the defective reading concealing the name Bani, see the Crit. Note.—Ver. 5. *And of the Shilonites, Asaiah the first-born*, etc. It seems pretty certain that הַשֵּׁלָנִי should be read here instead of הַשִּׁילֹנִי, as in Neh. xi. 5. We expect to find the descendants of Shelah (Num. xxvi. 20; comp. 1 Chron. ii. 3, iv. 21) mentioned between the sons of Perez and those of Zerah. Moreover, it is doubtful whether the Shelanite Asaiah (עֲשָׂיָה, "whom Jehovah has made") is to be at once taken as identical with the Maaseiah (מַעֲשֵׂיָה, "Jehovah's work"), as both names are of frequent occurrence (comp. for Asaiah, iv. 36, vi. 15, xv. 6, 11, 2 Kings xxii. 12, 14, and for Maaseiah, xv. 18, 20, 2 Chron. xxiii. 1, Jer. xxi. 1, xxix. 21). The existence of an Asaiah as head of a house in the family of Shelah before the exile does not preclude the appearance of a Maaseiah, son of Baruch, son of Col-hozeh, son of Hasaiah, etc., as head of this family after the exile.—Ver. 6. *And of the sons of Zerah: Jeuel and their brethren, six hundred and ninety.* This number refers, as the plur. suff. in אֲחֵיהֶם shows, not to Jeuel alone, but to the three chiefs named in vers. 4-6, and to their brethren, the remaining heads of houses of subordinate import. So it is also with the number 956 in ver. 9. Moreover, the name Jeuel (יְעוּאֵל), or its variant (יְעִיאֵל), occurs elsewhere; for example, v. 7, 2 Chron. xxvi. 11. In Neh. xi. no descendants of Zerah are given.—Vers. 7-9. Four Benjamite chiefs: Sallu, Ibneiah, Elah, Meshullam, of whom the first (and, as here, the son of Meshullam) occurs also Neh. xi., but the other three not; see the Preliminary Remark.—Ver. 9. *And their brethren*, etc.; comp. on ver. 6.—*All these men were chiefs of their father-houses.* This remark, which naturally refers, not to the brethren numbered, but to the chiefs named, applies to all that are named from ver. 4, both Jews and Benjamites. It serves thus to close the list of family chiefs, and lead to the following one of the priests and Levites.—Vers. 10-13. The priests of Jerusalem.—*Jedaiah, and Jehoiarib, and Jachin.* The names of these three priestly classes dwelling in Jerusalem (comp. xxiv. 7, 17) are found also in the parallel list in Neh. xi. 10 ff. (supposing that there, by a change of בֶּן־יוֹיָרִיב into יְהוֹיָרִיב, the true reading is restored).—Ver. 11. *And Azariah the son of Hilkiah . . . a prince of the house of God.* Instead of this prince or president of the temple, Azariah ben Hilkiah, certainly the same who, v. 40, was named as grandfather of the Jehozadak who was carried to Babel (comp. also 2 Chron. xxxi. 13), Neh. xi. 11 names rather a Seraiah son of Hilkiah. Yet the identity of this Seraiah with the Azariah of our passage is probable, as the other ancestors of both up to Ahitub (Meshullam, Zadok, Meraioth, Ahitub) are quite the same. Seraiah might indeed be a descendant of Azariah ben Hilkiah after the exile.—Ver. 12. *And Adaiah the son of Jeroham*, etc. This priestly chief Adaiah (belonging to the class of Malchijah; comp. 1 Chron. xxiv. 9) is given in Neh. xi. 12 in the same form and with the same line, up to Malchijah, as here. The following Maasai (מַעְשַׂי), belonging to the class of Immer (1 Chron. xxiv. 14), is called in Nehemiah Amashai (עֲמַשְׁסַי), and appears there connected by another line with Immer. Another priestly chief given by Nehemiah, Zabdiel, son of Haggedolim, who is designated the president or overseer of the last-named priestly family (that of Amashai), is wanting here.—Ver. 13. *And their brethren, heads of the father-houses*, 1760. This number cannot possibly refer to the heads; it rather denotes (like the number 1192 in Nehemiah) that of the brethren or the heads of houses standing under the heads of the great complex of families. The phrase appears thus inexact; per-

haps, with Keil, a transposition of the words is to be assumed, in such a way that "heads of father-houses" is placed before and drawn to ver. 12 as closing formula, while "and their brethren" (וַאֲחֵיהֶם) is immediately connected with the number 1760. Moreover, that all the priests dwelling in Jerusalem, or the priestly families of the six classes named, amount in our passage to 1760, and in Nehemiah only to 1192, tends to confirm our view of the present list as belonging to the period before the exile; we expect for the priesthood of Jerusalem after the exile, about 150 years after the restoration of the city and temple, not so great a number as here.—*Able men for the work of the service in the house of God.* Before מְלֶאכֶת, which may not be a mere accusative of reference ("able men with respect to the work"), the word עֹשֵׂי (comp. xxiii. 24; Neh. xi. 12), or perhaps a mere לְ (which might easily be overlooked after חַיִל), appears to have fallen out; see Crit. Note.—Vers. 14–16. *The Levites of Jerusalem.—Shemaiah the son of Hashub,* etc. This Merarite Shemaiah, as the descendant of Asaph (therefore Gershonite) Mattaniah named in ver. 15, recurs in Neh. xi. 15, and with substantially the same line of ancestors. Bakbakkar, Heresh, and Galal (ver. 15*a*) are wanting there; for the first name would have to be identified with Bakbukiah, Neh. xi. 17, of which there are grave doubts, as בַּקְבַּקַּר (=בַּקְבֵּק הָהָר) seems to mean "destruction of the hill;" but בַּקְבֻּקְיָה, "desolation from Jehovah." And of the names of Levites in ver. 16, only Obadiah can be identified with Abda, Neh. xi. 17 (as Jeduthun appears as the ancestor of both). Berechiah is wanting in Nehemiah; and the latter has two names, Shabbethai and Jozabad, which are foreign to our text.—*And Berechiah, the son of Asa, the son of Elkanah,* and so a Kohathite, as the name Elkanah is native in this family; comp. vi. 18–23.—*Who dwelt in the villages of the Netophathites,* thus near Bethlehem; comp. Neh. vii. 26. This clause refers, not to Berechiah, whose dwelling is in Jerusalem, but to his ancestor Elkanah. It is impossible to determine what the Kohathite so called in vi. 13 ff. was to this Elkanah.—Ver. 17. *And the porters: Shallum, and Akkub, and Talmon, and Ahiman, and their brethren; Shallum the head.* The four here named (of whom, in Neh. xi. 19, only two, Akkub and Talmon, recur) are to be regarded, as appears from the particulars following (vers. 24, 26), not as common porters, but as captains of the four companies of porters, who were to keep guard on the four sides and gates of the temple: they are designated, ver. 26, as "head keepers of the gates," a phrase reminding us of the στρατηγοὶ τοῦ ἱεροῦ in Luke xxii. 52. The number of all the doorkeepers, which is stated to be 172 in Neh. xi. 19, is wanting here, where it would, like that of the priests, have been considerably higher, because Jerusalem before the exile must have had a much more numerous staff of officers in every respect than that after the exile, to which the catalogue of Nehemiah refers. From all this, the correspondence of the two similar lists in the personal matters is only partial, and by no means such as to be inconsistent with the origin of the one before the exile and of the other after it. The resemblance and even sameness of the names in two or three generations does not of itself prove the identity of the persons, because we learn from the genealogy of Aaron (v. 29 ff.) that the series Amariah, Ahitub, Zadok repeats itself at different times (comp. vers. 33 f. and 37 f.). In general, the same names recur very often in genealogies, because it was the custom to give the children the names of their ancestors; comp. Luke i. 59; Winer, *Realw.* ii. 133; Hävernick, *Einl.* ii. 1, 179 ff. But if the likeness of names in the two lists furnishes no necessary ground for the identity of the lists, and in no way warrants us to identify the like sounding names by the assumption of errors of the pen, we must, on account of the great diversity in all points, understand our list of the inhabitants of Jerusalem before the exile, especially as the following remarks on the functions of the Levites demand this, because they relate throughout to the time before the exile.

3. Vers. 18–34. *The Ministerial Functions of the Levites, and first* (vers. 18–26*a*), *of the Levitical porters.—And hitherto* (he was, namely Shallum, who is called in ver. 17 the head of the porters) *in the king's gate eastward*; that is, till the present time the family of Shallum had to keep the guard at the east gate of the temple, that chief entrance to the inner court, by which the king alone entered (comp. 2 Kings xvi. 18; Ezek. xlvi. 1, 2). The "hitherto" scarcely gives a hint of the time when the present list was composed. It may point as well to a time before the exile as after it, as Shallum is here obviously named as a hereditary name of a house or collective personality, which Keil contravenes unnecessarily. For the circumstance that a pedigree of Shallum is given, not yet in ver. 18, but at length in ver. 19, shows that in this latter passage the person of the patriarch of the leading house of doorkeepers is first distinguished from his descendants; see also after.—*These are the porters for the camps of the sons of Levi.* This expression, having an antique ring, and reminding us of the wanderings of the people under Moses (Num. iii. 21 ff.), proves no more than the many other designations of this kind ("tent," ver. 20; "tent of meeting," ver. 21; "house of the tent," ver. 23*a*) that our list was composed before Solomon or near the time of Moses; comp. "camp of Jehovah" of Solomon's temple, 2 Chron. xxxi. 2.—Ver. 19. *And Shallum the son of Kore, the son of Ebiasaph, the son of Korah.* This reference of Shallum to Korah, the grandson of Kohath (v. 7), comes so close upon the ancestry of Shelemiah or Meshelemiah, the Korhite appointed by David over the east gate, 1 Chron. xxvi. 1, 14, that the Shallum of our passage can scarcely be different from him. It is also highly probable that the name of אֲבִיָסָף, the father or ancestor of Korah, should be restored there (see Crit. Note), so that the identity of the two persons and the merely formal diversity of their names (שַׁלּוּם, requital; מְשֶׁלֶמְיָהוּ, whom Jehovah requites) is almost certain; and the Meshelemiah, ver. 21, must be held to be identical with the Shallum belonging to the time of David: for there, as in xxvi. 2, a son Zechariah is ascribed to him. Thus the record goes back, as in ver. 20 to Phinehas the contemporary of Joshua, so in ver. 21 at

least to a contemporary of David; and the guard at the east gate (the king's gate), as it was hereditary in the family, is referred to a nomination by King David. The then mentioned brethren of Shallum, of the house of his father, the Korhites, are the heads of the other three families of porters, Akkub, Talmon, and Ahiman, living in the time of David, ver. 18.—*Were over the work of the service of the keepers of the thresholds of the tent.* This specifies the service performed by these Levites at the temple; they were threshold or gate keepers; comp. 2 Kings xii. 10; 2 Chron. xxiii. 4. The genit. "of the tent" (here expressed by לְ before אֹהֶל, because the preceding word having the article cannot be in the construct state) applies to the tent in Jerusalem erected by David, without, however, expressing any contrast to the temple of Solomon (which, in ver. 23, seems clearly to be included in the term "tent"); comp. on ver. 18.—*And their fathers in the camp of the Lord were keepers of the entry,* namely, in the time of Moses, to which there is reference here as in the following verse. "In the Pentateuch there is no mention of the Korhites keeping guard in the time of Moses; but as the Kohathites to whom they belonged were the first servants of the sanctuary, Num. iv. 4 ff., and especially had the charge of the tabernacle, it is in itself probable that they had to keep the entrance to the sanctuary (comp. Num. iv. 17-20); and therefore we cannot doubt that our statement follows an old tradition" (Berth.).—Ver. 20. *And Phinehas the son of Eleazar was formerly prince over them,* over the porters of the Korhite family. Phinehas cannot have been invested with this oversight of the Korhite porters when he was high priest, but only under the high-priesthood of his father Eleazar; as also Eleazar, as chief over the chiefs of Levi, Num. iii. 32, under the presidency of Aaron, had the oversight of the keepers of the sanctuary.—*The Lord with him.* This clause might be meant as a historical remark, and so completed by a הָיָה, "was," in which case the copula וְ was to be expected before יְהוָה, as in xi. 9. It is more natural to see in the two words a blessing, "God be with him," and to compare the German phrases, "God bless him," "Of blessed memory." We may remember also God's covenant of peace with Phinehas and his posterity, Num. xxv. 11 ff. [This goes to prove that the historical is the correct meaning, and not one that is nearly akin to an error of doctrine.—J. G. M.]—Ver. 21. *Zechariah the son of Meshelemiah,* that is, Shallum; see on ver. 19. The designation of this Shallum (before whose name we miss the copula וְ; see Crit. Note) as porter at the door of the tent of meeting has something indefinite needing explanation. But we can find nothing either from the present passage or from ch. xxvi. 2 to clear up this difficulty, or account for the prominence given to this Zechariah.—Ver. 22 returns to the description of the service of the porters, which was interrupted by the historical digression, vers. 19-21. What is now stated belongs to the time of the author of the list, with the exception of the remark applying to the time of David, ver. 22*b*.—*All these, that were chosen to be porters at the thresholds.* On בְּרוּרִים, "chosen," comp. vii. 40, xvi. 41; for construction with לְ, xxv. 1. The number 212 as the total of the porters agrees neither with the time of David, in which (xxvi. 8-11) 93 porters in all officiated at the tabernacle; nor with that of Zerubbabel, for which Ezra ii. 42 gives the number 139; nor, lastly, with that of Nehemiah, for which, Neh. xi. 19, the number 172 is set down. But it suits the time before the exile, to which also the numbers of the families and priests in vers. 6, 9, 13 most probably point.—*They were registered in their villages.* They dwelt, therefore, in villages (חֲצֵרִים, as vi. 41 ff.) around Jerusalem, and came to it on the days of their service, as the singers in the time after the exile, Neh. xii. 29 f.—*David and Samuel the seer* (ancient designation for prophet, נָבִיא; comp. 1 Sam. ix. 9) *had ordained them in their trust.* בֶּאֱמוּנָתָם, "in their trust," official trust or duty; comp. the same term without suffix, vers. 26, 31; 2 Kings xii. 16, xxii. 7; 2 Chron. xxxi. 12. The naming of Samuel with David (and after him, against the order of time; comp. Heb. xi. 32) the Chronist no doubt found in his source, and it is explained by the fact that the agency of Samuel in the religious institutions of Israel prepared the way for the reforms of David, and were therefore usually mentioned along with them. And perhaps some arrangement regarding the Levitical porters was made by Samuel which laid the foundation for that of David, though we have no information concerning this beyond the present passage.—Ver. 23. *And they and their sons,* the porters of the time of David and after it. The following phrase also, "at the house of the tent" (comp. on vers. 18, 19), is chosen, because the present statement applies to both—the tent-sanctuary before Solomon, and the stone temple built by him.—Ver. 24. *To the four winds* (quarters of the heaven; comp. Job i. 19; Matt. xxiv. 31) *were the porters,* יִהְיוּ, that is, according to the arrangement of David (xxvi. 14 ff.).—*By wards,* מִשְׁמָרוֹת of persons, as Neh. xii. 9, iv. 3, 16.—Ver. 25. *Were to come in seven days,* the seventh day from time to time, that is, on the Sabbath of the week, on which every family was in their rank to perform the service (לְ in לָבוֹא, to denote obligation, as v. 1).—*With them* (עִם אֵלֶּה), along with the heads or chiefs of the divisions, ver. 17, who dwelt in Jerusalem itself, and to whom the notice in ver. 26*a* refers.—*For they were in trust, the four head keepers of the gates;* comp. on ver. 17.—Vers. 26*b*-32 report on the duties of the other Levites besides the porters.—*These Levites, and were,* etc. It has been remarked in the Crit. Note that for this we are most probably to read (according to ver. 14), "And of the Levites were." At all events, the duties enumerated in the following passage (exclusive of ver. 27) belong to the Levites in common, and not to the porters. Accordingly, the words וְהֵם הַלְוִיִּם must be regarded either as a subscription to the whole preceding paragraph from ver. 14 (so Berth.), or amended (with Keil) in the way indicated.—

Over the chambers and treasuries of the house of God. These chambers (לְשָׁכוֹת) and treasuries (אֹצָרוֹת) were in the side buildings of the temple, over which the Levites presided; comp. Ezek. xl. 17, xlii. 1 ff.; Neh. x. 38; and Keil, *Bibl. Arch.* i. pp. 121, 124.—Ver. 27. *And they lodged around the house of God.* This notice, referring again to the porters, with the subjoined statement, that they had to open every morning (lit. "were set over the keys;" comp. מַפְתֵּחַ, Judg. iii. 25; Isa. xxii. 22), is strange in the present place: it had its place perhaps originally after ver. 26*a*.—Ver. 28. *And some of them were over the vessels of service*, the more valuable vessels of gold and silver, with the sacrificial bowls (xxviii. 13 f.; Dan. i. 2, v. 2 ff.), which required careful keeping, and as they were to be taken out of the treasuries for the public worship an exact "tale."—Ver. 29. *Over the vessels, even over all the holy vessels, and over the flour, and the wine*, etc. As the term כֵּלִים is used here as in ver. 28, the difference between the vessels here and there mentioned seems to depend on the articles which are here named in connection with the latter, namely, flour (סֹלֶת, Lev. ii. 1 ff.), wine, oil, frankincense, and spices (בְּשָׂמִים, as Ex. xxx. 23). They may be, therefore, the more ordinary, less costly vessels used in the daily incense, meat and drink offering (comp. on Ex. xxv. 6). For מנה, "order, appoint," in the *Piel*, comp. Dan. i. 5, 10, 11; the partic. *Pi.* only here.—Ver. 30. *And of the sons of the priests*, etc. To them belonged, Ex. xxx. 23 ff., the preparation of the holy anointing oil, by the compounding of several spices. This notice referring to the priests does not, strictly taken, belong to the functions of the Levites. The division of things has here for the moment overruled the division of persons. [The priests, however, were Levites.]—Ver. 31. *And Mattithiah of the Levites, who was the first-born of Shallum the Korhite:* thus an elder brother of that porter Zechariah, ver. 21, if this is actually to pass for the son of the Shallum here. But certainly, in ch. xxvi. 2, Zechariah is directly called first-born (בְּכוֹר) of Meshelemiah; and hence, to maintain the identity of this Meshelemiah with Shallum, we must assume "that in our passage Mattithiah bears the honourable title of first-born only in an improper sense, because he ranks high among the descendants of Shallum on account of his office" (Berth.). Nothing further is known to us concerning the person or time of Mattithiah.—*Was in trust over the baking in pans.* The term הַחֲבִתִּים, a baking in pans (comp. מַחֲבַת, an iron pan, Lev. ii. 5, vi. 14; 1 Chron. xxiii. 29; Ezek. iv. 3), is used only here.—Ver. 32. *And of the Kohathites their brethren*, the brethren of the last-mentioned Levites, at whose head was the Korhite Mattithiah. For the way of laying on the shew-bread, see Lev. xxiv. 6 ff.—*Every Sabbath.* For the phrase שַׁבַּת שַׁבָּת (the first with *Pattach* in the last syllable, for euphony), comp. Bertheau.—Ver. 33. *And these the singers, heads of the fathers for the Levites, were free in the chambers.* This is usually regarded as a first subscription to the foregoing, from ver. 14, to which a second still more general subscription is added in ver. 34. Yet in the mention of the singers (the families of which had been reported in vers. 14–16), the enumeration of the ministerial functions of the several classes of the Levites, which had begun ver. 26*b*, is rather continued; and therefore, instead of "these are the singers," the rendering is rather "these singers, etc.," and thus a force, extending to a rather remote point (ver. 14), is to be assigned to the demonstrative (Kamph. justly). The "being free" in their chambers is set forth very naturally, because their exclusive occupation with their art was to be indicated. Comp. Rashi's and Kimchi's interpretation of פְּטוּרִים, *immunes ab omni alio officio.*—*For they were over them in the service day and night.* This literal rendering of the Masoretic text (עֲלֵיהֶם בַּמְּלָאכָה) seems to express the sense: "they were placed over them, the subordinate singers, had to superintend them" (Berth.). But the comparison of the somewhat different passage, 2 Chron. xxxiv. 12, is insufficient to justify this view. It is more natural to take עֲלֵיהֶם to mean: "it lay upon them;" but then בַּמְּלָאכָה would have to be changed into הַמְּלָאכָה (ver. 27), and so the suitable sense restored: "for by day and night their service, their singing function, was incumbent on them."—Ver. 34. *These are the heads of the fathers for the Levites*, etc. Comp. the similar subscription, viii. 28. Since this precedes the first genealogy of Saul, as here the repetition of this genealogy immediately follows, Movers (p. 82 f.) conjectured that it had its place here originally, but was taken by an old transcriber erroneously for the beginning of the following genealogy of Saul, and therefore transposed with this (as he endeavoured to point out a more suitable place, as he thought, for it at the close of the genealogy of Benjamin, viii. 1–27) to that previous place, and thereby somewhat altered. This assumption would only be plausible if the double position of the genealogy of Saul must be regarded as resting on a mistake, and contrary to the plan of the writer, for which there is no manner of ground. He rather repeated this genealogy intentionally here to form a proper transition from his genealogical section to his following (introducing the historical section) account of the fall of Saul's house. This simple consideration removes all that was formerly adduced in the way of doubts, conjectures, and highly absurd and superfluous reflections on the supposed ground of this repetition, as, according to Mar Sutra in *Tr. Pesachim* 62*b*, 400 (or in another report, 1300) camel-loads of explanations are forthcoming on this repetition and on the present section; comp. Herzfeld, *Gesch.* p. 299.

4. *Repeated Genealogy of Saul:* vers. 34–44.—On the deviations of this list from viii. 29–39, see on that passage, where it has been already stated that our present passage seems to present the older and more correct text with respect to the forms of the names.

EVANGELICAL AND ETHICAL REFLECTIONS ON CH. I.–IX.

There is in many respects the impression of wandering in a wilderness, of walking among the stones in a graveyard, ranged in long rows, and more or less weathered, remaining on the mind after the exegetical examination of the genealogical contents of these chapters. But as in the wilds of Hauran, Idumæa, and Arabia Petræa, bristling with innumerable bare rocks, there is, notwithstanding all the drought and waste, a mysterious charm that acts with irresistible attraction on all Christian travellers animated by the spirit of biblical research; or as, to use another but kindred figure, the labyrinthine windings of the old Christian catacombs of Rome, with their thousands of sarcophagi, and the ever-varying inscriptions and manifold symbolic figures on them, prepare for the Christian antiquarian walking through them, not weariness, but an inexhaustible charm and ever new satisfaction; even so do the seemingly so dry and unrefreshing names of these nine chapters act upon the searchers of Scripture, not only the Jewish, but also the Christian. For it is from beginning to end holy ground through which we here pass. They are the grave-stones of the people of God, the monuments of a thousand years of the old covenant people, between the rows of which the Chronist leads us. They are the cities and places of the holy land, the origins of which are here presented to us in greater or briefer extent. And the same mysterious attraction that yearly impels thousands of Christian pilgrims, of all countries and confessions, to that land, in which not merely Israel after the flesh, but also the confessors of Christ, have to seek a right of home, insensibly influences every reader of this section who is led by a Christian and scientific interest. The same home-longing that comes upon us on beholding every chart of the country of the twelve tribes, on examining every plan and picture of Jerusalem, even on reading the plainest and simplest of the innumerable books of travels with which the present luxuriant literature of Palestine constantly floods us, seizes with irresistible power the biblical inquirer who turns his attention to these opening chapters of our work; it sweetens in many ways the hard labours that are occasioned by the deciphering of the often illegible text, the pondering on the import of so many isolated names, the reconciling of so many contradictory statements concerning places, persons, and genealogical lists. Considered in detail, there are four chief aspects in which the deeper significance of the history of salvation in our chapters is presented, and on which the attention of the historical inquirer, moved by higher motives than mere profane history and criticism can yield, will be concentrated.

1. The grouping and arrangement of the genealogical material, with all the complication, seeming inconnection and arbitrariness of the considerations involved, is highly attractive, as it affords a deep insight into the organic arrangement of the tribes of God's people, and the parts they are destined to perform in the history of the theocracy. The fundamental principle of division is neither purely genealogical nor politico-theocratic, but has reference to all these relations. The enumeration of the tribes is not arranged genealogically, according to the ages of the twelve sons of Jacob; otherwise it would have begun with Reuben and ended with Benjamin. It proceeds not according to the political relations of the time of the divided kingdom; otherwise Judah and Benjamin would have stood first, and Ephraim would have followed at the head of the northern kingdom. It follows not exclusively the geographical principle; for if it starts with Judah, the chief tribe of the south, and passing over the seats of the Simeonites, extending far to the south, bends round to the three eastern tribes, and enumerates them from south to north, in order to pass on to the remaining tribes of middle and northern Canaan, in the enumeration of the latter it abandons all geographical order, as the southern Benjamin and probably Dan are annexed to the northern Issachar, and then follows, not Ephraim, the more southern of the tribes of Joseph, but the more northern Manasseh, next to Naphtali; and lastly, after Ephraim and Asher, Benjamin reappears. In the midst of this not very geographical enumeration falls the copious genealogical details of Levi, to whom a definite territory was wanting, on account of its distribution over all the tribes. And yet in this apparently ungeographical and unhistorical order there lies a deeper sense. The author, as a strict theocratic legitimist, subordinates all the others to the two chief tribes, Judah and Benjamin, forming the kingdom of Judah, and adhering to the legitimate national sanctuary, as well as the tribe of Levi remaining in natural mutual connection with them. As he otherwise ignores, as far as possible, the northern kingdom, that had revolted from the legitimate worship, and subordinates the tribes belonging to it, on every occasion, to the orthodox tribes of the south, and regards them as mere dependencies of the latter (comp. ix. 3, where, along with Jews, Benjamites, and Levites, those belonging to the tribes of Ephraim and Manasseh are named as belonging to the inhabitants of Jerusalem; also the quite similar passage, 2 Chron. xxxiv. 9, and our remarks on it), here also is all that does not belong to the kingdom of Judah treated as accessory, and not only more briefly despatched (none of the tribes belonging to the north is given as fully as the tribe of Simeon belonging to Judah; some, as Dan and Naphtali, are almost wholly, and one, Zebulun, wholly omitted), but pushed in as subordinate, filling up between the tribes of Judah, Levi, and Benjamin, forming the beginning, the middle, and the end. What is especially conspicuous and beautiful is the central, all-pervading, embracing, and connecting position of the priestly tribe of Levi. "Over the whole distribution of the tribes is spread out as a connecting network the uniformly-distributed tribe of Levi, as the priestly mediator between God and His people, in its forty-eight cities, that belonged to all the tribes, but are not to be regarded as exclusively inhabited by Levites (comp. our remarks on vi. 65); whereby, according to Josh. xxi. (and our ch. vi.), a peculiar crossing of the families of Levi took place, partly in the east and partly in the north of Palestine, so that those akin in family appear removed as far asunder as possible (Kohathites in Judah and Simeon, but also in Ephraim and West Manasseh; Merarites in Reuben and Gad, but also in Zebulun, etc.). It is as if this tribe, provided it remained at the

height of its destiny, and the consciousness of God's people clung to it, should represent the strong sinews and muscles running through the body of the people, which bind the members into a living and moving whole" (Hoffmann, *Blicke in die früheste Geschichte des gelobten Landes*, p. 99 f.).

2. Prominent in this arrangement, with regard to the history of grace, is the passing over of two tribes in silence. That Dan is only indicated, not named, in vii. 12, can only be conceived as a critical judgment on this tribe, that early and almost wholly fell into idolatry (see on the passage, and comp. xxvii. 16 ff., where there is not so much an overpassing of the name as a transposition of it to the end of the twelve tribes, by which the same theocratico-critical judgment is passed upon it). On the contrary, it may be accidental that no mention is made of the tribe of Zebulun in giving the genealogy of the twelve tribes, though it occurs in the enumeration of the Levitical cities (vi. 48, 62). Yet a certain significance for the history of salvation cannot be denied to this accidental omission, as it was certainly the relative smallness of the tribe, the low number of famous and populous families, that occasioned its disappearance from the genealogical traditions of the later time. Yet this so small and obscure tribe[1] it was that included Nazareth, the dwelling-place of the earthly parents of Jesus. Zebulun, with its neighbour Naphtali, was, according to prophetic announcement (Isa. ix. 1; Ps. lxviii. 28), to prove to be "the people walking in darkness," the land overshadowed with heathen gloom, that was to see the great light of salvation go forth from its midst. In this contemporaneous omission, then, of Dan, the tribe typically pointing to the Antichrist, and of Zebulun, the tribe serving as the earliest scene of the earthly living and working of the Saviour, there is in our registers a certain significance for the history of salvation, that even if it rests upon accident, points to a higher guidance and a providential arrangement.

3. The investigator of all that is significant for the history of salvation and the defence of the truth, will take no less interest in the many historical and archæological notices that are interwoven in the genealogical text. With their now scanty, now copious, contributions to the special history of the tribe, their details, often truly surprising by the epic grandeur and dramatic life of the narrative (to which belong, in particular, the records of the conquests of the Simeonites, the successful raids of the three trans-jordanic tribes against the north Arabian Beduin, and the slaying of the two sons of Ephraim, Ezer and Elad, by the primeval inhabitants of Gath), their highly ancient colouring both in style and deed, which prompts us almost to generalize the remark once added by the author: "these are ancient things," and apply it to the whole of these accounts,[2] these notices delight us as petrifactions from the grey foretime imbedded in the strata of genealogical series; they resemble scattered gems or medals of antique stamp shining through the rubbish of ages, that give us accounts of otherwise unknown events of theocratic history, and open to us perspective views into remote epochs of the development of God's people, on which the darkness of absolute oblivion would otherwise have rested. From each of these, now shorter, now longer, documents concerning the older and oldest history of the tribe, goes forth the testimony of an unusually rich and many-sided individual impress of the Israelitish spirit, reminding us almost of the German nation in the multiplicity of its tribes, of a fresh but rude native power as a heritage more or less proper to each of the twelve tribes, and to each in peculiar modification, and thereby of a divine providence guiding and governing the life of the several tribes and of the whole nation with uninterrupted fatherly love as well as judicial integrity.

4. Of pre-eminent importance is finally the appearance, more or less clear in every tribe, of a preponderating repute and influence of one family over the rest. In the tribe of Judah, it is the family of Hezron the son of Perez, and grandson of Judah, that by its growth and power casts all the rest into the shade. In the tribe of Levi, the Kohathites predominate; in that of Benjamin, it is the house of Jeuel, or Abi-gibeon, the ancestor of Saul (viii. 29, ix. 35 ff.), that, obscuring all the rest, rises to kingly worth and power, and even in its later offshoots, especially the sons of Azel and the bold archers of Ulam (viii. 38–40), remains great and renowned. Among the Simeonites, Shimei, the descendant of Shaul, the last of the five sons of Simeon, becomes the ancestor of the most flourishing family (iv. 26 f.). Among the Reubenites, the family of Joel is conspicuous (v. 4 f., 8 f.); among the Gadites, that of Buz (v. 14); among the Manassites, that of Machir the father of Gilead (vii. 14 ff.); among the Ephraimites, that of Resheph the ancestor of Joshua (vii. 25); among the sons of Issachar, that of Izrahiah the son of Uzzi, the son of Tolah (vii. 3); among the sons of Asher, that of Heber the son of Beriah (vii. 32 ff.). It is obvious enough to explain this remarkable phenomenon naturally, and regard it as preservation and completion of the strong families in "the struggle for existence," or, if you will, as natural training. The statement of Palgrave, the English traveller, regarding the division of all the Arab tribes into two kinds of families, the townsmen or peasants, and the nomads or beduin, of which the former are the stronger and more developed, the latter the weaker, though patriarchally the more simply constituted, and therefore better fitted for handing down faithfully their genealogical recollections, should perhaps be regarded as pointing to a partial explanation of the present interesting phenomenon.[1] Neither of these two purely

[1] That Zebulun, in the times of Moses, and even David, sent into the field an army of 50,000 men (see xii. 33), is not in contradiction with its insignificance in the later times before and after the exile, and is historically quite conceivable.

[2] Thus J. Fürst (*Gesch. der bibl. Lit.* i. p. 318) conjectures that the raid of Elad and Ezer, the sons of Ephraim, against Gath, narrated vii. 21, is probably taken from "the old accounts (דברים עתיקים) mentioned iv. 22, which the Chronist had before him," but without adducing any direct proof for it.

[1] Palgrave, *Central Arabia*, i. p. 35: "Arab nationality is and always has been based on the divisions of families and clans. These clans were soon by the nature of the land itself divided each and every one into two branches, correlative indeed, but of unequal size and importance. The greater section remained as townsmen or peasants in the districts best susceptible of culture and permanent occupation, where they still kept up much of their original clannish denominations and forms, though often blended, and even at times obliterated, by the fusion inseparable from civil and social organization. The other and lesser portion

natural attempts at explanation can be called satisfactory. The last and deepest ground of the rise of one family or tribe to a physically, ethically, or intellectually distinguished preëminence, and to an illustrious name, obscuring kindred tribes or families, is the secret of the divine election, that, without respect to character or conduct, raises and glorifies the one people or family, and leaves the other to lowness and oblivion, according to the words, "Jacob have I loved, but Esau have I hated;" and, "I will have mercy on whom I will have mercy, and I will have compassion on whom I will have compassion" (Rom. ix. 13, 15; Mal. i. 2 f.; Ex. xxxiii. 19). As in the life of nations, so is this elective grace visible in the development of single tribes, clans, and families, and often in a way that directly contradicts the normal mode of growth and self-development, especially the law of the prevalence of the strong over the weak in "the struggle for existence," and rather proceeds according to the Pauline saying: "God hath chosen the weak things of the world to confound the things which are mighty; and base things of the world, and things which are despised, hath God chosen, and things which are not, to bring to nought things that are, that no flesh should glory in His presence" (1 Cor. i. 27–29). Above all, in the development of the forefathers of Christ, before David as well as after, in the times of the rise as in those of the decline, this election by grace has repeatedly asserted itself, and operated as the proper principle and inmost motive of that blessed historical process, embracing many thousands of years, which, as the divine education of the human race, is the counterpart of all natural training, and the ideal archetype of all human education.

devoted themselves to a pastoral life. They, too, retained their original clannish and family demarcations, but unsoftened by civilization, and unblended by the links of close-drawn society; so that in this point they have continued to be the faithful depositaries of primeval Arab tradition, and constitute a sort of standard rule for the whole nation. Hence, when genealogical doubts and questions of descent arise, as they often do among the fixed inhabitants, recourse is often had to the neighbouring beduins for a decision unattainable in the complicated records of the town life." Wellhausen (*De gentibus et familiis Jud.*, etc., p. 24 f.), setting out from the mainly correct presupposition, that these observations of Palgrave on the Arabs apply *mutatis mutandis* to the tribes of ancient Israel, has described the family of Caleb (ii. 18 ff., 42 ff.) as an example of a Jewish family dwelling in towns and tilling the ground, and therefore widely spread, but certainly difficult to reduce to a genealogy; and, on the contrary, that of his brother Jerahmeel, ii. 25–41, as an example of a nomad family, remaining certainly smaller and less renowned, but also provided with far more precise and correct genealogical recollections. *Etenim casu non factum est*, he thinks, with reference to ii. 25-41, *quod nusquam excultior invenitur articulatio corporis ethnologici, quam apud Jerachmeelem. Immo ut mos ille schemate genealogico depingendi res gentilicias fluxit primarie e tali societate, quæ magnæ familiæ erat similior quam artificiosæ ac contortæ structuræ civitatis quæ recte dici potest, ita postea etiam ibi sine dubio maxime viguit, ubi antiqua patriarcharum fidelius servabatur vitæ consuetudo, sic quidem ut sanguinis vis jungens et dirimens ceteris omnibus causis, quibus homines solent conciliari et abalienari, aut revera prævaleret aut certe secundum conscientiam popularem prævalere judicaretur*, etc.

---

§ 2. HISTORY OF THE KINGS IN JERUSALEM FROM DAVID TO THE EXILE.—1 CHRON. X.–2 CHRON. XXXVI.

1. DAVID.—1 CHRON. X.–XXIX.

a. INTRODUCTION: FALL OF THE HOUSE OF SAUL.—CH. X.

CH. X. 1. And the Philistines fought against Israel; and the men of Israel fled
2 before the Philistines, and fell down slain in Mount Gilboa. And the Philis-
tines pursued Saul and his sons; and the Philistines smote Jonathan and
3 Abinadab and Malchi-shua, sons of Saul. And the battle went sore against
4 Saul, and the archers found him, and he trembled for the archers. And Saul
said to his armour-bearer, Draw thy sword and thrust me through therewith,
lest these uncircumcised come[1] and insult me; but his armour-bearer would
5 not; for he was sore afraid: and Saul took the sword and fell upon it. And
his armour-bearer saw that Saul was dead, and he also fell on the sword and
6 died. And Saul died, and his three sons, and all his house died together.
7 And all the men of Israel that were in the valley saw that they fled, and
that Saul and his sons were dead; and they forsook their cities and fled, and
the Philistines came and dwelt in them.
8 And it came to pass on the morrow that the Philistines came to strip the slain,
9 and they found Saul and his sons fallen in Mount Gilboa. And they stripped
him, and took his head and his armour, and sent into the land of the Philistines
10 around, to bear tidings to their idols and to the people. And they put his
armour in the house of their god, and fastened his skull in the house of Dagon.
11, 12 And all Jabesh-gilead heard all that the Philistines had done to Saul. And
all the valiant men arose, and took the body of Saul and the bodies of his

sons, and brought them to Jabesh, and buried their bones under the oak in
Jabesh, and fasted seven days.
13 And Saul died for his transgression which he committed against the LORD,
for the word of the LORD which he kept not, and also for asking a necromancer
14 to inquire.[2] And inquired not of the LORD; and He slew him, and turned the
kingdom to David the son of Jesse.

[1] *Kethib:* יבאו. *Keri:* יבואו.

[2] After לדרוש the Sept. gives the superfluous addition: καὶ ἀπεκρίνατο αὐτῷ Σαμουὴλ ὁ προφήτης. Comp. Sir. xlvi. 20

EXEGETICAL.

PRELIMINARY REMARK.—This account of the downfall of Saul and his house agrees, except in subordinate details, literally with 1 Sam. xxxi. 1–13; only the vers. 13, 14 are an addition of the Chronist, designed to mark the history of the fall of Saul's family as the transition to the following history of David, that forms the proper centre of the whole work of our historian. For to this history of David points all that precedes, the whole of the genealogies in the first nine chapters, with their emphatic elevation of the tribe of Judah. And if these genealogies are so disposed that they close with the register of the Benjamite house of Saul, this serves to prepare for the contents of our chapter, which on its part is preparatory to the following special history of the reign of David, the ancestor and founder of the legitimate line of kings.

1. *Saul's Defeat and Death in the Battle with the Philistines on Mount Gilboa:* vers. 1–12 (comp. 1 Sam. xxxi. 1–12).—*And the men of Israel fled before the Philistines.* The fuller statement of the books of Samuel (1 Sam. xxix. 1; comp. xxviii. 4) shows that this flight of the defeated Israelites was directed from the plain of Jezreel, as the proper field of battle, to Mount Gilboa, their former post.—Ver. 2. *And the Philistines pursued Saul and his sons;* properly, "clung to Saul," a fit expression for the incessant and vehement pursuit (Sept.: συνάπτουσι τῷ Σαούλ; Luth.: "hingen sich an Saul"). The abridged form וַיַּדְבְּקוּ, for וַיַּדְבִּיקוּ, as in 1 Sam. xiv. 22, xxxi. 2. On Jonathan, Abinadab, and Malchishua, see ch. viii. 33.—Ver. 3. *And the archers found him,* overtook him (as ver. 8; comp. 1 Sam. xxx. 11).—*And he trembled for the archers.* וַיָּחַל, fut. apoc. *Kal* of חוּל, *torqueri, tremere;* so 1 Sam. xxxi. 3; comp. וַתָּחֵל, Ps. xcvii. 4. The present terror of Saul corresponds with that in 1 Sam. xxviii. 5. It is unnecessary here to prefer the reading of the Sept.: καὶ ἐπόνεσεν ἀπὸ τῶν τόξων (ἐπόνεσεν, perhaps resting on a וַיִּחַל, from חָלָה, πονεῖν), and so render (with Kamph.), "and he was pressed by the archers." For the ἐτραυματίσθη, "he was wounded," of the Sept. in the parallel 1 Sam. xxxi. 3, comp. Berth. and Wellh., *Text der Bücher Sam.* p. 147, who perhaps unnecessarily assumes that the Chronist may have read וַיֵּחָל, "and he was wounded" (*Niph.* of חלל), and therefore omitted מְאֹד, which did not suit this verb. The omission of this adverb is sufficiently accounted for by the abbreviating habit of the author, on which also the omission of the pleonastic אֲנָשִׁים after הַמּוֹרִים (1 Sam. xxxi. 3) rests, as also that of עִמּוֹ at the close of ver. 5, etc.—Ver. 4. *Lest these uncircumcised come and insult me.* Before וְהִתְעַלְּלוּ־בִי (comp. Jer. xxxviii. 19; 1 Sam. vi. 6) the parallel text in Samuel exhibits a וּדְקָרֻנִי, which perhaps did not originally stand in the text, but seems to be repeated by mistake from the foregoing imper. וְדָקְרֵנִי, so that the word is rightly omitted by the Chronist; comp. Berth. and Wellh.—Ver. 6. *And all his house died together.* Again an abbreviation for, "and his armour-bearer, and all his men on that day together," in Sam. xxxi. The design of this abbreviation was scarcely to remove the strong "exaggeration" (Wellh.) contained in גַּם כָּל־אֲנָשָׁיו, on account of which the Sept. perhaps left these words untranslated; for the וְכָל־בֵּיתוֹ of our author contains a like exaggeration, as Saul's whole house did not fall in this battle, as the author (ix. 35 ff.) knew very well. The expression is general and excessive, as the longer one in 1 Sam. xxxi. also.—Ver. 7. *And all the men of Israel that were in the valley,* or on the plain. More exactly, 1 Sam. xxxi., "the men of Israel that were beyond the valley and beyond the Jordan," that is, that dwelt west and east of Mount Gilboa. That our writer had a defective text (Thenius) is not to be assumed; rather the same process of abbreviation is found here, as immediately after, where the required subject אַנְשֵׁי יִשְׂרָאֵל is omitted after כִּי נָסוּ.—Ver. 9. *And they stripped him, and took his head and his armour.* Instead of this, 1 Sam. xxxi. 9 has, "and they cut off his head and stripped off his armour." The beheading, understood of itself (comp. Goliath, 1 Sam. xvii. 54), our author leaves unmentioned.—*And sent into the land of the Philistines around,* namely, these trophies, Saul's head and armour (comp. Judg. xix. 29 f.). Accordingly, the Sept. in 1 Samuel has translated καὶ ἀποστέλλουσιν αὐτά, where perhaps "messengers" (מְבַשְּׂרִים, צִירִים) is to be supplied; see Then. and Wellh.—*To their idols and to the people.* For אֶת־עֲצַבֵּיהֶם (where אֵת=with, before), the text in Samuel has בֵּית עֲצ׳, "in the house of their idols," a reading not confirmed by the Sept., which seems to owe its origin to the following verse (בית־אלהיהם).—Ver. 10. *And they put his armour in the house of their god;* according to

1 Sam. xxxi. 10, in the temple of Astarte. For the Ashtaroth, the same deity as the "queen of heaven" of the Canaanites, Jer. vii. 18 ff., or the Alilat of the Arabs, Herod. iii. 8 (perhaps also = the Phenician mother of gods, Astronoe of Damascius [*vit. Isid.* 302; comp. Döllinger, *Judenth.* p. 143], and the Spartan Venus *hastata victrix* of Cythera), was the chief deity of the Philistines, that Ἀφροδίτη Οὐρανία whose ancient and wealthy sanctuary at Askelon is mentioned by Herodotus i. 108. We are perhaps, therefore, to understand this Astarte temple at Askelon, as the next named temple of Dagon, the second chief divinity of the Philistines, will be that mentioned, 1 Sam. v. 3 ff., at Ashdod, which was especially frequented in the times of Saul (comp. Vaihinger, Art. "Philister" in Herzog's *Encycl.* xi. 576 f.). That "their god" and "Dagon" could not be opposed, as Wellh. thinks, is too much to assert. Rather was the Astarte of the Philistines a kind of androgynous being, that formed with Baal a syzygy or a supreme divine principle, and certainly one fundamentally different from the fish god Dagon (because the latter was both younger and less esteemed). Comp. Döllinger, p. 397 ff.; Müller, *Astarte*, a contribution to the mythology of oriental antiquity, Wien 1861 (in which also the Cretan Europa [= רַבָּה, the strong] is identified with Astarte), Vaihinger, as above.—*And fastened his skull in the house of Dagon.* These words are wanting in 1 Sam. xxxi., where, on the contrary (ver. 10), is found the following notice: "and they fastened his body to the wall of Bethshean." Here we must choose between the assumption, that our text arose from a corruption of this reading of Samuel (Wellh.), and such harmonizing attempts as that of Ewald and Thenius, who assume that originally after the words, "his skull in the house of Dagon," stood the following, "and they fastened his body to the wall of Bethshean," but they fell out on account of the similarity of ואת גלגלתו and ואת גויתו; or that of Bertheau, who explains the omission of the notice of the fastening of the body to the wall of Bethshean as an intentional one, that is to be judged in the same way as the other abbreviations of our writer. The latter assumption is the most probable, because in ver. 12 there is no mention of fetching the body from Bethshean.—Ver. 11. *And all Jabesh-gilead:* 1 Sam. xxxi.: "and the inhabitants of Jabesh-gilead." According to Berth., the יֹשְׁבֵי before יָבֵשׁ came into the text on account of the plur. וַיִּשְׁמְעוּ; but here again the easier supposition is that the Chronist has abbreviated the text of Samuel. Besides, it was gratitude for the deliverance wrought for them by Saul (1 Sam. xi.) that moved the citizens of Jabesh to this pious care for his burial.—Ver. 12. *And took the body of Saul.* גּוּפַת is a later phrase, usual in Aramaic, occurring only here in the O. T. for the גְּוִיַּת of Samuel. Whence the body was fetched, and what was done with it (for example, its incremation, 1 Sam. xxxi. 12), our author, true to his abbreviating habit, omits.

2. *Closing Reflection on the Fall of the Kingdom of Saul:* vers. 13, 14.—*And Saul died for his transgression.* Wherein this transgression (מַעַל, unfaithfulness, apostasy; comp. v. 25, ix. 1; Lev. v. 5) consisted, is added—1. In not following the word of the Lord, that is, His command to destroy Amalek (1 Sam. xv. 11; comp. xxviii. 18); 2. In inquiring of the necromancer.—*For the word of the Lord which he kept not.* Besides 1 Sam. xv., we are to understand here, also, that earlier case of disobedience in 1 Sam. x. 8, xiii. 13, and also 1 Sam. xxii. 18 f.—*And also for asking the necromancer to inquire*, to seek an oracle, a revelation; comp. 1 Sam. xxviii. 7, where דרשׁ is used in the same pregnant sense. On the quite superfluous gloss of the Sept., comp. Crit. Note.—Ver. 14. *And inquired not of the Lord*, sought not information. This is not inconsistent with the fact that, 1 Sam. xiv. 37, xxvi. 6, Saul had inquired of the Lord, but without effect (because the Lord had departed from him, xxviii. 15). It rests rather on the certainly correct and historical presupposition, that Saul had neglected to seek the favour of Jehovah with the proper zeal, and then inquire of Him. Comp. Starke: "he sought Jehovah not uprightly and in due order, and put not his trust in the Lord, in the order of true repentance;—he did not continue his inquiry of the Lord, when God refused him an answer on account of his sins, to the confession and entreaty for pardon of which he had not brought himself, but betook himself forthwith to the soothsayer."—*And He slew him* (in the battle, after Samuel's spirit had announced to him his doom, 1 Sam. xxviii. 19), *and turned the kingdom to David.* On ויסב, comp. xii. 23; 2 Sam. xiii. 12. On the significance of the present small section for the history of salvation, comp. the evangelical and ethical reflections on ch. x.-xxxix., No. 1.

b. David's Elevation to the Kingdom; Fixing of his Residence at Jerusalem; Wars and Numbering of the People.—Ch. xi.-xxi.

α. The Anointing of David in Hebron, and his Removal thence to Jerusalem: ch. xi. 1-9.

Ch. xi. 1. And all Israel gathered to David unto Hebron, saying, Behold, we are thy
2 bone and thy flesh. Also heretofore, even when Saul was king, thou wast he
that led Israel out and in; and the Lord thy God said unto thee, Thou shalt
3 feed my people Israel, and thou shalt be prince over my people Israel. And
all the elders of Israel came to the king to Hebron; and David made a covenant with them in Hebron before the Lord, and they anointed David over
Israel, according to the word of the Lord by Samuel.
4 And David went and all Israel to Jerusalem, that is, Jebus; and there

5 the Jebusites were the inhabitants of the land. And the inhabitants of Jebus
said to David, Thou shalt not come hither; and David took the castle of
6 Zion: this is the city of David. And David said, Whosoever smiteth the
Jebusites first shall be chief and captain; and Joab the son of Zeruiah went
7 up first, and became chief. And David dwelt in the castle; therefore they
8 called it the city of David. And he built the city around, from Millo to the
9 circuit; and Joab repaired the rest of the city. And David became greater
and greater; and Jehovah Zebaoth was with him.

β. List of David's Heroes: ch. xi. 10–47.

10 And these are the chiefs of the heroes of David, who held fast to him in
his kingdom, with all Israel, to make him king, by the word of the Lord con-
11 cerning Israel. And this is the number of the heroes of David: Jashobam
son of Hachmoni, the chief of the thirty;[1] he lifted his spear against three
12 hundred slain at one time. And after him Eleazar son of Dodo[2] the
13 Ahohite; he was among the three heroes. He was with David at Pas-dam-
mim, and the Philistines were gathered there for battle,[3] and there was a
plot of ground full of barley; and the people fled before the Philistines.
14 And they stood in the midst of the plot, and defended it, and smote the
Philistines; and the LORD granted them a great salvation.
15 And three of the thirty chiefs went down the rock to David, to the cave
of Adullam; and the camp of the Philistines was in the valley of Rephaim.
16 And David was then in the hold, and a post of the Philistines was then at
17 Bethlehem. And David longed, and said, Who will give me drink of the
18 water of the well of Bethlehem, that is at the gate? And the three brake
through the camp of the Philistines, and drew water out of the well of Beth-
lehem, at the gate, and took and brought it to David; but David would not
19 drink it, but poured it out to the LORD. And said, My God, forbid it me
that I should do this thing; shall I drink the blood of these men at the risk
of their lives? for at the risk of their lives they brought it: and he would not
drink it; these things did the three heroes.
20 And Abshai, Joab's brother, he was chief of the three; and he lifted up
his spear against three hundred slain, and had[4] a name among the three.
21 Above the three he was honoured among the two, and was their captain; but
22 he attained not to the three. Benaiah the son of Jehoiada, son of Ish-hail,
great in deeds, from Kabzeel; he smote two [sons] of Ariel of Moab, and he
23 went down and smote a lion in a pit in a snowy day. And he smote the
Egyptian, a man of stature,[5] of five cubits; and in the hand of the Egyptian
was a spear like a weaver's beam, and he went down to him with a staff, and
plucked the spear from the Egyptian's hand, and slew him with his own
24 spear. These things did Benaiah the son of Jehoiada, and had a name among
25 the three heroes. Before the thirty, behold, he was honoured; but he attained
not to the three; and David set him over his guard.
26 And the heroes of war were Asahel the brother of Joab, Elhanan the son
27, 28 of Dodo of Bethlehem. Shammoth the Harorite,[6] Helez the Pelonite. Ira
29 the son of Ikkesh the Tekoite, Abiezer the Antothite. Sibbechai the Husha-
30 thite, Ilai the Ahohite. Maharai the Netophathite, Heled the son of Baanah
31 the Netophathite. Ithai the son of Ribai of Gibeah, of the sons of Benjamin,
32 Benaiah the Pirathonite. Hurai of Nahale-gaash, Abiel the Arbathite.
33, 34 Azmaveth the Baharumite, Eliahba the Shaalbonite. The sons of Hashem
35 the Gizonite, Jonathan the son of Shageh the Hararite. Ahiam the son of
36 Sacar the Hararite, Eliphal the son of Ur. Hepher the Mecherathite, Ahijah
37, 38 the Pelonite. Hezro the Carmelite, Naarai the son of Ezbai. Joel the
39 brother of Nathan, Mibhar the son of Hagri. Zelek the Ammonite, Naharai
40 the Berothite, the armour-bearer of Joab the son of Zeruiah. Ira the Ithrite,
41, 42 Gareb the Ithrite. Uriah the Hittite, Zabad the son of Ahlai. Adina the
son of Shiza the Reubenite, a chief of the Reubenites, and thirty with him.[7]

43, 44 Hanan the son of Maachah, and Joshaphat the Mithnite. Uzziah the
45 Ashterathite, Shama and Jeiel the sons of Hothan the Aroerite. Jediael
46 the son of Shimri, and Joha his brother, the Tizite. Eliel the Mahavim,[8] and
47 Jeribai and Joshaviah the sons of Elnaam, and Ithmah the Moabite. Eliel,
and Obed, and Jasiel of Hammezobaiah.[9]

[1] For the *Keri* הַשָּׁלִישִׁים, the *Kethib* הַשְּׁלוֹשִׁים is to be retained; comp. vers. 15, 25, xii. 4, 18, xxvii. 6.

[2] For בֶּן־דּוֹדוֹ the Sept. seems to have read בֶּן־דֹּדַי; comp. xxvii. 4.

[3] For the not unimportant gap here, see Exeg. Expl.

[4] For וְלֹא is to be read וְלוֹ, one of the fifteen cases in which this form occurs in the Masoretic text, as Ex. xxi. 10, Isa. lxiii. 9, etc.

[5] For מִדָּה must apparently be read, with the Sept. (ἄνδρα ὅρατον), מַרְאֶה.

[6] Instead of הַהֲרוֹרִי read, 2 Sam. xxiii. 25, הַחֲרֹדִי, and, as there, supply אֱלִיקָא הַחֲרֹדִי. For the further conjectural corruption of the text till ver. 41, comp. Exeg. Expl.

[7] The Sept. and Vulg. appear to have read ועליו השלשים, like the Masoretic text, but the Syr. עַל השלשים; for it renders thus: "and even he (Adina) was a prince over thirty heroes."

[8] For הַמַּחֲוִים the Sept. gives ὁ Μαωί, the Vulg. *Mahumites*. The corruption of the name, under which, perhaps, הַמַּחֲנַיְמִי is concealed, seems indubitable.

[9] הַמְּצֹבָיָה is at all events corrupt. Sept. ὁ Μεσωβία, Vulg. *de Masobia*; comp. Exeg. Expl.

EXEGETICAL.

PRELIMINARY REMARK.—In the history of David, the author dwells chiefly on the bright and prosperous side of the Davidic kingdom; the troubles and disorders of his glorious career, occasioned by misfortune and his own guilt, he passes over as much as possible (comp. Introd. § 4, p. 11). Hence the mention of his anointing at Hebron, vers. 1–3, and yet the entire omission of the rival kingdom of Ishbosheth at Mahanaim, to which there is not even an indirect allusion in stating the seven years' duration of David's residence at Hebron. An account of the taking of Jerusalem, and the valour of Joab therein displayed, vers. 4–9, is then followed by a list of the other famous warriors of David, vers. 10–47, wherein again a shadow in the bright picture, the unprincipled and barbarous conduct of Joab (the murderer of Abner, Uriah, Absalom, etc.), is passed over in silence. And after this list, the appendix in ch. xii., containing the heroes devoted to David during the reign of Saul, and the proceedings in his elevation to the throne at Hebron, makes no reference to the rival kingdom of Ishbosheth, though many occasions of doing so were presented; so that it appears almost as if the statement in x. 6, that Saul and all his house together had fallen in the battle of Gilboa, were meant by the author to be literally true. But besides the conscious tendency to glorify as much as possible the kingdom of David, as the prototype of all theocratic excellence, his propensity to communicate long lists and mere enumerations, his statistical rather than historical mode of representation, also contributes more or less to the one-sidedness of his narrative. This method leads him to place the list of heroes, which in the books of Samuel (at least in its greater part; see 2 Sam. xxiii. 8–39) stands at the end of David's history, at the very head of it. Besides, not only this list, of which the closing verses only (41–47) are peculiar to Chronicles, but also the account of the anointing at Hebron, has its parallel in the books of Samuel, 2 Sam. v. 1–10. The agreement between the two is tolerably exact; comp. vers. 1–3 with 2 Sam. v. 1–3, and vers. 4–9 with 2 Sam. v. 6–10. Yet the note of the length of David's reign, 2 Sam. v. 4, 5, is wanting in our text, not from an oversight of the Chronist (Then.), but because he preferred to introduce it at the end of his report, xxix. 27.

1. *The Anointing of David at Hebron*: vers. 1–3.—*And all Israel gathered to David unto Hebron.* The phrase "all Israel" (comp. Ezra ii. 70) includes the northern and trans-jordanic tribes; it is therefore not the earlier anointing of David in Hebron by the tribes of Judah only, 2 Sam. ii. 4, which is here reported, but that which was performed after the deaths of Abner and Ishbosheth by all the tribes together, 2 Sam. v. 1 ff., to which there is a still fuller reference in xii. 23 ff.—*Behold, we are thy bone and thy flesh,* thy relatives by tribe and blood; comp. Gen. xxix. 14.—Ver. 2. *Also heretofore,* literally, "yesterday and ere yesterday," that is, a long time since; comp., besides 2 Sam. v. 2, also Gen. xxxi. 2; 2 Kings xiii. 5.—*That led Israel out and in,* out to the battle, and home after the victory; comp. 1 Sam. xviii. 13, 16.—*And the Lord thy God said unto thee,* by the mouth of Samuel the prophet; comp. 1 Sam. xvi. 1–3; 2 Sam. iii. 9, 18, etc.—Ver. 3. *And all the elders of Israel came,* as the representatives of the people, to establish the rights of the kingdom (1 Sam. viii. 11, x. 25) by contract (by making a covenant or elective treaty).—*According to the word of the Lord by Samuel.* These words, wanting in the corresponding place in 2 Sam. v. 3, appear to be an explanatory addition of our author; for it is not probable that they originally stood in the text of Samuel, and fell out by ὁμοιοτέλ. (שמואל—ישראל); comp. ver. 10 with 2 Sam. xxiii. 8 (against Then.). On the absence of the date here appended in the parallel text 2 Sam. v. 4 f. as intentional on the part of the writer, who reserves it for xxix. 27, comp. Preliminary Remark.

2. *The Taking of Zion, and the Change of Residence to Jerusalem*: vers. 4–9.—*To Jerusalem,* that is, *Jebus; and there the Jebusites were the inhabitants of the land.* For this circumlocution

2 Sam. v. 6 gives more briefly: "to Jerusalem, to the Jebusites, the inhabitants of the land." That the latter reading has been obtained by corruption of the text from the former (Berth., Then.) it is by no means needful to assume; the הִיא יְבוּס after יְרוּשָׁלַם seems rather to be an addition of the Chronist, serving as a transition from "Jerusalem" to the Jebusites, which then further necessitates the insertion of the notice: "and there the Jebusites were" (properly, the Jebusite was); comp. Wellh. p. 162 f.—Ver. 5. *And the inhabitants of Jebus said to David, Thou shalt not come hither.* Only the close of this threat, given in full in 2 Samuel, is here recorded, after the abbreviating manner of the author.—Ver. 6. *Whosoever smiteth the Jebusites first.* Only these first words of David's speech occur in 2 Sam. v. 8, where something quite different is given as spoken by him. "The highly peculiar account in 2 Sam. v. 8, clearly resting on strictly historical recollection, is obviously the more original and exact. It may well be conceived that in other accounts of the conquest of Jebus, the great captain of David, Joab (in like manner as Othniel, Judg. i. 12 ff., in the conquest of Kiriath-sepher), was mentioned; and a celebrated saying of David in the siege was referred to Joab, not from clear recollection, but from a conjecture which might rest on the account of Joab in ver. 8. Thus two different accounts of this saying might arise; the simpler, presenting apparently no difficulties, found its way into Chronicles." Such is Bertheau's view, at all events more probable than that of Then. on 2 Samuel, who makes the Chronist complete a critically corrupt text on the ground of tradition by conjecture.—*And Joab the son of Zeruiah* (comp. ii. 16) *went up first and became chief.* That this "becoming chief" is only a confirmation of Joab in his previous office is shown by 2 Sam. ii. 3.—Ver. 7. *And David dwelt in the castle.* מְצָד, the same as מְצוּדָה in ver. 5; comp. xii. 8, 16.—*Therefore they called it the city of David.* According to 2 Sam. v. 9, David himself gave it this name; but the one does not exclude the other.—Ver. 8. *And he built the city around, from Millo to the circuit,* beginning from Millo, and returning to it in a circuit. Somewhat different is 2 Sam. v. 9: "around from Millo and inward;" that is, from the circumference to the centre. For the fortress Millo, situated probably on the north-west corner of Zion, comp. Thenius and Bähr on 1 Kings ix. 11. The name מִלּוֹא signifies filling; that is, probably not wall or sconce, but a strong tower (bastion, castle); comp. בֵּית מִלּוֹא, 2 Kings. xii. 21 and 2 Chron. xxxii. 5.—*And Joab repaired the rest of the city,* properly, "quickened, made alive;" comp. חיה in the same sense, Neh. iii. 34, as the similar expression "heal," 1 Kings xviii. 30. On account of the supposed trace of ancient style contained in the use of חיה for בנה, "rebuild, Wellhausen, p. 164, declares this addition peculiar to the Chronist regarding Joab's co-operation in the building of Jerusalem, especially its fortification, to be not even historically credible. But that חיה in this sense occurs only here and in Nehemiah does not prove the lateness of this usage; and the circumstance that David's field-marshal took part in the fortification of the capital is so far from being improbable, that the statement seems a genuine trace of ancient history. Wherefore Kennicott's emendation, accepted by Thenius, is unnecessary: ויואב יהיה לְשַׂר העיר, "and Joab became governor of the city."—Ver. 9. *And David became greater and greater.* The construction with הָלַךְ is like that in Gen. viii. 3, 5, xii. 9, xxvi. 13, Judg. iv. 24; comp. Ew. § 280, *b*. On *b*, comp. ix. 20. The general remarks of the verse prepare very suitably for the following list of the numerous heroes of David.

3. *List of David's Heroes:* vers. 10–47; and first of Jashobam, Eleazar (and Shammah): vers. 10–14.—*And these are the chiefs of the heroes of David.* By these words, peculiar to the Chronist (the parallel text 2 Sam. xxiii. 8 opens the list merely with the clause: "and these are the names of the heroes of David"), the communication of the following list is justified, as standing in relation with David's elevation to the kingdom and confirmation in it. Hence the designation: "chiefs of the heroes," chief heroes, heroes of the first rank.—*Who held fast to him in his kingdom,* who stood bravely by him (in common with him) during his reign. הִתְחַזֵּק עִם, as in Dan. x. 21.—*To make him king.* Rightly Keil: "לְהַמְלִיכוֹ is not to be limited to the appointment to the kingdon, but includes also confirmation in it; for of the men named, heroic deeds are mentioned, which they performed in the wars which David as king waged with his foes, to maintain and extend his sway."—*By the word of the Lord concerning Israel.* Comp. on vers. 2 and 3; for the same word of God in and by Samuel is meant here also, as there.—Ver. 11. *And this is the number of the heroes of David.* In 2 Sam. xxiii. 8: "and these are the names of the heroes of David." The term מִסְפָּר instead of שְׁמוֹת is not surprising, especially after the plur. אֵלֶּה. If מִסְפָּר be the original, the expression must mean: "that these heroes at first formed a corps definite in number (the thirty)" (Keil). Moreover, Bertheau's conjecture, מִבְחַר for מספר ("and this is the choice, the *élite*, of the heroes"), deserves all attention.—*Jashobam son of Hachmoni, the chief of the thirty.* After the perhaps right reading here is to be corrected the corrupt ישב בשבת תחכמני, 2 Sam xxiii. 8. It remains doubtful, however, in this respect, that Jashobam in xxvii. 2 is called son of Zabdiel, not of Hachmoni, and that the MSS. of the Sept. differ surprisingly in the writing of the name, inasmuch as *cod. Alex.* presents 'Ισβαάμ (or 'Ισβοάμ, xxvii. 2), but *Vatic.*, the first time, xi. 11, 'Ιισαβαδά, the second time, xxvii. 2, 'Ισβοάζ. Hence Wellhausen (p. 212) might possibly be right in his conjecture, that the true name may have been "Ishbosheth the Hachmonite" (יִשְׁבֹּשֶׁת הַחַכְמוֹנִי), and that the ישבעם of our verse is corrupted from יִשְׁבַּעַל, the well-known by-form or rather primitive form of the name Ishbosheth. The "head of the thirty" (see

Crit. Note) is given as an epithet to Jashobam as leader of the thirty heroes of second rank who are set down by name in ver. 26 ff.—*He lifted his spear against three hundred slain at one time.* The same heroic deed is recorded, ver. 20, of Abshai; whence Thenius, Keil, and Wellh., starting from the supposition that Jashobam was a greater hero than Abshai, wish to correct our passage after 2 Sam. xxiii. 8, where the number of those slain at once by Jashobam is set down as 800 (otherwise Ew. *Gesch.* ii. p. 603, who defends the number 300 for both places; while Bertheau gives no decision).—Ver. 12. *And after him Eleazar son of Dodo the Ahohite.* הָאֲחוֹחִי is the correct reading, as appears from xxvii. 4, not בֶּן אֲחֹחִי, 2 Sam. xxiii. 9. Whether the name דּוֹדוֹ is to be changed, with the Sept. (as in ch. xxvii. 4), into דּוֹדַי appears less certain.—*He was among the three heroes,* among the three warriors of the first rank, Jashobam, Eleazar, and Shamma, of whom the name of the third has fallen out of the middle of ver. 13, as the parallel 2 Sam. xxiii. 11 shows. On the surprising but still grammatically admissible combination בִּשְׁלֹשָׁה הַגִּבֹּרִים instead of בִּשְׁלֹשֶׁת הַגִּ׳ (comp. v. 19), see Berth., who justly rejects as unnecessary the emendation of Thenius: בִּשְׁלִישֵׁי הַגִּבֹּרִים, "among the knights (Shalishim) of the heroes."—Ver. 13. *He was with David at Pas-dammim, and the Philistines.* These words refer still to Eleazar; see 2 Sam. xxiii. 9. Pas-dammim, or Ephes-dammim, 1 Sam. xvii. 1, is a place between Socho and Azekah, not otherwise known; in 2 Sam. xxiii. the name is wanting, from the great corruption of the text, which is otherwise fuller than our text here, as it describes more exactly the heroic deed of Eleazar. It is there said, vers. 9, 10, at the close of the sentence: "and the Philistines were gathered there for battle:" "and the men of Israel were gone away (to the mountain, fleeing before the Philistines); and he stood and smote the Philistines, until his hand was weary and clave unto the sword; and the Lord wrought a great victory that day; and the people returned after him only to spoil. And after him was Shammah the son of Age the Hararite; and the Philistines were gathered for battle," etc. This not inconsiderable gap in our text, by which that which follows in ver. 13*b* and ver. 14 seems to be a description of a heroic deed, not of Shammah, but of Eleazar, appears to have been occasioned by the eye of the transcriber wandering from בַּפְּלִשְׁתִּים נֶאֶסְפוּ שָׁם, 2 Sam. xxiii. 9, to וַיֵּאָסְפוּ פְלִשְׁתִּים, ver. 11.—*And there was a plot of ground full of barley.* For barley (שְׂעוֹרִים), in 2 Sam. xxiii. 11, the plot is said to be full of lentiles (עֲדָשִׁים); which is the original reading it is hard to decide, but it may be a mere slip of the pen (Movers, Wellh.).—*And they stood in the midst of the plot.* More correctly 2 Sam. xxiii.: "and he stood," namely, Shammah. The two following verbs also, "defended" and "smote," are to be changed into the sing., as, according to 2 Samuel, the one Shammah clearly achieved the successful defence of the plot. The three plurals have come into our text after the lines referring to Shammah had fallen out.

4. *Continuation.* The Three Heroes who fetched Water to David from Bethlehem: vers. 15–19 (comp. 2 Sam. xxiii. 13–17).—*And three of the thirty chiefs went down:* three other than those already named. The thirty chiefs or captains are those mentioned ver. 11 and given by name in ver. 26 ff.—*The rock to David, to the cave of Adullam.* This cave must have been either in the rock itself or in its immediate neighbourhood. On the rock itself, however, stood the hold (מְצוּדָה) mentioned ver. 16. The valley of Rephaim (valley of giants, κοιλὰς τῶν Γιγάντων; Joseph. *Antiq.* vii. 4. 1), mentioned as the camping ground of the Philistines, lies, according to Robinson, "between the present convent Mar-Elias and Jerusalem; is wide, bounded on the north by a small ridge of rock, that forms the margin of the valley of Hinnom, and sinks gradually to the south-west" (Winer, *Realwörterb.* ii. 322); comp. Josh. xv. 8, xviii. 16; 2 Sam. v. 18, 22.—Ver. 16. *And a post of the Philistines was then at Bethlehem,* which is therefore to be conceived as not far from Adullam and the valley of Rephaim.—Ver. 17. *Of the well of Bethlehem, at the gate.* On the dried-up cistern situated one-quarter hour north-east of Bethlehem, which tradition gives as the well of our passage, see Robinson, ii. 378, and Berth.—Ver. 18. *And the three brake through the camp of the Philistines,* namely, not through the main camp, but that of the post before Bethlehem.—*But poured it out to the Lord,* made a libation to God by pouring it on the ground; comp. 1 Sam. vii. 6.—Ver. 19. *My God forbid it me.* The same construction as in 1 Sam. xxiv. 7, xxvi. 11, 1 Kings xxi. 3, etc.—*Shall I drink the blood of these men at the risk of their lives,* literally, "in their souls;" comp. Gen. ix. 4; Lev. iii. 17, vii. 26, xvii. 10 ff., xix. 26 ff., especially xvii. 14. "As blood and soul are here made equal, the blood as the seat and bearer of the soul, the soul as moving in the blood, so David, according to our report of his words, makes the water which those heroes had brought at the price (or risk) of their souls equal to their souls, and the drinking of the water brought by them equal to the drinking of their souls, and the souls equal to the blood, in order to express his abhorrence of such drinking. So that we may express the meaning thus: Should I drink in the water the souls, that is, the blood, of these men; for they have fetched the water at the price of their souls?" (Keil). Moreover, בְּנַפְשׁוֹתָם appears to be put down twice only by an oversight; in the parallel 2 Sam. xxiii. 17 it stands only once, which is perhaps the original form of the text. That David pours the water out instead of drinking has its ground in this, that it was become blood in his eyes; for blood, if it cannot be put on the altar, must be "poured on the earth as water," Deut. xii. 16 (Berth.). With the Levitical prohibition of the use of blood, the saying of David has evidently nothing to do.

5. *Abshai and Benaiah:* vers. 20–25 (comp. 2 Sam. xxiii. 18–23).—*And Abshai, Joab's brother, he was chief of the three.* Abshai or Abishai (2 Samuel), one of the three sons of Zeruiah (ii. 16), is here designated as chief, and in the

following verse as captain, of the three, while it is said of him: "but he attained not to the three." This enigmatical saying has been explained in various ways: 1. So that two groups or classes of three are distinguished: those mentioned vers. 15–19, whose head or ruler Abshai may have been, and the three heroes, Jashobam, etc., mentioned before in vers. 11–14, to whom he was not so related (so in particular the ancients, and Starke). 2. So that it is sought to unite both, the being chief of the three and standing after them (in bravery), as possibly co-existent, though the same three, Jashobam, Eleazar, and Shammah, are still referred to; that is, Abshai has taken, along with Joab the field-marshal, the first place among David's captains; is therefore, as having a higher command, the chief and leader of the three heroes, while they excel him in personal bravery and famous deeds (Keil). 3. So that הַשְּׁלוֹשָׁה in vers. 20 and 21 is taken in two different senses, in that of the number three (so ver. 21), and in this of the abstract substantive, "body of thirty, Sheloshah-company" (so the three first times),—a sense that necessarily results from the comparison of ver. 21 with ver. 25, and of 2 Sam. xxiii. 19 with 2 Sam. xxiii. 23 (Berth.). We shall have the choice between these three modes, unless we prefer the three first times (ver. 20 and ver. 21*a*) to read the pl. הַשְּׁלוֹשִׁים for הַשְּׁלוֹשָׁה, as Wellhausen (supported by the numerous cases in which these like numbers are exchanged; see pp. 20, 81, 214 ff. of his work) declares to be necessary in the parallel 2 Sam. xxiii.—*And he lifted up his spear against three hundred slain;* comp. on ver. 11.—Ver. 21. *Above the three he was honoured among the two.* These enigmatical words in the present form can neither be explained, with the Vulg.: "Of the three of the second class" (*inter tres secundos*), nor, with the Sept.: "Of the three, above the two was he honoured" (ἀπὸ τῶν τριῶν ὑπὲρ τοὺς δύο ἔνδοξος). If the בַּשְּׁנַיִם is to be retained as genuine, it must be taken, with Ewald (*Lehrb.* § 269, *b*) and Keil, in the sense of "twofold, doubly," and so rendered: "above the three doubly honoured, he became their chief" (Keil). Or we may read, with Berth., הֲכִי for בַּשְּׁנַיִם, according to 2 Sam. xxiii. 19 (comp. 2 Sam. ix. 1; Gen. xxvii. 36, xxix. 15), and render: "Among the Sheloshah-company certainly he was honoured, and became their captain."—Ver. 22 ff. Benaiah's Heroic Deeds (comp. xviii. 17, xxvii. 6).—*Benaiah the son of Jehoiada, the son of Ishhail.* So, if we retain בֶּן before אִישׁ־חַיִל. There is much, however, for its erasure (Berth., Wellh., Kamph.), in which case the sense comes out: "Benaiah the son of Jehoiada, a valiant man of great deeds." For the home of this Benaiah, Kabzeel in the south of Judah, comp. Josh. xv. 21; Neh. xi. 25. —*He smote two* (sons) *of Ariel of Moab,* the king of Moab, who bore the epithet אֲרִיאֵל, "lion of God," as a title of honour. Before אריאל is to be inserted, with the Sept., בְּנֵי; comp. Then. and Wellh., 2 Sam. xxiii. 20.—*And he went down and smote a lion.* This feat of Benaiah, which happened on a snowy day, and therefore in winter, may have been performed during the great war of David with the Moabites, 2 Sam. viii. 2.—Ver. 23. *And he smote the Egyptian, a man of stature,* or probably, according to the Sept., "a man of repute." The following particulars of the successful combat of Benaiah with the giant nearly coincide with those of the conflict of David with Goliath, though the differences are not to be overlooked (there a Philistine, here an Egyptian; there a stature of six cubits and a span, here of five cubits; there the weapons are a staff and a sling, here only a staff; there the slaying of the fallen with his own sword, here with his own spear). If, with the Sept., in 2 Sam. xxiii. 21 be substituted for the weaver's beam a "bridge-beam" (ξύλον διαβάθρας), as an object of comparison to show the thickness of the spear, the difference of the two narratives would be still greater. But even without this, the similar feats are only so related as Shamgar's heroic deed to that of Samson (comp. Judg. iii. 31 with xv. 15), or as Jashobam's valiant deed (with the right reading 800 in ver. 11) to that of Abshai.—Vers. 24, 25. For "among the three heroes" and "above the thirty" Berth. would in both cases read "among the Sheloshah-company;" comp. on ver. 20.—*And David set him over his guard,* literally, "over his obedience," that is (*abstr. pro concr.*), over his obedient, his trusty men; comp., besides 2 Sam. xxiii. 23, also 1 Sam. xxii. 14; Isa. xi. 14. According to Bertheau's not improbable conjecture, by this guard of David is meant the corps of the Cerethi and Pelethi (see 2 Sam. viii. 18), from which, however, a second troop of guards, that of the 600 Gibborim (or Gittites, 2 Sam. xv. 18), 2 Sam. xvi. 6, xx. 7, etc., were no doubt different. Commander of the former was Benaiah, according to our passage and 2 Sam. viii. 18; over the 600 Gibborim, on the other hand, may have been placed the often named thirty, so that one of the thirty was leader to every twenty of the 600. This assumption of a difference of the Cerethi and Pelethi from the Gibborim is not certain; for as Benaiah, 2 Sam. viii. 28, appears as commander of the Cerethi and Pelethi, he is also, 1 Kings i. 10, connected with the Gibborim (Benaiah and the heroes).

6. *The Forty-eight Warriors:* and first the thirty-two enumerated in 2 Sam. xxiii.: vers. 26–41*a*. On the sixteen added by the Chronist, vers. 41*b*–47, see No. 7.—*And the heroes of war were,* or more precisely: "And heroes of war were;" for the phrase וְגִבּוֹרֵי הַחֲיָלִים without the article is a general superscription. The article before חֲיָלִים constitutes no real difference from גִּבּוֹרֵי חֲיָלִים, vii. 5, 7, 11, 40, or from גּ׳ חַיִל, vers. 2, 9, etc. [?] Here, as there, are meant: "heroes in action, valiant heroes," not "leaders of the divisions," as Berth. (appealing to 2 Kings xv. 20, 1 Chron. xii. 8, etc.) thinks.—*Asahel the brother of Joab.* For him, comp. ii. 16; for his murder by Abner, 2 Sam. ii. 19 ff. The parallel text 2 Sam. xxiii. 24 adds to his name בַּשְּׁלשִׁים, "among the thirty."—*Elhanan the son of Dodo,* different from Elhanan son of Jair, xx. 5.—Ver. 27 *Shammoth the Harorite.* In 2 Sam. xxiii. this hero is called "Shammah the Harodite," but in 1 Chron. xxvii. 8, "Shamhuth the Izrahite." In the *gentilic.* החרורי there ap-

pears at all events to be an error, which is to be corrected by הַחֲרֹדִי of Samuel; for in Judg. vii. 1 a Jewish place חֲרֹד is expressly mentioned. After the name of this Harodite Shammoth must have fallen out that of a second Harodite Elika (אֱלִיקָא), as 2 Sam. xxiii. 25 shows.—*Helez the Pelonite.* So xxvii. 10, whereas in 2 Sam. xxiii. 26 this Helez is originally designated as a Paltite (of Beth-pelet, בֵּית פֶּלֶט, Josh. xv. 27, Neh. xi. 26).—Ver. 28. *Ira and Abiezer;* comp. xxvii. 9, 12. —Ver. 29. *Sibbechai the Hushathite.* By the name סִבְּכַי the suspicious מְבֻנַּי of 2 Samuel must be corrected. Inversely, Ilai (עִילַי) must be amended after the צַלְמוֹן of Samuel.—Ver. 31. *Ithai the son of Ribai of Gibeah, of the sons of Benjamin.* For the situation of this Gibeah of Benjamin (near Ramah), comp. the expositor on Josh. xviii. 28 and on Judg. xiv. 19 ff.; for that of the following Pirathon (that occurs also, Judg. xii. 13–15, as the home of Abdon), *Zeitschr. der Deutschen morgenl. Gesellsch.* 1849, p. 55, and particularly Sandreczky in *Ausland*, 1872, No. 5, p. 97 ff.—Ver. 32. *Hurai* (so read also 2 Samuel for הִדַּי) *of Nahale-gaash.* This place, occurring only here (and 2 Sam. xxiii. 30), properly, "valleys of Gaash," is at all events to be sought near Mount Gaash in the Ephraimite range, not far from which was Joshua's grave; comp. Josh. xxiv. 30; Judg. ii. 9.—*Abiel the Arbathite*, of Beth-haarabah, Josh. xv. 6, 61, xviii. 18, 23. The name אֲבִיאֵל is in 2 Samuel אֲבִי־עַלְבוֹן, which form Berth. takes without ground to be original, while Wellh. rejects both forms, and makes the original to be אֲבִי־בַעַל.—Ver. 33. *Azmaveth the Baharumite*, that is, he of Bahurim (read הַבַּחֻרִימִי); comp. 2 Sam. xvi. 5, xix. 17.—The following *gentilic.* הַשַּׁעַלְבֹנִי is to be referred to שַׁעַלְבִים, Judg. i. 35, 1 Kings iv. 9 (or שַׁעֲלַבִּין, Josh. xix. 42), and so to be written הַשַּׁעַלְבִינִי.—Ver. 34. *The sons of Hashem the Gizonite.* בְּנֵי before הָשֵׁם appears to owe its origin to a repetition of the last three consonants of the foregoing *gentilic.* השעלבני; and thus originally there was only Hashem the Gizonite, after which 2 Samuel is to be amended: likewise in the following word the corrupt reading there is to be altered into our "Jonathan the son of Shageh the Hararite;" comp. Wellh. p. 216.—Ver. 35. *Eliphal the son of Ur.* 2 Sam. xxiii. 34: "Eliphelet the son of Ahasbai." The original was perhaps (comp. Then. and Berth. on the passage): "Eliphelet the son of Ur."—Ver. 36. *Hepher the Mecherathite;* perhaps the Maachathite (2 Samuel); as also "Ahijah the Pelonite" (comp. ver. 27) must perhaps be changed, as in 2 Samuel, into "Eliam, son of Ahithophel the Gilonite."—Ver. 37. *Naarai the son of Ezbai.* For נערי 2 Samuel has פערי; for בֶּן־אֶזְבָּי, הָאַרְבִּי, which is perhaps to be preferred on account of אֲרָב, Josh. xv. 52. —Ver. 38. *Joel the brother of Nathan.* If Nathan the prophet were meant, the אחי, "brother," by the side of the usual בֶּן־, would lose its strangeness. But in 2 Sam. xxiii. 36 we find a Nathan of Zobah. Hence אחי is perhaps to be changed into בן; and יִגְאָל might possibly be more original than our יואל.—*Mibhar the son of Hagri.* For these words 2 Sam. xxiii. 36 has "Bani the Gadite." מִבְחָר may have there fallen out; but it may also have been corrupted from מִצֹּבָה. In הגדי (if this, and not הגרי, is to be read) may possibly lie the name of the prophet Gad (Wellh.), so that here two relatives of prophets, a brother (son?) of Nathan and a son of Gad, may be named together.—Ver. 40. *Ira the Ithrite, Gareb the Ithrite.* The family of the Ithrites was enumerated, ii. 53, among those of Kiriath-jearim.—Ver. 41. *Uriah the Hittite*, the husband of Bathsheba, 2 Sam. xi. 3 ff. Here follows in 2 Sam. xxiii. 39 the closing subscription: "thirty and seven in all," as, according to the correct text, actually thirty-seven heroes are there enumerated, namely, twenty-nine others besides the eight mightiest heroes named in vers. 8-23 (Jashobam, Eleazar, Shammah, etc.). These twenty-nine should in the view of the author of the books of Samuel represent those thirty warriors (named in 2 Chron. xi. 25); whence he breaks off his enumeration after Uriah (or perhaps after Gareb, as Wellh. seeks to render probable), although most probably the same list, containing forty-eight names in all, lay before him, which our author has continued from this verse to the end. Moreover, for the criticism of both lists running parallel as far as our verse, the facts brought out by Wellh. (p. 215 f.) are to be considered:—1. "That the heroes are placed in pairs, and often every two from the same city (two Bethlehemites, ver. 26, two Netophathites, ver. 30, two Ithrites, ver. 40); 2. That the adjective of descent is always added, but not regularly the father's name, to the name of the hero; 3. That thorough corrections are only possible, if we have first collected the whole material of the proper names in the O. T. along with the variants in the Sept., and then elaborated them." The last rule applies also to the criticism of the following names preserved by the Chronist alone, which in this arrangement have no parallel.

7. *The last Sixteen of the Forty-eight Warriors*, whom the Chronist alone enumerates: vers. 41*b*-47.—Ver. 42. *Adina . . . a chief of the Reubenites, and thirty with him*, or besides him. So, according to the Masoretic reading, ועליו; but Berth. prefers that of the Syriac version (see Crit. Note), and so gets the sense: "leader of the Reubenites over thirty," that is, commander of the thirty captains or heroes of the Reubenites, to which may be compared the thirty leaders of the Benjamites, xxii. 4.—Ver. 44. *Uzziah the Ashterathite*, from Ashteroth (Karnaim) or Beth-Eshterah, a city of East Manasseh, vi. 56. Whether the "Aroerite" points to Aroer in the tribe of Reuben (Josh. xiii. 16), or in that of Gad (ver. 25), is doubtful.—Ver. 46. *Eliel the Mahavim.* We should probably read "the

Mahanaimite" (Josh. xiii. 26); comp. Crit. Note.—Ver. 47. *Eliel, and Obed, and Jasiel of Hammezobaiah.* The unmeaning הַמְּצֹבָיָה, that by its form cannot be a *gentilic.*, is either to be changed by omitting the article and the penult consonant into מִצֹּבָה, "from Zobah" (comp. 2 Sam. xxiii. 36) (so Bertheau), or to be regarded as corrupted from a longer name, such as מִגְדַּל צְבֻעִיא (a place, according to Rabbinic tradition, not far from Hebron), not, however, as a contraction or abbreviation of this name, as Reland (*Pal.* p. 899). Moreover, the Rabbinic Migdol Zebuiah could scarcely be contemplated, because almost all the sixteen names of our section, from ver. 41*b* on, belong to heroes from the east of Jordan. The Syrian Zobah would suit better in this connection.

γ. Supplementary List of Brave Men who held to David during the Reign of Saul: ch. xii. 1–22.

CH. XII. 1 And these are they that came to David to Ziklag, while banished from
Saul the son of Kish; and they were among the heroes, helpers of the war.
2 Armed with bows, using both right hand and left with stones and with
3 arrows on the bow:—Of the brethren of Saul of Benjamin. The chief Ahiezer
and Joash, sons of Hashmaah the Gibeathite; and Jezuel[1] and Pelet the
4 sons of Azmaveth; and Berachah, and Jehu the Antothite. And Ishmaiah
the Gibeonite, a hero among the thirty, and over the thirty;[2] and Jeremiah,
5 and Jahaziel, and Johanan, and Jozabad the Gederathite. Eluzai, and Jeri-
6 moth, and Bealiah, and Shemariah, and Shephatiah the Haruphite.[3] Elkanah,
7 and Ishiah, and Azarel, and Joezer, and Jashobam, the Korhites. And
Joelah and Zebadiah the sons of Jeroham of Gedor.[4]
8 And of the Gadites, separated themselves unto David at the hold in the
wilderness, valiant heroes, men of the host for battle, handling shield and
spear,[5] with faces like lions, and like roes on the mountains for swiftness.
9, 10 Ezer the chief, Obadiah the second, Eliab the third. Mishmannah the
11 12 fourth, Jeremiah the fifth. Attai the sixth, Eliel the seventh. Johanan
13 the eighth, Elzabad the ninth. Jeremiah the tenth, Machbannai the
14 eleventh. These were of the sons of Gad, heads of the host: one for a
15 hundred, the least, and the greatest for a thousand. These are they that
went over Jordan in the first month, when it had overflown all its banks;[6]
and they put to flight all the valleys to the east and to the west.
16 And there came of the sons of Benjamin and Judah to the hold unto David.
17 And David went out before them, and answered and said unto them, If ye
be come peaceably unto me to help me, my heart shall be at one with you;
but if to betray me to my enemies, with no wrong in my hands, the God of
18 our fathers look on and rebuke it. And the spirit came upon Amasai the
chief of the thirty,[7] Thine are we, David, and with thee, son of Jesse; peace,
peace be to thee, and peace to thy helpers; for thy God helpeth thee; and
David received them, and made them captains of the troop.
19 And of Manasseh some fell to David, when he came with the Philistines
against Saul to battle; but they helped him not: for on advisement, the
lords of the Philistines sent him away, saying, At the peril of our heads he
20 will fall to his master Saul. When he went to Ziklag, there fell to him of
Manasseh, Adnah, and Jozabad, and Jediael, and Michael, and Jozabad, and
21 Elihu, and Zillethai, captains of the thousands of Manasseh. And they
helped David against the troop; for they were all valiant heroes, and they
22 became captains in the host. For day by day they came to David to help
him, until the camp was great, like a camp of God.

δ. Supplementary Data concerning the Number of the Warriors who made David King in Hebron: vers. 23–40.

23 And these are the numbers of the heads of those armed for the host who
came to David to Hebron, to turn the kingdom of Saul to him, according to
24 the word of the LORD. The sons of Judah, bearing shield and spear, were
25 six thousand and eight hundred, armed for the host. Of the sons of Simeon,
26 valiant heroes for the host, seven thousand and one hundred. Of the sons of

27 Levi, four thousand and six hundred. And Jehoiada was the leader of the
28 Aaronites, and with him three thousand and seven hundred. And Zadok, a
29 valiant young man, and his father's house twenty and two captains. And of
the sons of Benjamin, brethren of Saul, three thousand; for hitherto the
30 most part of them kept the ward of the house of Saul. And of the sons of
Ephraim, twenty thousand and eight hundred valiant heroes, famous men of
31 their father-houses. And of the half-tribe of Manasseh, eighteen thousand,
32 who were expressed by name, to come to make David king. And of the sons
of Issachar, men having understanding of the times, to know what Israel had
to do, their heads were two hundred, and all their brethren were at their
33 command. Of Zebulun, those going to the host, ordering the battle with all
weapons of war, fifty thousand, arraying themselves[8] with a single heart.
34 And of Naphtali, a thousand captains, and with them, with shield and spear,
35 thirty and seven thousand. And of the Danites, ordering the battle, twenty
36 and eight thousand and six hundred. And of Asher, those going to the host
37 to order the battle, forty thousand. And beyond the Jordan, of the Reubenites, and the Gadites, and the half-tribe of Manasseh, with all weapons
of war for the battle, a hundred and twenty thousand.
38 All these men of war, keeping rank,[9] came with true heart to Hebron to
make David king over all Israel; and all the rest[10] of Israel also were of one
39 heart to make David king. And they were there with David three days eat-
40 ing and drinking; for their brethren had prepared for them. Moreover,
they that were nigh them, even to Issachar, and Zebulun, and Naphtali,
brought bread on asses, and on camels, and on mules, and on oxen, bread of
meal, fig and raisin cakes, and wine, and oil, and oxen, and sheep abundantly;
for there was joy in Israel.

[1] *Keri:* Jeziel (יְזִיאֵל).

[2] With וְעַל הַשְּׁלֹשִׁים the fourth verse closes in the MSS. and older editions, even that of R. Norzi, so that the whole chapter contains forty-one verses.

[3] *Keri:* "the Hariphite" (הַחֲרִיפִי); comp. בְּנֵי חָרִיף, Neh. vii. 24.

[4] For הַגְּדוּד is certainly to be read הַגְּדוֹר; comp. iv. 4.

[5] For וָרֹמַח the *Bibl. Venet. Rabb.* has וּמָגֵן: so some old prints, but not the MSS.

[6] The *Kethib* גְּדִיֹתָיו, if correct, would be the plur. of גְּדִיָּה, and occur only here. With the *Keri* גְּדוֹתָיו comp. Josh. iii. 15, iv. 18; Isa. viii. 8.

[7] *Kethib:* הַשְּׁלוֹשִׁים; *Keri*, as usual: הַשָּׁלִישִׁים. The Sept. and Vulg. agree with the *Kethib*.

[8] For וְלַעְדֹר nine MSS., the Sept. (βοηθῆσαι), and the Vulg. read וְלַעְזֹר.

[9] Three MSS. change עֹדְרֵי into עֹרְכֵי unnecessarily. See Exeg. Expl.

[10] שֵׁרִית, defective for שְׁאֵרִית, occurring only here; hence some MSS. have the *scr. plena*.

EXEGETICAL.

PRELIMINARY REMARK.—The whole of the twelfth chapter is peculiar to the Chronist. Standing after that which is related in xi. 4 ff., it has th nature of an appendix, in the form of several military lists referring to the force of David before and at his accession to the sole sovereignty. The first of these lists consists properly of three smaller ones—*a*. That of the Benjamites and Jews that came to David during his residence at Ziklag: vers. 1–7; *b*. That of the Gadites and some other men from Judah and Benjamin who passed over to him during his residence in the hold: vers. 8–18; *c*. That of the Manassites who joined themselves to David shortly before the battle with the Philistines, and the death of Saul at Gilboa: vers. 19–22. To these lists referring to the Sauline period is then subjoined that of the contingents from all the tribes present at the anointing in Hebron: vers. 23–40.

1. The Benjamites and Jews who came to Ziklag: vers. 1–7.—*And these are they that came to David to Ziklag.* Ziklag, belonging to the tribe of Simeon (iv. 30; Josh. xix. 5), assigned by Achish to David as a residence, was in a site not certainly determined. The sojourn of David there until his anointing at Hebron lasted (1 Sam. xxvii. 7) a year and four months.—*While banished from Saul* (עוד עצור), that is, while his return to Israel as king was still hindered by Saul: *inter Israelitas publice versari prohibitus* (J. H. Michaelis).—*And they were among the heroes, helpers of the wars.* They belonged to the heroes

who served and stood by him in his earlier wars; comp. vers. 17, 18, 21, 22.—Ver. 2. *Armed with bows*, or "aiming with the bow;" not really different from bending the bow (דֹּרְכֵי קֶשֶׁת), viii. 40; comp. 2 Chron. xvii. 17 and Ps. lxxviii. 9.—*Using both right and left with stones* (in slinging, Judg. xx. 16) *and with arrows on the bow*, namely, to shoot and surely hit with them.—*Of the brethren of Saul of Benjamin.* The second restriction serves to explain the first: אֲחֵי־שָׁאוּל do not mean near or blood relations. Comp. Gibeath-Saul, 1 Sam. xi. 4, Isa. xv. 29, and as denoting the same place, Gibeath-Benjamin, 1 Sam. x. 16, xv. 34, or Gibeah of the sons of Benjamin, 1 Chron. xi. 31.—Ver. 3. *Sons of Hashmaah the Gibeathite*, from the Gibeah of Benjamin just mentioned.—Ver. 4. *And Ishmaiah the Gibeonite.* That this Gibeonite (this Benjamite of Gibeon; comp. viii. 29, ix. 35, with 2 Sam. xxi. 2 ff.) Ishmaiah is described first as a hero among the thirty, and then as a leader over the thirty, may be explained by assuming a temporary command over this company. The absence of his name in ch. xi. must be explained by this, that he was no longer alive at the time when this list was composed, and was therefore among the earliest members of the corps of the thirty.—*And Jozabad the Gederathite;* perhaps from Gederah (now Ghedera, one hour south-west of Jabneh), a Jewish locality in the Shephelah, Josh. xv. 36. That Jozabad, though coming from Gederah, belonged to some family of Benjamites dwelling there, is an unnecessary assumption of Keil. The following verses, especially the Geder, ver. 7, rather show that those here enumerated were by no means exclusively Benjamite.—Ver. 6. *Elkanah . . . the Korhites.* To think of another Korah as the ancestor of the Korhites than the known descendant of Levi is unnecessary; these may be Korhitic Levites settled in Benjamin who are here in question; and the names Elkanah and Azarel having a genuine Levitical ring, make it very probable that they are such; comp. Keil on the p. and Del. *Psalter*, p. 300. Yet it is possible that they may be descendants of the Jewish Korah mentioned ii. 43 (so Berth., Kamph., etc.).—Ver. 7. *And Joelah . . . of Gedor*, without doubt the Jewish city mentioned iv. 4, south-west of Bethlehem; so that here also non-Benjamites are included in the series, notwithstanding the announcement, ver. 2, which leads us to expect only Benjamites. Whether this contradiction between the announcement and the contents of the list arises from the whole series of names being greatly abridged and composed out of two originally distinct lists, one of pure Benjamites, and another containing Jews, as Berth. thinks, appears doubtful; comp. Keil, p. 134.

2. The Gadites and some other Jews and Benjamites who joined themselves to David while in the Hold: vers. 8–18.—*a.* The Gadites: vers. 8–15.—*And of the Gadites* (that is, of those belonging to the tribe of Gad, while the others adhered to Saul) *separated themselves unto David at the hold in the wilderness.* This was during the first year of his flight before Saul, 1 Sam. xxii. ff.—לַמְצַד מִדְבָּרָה (so pointed for לַמְצַד מ׳, on account of the close connection of the two following words) denotes properly: "to the hold towards the wilderness." A definite single hold (מָצַד = מְצוּדָה; comp. xi. 16) is here as little intended as in ver. 16, but rather the greater number of those holds of the wilderness of Judah (comp. בַּמִּדְבָּר בַּמְּצָדוֹת, 1 Sam. xxiii. 14, xxiv. 1) in which David dwelt at that time; thus מצד is here general, as מְצוּדָה, 1 Sam. xxiv. 23.—*Men of the host for battle*, practised in war; comp. vii. 11. On the following "handling (עֹרְכֵי) shield and spear," comp. ver. 24 ("bearing shield and spear") and Jer. xlvi. 3; for the comparison of the warriors with lions and roes, 2 Sam. i. 23, ii. 18. "The expressions in the description of their power and fleetness, ver. 8, remind us of such as are used in the historical books of heroes in the time of David, and are without doubt drawn from the source which our author here used" (Berth.).—Ver. 13. *Machbannai the eleventh*, literally, the eleven; comp. xxiv. 12.—Ver. 14. *Heads of the host* (so ver. 21*b*), that is, chief warriors, not leaders.—*One for a hundred the least, and the greatest for a thousand.* The smallest of them was equal to one hundred other warriors, and the strongest to a thousand,—an expression of manifestly poetical colouring, reminding us of Lev. xxvi. 8 and of 1 Sam. xviii. 7, xxi. 11, which our author certainly found in his source. The Sept. and the most of the older Rabbis rightly understood the passage, but the Vulg. wrongly: *novissimus centum militibus præerat et maximus mille*, for which עַל instead of לְ, and another order of words, should be expected.—Ver. 15. *These are they that went over Jordan*, at the time when they separated themselves from the other Gadites of the host of Saul, and were forced to break through this to reach David. Their flight fell "in the first month," that is, in the spring, when the Jordan was greatly swollen, and had overflown its bank. So much greater was the heroic deed.—*And put to flight all the valleys to the east and to the west*, on both sides of the river, just as if its overflowing waters were not present. עמקים, properly "valleys," here inhabitants of the valleys, Hitzig (*Gesch. Isr.* p. 29) conceives to be the name of a people, that occurs also Jer. xlix. 4 (comp. xlvii. 5), and is identical with the Anakim, Josh. xv. 14, and with the Amorites—with the latter really, with the former even in name (?). See, on the contrary, Keil on *Jer.* p. 480.—*b.* The men of Benjamin and Judah: vers. 16–18.—*And there came of the sons of Benjamin and Judah.* The names of these other followers of David when persecuted by Saul the Chronist does not give, either because his source did not contain them, or because they may have been included for the most part in the lists already communicated in ch. xi. Amasai only, the leader of this troop, is named.—Ver. 17. *And David went out before them*, or to meet them; comp. xiv. 8.—*My heart shall be at one with you.* לֵב לְיָחַד, a phrase occurring only here, not essentially different from לֵב אֶחָד, ver. 38 (comp. ver. 33).—*But if to betray me to my enemies.* רִמָּה, with accus. of the object, means, "to practise fraud on any one." For the following, compare, on the one hand, Job xvi. 17, Isa. liii. 9; on the other

hand, 2 Chron. xxiv. 22. For the phrase: "the God of our fathers," namely, of the patriarchs Abraham, etc., comp. Ex. iii. 13; Ezra vii. 27; 2 Chron. xx. 6; Matt. xxii. 32.—Ver. 18. *And* (the) *Spirit came upon Amasai the chief of thirty.* Here, as in the parallel Judg. vi. 34, the Spirit of God is meant (comp. 2 Chron. xxiv. 20), as the principle of higher inspiration to great and bold deeds. The Amasai of our passage is perhaps not different from Amasa (with א instead of י at the end) the son of Abigail, sister of David, ii. 17, who, at a later period, in the time of Absalom, performed a not unimportant part as commander (first under Absalom, and then under David), till Joab murdered him (2 Sam. xvii. 25, xix. 14, xx. 4 ff.). Much less probable is the identity assumed by others of this Amasai with Abshai the brother of Joab (ii. 16, xi. 20).—*Thine are we, David,* to thee we belong, *and with thee,* we hold. Notwithstanding this simple and obvious completion, the Sept. has wholly misunderstood the words לך דויד ועמך, and made of them πορεύου καὶ ὁ λαός σου.—*For thy God helpeth thee.* This עֲזָרְךָ refers to the past aid which David had received from God (1 Sam. xviii. 12 ff.), but also to the further aid in prospect, which was to be imparted to him in future.—*And made them captains of the troop,* appointed them leaders of the several divisions of his army,—that army (גְּדוּד) of all kinds of people that had gathered about him; comp. 1 Sam. xxii. 2, xxvii. 8, etc.

3. The Seven Manassites who joined themselves to David before the Last Battle of Saul with the Philistines: vers. 19-22.—*And of Manasseh some fell to David.* נָפַל עַל, as in 2 Kings xxv. 11; 1 Sam. xxix. 3; comp. נָפַל אֶל at the close of the verse. For the historical situation, comp. 1 Sam. xxix. 2-11.—*For on advisement,* בעצה, on consultation, as Prov. xx. 18.—*At the peril of our heads,* literally, "for our heads, for the price of them;" comp. 1 Sam. xxix. 4.—Ver. 20. *When he went to Ziklag,* and thus before the great battle of Gilboa in which Saul fell; comp. 1 Sam. xxix. 11.—*Captains of the thousands of Manasseh,* of the great military divisions (regiments) into which the tribe of Manasseh was divided; comp. Num. xxxi. 14, 26, xxvii. 1, and ch. xv. 25.—Ver. 21. *And they helped David against the troop,* namely, his present foes, the Amalekites; comp. 1 Sam. xxx. 8, 15, where the גְּדוּד here used (for which the Sept. perversely read a *n. pr.* Γεδδούρ) appears more definitely as the army of the Amalekites. Moreover, the seven here named Manassites only are the immediate and direct subject of the sentence, not all the heroes named from ver. 1 to ver. 20 (as Berth. thinks), though certainly the whole force of David (600 strong, 1 Sam. xxx. 9) was drawn out to fight with Amalek. But that by וְהֵמָּה only the seven Manassites can here be meant is shown by the following words: "and they became captains in the host," which cannot apply to the whole troop.—Ver. 22. *Until the camp was great, like a camp of God;* comp. Gen. xxxii. 2 and phrases like mountains, cedars of God, Ps. xxxvi. 7 lxxx. 11. The phrase is "only rhetorical, not idealizing or exaggerating" (Keil); it extends also clearly beyond the time when David had only 600 followers to the time when thousands, and then hundreds of thousands, followed him. The following description seizes the moment when out of the thousands of the first seven years of his reign at Hebron came the hundred thousands and more.

4. The Number of the Warriors who made David King over all Israel: vers. 23-40.—*And these are the numbers of the heads of those armed for the host,* or for military service (comp. Num. xxxi. 5; Josh. iv. 13). The "heads of those armed" are here not the captains or leaders (Vulg. *principes exercitus,* Berth., etc.), but the sums or masses of the warriors, as Judg. vii. 16, 20, ix. 34, 37, 44, 1 Sam. xi. 11, or perhaps also the polls (Judg. v. 30); so that מִסְפַּר רָאשֵׁי would be the number of polls. For it cannot be proved (against Berth.) that only גֻּלְגֹּלֶת, and not also ראש, can have this sense; and the following is not a list of leaders, but a poll list, that also originally bore this form, though the abbreviating changes of our author make it difficult to prove. —*To turn the kingdom of Saul to him;* comp. x. 14, and for the following, xi. 3, 10.—Ver. 24. *The sons of Judah, bearing shield and spear;* comp. on ver. 8. The enumeration begins with the two southern tribes, Judah and Simeon; next gives the priestly tribe of Levi, whose chief force lay at that time in and about Judah; and then, proceeding from south to north, names first the other western tribes, and then the three eastern ones.—Ver. 26. *And Jehoiada was the leader of the Aaronites,* literally, "the leader of Aaron," that is, not the high priest (who was at that time Abiathar, 1 Sam. xxiii. 9), but the head of the family of Aaron. Perhaps this was Jehoiada the father of Benaiah, xi. 22.—Ver. 28. *And Zadok, a valiant young man,* perhaps that descendant of Eleazar (v. 34) whom Solomon, 1 Kings ii. 26, made high priest. That the house of this Zadok, at the time of David's elevation, counted twenty-two chiefs or heads of families, proves how flourishing this branch of the Aaronites was at that time. —Ver. 29. *And of the sons of Benjamin, brethren of Saul, three thousand.* This number is indeed surprisingly small, but certainly original. The writer accounts for it also, first briefly, by the characteristic addition אֲחֵי שָׁאוּל, then more fully by the remark, "for hitherto (וְעַד הֵנָּה, as ix. 18) the most part of them kept the ward of Saul's house;" that is, the most of them were still devoted to the interest of the kindred house of Saul (שֹׁמֵר מִשְׁמֶרֶת, as Num. iii. 38; comp. 1 Chron. xxiii. 32; 2 Chron. xxiii. 6), so that they turned to David only slowly, and when Ishbosheth was dead.—Ver. 30. *Famous men of their father-houses,* arranged according to their father-houses. The Ephraimites, on the whole, though their number was above 20,000, are called celebrated, famous men (comp. Gen. vi. 4), perhaps because they were distinguished by their warlike bravery, and had not merely a few able heroes or leaders.—Ver. 31. *And of the half-tribe of Manasseh,* the western half. The "being expressed by name" (נִקְּבוּ בְּשֵׁמוֹת, as Num. i. 17;

1 Chron. xvi. 41) points to the formation of a list by the tribe authorities, in which all those warriors of the tribe were entered who were chosen to take part in the elevation of the new king at Hebron. All the other tribes may have formed similar lists for this purpose.—Ver. 32. *And of the sons of Issachar, men having understanding of the times, to know what Israel had to do.* This applies, not to the whole tribe, but only to the 200 heads of their forces; and it denotes, not every kind of activity in astronomical or physical science (Chald., several Rabbis, Cleric.), but only that those leaders "saw what was most advisable to be done in the condition of the times" (Starke), that they were *prudentes viri, qui quid, quando et quomodo agendum esset, varia lectione* (?) *et usu rerum cognoscebant* (L. Lavater). "Men understanding," literally, knowing judgment, יֹודְעֵי בִינָה; comp. 2 Chron. ii. 12 and the similar יֹודְעֵי דַעַת, Dan. i. 4. "To know what Israel had to do," in the present case, means to whom it had to apply as its king and supreme ruler. These men of Issachar were not dull and narrow "bony asses" (Gen. xlix. 14), but prudent "judges of the signs of their time" (Matt. xvi. 3).—*And all their brethren were at their command.* עַל פִּיהֶם, literally, "by their mouth," namely, guided; comp. Gen. xli. 40; Num. iv. 27; Deut. xxi. 5.—Ver. 33. *Ordering the battle with all weapons of war*, practised in the conflict with all kinds of weapons; comp. ver. 6.—*Arraying themselves with a single heart*, literally, "and to band together with not heart and heart." For וְלַעֲדֹר, with some critical evidence (see Crit. Note), to read וְלַעְזֹר is unnecessary and untenable, from the recurrence of עדר in ver. 38. From this parallel passage, this verb must mean, "to take rank for war, to stand in order of battle." For לֵב וָלֵב, to denote double-mindedness or a divided heart, comp. Ps. xii. 3 and ver. 38; לֵבָב שָׁלֵם and לֵב אֶחָד.—Ver. 38. *All these men of war, keeping rank;* Sept. παρατασσόμενοι παράταξιν. The change of עֹדְרֵי into עֹרְכֵי (see Crit. Note) is unnecessary, and as little demanded by עָרַךְ in vers. 33, 35, 36 as by מַעֲרָכָה; comp. on ver. 33. "All these" points naturally to the whole troops enumerated from ver. 24 on.—*And all the rest of Israel*, etc. On לב אחד, "one, united heart," comp 2 Chron. xxx. 12.—Ver. 39. *And they were there with David three days, eating and drinking.* Comp. the festivals described 1 Sam. xxx. 16, 1 Kings i. 25, 40, etc., and also from the most recent oriental history; for example, the enormous feast (100,000 sheep and wethers, 20,000 oxen, 40,000 gallons honey-wine, etc.) that was given in connection with the elevation of Kassai to be emperor (negus) of Abyssinia (Feb. 1872).—*For their brethren had prepared for them* (victuals), namely, the Jews about Hebron. Comp. on this הֵכִין, Gen. xliii. 16; 2 Chron. xxxv. 14, etc.—Ver. 40. *Moreover, they that were nigh them* (comp. Deut. xiii. 8), all the neighbouring tribes of Judah on this side the Jordan; and not merely those immediately adjacent, but also the tribes in the middle, and some of those in the north of Palestine.—*Brought bread* (victuals) *on asses, and camels, and mules*, etc. Observe the purely epical character of the representation, that points to a very ancient historical source used by the Chronist.—*Fig and raisin cakes.* For the masses of dried figs (דְּבֵלִים) and raisins (צִמֻּקִים), as indispensable dainty additions to feasts, comp. 1 Sam. xxv. 18, xxx. 12; Jer. xl. 10, 12; Amos viii. 1 f.; also Celsius, *Hierobot.* i. 377 ff.; Winer, *Realw.*, Art. "Feigenbaum."

Apologetic on Ch. xii. 23 ff.

With respect to the credibility of the numbers of our section, it is to be remarked in general, that the sum total of about 340,000 men,[1] resulting from the data relative to the military contingents of the several tribes, agrees, on the whole, with other known data concerning the sum of the people of Israel equipped for war (for example, the 600,000 men in the time of Moses, the 800,000 Israelites and 500,000 Jews in the census of David), as, indeed, a full call of all those fit to bear arms could not be expected on the present occasion. On the contrary, the relation of the numbers in the several tribes presents much that is surprising. The strength of the three eastern tribes (120,000), exceeding a third of the sum total, and the likewise considerable strength of Zebulun (50,000), Naphtali (37,000), and Asher (40,000), seem to contrast in a manner scarcely conceivable with the small contingents of Judah, Simeon, Levi, and Benjamin. But—1. With regard to Benjamin, the ground of his only small share in the festivities at Hebron is expressly stated, and in a way entirely satisfactory, and admitting of no further objection. 2. The number of the Levites is, in vers. 27, 28, not fully given, inasmuch as of the third division of them, the house of Zadok, only the number of the chiefs (22) and not that of the common order is stated (as in Issachar only the

[1] Namely,

from Judah,	6,800 men.	
" Simeon,	7,100 "	
" Levi,	4,600 "	
Also with Jehoiada,	3,700 "	(with 22 chiefs of the house of Zadok).
From Benjamin,	3,000 "	
" Ephraim,	20,800 "	
" Half-Manasseh,	18,000 "	
" Issachar,	? "	(200 chiefs "and all their brethren").
" Zebulun,	50,000 "	
" Naphtali,	37,000 "	(with 1000 chiefs).
" Dan,	28,000 "	
" Asher,	40,000 "	
From the three eastern Tribes,	120,000 "	
Sum,	339,000 men	(with 1222 chiefs and heads).

number of the chiefs or heads is expressed, ver. 32). 3. Of Judah and Simeon are certainly only comparatively very small numbers given, for this reason, that the warriors of this tribe had long since, seven years before, ranged themselves on the side of David, and therefore, in the review on the occasion of the solemnities of his anointing, did not need to be represented in their full military strength (which would have reached in itself to between 100,000 and 200,000 men). These warriors of Judah and Simeon had rather to act as commissaries, to make provision for the greater bodies of troops; and most of them were to be sought, not among the רָאשֵׁי הֶחָלוּץ לַצָּבָה (vers. 24, 25 ff.), but among the אֲחֵיהֶם הַמְּכִינִים. 4. Yet highly surprising is the numerical relation of the middle and northern tribes west of the Jordan, namely, the smallness of Ephraim (20,800) beside Zebulun and Naphtali. "But if we consider that Ephraim, which had 40,500 men at the first census under Moses at Mount Sinai, had diminished to 32,500 at the second on the steppes of Moab, this tribe may not at this time have been very strong in men-at-arms, as it may have suffered and been weakened most of all the tribes in the last wars of Saul with the Philistines, and in the battles of Abner for the recovery of the region occupied by the Philistines for Ishbosheth. Moreover, perhaps Ephraim, in his jealousy of Judah, dating from the time of the Judges, might not be altogether inclined to make David king over all Israel. That, however, Zebulun and Naphtali are here so numerously represented, though they played no important part in the history of Israel, is not enough to cast suspicion on the numbers given. As Zebulun under Moses numbered 57,400, and afterwards 60,500, and Naphtali then 53,400, afterwards 45,400 men-at-arms (comp. Num. i.–iii. with Num. xxvi.), the former might send 50,000, the latter 37,000, men to David at Hebron" (Keil). The subsequent smallness and insignificance of these tribes (comp Evangelical-Ethical Reflections on ch. i.–ix., No. 2, p. 92) is simply explained by their only imperfect restoration after the destruction of the kingdom of Israel by Shalmaneser.—The credibility of the data of our list cannot in general be doubted according to all this, that is, irrespective of particular corruptions of the text that are always to be admitted as possible. It would much more present matter for well-founded doubts if the numerical strength of the several tribes attested in it were exactly proportional to the data of Numbers regarding the early relations of the military divisions. The appearance of something surprising in the present numerical data speaks directly for their true historical origin, and imposes the greatest caution on the modern critic of the contents of our chapter, that exhibit so many traces of fresh originality and high antiquity. This also may perhaps be urged as a proof of the essentially unchanged transmission of the present documents from the author, that the tribe of Dan, which is elsewhere often omitted, as it seems intentionally, by the Chronist, is here expressly mentioned, and in no disparaging way; comp. ver. 35 with Introd. § 6, No. 1, p. 24, and with the remarks on vi. 46 and vii. 12.

ε. *The Removal of the Ark from Kiriath-jearim:* ch. xiii.

CH. XIII. 1. And David consulted with the captains of thousands and of hundreds,
2 with every leader. And David said unto all the congregation of Israel, If it
seem good to you, and it be of the LORD our God, let us send quickly unto our
brethren remaining in all lands of Israel, and with them the priests and Levites
3 in the cities of their suburbs, that they gather unto us. And let us bring again
4 the ark of our God to us; for we inquired not at it in the days of Saul. And
all the congregation said, We must do so; for the thing was right in the eyes of
5 all the people. And David gathered all Israel, from Shihor of Egypt even unto
Hamath, to bring the ark of God from Kiriath-jearim.
6 And David went up, and all Israel, to Baalah, unto Kiriath-jearim, which belonged to Judah, to bring up thence the ark of God the LORD, that sitteth over
7 the cherubim, as He is called by name. And they carried the ark of God on a
new waggon from the house of Abinadab; and Uzza and Ahio drove the
8 waggon. And David and all Israel played before God with all their might, and
with songs and with harps, and with psalteries, and with timbrels, and cymbals,
and trumpets.
9 And they came to the threshing-floor of Chidon; and Uzza put forth his
10 hand to hold the ark; for the oxen shook it. And the anger of the LORD was
kindled against Uzza, and He smote him, because he put his hand to the ark; and
11 he died there before the Lord. And David was angry, because the LORD had
12 made a breach upon Uzza; and that place is called Perez-uzza to this day. And
David was afraid of God that day, saying, How shall I bring the ark of God to
13 me? And David removed not the ark to him to the city of David, but placed
14 it in the house of Obed-edom the Gittite. And the ark of God remained in the
house of Obed-edom in his house three months; and the LORD blessed the house
of Obed-edom, and all that he had.

EXEGETICAL.

Preliminary Remark.—In the second book of Samuel, where ch. vi. 1-11 corresponds to the present section, the history of the transference of the ark from Kiriath-jearim to the house of Obed-edom (which is there related, irrespective of the somewhat shorter introduction, almost word for word as here; comp. 2 Sam. vi. 2-11 with vers. 6-14 of our chapter) is immediately followed by the account of the removal three months later of the ark from that house to Zion. Our author, on the contrary, inserted (ch. xiv.) an account of David's house-building, his family, and his victory over the Philistines, which in 2 Sam. v. 11-25 follows the narrative of the taking of Zion, between the history of the removal of the ark to the house of Obed-edom and its introduction into Zion, and, moreover, on the ground of an old Levitical document, has treated this latter part of the history with vastly greater detail and fulness (see ch. xv. and xvi.). The more circumstantial introduction of our chapter, vers. 1-5, to which there is only one verse parallel in 2 Sam. vi., may spring from the same source as the following full detail in ch. xv., xvi.

1. Description of the Assembly in which the Removal of the Ark from Kiriath-jearim was resolved upon: vers. 1-5.—*And David consulted* (comp. 2 Chron. x. 6, xxx. 2) *with the captains of thousands and of hundreds* (comp. xv. 25), *with every leader.* לְ before לְכָל־נָגִיד serves here for the brief recapitulation of the fore-mentioned, thus, "in short, namely;" comp. Gen. xxiii. 10. —Ver. 2. *And David said unto all the congregation of Israel,* that is, to those princes as the representatives of the community (to the *ecclesia repræsentativa*); comp. קהל in Lev. xiv. 3; Deut. xxxi. 30, etc.—*If it seem good to you,* properly, "if it be good with you;" comp. Neh. ii. 5, 7; Esth. i. 19, iii. 19. For the following: "and it be of the Lord our God," comp. Gen. xxiv. 50; Acts v. 39.—*Let us send quickly,* properly, "let us break through (פרץ) and send," that is, with all diligence, and instant suppressing of all hesitation; comp. 1 Sam. xxviii. 23. Less certain is the interpretation, flowing from the notion of spreading out (so פרץ, for example, Isa. liv. 3): "send far and wide."—*Unto our brethren remaining in all lands of Israel,* in all lands of the several tribes; comp. כָּל־אֲרָצוֹת in Gen. xxvi. 3, 4; 2 Chron. xi. 23, xxxiv. 33. The preposition עַל before אַחֵינוּ, because in the sending is implied at the same time the commanding (comp. צִוָּה עַל). After עִמָּהֶם ("with them," that is, here, "likewise, besides"), this עַל, or even נִשְׁלְחָה עַל, is to be repeated.—Ver. 4. *We must do so,* literally, "to do so;" לַעֲשׂוֹת כֵּן, the infin. with לְ, as in v. 1, ix. 25.—Ver. 5. *All Israel, from Shihor of Egypt even unto Hamath,* that is, not all the individuals, but a large representation of the whole people (according to 2 Sam. vi. 1, a select number of 30,000). "From Shihor of Egypt even unto Hamath" means essentially the same as "from Dan to Beersheba," namely, Palestine from the south to the north border; comp. Judg. xx. 1; 2 Sam. iii. 10, xvii. 11. שִׁיחוֹר מִצְרַיִם is abbreviated for שִׁיחוֹר אֲשֶׁר עַל־פְּנֵי מִצְרַיִם, Josh. xiii. 3. It means the small stream between Palestine and Egypt, which is otherwise called the river of Egypt (נחל מצ', Josh. xiii. 4, 47; 1 Kings viii. 65; 2 Chron. vii. 8, etc.), the Rhinokorura of old, and the Wady el Arish of the present. The Nile certainly bears the name שִׁחֹר, that is, "black water" (Isa. xxiii. 3; Jer. ii. 18); yet smaller waters are also so named, as Josh. xix. 26, the Shihor Libnath, in the tribe of Asher, which, however, casts no doubt on our interpretation. On לְבוֹא חֲמָת, to denote the northern border of Palestine, comp. Num. xxxiv. 5, 8; 2 Kings xiv. 25. Hamath, on the river Orontes, on the southern slope of Antilibanus or Hermon, an old Canaanitish colony (Gen. x. 8), which the prophet Amos (vi. 2), in the 9th century B.C., designated "the great" (חֲמַת רַבָּה), and which still, in the Seleucidic and Roman times, when it was called Ἐπιφάνεια, belonged to the most considerable Syrian cities, was in David's time the seat of a king friendly to David, but independent of him, and tolerably powerful; see xviii. 9 f.; 2 Sam. viii. 9 ff.

2. The Execution of this Resolve: vers. 6-14. —*And David went up, and all Israel.* By "all Israel" is undoubtedly to be understood here, as well as in the foregoing verse, that assembly of select representatives of the people from every tribe, which amounted, 1 Sam. vi. 1, to 30,000 men. Neither the assumption that here, in the fetching of the ark, the participation of a much greater number is presupposed than in that preparatory assembly, nor the hypothesis that 2 Sam. vi. 1 originally conveyed the sense: "And David multiplied all the men of war in Israel, the Sheloshim and the captains of thousands" (instead of 30,000), is necessary (against Berth.), as the indefinite "all Israel" would suit even a smaller number of representatives than 30,000.—*To Baalah, unto Kiriath-jearim.* For בַּעֲלָתָה אֶל קִרְיַת י' might be expected, from Josh. xv. 9, perhaps בַּעֲלָתָה הִיא ק' י'; for Baalah is the older Canaanitish name for Kiriath-jearim, which is also called Kiriath-baal (Josh. xv. 60, xviii. 14). Yet the thing is expressed intelligibly enough; the "to Baalah" is sufficiently explained by the addition, "unto Kiriath-jearim." For the addition, "which belonged to Judah," comp. on Judg. xviii. 12, and for the situation of Kiriath-jearim, the present Kureyet el Enab, on the way from Jerusalem to Ramleh and Lydda (three hours from Jerusalem), comp. Rob. *Pal.* ii. 589.—*That sitteth over the cherubim, as He is called by name.* אֲשֶׁר, here ὡς, "as" (comp. Ew *Lehrb.* § 333, *a*); the acc. of reference שֵׁם belongs not merely to יהוה, but to יהוה ישב הכרובים, and designates the whole phrase as a usual epithet of God in religious worship; comp. Isa. xxxvii. 16; Ps. lxxx. 2. Others would refer אֲשֶׁר to אֲרוֹן, and

change שֵׁם into בְּשֵׁם (Kamph.: "which is called by the name"), or even change שֵׁם into שָׁם (with reference to 2 Sam. vi. 2, where also שָׁם is once to be read), and so get the sense: "who was there, at the ark, addressed" (Berth.; comp. Then. on 2 Sam. vi.). See, on the contrary, and in favour of our interp., Keil, p. 144.—Ver. 7. *And they carried . . . from the house of Abinadab.* This house lay on a hill in Kiriath-jearim (בַּגִּבְעָה, 1 Sam. vii. 1), not in a place Gibeah, near Kiriath-jearim, as the passage 1 Sam. vii. 1 seems to say in the faulty translation of the Vulg. and Luther (comp. C. Hoffmann, *Blicke in die früh. Gesch. d. gelobten Landes*, i. p. 156). Uzza and Ahio, the drivers of the waggon with the ark, are, 2 Sam. vi., expressly called the sons of Abinadab.—Ver. 8. *With all their might, and with songs, and with harps*, etc. The parallel: "with all woods of cypresses," in 2 Sam. vi. 5, rests on a corruption of the text, and is, as ἐν ἰσχύϊ of the Sept. there shows, to be amended by our passage (בְּכָל־עֹז); comp. 2 Sam. vi. 14. For the instruments here named, particularly the harps, psalteries, and cymbals, see on xv. 16.—*Cymbals and trumpets.* The words presented instead of במצלתים ובחצצרות in 2 Sam. vi. 5: וּבִמְנַעַנְעִים וּבְצֶלְצְלִים, "and with rattles and with cymbals," are perhaps more original; at least the מנענעים (Vulg. *sistra*), occurring nowhere else, might easily have been suppressed by the alleviating correction of a later hand (comp. Wellh. p. 167 f.).

3. Uzza's Fall, and the Placing of the Ark in the House of Obed-edom: vers. 9–14.—*And they came to the threshing-floor of Chidon.* The name כִּידֹן is written, in 2 Sam. vi. 6, נָכוֹן (Sept. Ναχώρ), a reading scarcely preferable to our own.—*For the oxen shook it*, were on the point of upsetting it (Sept. ἐξέκλινεν αὐτήν; Vulg. *paululum inclinaverant eam*); the ark of itself supplies the subject to שָׁמְטוּ. Others give "the oxen let go" (Berth.), or "stept aside" (Luther and many ancients), or "flung on every side," Ew., etc.—Ver. 10. *And the anger of the Lord was kindled against Uzza*, whose error might lie less in the accidental and involuntary touching of the ark, as in his conveying this sacred thing on an ox waggon, instead of having it borne according to the law (Num. vii. 9, x. 17); comp. what David afterwards did, xv. 2. For the parallel text of Samuel to be amended by our passage, comp. Thenius and Wellhausen. —Ver. 13. *In the house of Obed-edom the Gittite;* according to xv. 18, 24, this Obed-edom was one of the Levitical porters; whence we are not to think of the Philistine Gath, but the Levitical city Gath-rimmon (Josh. xix. 45, xxi. 24), as his birth-place.—Ver. 14. *In the house of Obed-edom in his house*, in his own tent, which was spread over it in the court of this Levite (thus, in his dwelling-house, עִם־בֵּיתוֹ). This text appears more correct than that in 2 Sam. vi., which only states that the ark remained "in the house of Obed-edom the Gittite."—*And all that he had.* For this 2 Sam. vi. has: "and all his house." The various reading of our passage "is well chosen, because, just before, בֵּיתוֹ was used of the tent of the ark" (Berth.). That the blessing which God gave to Obed-edom consisted chiefly in numerous offspring, appears from xxvi. 4–8. Yet, even during the three months mentioned in our passage, David must have clearly perceived that the Lord's anger was sufficiently appeased by the death of Uzza, and that the removal of the ark to Jerusalem involved no danger, but would be attended with blessed effects.

ζ. David's House-Building, Family, and Victories over the Philistines: ch. xiv.

CH. XIV. 1. And Hiram[1] king of Tyre sent messengers to David, and cedar-wood,
2 and masons, and carpenters, to build him a house. And David perceived that
the LORD had confirmed him king over Israel; for his kingdom was lift up on
high, because of his people Israel.
3 And David took more wives in Jerusalem; and David begat more sons
4 and daughters. And these are the names of those born to him in Jerusalem:
5 Shammua and Shobab, Nathan and Solomon. And Ibhar, and Elishua, and
6, 7 Elpelet. And Nogah, and Nepheg, and Japhia. And Elishama, and Beeliada,
and Eliphelet.
8 And the Philistines heard that David was anointed king over all Israel;
and all the Philistines went up to seek David: and David heard it, and went
9 out against them. And the Philistines came and spread themselves in the
10 valley of Rephaim. And David inquired of God, saying, Shall I go up against
the Philistines, and wilt Thou give them into my hand? And the LORD said
11 unto him, Go up, and I will give them into thy hand. And they went up to
Baal-perazim; and David smote them there: and David said, God hath
broken my enemies by my hand, like the breaking of waters; therefore they
12 called the name of that place Baal-perazim. And they left their gods there;
and David ordered, and they were burnt with fire.
13, 14 And the Philistines came again and spread themselves in the valley.[2] And
David inquired again of God; and God said unto him, Go not up after them;
15 turn away from them, and come upon them by the bacas. And it shall be,
when thou hearest the sound going on the tops of the bacas, then go out to

the battle: for God is gone out before thee to smite the camp of the Philistines.
16 And David did as God commanded him: and they smote the camp of the
17 Philistines, from Gibeon even unto Gezer. And David's fame went out into
all lands; and the LORD brought his fear upon all nations.

[1] *Kethib*· חִירָם. *Keri:* חוּרָם, as always in Chronicles (Sept. Χειράμ, as ever).

[2] For בעמק the Sept. and Syr. read בעמק רפאים, which is perhaps original; comp. 2 Sam. v. 22.

EXEGETICAL.

PRELIMINARY REMARK.—On the different position of this section in 2 Sam. v. 11–25, namely, before the history of the removal of the ark from Kiriath-jearim, comp. the Preliminary Remark on ch. xiii. The motive of the Chronist for the transposition is evidently the wish to represent the preparations for the removal of the national sanctuary to Jerusalem as the first undertaking of the king after the taking of the capital, to exhibit the building of his own palace as a work certainly taken in hand soon after, but still standing behind that all-important concern. To the history of the beginning of the palace-building is attached in the sources common to both historians a description of the blessing which attended David as a father and a captain in the battles with the Philistines. Our author took this description, in the main unaltered, along with the notice of the beginning of the palace-building, over into his narrative, undeterred by the appearance thence arising of the events in question, especially the two successful battles with the Philistines, having fallen in the three months between the removal of the ark to the house of Obed-edom and its introduction into Jerusalem. This grouping is here, as often in his representation of the history of David, determined by the order of thought rather than of time.

1. David's Palace-building and Family: vers. 1–7.—The text of the older parallel, 2 Sam. v. 11–16, agrees in the main with the present, only here and there more precise.—*And cedar-wood, and masons, and carpenters,* literally, "and timbers (beams) of cedars, and craftsmen of walls, and craftsmen of timbers" (Vulg. *artifices parietum lignorumque*).—Ver. 2. *And David perceived* (concluded from the high honour which was conferred upon him by this message from the Phenician king) *that the Lord had confirmed him king over Israel,* definitely transferred the kingdom to him, established ("bestätigt," Luther) him as king.—*For his kingdom was lift up on high.* נִשֵּׂאת, if genuine, would be an irregularly formed 3 fem. perf. *Niph.* (not, as 2 Sam. xix. 43, an *inf. abs. Niph.*) from נשׂא, intensified by the לְמַעְלָה, "on high;" comp. xxii. 5, xxiii. 17, xxix. 3–25. But perhaps, as in 2 Sam. v. 12, the perf. *Piel* נִשֵּׂא is to be read, and Jehovah taken as the subject: "and that He had exalted his kingdom." For מַמְלַכְתּוֹ, 2 Sam. v., our text presents the later (occurring also xvii. 11, 14) form מַלְכוּתוֹ, perhaps merely by a slip of the pen; see Wellh. p. 164.—Ver. 3. *And David took more wives in Jerusalem.* Before נָשִׁים in 2 Samuel stands פִּלַגְשִׁים, which may have fallen accidentally out of our passage, as the concubines of David are mentioned in iii. 9. Comp. on iii. 5–9, where the names of the thirteen sons of David born in Jerusalem, and the partly different spelling here and there, are fully handled.

2. The First War with the Philistines: vers. 8–12 (comp. 2 Sam. v. 17–21).—*To seek David,* to attack, לְבַקֵּשׁ, *sensu hostili,* as in 1 Sam. xxiii. 15, 25, xxiv. 3, xxvi. 2.—*And David heard it, and went out against them,* properly, "before them;" comp. xii. 17. Into this general and indefinite expression our author has changed the more concrete, but also more obscure, statement of Samuel: "and went down to the hold" (the hold of Zion), perhaps designedly.—Ver. 9. *And spread themselves in the valley of Rephaim;* comp. on xi. 15, 2 Sam. v. 18: "sat down in the valley of Rephaim." The perhaps more original וַיִּנָּטְשׁוּ, 2 Sam. v. 18, 22, the Chronist has here and ver. 13 exchanged for the simpler and more intelligible וַיִּפְשְׁטוּ.—Ver. 11. *Like the breaking of waters,* like an outburst of water (כְּפֶרֶץ מַיִם). We may think of the rending or outbursting of enclosing dams by rapid floods, perhaps after a water-spout. The situation of Baal-perazim cannot be exactly ascertained. Mount Perazim, Isa. xxviii. 21, is not essentially different from it.—Ver. 12. *And they left their gods there.* 2 Sam. v.: "their idols" (עצביהם). The present phrase is the stronger; it yields, along with the following statement regarding the burning of these gods, a bitterly sarcastic sense. The burning took place, moreover, on the ground of the divine command in Deut. vii. 5, 25. The text of Samuel weakens the statement in a strange way: "and David and his men took them away." If the more concrete and stronger statement of our author is a traditional expansion of that text, the tradition on which it rests is at all events credible; comp. Movers, p. 224. By this victory, David wiped out the old disgrace of Israel, which rested on the people since Eli's time. "As then Israel lost the ark, 1 Sam. iv. 11, so now the sacred things of the Philistines fell into the hands of the Israelites" (Berth.).

3. The Second War with the Philistines: vers. 13–17 (comp. 2 Sam. v. 22–25).—*And spread themselves in the valley,* that is, as the parallel text (so as the Sept. and Syr.; see Crit. Note) shows, in the same valley as above, ver. 9, scarcely in another at Gibeon, as Movers, p. 243, thinks.—Ver. 14. *Go not up after them,* that is, as Samuel shows: "go not directly towards them; seek not to drive them before thee by a direct attack." Perhaps also our text is somewhat faulty, and to be amended, according to 2 Sam. v. 23: לֹא תַעֲלֶה הָסֵב אֶל אַחֲרֵיהֶם, by the change of אחריהם in עֲלֵיהֶם (Berth.).—*And come upon*

them by the bacas, literally, over against the bacas. These we must suppose, as the divine command implies a going round the Philistine army, to be behind them. The baca, mentioned only here and 2 Sam. v., and perhaps Ps. lxxxiv. 7, is, according to Abulfadi (in Celsius, *Hierobot.* i. 339), a plant related to the balsam tree, and resembling it, which, when cut, discharges a white, sharp, and warm resin in the manner of tears, and appears to have received its name from בכא, *flare.* The older expositors, wavering uncertainly, render the term variously: Sept. ἄπιος, Vulg. *pyrus;* Luther, after the Jewish expositors, mulberry tree.—Ver. 15. *The sound going on the tops of the bacas*, namely, the rustling of their leaves in the wind (Sept.: τὴν φωνὴν τοῦ συσσεισμοῦ αὐτῶν), not the sound occasioned by the entrance of God (supernatural, as in Gen. iii. 8). As the baca has much larger leaves than the ordinary balsam, the rustling of them may occasion a sufficiently loud sound; the rendering "baca trees" (Kamph.) is therefore unnecessary.—Ver. 16. *And they smote the camp of the Philistines, from Gibeon even unto Gezer.* Two places of this name lie to the north-west of Jerusalem, the former (now el Jib) 2½, the latter 4½, hours distant from it. If the battle-field is to be sought between the two, in the region of Upper and Nether Beth-horon, the valley, ver. 13, may still be the valley of Rephaim; only the site of it should be sought not so far south, as Thenius and Bertheau suppose (who also read for Gibeon in our passage, "Geba," according to 2 Sam. v. 25), and the battle must be regarded as moving in a north-westerly direction from its starting-point (comp. Wellh. on 2 Sam. v. 25, also Ew. *Gesch. d. V. Isr.* ii. 610).—Ver. 17. *And David's fame went out into all lands; and the Lord brought his fear upon all nations*, literally, "gave his fear upon all nations;" comp. Esth. viii. 17. A pragmatic reflection of our author added to the original text, as its absence in 2 Sam. v. 25 shows. Comp. the similar reflections in 2 Chron. xvii. 10, xx. 29. On וַיֵּצֵא שֵׁם especially, comp. 2 Chron. xxvi. 15.

η. The Removal of the Ark to Jerusalem, with the Solemn Hymn sung on this occasion:
ch. xv., xvi.

CH. XV. 1. And he made him houses in the city of David, and he prepared a place
for the ark of God, and pitched for it a tent.
2 Then David said, None should carry the ark of God but the Levites; for
the LORD hath chosen them to carry the ark of God, and to minister to Him
3 for ever. And David gathered all Israel to Jerusalem, to bring up the ark of
4 the LORD unto its place which he had prepared for it. And David assembled
5 the sons of Aaron, and the Levites. Of the sons of Kohath: Uriel the chief,
6 and his brethren a hundred and thirty. Of the sons of Merari: Asaiah the
7 chief, and his brethren two hundred and twenty. Of the sons of Gershom: Joel
8 the chief, and his brethren a hundred and thirty. Of the sons of Elizaphan:
9 Shemaiah the chief, and his brethren two hundred. Of the sons of Hebron:
10 Eliel the chief, and his brethren eighty. Of the sons of Uzziel: Amminadab the
11 chief, and his brethren a hundred and twelve. And David called Zadok and
Abiathar the priests, and the Levites Uriel, Asaiah, and Joel, Shemaiah, and
12 Eliel, and Amminadab. And said unto them, Ye chiefs of the Levites, sanctify
yourselves with your brethren, and bring up the ark of the LORD God of Israel
13 to the place I have prepared for it. For because ye were not at the first, the
14 LORD our God broke out upon us, because we sought Him not aright. And the
priests and Levites sanctified themselves to bring up the ark of the LORD God of
15 Israel. And the sons of the Levites bare the ark of God, as Moses commanded
by the word of the LORD, upon their shoulders, with staves upon them.
16 And David said to the chiefs of the Levites, to appoint their brethren the
singers with instruments, psalteries, and harps, and cymbals, sounding, to lift up
17 the sound with gladness. And the Levites appointed Heman son of Joel; and
of his brethren, Asaph son of Berechiah; and of the sons of Merari their brethren,
18 Ethan son of Kushaiah.[1] And with them their brethren of the second degree:
Zechariah,[2] and Jaaziel, and Shemiramoth, and Jehiel, and Unni, Eliab, and
Benaiah, and Maaseiah, and Mattithiah, and Elipheleh, and Mikneiah, and Obed-
19 edom, and Jeiel, the porters. And the singers, Heman, Asaph, and Ethan, with
20 cymbals of brass to sound aloud. And Zechariah, and Aziel, and Shemiramoth,
and Jehiel, and Unni, and Eliab, and Maaseiah, and Benaiah, with psalteries,
21 in the way of maidens. And Mattithiah, and Elipheleh, and Mikneiah, and
Obed-edom, and Jeiel, and Azaziah, with harps after the octave to lead.
22 And Chenaniah, chief of the Levites;[3] for he instructed in bearing, for he
23 was skilful. And Berechiah and Elkanah were door-keepers for the ark.
24 And Shebaniah, and Joshaphat, and Nathaneel, and Amasai, and Zechariah,

and Benaiah, and Eliezer, the priests, blew[4] with the trumpets before the ark of
God; and Obed-edom and Jehiah were door-keepers for the ark.
25 And David, and the elders of Israel, and the captains of thousands, were
going to bring up the ark of the covenant of the LORD out of the house of Obed-
26 edom with gladness. And when God helped the Levites bearing the ark of the
27 covenant of the LORD, then they offered seven bullocks and seven rams. And
David was clothed with a robe of byssus, and all the Levites bearing the ark,
and the singers, and Chenaniah the master of the bearing [the singers];[5] and upon
28 David was a linen ephod. And all Israel brought up the ark of the covenant of
the LORD with shouting, and with sound of cornet, and with trumpets, and with
29 cymbals sounding, with psalteries and harps. And when the ark of the covenant
of the LORD came to the city of David, then Michal, daughter of Saul, looked out
from the window, and saw King David leaping and playing; and she despised him
in her heart.

CH. XVI. 1. And they brought the ark of God, and set it in the tent that David had
pitched for it; and they offered burnt-offerings and peace-offerings before God.
2 And David made an end of offering burnt-offerings and peace-offerings, and blessed
3 the people in the name of the LORD. And he dealt to every one of Israel, both
man and woman, to every one a loaf of bread, and a measure [of wine], and a grape
cake.
4 And he appointed before the ark of the LORD ministers of the Levites, to
5 record, and to thank and to praise the LORD God of Israel. Asaph the chief, and
next to him Zechariah, Jeiel,[6] and Shemiramoth, and Jehiel, and Mattithiah, and
Eliab, and Benaiah, and Obed-edom, and Jeiel, with psalteries and harps; and
6 Asaph sounding with cymbals. And Benaiah and Jahaziel the priests with
7 trumpets continually before the ark of the covenant of God. On that day then
David ordered for the first time to thank the LORD by Asaph and his
brethren.[7]

8 Thank ye the LORD, call on His name,
Make known His deed among the peoples.
9 Sing ye to Him, play ye to Him;
Muse on all His wonders.
10 Glory ye in His holy name;
Let the heart of them that seek the LORD be glad.
11 Seek ye the LORD and His strength,
Seek ye His face continually.
12 Remember His wonders that He hath done,
His signs, and the judgments of His mouth.
13 O ye seed of Israel His servant,
Ye sons of Jacob, His chosen.
14 He the LORD is our God,
His judgments are in all the earth.
15 Remember His covenant for ever—
The word He commanded to a thousand ages.
16 Which He made with Abraham,
And His oath unto Isaac.
17 And appointed it to Jacob for a statute,
To Israel for an everlasting covenant.
18 Saying, To thee I give the land of Canaan,
The line of your inheritance.
19 When ye were small in number,
Few, and strangers in it.
20 And they went from nation to nation,
And from one kingdom to another people.
21 He let no man do them wrong,
And reproved kings for their sake.
22 "Touch not mine anointed,
And do my prophets no harm."

23 Sing ye to the LORD, all the earth;
Proclaim from day to day His salvation.
24 Tell ye among the nations His glory,
His wonders among all the peoples.
25 For great is the LORD, and greatly to be praised;
And He is to be feared above all gods.
26 For all the gods of the peoples are idols;
But the LORD made the heavens.
27 Majesty and honour are before Him,
Strength and gladness are in His place.

28 Give unto the LORD, ye kindreds of the people,
Give unto the LORD glory and strength.
29 Give to the LORD the glory due to His name;
Bring an oblation, and come before Him;
Worship the LORD in the beauty of holiness.
30 Tremble before Him, all the earth:
The world will also stand fast without moving.

31 Let the heavens be glad, and let the earth rejoice;
And let them sing among the nations, The LORD reigneth.
32 Let the sea roar, and the fulness thereof;
Let the field rejoice, and all that is therein.
33 Then shall the trees of the wood sing out
Before the LORD; for He cometh to judge the earth.

34 Thank ye the LORD; for He is good;
For His mercy endureth for ever.
35 And say ye, Save us, O God of our salvation,
And gather us and deliver us from the heathen,
To thank Thy holy name,
To glory in Thy praise.
36 Blessed be the LORD, the God of Israel,
For ever and ever.
And all the people said, Amen, and praised the LORD.
37 And he left there, before the ark of the covenant of the LORD, Asaph and
his brethren, to minister before the ark continually, for the day's work in its day.
38 And Obed-edom[8] and their brethren sixty and eight; and Obed-edom, son of
39 Jedithun, and Hosah, to be porters. And Zadok the priest, and his brethren
the priests, before the tabernacle of the LORD, in the high place that was at
40 Gibeon. To offer burnt-offerings to the LORD on the altar of burnt-offering con-
tinually morning and evening, and for all that is written in the law of the LORD,
41 which He commanded Israel. And with them Heman and Jeduthun, and the
rest that were chosen, who were expressed by name, to thank the LORD, that His
42 mercy endureth for ever. And with them, Heman and Jeduthun,[9] were trumpets
and cymbals for loud sounding, and [other] instruments of God; and the sons of
43 Jeduthun were at the gate. And all the people went every man to his house;
and David turned in to bless his house.

1 קוּשָׁיָהוּ, without variation, while in vi. 29 the name is קוּשִׁי, and so the Sept. read here Κισαίου (Vulg. *Casajæ*).

2 בֵּן after זְכַרְיָהוּ has come into the text by a mistake of the pen, as the ו before the next name shows. On the contrary, the name עֲזַזְיָהוּ seems to have fallen out at the close of ver. 18 (see Exeg.).

3 בְּמַשָּׂא. So most editions, in the first place; whereas R. Norzi has בַּמַּשָּׂא even the first time.

4 *Kethib*: מַחְצְצְרִים. *Keri*: מַחְצְרִים (*partic. Hiph.*). The same variation recurs 2 Chron. v. 13, where, however, the *Keri* is to be read as *partic. Pi.* (לְמַחַצְּרִים).

[5] The words וּכְנַנְיָה הַשַּׂר הַמַּשָּׂא הַמְשֹׁרְרִים are wanting in the *Pesh.* At least, הַמְשֹׁרְרִים should apparently be erased as unmeaning (comp. Exeg.); though the Sept. and Vulg. have it.

[6] Instead of יְחִיאֵל after xv. 18 is certainly to be read here, in the first place (after שְׁמִירָמוֹת), יְעִיאֵל.

[7] The variants in this song, from its parallel in the Psalter (Ps. cv., xcvi., cvi.), see in Exeg.

[8] After עֹבֵד אדם, as the plur. suff. in ואחיהם shows, must at least one name, probably וְחֹסָה (see the following), have fallen out.

[9] The names הֵימָן וִידוּתוּן were not read by the Sept. (*καὶ μετ' αὐτῶν σάλπιγγες καὶ κύμβαλα τοῦ ἀναφωνεῖν, κ.τ.λ.*), and appear to be repeated by mistake from the preceding verse, which also begins with וְעִמָּהֶם.

EXEGETICAL.

Preliminary Remark.—Instead of the brief description of the parallel text 2 Sam. vi. 11-23, our author gives a detailed account: 1. Of the preparations for the solemn act of transferring the ark into its new sanctuary in Jerusalem, xv. 1-24, including *a*. The erection of the tent for the reception of the ark, ver. 1; *b*. a conference of the king with the priests and Levites, vers. 2-16; and *c*. the selection of the Levites appointed for the chief part in the solemnity (and therefore designated by name), vers. 16-24. 2. Then follows the execution of the so prepared holy act itself, xv. 25-xvi. 3; at the close of which comes the description of the first solemn service before the ark in its new sanctuary on Zion, xvi. 4-43, including the psalm of praise and thanks then sung, vers. 8-36. This long closing section is (except the last verse) peculiar to the Chronist. On its credibility, and especially on the genuineness and age of the psalm of praise and thanks, see at the close of these expositions.

1. *The Preparation for the Removal;* and first, *a*. The erection of the tent on Zion: xv. 1.—*And he made him houses in the city of David.* This may be understood of the building of other houses besides the palace built with the aid of Hiram of Tyre, xiv. 1 (Berth., Kamph.); but as the verb used is עָשָׂה, not בנה, it appears rather to refer to the internal finishing of a palace for the abode of the king and his wives.—*And he prepared a place for the ark of God.* This was probably in the immediate neighbourhood of the king's house adjoining it; for here the one of the two existing high priests, Abiathar the Ithamaride, who, since the massacre at Nob, was constantly about David (as it were his court or domestic priest, while Zadok of the house of Eleazar officiated at Gibeon), was to exercise his functions.—*And pitched for it a tent,* we may suppose, after the model of the old tabernacle still existing at Gibeon (xvi. 39 f., xxi. 29; 1 Kings iii. 4 ff.), but only as a provisional sanctuary.

2. *Continuation.* *b*. The conference with the priests and Levites: vers. 2-15.—*Then David said,* namely, at the end of the three months, xiii. 14.—*None should carry,* properly, "it is not to carry." With this confession of the sole right of the Levites to carry the ark (comp. Num. i. 50, iv. 15, vii. 9, x. 17), David acknowledges that it was unlawful to convey it on a waggon, xiii. 7.—Ver. 3. *And David gathered all Israel,* by its natural representatives, the elders and captains of thousands; see ver. 25, and comp. 2 Sam. vi. 15: "all the house of Israel." Of this summons to a previous consultation in Jerusalem nothing further is reported, 2 Sam. vi.—Ver. 4. *And David assembled the sons of Aaron, and the Levites;* he formed of these representatives of the priesthood an inner circle in the assembly of the people, to hear their counsel regarding the order of the solemnities. "The sons of Aaron" are the high priests Zadok and Abiathar, ver. 11; the "Levites" are the six chiefs named in vers. 5-10, with their brethren.—Ver. 5. *Of the sons of Kohath: Uriel the chief;* see vi. 9. The Kohathite chief is named first, because the ministry of the most holy, the carrying of the most holy vessels of the tabernacle, belonged to the Kohathites, the family from which Aaron the high priest sprang, Num. iv. 4, 15, vii. 9 (Keil).—On the Merarite chief Asaiah, comp. vi. 15; on Joel, the chief of the sons of Gershom, vi. 21.—Vers. 8-10 name the chiefs of three other Kohathite families, those of Elizaphan (=Elzaphan son of Uzziel, Ex. vi. 22), of Hebron (son of Kohath, Ex. vi. 18; comp. 1 Chron. v. 28), and of Uzziel. The last named is probably not different from the Kohathite Uzziel, father of Elizaphan, Ex. vi. 22; there are thus formed of the sons of this Uzziel two houses, of which one is named after Elizaphan, the other after Uzziel himself, and not any of his other sons. There are then in all four Kohathite houses, with one Merarite and one Gershomite, here represented: a strong preference of the house of Kohath, which is not surprising, because the conveyance of the ark specially belonged to them.—Ver. 11. *And David called Zadok* (of Eleazar, v. 27 ff.) *and Abiathar* (of Ithamar), the high priests, who then acted together; see above on ver. 1, and comp. xxiv. 3; 2 Sam. xv. 24 ff., xx. 25.—Ver. 12. *Ye chiefs of the Levites,* literally, "ye chiefs of the fathers of the Levites;" comp. viii. 6, 10.—*Sanctify yourselves with your brethren,* properly, "ye and your brethren." The "sanctifying" consisted in keeping from their wives, from contact with unclean things, and also in washing the body and the clothes; comp. Gen. xxxv. 2 with Ex. xix. 10, 15, also 2 Chron. xxx. 3.—*To* (the place) *I have prepared for it,* אֶל־הֲכִינוֹתִי לוֹ. The same elliptical construction (with omitted אֲשֶׁר, or immediate connection of the relative sentence with the preposition) see in 2 Chron. i. 4; comp. 1 Chron. xxix. 3; 2 Chron. xvi. 9, xxx. 18; Neh. viii. 10 (Ew. § 333, *b*).—Ver. 13. *For because ye were not at the beginning,* or "ye were not those who bare the ark." "At the beginning," on the former occasion, when three months before the ark was brought from Kiriath-jearim, xiii. On the peculiar construction לְמַבָּרִאשׁוֹנָה (from לָמָה and בָּרִאשׁוֹנָה), comp. מַה־תְּלָאָה = מַתְּלָאָה, Mal. i. 13, and Ew. § 91, *d*. לָמָה in this compound signifies "for this, that," "because;"

comp. Ew. § 222, *a*, 353, *a*.—*The Lord our God broke out upon us* (xiii. 11), *because we sought Him not aright*, because we approached Him not in the manner prescribed by law, had neglected to testify our reverence to Him by keeping the legal regulation, that only Levites should bear the holy things. —Ver. 15. *And the sons of the Levites bear the ark of God.* An anticipation, occasioned by that which was said in the verse before of the immediate execution of the order for the purification of the Levites. See the particulars, ver. 25 ff.—*Upon their shoulders, with staves upon them*, upon their shoulders. On מוֹטָה (from מוּט, "waver"), the pole, comp. Num. xiii. 23 (also Lev. xxvi. 13; Ezek. xxxiv. 27). In the Pentat. the poles are besides called בַּדִּים, Ex. xxv. 13 ff., etc.

3. *Close.* *c.* The appointment of the Levitical singers for the solemnity: vers. 16–24.—*To appoint their brethren the singers with instruments*, properly, "with instruments of song," that is, to accompany the singing. Such כְּלֵי שִׁיר (comp. Neh. xii. 36) are now named in three classes: 1. נְבָלִים, ψαλτήρια (Sept.), or *nablia* (Vulg.), guitar-like instruments, consisting of an oblong chest with flat bottom and convex sounding board, over which strings of wire were stretched, called by Luther, in accordance with the Sept. (and the Arab. *santir*), psalteries, by others "harps" or nablia; 2. כִּנֹּרוֹת (Sept. κίνυραι, Vulg. *lyræ*), harps or lute-like instruments, rendered by Luther not unsuitably, "harps," though lutes would perhaps be more correct [rather should the former be called lutes]; 3. מְצִלְתַּיִם (equivalent to the older term צֶלְצְלִים, 2 Sam. vi. 5; Ps. cl. 5), here more fully defined by the epithet מַשְׁמִיעִים, "clear-sounding" (making to hear), which belongs neither to all the three instruments (Berth.), nor to the too remote "their brethren the singers" (Kamph.), but, as in vers. 19, 28, and xvi. 5, 42, only to מְצִלְתַּיִם; comp. Böttch. *Neue exeg.-krit. Aehrenl.* iii. 223 f. (who, however, assigns to the term the unsuitable meaning, "beating time").—*To lift up the sound with gladness*, to express or signify joy; comp. ver. 25; 2 Chron. xxiii. 18, xxix. 30. This telic clause refers not merely to the clear-sounding cymbals, but to the chief sentence.—Ver. 17. *And the Levites appointed Heman son of Joel.* That this Heman was of the family of the Kohathites, and Asaph of the Gershonites (comp. vi. 18, 24), is not here stated; only of the third song-master Ethan is his family, or his descent from Merari, expressly mentioned. On the name of Ethan's father, Kushaiah, see Crit. Note.—Ver. 18. *And with them their brethren of the second degree.* On הַמִּשְׁנִים, "the second in rank," comp. the sing. הַמִּשְׁנֶה, 2 Kings xxiii. 4 and 1 Chron. xvi. 5.—*Zechariah and Jaaziel.* For the certainly spurious בֵּן after זְכַרְיָהוּ, see Crit. Note. The here named Jaaziel is certainly identical with the Aziel, ver. 20, and with the Jeiel, xvi. 5, or rather these names are to be changed into the present one.—*And Obed-edom and Jeiel the porters.* The office of doorkeeper does not exclude their acting also as musicians, as ver. 21 shows. After Jeiel, as the same verse teaches, the name Azaziah must have fallen out, so that originally there were not thirteen but fourteen persons named as musicians of the second order. After these singers and musicians have been mentioned by name (and in two orders or ranks, vers. 17 and 18), they are again brought forward, vers. 19–21, divided into three choirs, after the musical instruments on which they played.—Ver. 19. *The Cymbal Players: Heman, Asaph, and Ethan.—With cymbals of brass to sound aloud*, they were bound, had this to do. The cymbals were wholly of brass; comp. 1 Cor. xiii. 1: χαλκὸς ἠχῶν, and Joseph. *Antiq.* vii. 12. 3: κύμβαλά τε ἦν πλατέα καὶ μεγάλα χάλκεα. The "loud-sounding" (הַשְׁמִיעַ) of the three cymbal players was designed to beat time or direct; for in ver. 17 they are placed before as leaders.—Ver. 20. The Players on Psalteries or Nablia: Zechariah and Seven Others. Of these, who are here repeated with slight changes from ver. 18 (instead of Jaaziel, the second is here called Aziel; and at the end of the first series stands here Maaseiah before Benaiah, there inversely), it is here stated that they played *with psalteries in the way of maidens.* עַל־עֲלָמוֹת is certainly the name of that tone, which sounds in a high, clear voice, that is, the soprano, as the following עַל־הַשְּׁמִינִית, "after (or on) the octave," is equivalent to "on the bass," *al ottava bassa.* Comp. Del. on Ps. vi. 1, xlvi. 1.—Ver. 21. The Harp or Lute Players: Mattaniah and Five Others.—*With harps after the octave to lead.* How this leading or directing expressed by נצח is distinct from that which is expressed, ver. 19, by השמיע, we can no longer define; at all events, it was not such directing as could belong only to the music-master. Comp. Delitzsch on Ps. iv. 1.—Vers. 22–24 bring forward the other Levites engaged in the solemn procession. —*And Chenaniah, chief of the Levites, for bearing.* בְּמַשָּׂא (or as perhaps is to be read, with R. Norzi, בַּמַּשָּׂא) is scarcely to be understood of any presiding or overseeing action of Chenaniah (as the Sept. ὁ ἄρχων τῶν ᾠδῶν, Vulg. *prophetiæ præerat ad præcinendam melodiam;* Luth. "to instruct in singing;" L. Lavater, *supremus musicus;* Kamph. and others, "the leader in execution," etc.). The phrase is rather to be referred to the bearing of the ark, which, according to ver. 23 f., is here in question (comp. also מַשָּׂא in 2 Chron. xxxv. 3 and Num. iv. 19). With this agrees, rightly conceived, ver. 27, as well as the later mention of Chenaniah in xxvi. 29, where he is placed over the outward business of the Levites (rightly Berth. and Keil; undecided Kamph.).—*Instructed in bearing; for he was skilful*, acquainted with the ritual, experienced in the ceremonial relative to the bearing of the ark. Whether we take יָסֹר as *inf. abs. Kal* in the sense of the *verb. fin.* יִסֹּר, "instruct" (J. H. Mich., Gesen., etc.), or as imperf. of סרר = שָׂרַר, "be chief, command" (Berth., etc.), or as a subst. in the sense of "instructor" (Keil), the meaning of presiding, directing, leading, is at all events ex-

pressed by the word.—Ver. 23. *And Berechiah and Elkanah were doorkeepers for the ark*, who were to guard not so much the doors of the ark itself as those of the tent that gave access to it; thus, in general, to guard the ark. As these two at first, and then at the close of the following verse, Obed-edom and Jehiah also, are named as doorkeepers of the ark, we must regard the former two as going before the ark during the solemn procession, and the latter two as following after. Close by the ark, however, either immediately before it or on the two sides, the seven priests blowing trumpets, ver. 24, may be supposed to go. —Ver. 24. *And Shebaniah . . . blew with trumpets before the ark of God.* Whether the *Kethib* מַחְצְצְרִים (*denom.* from חֲצֹצְרָה) or the *Keri* מַחְצְרִים (*Hiph.* of חצר) is read does not affect the sense. The blowing of trumpets here is according to the prescription, Num. x. 1–10, and the example of the compassing of Jericho, Josh. vi. 4–6.—*And Obed-edom and Jehiah were doorkeepers for the ark.* Of these, Obed-edom was a son of Jeduthun, xvi. 38, and so perhaps different from him of the same name among the singers, vers. 18, 21 (though he also, ver. 18, is called a doorkeeper). Perhaps also the Jehiah named with him is not to be identified with Jehiel there (vers. 18 and 21) named with Obed-edom (against Raschi, Berth., etc.). It is plain that according to all this the whole procession included the following divisions:—1. The singers arranged in three choirs; 2. Chenaniah the captain of the bearers (as it were marshal); 3. Two doorkeepers; 4. Seven priests blowing trumpets close by the ark; 5. Two doorkeepers. After these followed, ver. 25, the king, with the elders and captains of thousands.

4. The Execution of that which was resolved in the Assembly: xv. 25–xvi. 3.—*And David and the elders of Israel, and the captains of thousands* (commanders over the thousands, chiliarchs). וַיְהִי דָוִיד וגו׳ connects this with ver. 3, after the details concerning the preparations have intervened. The parallel 2 Sam. vi. 12 wants this connecting וַיְהִי, and does not mention the elders and chiliarchs along with David.—Ver. 26. *And when God helped the Levites*, permitted them without danger or harm to convey the ark, thus to escape the fate of Uzza. The offering of seven bullocks and seven rams seems to have been made at the close of the procession, after the conveyance had been successfully conducted. Otherwise 2 Sam. vi. 13, where (at least in the Masoretic text) David, after the bearers of the ark had made the first six steps, offered a sacrifice. It is probable that both accounts are original, and that the two must be harmonized and combined.—Ver. 27. *And David was clothed with a robe of byssus.* Instead of these words (וְדָוִיד מְכֻרְבָּל בִּמְעִיל בּוּץ), 2 Sam. vi. 14 presents וְדָוִיד מְכַרְכֵּר בְּכָל־עֹז (with the addition לִפְנֵי יְהוָֹה). That מכרבל is corrupted from מכרכר, and במעיל בוץ from בכל־עז (Berth., etc.; also Böttcher, *Neue Aehrenlese*, iii. 224), might be assumed, if the לפני יהוה, wanting in our text, did not create a difficulty. For this assumption, according to which the Chronist shall have thought it unbecoming to speak of David (and, with Berth., the Levites also) dancing, though in ver. 29 and xiii. 8 he states, or at least implies, this fact quite freely, it is at all events easier to regard both texts as abbreviations of one and the same narrative contained in the common sources of our author, which, besides the dancing of David (which the Chronist merely presupposes, while the author of 2 Samuel gives it prominence), contained full reports of the clothing of David, and of the Levites around him. It is accordingly to be supposed that the Chronist has taken only these latter reports in full, "because the statement concerning the clothing of the king and the Levites appeared more important for the purpose of describing fully the religious aspect of the procession, as this import of it was more conspicuous here; for the dress which the king wore had a priestly character" (Keil; comp. Movers, p. 168). That the verb כרבל, "to be wrapt up," belongs to the later usage of speech, or rather, is properly Chaldaic (Dan. iii. 21), can scarcely bring into question the justice of this harmonistic assumption (against Böttch.).—*And all the Levites . . . and the singers, and Chenaniah.* To these also obviously applies the being "clothed with a robe of byssus," which is first said of David. All these, who are here in apposition with David, are described as adorned with priestly attire, with the meïl of byssus (comp. the byssus attire of the Levites and singers in the dedication of the temple by Solomon, 2 Chron. v. 12, and for the meïl, the upper garment of distinguished persons, 1 Sam. ii. 19, xv. 27, xviii. 4, xxiv. 5; Ezra ix. 3; Job xxix. 14). The closing sentence, "and upon David was a linen ephod," first names the distinguishing part of the clothing of the king as the sovereign of the priestly people (comp. 2 Sam. vi. 14). The designation of Chenaniah as "the master of the bearing" (הַשַּׂר הַמַּשָּׂא with the double article; comp. Ew. § 290, *d*) is to be understood according to ver. 22; the unmeaning: "the singers," after הַמַּשָּׂא, appears spurious (see Crit. Note); even if we understood מַשָּׂא of musical performance, this addition would be disturbing.—Ver. 28. *With shouting, and with sound of cornet*, etc. Shorter and simpler 2 Sam. vi. 15, without naming the several instruments.—Ver. 29. *Then Michal . . . saw King David leaping and playing.* Instead of מרקד ומשחק, 2 Sam. vi. 16 has מְפַזֵּז וּמְכַרְכֵּר. This brief reference to the well-known history, fully reported in 2 Sam. vi. 16, 20–23, of the dispute between David and Michal, shows sufficiently that the Chronist did not wish to be silent concerning this matter from dogmatic or æsthetic considerations. Moreover, ver. 29–xvi. 3 agrees in all essentials with 2 Sam. vi. 16–19*a*.—Ch. xvi. 3: *To every one a loaf of bread* (כִּכַּר לֶחֶם, the more usual phrase for the rarer חַלַּת ל׳ used in 2 Sam. vi. 19), *and a measure* (of wine), *and a grape cake.* The אֶשְׁפָּר, occurring only here and 2 Samuel, is explained by the Vulg., Chald., and Syr., and by several Rabbis and moderns (Ew., Berth., Kamph.), as "a piece

of flesh" (roast), as if from פַּר, ox, and אֵשׁ, fire, or rather from שׁפר = שׂרף, "to burn." But the reference of the word to שׁפר, in the sense of the Aethiopic *safara = metiri*, "to measure," is better ascertained, according to which, אשׁפר (with א *prosthet.*) signifies a portion of drink, a measure of wine (de Dieu, Gesen., Rödiger, Keil, etc.). On אֲשִׁישָׁה, "grape or raisin cake" (from אשׁשׁ, to make firm, press), comp. Song ii. 5, Hos. iii. 1, and the equivalent צמוקים, xii. 40.

5. *The First Solemn Service before the Ark in Jerusalem, and the Institution of Divine Service in general:* vers. 4–43.—*a.* The Levites appointed for service by David: vers. 4–6.—*And he appointed* (properly, "gave;" comp. ver. 7) *before the ark of the Lord ministers of the Levites,* namely, as the addition "to record, etc." shows, singers and players for the purpose of sacred singing, Levitical ministers (λειτουργοῦντας, Sept.).—*To record, and to thank, and to praise.* לְהַזְכִּיר, literally, "to bring to remembrance, to pray at the אַזְכָּרָה of the meat-offering" (Lev. ii. 2; comp. Ps. xxxviii. 1, lxx. 1, and Del. on the first passage). לְהוֹדוֹת, properly, "to confess" (Sept., ἐξομολογεῖσθαι), refers to the singing of psalms that prominently confess and express thanks to God, as לְהַלֵּל refers to the praises of the hallelujah songs. —Ver. 5. *Asaph the chief, and next to him Zechariah,* literally, "and as his second, his next man (follower);" comp. Esth. x. 3. Of the three song-masters and fourteen musicians named in the list xv. 19–21, a part only are named again: of the song-masters only Asaph, and of the musicians only nine (namely, six of the eight nebel-players and three of the six kinnor-players), and also, ver. 6, of the seven trumpet-blowers, only two, Benaiah and Jahaziel, the latter of whom did not appear in xv. 24. As we possess no parallel report to compare with the contents of our section, nothing definite can be conjectured of the relation of the present names to those of the longer series, and it must be left uncertain whether Jahaziel be identical with the Eliezer named, ver. 24, along with Benaiah.

6. *Continuation. b.* The song of praise and thanks by Asaph and his brethren: vers. 7–36.—*On that day then David ordered for the first time . . . by Asaph,* etc. Properly, "then David gave over . . . by the hand of Asaph;" נָתַן בְּיַד, here "to hand over, arrange." בָּרֹאשׁ, not "by the chief, by Asaph," but "first, for the first time;" comp. מֵרֹאשׁ, Isa. xl. 21. This is the first introduction of the new cultus. Along with Asaph are named "his brethren," the Levites arranged with (and under) him, enumerated in vers. 5, 6. We may observe, moreover, how clearly this verse, especially by its בָּרֹאשׁ, announces the following song as an ideal composition, characterizing only in general that which was to be sung by the musicians, but not expressing a stereotype form. Had the author wished to convey the sense that the song was sung for all time so as he communicated it, and not otherwise, he would have added, "and he commanded them *thus* to sing," or, "to sing this song."—Ver. 8 ff. *Thank ye the Lord, call on His name,* etc. Of the eight strophes of the song, the first four (vers. 8–22) correspond to the opening of Ps. cv. (vers. 1–15); the next three (vers. 23–33) to Ps. xcvi.; the last (vers. 34–36) to the first and last two verses of Ps. cvi., with some unimportant variations which are here to be noted.—*First Strophe:* vers. 8–11 (= Ps. cv. 1–4): Summons to sing praise to the Lord and to seek His face.—*Second Strophe:* vers. 12–14 (= Ps. cv. 5–7): Summons to think of the wonders of the Lord and His judgments. Here are the first variants, namely, ver. 12, פִּיהוּ instead of פִּיו, and, ver. 13, זֶרַע יִשְׂרָאֵל instead of ז׳ אַבְרָהָם, of which the latter only is of any consequence. On account of the parallelism with the "sons of Jacob," the "seed of Israel" appears the better reading.—*Third Strophe:* vers. 15–18 (= Ps. cv. 8–11): Summons to think of the covenant made by the Lord with the fathers.—*Remember His covenant for ever.* Ps. cv. rather: "He remembereth, etc." (זָכַר for זִכְרוּ). Our reading, corresponding better with the application of the song to the end proposed in ver. 7, appears to be substituted for the more original one of the Psalm.—Ver. 16. *And His oath unto Isaac.* For לְיִצְחָק Ps. cv. 9 presents the weaker form לְיִשְׂחָק (found also in Amos vii. 9; Jer. xxxiii. 26), a critically unimportant variant, like that in ver. 18*a*, where אֶרֶץ כְּנַעַן stands for את־ארץ־כ׳.—*Fourth Strophe:* vers. 19–22 (= Ps. cv. 12–15): Reason of the summons to remember the covenant of the Lord with the fathers, because the Lord has so truly and mightily protected them according to His promise.—*When ye were small in number.* Instead of בִּהְיוֹתְכֶם Ps. cv. 12 presents בִּהְיוֹתָם. To address the children of Israel again corresponds better with the aim of the Psalm; this variant is thus similar to that in ver. 15, but affords no presumption in favour of the priority of this or that reading.—Ver. 20. *And from one kingdom.* Ps. cv. omits the "and" (ו before מִמַּמְלָכָה); critically unimportant, as also the two following variants (ver. 21, לְאִישׁ for אָדָם, and, ver. 22, וּבִנְבִיאַי for וְלִנְבִיאַי).—*Fifth Strophe:* vers. 23–27 (= Ps. xcvi. 1–6): All the world shall concur in praise of the greatness and glory of God.—The first verse of this passage seems compounded of the first two verses of Ps. xcvi., the first members being omitted. Whether this be an abbreviating process of the Chronist, or an amplifying one of the Psalmist, it is hard to determine; much may be said for each of the two assumptions (see Keil).—Ver. 27. *Strength and gladness are in His place* (וְחֶדְוָה בִּמְקֹמוֹ; comp. for this late, but in Aram. frequent, חֶדְוָה, Ezra vi. 16; Neh. viii. 10). On the contrary, Ps. xcvi. 6: "strength and beauty in His sanctuary" (וְתִפְאֶרֶת בְּמִקְדָּשׁוֹ).—*Sixth Strophe:* vers. 28–30 (= Ps. xcvi. 7–9): All nations shall worship God

with offerings and confessions.—Ver. 29. *Give to the Lord the glory due to His name*, etc. Instead of two, this verse has, to our surprise, three members: the first two correspond to Ps. xcvi. 8; ver. 9 there to our ver. 29*c* and ver. 30*a*. The disturbance of the parallel in our verse rests on this, that after ver. 31*a* (=Ps. xcvi. 11*a*) the verse-member Ps. xcvi. 10*a* is placed, but Ps. xcvi. 10*c* is altogether omitted. Thus, in our text, the verse beginning with "give to the Lord the glory;" on the contrary, in Ps. xcvi., that beginning with "say among the heathen" (ver. 10), forms the exception to the otherwise constant bipartition of the verse. It is impossible, however, to arrive at a certain result on which side the priority lies (see on ver. 31).—*Bring an oblation, and come before Him.* Ps. xcvi. 8*b*: "and come to His courts" (לְחַצְרוֹתָיו for לְפָנָיו). This variant is similar to that in ver. 27, where "in His sanctuary" of the Psalm is changed into the more general "in His place," because the mention of the "sanctuary" (as here of the "courts") does not seem to comport well with the time and aim of the present song, which was sung before the erection of the temple.—Ver. 30. *Tremble before Him, all the earth.* For מִלְּפָנָיו Ps. xcvi. 9 has מִפָּנָיו, an unimportant difference.—*Seventh Strophe:* vers. 31–33 (=Ps. xcvi. 10–13): Even the inanimate creation will exult before the Lord of all nations coming to judgment. Ver. 31*a* corresponds to Ps. xcvi. 11*a*, but ver. 31*b* to Ps. xcvi. 10*a*.—*And let them say among the nations*, etc., is in Ps. xcvi. 10*a*: "say among the nations" (אִמְרוּ instead of וְיֹאמְרוּ). It is too much to say that this summons, addressed to the Israelites after the words "tremble before Him, all the earth" (which there go immediately before, as ver. 9*b*), yields a "rather tame thought," and speaks for the priority of the text of Chronicles (Keil). The position of the present summons among mere appeals to the representatives of inanimate nature, as the heavens, the earth, the sea, the field, may appear surprising and disturbing. There is something excited and wavering in the line of thought and mode of expression, there as well as here.—Ver. 32*b*. *Let the field rejoice*, etc. For יַעֲלֹץ הַשָּׂדֶה Ps. xc. 12*a* presents יַעֲלֹז שָׂדַי, in which the poetic and archaic שָׂדַי, instead of the prosaic הַשָּׂדֶה, seems not without significance.—Ver. 33. *Then shall the trees of the wood sing out.* For this Ps. xcvi. 12*b* has "all trees of the wood." The second member of this verse corresponds to the first in Ps. xcvi. 13, as far as the repetition of "for He cometh" (כִּי בָא), which occurs only once here. Ps. xcvi. 13*b*, the close of the whole Psalm, is wanting in our text, which the defenders of the priority of the latter explain thus: that when the contents of our verses 23–33 were made a distinct Psalm, it was found necessary to make at the close a suitable addition; whereas the matter may as well be explained by the abbreviating habit of our author (as the later compiler of the present song).—*Eighth Strophe:* vers. 34–36 (=Ps. cvi. 1, 47, 48): Repeated summons to thank God, and to pray for His further help, with the closing doxology.—*Thank ye the Lord; for He is good*, etc. This verse is found not merely at the head of Ps. cvi., but also of Ps. cvii., cxviii., cxxxvi. (comp. also Ps. cxviii. 29 and Jer. xxxiii. 11); as an old and favourite liturgical form, it is not necessarily to be regarded as taken from Ps. cvi. in particular.—Ver. 35. *And say ye, Save us, O God of our salvation.* Similar, but not verbally so, Ps. cvi. 47, where "and say ye" is wanting, and for "God of our salvation" stands "the Lord our God."—*And gather us and deliver us from the heathen.* For this Ps. cvi. 47 has: "and gather us from the heathen." The two following members agree verbally with the parallel verse of the Psalm.—*Blessed be the Lord*, etc. This closing doxology, which recurs exactly in Ps. cvi. 48, forms there the close of the fourth book of the Psalter, together with the words: "and let all the people say, Amen. Praise ye the Lord," which are here changed into the historical notice: "and all the people said, Amen, and praised the Lord" (וַיֹּאמְרוּ for the jussive וְאָמַר, and וְהַלֵּל יְהוָֹה for הַלְלוּ יָהּ). Even in these last deviations from the similar passages of the Psalter there is nothing that could prove with certainty the priority of our text, and a partly imitative, partly devious, procedure of the Psalmist. With regard to the doxology בָּרוּךְ יהוה וגו׳, which was originally nothing else than the liturgical close of the fourth book (analogous to those at the close of Ps. xli., lxxii., and lxxxix.), it is much more probable that our author changed, for his own purpose, this doxological formula, which may have been attached to Ps. cvi. long ago, from liturgical use. And the more probable this must appear to the unprejudiced mind, the more clearly all the other differences between our text and that of the corresponding Psalms appear as alterations, occasioned by the revising and compiling habit of the Chronist, of that which was before him in the Psalter. Comp. the closing remarks.

7. Division of the Levites and Priests for Divine Service (as continuation and close of the list of Levitical singers and players in vers. 4–6): vers. 37–43.—*Asaph and his brethren.* The לְ before the accus. of the object, according to later usage.—*For the day's work in its day*, literally, "for the matter of the day on its day," that is, according to the service required for every day; comp. 2 Chron. viii. 14, xxxi. 16.—Ver. 38. *And Obed-edom and their brethren sixty and eight.* That here should be read, according to what follows: "and Obed-edom and Hosah and their brethren," see Crit. Note. If, indeed, in the next clause of our verse: "and Obed-edom . . . and Hosah to be porters," another Obed-edom were meant, as the distinction of this as "son of Jedithun" (possibly, xxvi. 4, a Korhite Jedithun, and not the Merarite singer Jeduthun) appears to indicate, some other name than that of Hosah must be supplied along with the former Obed-edom. Even in xv. 21, 24 there seem to be two different Obed-edoms, a singer, ver. 21, and a porter, ver. 24. Yet the diversity of the two named in our verse is by no means certain; for in xxvi. 4–8, of Obed-edom with his sons and brothers, sixty-two men are mentioned as porters, which nearly agrees with the present number sixty-eight, and seems

to point to the identity of the first-mentioned and the second Obed-edom. Ver. 42 of our chapter also shows clearly enough the identity of the present Jedithun with Jeduthun. In the notorious defectiveness of the text, besides, we cannot attain to a certain decision.—Ver. 39. *And Zadok the priest, and his brethren the priests.* ויעזב, ver. 37, still acts as the governing verb. For the continued religious use of the sanctuary at Gibeon under David, see on xv. 1. It is to be remarked that Zadok is designated only as priest, not as high priest, as he was made first by Solomon; see 1 Kings ii. 27, 35.—Ver. 40. *To offer burnt-offerings to the Lord on the altar of burnt-offering.* The mention here of burnt-offerings only at Gibeon proves nothing against the assumption that they were also offered in the sanctuary at Jerusalem; and ch. xxi. 26, 30 shows directly and expressly that these offerings were made here also, no doubt under the direction of Abiathar (comp. xviii. 16).—*Continually morning and evening.* Comp. the prescriptions of the law, Ex. xxix. 38; Num. xxviii. 3, 6.—*And for all* (that was prescribed besides the daily burnt-offering; comp. Num. xxviii.) *that is written.* לְכָל־הַכָּתוּב, briefly for לַעֲשׂוֹת כָּל־הכ׳.—Ver. 41. *And with them*, etc., with Zadok and his brethren. This refers to the singers at the sanctuary in Gibeon, where Heman, Jeduthun (Ethan), and a number of subordinates were appointed. The Chronist points indeed to a list before him, in which the Gibeonite singers were named (on נִקְּבוּ בְּשֵׁמוֹת, comp. xii. 31), but does not specify them, because the singers under Asaph at Jerusalem, who are enumerated vers. 4–6, interested him most. — Ver. 42. *And with them, Heman and Jeduthun, were trumpets and cymbals.* So, according to the Masoretic reading, which, however, appears suspicious, from the absence of the names Heman and Jeduthun in the Sept. (comp. Crit. Note), and gives no very suitable sense. If we erase the two names, the sense comes out: "and with them were, that is, they had trumpets and cymbals," a phrase somewhat strange, but still affording a suitable sense, which is at all events to be preferred to the artificial and forced emendation of Bertheau ("And Heman and Jeduthun were playing aloud with trumpets and cymbals, and with them the others chosen, with song-instruments of God"). — *For loud sounding,* לְמַשְׁמִיעִים. This epithet belonging to the מְצִלְתַּיִם defines the cymbals as giving the tone, or intoning the melody, and thus being a means of leading the song for the song-masters Heman and Jeduthun; comp. on xv. 16, 19. —*And* (other) *instruments of God*, other instruments of religious music besides those named, especially psalteries and harps.—*And the sons of Jeduthun were at the gate;* they were appointed to guard the entrance of the Gibeonite tabernacle. These are obviously Obed-edom, Hosah, and their brethren, who had been designated, ver. 38, as doorkeepers. — Ver. 43. *And all the people went every man to his house;* essentially as in 2 Sam. vi. 19, 20, where this closing verse of our chapter has its parallel in an otherwise much more concise report. The narrative there added, of David's altercation with Michal (comp. xv. 29), our author omits as a scene of a purely domestic character, unsuitable to his purpose.—*And David turned in to bless his house,* on this festive day, as he had before (ver. 2) blessed the whole people in the name of the Lord.

Appendix: On the Credibility of the Contents of ch. xvi.

As ch. xii., notwithstanding its exclusive transmission by our author, makes the impression of the highest credibility, the statistical data and registers also of our section, just because they are mostly of a concrete and detailed kind, afford the warrant of a true rendering of the historical facts. Important there as well as here is the reference to greater and richer registers, that must have served the Chronist as sources, without being exhausted by him; comp. the characteristic אֲשֶׁר־נִקְּבוּ בְּשֵׁמוֹת, xii. 31, xvi. 41, and such specifications of names as vers. 4–6 and ver. 38 ff., which clearly indicate in the author a process of abstracting and contracting more copious lists. It is manifest enough that he was in a position, as belonging himself to the corps of Levitical singers after the exile (Introd. § 3), to draw these statements from the full fountains, and to depend on copious written and oral traditions.

Only with respect to the song given in vers. 8–36, at the dedication, the assumption of strict historical accuracy appears to be given up on account of its relation to several parallel Psalms; and an ideal composing process of the writer, similar to that of Livy and Thucydides in their speeches, is assumed as necessary. We know not, in fact, what could stand against the admissibility of this assumption, defended by Bertheau, Kamph., Dillmann, Davidson, Ewald (*Bibl. Jahrb.* vi. 24), Delitzsch (*Komm. zum Psalter*, ii. p. 93 f.), A. Köhler (*Zeitschr. für luth. Theol.* 1867, p. 295 ff.), C. Ehrt (*Abfassungszeit und Schluss des Ps.*, Leipzig 1869, p. 41 ff.), Hupfeld, and others. If, of recent scholars, on the one hand Hitzig (*Die Psalmen*, 2 Bd. 1865, p. viii. ff.), on the other Keil (*Komm.* p. 155 ff.),—the former impelled by a hypercritical zeal to show the Maccabean origin of those Psalms to be probable, the latter by an apologetic motive in favour of the Chronist,—have endeavoured to prove our form to be original, and the passages of the Psalms cv. 1–15, xcvi. 1–13, cvi. 1, 47, 48, to be mere fragments of the original song, against this the following considerations remain still in force:—

1. The constitution of both the texts, even if the greater number of defects and corruptions occur in the Psalms, and the text of Chronicles be comparatively older and better, admits of no certain conclusion with respect to the greater or less age of the one or the other recension. For, irrespective of the many cases in which Chronicles most probably contains the later readings (for example, ver. 27, חֶדְוָה; ver. 32, הַשָּׂדֶה; ver. 29, לְפָנָיו for לַחֲצֵרוֹתָיו; and again, ver. 27, בִּמְקֹמוֹ for בְּמִקְדָּשׁוֹ), the more archaic form of the text cannot of itself decide in favour of priority, as younger MSS., and certainly Hebrew as well as Greek and Latin, often enough present a more original text than older ones, and the text of the passages in the Psalms are not to be judged according to their external written form. For

"the text of the Psalms, while they were in liturgical use, was more exposed to alterations from the influence of the later speech than that of a historical book; and on this ground, more ancient turns and phrases in Chronicles could not be at once maintained as proofs that Chronicles was original and the Psalms an imitation" (Berth.).

2. If we consider the matter and line of thought in our song, and compare it with the corresponding Psalms, the latter appear simple, well connected, and well-ordered wholes in a higher degree than the former. The transition from strophe four to strophe five of our song (see vers. 22, 28) is abrupt and sudden. We expect that after ver. 22, either the agency of Jehovah in the early time of Israel will be further depicted, as is done in Ps. cv., where complete connection and unity of thought prevails,[1] or at least, by a description of His agency in the heathen world or in inanimate nature (comp. Ps. civ.), the way will be prepared for the summonses contained in vers. 23–33. A similar hiatus again appears between vers. 33 and 34 (or between strophes seven and eight), and also after the section parallel with Ps. xcvi. For the summons of ver. 34, as appears undeniable from ver. 35, is to be regarded as specially directed to Israel; but Israel is not spoken of either in ver. 34 or in the whole preceding paragraph, vers. 23–33. If Hitzig thinks that here the end of the song only returns to its beginning, he has not sufficiently considered that petitions such as those contained in ver. 35, for the deliverance and gathering of Israel from the heathen, do not occur at the beginning of the song, and that these petitions come in here quite unexpectedly after the previous line of thought in vers. 8–33; whereas they are very well introduced in Ps. cvi. 47, after vers. 40–46.

3. Decisive for the priority of the Psalter is the transference of the closing doxology of the fourth book of Psalms (Ps. cvi. 48) by the redactor of our song; see on this passage, and comp. Delitzsch on the Psalm.

4. The manner in which the song is introduced (see on ver. 7) points also to an ideal composing activity of the author of it.

5. Our combining of a number of passages from the Psalms into one whole should not be regarded as a product of mere trifling and insipid compilation, like the Homeric or Virgilian cantos of the declining old classical poetry, because it applies to a festal song to be used for a definite liturgical purpose, and because nothing certain can be opposed to the assumption, that not the Chronist in the times after the exile, but the writer of his source, the older report (certainly before the exile) which he follows throughout the section vers. 4–42, is to be regarded as the author of the present composition.

6. Whether the present attempt to exhibit the opening of the worship on Zion in Davidic strains is to be considered older than the composition of our book, or contemporary with it, we are not to find an offence against the obligation of historical fidelity in this ideal composition, which seeks to reproduce the fundamental tone of the song sung on that occasion. The author knew that in the religious festivals of his people songs were sung of the tone of Ps. xcvi., cv., cvi., from the oldest times; hence he puts in the mouth of the Levitical singers in David's time a song formed out of these Psalms as a probable expression of the spiritual thanksgiving presented to the Lord by the community of that day, without in the least making himself guilty of a falsehood. He appears on this ground as little a falsifier as the author of the song of Mary, of Zacharias, or of Simeon in the introductory chapter of Luke's Gospel, the verbal recitation of which, according to the form there given, need scarcely be insisted on, and the harmony of which with so many characteristic phrases of the Psalms and Prophets, has its historical precedent in the relations of our song to the Psalms in question.

[Ps. xcvi., cv., and cvi. are anonymous in the Hebrew; but on examination, there is no convincing reason why they may not have been composed by David. Ps. xcvi. is actually ascribed to him in the Sept., with the following remarkable addition: "when the house was built after the captivity." Here the captivity seems to refer to the captivity of the ark when far from the sanctuary, 1 Sam. iv., and the house to the tabernacle which David erected on Zion. The other two Psalms may be as old as David; and there is therefore no reason to doubt the historical veracity of the statement made by the Chronist, that David selected from these Psalms the piece that was actually sung at the dedication of the tabernacle on Zion.—J. G. M.]

[1] For the picture of the benign sway of God over Abraham, in vers. 10–15 of this Psalm, forms only the beginning of that which is said in the further course of the same picture, of Jacob, of Joseph and his brethren, of Moses, and of the whole of God's people in the patriarchal and Mosaic times.

θ. The Purpose of David to build a Temple, and the Objection raised by the Prophet Nathan. ch. xvii.

CHAP. XVII. 1. And it came to pass, as David sat in his house, he said unto Nathan
the prophet, Lo, I dwell in a house of cedars, and the ark of the covenant of the
2 LORD is under curtains. And Nathan said unto David, Do all that is in thine
3 heart; for God is with thee. And it came to pass in that night, that the word of
4 the LORD came to Nathan, saying, Go and say unto David my servant, Thus
5 saith the LORD, Thou shalt not build me a house to dwell in. For I have not
dwelt in a house from the day that I brought up Israel unto this day; but I was
6 from tent to tent, and from one tabernacle to another. As long as I have walked
in all Israel have I spoken a word with any of the judges of Israel, whom I com-
7 manded to feed my people, Why have ye not built me a house of cedars? And
now, thus shalt thou say unto my servant David, Thus saith the LORD of hosts,

I took thee from the common, from behind the sheep, to be ruler over my people
8 Israel. And I was with thee, whithersoever thou wentest; and I cut off all thy
enemies from before thee, and made thee a name like the name of the great on
9 the earth. And I ordained a place for my people Israel, and planted them, and
they dwelt in it, and were no more troubled; and the sons of evil no more wasted
10 them as before. And since the days that I appointed judges over my people
Israel: and I subdue all thy enemies; and I tell thee that the Lord will build
11 thee a house. And it shall come to pass, when thy days are fulfilled to go unto
thy fathers, that I will raise up thy seed after thee, which shall be of thy sons,
12 and I will establish his kingdom. He shall build me a house, and I will estab-
13 lish his house for ever. I will be his father, and he shall be my son; and I will
14 not take my mercy from him, as I took it from him who was before thee. But
I will settle him in my house and in my kingdom for ever; and his throne shall
be established for ever.
15 According to all these words and all this vision, so Nathan spake unto David.
16 And King David went and sat before the LORD, and said, Who am I, O LORD
17 God, and what is my house, that Thou hast brought me hitherto? And this was
a small thing in Thine eyes, O God; and Thou hast spoken of the house of Thy
servant for a great while to come, and regardest me after the way[1] of man that
18 raiseth up, O LORD God. What shall David add to Thee of the glory of Thy
19 servant?[2] and Thou knowest Thy servant. O LORD, for Thy servant's sake, and
after Thy heart, hast Thou done all this greatness, to make known all these great
20 things. O LORD, there is none like Thee, and no God besides Thee, according to
21 all that we have heard with our ears. And what one nation in the earth is like
Thy people Israel, whom God went to redeem to Himself as a people, to make
Thee a name of great and terrible deeds, to drive out nations before Thy people,
22 whom Thou didst redeem from Egypt? And madest Thy people Israel a people
23 to Thee for ever; and Thou, LORD, becamest their God. And now, LORD, let the
word which Thou hast spoken of Thy servant and of his house be maintained for
24 ever, and do as Thou hast said. Yea, let it be maintained, and let Thy name be
magnified for ever, saying, JEHOVAH Zebaoth, the God of Israel, is God to Israel;
25 and the house of David Thy servant is established before Thee. For Thou, O my
God, hast opened the ear of Thy servant, that Thou wilt build him a house; there-
26 fore Thy servant hath found [courage] to pray before Thee. And now, LORD,
27 Thou art God, and hast spoken this goodness concerning Thy servant. And now
Thou art pleased to bless the house of Thy servant, that it may be before Thee
for ever; for Thou, LORD, hast blessed, and it is blessed for ever.

[1] For כְּתוֹר a good many MSS. read בְּתוֹךְ, which is as unsatisfactory as the obscure כְּתוֹר, or as תּוֹרַת, 2 Sam. vii. 19, or as the reading of the **Sept.**: *καὶ ἐπεῖδές με ὡς ὅρασις ἀνθρώπου, καὶ ὕψωσάς με*, or that of the Vulg.: *et fecisti me spectabilem super omnes homines.*

[2] אֶת־עַבְדֶּךָ, wanting in the Sept. and in 2 Sam. vii. 21, is perhaps spurious. But see Exeg. Expl.

EXEGETICAL.

PRELIMINARY REMARK.—After the history of the transplanting of the ark to Jerusalem, the author of the books of Samuel has given the account of David's purpose to build a temple, and of the word of God communicated to him by Nathan, 2 Sam. vii., and, indeed, in a form substantially agreeing with the present text, though occasionally deviating from it in words. Besides the expositors of Chronicles are therefore here to be compared also those of the corresponding parts of the books of Samuel, namely, C. A. Crusius (*Hypomnemata*, ii. pp. 190-219), Thenius, Keil, Hengstenberg (*Christol.* 2d edit. i. 143 ff.), L. Reinke (*Die Weissagung des Propheten Nathan*, in his contributions to the explanation of the O. T., vol. iv. p. 427 ff.), and, in a critical respect, Wellhausen (p. 170).

1. David's Purpose, and Nathan's Consent at first to it: vers. 1, 2.—*As David sat in his house*, in that cedar palace described in xiv. 1, xv. 1 ff. After בְּבֵיתוֹ 2 Sam. vii. 1 has the further chronological determination: "and the Lord had given him rest round about from all his enemies." Our author leaves out this determination intentionally, to avoid the apparent contradiction with the circumstance that the severest wars of David are introduced afterwards, and so, according to his arrangement of the material, following the order of thought rather than of time.—Ver. 2. *Do all . . . for God is with thee.* In 2 Sam.: "Go and do . . . for the Lord is with thee." The omission of לֵךְ before עֲשֵׂה rests on the strong abbreviating and simplifying tendency of our author; the substitution of אֱלֹהִים for

יְהוָה on his aim to choose the current expressions of his day. The older practical expositors justly designate this preliminary consent of Nathan as proceeding "from his merely human judgment" (*bona intentione et sincero animo, non tamen ex divina revelatione*, J. H. Mich.).—Luth.: "The prophets themselves occasionally err and sin, as Nathan when he says to David of his own spirit that he shall build a house to the Lord, which is soon after altered by a divine revelation."

2. God's Revelation to Nathan: vers. 3–15.—On the night as the time of divine revelations by dreams, visions, etc., comp. our remarks on Job iv. 13 (pp. 75, 84).—*Thou shalt not build me a house to dwell in.* In 2 Samuel this prohibition is put in the form of a question: "Shalt thou build me a house?"—Ver. 5. *But I was from tent to tent, and from tabernacle;* that is, from one tabernacle to another. For this sentence, which is obscure from its pregnant brevity, 2 Samuel gives: "but have walked (have been walking) in a tent and in a tabernacle." The tabernacle (משכן) is presented along with the tent (אהל) as the more comprehensive notion, including court, altar of burnt-offering, etc.—Ver. 6. *With any of the judges of Israel.* 2 Samuel: "with any of the tribes of Israel" (שִׁבְטֵי for שֹׁפְטֵי). Our reading is perhaps the older; comp. Berth. and Wellh.—Ver. 7 ff. give the proper contents of the divine revelation, as far as it concerns David's relation to the building of the temple.—Ver. 8. *And made thee a name, like the name of the great on the earth,* referring to the kings of the heathen monarchies. These words (ver. 8*b*) formed the text of the memorial sermon preached in all the churches of the Prussian state on the death of Frederick II. (1786).—Ver. 9. *And I ordained a place for my people Israel.* The perfects (with ו *consec.*) וּנְטַעְתִּיהוּ, וְשַׂמְתִּי, etc., may be taken as future statements of that which God will further show to His people. Yet it seems better to make these promises of future salvation begin with ver. 11.—*And the sons of evil no more wasted them as before.* The Egyptians are no doubt chiefly intended; comp. xvi. 20. On בַּלֹּה in the sense of wasting (= עַנֹּה in 2 Samuel), comp. Dan. vii. 25.—Ver. 10. *And since the days that I appointed judges over my people Israel.* וּלְמִיָּמִים, "and until the days" (Ew. § 218, *b*); comp. the still more definite phrase: וּלְמִן־הַיּוֹם, 2 Sam. vii. 11. The whole time from Joshua to Saul is here included.—*And I subdue all thy enemies.* 2 Samuel: "and I give thee rest from all thy enemies" (וַהֲנִיחֹתִי לְךָ for וְהִכְנַעְתִּי), perhaps more original. The change of the suffix of the 2d pers. into that of the 3d (Berth., Ew.) is not necessary, either in our passage or there, as the enumeration of the divine benefits extends to the present, and even to that which was experienced by David himself.—*And I tell thee that the Lord will build thee a house,* and not inversely: thou build Him a house. The building of the house is here naturally figurative of the bestowment of a blessed posterity, etc. There is no allusion to David's house of cedar (ver. 1, xiv. 1). Inadmissible is the past meaning of וָאַגִּד, "and I have told them," etc. (Berth., Wellh.); for we cannot discover that such an announcement was made before, as our historical books nowhere mention it. Even 2 Sam. (וְהִגִּיד) speaks of an announcement in the present or immediate future.—Ver. 11. *To go unto thy fathers.* 2 Sam. vii.: "to lie with thy fathers." For the phrase, comp. Deut. xxxi. 16; 1 Kings ii. 2.—*Thy seed . . . which shall be of thy sons.* Instead of this somewhat pleonastic reference to Solomon, 2 Samuel presents perhaps the original: "which shall proceed out of thy bowels" (אֲשֶׁר יֵצֵא מִמֵּעֶיךָ; comp. 1 Sam. xvi. 11; Gen. xv. 4). Probably the chronological difficulty contained in this phrase, according to which Solomon appeared to be not yet born at the time of this promise, led our author to choose the more general expression, as he had in ver. 1 altered the text for a chronological reason by means of an omission. That here, as in the two following verses, he meant to designate not so much Solomon as the Messiah, is asserted by the older orthodox exegesis (for example, L. Lavater: "*Si tantum de Salomone h. l. intelligendus esset, non dixisset semen quod erit de filiis tuis, sed quod erit de te;*" and so Starke and others), and recently still by Keil. But the very next prediction: "He shall build me a house" (ver. 12), applies clearly to Solomon only, as in 2 Chron. vii. 18 his person, and not that of some future Messianic descendant, is manifestly designated. Accordingly, as in 2 Samuel, so also in Chronicles the Messianic element is limited essentially to the eternal duration that is promised (vers. 12–14) to the kingdom of Solomon; comp. Hengstenb. *Christol.* i. 152 ff.—Ver. 13. *And he shall be my son.* The words following this promise: "whom I will chasten with the rod of men, and with the stripes of the sons of men," the Chronist has designedly omitted, to bring out more sharply the thought of the everlasting divine favour, in harmony with his usual practice to set the light before the shade of the house of David.—*From him who was before thee,* from Saul, whose name is added, 2 Sam. vii., perhaps by the hand of a glossator. The present text is certainly more original, even with respect to the foregoing לֹא אָסִיר (for לֹא יָסוּר), as Bertheau and Wellh. justly assert against Thenius.—Ver. 14. *But I will settle him in my house and in my kingdom for ever;* הֶעֱמִיד לְעוֹלָם, as in 2 Chron. ix. 8, 1 Kings xv. 4, of enduring foundation or preservation, causing perpetual existence. The "house" or "kingdom" of God, in which this preservation or confirming of the seed of David is to take place, is first the Old Testament theocracy, then the Messianic kingdom of the new covenant. The text of Samuel differs: "and thy house and thy kingdom shall endure for ever before thee, and thy throne shall be established for ever," of which form it can scarcely be so absolutely asserted, as is done by Bertheau and others, that it is the more original. Moreover, the sense of the one as of

the other form is Messianic.—Ver. 15. *According to all these words and all this vision.* A hendiadyoin, by which the words addressed by Jehovah to Nathan are characterized as spoken, בְּחָזוֹן (comp. 1 Sam. iii. 1) or בְּחִזָּיוֹן (2 Sam. vii. 17), as a divine revelation or prophetic message from God. It is to be observed also that this prophetic message is communicated not as it was related by Nathan before the king, but as it was revealed to him of the Lord by night, which is a plain indication that we are to hold by the matter rather than the form of the words in question. The case is the same as in 1 Sam. iii. 10–14 (the disclosure made to the young Samuel concerning the fate of Eli) and in 1 Sam. viii. 7–9 (God's word to Samuel on the introduction of the kingdom in Israel).

3. David's Thanksgiving for the Promise made to him through Nathan: vers. 16–27.—*And King David went,* into the sanctuary erected by him, as the following words: "and sat before the Lord," show.—*Who am I, O Lord God?* 2 Samuel: "my Lord God," a difference actually not existing for the Masoretic reader, as our יהוה is to be read by אֲדֹנָי.—Ver. 17. *And this was a small thing in Thine eyes.* This is the literal rendering.—*And Thou hast spoken of the house of Thy servant for a great while to come,* literally, "hast spoken that which points far away;" לְמֵרָחוֹק is an accusative depending on תדבר, of the same force as in Prov. vii. 19, Job xxxix. 29; comp. ver. 14.—*And regardest me after the way of man that raiseth up.* So should the obscure וּרְאִיתַנִי כְּתוֹר הָאָדָם הַמַּעֲלָה perhaps be rendered; "the way of man leading upwards" (תּוֹר, abbreviated from תּוֹרָה) would then be the gracious and upholding (thus not merely condescending, but positively furthering and improving) disposition and conduct of human benefactors, with which the gracious procedure of God towards David is here compared. Nearly so Keil, who makes הַמַּעֲלָה correspond to the parallel לְמֵרָחוֹק, whereas Hengstenberg, like many ancients, conceives the phrase to be an address to God: "Thou highest Lord God;" and other expositors take it as an adverb of place equivalent to בַּמָּרוֹם (*et me intuitus es more hominum in cœlis*). It is natural enough to assume some corruption of the text here, as in the parallel reading of Samuel: וְזֹאת תּוֹרַת הָאָדָם, though none of the proposed emendations give satisfaction, neither Ewald's and Bertheau's change of the *Kal* ראיתני into the *Hiph.* הראיתני, and of המעלה into למעלה (resulting in the sense: "and hast caused me to see, as it were, the order of men upwards"), nor Böttcher's reading וּרְאִיתִינִי, "so that I saw myself as the order of men that is upwards" (saw myself as the after-age at the head of a ruling race), nor Wellhausen's conjecture that וַתַּרְאֵנִי דֹרוֹת (at least in 2 Samuel) should be read. That the בְּתוֹךְ of some Heb. MSS. affords no sufficient help, see Crit. Note.—Ver. 18. *What shall David add to Thee of the glory of Thy servant,* of the honour pertaining to Thy servant, of the high honour which Thou hast vouchsafed to Thy servant (me, David). So conceived, אֶת־עַבְדֶּךָ gives a tolerable sense, and need not be erased, with the modern critics, though its absence in the Sept. and in 2 Samuel (where there is merely: "what shall David say further to Thee?") is fitted to create suspicion.—Ver. 19. *O Lord, for Thy servant's sake.* 2 Sam. vii. 21: "for Thy word's sake." The original reading is not necessarily to be sought in the text of Samuel (see Wellh.). In *b* our author has contracted the longer form of the other text.—Ver. 21. *Whom God went to redeem to Himself as a people.* After this certainly correct reading (הלךְ האלהים) is that in 2 Samuel (אֲשֶׁר הָלְכוּ אלהים) to be altered. — *To make Thee a name of great and terrible deeds.* The words גְּדֻלּוֹת וְנוֹרָאוֹת appear to be loosely annexed to שֵׁם, to define the way in which God made him a name (comp. Ew. § 283). If this construction seem too harsh, לַעֲשׂוֹת must be inserted (as in 2 Sam. vii. 23) after שֵׁם: "that Thou makest Thee a name, and doest great and terrible things."—*To drive out nations before Thy people.* The here much deviating text in 2 Samuel should be altered partly according to the present text, namely, by inserting the certainly original לְגָרֵשׁ; see Geiger, *Urschrift und Uebersetzung des A. T.*, and Wellh., who follows him. —Ver. 24. *Yea, let it be maintained,* etc. This וְיֵאָמֵן is wanting in 2 Samuel, and is perhaps repeated from ver. 23, to set forth more clearly the connection with the following: "and let Thy name be magnified." On the copula וְ, in the sense of our "yea," comp. Dan. x. 19.—Ver. 25. *For Thou, O my God, hast opened the ear of Thy servant,* revealed, disclosed, made known to him; comp. 1 Sam. ix. 15.—*That Thou wilt build him a house,* figuratively, by the increase of his posterity and the prosperity of his dynasty; comp. ver. 10.—*Therefore Thy servant hath found to pray before Thee,* namely, "the courage, the heart to do so" (אֶת־לִבּוֹ, 2 Sam. vii. 28), which is, at all events, here to be supplied, if not necessarily inserted in the text.—Ver. 27. *For Thou, Lord, hast blessed, and it is blessed for ever;* comp., for the sentence and the expression, Ps. xxxiii. 9. On the credibility of the thanksgiving of David given here and 2 Sam. vii. 18 ff., Thenius and Bertheau express themselves very favourably. They refer its main elements to David, on account of its many properties harmonizing with other genuine Davidic documents. In particular the last words of David (2 Sam. xxiii. 5 ff.), in which the joyful confidence founded on the divine promises in the happy continuance of his house has found a quite similar expression, count with them as a proof that our verses rest on a definite recollection of the utterance of David, and that exact reports of important expressions

concerning the history of salvation, as they were handed down partly by David, partly concerning him, must have been contained in the sources f the books of Samuel and of Chronicles.

c. *David's Wars and Officers of State, especially his Victorious Battles with the Ammonites and the Philistines:* ch. xviii.–xx.

CH. XVIII. 1. And after this it came to pass, that David smote the Philistines, and
subdued them, and took Gath and her daughters out of the hand of the
2 Philistines. And he smote Moab; and the Moabites became David's servants,
and brought gifts.
3 And David smote Hadadezer[1] king of Zobah towards Hamath, as he went
4 to set up his sign at the river Euphrates. And David took from him a thousand
chariots, and seven thousand horsemen, and twenty thousand footmen: and
5 David lamed all the teams, but reserved of them a hundred teams. And the
Syrians of Damascus[2] came to help Hadadezer king of Zobah; and David slew
6 of the Syrians twenty and two thousand men. And David put [men[3]] in Syria
Damascus; and the Syrians became David's servants, and brought gifts: and
7 the LORD preserved David wherever he went. And David took the arms of
gold that were on the servants of Hadadezer, and brought them to Jerusalem.
8 And from Tibhath and from Chun, cities of Hadadezer, David took very much
brass, of which Solomon made the brazen sea, and the pillars, and the brazen
vessels.
9 And Tou king of Hamath heard that David had smitten all the host of
10 Hadadezer king of Zobah. And he sent Hadoram his son to King David, to
greet him and to bless him, because he had fought against Hadadezer and
smitten him; for Tou was at war with Hadadezer; and [with him] all manner
11 of vessels of gold, and silver, and brass. These also King David dedicated unto
the LORD, with the silver and the gold that he had taken from all the nations,
from Edom, and from Moab, and from the sons of Ammon, and from the Philis-
tines, and from Amalek.
12 And Abshai the son of Zeruiah slew of Edom in the valley of salt eighteen
13 thousand. And he put garrisons in Edom; and all the Edomites became
servants of David: and the LORD preserved David wherever he went.
14 And David reigned over all Israel, and executed judgment and justice for all
15 his people. And Joab the son of Zeruiah was over the host; and Jehoshaphat
16 the son of Ahilud was recorder. And Zadok the son of Ahitub, and Abimelech[4]
17 the son of Abiathar, were priests; and Shavsha was scribe. And Benaiah the
son of Jehoiada was over the Cherethi and Pelethi; and David's sons were the
chief beside the king.
CH. XIX. 1. And it came to pass after this, that Nahash king of the sons of Ammon
2 died, and his son reigned in his stead. And David said, I will show kindness
unto Hanun the son of Nahash, because his father showed kindness to me; and
David sent messengers to comfort him concerning his father: and the servants of
3 David came to the land of the sons of Ammon, to Hanun, to comfort him. And
the princes of the sons of Ammon said to Hanun: Thinkest thou that David
doth honour thy father, that he hath sent comforters unto thee? are not his
servants come to thee to search and to turn over, and to spy out the land?
4 And Hanun took David's servants, and shaved them, and cut off half their
5 garments by the breech, and sent them away. And they went, and they told
David about the men, and he sent to meet them; for the men were greatly
ashamed: and the king said, Tarry at Jericho until your beard be grown, and
then return.
6 And the sons of Ammon saw that they had made themselves stink with David:
and Hanun and the sons of Ammon sent a thousand talents of silver to hire
them chariots and horsemen out of Mesopotamia, and out of Syria-maachah, and
7 out of Zobah. And they hired them thirty and two thousand chariots, and the
king of Maachah and his people; and they came and pitched before Medeba:
and the sons of Ammon gathered together from their cities, and came to battle.

8, 9 And David heard, and sent Joab, and all the host of the mighty men. And the
sons of Ammon came out, and set the battle in array at the gate of the city; and
the kings that were come stood by themselves in the field.
10 And Joab saw that the battle was directed against him before and behind;
and he chose out of all the choice in Israel, and drew up against the Syrians.
11 And the rest of the people he gave into the hand of Abshai his brother, and
12 they drew up against the sons of Ammon. And he said, If the Syrians be too
strong for me, then thou shalt come to my help; and if the sons of Ammon be
13 too strong for thee, then I will help thee. Be courageous, and let us do valiantly
for our people and for the cities of our God; and the LORD do that which is good
14 in His sight And Joab, and the people that were with him, drew nigh before
15 the Syrians to the battle; and they fled before him. And the sons of Ammon
saw that the Syrians fled, and they also fled before Abshai his brother, and went
into the city; and Joab went to Jerusalem.
16 And when the Syrians saw that they were smitten before Israel, they sent
messengers, and drew forth the Syrians that were beyond the river; and Sho-
17 phach, captain of the host of Hadadezer, went before them. And it was told
David; and he gathered all Israel, and passed the Jordan, and came to them,[5]
and drew up against them; and David drew up against the Syrians for battle,
18 and they fought with him. And the Syrians fled before Israel; and David slew
of the Syrians seven thousand teams, and forty thousand footmen; and he killed
19 Shophach, captain of the host. And when the servants of Hadadezer saw that
they were smitten before Israel, they made peace with David, and served him;
and the Syrians would not help the sons of Ammon any more.
CH. XX. 1. And it came to pass, when the year was ended, at the time when the
kings go out, that Joab led forth the strength of the host, and wasted the land
of the sons of Ammon, and came and besieged Rabbah; but David tarried in
2 Jerusalem; and Joab smote Rabbah, and destroyed it. And David took the
crown of their king from his head, and found it in weight a talent of gold, and
set with precious stones; and it was put upon David's head, and he brought
3 very much spoil out of the city. And he brought out the people that were in
it, and cut them with saws, and iron threshing-carts and saws;[6] and so David
did to all the cities of the sons of Ammon; and David returned with all the
people to Jerusalem.
4 And it came to pass after this, that a war arose at Gezer with the Philis-
tines; then Sibbecai the Hushathite slew Sippai, one of the sons of Rapha; and
5 they were subdued. And there was a war again with the Philistines; and
Elhanan the son of Jair slew Lachmi, brother of Goliath the Gittite; and his
6 spear's staff was like a weaver's beam. And again there was war in Gath, where
was a man of [great] stature, and his fingers were six and six, twenty and four
7 [in all]; and he also was born to Rapha. And he reproached Israel; and Jona-
8 than the son of Shima, David's brother, slew him. These were born to Rapha
in Gath; and they fell by the hand of David, and by the hand of his
servants.

[1] הֲדַרְעֶזֶר is the *Kethib* in all passages of our chapter, but the *Keri*: הֲדַדְעֶזֶר (so in 2 Sam. x. 16-19). The first form, the more usual in the books of Samuel and Kings, is also the more original, because הֲדַד, a Syrian idol name, occurs in other Syrian proper names.

[2] Properly Darmascus (דַּרְמֶשֶׂק—so here and ver. 6, also 2 Chron. xvi. 2, xxiv. 23, without variation; elsewhere always דַּמֶּשֶׂק).

[3] After וַיָּשֶׂם דָּוִיד there seems to have fallen out נְצִיבִים; comp. Sept. (φρουράν) and Vulg. (*milites*), and see Exeg. Expl.

[4] For אבימלך read rather (with the Sept., Vulg., and xxiv. 3, 6) אֲחִימֶלֶךְ.

[5] For וַיָּבֹא אֲלֵהֶם the text in Samuel (2 Sam. x. 17) has וַיָּבֹא חֵלָאמָה, "and went to Helam," perhaps more correct and original (comp. Exeg. Expl.), though all the translations and MSS. confirm the אֲלֵיהֶם of our passage.

[6] Rather, perhaps, "and scythes," as for וּבַמְּגֵרוֹת is (with 2 Sam. xii. 31) no doubt וּבְמַגְזְרוֹת to be read.

EXEGETICAL.

Preliminary Remark.—The present group of war reports runs parallel to four sections of 2 Samuel, separated from one another by other accounts. To the present summary accounts of the victorious warfare of David with all surrounding enemies in general, in ch. xviii., corresponds 2 Sam. viii.; to the more copious description of the peculiarly difficult war with Ammon, in ch. xix., corresponds 2 Sam. x.; the close of this war, described in ch. xx. 1–3, by the taking of Rabbah, has its parallel in 2 Sam. xii. 26–31; the shorter reports of the several heroic acts of David's warriors in conflict with giants from the land of the Philistines, ch. xx. 4–8, corresponds with the section 2 Sam. xxi. 18–22. The statements of 2 Samuel coming between these sections (namely ch. ix. and xi. 1–12, 25; but also ch. xiii. and xiv.–xviii.) are particulars from the private life and domestic history of David, which the Chronist, in conformity with his plan, neither could nor would take up.

1. *General Report of David's Victorious Wars with his Neighbours:* ch. xviii. 1–13. Ver. 1 treats of the victories over the Philistines.—*And took Gath and her daughters out of the hand of the Philistines.* This statement is surprising, because 2 Sam. viii. 1 has the more general and withal poetical expression: "and David took the arm-bridle from the hand of the Philistines" (מֶתֶג הָאַמָּה for גַּת וּבְנֹתֶיהָ). To assume a purely arbitrary change of text on the part of our author is questionable; and against, at least, a passing seizure of the metropolis Gath with its daughter towns (vii. 28) by David, it can scarcely be maintained that in Solomon's time Gath was again an independent city under its own king.—Ver. 2. *And the Moabites became David's servants, and brought gifts,* in short, became tributary subjects (ver. 6). Why our author has omitted the notice, following here in 2 Sam. viii. 2, of the severe handling of the Moabites by David, is uncertain. It scarcely rests on an apologetic tendency in favour of David; comp. in xx. 3 the account of the cruel punishment of Rabbath Ammon. Moreover, this war of David with Moab seems to be that in which Benaiah slew the two sons of the king of Moab, xi. 22.—Vers. 3–8. The War with Hadadezer of Zobah.—*King of Zobah towards Hamath.* This closer determination of the situation of Zobah (חֲמָתָה), which is peculiar to our text, places it pretty far north, not far from Hamath, the later Epiphania, on the Orontes; scarcely Haleb or Nisibis, both of which lay farther north than Hamath, and can scarcely, from an Israelitish point of view, be described as lying "towards Hamath" (against the Rabbis of the middle ages on the one hand, and J. D. Mich. on the other). Zobah is perhaps = Zabe of Ptolemy; at all events, it is to be sought north or north-east of Damascus (with Ew., Then., Berth., etc.).[1] On the spelling peculiar to Chronicles and 2 Sam. x. 16–19, Hadarezer (Sept. Ἀδρααζάρ), see Crit. Note.—*As he went to set up his sign at the river Euphrates,* to establish his power (properly "hand") there; comp. 1 Sam. xv. 12. Whether these words refer to David or Hadadezer is doubtful; the latter (which J. H. Mich., Ew., Berth., etc., assume) may be the more probable, on account of the mention of David as subject at the beginning of the following verse. The various reading in 2 Sam. viii. 3: לְהָשִׁיב יָדוֹ, "to turn his hand," is perhaps to be amended from our passage, as it gives a less suitable sense.—Ver. 4. *And David took from him a thousand chariots, and seven thousand horsemen, and twenty thousand footmen.* For this 2 Sam. viii. 4 has "1700 horsemen and 20,000 footmen," perhaps defectively; after אֶלֶף, and before וּשְׁבַע־מֵאוֹת, it appears necessary to insert רֶכֶב there, for which also the Sept. speaks. Yet comp. Wellh. on this passage, who questions the insertion of רֶכֶב, on account of the close of the verse.—*And David lamed all the teams, but reserved of them a thousand teams,* for his own use; in fact, therefore, he lamed only 900. For this custom of laming (עִקֵּר) war-horses, comp. Josh. xi. 6, 9.—Ver. 6. *And David put in Syria Damascus,* men, soldiers, garrison troops. From 2 Sam. viii. 6 and ver. 13 of our chapter the word נְצִיבִים appears to have fallen out after וַיָּשֶׂם דָּוִיד; comp. also xiii. 3; 1 Sam. x. 5.—Ver. 7. *And David took the arms* (or equipments) *of gold,* שִׁלְטֵי־הַזָּהָב; so rightly the moderns, instead of the golden collars (χλοιοί) of the Sept., the quivers (*pharetræ*) of the Vulg., and the golden shields of the Chald., of some Rabbis, and of Luther.—*Which were on the servants of Hadadezer,* his military servants, soldiers. On the addition of the Sept., in 2 Sam. viii. 7 relative to the later capture and carrying away of these golden arms by Shishak of Egypt, under Rehoboam, comp. the expositors of that passage.—Ver. 8. *And from Tibhath and from Chun,* etc. Tibhath (טִבְחַת), or, as it is perhaps to be read, Tebah (טֶבַח, for which, 2 Sam. viii., stands erroneously בֶּטַח), appears to be identical with the family mentioned, Gen. xxii. 24, among the descendants of Nahor; whether it be the present Taibeh, on the caravan road between Aleppo and the Euphrates, is questionable. In place of כּוּן 2 Samuel gives בֵּרֹתַי (= *Barathena,* Ptol. v. 19? or בֵּרֹתָה, Ezek. xlvii. 16?). On what this diversity of name rests, whether on the corruption of the original בֵּרֹתַי into כּוּן, as Berth. thinks, or on a double name of the place in question, must remain doubtful.—*Of which Solomon made the brazen sea, and the pillars, and the brazen vessels.* These words, wanting in 2 Sam. viii. 8 in the Masoretic text, are perhaps to be restored according to our passage, and according to the Sept. and Vulg.—Vers. 9–11. Embassy and Present of Tou King of Hamath to David. In the parallel account, 2 Sam. viii. 9–12, this Tou is called Toi (תֹּעִי).—Ver. 10. *And he sent Hadoram his son.* 2 Samuel: "Joram," at all

[1] Recently Th. Bischoff (*Das Ausland*, 1873, p. 136) thinks he has found the ruins of Zobah south-east of Aleppo, near the salt lake Jabul. He appears to mean the same ruins which J. W. Helfer (*Helfer's Reisen in Vorderasien*, by Countess Pauline Nostitz, Leipz. 1873, i. p. 174 ff.) saw in 1830.

events incorrect, as a name compounded with יְהוָֹה would scarcely have suited a member of a Syrian royal house; and the Sept. gives there Ἰεδδουράμ (here Ἀδουράμ).—*To greet him*, to wish him health. So is לִשְׁאָל־לוֹ לְשָׁלוֹם to be taken, according to the parallel passages, as Gen. xliii. 27, not, with the Sept. and Vulg., in the sense of a prayer for peace (*ut postulant ab eo pacem*).—*For Tou was at war with Hadadezer*, literally, "For Hadadezer was a man of wars of Tou," a constant assailant and adversary to him; comp. xxviii. 3; Isa. xlii. 13. After these words, which form a parenthetical explanation to the foregoing, follows the wider object of וַיִּשְׁלַח: "and all manner of vessels of gold and silver and brass," which Luther erroneously refers to ver. 11.—Ver. 11. *With the silver and the gold that he had taken.* For אֲשֶׁר נָשָׂא 2 Samuel presents אֲשֶׁר הִקְדִּישׁ, perhaps the original form.—*From all the nations . . . and from Amalek.* In 2 Samuel a more complete and probable text is found (in which, besides, מֵאֱדֹם is to be read for מֵאֲרָם).—Vers. 12, 13. *Abshai's Victory over the Edomites in the Valley of Salt.—And Abshai . . . slew of Edom* (literally, "slew Edom") *in the valley of salt*, 18,000 *men*. In Bertheau's combination of the very different reading in 2 Sam. viii. 13 with our passage, for "Abshai son of Zeruiah" would have to be read "Joab, etc.," and after "slew of Edom" would have fallen out the words "when he (Joab) returned from the conquest of Aram." Otherwise Ew., Then., Wellh., Keil, etc., the latter of whom upholds the statement of Chronicles, that Abshai gained this victory, by reference to ch. x. 10 ff. of our book (where Abshai appears as commander under his brother Joab), and declares it consistent as well with Ps. lx. 2 as with 1 Kings xi. 15.—Ver. 14. *And all the Edomites became servants of David.* For this 2 Samuel has more fully, and perhaps originally: "and in all Edom he appointed officers; and all the Edomites became David's servants."

2. *David's Officers of State:* vers. 14–17,—a list in 2 Sam. viii. also appended to the above summary war reports (= 2 Sam. viii. 15–18), that was certainly found here in the old common sources of both authors, introduced by the general remark on the ability and excellence of the government of David (ver. 14).—Ver. 15. For Joab, comp. on ii. 16.—*Jehoshaphat the son of Ahilud was recorder.* מַזְכִּיר, properly "remembrancer," that is, not annalist (Sept. ὁ ἐπὶ τῶν ὑπομνημάτων; Vulg. *a commentariis*), but chancellor, who makes to the king a report of all that takes place in the kingdom, and conveys his commands; comp. the *magister memoriæ* of the later Romans, and the *Waka Nuvis* in the Persian court (Chardin, *Voyages*, v. p. 258).—Ver. 16. For Zadok, comp. on v. 30 ff.—*Abimelech the son of Abiathar.* For אבימלך is certainly to be read, with the Sept., Vulg., and 2 Sam. viii. 17, אחימלך; for so is this priest called in xxiv. 3, 6, 31, where he is likewise named as the representative of Ithamar with Zadok of Eleazar, and where he appears as the son of Abiathar. That Abiathar's father was also called Ahimelech, 1 Sam. xxii. 20, does not warrant the assumption that in our passage, as in xxiv., there is an exchange of the father and the son; and thus a transposition of the names into "Abiathar the son of Ahimelech" is necessary (as Movers, Then., Ew., Wellh. think). Rather is our Ahimelech to be regarded as a son of the same name with his grandfather, according to the known Hebrew custom, who, even during his father's lifetime, acted in the priestly office. Comp. the frequent recurrence of the grandfather's name in the grandson in v. 30–41.—*And Shavsha was scribe*, that is, secretary of state. This Shavsha (Luth. "Sausa") is called in 1 Kings. iv. 3 Shisha (שִׁישָׁא, differing only in spelling from שַׁוְשָׁא), but in 2 Sam. xx. 25 שְׁוָא (שְׁיָא). If 2 Sam. viii. 17 exhibits שְׂרָיָה, this is to be considered, perhaps, an error of the pen.—Ver. 17. *And Benaiah . . . was over the Cherethi and the Pelethi.* So also 2 Sam. viii. 18, with the more correct reading עַל הַכְּרֵתִי for וְהַכְּ׳, as in 2 Sam. xx. 23. That "Cherethi and Pelethi" denote the two divisions of the royal guard (the σωματοφύλακες, Joseph. *Antiq.* vii. 5. 4) is undoubted, though, with Gesen., Then., Bähr (on 1 Kings i. 36), Keil, etc., the former name be explained by *confossores, lictores*, executioners, the latter by *celeres*, ἄγγαροι, runners (couriers), and thus both appellatively, for which the passages 1 Kings ii. 25, 2 Kings xi. 4 appear to speak, or though (with Lakemacher, Movers, Ew., Berth., Hitz., etc.) they be regarded as the nationalities of the Cretans (Carians) and the Philistines. Comp. the latest discussion of this controversy by J. G. Müller (*Die Semiten in ihrem Verhältniss zu Chamiten und Japhetiten*, 1872, p. 263 ff.), who decides for the latter interpretation. For Benaiah, comp. also xi. 22 ff.—*And David's sons were the chief beside the king*, the next to him. In 2 Sam. viii. 18 the ancient term כֹּהֲנִים, privy counsellors, is chosen to designate the high rank of the royal princes (comp. 1 Kings iv. 5).

3. *The War with Ammon and Syria:* ch. xix. 1–xx. 3; comp. 2 Sam. x.—*And it came to pass after this.* The loose form of connection וַיְהִי אַחֲרֵי כֵן serves sometimes to introduce new reports, even if there be no strict chronological order, or if, as here (comp. xviii. 3–5 with xix. 16 ff.), that which is to be related has been partly mentioned before. Comp. for example, 2 Sam. viii. 1, x. 1, xiii. 1. For the Ammonite king Nahash, and his war with Saul, see 1 Sam. xi.—*And his son reigned in his stead.* The following certainly shows that this son was called Hanun; yet the name חָנוּן, from 2 Sam. x. 1, appears to have originally stood in the text after בְּנוֹ, as inversely there, the omitted name נָחָשׁ must apparently be supplied from our passage.—Ver. 3. *Thinkest thou that David doth honour thy father?* literally, "Does David honour thy father in thine eyes?" The emphasis in this question rests on the notion of honouring, of which the questioners doubt whether it really forms the object of David's embassy.—*To search and to turn over* (turn up-

side down, examine thoroughly), *and to spy out the land.* This sentence is also in Hebrew a question, but, as an affirmative answer is expected, introduced, not with הֲ, but with הֲלֹא: "Are they not come to search, etc.?" In 2 Sam. x. 3, the sentence runs somewhat different, so that not the land (הארץ), but the city (הָעִיר), is the object of the verbs, and the הָפַךְ removed to the end has the sense, not of turning over, but of destroying. But it is scarcely necessary to change our text accordingly (against Berth.).—Ver. 4. *And shaved them.* 2 Samuel more exactly: "shaved off the half (the one side) of their beard." —*And cut off half their garments by the breech.* הַמִּפְשָׂעָה, properly, "the step, the step-region in the middle of the body," here euphemistic for שְׁתוֹת, *nates*, which is used in 2 Samuel.—Ver. 5. *And they went.* This is wanting in 2 Samuel, but not therefore to be erased as superfluous (against Berth.).—*And the king said, Tarry at Jericho.* So far they were then come on their way to Jerusalem. The following "then return" is naturally completed by adding "to Jerusalem" or "hither."—Ver. 6. *That they had made themselves stink with David,* had drawn his hatred on them. For the *Hithp.* התבאשו 2 Samuel has the *Niph.* of the same verb, in the same reflexive sense.—*Hanun . . . sent a thousand talents of silver to hire,* etc. The statement that this hiring of auxiliaries took place is wanting in 2 Samuel, but is certainly genuine. — For Mesopotamia = Aram-naharaim, 2 Samuel names, as the first of the countries from which Hanun hired his auxiliaries, Aram-beth-rehob, which can scarcely be only another name of Mesopotamia (as some ancients have assumed, identifying the city Beth-rehob with Rehobath, now Rahabe, on the Euphrates, Gen. xxxvi. 37), but the kingdom or territory of Beth-rehob, a Syrian city, Num. xiii. 21, Judg. xviii. 28, lying south of Hamath. For the following name, Aram-Maachah, 2 Sam. x. (as ver. 7 of our ch.) has only Maachah (on which region, bordering northward on the trans-jordanic Palestine, comp. Deut. iii. 14; Josh. xii. 5, xiii. 11). On the contrary, Zobah is there called more fully: Aram-Zobah (comp. on xviii. 3).—Ver. 7. *And they hired them* 32,000 *chariots*, that is, chariots with riders, רֶכֶב וּפָרָשִׁים, as the foregoing verse shows. The number 32,000 agrees substantially with the deviating statement in 2 Samuel, in which these auxiliaries appear rather as footmen, and, indeed, consisting of 20,000 footmen from Aram and Aram-beth-rehob, 1000 men from Maachah, and 12,000 men from the kingdom of Tob (Judg. xi. 3), which latter our author has left undistinguished.—*And they came and pitched before Medeba,* the city of the tribe of Reuben mentioned Josh. xiii. 16, two miles (about nine English miles) south-east of Heshbon. This statement as well as the following, relative to the simultaneous assembling of the Ammonite troops, is wanting in 2 Sam. x., but was found no doubt in the old sources used by our writer, in common with the author of the books of Samuel.—Ver. 8. *And all the host of the mighty.* Different, but merely in expression, from 2 Samuel: "the whole host, the mighty men."—Ver. 9. *And the sons of Ammon . . . at the gate of the city,* before the gates of Rabbah, their capital. This reading: פֶּתַח הָעִיר, is to be preferred, as clearer than that in 2 Sam. x.: פֶּתַח הַשַּׁעַר, "at the gate, outside the gate."—Ver. 10. *And Joab saw that the battle was directed against him before and behind,* literally, "that the face of the battle (= the front of the line) was before and behind him:" that before him stood the Ammonites, and in his rear the Syrians. Opposite the latter, as the stronger foe, Joab took his ground, while, ver. 11, he entrusted the engagement with the Ammonites to his brother Abshai. —Ver. 13. *For our people, and for the city of our God:* that these may not fall into the hands of the heathen, and from cities of the Lord become cities of idols.—Ver. 15. *And went into the city,* fled into their capital Rabbah, while Joab first returned to Jerusalem, reserving the siege and capture of this strong fortress for the following campaign. — Vers. 16–19. The Conquest of the Syrians allied with the Ammonites.—*They sent messengers, and drew forth the Syrians that were beyond the river Euphrates,* the Mesopotamians, who must have been somehow subject to Hadadezer, and laid under tribute; comp. 2 Sam. x. 16. —Ver. 17. *And came to them.* Instead of this notice, which is superfluous, along with the following words: "and drew up against them," should be read, with 2 Sam. x. 16 (see Crit. Note): "and he came to Helam." This elsewhere not occurring local name חֵילָם or חֵלָאם (Sept. Αἰλάμ, Vulg. *Helam*) the Chronist quite omits in its first place (in 2 Sam. x. 16 = ver. 16 of our ch.), and changes it the second time, whether intentionally or not, into אליהם. Comp. Joseph. *Antiq.* vii. 6. 3, where the name is regarded as a proper name of a king beyond the Euphrates, the master of the general Shophach (Sabekos). It is, moreover, not impossible that the local name Helam corresponds to the Alamatha on the Euphrates in Ptolem. xv. 5, in which case ch. xviii. 3 might be combined with our passage, if the same war with Hadadezer and the Syrians be spoken of there as here.—Ver. 18. *And David slew of the Syrians* 7000 *teams* (chariot horses) *and* 40,000 *footmen.* On the contrary, 2 Samuel has 700 teams and 40,000 horsemen. Perhaps the smaller number of teams in 2 Samuel and the designation of the 40,000 as footmen in our text deserve the preference; comp. Wellh. p. 180.—Ver. 19. *And when the servants of Hadadezer,* here not his warriors, but his allies or subject kings (vassals); comp. 2 Sam. x. 19: כָּל הַמְּלָכִים עַבְדֵי הֲדַדְעֶזֶר.—Ch. xx. 1–3. The Siege and Conquest of Rabbah, here more briefly related than in 2 Sam. xi. 1, xii. 26–31, and therefore without any reference to the death of Uriah.—*When the year was ended, at the time when the kings go out,* in the spring, as most suitable for re-opening the campaign. The last described battle with the Syrians appears accordingly to have fallen in the autumn of the previous year.—*Joab led forth the strength of the host;* more circumstantially 2 Sam. xi. 1: "David sent Joab, and his servants with him, and all Israel." On חֵיל הַצָּבָא, comp.

the similar חֵיל צָבָא, 2 Chron. xxvi. 13.—*And Joab smote Rabbah, and destroyed it*, properly, pulled it down; comp. Ezek. xvi. 39, xxvi. 4, 12; Lam. ii. 2, 17. Compared with 2 Sam. xii. 26 ff., where it is reported that Joab first only took the so-called city of waters, but called King David to the taking of the proper fortress (citadel, acropolis), that the honour of completing the conquest and destruction of the city might be his, the present report appears brief and summary. —Ver. 3. *And cut them with saws, and iron threshing-carts and saws.* וַיָּשַׂר, *ἅπ. λεγ.*, from the root שׂוּר, "cut"; comp. מְשׂוֹר, "saw," from the cognate root נשׂר. In 2 Sam. xii. 31, וַיָּשֶׂם is perhaps only an error of the pen for וַיָּשַׂר or וַיְשָׂרֵם (Böttcher).—For וּבַמְּגֵרוֹת, as in 2 Samuel, וּבְמַגְזְרוֹת, "and with scythes" (or like iron-cutting instruments, scarcely "wedges," as Luther, or "axes," as Kamph., thinks), is perhaps to be read. A twofold mention of saws, first in the sing., then in plur., would be an intolerable tautology. Moreover, this cutting and grinding of the vanquished Ammonites with iron saws, threshing sledges, and the like, is in itself horrible and barbarous enough (comp. Prov. xx. 26; Amos i. 3); and we need not assume that the Chronist intentionally, and from an apologetic tendency, passed over a still more horrid kind of punishment then inflicted on the vanquished Ammonites, burning in tile-kilns (2 Sam. xii. 31); comp. on xviii. 2.

4. *Appendix: Briefer Report of the Heroic Deeds of some of David's Warriors in the Conflict with Philistine Giants:* vers. 4–8.—This report is also treated as an appendix in 2 Samuel, where it is found quite at the end of the history of David, ch. xxi. 15–22, and, indeed, enlarged by a fourth heroic deed (vers. 15–17), there related in the first place, but here wanting—the dangerous conflict of David with the giant Ishbi-benob, whom Abshai at length slew. It appears as if the Chronist had omitted this story intentionally, because it might have lessened the military fame of David. Comp. Lightfoot, *Chronol. V. T.* p. 68: *Illud prœlium, in quo David in periculum venit et unde decore et illæsus prodire nón potuit, omissum est;* as Starke: "The dangerous combat of David with Ishbi is not mentioned here, as the book of Chronicles, as some remark, conceals or passes over the shame of the saints; whence also nothing occurs here of the adultery and murder by David, or of the idolatry of Solomon." —Ver. 4. *And it came to pass after this.* This formula stood here originally not so unconnected as in xix. 1; but the event to which it referred, 2 Sam. xxi. 18, was that history of the combat with Ishbi which is intentionally omitted by our author, on which account the formula does not now appear very suitable.—*A war arose at Gezer.* וַתַּעֲמֹד (perhaps arising out of וַתְּהִי עוֹד, 2 Sam. xxi. 18), here = וַתָּקָם, according to later usage. For Gezer (in the tribe of Ephraim, to the south-west, near the north border of the Philistines), see vii. 28. For בְּגֶזֶר, moreover, we should apparently (2 Sam. xxi. 18) read בְּגֹב, or perhaps בְּנֹב; that passage is not inversely to be amended from ours (against Berth.).—*Then Sibbecai the Hushathite* (one of David's Gibborim; see xi. 29 and xxvii. 11) *slew Sippai, one of the sons of Rapha*, one of the Rephaites or descendants of Rapha, that gigantic tribe that before the invasion of the Philistines inhabited the south-west of Canaan, and of which several families of gigantic size still lived among the Philistines; comp. Josh. xi. 22; Deut. ii. 6, 23.—*And they were subdued*, namely, by the conquest of this giant; comp. Judg. xi. 33; 1 Sam. vii. 13. The absence of this remark in 2 Samuel does not make its originality suspicious.—Ver. 5. *And there was a war again with the Philistines*, namely, 2 Sam. xxi. 19, at Gob (or Nob), and so at the same place as the former.—*Elhanan the son of Jair slew Lachmi, brother of Goliath the Gittite.* According to this certainly original reading is the defective text, 2 Sam. xxi. 19: "Elhanan the son of Jaare-oregim, a Bethlehemite, slew Goliath the Gittite," to be amended (with Piscat., Cleric., Mich., Mov., Then., Keil, Wellh.). "The form יערי, instead of יָעִיר of Chronicles, would be caused by the following ארגים, the accidental insertion of which from the line underneath is easily understood" (Wellh.). Besides, the here quite unexplained mention of the celebrated captain of David, Elhanan of Bethlehem (xi. 26), will have occasioned a change of אֶת־לַחְמִי into בית הלחמי. Accordingly, the question started by Berth., as defender of the originality of the text of Samuel: "Have there been two Goliaths?" falls to the ground as an idle one.—Ver. 6 ff. The Last of the Four Heroic Deeds.—*Where was a man of* (great) *stature:* אִישׁ מִדָּה = the אִישׁ מָדִין, *vir mensurarum*, in 2 Samuel.—*And his fingers were six and six* (namely, on the hands and the feet, therefore in all), *twenty and four.* Comp. the *sedigiti* mentioned by Plin. *H. N.* xi. 43; also Trusen, *Sitten, Gebräuche, und Krankheiten der alten Hebräer*, p. 198 f.; Carlisle, "An account of a family having hands and feet with supernumerary fingers and toes" (in *Philos. Transac.* 1814, part 1, p. 94); Rosbach, *Diss. de numero digitorum adaucto*, Bonn 1838; Blasius, *Fall von Ueberzahl der Zehen*, in Siebold's *Journ. für Geburtshülfe*, vol. xiii. Art. 1; also *Lond. Medic. Gaz.* vol. xiv. Apr. 1834, and Friedrich, *Zur Bibel*, i. p. 298 f. Recently the well-known Arabian traveller F. v. Maltzan, in the Berlin Anthropological Society, reported as follows: "Among the Himyarites (in South Arabia), in the dynasty of Forli, the six fingers are hereditary, and the pride of the ruler and the people. Indeed, this property of six fingers, a sign of bodily or, if not bodily, of mental strength among the Arabs, is still kept up artificially, as the six-fingered princes of the reigning house are allowed to marry only six-fingered members of the family, to avoid as much as possible the appearance of five fingers. In short, the twenty-four fingers and toes of the ruler are the pride of the country; and any one out of the country might prove his nearer or further connection with the ruling house by a greater or smaller superfluity of fingers" (*Correspondence Sheet* of the German Society for Anthropology, Ethnol., etc., 1872,

No. 8, p. 60).—Ver. 7. *Jonathan the son of Shima, David's brother, slew him.* Comp., on this Shima, ii. 13.—Ver. 8. *These were born.* אֵל for אֵלֶּה is an archaism, that occurs eight times in the Pentateuch, but always with the article (הָאֵל), and stands only here without it, for which reason it appears suspicious; the following נוּלְדוּ also probably contains an error; comp. the regular אֵלֶּה יֻלְּדוּ in 2 Sam. xxi. 22, where it is preceded by the number "four" (which is naturally omitted by the Chronist).—*And they fell by the hand of David, and by the hand of his servants,* namely, by David's hand in a mediate way, as he was the supreme commander and military chief of the victorious Israelites, but immediately by the hand of his so-called servants or heroes. The whole remark forms a concluding subscription, that appears no less suitable in our passage than in 2 Sam. xxi. 22 (against Berth.).

x. The Census and the Plague: ch. xxi.

CH. XXI. 1. And Satan stood up against Israel, and provoked David to number
2 Israel. And David said unto Joab, and to the rulers of the people, Go,
number Israel from Beersheba even to Dan; and bring it to me, that I may
3 know their number. And Joab said, The LORD add to His people an hundred-
fold as many as they are. Are they not, my lord the king, all my lord's ser-
vants? Why doth my lord require this thing? Why shall it be a trespass
4 to Israel? But the word of the king prevailed against Joab; and Joab de-
5 parted, and went through all Israel, and came to Jerusalem. And Joab gave
the sum of the number of the people unto David; and all Israel were a
thousand thousand and a hundred thousand men that drew sword; and
6 Judah was four hundred and seventy thousand men that drew sword. But
Levi and Benjamin he counted not among them; for the king's word was
abominable to Joab.
7, 8 And God was displeased with this thing; and He smote Israel. And
David said unto God, I have sinned greatly, because I have done this thing:
but now take away the iniquity of Thy servant; for I have done very foolishly.
9, 10 And the LORD spake unto Gad, David's seer, saying, Go and tell David,
saying, Thus saith the LORD, Three things I lay before thee; choose thee one
11 of them, that I may do it unto thee. And Gad came to David, and said unto
12 him, Thus saith the LORD, Choose thee either three years of famine; or three
months to be driven[1] before thy foes, and the sword of thy enemies to over-
take thee; or three days the sword of the LORD and pestilence in the land,
that the angel of the LORD may destroy in all the border of Israel; and now
13 consider what word I shall return to Him that sent me. And David said
unto Gad, I am in a great strait: let me now fall into the hand of the
LORD; for very great are His mercies: but let me not fall into the hand of
man.
14 And the LORD sent pestilence upon Israel; and there fell of Israel seventy
15 thousand men. And God sent an angel to Jerusalem to destroy it; and as
he was destroying, the LORD beheld, and repented of the evil, and said to the
destroying angel, It is enough now, stay thy hand: and the angel of the
16 LORD stood by the floor of Ornan[2] the Jebusite. And David lifted up his
eyes, and saw the angel of the LORD standing between the earth and the
heaven, having a drawn sword in his hand stretched over Jerusalem; and
17 David and the elders, clothed in sackcloth, fell on their faces. And David
said unto God, Have not I commanded to number the people? it is I that
have sinned, and done evil indeed; and these sheep, what have they done?
O LORD my God, let Thy hand now be on me and on my father's house, and
not on Thy people to smite.
18 And the angel of the LORD commanded Gad to say unto David, that
David should go up and set up an altar unto the LORD in the floor of Ornan
19 the Jebusite. And David went up at the word of Gad, which he spake in
20 the name of the LORD. And Ornan turned, and saw the angel; and his four
21 sons with him hid themselves: and Ornan was threshing wheat. And David
went to Ornan; and Ornan looked, and saw David, and came out of the floor,

22 and bowed to David with his face to the ground. And David said unto
Ornan, Give me the place of this floor, that I may build therein an altar
unto the LORD: thou shalt give it me for the full price, that the plague be
23 stayed from the people. And Ornan said unto David, Take thee, and let my
lord the king do that which is good in his eyes: lo, I give thee the oxen for
burnt-offerings, and the threshing-rollers for wood, and the wheat for the
24 meat-offering: I give all. And King David said unto Ornan, Nay; but I will
verily buy it for the full price; for I will not take that which is thine for the
25 LORD, nor offer burnt-offerings without cost. And David gave to Ornan for
26 the place six hundred shekels of gold by weight. And David built there
an altar unto the LORD, and offered burnt-offerings and peace-offerings; and
he called upon the LORD, and He answered him by fire from heaven on the
27 altar of burnt-offering. And the LORD commanded the angel; and he put
his sword again into its sheath.
28 At that time, when David saw that the LORD had answered him in the floor
29 of Ornan the Jebusite, he sacrificed there. For the tabernacle of the LORD,
which Moses made in the wilderness, and the altar of burnt-offering, were at
30 that time in the high place at Gibeon. And David could not go before it
to inquire of God; for he was afraid before the sword of the angel of
the LORD.

according to the parallel text 2 Sam. xxiv. 13 (נִסְךָ for נִסְפֶּה), rather "flight." So the Sept., Vulg., and Luther.

[2] אָרְנָן the Sept. renders here and in the whole chapter by 'Ορνά, as it conforms to אוֹרְנָה, the *Kethib* in 2 Sam. xxiv. 16 (for which elsewhere there the *Keri* אֲרַוְנָה always stands). Our text has throughout invariably אָרְנָן, which the Vulg. gives rightly Ornan, Luther wrongly "Arnan."

EXEGETICAL.

PRELIMINARY REMARK. *Relation of the Foregoing Account of Chronicles to* 2 Sam. xxiv.—As clearly as the mostly verbal agreement of our account with the parallel text of Samuel points to one common source of both, so numerous and important are also their deviations from one another. They chiefly consist of the following:—*a.* The position of the history of the census in 2 Samuel is that of an appendix to the history of David's reign already in the main completed. In our book, on the contrary, it closes only that section of the history of this king which refers to the external security and enlargement of his power by wars, buildings, etc.; but it thereby leads (in connection with the following description of his preparation for the building of the temple, xxii.) to a new section, that by means of full details of his temple, state and war officers, is fitted to present a picture of the inner character of his government. *b.* The event is so introduced in 2 Samuel, that reference is made to a former plague, a famine (2 Sam. xxi. 1–14) which God had brought on the kingdom, so that David's pernicious project of a census is represented as the direct effect of the divine anger ("And again the anger of the Lord was kindled against Israel; and He moved David, etc."), but, in our account, so that the whole is referred to a tempting influence of Satan on David, and connected neither with that famine nor any former visitation of Israel under David (not, for example, with the insurrections of Absalom and Shebna, which, like the famine, are entirely unnoticed by our author). For the question, whether the representation of Satan as the moral originator of the census rests on the influence of the religious ideas of a later time, see on ver. 1. *c.* The census executed by Joab at the command of David is described pretty fully in 2 Sam. xxiv. 4–9, but only summarily in our chapter, with the chief emphasis on the numerical result, and the notice of a special circumstance unmentioned in 2 Samuel, namely, that Joab, because the royal commission was repugnant to him, neglected to enumerate the tribes of Levi and Benjamin (vers. 4–6). *d.* On the purchase of Ornan's (or, as the *Keri* is in 2 Samuel, Araunah's) floor and the sacrifice by David, our text (vers. 19–27) is more full than 2 Sam. xxiv. 19–25. *e.* The statement, forming the close of our account and its connection with what follows, regarding the selection of the floor of Ornan for the constant place of sacrifice by David (and for the site of the temple), in vers. 28–30, is wholly wanting in 2 Sam. xxiv., as, indeed, an express reference to the fact that that place attained a special sacredness under David by the angelic appearance and the sacrifice during the plague is absent there, while the whole occurrence is presented under the prevailing view of such a judicial punishment as the rebellions of Absalom and Shebna, and the famine already reported there, but by our author entirely omitted. That the most of these deviations are occasioned by the peculiar pragmatism and the special tendency of the author of the books of Samuel on the one hand and of the Chronist on the other, is already apparent from this brief survey, and will receive further confirmation from the following exposition.

1. *The Census, its Occasion and Effect:* vers. 1–6.—*And Satan stood up against Israel.* That, instead of the divine anger, here Satan, the personal evil principle (see on Job i. 6, ii. 1), is named as the hostile power that occasioned the pernicious expedient of the census, is now usually explained (even by Keil) as a later idea of the

Israelites, and accordingly reckoned among the proofs that our book was composed after the exile. That this view is at least hasty, if it does not involve an error, is plain when we reflect—1. That the way in which the prologue of the book of Job presupposes the idea of Satan, as long naturalized in the belief of Israel, speaks for the origin of this idea, not only before the exile, but before the time of Solomon; 2. That passages such as Gen. iii. 1 ff. and 1 Kings xxii. 19 ff., though the name שָׂטָן does not occur in them, show that the materials of this idea arose from that early time; and 3. That to the parallel passage 2 Sam. xxiv., though not using the name, the notion of an intervention of Satan in the temptation of David is by no means foreign; indeed, even a positive hint of this is implied in it. Ew. and Wellh. justly assume that in the verb used, 2 Sam. xxiv. 1, ויסת, "provoked," lies an allusion to a personal tempting power, which cannot be God or the divine anger;[1] that, indeed, according to the original, now mutilated, text of Samuel, probably הַשָּׂטָן was the subject of ויסת.—*And provoked David to number Israel.* The injury of the census, indicated by this expression, rests on this, that such an undertaking in and of itself counted as an act exciting the anger of God, and therefore demanding propitiation (comp. the expiatory customs in the enumerations of the Romans, according to Valerius, Maximus, Varro, and Livius, as also that census instituted by Moses, Ex. xxx. 11–16, which did not provoke God, only because the money collected by it as a gift to the tabernacle had a holy purpose, and therefore an expiating significance in itself). But a special wrong and blame was attached to the census of David, because it was a work of proud boastfulness and wicked haughtiness, not valuing, but over-valuing, his own power and greatness (comp. Joab's warning, ver. 3). The measure can scarcely be regarded as an expression of despotic wilfulness and tyrannic oppression of the people, or as a preparation for the imposition of an oppressive war tax or other tribute (Berth., etc.), or even as expressive of a lust for warlike conquest in the king (J. D. Mich.; comp. Kurtz in Herzog's *Real-Encyl.* iii. 306); at least the text in nowise indicates that blame was attached to it on any of these grounds.—Ver. 2. *Go, number Israel from Beersheba even to Dan,* the usual formula to designate the land of Israel in all its length; comp. Judg. xx. 1; 1 Sam. iii. 20; 1 Kings iv. 25, etc. The plain customary phrases: "Go, number" (לְכוּ סִפְרוּ), are simplifying and explanatory for those selected in 2 Samuel: שׁוּט־נָא (specially addressed to Joab) and פִּקְדוּ (including the assistants of Joab in the enumeration, the captains or commanders of the army).—*And bring it to me, that I may know their number,* the number of the Israelites.—Ver. 3. Joab's Warning.—*The Lord add to His people a hundredfold as many as they are.* In 2 Samuel stands, in accordance with the preference of this author for repetitions of the same phrase (comp. 1 Sam. xii. 8), a double כָּהֵם, "so many as they are, so many as they are, a hundredfold," or more briefly: "so and so many as they are a hundredfold." For the present simpler expression, comp. Deut. i. 11.—*Are they not all . . . my lord's servants?* Does any one doubt that this great multitude of people is subject to thee? Will any one check thy joy in the greatness and power of thy kingdom? This question is wanting in the often deviating text of Samuel, in place of which are the words: "that the eyes of my lord the king may see it" (the hundredfold increase of the people).—*Why shall it be a trespass to Israel?*—a trespass (אַשְׁמָה) that brings divine punishment on the people instead of thee, the king, who art guilty of this wicked haughtiness.—Ver. 4. *But the word of the king prevailed against Joab,* literally, "was strong above Joab" (which form חזק על is perhaps to be restored in 2 Samuel in place of the present ח' אֶל), overcame his resistance (Luth.: "succeeded against Joab"); comp. 2 Chron. viii. 3, xxvii. 5.—Ver. 5. *And all Israel were a thousand thousand and a hundred thousand men that drew sword,* literally, "that bare the sword;" comp. Judg. viii. 10, xx. 2, 15, 17, 46, etc. The number 1,100,000, compared with the 800,000 men-at-arms in 2 Sam. xxiv. 9, involves an actual deviation, which either depends on an ancient variety in the traditions concerning the numerical result of the census, or what is more probable, must be derived from a confusion of the numbers; comp. the cases of this kind cited in the Introd. § 6, No. 5. The difference in the number of the Jewish men-at-arms is smaller, in which the 500,000 in 2 Samuel is merely a round number, for the more exact one, 470,000, contained in our text. Moreover, differences in the later traditions might the more easily arise in this Davidic census, because it was merely oral, as, according to 1 Chron. xxvii. 24, the result was not entered in the annals of the kingdom. The general correctness of the account, that Israel then numbered about a million, and Judah about half a million warriors, is warranted by the communications of the author, which attest even for much later times the extraordinary density of the population in the formerly so fruitful land of promise. And that the actual army of David, 1 Chron. xxvii. 1 ff., amounted only to 288,000 men, by no means contradicts the present statement relative to the total number of men fit to bear arms; comp. our remark on iv. 18.—Ver. 6. *But Levi and Benjamin he counted not among them; for the king's word was abominable to Joab;* on account of the reluctance with which he obeyed the command of the king, the numbering was not quite completed: it was stopped, perhaps at the king's command, before Benjamin, the last of the tribes to be numbered, was taken in hand; comp. the more exact statements in 2 Sam. xxiv. 5 ff. concerning the order pursued by the commission under Joab, that, starting from the southern tribes east of Jordan, went round over the north of the land to the south of Judah, and thence arrived at Jerusalem. As no time remained for the numbering of Benjamin

[1] Comp. Volck, *De summa carminis Jobi sententia,* p. 33 sqq.: *Hoc si tenes, Deum non sine causa populo suo atque ejus regi, superbienti illi quidem, succensuisse, Satanumque eum esse, qui, ut homines propter delicta apud Deum accuset eorum pœnas repetiturus, ita hoc efficiat, ut peccati pullulantis vis erumpat: difficultatem ita expedies, ut Davidem, quia Deus iratus pravitatis pœnam irrogare voluerit, ad infelix illud consilium adductum fuisse dicas diaboli divinæ voluntati inservientis impulsu,* etc.—Comp. also Hofmann, *Schriftbew.* ii. p. 437 ff., and Schlottmann, *Das Buch Hiob,* p. 38 ff.

(comp. xxvii. 23 f.—the express statement that the numbering was not completed; also Josephus, *Antiq.* vii. 13. 1: χωρὶς τῆς Βενιαμίτιδος φυλῆς. ἐξαριθμῆσαι γὰρ αὐτὴν οὐκ ἔφθασεν), so the tribe of Levi was omitted on account of its legal exemption from numerations for political or military objects (comp. Num. i. 47–54). In the present statement, therefore, there is nothing incredible; and neither its absence in 2 Samuel, nor the circumstance that the Chronist, instead of the unfinished state of the census, puts forward in his subjective pragmatism the reluctance of Joab as the cause of the omission of those tribes, justifies the suspicions entertained by de Wette and Gramberg against it. Comp. Keil, *Apologet. Versuch*, p. 349 ff.

2. *The Divine Displeasure with the Numbering of the People by the Voice of the Seer Gad:* vers. 7–13. —*And God was displeased with this thing*, literally, "and it was evil (וַיֵּרַע) in God's eyes for this thing:" the same construction appears in Gen. xxi. 22; usually without עַל before the displeasing object, Gen. xxxviii. 10; 2 Sam. xi. 27, etc.—*And He smote Israel.* This is not so much an anticipation of that which is narrated ver. 14 ff., as a generalizing description of the mode in which God's anger took effect on Israel. It does not appear that the words are to be amended (Berth.), according to 2 Sam. xxiv. 10: וַיַּךְ לֵב־דָּוִד אֹתוֹ, "and the heart of David smote him." We have here simply two modes of narrative, one of which regards more the human thought and deed, the other more the divine.—Ver. 10. *Three things I lay before thee*, concerning thee, with thee, laying the choice before thee. Wellh. justly declares, not the strange נטל of Samuel, but our נטה to be original (against Berth.).—Ver. 12. *Either three years of famine.* This time is certainly the original, not the seven years of the text in Samuel, which has arisen by the easy change of the letters (שֶׁבַע for שָׁלֹשׁ), and finds its emendation in the Sept.—*Or three months to be driven before thy foes.* What is here original, whether נִסְפֶּה of our text (*nom. particip. Niph.*: "to perish, be swept away") or נֻסְךָ in 2 Samuel, must remain doubtful. On the contrary, the following וְחֶרֶב אוֹיְבֶיךָ לְמַשֶּׂגֶת, "and the sword of thy foes to overtake" (= so that the sword of thy foes overtake thee), is certainly to be preferred to the reading וְהוּא רֹדְפֶךָ in 2 Samuel.—*That the angel of the Lord destroy in all the border of Israel.* This enforcing addition to the third question is wanting in 2 Samuel, but must be no less original than that parallel addition to the second question. And the hendiadyoin: "the sword of the Lord and pestilence," for the simple pestilence (דֶּבֶר) in 2 Samuel, can scarcely be regarded as an arbitrary addition of the Chronist. Comp., moreover, with respect to the triad of divine judgments—famine, sword, and pestilence—the parallels, Lev. xxvi. 25 f.; 1 Kings viii. 37; 2 Chron. xx. 9; Jer. xiv. 12 ff., xxi. 7–9, xxiv. 10, xxvii. 8, 13, xxix. 17 f., xxxii. 24–36, xxxiv. 17, xxxviii. 2, xlii. 17, 22, xliv. 13; Ezek. v. 12, vi. 11 f., vii. 15, xii. 16; also Ezek. xxi. 19, where this woful triad is indicated by the figure of three swords; likewise Ezek. v. 17, xiv. 13–19, Rev. vi. 8, where the triad is extended to a quatrain by the addition of beasts of prey (comp. still other appropriate parallels in my *Theol. naturalis*, i. p. 637).

3. *The Judgment, and David's Repentant Entreaty for its Removal:* vers. 14–17.—*And the Lord sent pestilence upon Israel.* That this pestilence continued "from the morning even to the time appointed" is stated in the precise account in 2 Samuel; likewise that it affected all the people "from Dan even to Beersheba." Wellh. (p. 220) defends, perhaps not unjustly, the extended form of our first verse-member, which the Sept. presents, as original: "And David chose the pestilence; and when the days of wheat harvest came (comp. ver. 20), the plague began among the people."—Ver. 15. *And God sent an angel to Jerusalem.* The מַלְאָךְ without the article, "an angel," is strange, as the angel in question, ver. 12, was named before. Berth. gives the preference to the text 2 Sam. xxiv. 16: "And the angel stretched out his hand to Jerusalem," whereas Movers (p. 91) defends our text as original. Perhaps neither text now contains exactly and fully the original, whether we amend, with Keil: "And the angel of God stretched out his hand toward Jerusalem," or declare the restoration of the original now impossible (with Wellh.).—*And as he was destroying, the Lord beheld, and repented of the evil;* that is, as soon as the angel had begun to destroy, Jehovah considered, and repented that He had decreed the heavy stroke. On this repentance of God, comp. Gen. vi. 16; Ex. xxxii. 14; Jer. xlii. 10; Jon. iii. 10; Ps. cvi. 23.—*It is enough now, stay thy hand.* Notwithstanding the *acc. distinct.* over רַב, this word is to be connected with the following עַתָּה, and taken in the sense of "enough" (*sufficit*); comp. Deut. i. 6; 1 Kings xix. 4. Against Berth., who in 2 Sam. xxiv. 16 connects רב with בָּעָם, and regards this "a great mass of people" as the original reading, see not only Keil, but also Wellh.—*And the angel of the Lord stood by the floor of Ornan the Jebusite.* That this Ornan (or Araunah, as the *Keri* writes his name in 2 Samuel; comp. Crit. Note here) had been king of the Jebusites cannot be inferred from 2 Sam. xxiv. 23, as the word הַמֶּלֶךְ there is either to be erased, with Then., or (with Böttcher and Wellh.) to be referred by emendation to David (there addressed by Araunah). That the floor of Ornan was on Mount Moriah, the subsequent site of the temple, north-east of Zion, is stated in the sequel; see ver. 28 ff.—Ver. 16. *And David . . . saw the angel of the Lord standing between the earth and the heavens.* This whole verse, as also ver. 20, with the statement of the hiding of Ornan and his four sons before the angel, and ver. 26, with the mention of the fire coming down from God on David's offering, are wanting in the shorter and simpler account in 2 Samuel. These may be called embellishments of tradition, but they are not to be regarded as inventions of our historian (against Berth., etc.).—*And David and the elders . . . fell on their faces.* The mention of the elders is wanting in 2 Samuel, but is not the least strange, as it was a solemn act of expiation

and penitence on behalf of the whole nation. Comp. also the mention, 2 Sam. xxiv. 20, of the retinue of servants accompanying the king when he went to Ornan.—Ver. 17. *Have not I commanded to number the people?* In 2 Samuel the prayer of David is much briefer. But for this very reason the attempt of Bertheau to show that our text here and in the sequel arises from the effort to explain and improve the other text is altogether unjustified. Neither are the present words הלא אני אמרתי למנות בעם corrupted from those in Samuel: בראתו את־המלאך המכה בעם, nor is וְהָרֵעַ הֲרֵעוֹתִי to be changed into a supposed original וְאָנֹכִי הָרֹעֶה הֲרֵעוֹתִי, "and I, the shepherd, have done wrong;" for the question: "but these sheep, what have they done?" is easily understood without the previous mention of the shepherd; comp. Ps. xcv. 7, c. 3, etc.

4. *The Purchase of Ornan's Floor, and the Offering of the Burnt-Sacrifice there:* vers. 18–27.—Ver. 20. *And Ornan turned.* So וַיָּשָׁב is certainly to be translated (comp. 2 Kings xx. 5; Isa. xxxviii. 5; and such New Testament passages as Luke xxii. 61, etc.), not "returned," as Bertheau does against the context, at the same time defending the conjecture that וישב is corrupted from וַיַּשְׁקֵף.—*And Ornan was threshing wheat,* a clause wanting in 2 Samuel, but certainly original, which is confirmed by the notice of the Sept. already mentioned on ver. 15 concerning the wheat harvest as the time when the pestilence began.—Ver. 22. *Give me the place of this floor.* So it is to be translated, not as in Luther: "Give me space in this floor." The whole floor was necessary for the king's object; it is also all bought by him. The history of this purchase recalls in general the similar incident in the life of Abraham, Gen. xxiii., but does not necessitate the assumption that the recollection of Gen. xxiii. 9 affected the forms of the text, nor in particular that the twofold בכסף מלא was taken thence.—Ver. 23. *Lo, I give the oxen for burnt-offerings.* Along with וְהַמּוֹרִגִּים stands also 2 Samuel: וכלי הבקר, "and the harness of the oxen," their wooden yokes, a certainly original phrase, that has only fallen out of our text by a mistake. The other text also requires the mention of "the wheat for the meat offering," which can be no late addition.—Ver. 24. *Nor offer burnt-offerings without cost,* that is, without having paid the full price for them. The infin. וְהַעֲלוֹת after the finite verb as a continuation is not surprising; comp. Ew. § 351, *c.* Here also Bertheau's emendations are superfluous. —Ver. 25. *And David gave to Ornan for the place six hundred shekels of gold by weight.* Otherwise 2 Samuel xxiv. 24, where David purchases the floor with the oxen for fifty shekels of silver. The one of these two contradictory statements is certainly corrupt, and more probably that in 2 Samuel, as fifty shekels of silver is too low a price; comp. Abraham's 400 shekels of silver for the cave of Machpelah, Gen. xxiii. 15. The sum of 600 shekels of gold appears, indeed, too high; but an over-payment corresponds better with the crisis than a much smaller price, which might have been interpreted as an act of mean covetousness. That the Chronist has "intentionally exaggerated" (Then.) is a conjecture as little to be justified as the different harmonizing attempts of the ancients; for example, that each of the twelve tribes must have given fifty shekels, whereby the 600 shekels mentioned by the Chronist were raised (Raschi), or that the 600 shekels are to be reckoned as silver, but to be paid in gold, and with fifty pieces of gold, of which each was = twelve silver shekels (Noldius, *ad concord. Part. not.* 719), etc.—Ver. 26. *And David . . . offered burnt-offerings and peace-offerings.* After the sentence corresponding to these words in 2 Sam. xxiv. 25 is found in the Sept. an addition that anticipates in brief the contents of xxii. 1–6.—*And he called upon the Lord, and He answered him by fire* (or heard him with fire) *from heaven on the altar of burnt-offering.* For these words, to be understood according to Lev. ix. 24, 1 Kings xviii. 24, 38, 2 Kings i. 12, and 2 Chron. vii. 1, 2 Samuel has simply: "and the Lord was entreated for the land" (comp. on ver. 16); likewise for our ver. 27, with its mention of the angel's sword returned into its sheath, the plainer and less poetical: "and the plague was stayed from Israel."

5. *David's repeated Offering on the Floor of Ornan, with the Reason:* vers. 28–30.—*At that time . . . he sacrificed there;* that is, repeatedly, frequently; Luther rightly: "was wont to offer there." Only this sense of ויזבח שם agrees with the sequel, especially with xxii. 1.—Vers. 29, 30 explain this selection of Ornan's floor for the regular place of sacrifice for the king more precisely, by referring to the older sanctuary at Gibeon, and to the apparent neglect of it; comp. on ch. xv. 1, xvi. 39 f.—*And David could not go before it,* the tabernacle at Gibeon, and the altar there; comp. for לִפְנֵי in this connection, xvi. 4, 37, 39.—*For he was afraid before the sword of the angel of the Lord;* the appearance of the angel, with its desolating effects, had left in his mind an awfully strong impression of the holiness of the place, so that he did not venture to sacrifice in any other place. This interpretation only (comp. Berth.) suits the fact and the context, not that of various recent expositors, who wish to extract strange motives out of the words; for example, J. H. Mich.: "*quia ex terrore visionis angelicæ infirmitatem corporis contraxerat,*" or O. v. Gerlach: "because Gibeon was too far away," or Keil: "because Gibeon, notwithstanding the sanctuary existing there with the Mosaic altar, was not spared by the plague," etc.

Comp., moreover, for the various details of the present account, the evangelical and ethical reflections at the close of the exposition of this book.

c. David's Arrangements for the Building of the Temple; other Spiritual and Temporal Regulations; last Will and Death.—Ch. xxii.–xxix.

α. *Provisions for the Building of the Temple:* ch. xxii.

Ch. xxii. 1. And David said, This is the house of the Lord God, and this is the
altar of burnt-offering for Israel.
2 And David commanded to gather the strangers that were in the land of
Israel; and he appointed masons to hew square stones to build the house of
3 God. And David prepared iron in abundance for the nails for the doors of
4 the gates, and for braces; and brass in abundance without weight. And
cedar-trees without number; for the Zidonians and Tyrians brought much
5 cedar-wood to David. And David said, Solomon my son is young and
tender, and the house to be builded for the Lord must be highly magnifical
for name and glory in all countries: I will now prepare for it: and David
prepared abundantly before his death.
6 And he called for Solomon his son, and charged him to build a house for
7 the Lord God of Israel. And David said to Solomon, My son,[1] I had it in
8 mind to build a house unto the name of the Lord my God. But the word of
the Lord came unto me, saying, Thou hast shed much blood, and made great
wars; thou shalt not build a house unto my name, because thou hast shed
9 much blood on the earth in my sight. Behold, a son shall be born to thee,
who shall be a man of rest; and I will give him rest from all his enemies
around; for Solomon shall be his name, and I will give peace and rest unto
10 Israel in his days. He shall build a house to my name; and he shall be my
son, and I will be his father; and I will establish the throne of his kingdom
11 over Israel for ever. Now, my son, the Lord be with thee; and prosper
12 thou, and build the house of the Lord thy God, as He hath said of thee. Also
the Lord will give thee wisdom and understanding, and ordain thee over
13 Israel, that thou mayest keep the law of the Lord thy God. Then shalt thou
prosper, if thou takest heed to fulfil the statutes and judgments which the
Lord commanded Moses concerning Israel: be firm and strong; fear not, nor
14 be dismayed. And, behold, in my trouble I have prepared for the house of
the Lord a hundred thousand talents of gold, and a thousand thousand
talents of silver, and of brass and of iron without weight; for it is in abun-
dance: and I have prepared timber and stone, and thou shalt add thereto.
15 And with thee are workers in abundance, hewers and carvers of stone and of
16 timber, and all skilful men in all work. Of the gold, the silver, and the brass,
and the iron there is no number: arise and do, and the Lord be with thee.
17 And David commanded all the princes of Israel to help Solomon his son:
18 Is not the Lord your God with you? and hath He not given you rest on
every side? For He hath given the inhabitants of the land into my hand;[2]
19 and the land is subdued before the Lord, and before His people. Now give
your heart and your soul to seek the Lord your God; and arise and build
the sanctuary of the Lord God, to bring the ark of the covenant of the Lord,
and the holy vessels of God, into the house that is to be built to the name of
the Lord.

[1] בְּנִי, according to the *Keri;* the *Kethib* has בְּנוֹ, "unto Solomon his son;" but it scarcely deserves the preference, as בְּנוֹ might easily arise from לִשְׁלֹמֹה בְּנוֹ, ver. 6.

[2] So the Masoretic text and a part of the MSS. of the Sept. (A^2 F X: ἐν χειρί μου). But the Sept. *cod. Vat.*, Vulg., Luther, etc.: "into your hands."

EXEGETICAL.

1. *Connection with the Foregoing Section:* ver. 1.—The present chapter, which opens the second half of David's history referring to the inner side of his government, is, by its introductory verse, closely connected with the foregoing account of the pestilence, and the consequent elevation of

the floor of Ornan to be the place of sacrifice for the king. The further accounts, relating directly or indirectly to the security of David's kingdom for his successor, to the end of the book, are thus in a suitable way connected with the last-mentioned important event in the external history of the government of David.—*This is the house of the Lord God*, or: "shall be a house of the Lord God." David gives this determination to the former threshing-floor on the same ground that moved Jacob to consecrate his resting-place at Luz to be a Bethel (Gen. xxviii. 17), because Jehovah had there revealed to him His saving presence.

2. *The Preparation of Materials for the future Temple:* vers. 2–5.—*And David commanded to gather the strangers that were in the land of Israel*, the descendants of the Canaanites subdued in the conquest of the land, who lived as bondmen under his government; comp. 2 Chron. viii. 7–10 and ch. ii. 16, 17, where the number of these bondmen under Solomon is stated to be 150,000, whom he employed as bearers and workmen in building the temple.—*Masons to hew square stones.* Comp. 1 Kings v. 17, 31; also the simple גָּזִית, square stones, 1 Kings vi. 36, vii. 9 ff.; Ex. xx. 25; Isa. ix. 9.—Ver. 3. *For the nails for the doors of the gates, and for braces.* לַמְחַבְּרוֹת, properly, "for joining things" (Sept. στροφεῖς; more correctly Vulg. *commissuræ atque juncturæ*); comp. 2 Chron. xxxiv. 11, where, however, braces of wood are meant.—Ver. 4. *For the Zidonians and Tyrians* (= Phenicians; comp. Ezra iii. 7) *brought much cedar-wood to David;* this at first naturally, as an article of trade for the exports of Palestine, corn, wine, fruit, etc., not yet by a contract of supply for building the temple, such as Solomon afterwards made with Hiram, 1 Kings v. 15 ff.—Ver. 5. *Solomon my son is young and tender.* So (נַעַר וָרָךְ, *parvulus et delicatus*, Vulg.) David names Solomon also, ch. xxix. 1, in one of his last speeches to the people, although, born shortly after the Syrian Ammonite wars (2 Sam. xii. 24), he must have been at this time, shortly before David's end, above twenty years of age. But even shortly after the beginning of his reign, Solomon calls himself נַעַר קָטֹן, 1 Kings iii. 7; comp., for example, also Benjamin, Gen. xliii. 44; Joshua, Ex. xxxiii. 11; Rehoboam, 2 Chron. xiii. 7, etc.—*And the house to be builded for the Lord must be highly magnifical* (properly, "great to make"). לְמַעְלָה, properly, "upward," "above measure great;" comp. on xiv. 2.—*For name and glory in all countries*, that it tend to the glory of the Lord in all countries; comp. xiv. 17.—*I will now prepare for it.* The meaning of this cheerful offering is somewhat weakened, if, with the Vulg. (*præparabo ergo*, etc.) and Luther ("therefore will I make preparation"), we take נָא as a particle of inference.

3. *The Charge to Solomon to build the Temple:* vers. 6–16. This charge is obviously to be regarded as given to Solomon shortly before the death of David; see the לִפְנֵי מוֹתוֹ at the close of ver. 5. The whole address on to ver. 16, besides being a legacy of the predecessor to his successor, is therefore to be regarded in some measure as parallel to 1 Kings ii. 2–9, and as essentially contemporary with the contents of ch. xxviii. and xxix. of our book. On its perhaps not strictly historical but ideal character, which is common to it with those addresses of David in ch. xxviii. and xxix., see Introd. § 6, No. 6.—Ver. 7. On the *Keri* בְּנִי to be preferred to the *Kethib* בְּנוֹ, see Crit. Note.—*I had it in mind*, literally, "I, it was in my heart;" quite so (with the same emphatic position of אֲנִי before עִם לְבָבִי) also ch. xxviii. 2. The phrase: "it is or was in my heart," for: "I have (had) in mind," appears also in 2 Chron. i. 11, vi. 7 f., ix. 1, xxiv. 4, xxix. 10, as in other historical books, Josh. xiv. 7; 1 Kings viii. 17 f., x. 2.—Ver. 8. *But the word of the Lord came unto me, saying.* What was a historical necessity in the course of David's government is by this concrete description referred to a definite word of the Lord communicated somewhere and sometime to David, as in ch. xxviii. 3 (comp. 1 Kings v. 17). It is not necessary to seek a definite place, where such a divine command was at least intimated to him. What Nathan says, xvii. 4 ff., of David's wars, concerns only the help which God gave him in these, but does not give prominence to the circumstance that he was by those frequent wars unfitted for building the temple. Comp. also Hengstenb. *Gesch. des Reiches Gottes*, iii. 124.—Ver. 9. *Behold, a son shall be born to thee.* The participle (נוֹלָד) is here in the sense of the future; comp. ver. 19 and 1 Kings xiii. 2.—*Who shall be a man of rest*, not a man who makes rest (Jer. li. 59; comp. Hitzig on this passage), but, as the sequel shows, a man who enjoys rest, who has the blessings of peace, and therefore rightly bears his name שְׁלֹמֹה. Comp. the description of the profound peace during the reign of Solomon, 1 Kings v. 4 f.—On ver. 10, comp. ch. xvii. 12 f., which prediction of Nathan is briefly repeated in our passage.—Ver. 11. *The Lord be with thee* (comp. vers. 16, 18); *and prosper thou;* comp. ver. 13; Josh. i. 8; and lastly, on דִּבֶּר עַל, to charge any one, ver. 8 (עָלַי) and xi. 10.—Ver. 12. *Also the Lord will give thee wisdom and understanding;* the same terms are so connected in 2 Chron. ii. 11. The fulfilment of this prophecy, as of the similar one of Nathan (2 Sam. vii. 11), see in 1 Kings iii. 5 ff.—*That thou mayest keep the law of the Lord*, properly, "and to keep the law," etc. Comp., on this continuation of the *verb fin.* by the *infin.* with לְ, Ew. § 351, *c.*—Ver. 13. *If thou takest heed to fulfil* ("to do") *the statutes and judgments.* The language here frequently coincides with the prescriptions and promises of Deuteronomy; comp. Deut. iv. 1, v. 1, vii. 4, 11, xi. 32; and respecting the closing admonition: "be firm and strong," Deut. xxxi. 6, 8; Josh. i. 7, etc.—Ver. 14. *And behold, in my trouble*, etc. So is בְּעָנְיִי to be taken here (comp. Gen. xxxi. 42, and the parallel meaning, ch. xxix. 2), not "in my labour," as the Sept.,

Vulg., and Luther have misunderstood the phrase. The following numbers, 100,000 talents of gold and 1,000,000 talents of silver, are only free from the suspicion of wilful exaggeration by the Chronist or an error of transcription, if we are permitted to introduce a reckoning according to other, that is, smaller units than those customary in the O. T. (comp. Introd. § 6, No. 5). If we reckon the talent (כִּכָּר) of silver at 3000 shekels of silver, according to the usual Mosaic or sacred value of about 2s. 3⅜d. each, it would amount to £342, and therefore 1,000,000 such silver talents would make the large sum of £342,000,000; and 100,000 talents of gold, if the gold shekel be sixteen times that of silver, would reach the still higher sum of £547,500,000. The gold and silver thus gathered by David would amount to £889,500,000, a sum incredibly high for the requirements of worship at that time. On the contrary, if we assume, with Keil, that the present shekel is not the sacred (Mosaic) but the civil so-called shekel, after the king's weight, and that these royal shekels were only half as weighty as the others, and so equal in weight and value to the bekah or Mosaic half-shekel (Ex. xxxviii. 26),—an assumption that seems to be corroborated by the comparison of 1 Kings x. 17 with 2 Chron. ix. 16,[1] the sum named is reduced by at least a half. That so large a sum gathered and saved by David is not inconceivable, but has its parallel in other high sums of oriental antiquity, Movers (*Die Phönizier*, ii. 3, p. 45 ff.) and Keil (p. 182 f. of his *Comment.*) have rendered probable by examples from the history of Persia and Syria, those exceedingly rich countries adjacent to the kingdom of David; comp. the £34,000 of gold and 500,000 talents of silver which Cyrus seized in the conquest of Athens (Varro, in Plin. *Hist. Nat.* xxxii. 15), the 40,000 talents of uncoined gold and silver and 9000 talents of coined silver which Alexander seized in Susa alone, the 120,000 talents which the same conqueror acquired in Persepolis; likewise the colossal treasures of Syria, with its numerous great idols of solid gold, its gold shields for the servants of Hadadezer, 2 Sam. viii. 7 ff., its gold pins as ornaments of the boots of the common soldiers of an Antiochus the Great, etc. At all events, it is hasty in Bertheau, who, besides, commits a great error in asserting that 5000 millions of thalers (about £750,000,000) would suffice to pay off the debt of all European states, to deny the credibility of the present high numbers, and suppose that they could be "nothing but the first circumlocution of the notion, 'great, exceedingly great,'—a circumlocution that may still be heard in the mouth of those who have not reflected on the value and import of the numbers, and therefore deal quite freely with thousands and hundred thousands." Neither the fact that Solomon's annual revenue amounted only to 666 talents of gold, nor that the queen of Sheba made him a present of 120 talents of gold (comp. 1 Kings x. 10, 14; 2 Chron. ix. 9), is sufficient to confirm this suspicion of a boastful exaggeration as the ground of the present statements. For, besides the 666 talents in gold expressly mentioned in those passages, Solomon must have had still other revenues considerably higher in their total amount (especially from tolls and tributes of the subject nations); but the value of a single gift in money and precious metals cannot in itself be compared with that of a great treasure amassed during several years. And should not David have actually contemplated the foundation of a temple treasure, of which the surplus remaining after defraying the cost of building should be kept in the sanctuary, and saved for covering the future expenses of it (as Solomon actually did after the building was finished with the money remaining over, 2 Chron. v. 1; 1 Kings vii. 51), and therefore have accumulated so vast a sum? Comp. that which is expressly reported to this effect, and see Keil's full discussion of all questions and opinions on this matter (pp. 181–184).—*And thou shalt add thereto.* That Solomon followed this advice of his father, to add to the building materials, is clear from 2 Chron. ii., where also the activity of the here (ver. 15, and in ver. 2) mentioned workers in stone and wood, as well as the "skilful men in all work" (חָכָם, to denote the ingenious mastery in the crafts of building and figuring, as in Bezaleel, Ex. xxxi. 3), is again mentioned.—Ver. 16. *Of the gold, the silver, and the brass, and the iron, there is no number*, properly, "for gold," etc. The לְ before the several words serves to make more prominent that which is hitherto enumerated (Ew. § 310, *a*). On the following קוּם וַעֲשֵׂה, "arise and do," comp. Ezra x. 4.

4. *Invitation to the Princes of Israel to aid in the building of the Temple:* vers. 17–19.—*Is not the Lord your God with you?* The remembrance of God's former grace toward the people is a ground for the invitation. That the words communicated here and in ver. 19 are David's words to the princes, is sufficiently clear even without לֵאמֹר from the foregoing וַיְצַו; comp. the same immediate introduction of the address in xxiii. 4. *He hath given the inhabitants of the land into my hand*, the Canaanites, Jebusites, Philistines; comp. xiv. 10 f., Josh. ii. 24; as on the following: "the land is subdued," Josh. xviii. 1, Num. xxxii. 22, 29.—Ver. 19. *Now give your heart and soul to seek the Lord your God;* comp. 2 Chron. xvii. 4, Ezra iv. 2, where the same construction of דרשׁ with לְ is found, whereas elsewhere it usually has the simple acc. of the object after it (xvi. 12, xxi. 30, etc.).—*To bring the ark of the covenant* (xv. 1; 2 Chron. v. 2) . . . *into the house*, etc. לְ in לְבֵית stands (as in Josh. iv. 5) for אֶל, and is not perhaps *nota accusativi* (Berth.), as הֵבִיא is never constructed with the *acc. loci*, but with אֶל, or with the acc. and ה local. For the future sense of הַנִּבְנֶה, comp. on ver. 9.

[1] See Mosis Maimon. *Constitutiones de siclis,—quas illustravit*, Jo. Esgers, Lugd. Bat. 1718, p. 19, and comp. the remarks on 2 Chron. iii. 3 concerning the relation of the older (sacred or Mosaic) cubit to the shorter civil cubit of later times. [In the text, English money has been substituted for foreign.]

β. Distribution of the Levites and Priests, and Order of their Service: ch. xxiii.–xxvi.

CH. XXIII. 1. And David was old and full of days, and he made his son Solomon
king over Israel.

1. *Enumeration of the Levites, and Arrangement of their Work:* vers. 2–5.

2 And he gathered all the princes of Israel, and the priests and the Levites.
3 And the Levites were numbered from the age of thirty years and upwards;
4 and their number by their polls in men was thirty and eight thousand. Of
these, twenty and four thousand were to oversee the work of the house of the
5 Lord, and six thousand were to be officers and judges. And four thousand
porters; and four thousand praising the LORD with instruments which I have
made[1] for praise.

2. *The Twenty-four Houses of the Levites:* vers. 6–23.

6 And David divided them[2] into courses for the sons of Levi, for Gershon,
Kohath, and Merari.
7, 8 Of the Gershonites were Ladan and Shimi. The sons of Ladan were the
9 chief Jehiel, and Zetham, and Joel, three. The sons of Shimi were Shelomith,[3]
and Haziel, and Haran, three: these were the chiefs of the fathers for Ladan.
10 And the sons of Shimi were Jahath, Zina, and Jeush, and Beriah: these four
11 were Shimi's sons. And Jahath was the chief, and Zizah the second; and
Jeush and Beriah had not many sons; and they formed one father-house and
one class.
12, 13 The sons of Kohath: Amram, Izhar, Hebron, and Uzziel, four. The sons
of Amram: Aaron and Moses; and Aaron was separated to sanctify him as
most holy, he and his sons for ever, to burn incense before the LORD, to
14 minister to Him, and to bless in His name for ever. And Moses, the man of
15 God, his sons were called after the tribe of Levi. The sons of Moses were
16, 17 Gershom and Eliezer. Of the sons of Gershom, Shebuel was the chief. And
the sons of Eliezer were Rehabiah the chief: and Eliezer had no other sons;
18 but the sons of Rehabiah were very many. The sons of Izhar, Shelomith the
19 chief. The sons of Hebron: Jeriah the first, Amariah the second, Jahaziel
20 the third, Jekamam the fourth. The sons of Uzziel: Micah the first, and
Jesiah the second.
21 The sons of Merari: Mahli and Mushi; the sons of Mahli: Eleazar and
22 Kish. And Eleazar died, and had no sons, but only daughters; and their
23 brethren, the sons of Kish, took them. The sons of Mushi: Mahli, and
Eder, and Jeremoth, three.

3. *Closing Remarks on the Levites:* vers. 24–32.

24 These are the sons of Levi after their father-houses; the chief of the
fathers for those mustered by the number of the names for their polls, doing
the work for the service of the house of the LORD from twenty years old and
25 upwards. For David said, The LORD God of Israel hath given rest to His
26 people, and He dwelleth in Jerusalem for ever. And also the Levites have
27 no more to carry the tabernacle, with all its vessels for its service. For, by
the last words of David, these were the number of the Levites from twenty
28 years old and upward. For their post was at the hand of the sons of Aaron,
for the service of the house of the LORD, for the courts, and for the chambers,
and for the purifying of everything holy, and the work of the service of the
29 house of God. And for the shew-bread, and the fine flour for meat-offering,
and the unleavened cakes, and pancakes, and that which is fried, and all
30 measures of capacity and length. And to stand every morning to thank and
31 praise the LORD, and so in the evening. And to offer all burnt-offerings to
the LORD for the Sabbaths, for the new moons, and the set feasts by number,

32 after the order of them, continually before the LORD. And they shall keep
the charge of the tent of meeting, and the charge of the sanctuary, and the
charge of the sons of Aaron their brethren, for the service of the house of the
LORD.

4. *The Twenty-four Classes of Priests:* ch. xxiv. 1–19.

CH. XXIV. 1. And for the sons of Aaron, these are the divisions: the sons of Aaron:
2 Nadab and Abihu, Eleazar and Ithamar. But Nadab and Abihu died before
3 their fathers, and had no sons; and Eleazar and Ithamar became priests. And
David distributed them, so that Zadok of the sons of Eleazar and Ahimelech
4 of the sons of Ithamar were for their office in their service. And the sons of
Eleazar were found more numerous in chief men than the sons of Ithamar;
and they were thus divided: for the sons of Eleazar sixteen chiefs of father-
5 houses; and eight of father-houses for the sons of Ithamar. And they
divided them by lot, one with the other; for the holy princes and the princes
6 of God were of the sons of Eleazar, and of the sons of Ithamar. And
Shemaiah son of Nethaneel, the scribe of the Levites, wrote them before the
king and the princes, and Zadok the priest, and Ahimelech the son of Abiathar,
and the chiefs of the fathers for the priests and for the Levites: one father-
house being taken for Eleazar, and one[4] taken for Ithamar.
7, 8 And the first lot came out to Jehoiarib, the second to Jedaiah. The third
9 to Harim, the fourth to Seorim. The fifth to Malchijah, the sixth to
10, 11 Mijamin. The seventh to Hakkoz, the eighth to Abijah. The ninth to
12 Jeshuah, the tenth to Shecaniah. The eleventh to Eliashib, the twelfth to
13, 14 Jakim. The thirteenth to Huppah, the fourteenth to Jeshebab. The
15 fifteenth to Bilgah, the sixteenth to Immer. The seventeenth to Hezir, the
16 eighteenth to Hapizez. The nineteenth to Pethahiah, the twentieth to
17 Jehezkel. The one and twentieth to Jachin, the two and twentieth to Gamul.
18 The three and twentieth to Delaiah, the four and twentieth to Maaziah.
19 These are their offices for their service, to go into the house of the LORD
according to their order by Aaron their father, as the LORD God of Israel had
commanded him.

5. *The Classes of the Levites:* vers. 20–31.

20 And for the remaining sons of Levi: for the sons of Amram, Shubael; for
21 the sons of Shubael, Jehdeiah. For Rehabiah: for the sons of Rehabiah, the
22 chief was Isshiah. For the Izharites, Shelomoth; for the sons of Shelomoth,
23 Jahath. And the sons [of Hebron][5]: Jesiah [the first], Amariah the second,
24 Jahaziel the third, Jekamam the fourth. The sons of Uzziel, Micah; for the
25 sons of Micah, Shamir.[6] The brother of Micah was Isshiah; for the sons of
26 Isshiah, Zechariah. The sons of Merari were Mahli and Mushi: the sons of
27 Jazziah, Beno.[7] The sons of Merari, by Jaaziah his son: Shoham,[8] and
28, 29 Zaccur, and Ibri. To Mahli belonged Eleazar;[9] and he had no sons. Con-
30 cerning Kish, the sons of Kish, Jerahmeel. And the sons of Mushi: Mahli,
and Eder, and Jerimoth: these were the sons of the Levites after their
31 father-houses. And these also cast lots like their brethren the sons of Aaron,
before David the king, and Zadok, and Ahimelech, and the chiefs of the
fathers for the priests and for the Levites: the fathers, the chief like his
younger brother.

6. *The Twenty-four Classes of Singers:* ch. xxv.

CH. XXV. 1. And David and the captains of the host separated for service the sons
of Asaph, and Heman, and Jeduthun, who prophesied[10] with harps, with
psalteries, and with cymbals: and the number of the workmen for the service
2 was. For the sons of Asaph: Zaccur, and Joseph, and Nethaniah, and
3 Asharelah sons of Asaph, under Asaph, who prophesied under the king. For
Jeduthun: the sons of Jeduthun were Gedaliah, and Zeri, and Jeshaiah,
Hashabiah, and Mattithiah, six, under their father Jeduthun, on the harp who

4 prophesied to thank and praise the LORD. For Heman: the sons of Heman
Bukkiah, Mattaniah, Uzziel, Shebuel, and Jerimoth, Hananiah, Hanani,
Eliathah, Giddalti, and Romamti-ezer, Joshbekashah, Mallothi, Hothir,
5 Mahazioth. All these were the sons of Heman, the king's seer in the words
of God, to lift up the horn: and God gave Heman fourteen sons and three
6 daughters. All these were under their father for song in the house of the
LORD, with cymbals, psalteries, and harps for the service of the house of God
7 under the king, with Asaph, and Jeduthun, and Heman. And their number
with their brethren that were instructed in singing to the LORD, all that
8 were cunning were two hundred eighty and eight. And they cast lots for the
charge, the small as the great, the teacher with the scholar.
9 And the first lot came forth for Asaph to Joseph:[11] the second to
10 Gedaliah; he and his sons and his brethren were twelve. The third to
11 Zaccur, his sons and his brethren, twelve. The fourth to Izri, his sons and
12 his brethren, twelve. The fifth to Nethaniah, his sons and his brethren,
13, 14 twelve. The sixth to Bukkiah, his sons and his brethren, twelve. The
15 seventh to Jesharelah, his sons and his brethren, twelve. The eighth to
16 Jeshaiah, his sons and his brethren, twelve. The ninth to Mattaniah, his
17 sons and his brethren, twelve. The tenth to Shimei, his sons and his
18 brethren, twelve. The eleventh to Azarel, his sons and his brethren, twelve.
19, 20 The twelfth to Hashabiah, his sons and his brethren, twelve. The thirteenth
21 to Shubael, his sons and his brethren, twelve. The fourteenth to Mattithiah,
22 his sons and his brethren, twelve. The fifteenth to Jerimoth, his sons and
23 his brethren, twelve. The sixteenth to Hananiah, his sons and his brethren,
24 twelve. The seventeenth to Joshbekashah, his sons and his brethren, twelve.
25, 26 The eighteenth to Hanani, his sons and his brethren, twelve. The nineteenth
27 to Mallothi, his sons and his brethren, twelve. The twentieth to Eliathah,
28 his sons and his brethren, twelve. The one and twentieth to Hothir, his sons
29 and his brethren, twelve. The two and twentieth to Giddalti, his sons and
30 his brethren, twelve. The three and twentieth to Mahazioth, his sons and
31 his brethren, twelve. The four and twentieth to Romamti-ezer, his sons and
his brethren, twelve.

7. *The Classes of Porters:* ch. xxvi. 1–19.

CH. XXVI. 1. Concerning the divisions of the porters: to the Korhites was Meshele-
2 miah son of Korah, of the sons of Asaph.[12] And Meshelemiah had sons:
Zechariah the first-born, Jediael the second, Zebadiah the third, Jathniel the
3, 4 fourth. Elam the fifth, Jehohanan the sixth, Elioenai the seventh. And
Obed-edom had sons: Shemaiah the first-born, Jehozabad the second, Joah
5 the third, and Sacar the fourth, and Nathaneel the fifth. Ammiel the sixth,
6 Issachar the seventh, Peulthai the eighth; for God blessed him. And to
Shemaiah his son were born sons, that ruled in the house of their father; for
7 they were valiant men. The sons of Shemaiah: Othni, and Rephael, and
8 Obed, Elzabad,—his brethren, strong men,—Elihu, and Semachiah. All these
of the sons of Obed-edom, they and their sons and their brethren, strong men
9 of ability for service, were sixty and two of Obed-edom. And Meshelemiah
10 had sons and brethren, strong men, eighteen. And Hosah, of the sons of
Merari, had sons: Shimri the chief; for he was not the first-born, but his
11 father made him chief. Hilkiah the second, Tebaliah the third, Zechariah
the fourth: all the sons and brethren of Hosah were thirteen.
12 To these divisions of the porters, to the chiefs of the men, were the wards
13 like their brethren, to minister in the house of the LORD. And they cast
14 lots, the small as the great, after their father-houses, for every gate. And
the lot eastward fell to Shelemiah: and for Zechariah his son, a wise coun-
15 sellor, they cast lots, and his lot came out northward. To Obed-edom south-
16 ward; and to his sons the house of Asuppim. To Shuppim[13] and to Hosah
westward, at the gate Shallecheth, by the causeway of ascent, one ward like
17 another. Eastward were six Levites, northward four a day, southward four

18 a day, and towards Asuppim two and two. At Parbar westward, four on
19 the causeway, and two at Parbar. These were the divisions of the porters
for the sons of Kore, and for the sons of Merari.

8. *The Administrators of the Treasures of the Sanctuary, with the Officers for the External Business:* vers. 20–32.

20 And the Levites their brethren[14] were over the treasures of the house of
21 God, and over the treasures of the holy things. The sons of Ladan, the sons
of the Gershonite of Ladan, chiefs of the father-houses of Ladan the Ger-
22 shonite, Jehieli. The sons of Jehieli: Zetham, and Joel his brother, over the
23 treasures of the house of the LORD. Of the Amramites, the Izharites, the
24 Hebronites, and the Uzzielites. Shebuel son of Gershom, the son of Moses,
25 was ruler of the treasures. And his brethren by Eliezer were Rehabiah his
son, and Jeshaiah his son, and Joram his son, and Zichri his son, and Shelo-
26 moth[15] his son. This Shelomoth and his brethren were over the treasures of
the holy things, which David the king had dedicated, and the chiefs of the
fathers, and[16] the captains of thousands and hundreds, and the captains of
27 the host. Out of the wars and of the spoil they dedicated to maintain the
28 house of the LORD. And all that Samuel the seer, and Saul the son of Kish,
and Abner the son of Ner, and Joab the son of Zeruiah, had dedicated; every-
thing dedicated was under Shelomoth and his brethren.
29 Of the Izharites was Chenaniah with his sons, for the outer business over
30 Israel, for officers and judges. Of the Hebronites were Hashabiah and his
brethren, valiant men, a thousand and seven hundred, for the oversight of
Israel on this side Jordan westward, for all the business of the LORD, and for
31 the service of the king. Of the Hebronites was Jeriah the chief; for the
Hebronites, in their generations for the fathers, in the fortieth year of the
reign of David, they were sought, and there were found among them men of
32 valour in Jazer of Gilead. And his brethren, valiant men, two thousand and
seven hundred fathers of families; and David the king appointed them over
the Reubenites, the Gadites, and the half-tribe of Manasseh, for every matter
of God, and of the king.

[1] For עָשִׂיתִי the Sept. (ἐποίησεν) and Vulg. (fecerat) have the 3d person. But see Exeg. Expl.

[2] For וַיֶּחָלְקֵם read (here and xxiv. 3) וַיַּחְלְקֵם. See Exeg. Expl.

[3] So the *Keri:* in the *Kethib* the name is Shelomoth. The same difference appears in another Shelomith, xxvi. 25.

[4] For וְאֶחָז is perhaps to be read וְאֶחָד (with L. Cappell., H. Grotius, Gesen., etc.), as some late and unimportant MSS. in de Rossi exhibit in the *var. lect.*

[5] The insertion of חֶבְרוֹן after בְּנֵי (Luther., Berth., and most moderns) is certainly confirmed neither by the Hebrew *Cod.* nor by the old translations (Sept., Vulg., etc.), but appears necessary from xxiii. 19.

[6] So the *Keri*· the *Kethib* has Shamur: the old Vers. (Sept. Σαμήρ, Vulg. *Samir*) as the *Keri*.

[7] Before בְּנוֹ a name seems to have fallen out. The text in vers. 26 and 27 is corrupt. See the Exeg. Expl.

Properly "and Shoham" (וְשֹׁהַם).

[9] After the name of Eleazar the Sept. (*cod. Vat.*) adds καὶ Ἰθάμαρ, καὶ ἀπέθανεν Ἐλεάζαρ, a gloss which is wanting in A E F X.

[10] The *Kethib* הנביאים is an error of transcription for the certainly correct *Keri* הַנִּבָּאִים (partic. *Niph.*); comp. the sing. הַנִּבָּא in vers. 2 and 3, and see Exeg. Expl.

[11] After לְיוֹסֵף, the notice constantly recurring in the following verses: "his sons and his brethren, twelve," appears to have fallen out by an oversight. Yet it is to be observed that this notice in ver. 9*b*, after גְּדַלְיָהוּ הַשֵּׁנִי, is different from that in all subsequent cases, namely, "he and his brethren and his sons" (אֶחָיו before, not בָּנָיו, as afterwards) whence it is probable that the writer did not mention with the first singer the eleven companions, whom he preceded as the twelfth.

[12] For אסף, according to ch. ix. 19, אֶבְיָסָף appears to have been read, though no external evidence confirms this conjecture.

[13] לְשֻׁפִּים (Sept. τῷ Σεφιείν; but *cod. Vat.* εἰς δεύτερον) appears to have come into the text by the repetition of the last two syllables of the foregoing הָאֲסֻפִּים, which was perhaps aided by an obscure remembrance of the root שֻׁפִּים, vii. 12.

[14] So according to the Sept. (Καὶ οἱ Λευῖται ἀδελφοὶ αὐτῶν), which has here certainly the right text; comp. הַלְוִיִּם אֲחֵיהֶם, 2 Chron. xxix. 34. If the אֲחִיָּה of the Masoretic text be original, מֵהַלְוִיִּם must have stood in place of וְהַלְוִיִּם (comp. the Vulg., which has wholly omitted that והלוים).

[15] *Kethib:* שְׁלֹמוֹת; *Keri:* שְׁלֹמִית (comp. xxiii. 9). The *Kethib* is proved by ver. 26 to be more correct, though the name recurs, ver. 28, as שְׁלֹמִית without variation.

[16] For לְשָׂרֵי־הָאֲלָפִים should apparently be read וְשָׂרֵי־ה׳; comp. xxix. 6.

EXEGETICAL.

Preliminary Remark, especially regarding the introductory notice, ch. xxiii. 1.—The connected survey of the condition, distribution, and ministerial functions of the tribe of Levi at the end of the reign of David, which fills the four ch. xxiii.-xxvi. (and falls into eight subdivisions, as is noted in the superscriptions of the above translation), is introduced by the statement, ch. xxiii. 1, that the aged and life-weary King David appointed his son Solomon to be king over Israel, formally appointed him his successor on the throne, and regularly delivered over the kingdom to him. The numbering and classification of the Levites, and the order of their service in the sanctuary, appears accordingly to be the principal measure by which David introduces the transference of the kingdom to his successor. A survey of the state of his army and of his military and civil officers (ch. xxvii.) is appended as the second of these measures, after which the final arrangements committed in solemn assembly to Solomon and the heads of the people, referring chiefly to the building of the temple (ch. xxviii., xxix.), form the close of these measures, and the immediate transition to the death of the king (ch. xxix. 26 ff.). As sources in communicating these accounts of the order of the Levites and their service, the Chronist had no doubt liturgical precepts and statistical notes proceeding (mediately or immediately) from David, that כְּתָב דָּוִיד, which he mentions, 2 Chron. xxxv. 4, along with a מִכְתַּב שְׁלֹמֹה, and which we may regard either as part of the royal annals of this king or as an independent document. Comp. Introd. § 5. —*And David was old and full of days.* זָקֵן is here not an adjective, but 3d p. perf. of the verb, as in Gen. xviii. 12; and so שָׂבַע with its accusative of restriction יָמִים, for which elsewhere usually the adj. שְׂבַע יָמִים (Gen. xxxv. 29; Job xii. 17), or even שָׂבֵעַ alone (Gen. xxv. 8). —*He made his son Solomon king over Israel.* This notice does not perhaps forestall the more precise and definite statement of the appointment of Solomon to be king in ch. xxix. 22 (which reports also the mode of appointment, by the anointing of the successor), but forms a general introduction to all that follows to the end of our book (comp. the similar general but not forestalling statement in ch. xxii. 7), and serves to place all that is here related of the Levites, the military and civil officers, under the head of the last will and concluding acts of the king. A statement in many respects similar occurs in John xiii. 1, which characterizes all that follows to the end of this Gospel as a "loving of his own unto the end." Against the opinion of Bertheau, that the Chronist has in our verse given briefly the contents of the narrative 1 Kings i., the remarks of Keil suffice; comp. also our exegetical exposition of ch. xxix. 22.

1. *Enumeration of the Levites, and Arrangement of their Work:* ch. xxiii. 2–5.—*And he gathered all the princes of Israel.* These, the representatives of the tribes, had to co-operate in this mustering and regulation of the Levites, because this was a general concern of the kingdom. The present account concerning the holding of a great *census Levitarum* in a solemn assembly of the spiritual and temporal chiefs of the people, shortly before the end of David, is confirmed by the passage xxvi. 30 f., which speaks specially of the result of this muster "in the fortieth year of the reign of David" with regard to the family of Hebronites in Gilead.—Ver. 3. *And the Levites were numbered from the age of thirty years and upwards.* This accords with the proceeding of Moses, who, Num. iv. 3, 23, 30, 39 ff., likewise numbers the Levites from thirty years of age (to fifty) for service in the sanctuary. But as he had already included younger men, namely, from twenty-five years of age (Num. viii. 23–26), David's muster may also have extended not merely to those of thirty years and upwards, but rather, according to the express statement of ver. 24, reached the Levites of twenty years and upwards. That this later statement does not contradict the present one, and that it is not necessary to amend our passage by inserting עֶשְׂרִים for שְׁלֹשִׁים (Keil), see on ver. 24.—*By their polls in men,* thus excluding women and children; the לִגְבָרִים defining more exactly the לְגֻלְגְּלֹתָם.—Ver. 4 f. contain the words of the king, as appears from the 1st perf. עָשִׂיתִי at the end of ver. 5, for which the Sept. and Vulg. have unnecessarily, and only from ignorance of the true state of the matter, substituted the third person.—*Of these, twenty and four thousand were to oversee the work of the house of the Lord,* the duties of the Levitical temple service in general, to which belonged not—*a.* the proper priestly

functions (xxiv. 1–19); *b.* those of the Levitical civil and judicial officers (the שֹׁטְרִים and שֹׁפְטִים, ver. 4*b*; comp. xxvi. 29–32); *c.* those of the porters (ver. 5*a*; comp. xxvi.); *d.* those of the singers and musicians (ver. 5; comp. xxv.).—*With instruments, which I have made for praise*, which I have introduced to accompany the sacred singing in the service of God; comp. 2 Chron. xxix. 26; Neh. xii. 36; also Amos vi. 5, where David is mentioned as inventor of sacred musical instruments.

2. *The Twenty-four Houses of the Levites*: ch. xxiii. 6–23.—*And David divided them into courses for the sons of Levi.* In his new muster and order of the Levitical houses he thus founded upon the three old well-known branches of this tribe (comp. v. 27–vi. 15). וַיֶּחָלְקֵם, for which, here and xxiv. 3, R. D. Kimchi would read rather וַיְחַלְּקֵם (see Crit. Note), stands for וַיַּחְלְקֵם (comp. ch. xxiv. 4, 5), and is merely a by-form of the *imperf. Kal*, not *Piel*, as Ges. and Ew. think. Bertheau asserts that not all the Levites, but only the 24,000 specially appointed for the service in the house of the Lord, are to be regarded as the object of ויחלקם; and, in fact, ver. 24 appears to favour this, as well as the circumstance that a great part of the names here enumerated recur in xxiv. 20–31 and xxvi. 20–28; whereas in the enumeration of the twenty-four classes of singers (xxv.), porters (xxvi. 1–19), and officers, and judges (xxvi. 29–32), quite other names occur. What Keil adduces against this (p. 188) is by no means sufficient to invalidate it.—*a.* The Houses of the Gershonites: vers. 7–11.—*Of the Gershonites were Ladan and Shimi.* In ch. vi. 2, as already in Ex. vi. 17, Num. iii. 18, these two sons and founders of the two chief branches of the Gershonites are called Libni and Shimi. Our Ladan appears not to be identical with Libni, but rather to have been a descendant of this son of Gershon, after whom, in David's time, a greater branch of the family was named. Vers. 8, 9 analyze this branch of the Ladanites as falling into the two chief stems of the sons of Ladan and the sons of Shimi, a descendant of Libni, by name Shimi, not the brother of Ladan or Libni named in ver. 7, whose branch is more fully described in vers. 10, 11. Those belonging to the branch of Ladan fall altogether into six houses, namely, three of the sons of Ladan (ver. 8) and three of the sons of Shimi (ver. 9). On the contrary, the descendants of the other Shimi (brother of Ladan, ver. 10) form only four, or rather only three, houses, as the two youngest of the families belonging to them, Jeush and Beriah, from their numerical weakness, are included in one house, and also in one class (פְּקֻדָּה, ver. 11). The Gershonites, therefore, in David's time counted in all nine houses.—*b.* The Houses of the Kohathites: vers. 12–20.—*Amram, Izhar, Hebron, and Uzziel.* So are the four sons of Kohath named also in v. 28, vi. 3, and previously in Ex. vi. 18; Num. iii. 27. —*Aaron was separated to sanctify him as most holy.* So is לְהַקְדִּישׁוֹ קֹדֶשׁ קָדָשִׁים to be understood of Aaron's choice and anointment to be the most holy person of a high priest, not from his ministering in the most holy place (Vulg. *ut ministraret in sancto sanctorum;* likewise the Peschito), nor from his appointment to consecrate the most holy utensils (Clericus, against which see Hengsten. *Christol.* ii. 50, and Keil on the passage).—*And to bless in His name for ever*, in Jehovah's name, to pronounce the blessing on the community (after the prescription of Moses, Num. vi. 23, xvi. 2; Deut. xxi. 5); not to bless the name of Jehovah, or call upon Him, as Ges. and Berth. think.—Ver. 14. *And Moses the man of God, his sons were called after the tribe of Levi*, were reckoned among the simple Levites, and not among the priests. On נִקְרָא עַל, comp. Gen. xlviii. 6; Ezra ii. 61; Neh. vii. 63.—Ver. 15. *Of the sons of Gershom, Shebuel was the chief*, properly, "Gershom's sons, Shebuel the chief;" comp. the numerous cases in which "sons" are announced, and yet only one follows, as ch. ii. 31, etc. That, moreover, Gershom had other sons, who were reckoned with the house of Shebuel (or Shubael, as he is called in ch. xxiv. 20), appears to follow from ver. 17, where it is expressly said of Eliezer that he had no sons besides Rehabiah. Shebuel and Rehabiah therefore were the names of the houses of the family of Amram that sprang from Moses. To these two non-sacerdotal houses of the Kohathites are to be added, according to vers. 18–20, of the family of Izhar, the house of Shelomith (or Shelomoth, ch. xxiv. 22); of the family of Hebron four houses, Jeriah, Amariah, Jahaziel, and Jekamam; of the family of Uzziel two, Micah and Jesiah,—in all, nine Levitical houses of Kohathite origin.—*c.* The Houses of the Merarites: vers. 21–23—*The sons of Merari: Mahli and Mushi.* So are called the two sons of Merari also, vi. 4; Ex. vi. 19; Num. iii. 33; whereas in xxiv. 27 a third son of Merari is named, Jaaziah, the founder of the three houses of Shoham, Zaccur and Ibri. The conjecture is obvious, that the name of this Jaaziah with his three sons has fallen out of our passage by an old oversight, as Bertheau assumes when he supplements the text of our passage from ch. xxiv. 26, 27. But, 1. The Sept., Vulg., and Syr. present our text, that gives only two sons of Merari; 2. The books of Moses, and indeed the whole of the Old Testament elsewhere, know nothing of a third son of Merari and his descendants; 3. The passage xxiv. 26, 27 bears manifest traces of an interpolation in itself, by which the name Jaaziah must have come into the text; 4. The names of the supposed sons of Jaaziah occur nowhere else, with the exception of Zaccur alone (see xxv. 2); 5. The only gain that the assumption of the names in question into our text could be,—that, namely, the number of the Merarite houses should be brought up to six, and so a total of twenty-four houses of Levites should be shown in our section (nine Gershonite, nine Kohathite, and six Merarite), analogous to the number of twenty-four houses and classes of priests (ch. xxiv.), and of twenty-four classes of singers (ch. xxv.), and corresponding with the express assertion of Josephus (*Antiq.* vii. 14. 7), that David divided the Levites into twenty-four classes,—this single gain is lost by this, that there should be not twenty-four but twenty-five houses resulting from the addition of the three sons of Jaaziah, as our passage (vers. 21–23) derives not three but four houses from Merari: one from Mahli (named

after Eleazar the father of the heiress, or after his brother Kish, and then after Jerahmeel, chief son of this Kish; see xxiv. 29), and three from Mushi, namely, Mahli, Eder, and Jeremoth. Now of these three sons of Mushi, Bertheau will certainly exclude from the text the first, Mahli, on account of his identity of name with Mahli the brother of Mushi, to obtain the desired result of six Merarite houses; but the arbitrariness of this procedure is obviously greater and more unjustifiable than the boldness of our condemnation of the vers. 26 and 27 in ch. xxiv. as interpolated, that has sufficient ground in the clearly corrupt text of this verse. It necessarily follows that our section yields only four Merarite, and therefore in all only twenty-two Levitical houses.

3. *Closing Remarks respecting the Levites:* ch. xxiii. 24-32.—*These are the sons of Levi . . . for those mustered,* לִפְקוּדֵיהֶם (comp. Ex. xxx. 14, Num. i. 21 ff., as on the following words: "by the number of the names," Num. i. 18, iii. 43).—*Doing the work for the service of the house of the Lord.* עֹשֵׂה הַמְּלָאכָה is, as also in 2 Chron. xxxiv. 10, 13, Ezra iii. 9, Neh. ii. 16, not sing. but plur. = עֹשֵׂי הַמְּל׳, and differing only in writing from this regular form (that occurs, for example, 2 Chron. xxiv. 13); comp. Ew. § 16, *b.*—*From twenty years old and upwards.* This statement, that the twentieth year is fixed as the starting-point for the entrance of the Levites on their official duties, is more exactly explained in the following words, by reference to the lighter labour which fell upon the Levites when the wandering life of the wilderness ceased,—a conclusion that is not fully expressed, but indicated clearly enough by vers. 25, 26.—Ver. 27. *For by the last words of David these were,* etc. Thus it is obvious we are to understand the orders of David issued shortly before his end by the words בְּדִבְרֵי דָוִיד הָאַחֲרוֹנִים (with the Vulg.: *juxta præcepta David novissima,* and so Clericus, J. H. Mich., Keil, etc.), not "in the later histories of David" (Kimchi, Berth.),—a conception which imports into the text a thought quite foreign to the context, and by no means justified by referring to ch. xxix. 29. Even because a last arrangement of David is now expressly named as the ground of the introduction of Levites of twenty years into the sacred service, it is to be assumed that that statement in ver. 3 respecting the entrants at the age of thirty years refers to an earlier numeration, in which David had adhered to the legal determination in Num. iii. 23, 30 (so Kimchi, J. H. Mich., and others), though the words and the connection of that passage, especially the circumstance that there the number 38,000 is given as the result of the muster, and that here no greater number takes its place, may not appear to favour such a distinction between an earlier and a later muster. It is conceivable, though not indicated by our author, that David may have established a distinction of classes, in such a way that he introduced the Levites of twenty years to the lower and easier duties, and those of thirty years to the higher and holier functions. At all events, any mode of harmonizing the two accounts appears more reasonable than the expedient of Bertheau, that the Chronist placed side by side two different accounts, the one giving twenty, the other thirty, years, without explanation as they were found in his sources, or than the emendation of Keil, who changes שְׁלֹשִׁים, ver. 3, into עֶשְׂרִים.—Vers. 28-31. Here follows an enumeration of the duties to be performed by the Levites, rising from the lower and more external (referring to the court and its chambers, to purification and the like) to the higher, and closing with the assistance given in the sacrifices of the great feasts.—*And for the shew-bread,* that is, the preparation, not the presentation of it, which belonged exclusively to the priests (Lev. xxiv. 8 ff.).—*And pancakes,* properly, "the pan," comp. Lev. ii. 5.—*And that which is fried* (Lev. vi. 14), *and all measures of capacity and length,* for measuring flour, oil, and wine, which were added to the sacrifices, which the Levites had to clean and keep (comp. Ex. xxix. 40, xxx. 24; Lev. xix. 35).—*And to stand every morning to thank and praise the Lord.* This naturally refers to the duties of the 4000 Levitical singers and musicians (ver. 5; comp. ch. xxv.); for here are enumerated the offices of all classes of the Levites, not merely of the 24,000 (against Berth.).—*And to offer all burnt-offerings to the Lord.* "Hereby the Levites were obliged to prepare the requisite number of victims, to examine the fitness of them, to slay the animals, to flay them, etc." (Keil.)—*By number after the order of them continually before the Lord,* that is, by number as they are to be presented continually before the Lord, according to the prescriptions of the law regarding them. The תָּמִיד continually refers to "the offering" (הַעֲלוֹת עֹלוֹת) as a business recurring regularly on the appointed day; comp. עֹלוֹת תָּמִיד, Num. xxvii. 6, etc.—Ver. 32. *And they shall keep the charge of the tent of meeting* ("the temple," comp. Num. xviii. 4), *and the charge of the sanctuary* (of all holy things connected with worship, Num. xviii. 5), *and the charge of the sons of Aaron* (the care of all that the priests enjoin upon them, all the help given to the priests). On this particular recapitulation of all the functions of the Levites, comp. the similar passage, Num. xviii. 3 ff.

4. *The Twenty-four Classes of Priests:* ch. xxiv. 1-19.—The enumeration of these follows quite suitably after the foregoing passage, particularly after ch. xxiii. 32; comp. the "sons of Aaron" with that in ver. 1 of our chapter.—*The sons of Aaron: Nadab and Abihu,* etc. Comp. on this introduction to the Davidic regulations referring to the Mosaic time in vers. 1 and 2, ch. v. 29, and Ex. vi. 23; Lev. x. 1; Num. iii. 4.—Ver. 3. *And David distributed them, so that Zadok of the sons of Eleazar.* For ויחלקם, comp. on xxiii. 6; for Zadok and Abiathar, on v. 30, xvi. 39, xviii. 16; for פְּקֻדָּה, official class, on xxiii. 11.—Ver. 4. *And the sons of Eleazar were found more numerous in chief men.* These "men" (גְּבָרִים), of whom Eleazar had twice as many in heads or chiefs (רָאשִׁים) as Ithamar, are the chiefs, not of the great complex of families or houses (Berth.), but of the several families, the fathers, chiefs of

the several priestly homes.—Ver. 5. *And they divided them.* The subject is David, Zadok, and Ahimelech, to whom naturally this matter belonged.—*One with the other*, literally, "these with those," those of Eleazar with those of Ithamar; comp. xxv. 8.—*For the holy princes and the princes of God.* On the former phrase, comp. Isa. xliii. 28, and the parallel phrase: "princes of the priests," שָׂרֵי הַכֹּהֲנִים, 2 Chron. xxxvi. 14; on the second (Sept. ἄρχοντες κυρίου), the equivalent: "high priests, upper priests." For the princes of priests and high priests from Ithamar, who were far behind those of the line of Eleazar in number and importance, comp. on v. 30.—Ver. 6. *Wrote them*, namely, the classes, as the lot determined.—*One father-house being taken for Eleazar and one for Ithamar*, that is, alternately, from the urn containing the lots for Eleazar, and then from that containing the lots for Ithamar (so אָחֻז signifies; comp. Num. xxxi. 30, 47), that none might seem preferred before the other. And, indeed, this alternation in drawing the lots might have been so managed, that, on account of the double number of the families of Eleazar, two lots for Eleazar might be drawn for every one for Ithamar (comp. Berth.). Whether this mode of drawing lots be indicated by the doubling of the אָחֻז in the second place (וְאָחֻז אָחֻז לְאִיתָמָר), as Berth. thinks, is more than doubtful. Notwithstanding the almost universal agreement of the MSS. respecting this double אָחֻז, and the fact that the old translators and the Rabbis did not understand the passage, the alteration of the first אָחֻז into אֶחָד (see Crit. Note) appears to be the only means of obtaining a correct conception of these otherwise dark words.—Ver. 7 ff. The names of the twenty-four classes are now given in order, as they were settled by lot.—*And the first lot came out* of the urn; comp. for יצא in this sense, Josh. xvi. 1, xix. 1. Jehoiarib and Jedaiah, the names of the first two classes, are so named together in ch. ix. 10. For Jedaiah, comp., besides Ezra ii. 36, Neh. vii. 39; for Jehoiarib, as the class from which Mattathias and the Maccabees sprang, 1 Macc. ii. 1; for Abijah, as the class of Zacharias the father of John the Baptist, Luke i. 5; for the classes of Immer (ver. 14) and Jachin (ver. 17), ch. ix. 10, 12. Some of the twenty-four classes never occur again, namely, Seorim (ver. 8), Jeshebab (ver. 13), and Hapizez (ver. 15), some at least not among the priests, as Mijamin (ver. 9), Huppah (ver. 13), and Gamul (ver. 17). With respect to the name Pethahiah (ver. 16), Holzhausen (*Die Weissagungen des Joel übers. und erklärt*, Gött. 1829) has propounded the quite arbitrary conjecture that it is identical with Pethuel (פְּתַחְיָה = פְּתוּאֵל) the father of the prophet Joel,—a conjecture which is of almost as much value as that of Raschi, who would identify Pethuel the father of Joel with Samuel (comp. R. Wünsche, *Die Weissagungen des Joel*, 1872, p. 1).—Ver. 19. *According to their order by Aaron their father, as the Lord . . . had commanded him.* Comp. the words occurring so often in the law: "And the Lord said unto Moses and Aaron" (for example, Num. iv. 1, 17), and similar Pentateuchic testimonies for the regulation of the priestly service according to the divine command.—The credibility of the present statements of the Chronist regarding the origin of the twenty-four classes of priests, and their order in the service by David, is attested by Ezek. viii. 16–18 (see the exposition of the passage), Neh. xii. 1–7, 12–21, and by Josephus, *Antiq.* vii. 14. 7: διέμεινεν οὗτος ὁ μερισμὸς ἄχρι τῆς σήμερον ἡμέρας. Against the assertion made by de Wette and Gramberg, and defended by Herzberg (*Gesch. des V. Israel*, i. 381 ff.), that the twenty-four classes originated after the exile, see Movers, *Chronik*, p. 279 ff., and Oehler in Herzog's *Real-Encycl.* xii. 185 ff.

5. *The Classes of the Levites*: ch. xxiv. 20–31. —*And for the remaining sons of Levi*, after the enumeration of the priests. By this might be understood all the Levites except the family of Aaron or the priests; but as in the two following chapters the twenty-four orders of singers and the divisions of the porters and of those charged with external duties are enumerated apart, it seems necessary to suppose that the present section speaks only of the Levites employed in worship, and not of the whole body. They are "the brethren of Aaron," the Levites specially assigned to the priests as assistants in divine service, whose division into classes is here described. Only on this assumption is explained the otherwise very surprising, indeed inconceivable, incompleteness of the present list of Levitical classes, compared with that of the Levitical houses named in xxiii. 6–23, which embraces all the three families, the Kohathites, the Merarites, and the Gershonites, whereas the Gershonites are wholly excluded from the present list. This exclusion seems to have its ground in this, that, xxvi. 20 ff., several Gershonite houses had the charge over the treasures of the sanctuary, and also the duties of officers and judges (although this is not expressly stated) were partly discharged by the Gershonites. So at least Keil, whereas others certainly, as Berth., regard our list as laid out for a full enumeration of all the Levitical classes or houses, but from some cause (perhaps "because the author was not able to make out all the names of the classes") no longer fully preserved. The list, for the at least often defective character of which the elucidation of the details will afford more than one proof, begins after omitting the Gershonites, ver. 20, at once with the classes of the Kohathites.—*For the sons of Amram, Shubael* was the chief or head of a class; obviously the son of Gershom son of Moses, therefore grandson of Amram, who is called Shebuel xxiii. 16. The same double spelling of this name is found also xxv. 4, 20, in a family of singers of the house of Heman. As chief of the class springing from Shubael was, in David's time, Jehdeiah, a person otherwise unknown, whose name, xxvii. 30, is also borne by an officer of David.—Ver. 21 ff. Other chiefs of classes are now named—1. For the Amramite class, Isshiah (different from the one named ver. 25). 2. For the Izharite class, Jahath (ver. 22). 3. For the Uzzielite class of Micah, Shamir (ver. 24). 4. For the Uzzielite class of Isshiah, Zechariah (ver. 25). In this kind of enumeration, it is strange that in ver. 23, where we should expect to find the chiefs of some classes of the great Hebronite family (xxiii. 19), only the names of the four chiefs or

founders of the Hebronite houses, Jeriah, Amariah, Jahaziel, and Jekamam, are mentioned, quite as in xxiii. 19, and indeed introduced by a mere וּבְנֵי before the name of the first יְרִיָּהוּ. There can be no doubt that the text is here defective. It is probable that not merely the name חֶבְרוֹן is to be inserted after וּבְנֵי (see Crit. Note), but that also the names of the four chiefs in David's time have fallen out after those of the four classes.—Vers. 26, 27 bear still clearer marks of the corruption of the present text, perhaps even of its complete spuriousness, than ver. 23 (comp. partly the Crit. Notes and partly the Exeg. Expl. of xxiii. 21–23). Especially strange is—1. The בְּנֵי יַעֲזִיָּהוּ in ver. 26*b*, detached from that which goes before (instead of "וּבְנֵי י). 2. The בְּנוֹ in the same place, that cannot possibly be taken for a proper name (with some older exegetes), but rather indicates that a proper name had fallen out before it. 3. The repetition of בְּנֵי מְרָרִי at the beginning of ver. 27, which appears to presume a wholly different mode of enumeration from that which is usual from ver. 20 on. 4. The copula וְ before שֹׁהַם, as first of the sons of Jaaziah, in ver. 27*b*. To all this are to be added the reasons which make improbable the existence of a Jaaziah as third son of Merari along with Mahli and Mushi; see on xxiii. 21 f. The spurious character of the two verses appears therefore almost certain, though they are attested by the Sept., Syr., and the Vulg.—For vers. 28, 29, comp. likewise the remark on xxiii. 21 ff.—Ver. 30. *And the sons of Mushi: Mahli, and Eder, and Jerimoth.* As in ver. 23, so here it is strange to name the houses without stating the chiefs of the classes taken from them. The text appears here also to be defective.—Ver. 31. *And these also cast lots like their brethren the sons of Aaron.* From this manifestation of the quite analogous character of the allotment of the Levites and the priests (vers. 1–19), it is highly probable that the number of the Levitical classes (as also that of the singers in the following chapter) was likewise twenty-four, although in the present text, the partial defectiveness of which is obvious, and needs no further proof, only fifteen chiefs of classes are expressly named. —*The fathers, the chief like his younger brother;* that is, the eldest brother representing the house, as well as his younger brother (for הָרֹאשׁ, in apposition with the father-house, comp. on xxiii. 17, 18). Quite correct in sense the Vulg.: "*tam minores, quam majores; omnes sors æqualiter dividebat.*" That nothing is communicated to us of the order of the several classes, as they were settled by lot, completes the impression of the great defectiveness which characterizes this section.

6. *The Twenty-four Classes of Singers:* ch. xxv.—*And David and the captains of the host separated.* "Captains of the host" (שָׂרֵי הַצָּבָא) are those partakers in the legislative and judicial government of David who were designated, xxiv. 6, merely as "princes," xxiii. 2, as "princes of Israel." The designation explains itself from the conception of Israel as the host of the Lord (Ex. xii. 17, 41), not from that of the Levites as an army, or their doings as a military service (Num. iv. 23).—*The sons of Asaph, and Heman, and Jeduthun.* The לְ before אָסָף is here *nota accusativi;* comp. Ezra viii. 24. For the genealogy of the three song-masters, of whom Asaph was a Gershonite, Heman a Kohathite, and Jeduthun a Merarite, see vi. 18, 24, 29 ff.—*Who prophesied with harps,* or showed themselves inspired with harps; for "the really artificial play is, like every art, an expression of inspiration or enthusiasm" (Berth.); comp. Ex. xxxi. 3, and for the *Keri* הַנִּבְּאִים as alone admissible, the Crit. Note.—*And the number of the workmen for the service was.* For the position of the genitive 'אַנְשֵׁי וגו after the governing מִסְפָּר with suffix, comp. the similar construction נַפְשׁוֹ עָצֵל, "his the sluggard's soul," Prov. xiii. 4 (Ew. § 309, *c*). That statements are actually made in the sequel concerning the number of the Levitical musicians appears from vers. 3–5, where the families of them are referred to: four sons of Asaph (ver. 2, without express mention of the number four), six sons of Jeduthun, and fourteen sons of Heman; and also from ver. 7, where the sum of all the singers of these families is stated to be 288.—Ver. 2. *Sons of Asaph under Asaph,* literally, "by the hand," or "at the hand," of Asaph, that is, led by him. עַל־יַד here means the same as in the vers. 3 and 6, עַל־יְדֵי, "at the hands," under the guidance or order.—Ver. 3. *For Jeduthun, the sons of Jeduthun were Gedaliah,* or, "as to Jeduthun (the family of Jeduthun), the sons of Jeduthun," etc. As the number of these "sons of Jeduthun" (perhaps disciples trained by him; comp., for this figurative import of the term "sons" in our section, on ver. 7) is expressly stated to be six, and yet only five are here named, hence one name must have fallen out, and, indeed, according to ver. 17, that of Shimi, the only one that is wanting in our verses, while all the other twenty-three names recur (vers. 9–31).—*Under their father Jeduthun on the harp,* or "under the guidance of their father Jeduthun on the harp;" בַּכִּנּוֹר belongs to יְדוּתוּן. For the following: "who prophesied (or 'was inspired") to thank and praise the Lord,' comp. xvi. 4; 2 Chron. v. 13.—Ver. 4. *Giddalti and Romamti-ezer.* The genitive עֶזֶר probably belongs also to גִּדַּלְתִּי, so that the full name of this son of Heman is Giddalti-ezer (though in ver. 9 this is not expressly stated).—Ver. 5. *All these were the sons of Heman, the king's seer in the words of God.* Heman is so called as mediator of divine revelations for the king; comp. 2 Chron. xxxv. 15, where the same predicate is applied to Jeduthun, and ch. xxi. 9, where Gad is introduced as David's seer.—*To lift up the horn; and God gave to Heman fourteen sons and three daughters.* The rich blessing of descendants is here, as elsewhere (for example, Job xlii. 13; Ps. cxxvii. 3 f.; also ch. xxvi. 5), represented as a lifting up of the horn, that is, the might and consequence of the person con-

cerned; comp. for הֵרִים קֶרֶן (which does not mean to "sound the horn," as Berth., misled by the certainly erroneous Masoretic accentuation, supposes) in this figurative sense, for example, 1 Sam. ii. 10 (Luke i. 78); Lam. ii. 17; Ps. lxxxix. 18, xcii. 11, cxlviii. 14.—Ver. 6. *All these were under their father*, literally, "under the guidance of their father." The genitive אֲבִיהֶם is distributive, and does not refer specially to Heman (Berth.); for by "all these" our verse clearly points to all enumerated from ver. 2, and not merely to Heman's sons, vers. 4, 5.—*Under the king, with Asaph, and Jeduthun, and Heman.* That here, by the עַל־יְדֵי referring to הַמֶּלֶךְ and the three following names, David appears co-ordinated with the three song-masters, is explained by his having co-operated with them in the first arrangement and institution of the service of song.—Ver. 7. *And their number . . . all that were cunning, were two hundred eighty and eight.* This total of 288, or 24 × 12, as the sequel (ver. 9 ff.) shows, is explained by this, that each of the twenty-four (4 + 6 + 14) sons of Asaph, Jeduthun, and Heman, with his eleven "brethren," not his nearest kindred, but rather his companions in calling, was incorporated into one class or choir of twelve musicians, so that thus there were twenty-four such dodecades. These 288 musicians were designated "all the cunning" (כָּל־הַמֵּבִין), as by instruction and practice they were entrusted with the art of sacred singing, and were able to train the great body of singers (the 4000 who, ver. 8, are distinguished from them as "scholars," תַּלְמִידִים).—Ver. 8. *And they cast lots for the charge*, גּוֹרָלוֹת מִשְׁמֶרֶת, properly, "lots of service" (κλήρους ἐφημεριῶν, Sept.).—*The small as the great, the teacher with the scholar.* To לְעֻמַּת belongs כַּקָּטֹן כַּגָּדוֹל as genitive: "in the way of as the small so the great" (comp. Eccl. v. 15 and Ew. § 360, *a.*). The repetition of a מִשְׁמֶרֶת after לְעֻמַּת, which some MSS. present, and some Rabbinical expositors, as Raschi and Kimchi, demand, is an unnecessary attempt to amend and interpret. The passage says that the whole of the Levites destined for the service of song, the leaders as well as the choristers, the 288 מְבִינִים as well as the 3712 תַּלְמִידִים, were chosen by lot; and so the regularly exchanging classes, or ἐφημερίαι, included both kinds of singers.—Vers. 9–31. The Result of the Lot.—*And the first lot came out for Asaph to Joseph*, literally, "for Asaph, (namely) for Joseph" his son. The לְ, "for" or "on," is usually omitted in the following. For the question whether the words "his son and his brethren twelve" (or, "he and his sons and his brethren"—together—"twelve"), which stand after the following twenty-three names, have fallen out after לְיוֹסֵף, or were intentionally omitted, see Crit. Note.—Ver. 11. *The fourth to Izri, his sons.* This Izri is called Zeri in ver. 3, as several other names in this list vary in spelling and form from those in vers. 2–4,—namely, Nethanjahu and Hananjahu, vers. 12, 23 (for Nethaniah, Hananiah, vers. 2, 4); Hashabiah, ver. 19 (for Hashabjahu, ver. 3); Jesharelah, ver. 14 (for Asharelah, ver. 2); Azarel, ver. 18 (for Uzziel, ver. 4; comp. the various forms of the royal name Uzziah-Azariah, 1 Chron. iii. 12; 2 Chron. xxvi. 1); Shubael, ver. 20 (for Shebuel, ver. 4); Jeremoth, ver. 22 (for Jerimoth, ver. 4); Elijathah, ver. 27 (for Eliathah, ver. 4). For the absence of Shimi, ver. 17, in the former list, see on ver. 3. The various deviations in the spelling and formation of the names deepen the impression of the historical character, for which the whole account of singing-classes vouches. That of the twenty-four names of the leaders only one, that of Mattithiah, ver. 21, occurs elsewhere (xv. 18, 21, in the account of the removal of the ark), proves nothing against the credibility of the present double list, the arbitrary invention of which would be far more difficult to conceive than the assumption of its resting on ancient and genuine documents.

With regard to the series of names in vers. 9–31, what is remarked by Keil suffices for its explanation:—"The series is so determined by lot, that the four sons of Asaph hold the first, third, fifth, and seventh places; the six sons of Jeduthun, the second, fourth, eighth, tenth, twelfth, and fourteenth places; lastly, the four sons of Heman mentioned in ver. 4, the sixth, ninth, eleventh, and thirteenth places; and the remaining places, 15–24, fall to the remaining sons of Heman. Hence it follows that the lots of the sons of the three song-masters were not put in separate urns, and one lot drawn from each urn in succession, but all the lots were united in one urn, and, in drawing, the lots of Asaph and Jeduthun so came out, that after the fourteenth drawing only the sons of Heman remained." This simple explanation of the order of the names is certainly preferable to the artificial assumption of Bertheau, that "two series of seven each were first put in the urns, and one drawn from each of these alternately, and then the remaining ten sons of Heman were put in."

7. *The Classes of Porters*: ch. xxvi. 1–19.—*To the Korhites was Meshelemiah.* Comp. ver. 14, where the name is Shelemiah. On the patronymic הַקָּרְחִים, "the Korhites," comp. ix. 19, where also the names Kore and Abiasaph occurred. That "Asaph" is a slip of the pen appears from this, that, vi. 24 ff., Asaph belongs to the descendants of Gershon, not, as the Korhites, to that of Kohath.—Ver. 2. *Zechariah the first-born.* This son of Meshelemiah occurs also ix. 21 and in ver. 14.—Vers. 4–8. Obed-edom and his Descendants.—*And Obed-edom had sons.* This Obed-edom, already occurring xv. 18, 24, and xvi. 38, is called in the latter place a son of Jeduthun, not of the well-known song-master of the house of Merari, for the account of the Merarite porters begins in ver. 10, but of some other unknown Korhite of the same name, as appears from ver. 1 comp. with ver. 19.—Ver. 6. *And to Shemaiah . . . were born sons that ruled in the house of their father*, properly, "the lordships (הַמִּמְשָׁלִים, *abstr. pro concr.* for הַמּשְׁלִים; comp. Ew. § 160, *b*) of the house of their father."—Ver. 7. *And Obed,*

Elzabad, his brethren. The missing copula ו is to be supplied before אֶלְזָבָד as before אֶחָיו. Then the strong men, Elihu and Semachiah, are named as Elzabad's brethren. That the names of the brethren are not stated (Berth.) is less probable. —Ver. 8. *Strong men of ability for service.* The sing. אִישׁ־חַיִל is in apposition with the כֹּל standing at the beginning of the verse (or such a כֹּל is to be supplied before it).—Ver. 9. *And Meshelemiah . . . eighteen.* By this appended statement of the number of Meshelemiah's family, the sum of the Korhite porters is fixed at eighty.—Vers. 10, 11. *And Hosah, of the sons of Merari.* This Hosah occurred before, xvi. 38, along with Obed-edom as porter.—*Shimri the chief; for he was not the first-born,* that is, because none of the families springing from Hosah possessed the birthright (perhaps because the eldest son had died without male heirs), the father named Shimri, the strongest and cleverest of his sons, chief of the family. —Ver. 11. *All the sons and brethren of Hosah were thirteen.* Hence the whole number of all the porters here named is ninety-three (62 + 18 + 13). On the relation of this number to the statement in ix. 22, that the porters were in all 212, see on the passage; comp. also xvi. 38. — Vers. 12–19. The Division of Porters according to the several Stations at which they were to serve.—*To these divisions of the porters, to the chiefs of the men.* For this explicative לְרָאשֵׁי הַגְּבָרִים, comp. on xxiv. 4; for the following statement respecting the division of the stations by lot, xxv. 8.—*For every gate,* literally, "for gate and gate." These are the gates of the four-sided temple, facing the four quarters of heaven.—Ver. 14. *And for Zechariah his son, a wise counsellor,* literally, "one counselling with prudence;" on what this strange predicate rests is unknown. Before זְכַרְיָהוּ we are to repeat לְ.—Ver. 15. *To Obed-edom . . . and to his sons the house of Asuppim,* namely, to guard. This בֵּית־הָאֲסֻפִּים, "house of collections" (comp. Neh. xii. 25), must have been a place for keeping the sacred stores for the temple service, a temple magazine, situated in the court near the south gate, and, as appears from ver. 17, had two entrances to guard. No particulars of it are known. "The translation of the Vulg.: *in qua parte erat seniorum concilium,* appears to rest upon the explanation of the word אספים by 'assembly of men'" (Berth.).—Ver. 16. *To Shuppim and to Hosah.* On the probable spuriousness of "Shuppim," see Crit. Note. The "gate Shallecheth by the causeway of ascent," the keeping of which was committed to Hosah, is to be regarded as turned, because toward the west, also to the lower city (east of which lay the temple mount). Thus, "the causeway of ascent," by this gate is the way that led from the lower city up to the higher temple mount. The name "gate Shallecheth" is perhaps to be explained, with Böttcher and Thenius, by "refuse gate."—*One ward like another,* literally, "ward beside ward" (לְעֻמַּת as in ver. 12 and xxv. 8), not "ward over against ward," as Berth. thinks, who, on the ground of this precarious interpretation, assumes a diversity of the west gate and the Shallecheth gate as two entrances placed over against each other. Even ver. 18 does not confirm this interpretation, as here the guard stationed on the west side is represented certainly as double, consisting of four guards standing at "Parbar," and two on the causeway, but not as a guard divided between two gates. Far-fetched and contrary to the Masoretic division is the attempt of Clericus to refer the words מִשְׁמָר לְעֻמַּת מִשְׁמָר to all the stations, and so to the contraposition of the four temple gates.—Ver. 17. *Eastward were six Levites, northward four a day.* These (6 + 4) ten daily guards the house of Meshelemiah (with his eighteen sons and brothers), ver. 14, had to set, as the (4 + 2 + 2) eight guards stationed southward, ver. 15, belonged to the house of Obed-edom (with his sixty-two sons and brothers), and on Hosah (with his thirteen sons and brothers) was imposed the setting of the (4 + 2) six guards for the west side; comp. ver. 16 with ver. 18. A uniform and systematic division we cannot discover; probably it was arranged by lot. Moreover, not (6 + 4 + 8 + 6) twenty-four single men are meant, but so many leaders or guarding officers; for the strength of the several stations was certainly greater, as the sum total of all the porters is said in ch. xxiii. 6 to be 4000 men. There is nothing in the text to show that the number twenty-four points to a division of the whole body of porters into twenty-four classes, analogous to the twenty-four classes of priests and singers.—Ver. 18. *At Parbar westward, four on the causeway, and two at Parbar.* This פַּרְבָּר (= פַּרְוָרִים, 2 Kings xxiii. 11) is, as the statement of its situation to the west shows, to be regarded as a part of the temple buildings, near the Shallecheth gate, an addition with cells for depositing the stores and utensils of the temple, similar to the house of Asuppim, ver. 15, on the south side. The "causeway" is naturally the "causeway of ascent," ver. 16.

8. *The Administrators of the Treasures of the Sanctuary, with the Officers for the External Business:* vers. 20–32. *a.* The Lord Treasurers (Stewards): vers. 20–28.—*And the Levites their brethren.* That instead of the unmeaning וְהַלְוִיִּם אֲחִיָּה of the Masoretes we are to read thus (after the Sept. and the analogy of such passages as 1 Chron. vi. 29, 2 Chron. xxix. 34), is maintained by most modern expositors since J. D. Mich.—*Were over the treasures of the house of God, and over the treasures of the holy things.*—This general statement is specialized by the following passage in this way, that the sons of the Gershonite Ladan were placed over the treasures of the house of God, that is, in a strict sense the temple treasures (ver. 22 ff.), but the sons of Shelomoth over the treasures of the holy things, that is, the spoils consecrated by David (ver. 26 ff.).—Ver. 22. *Jehieli, the sons of Jehieli: Zetham, and Joel his brother.* The sense is, as appears from xxiii. 7 f., that Zetham and Joel, the heads of the house of Jehieli (or Jehiel), belonging to the Gershonite line of Ladan, had to administer the treasures of the house of God (the proper treasures of the temple, ver. 20).—Ver. 23 f. *Of the Amramites, the Izharites, the Hebron-*

ites, and the Uzzielites, the four branches of the family of the Kohathites, xxiii. 15 ff.—*Shebuel . . . ruler over the treasures* (ו before שְׁבוּאֵל continuing the sentence). As "son of Gershom son of Moses," this Shebuel (or Shubael, as in xxiv. 20) belongs to the Amramites. And indeed this Amramite Shebuel appears, as the general phrase: "ruler (נָגִיד) of the treasures," shows, to be chief superintendent or administrator of all the sacred treasures, the president or administrator of the two departments of these treasures mentioned in ver. 20 (not merely as superintendent of such sums as flowed regularly into the sanctuary, as Berth., limiting the word אוֹצָרוֹת, thinks).—Ver. 25. *And his brethren by Eliezer were Rehabiah his son* (Eliezer's), *and Jeshaiah his son,* etc. These are called brethren of Shebuel, because they sprang from Moses by Eliezer, as this by his brother Gershom (xxiii. 16).—Ver. 26. *This Shelomoth and his brethren.* As a descendant of Eliezer, and therefore an Amramite, this Shelomoth (or Shelomith; see Crit. Note) is different from the two Shelomiths of ch. xxiii., the Gershonite (ver. 9) and the Izharite (ver. 18; comp. xxiv. 22). As he with his brethren has charge over the treasures of the holy things of David (that is, over the consecrated gifts from the spoils of the wars of this king), he appears co-ordinate with the Jehielites Zetham and Joel, but subordinate to the ruler Shebuel.—*And the captains.* These last-named שָׂרֵי הַצָּבָא are the field-officers or generals of David's army, as Joab, Amasa, as distinct from the before-mentioned captains of thousands and hundreds, or officers in general.—Ver. 27. *Out of the wars and of the spoil they dedicated to maintain the house of the Lord,* not to keep it in good condition or to repair it (according to the meaning which חִזֵּק has in 2 Kings xii. 7; Neh. iii. 7 ff.), but "to make it great" (comp. xxix. 12, where חִזֵּק stands by גַּדֵּל, and is synonymous with it). Only this view agrees with the circumstance that the temple, at the time now in question, was not built, but only about to be built. For לְ in לְבֵית as *nota accus.*, comp. xxix. 12.—Ver. 28*a* belongs still to the parenthetical explication of the dedicated gifts which began with ver. 27.—*And all that Samuel . . . had dedicated.* The article in הַהִקְדִּישׁ stands for the relative אֲשֶׁר, as in xxix. 17; 2 Chron. xxix. 36; Ezra viii. 25, x. 14, 17.—*Everything dedicated,* literally, every one who had dedicated (כֹּל־הַמַּקְדִּישׁ), who placed that which was dedicated by him *under Shelomoth and his brethren.* The enumeration of the several gifts derived from war, which began with ver. 27, or properly with ver. 26*b*, is here concluded, and referred to ver. 26*a*. עַל־יַד, properly, "on the hand," entrusted for keeping, committed to the charge of any one.—*b.* Officers for the External Business: vers. 29–32. Only one Izharite and two Hebronite families are mentioned in this category, consequently only those belonging to two lines of the family of Kohath, and no Gershonites or Merarites (as also, vers. 20–28, to the treasurers belong no Merarites and the Gershonites play only a subordinate part).—*Of the Izharites was Chenaniah . . . for the outer business.* In what this outer business consisted the more definite addition shows: "for officers (scribes) and judges." Although, xxiii. 4, the whole number of the Levites assigned to these functions is stated to be 6000, a number so high that all the situations of this kind in Israel might apparently be filled by them, yet we should include, according to Neh. xi. 16, the administration of the external business specially for the temple and its servants, the exaction of the taxes for the temple, the collection of tithes, etc.—Ver. 30. *Of the Hebronites . . . for the oversight of Israel on this side the Jordan westward,* of the west-land of Israel; comp. Josh. v. 1, xxii. 7. עַל פְּקֻדַּת the Sept. correctly renders: ἐπὶ τῆς ἐπισκέψεως τοῦ Ἰσραήλ (*ad inspectionem Israel*). The view of Berth.: "were over the gifts," that is, the taxes, is unsupported by the usage, and scarcely reconcilable with the explanation of the contents of the foregoing verses on such taxes. Comp. also הִפְקִיד עַל in ver. 32, which signifies nothing but "appoint as overseers," give the oversight.—Ver. 31. *Of the Hebronites was Jeriah the chief.* This Jeriah occurred in xxiii. 19, but not in his present character as chief of the Hebronite family appointed over the land east of the Jordan.—*For the Hebronites.* This parenthesis, extending to the end of the verse, explains the surprising circumstance that the oversight of both sides of the Jordan was committed to the Hebronites. Why Jazer of Gilead, according to Josh. xxi. 39, a Merarite city, served as a chief residence to these Hebronites, remains obscure in the brevity of the present notice.—Ver. 32. *And his brethren, valiant men, two thousand and seven hundred fathers of families.* So in the sense of house or family fathers is רָאשֵׁי הָאָבוֹת here without doubt to be understood, as the very great number 2700 teaches (not "heads of father-houses"). The phrase is essentially equivalent to the shorter אָבוֹת, "fathers," in ver. 31. Moreover, the conjecture is natural, that as the Hebronite family of Hashabiah numbered 1700, and the Hebronite family of Jeriah 2700, house-fathers, so to the Izharite family of Chenaniah (ver. 29) belonged the 1600 still wanting to the sum total of 6000 (xxiii. 4), and that this number has fallen out by some oversight. The present list of officers for the outer business appears not to have been preserved entire (comp. Keil, p. 209).

γ. *Division of the Military Officers; Order of the Service and of the Royal Househould:* ch. xxvii.

1. *The Twelve Divisions of the Army:* vers. 1–15.

CH. XXVII. 1. And the sons of Israel after their number, the heads of the houses and the captains of thousands and hundreds, and their officers that served the

king in any matter of the courses, that which came in and that which went
out month by month for all the months of the year, the one course was
2 twenty and four thousand. Over the first course, for the first month, was
Jashobam son of Zabdiel; and in his course were twenty and four thousand.
3 Of the sons of Perez, the chief of all the captains of the host for the first
4 month. And over the course of the second month was Dodai[1] the Ahohite,
and his course, and Mikloth the commander; and in his course were twenty
5 and four thousand. The third captain of the host, for the third month, was
Benaiah son of Jehoiada the priest as chief; and in his course were twenty
6 and four thousand. This is Benaiah the hero of the thirty, and above the
7 thirty; and his course was for Ammizabad his son. The fourth, for the fourth
month, was Asahel Joab's brother, and Zebadiah his son after him; and in
8 his course were twenty and four thousand. The fifth, for the fifth month, was
the captain Shamhuth the Izharite; and in his course were twenty and four
9 thousand. The sixth, for the sixth month, was Ira son of Ikkesh the Tekoite;
10 and in his course were twenty and four thousand. The seventh, for the
seventh month, was Helez the Pelonite, of the sons of Ephraim; and in his
11 course were twenty and four thousand. And the eighth, for the eighth month,
was Sibbechai the Hushathite, of the Zarhites; and in his course were twenty
12 and four thousand. And the ninth, for the ninth month, was Abiezer the
Anthothite, of the Benjamites; and in his course were twenty and four
13 thousand. The tenth, for the tenth month, was Maharai the Netophathite, of
14 the Zarhites; and in his course were twenty and four thousand. The eleventh,
for the eleventh month, was Benaiah the Pirathonite, of the sons of Ephraim;
15 and in his course were twenty and four thousand. The twelfth, for the twelfth
month, Heldai the Netophathite, of Othniel; and in his course were twenty
and four thousand.

2. *The Princes of the Twelve Tribes:* vers. 16–24.

16 And over the tribes of Israel: of the Reubenites, Eliezer son of Zichri was
17 ruler: of the Simeonites, Shephatiah son of Maachah. Of Levi, Hashabiah
18 son of Kemuel: of Aaron, Zadok. Of Judah, Elihu,[2] of the brethren of
19 David: of Issachar, Omri son of Michael. Of Zebulun, Ishmaiah son of
20 Obadiah: of Naphtali, Jerimoth son of Azriel. Of the sons of Ephraim,
Hoshea son of Azariah: of the half-tribe of Manasseh, Joel son of Pedaiah.
21 Of the half-tribe of Manasseh in Gilead, Iddo son of Zechariah: of Benjamin,
22 Jaasiel son of Abner. Of Dan, Azarel son of Jeroham: these are the princes
23 of the tribes of Israel. But David took not their number from twenty years
old and under, because the LORD had promised to increase Israel as the stars
24 of heaven. Joab the son of Zeruiah began to number, but did not finish,
because for this there was wrath against Israel; and the number was not put
in the account of the chronicles of King David.

3. *The Lords of the Treasures and Possessions of David:* vers. 25–31.

25 And over the king's treasures was Azmaveth son of Adiel: and over the
stores in the country, in the cities, and the villages, and the towers, was
26 Jonathan son of Uzziah. And over the field-labourers for tillage of the ground
27 was Ezri son of Chelub. And over the vineyards was Shimi the Ramathite;
and over that which was in the vineyards of stores in wine was Zabdi the
28 Shiphmite. And over the olive-trees and the sycamores which were in the
Shephelah was Baal-hanan the Gederite: and over the cellars of oil was
29 Joash. And over the herds that fed in Sharon was Shitrai[3] the Sharonite:
30 and over the herds in the valleys was Shaphat son of Adlai. And over the
camels was Obil the Ishmaelite: and over the asses was Jehdeiah the
31 Meronothite.[4] And over the flocks Jaziz the Hagrite: all these were rulers
of the substance which belonged to King David.

4. *The State Counsellors of David:* vers. 32–34.

32 And Jonathan, David's kinsman, was a counsellor, a wise man, and a
33 scribe; and Jehiel son of Hachmoni was with the king's sons. And Ahithophel
was the king's counsellor; and Hushai the Archite was the king's friend.
34 And after Ahithophel was Jehoiada son of Benaiah, and Abiathar; and the
general of the king's army was Joab.

[1] For דּוֹדַי, according to xi. 12, is to be read אֶלְעָזָר בֶּן־דּוֹדַי.

[2] For אֱלִיהוּ the Sept., in accordance with ii. 13 and 1 Sam. xvi. 6, xvii. 13, exhibits Ἐλιάβ.

[3] So the *Kethib:* the *Keri* has Shirtai (שִׁרְטַי).

[4] Sept. ὁ ἐκ Μεραθών; but מֵרֹנוֹת occurs also, Neh. iii. 17, as the name of a place near Mizpah; a מֵרָתוֹן nowhere.

EXEGETICAL.

Preliminary Remark.—In this list of the military and civil officers of David, the collocation of ministers and associates of the army, domains, and kingdom of this king is connected with the survey contained in ch. xxiii.–xxvi. of the Levites and priests in his reign, and also with the account of the census of the people in ch. xxi. To the latter vers. 23, 24 distinctly refer, which show the fore-mentioned captains of the military divisions and princes of the tribes as included in that census, and thereby indicate the political and military import of that measure (comp. on xxi. 1, 6). With the registers of Levites and priests in ch. xxiii.–xxvi., however, our section is connected partly by its position and the similarity of its contents, partly by the circumstance that both the spiritual (Levitical) and the temporal hierarchy of officers had obtained their more permanent regulation and organization in the last year of his government, and, indeed, in connection with the census of the people, as appears again from ver. 23.

1. *The Twelve Divisions of the Army:* vers. 1–15.—*And the sons of Israel after their number.* Ver. 1 forms the full superscription to the following list. As this contains only the twelve divisions of the army of 24,000 men each, with the names of their commanders, this circumstantial superscription seems to promise too much; the detailed description of the army divisions announced in it, and of their officers, appears in vers. 2–15 to be no longer complete, but only preserved in the form of an abstract (Berth.). But the chief stress rests on "after their number" (לְמִסְפָּרָם), as the determination of the monthly changing military courses at the strength of 24,000 each, immediately after the close of this superscription, clearly shows. Hence all else that is here indicated, the mention of the captains of the thousands and hundreds, the officers, etc., is to be regarded as of mere secondary account.—*That which came in and that which went out month by month,* properly, "the coming in and outgoing," namely, the course going in and out of service at the beginning of every month; comp. 2 Kings xi. 5, 7, 9, and 2 Chron. xxiii. 4, 8. Here naturally only the monthly attendance of each of the twelve divisions or corps is spoken of, not that they had changed places every month, and were stationed one after another in Jerusalem, which would have been quite impossible for so large a corps.—*The one course;* הָאַחַת, taken distributively, as Num. xvii. 18; Judg. viii. 18.—Ver. 2. *Over the first course . . . Jashobam.* Concerning this Jashobam (perhaps "Ishbosheth") son of Zabdiel, see on xi. 11.—*And in his course were twenty and four thousand,* literally, "on (עַל) his course went 24,000 men."—Ver. 3. *Of the sons of Perez:* he was descended from that distinguished Jewish family from which David sprang; comp. ii. 4 ff.—*The chief of all the captains of the host for the first month,* stood as first in the series of twelve commanders relieving each other monthly, but was still subordinate to the commander of the whole army (generalissimo), namely, to Joab (ver. 34).—Ver. 4. *Dodai the Ahohite.* On the omission of "Eleazar son of" before Dodai, see the Crit. Note.—*And his course, and Mikloth the commander.* ו before מִקְלוֹת appears to introduce the consequent, and seems to be superfluous, as it is wanting before עַמִּיזָבָד, ver. 6, in a similar connection. At all events, Mikloth is a proper name, as viii. 32, ix. 37 f. prove; whether the there named Benjamite be identical with the present Mikloth must remain doubtful.—Ver. 5. *The third captain . . . was Benaiah . . . as chief.* רֹאשׁ, predicate to Benaiah, not attribute to הַכֹּהֵן. Concerning this Benaiah and his distinguished position as "hero of the thirty, and above the thirty" (more honoured than all of them), see xi. 22, 25; 2 Sam. xxiii. 23. For the construction in ver. 6*b*, comp. on ver. 4*b*.—Ver. 7. *Asahel . . . and Zebadiah his son after him.* This form of expression contains a plain reference to the early death of Asahel (xi. 26), his tragic end, which Abner prepared for him, 2 Sam. ii. 18–23. The fourth course would thus, at least for the late time now in question, have to be designated properly after Asahel's son Zebadiah, its then living leader. But it is called (*honoris causa*) *de patris defuncti nomine,* as Clericus well remarks, just as the family of the Maccabees is distinguished by the name Asmonæans.—Ver. 8 ff. The following names Shamhuth (earlier, xi. 27, Shammoth; 2 Sam. xxiii. 11, Shammah), Ira, Helez, Sibbechai, Abiezer, Maharai, Benaiah, and Heldai occurred together already, though in a somewhat different order, in the list of heroes in xi. 27–31.—*Shamhuth the Izrahite,* the descendant of Zerah son of Judah, ch. ii. 4, 6; הַיִּזְרָח stands for הַיִּזְרָחִי, and this is equivalent to הַזַּרְחִי, vers. 11 and 13.—Ver. 15. *Heldai the*

Netophathite, of Othniel, belonging to the family of Othniel, incorporated by his connection with Caleb into the tribe of Judah, Josh. xv. 17; Judg. i. 12-15. The name Heldai is besides in xi. 30 Heled, and in 2 Sam. xxiii. 29, by an error of the pen, Heleb.

2. *The Princes of the Twelve Tribes*: vers. 16-24.—In this list the twelve tribes are enumerated in quite a different order from that in Genesis, and even that in iv.-vii. of our book. A fundamental ground for the order here exhibited—Reuben, Simeon, Levi, Judah, Issachar, Zebulun, Naphtali, Ephraim, Manasseh, Benjamin, Dan—can the less be ascertained, because the names of two tribes (Gad and Asher) have fallen out probably by an old corruption of the text; and there is no means even of conjecturing what was their original place in the list. There remains, therefore, only an uncertain surmise that Dan has been assigned the last place on account of his fall into idolatry; comp. evangelical and ethical reflections on ch. i.-ix., No. 3.—Ver. 17. *Of Aaron, Zadok.* Whether this naming of a prince of the Aaronites, namely, the high priest Zadok, of the line of Eleazar, along with that of the Levite was to make amends for the omitted princes of Gad and Asher is uncertain.—Ver. 18. *Of Judah, Elihu.* That "Eliab" (ii. 13) is to be read, with the Sept., for "Elihu" is most probable, even for this reason, that Eliab was the first-born of Jesse, to whom the dignity of prince must have naturally fallen.—Ver. 21. *Of the half . . . in Gilead,* literally, "toward Gilead" (גִּלְעָדָה), a suitable designation of the east half of Manasseh.—Vers. 23, 24. Closing Remark on the Two Lists referring to the Army of Israel, vers. 2-15 and vers. 16-22.—*But David took not their number from twenty years old and under;* he had only those above twenty years numbered. On נָשָׂא מִסְפָּר, to take, determine, a number, comp. Num. iii. 40, and Ex. xxx. 12; Num. i. 49.—*Because the Lord had promised to increase Israel as the stars of heaven.* This ground for the remark that David included only those above twenty years in his census of the people obviously means that to number the whole mass of the people, which God's promise to the patriarchs (Gen. xxii. 17, etc.) had designated as innumerable, was not intended by David; he had only wished to ascertain the number of those able to bear arms for the organization of his army. On ver. 24*a*, comp. xxi. 6.—*And the number was not put in the account of the chronicles of King David,* literally, "and the number went not up," etc.; comp. העלה על ספר, 2 Chron. xx. 34, on account of which parallel, moreover, בְּסֵפֶר is not to be read for בְּמִסְפַּר, especially as the phrase ספר דברי הימים does not occur in Chronicles. The second מִסְפָּר is rather to be understood in the sense of "reckoning, register of numbers," and therefore we are to think of the statistical section of the annals of David's reign (Berth., Kamph., etc.). In these the result of that great census of the people had no place according to our passage; and if, xxi. 5, a communication regarding this result is made, it must have been derived from some other source.

3. *The Lords of the Treasures and Possessions of David:* vers. 25-31.—*And over the king's treasures was Azmaveth.* These first-mentioned treasures in general (אֹצָרוֹת; comp. xxvi. 20; Job xxxviii. 22) were perhaps, as the contrast with the "treasures in the country" teaches, the stores or spoils of war preserved in Jerusalem, so far as they were crown and not temple property (xxvi. 22); thus rightly Luther: "over the treasure of the king."—*And over the stores in the country, in the cities, and the villages, and the towers,* that is, in the forts or keeps; comp. the notice of such towers in 2 Chron. xxvi. 10; Mic. iv. 8; Song iv. 4.—Ver. 26. *And over the field-labourers for tillage of the ground was Ezri.* Here begins the specification of the stores in the field, with the royal domains or fields (שׂדה here in the strict or proper sense, not as in ver. 25).—Ver. 27. *And over the vineyards was Shimi the Ramathite,* of Ramah in the tribe of Benjamin, Josh. xviii. 25. The next following officer, Zabdi, the manager of the wine-stores in the vineyards, is called הַשִּׁפְמִי, "the Shiphmite," coming perhaps from שְׁפָם, a place mentioned in Num. xxxiv. 10 f., on the north border of Canaan. But perhaps it is more natural to refer to שִׂפְמוֹת in the south of Judah (1 Sam. xxx. 28), as the south produced the most wine, and of course the most vineyards and vine cultivators.—Ver. 28. *And over the olive-trees and the sycamores in the Shephelah,* in the lowlands of the fruitful plain, between the hills of Judah and the Mediterranean, Josh. xv. 53. זֵיתִים, olive plantations and gardens; comp. Deut. vi. 11, 1 Kings v. 25; and so the following שִׁקְמִים. How important the produce of the sycamores must have been in the times of David and Solomon appears from the proverbial expression, 1 Kings x. 27, 2 Chron. i. 15: "Cedar-wood as plentiful as the sycamores that grew in the Shephelah." Comp. C. Hoffmann, *Blicke in die frühere Geschichte des gelobten Landes,* p. 171: "None of the plants adorning the country in that time is so fallen as those oft-mentioned sycamores, of which only a few still stand in the gardens of Jaffa as tokens of bygone beauty. On the coast, on the hot soil, moistened by under water, stood in broad plantations these mighty, shady, leafy crowns, the native land of which is Egypt. They are mentioned at Jericho in the time of Christ (Luke xix. 4). Did they, as the herdsman Amos, who plucked their figs, intimates Amos vii. 14, extend to the now so cool and dry valleys of Tekoa, about the Frank Mountains, that now bear among the Arabs the name of paradise, as a monument of vanished glories? At all events, they were proverbially common in Solomon's time; and this leads to one of those numerous indications of a former abundance of water," etc.—*Baal-hanan the Gederite,* of Geder or Gederah, situated in the lowlands south-east of Jabneh (comp. Josh. xii. 13, xv. 36, and our remark on Beth-geder, ii. 51); הַגְּדֵרִי is thus not really different from הַגְּדֵרָתִי, xii. 4. Keil would derive הַגְּדֵרִי rather from Gedor (גְּדוֹר), on the hills of Judah, Josh. xv. 58; but the form of the

Gentilicium is against this.—*And over the herds in the valleys*, namely, those in the hill country of Judah towards the Dead Sea and the Jordan; comp. xii. 15.—Ver. 30. *And over the camels was Obil the Ishmaelite.* As the riches of the king consisted in camels (comp. Job i. 3; Judg. vii. 12) in the south country, where the Ishmaelites formerly wandered, a descendant of this race was appointed overseer of them. So it might be with the Hagarite Jaziz, who was placed over the flocks (comp. v. 10, 19; Ps. lxxxiii. 7). For Jehdeiah the Meronothite, see Crit. Note.—Ver. 31. *All these were rulers of the property which belonged to King David.* רְכוּשׁ, "property," a wider notion than that of the "treasures of the king," ver. 25, including these (the treasures in Jerusalem) and "the treasures in the country." The total number of the officers appointed to take charge of all this property, as they are named above, is twelve, namely, the two head officers, ver. 25 (for the city, Azmaveth; for the country, Jonathan), and the ten overseers of the tillage and pasturage, the latter of whom were to give a yearly account of the produce of the stock under their charge to the former. The number twelve can scarcely be accidental here, though it is not expressly noticed.

4. *The State Counsellors of David*: vers. 32–34; comp. the similar lists of the chief officers of state in xviii. 15–17 (2 Sam. viii. 15–18) and in 2 Sam. xx. 23–26, with which, however, the present has only Joab the commander-in-chief in common, whereas, otherwise, here partly other persons, partly other functions, appear; and, indeed, its chief aim is to name the counsellors (יֹעֲצִים) of the king: it is a list of the chief counsellors of David (as it were his private council of state or cabinet).—*And Jonathan David's kinsman was a counsellor;* דּוֹד (properly favourite, friend, Song i. 13, etc.) may signify the father's brother, Jer. xxxii. 7, in which sense it appears to be taken by the Sept. (πατράδελφος) and Vulg. (*patruus*). Yet it signifies also (Jer. xxxii. 12) "kinsman, cousin" in general, and appears here also to convey this wider sense, where scarcely any other Jonathan than the son of Shima is meant, and therefore a nephew of David. On יוֹעֵץ, counsellor, comp. xxvi. 14; on the following attribute, "wise," xv. 22; on a "scribe" (סוֹפֵר, here not a name of office, as in xviii. 16), ii. 55; Ezra vii. 6.—*And Jehiel . . . was with the king's sons*, as their instructor or tutor, an office mentioned only here. Whether Hachmoni the father of this Jehiel be the same with the Hachmoni father of Jashobam mentioned xi. 11 must remain uncertain.—Ver. 33. *And Ahithophel was counsellor of the king*, without doubt the same who became notorious from the history of the revolt of Absalom—comp. 2 Sam. xv. 31, xvi. 23, xvii. 1 ff.; Ps. xli. 10—as Hushai the Archite is the well-known opponent of this Ahithophel, 2 Sam. xv. 32, 37, xvi. 16.—Ver. 34. *And after Ahithophel was Jehoiada son of Benaiah and Abiathar.* That by the latter the well-known high priest of the family of Ithamar (v. 27) is meant cannot well be doubted; whether with regard to the previous name we are to think of the Benaiah named ver. 5, captain of the third division, son of Jehoiada the priest, so that here a transposition of the names has taken place (Berth.), appears doubtful. It is perhaps simpler to take the Jehoiada named as successor to Ahithophel in the privy council of the king for a son of that Benaiah who, after the well-known Hebrew custom, bore the name of his grandfather. We may observe, moreover, how clearly the Chronist here again (as in ver. 7) betrays his acquaintance with certain episodes in the history of David, the special course of which it does not lie within the scope of his plan to narrate.—*And the general of the king's army was Joab;* as such generalissimo, at the same time in some sense minister of war, and therefore *eo ipso* belonging to the rank of king's counsellors. Accordingly he appears, xxi. 2 ff., in the exercise of his office of counsellor in regard to the census of the people.

In an apologetic respect, it is worthy of remark, in regard to this list of the counsellors of David, that, with the exception of Jehiel, names of persons about David occurring also in the books of Samuel and elsewhere in our books are contained in it, but that it cannot be compiled by the Chronist from the other accounts of the history of this king, because it exhibits something peculiar, not elsewhere occurring, in its statements of the functions of these men. "We must therefore assume that this list comes from the same source from which our historian has drawn the previous lists (xxiii.–xxvi. and xxvii. 1–31)" (Berth.).

δ. *The Last Directions of David concerning the building of the Temple and the Succession of Solomon, and his own Death:* ch. xxviii., xxix.

1. *Directions to Solomon concerning the building of the Temple:* ch. xxviii.

CH. XXVIII. 1. And David assembled all the princes of Israel, the princes of the
tribes, and the captains of the divisions, that served the king, and the
captains of thousands, and captains of hundreds, and the stewards of all the
property and cattle of the king and his sons, with the courtiers and the heroes,
2 and all the valiant men in Jerusalem. And David the king stood up on his
feet, and said, Hear me, my brethren and my people. I had it in my heart
to build a house of rest for the ark of the covenant of the Lord, and for the
3 footstool of our God; and I made ready for the building. But God said to
me, Thou shalt not build a house for my name, because thou hast been a
4 man of war, and hast shed blood. And the LORD God of Israel chose me out

of all my father's house to be king over Israel for ever: for He hath chosen
Judah to be the ruler, and in the house of Judah the house of my father; and
among the sons of my father He liked me, to make me king over all Israel.
5 And of all my sons—for the LORD hath given me many sons—He hath chosen
Solomon my son to sit upon the throne of the kingdom of the LORD over
6 Israel. And He said unto me, Solomon thy son, he shall build my house and
my courts; for I have chosen him to be my son; and I will be his father.
7 And I will establish his kingdom for ever, if he be strong to do my com-
8 mandments and my judgments as at this day. And now in the eyes of all
Israel, the congregation of the LORD, and in the ears of our God, keep and
seek all the commandments of the LORD your God, that ye may possess
9 the good land, and bequeath it to your sons after you for ever. And thou,
Solomon my son, know the God of thy father, and serve Him with a whole
heart, and with a willing mind; for the LORD searcheth all hearts, and
understandeth all the imagination of the thoughts: if thou seek Him, He
will be found of thee; and if thou forsake Him, He will cast thee off for ever.
10 Take heed now; for the LORD hath chosen thee to build a house for the
sanctuary: be strong, and do it.
11 And David gave Solomon his son the pattern of the porch, and of its
buildings and its treasuries, and its upper rooms, and its inner parlours, and
12 the house of the mercy-seat. And the pattern of all that his spirit had in
thought for the courts of the house of the LORD, and for all the chambers
around for the treasures of the house of God, and for the treasures of the
13 holy things. And for the courses of the priests and the Levites, and for all
the work of the service of the house of the LORD, and for all the vessels of
14 the service of the house of the LORD. For gold by weight, for gold for all
instruments of every service; and for all instruments of silver by weight, for
15 all instruments of every service. And the weight for the golden candlesticks,
and their lamps of gold; by the weight of every candlestick and its lamps;
and for the silver candlesticks, by weight for the candlestick and its lamps,
16 according[1] to the use of each candlestick. And the gold by weight for the
17 tables of shew-bread for every table; and silver for the tables of silver. And
the forks, and the sprinkling bowls, and the cans of pure gold; and for the
golden tankards by weight for every tankard, and for the silver tankards by
18 weight for every tankard. And for the altar of incense, refined gold by
weight; and for the pattern of the chariot; the cherubim of gold that
spread out (their wings) and cover[2] the ark of the covenant of the LORD.
19 "All this has He taught me in writing from the hand of the LORD upon me,
even all the works of the pattern."
20 And David said to Solomon his son, Be strong and active, and do it:
fear not, nor be dismayed, for the LORD God, my God, is with thee; He will
not fail thee, nor forsake thee, till all the work of the service of the house of
21 the Lord is completed. And, behold, the courses of the priests and the
Levites for all the service of the house of God; and with thee is in every
work every willing man of wisdom for all service; and the princes and all
the people for all thy matters.

2. *Contributions of the assembled Princes for building the Temple:* ch. xxix. 1–9.

CH. XXIX. 1. And David the king said unto all the congregation, Solomon my son,
whom alone God hath chosen, is young and tender, and the work is great;
2 for the palace is not for man, but for the LORD God. And with all my
might I have prepared for the house of my God, gold for golden things, and
silver for silver, and brass for brazen, and iron for iron, and wood for wooden;
onyx-stones and set stones, rubies and mottled stones, and all kinds of pre-
3 cious stones, and marble stones in abundance. And, moreover, because I
delight in the house of God, I have a treasure of gold and silver which I have
given to the house of my God over and above all that I have prepared for

4 the holy house. Three thousand talents of gold, of the gold of Ophir, and
seven thousand talents of refined silver, to overlay the walls of the houses.
5 The gold for golden, and the silver for silver, and for all work by the hand of
artificers; and who is willing to fill his hand this day unto the LORD?
6 And the princes of the houses, and the princes of the tribes of Israel, and
the captains of thousands and of hundreds, with the rulers of the king's work,
7 showed themselves willing. And gave, for the service of the house of God,
of gold, five thousand talents and ten thousand darics; and of silver, ten
thousand talents; and of brass, eighteen thousand talents; and of iron, a
8 hundred thousand talents. And they with whom stones were found gave
them for the treasure of the house of the LORD, by the hand of Jehiel the
9 Gershonite. And the people were glad, because they were willing, because
with a perfect heart they offered willingly to the LORD; and David the king
also was exceedingly glad.

3. *David's Thanksgiving:* vers. 10–19.

10 And David blessed the LORD in the eyes of all the congregation; and
David said, Blessed be Thou, LORD God of Israel our father, for ever and
11 ever. Thine, O LORD, is the greatness, and the power, and the beauty, and
the lustre, and the majesty; for all in the heaven and in the earth is Thine:
12 Thine, O LORD, is the kingdom, and Thou art exalted as head over all. And
the riches and the glory come of Thee, and Thou rulest over all; and in Thy
hand is might and power; and in Thy hand it is to make all great and strong.
13, 14 And now, our God, we thank Thee, and praise Thy glorious name. For who
am I, and what is my people, that we should be able to offer so willingly in
15 this way? for all comes of Thee, and of Thy hand have we given Thee. For
we are strangers before Thee, and sojourners, as all our fathers: our days on
16 the earth are as a shadow, and there is no hope. O LORD our God, all this
store that we have prepared to build Thee a house for Thy holy name, it[3]
17 cometh of Thy hand, and is all Thine own. And I know, O my God, that
Thou triest the heart, and hast pleasure in uprightness: I, in the integrity of
my heart, have willingly offered all these things: and now Thy people who
18 are present I have seen with gladness to offer willingly unto Thee. O LORD
God of Abraham, Isaac, and Israel, our fathers, keep this for ever in the
imagination of the thoughts of the heart of Thy people, and stablish their
19 heart unto Thee. And give to Solomon my son a perfect heart, to keep Thy
commandments, Thy testimonies, and Thy statutes, and to do all, and to
build the palace which I have prepared.

4. *Close of the Public Assembly; Solomon's Elevation to the Throne:* vers. 20–25.

20 And David said to all the congregation, Bless now the LORD your God:
and all the congregation blessed the LORD God of their fathers; and they
21 bent and bowed down to the LORD, and to the king. And they killed sacri-
fices unto the LORD, and offered burnt-offerings unto the LORD, on the morrow
of that day, a thousand bullocks, a thousand rams, a thousand lambs, with
22 their drink-offerings, and sacrifices in abundance for all Israel. And they
ate and drank before the LORD on that day with great gladness, and the
second time made Solomon the son of David king, and anointed him unto
23 the LORD to be ruler, and Zadok to be priest. And Solomon sat on the
throne of the LORD as king, instead of David his father; and he prospered,
24 and all Israel obeyed him. And all the princes, and the heroes, and also all
25 the sons of King David, submitted to Solomon the king. And the LORD
magnified Solomon exceedingly in the eyes of all Israel, and bestowed on him
the majesty of the kingdom, which had not been on any king over Israel
before him.

5. *Close of the History of David:* vers. 26–30.

26, 27 And David the son of Jesse reigned over all Israel. And the time that

he reigned over all Israel was forty years; in Hebron he reigned seven years,
28 and in Jerusalem he reigned thirty and three. And he died in a good old
age, full of days, riches, and glory; and Solomon his son reigned in his stead.
29 And the acts of David the king, first and last, behold, they are written in the
words of Samuel the seer, and in the words of Nathan the prophet, and in
30 the words of Gad the seer. With all his reign and his might, and the times
that went over him, and over Israel, and over all the kingdoms of the
countries.

[1] For כַּעֲבֹדַת a number of MSS. and old editions read בַּעֲבֹדַת ("for the service").

[2] For לְפֹּרְשִׁים וְסֹכְבִים the Sept. and Vulg. read הַפֹּרְשִׁים וְהַסֹּכְבִים; comp. Exeg. Expl

[3] So the *Kethib* (הִיא); the *Keri* has הוּא, referring to הֶהָמוֹן.

EXEGETICAL.

1. Directions to Solomon concerning the building of the Temple: ch. xxviii. 1–21.—These directions for building the temple David announces in a solemn assembly of the states or representatives of the people, or as they are designated in general: "all the princes of Israel" (שָׂרִים). The several classes of these representatives of the kingdom are there specified:—1. "the princes of the tribes" (see their enumeration in xxvii. 16–22); 2. "the captains of the divisions that served the king;" see xxvii. 1–15; 3. "the captains of thousands and captains of hundreds," the officers of the army, and those captains of divisions, the commanders and chiefs of the twelve corps of the army (xxvii. 1); 4. "the stewards of all the property and cattle of the king and his sons," the officers of the royal domains (xxvii. 25–31), who are here extended by the addition (misunderstood by the Vulg.) וּלְבָנָיו to the royal princes and their possessions; 5. "the courtiers," סָרִיסִים, properly, eunuchs (so the Sept. and Vulg. in our passage), but here obviously in a wider sense, of officers of the royal court, or chamberlains in general; comp. 1 Sam. viii. 15; 1 Kings xxii. 19; 6. the "heroes," that is, the distinguished champions enumerated in xi. 10 ff., so far as they not merely (as captains of the divisions or over the thousands, etc.) belonged to the active service, but perhaps as occasional counsellors of the king, or otherwise influential persons, were entitled to a prominent position in the kingdom (hence the Sept. not unsuitably: τοὺς δυνάστας); 7. all "the valiant men" (וּלְכָל־גִּבּוֹר חָיִל with לְ as *nota acc.*), every other person of note or importance,—a wide phrase reverting to the general notion of the "princes of Israel."—Ver. 2. *And David the king stood up on his feet*, in order to speak; for before he was sitting from the weakness of age (not reclining, as the Rabbinical expositors would infer from 1 Kings i.). For the kindly humble address, "my brethren," in the king's mouth, comp. 1 Sam. xxx. 23; 2 Sam. xix. 13.—*I had it in my heart to build*, literally, "I, in my heart it was to build;" comp. xxii. 7.—*A house of rest*, a house where the ark might abide at rest. Along with the ark, on account of its special holiness, is mentioned the mercy-seat (ver. 11), and, indeed, described in a figurative way as "the footstool of our God," as Jehovah is regarded as sitting on the cherubim of the capporeth.—*And I made ready for the building*, I prepared workmen and materials for it; comp. xxii. 2 ff., 14 ff.; as for the following verse xxii. 8, and for ver. 4, ch. xi. 2, v. 2.—Ver. 5. *To sit upon the throne of the kingdom of the Lord over Israel*, the theocratic kingdom; comp. the equivalent briefer phrase: "to sit on Jehovah's throne," xxix. 23 and Ps. xlv. 7, where the correctly interpreted כִּסְאֲךָ אֱלֹהִים, "thy God's throne," yields practically the same notion (see Moll, *Der Psalter*, p. 237). God is the proper king of Israel; but David, Solomon, etc., are only the earthly representatives of His royalty.—Ver. 7. *And I will establish His kingdom.* Comp. in general xxii. 10 and xvii. 11 f., and for the condition: "if he be strong," etc., the quite similar conditions which God, 1 Kings iii. 14, ix. 4, imposes on Solomon; also 1 Kings viii. 61 (where also the כַּיּוֹם הַזֶּה).—Ver. 8. *Keep and seek all the commandments*, keep them earnestly, seek to keep them with zeal.—*That ye may possess the good land.* Comp. Deut. iv. 21; Lev. xxv. 46; Jer. iii. 18.—Ver. 9. *And thou, Solomon my son, know the God of thy father*, the God who so truly helped me, thy father, in all troubles; comp. the emphatic "my God," ver. 20 and Ps. xviii. 3, and similar passages.—*And serve Him with a whole heart*, with an undivided mind, without διψυχία; comp. xxix. 9; also xxix. 19 and 1 Kings viii. 61.—*Understandeth all the imagination of the thoughts.* The phrase: "imagination of the thoughts," as in Gen. vi. 5; the reference to the omniscience of God, as in 1 Sam. xvi. 7; Ps. vii. 10, cxxxix. 1 ff.—*If thou seek Him, He will be found of thee;* comp. Deut. iv. 29; Isa. lv. 6; Jer. xxix. 13 f. On the following strong expression: "He will cast thee off" (יַזְנִיחֲךָ), comp. 2 Chron. xi. 14, xxix. 19, and Lam. iii. 17.—Ver. 10. *Be strong, and do it.* In essentially the same words, ver. 20, David again addresses Solomon, after the interruption, vers. 11–19, occasioned by delivering the draft and plan of the holy buildings.—Vers. 11–19. The Details of the Outline and Plan for the Temple, as David laid it before his Son in the public Assembly. We may imagine the architects and other craftsmen, by whose help he had this outline and plan drawn out, present in the assembly, and explaining it at the king's order.—*And David gave . . . the pattern of the court.* תַּבְנִית, pattern, model, as Ex. xxv. 40;

הָאוּלָם, the porch before the sanctuary, 2 Chron. iii. 4; 1 Kings vi. 3.—*And of its buildings*, those of the temple. The suffix must refer, not to the אוּלָם, but only to הבית, "the temple, the house," to be supplied from the context. The buildings of the house are the holy place and the most holy.—*And its treasuries* (גַּנְזַכִּין, cognate with גְּנָזִין, Ezra vii. 20, Esth. iii. 9, iv. 7, occurs only here), *and its upper rooms* (above the most holy place, 2 Chron. iii. 9), *and its inner parlours*, namely, the porch and the holy place; for only to these can the phrase refer, as immediately after follows the special mention of the most holy place, designated as the "house of the mercy-seat" or "abode of the capporeth."—Ver. 12. *And the pattern of all that his spirit had in thought* (or what was before his mind) *for the courts . . . and all the chambers around*, the cells or rooms on the four sides of the court, that served to keep "the treasures of the house of God," that is, the treasure of the temple and the "treasures of holy things," the stores of dedicated things collected from the spoils of war (the same distinction as in xxvi. 20).—Ver. 13 continues the statement of that for which the chambers or cells of the court were designed.—*And for the courses of the priests and the Levites*, for their sojourn during their service, likewise for the works belonging to this service (cooking of flesh, preparing of shew-bread, etc.), and for the keeping of the requisite utensils, which last are enumerated in detail from ver. 14 on.—Ver. 14. *For gold.* The לְ in לַזָּהָב corresponds to that in לְכָל־הַלְּשָׁכוֹת, ver. 12; the sentence begun in ver. 11 thus extends to the close of this verse. A new construction begins first in ver. 15, which may be regarded as a continuation of that begun in ver. 11. As to the object וּמִשְׁקָל, a וַיִּתֵּן must be supplied from ver. 11, but not certainly in the same sense of giving, but in that of stating or defining. Thus: "And (he stated) the weight for the golden candlesticks and their lamps of gold;" זהב is freely subordinated to וְנֵרוֹתֵיהֶם (comp. 2 Chron. ix. 15). For the golden candlesticks of the sanctuary, comp. Ex. xxv. 31 f.; 2 Chron. iv. 7.—*According to the use of each candlestick*, according to its set service, its import for the holy service. For the var.: "for the service of every one" (כַּעֲבוֹדַת), see Crit. Note.—Ver. 16. *And the gold by weight;* מִשְׁקָל, accus. of free subordination.—*For the tables of shew-bread for every table; and silver for the tables of silver.* Whereas elsewhere (Ex. xxv. 23 ff.; 1 Kings vii. 48; and 2 Chron. xxix. 18) only one table of shew-bread is spoken of, here several tables of this kind are mentioned. As also, 2 Chron. iv. 8, a greater number of golden tables, namely, ten, destined as it appears for the ten golden candlesticks, is spoken of, so in our passage (as in 2 Chron. iv. 19) a synecdoche appears to be used, and the one golden table of shew-bread to be included with the tables for the golden candlesticks. Silver tables (as silver candlesticks, ver. 15) are only here expressly mentioned: such may be understood as included among the silver articles mentioned on the occasion of the repair of the temple by Joash (2 Chron. xxiv. 14; comp. also 2 Kings xxv. 15). The statements of the Rabbis, that the silver tables stood in the court, and the silver candlesticks in the chambers of the priests, may rest on an old tradition.—Ver. 17. *And* (gave him in pattern: the same supplement as in ver. 15) *the forks*, namely, the flesh-forks used in cooking the pieces of the sacrifices; comp. Ex. xxvii. 3; 1 Kings vii. 50. For the sprinkling-bowls (מִזְרָקוֹת), comp. also 2 Chron. iv. 11, 22; for the "cans" or "cups" (קְשָׂוֹת, σπονδεῖα) that were used in libations, Ex. xxv. 29, xxxvii. 16; Num. iv. 7.—*Of pure gold;* accus. of free subordination, as in vers. 15, 16.—*And for the golden tankards.* כְּפוֹרִים, from כָּפַר, cover, are covered vessels, and so tankards (not cups); comp. Ezra i. 10, viii. 27, the only other passages in which it occurs.—Ver. 18. *The pattern of the chariot, the cherubim of gold.* The term pattern, תַּבְנִית, recurs here, near the close of the whole enumeration, from vers. 11 and 12, but with לְ as *nota accusat.* The mercy-seat with its cherubim appears here symbolized as the chariot on which Jehovah sits or moves (comp. Ex. xxv. 22; Ps. xviii. 11, xcix. 1),—a very important passage for the right understanding of Ezek. i. 15 ff. The cherubim themselves, though only two in number, according to the present description, which represents the older and simpler idea, exhibit as it were a chariot (observe that הַכְּרוּבִים is not subordinate to מֶרְכָּבָה as a genitive, but co-ordinate with it, as in apposition); of a wheel-work connected with it, an external exhibition of the chariot idea, as Ezekiel depicts it, nothing is indicated in the passage; the Sept. and Vulg. only, by taking הַכְּרוּבִים as a genitive (ἅρμα τῶν Χερουβίμ: *quadriga cherubim*), have introduced this foreign element.—*That spread out* (their wings) *and cover the ark of the covenant of the Lord*, literally, "for spreading and covering," that is, they are represented spreading and covering with their wings. Comp. for this use of לְ in the sense of becoming something, or appearing as somewhat, ch. xxix. 33 (לְמֶלֶךְ, "as king"), also Gen. ix. 5, Job xxxix. 16, and other passages, in Ew. § 217, *d* (p. 553). The change of לְפֹרְשִׂים וְסֹכְכִים into הַפֹּרְשִׂים וְהַסֹּכְכִים (Sept., Vulg., and recent expositors, as Berth., Kamph., etc.) is therefore unnecessary. J. H. Mich. correctly: *ut essent expandentes*, etc. To לְפֹרְשִׂים it is easy to supply הַכְּנָפַיִם, "the wings," as object; comp. Ex. xxv. 20, and 1 Kings viii. 7; 2 Chron. v. 8.—Ver. 19 contains again words of David, as the עָלַי, "upon me," and the whole sense and contents teach.—*All this has He taught me in writing from the hand of the Lord upon me.* So it seems the difficult and perhaps corrupt words

הַכֹּל בִּכְתָב מִיַּד יְהוָה עָלַי הִשְׂכִּיל must be taken. To הִשְׂכִּיל we are to understand יהוה as subject, and "me" (or perhaps "us") as object. Possibly also עָלַי might be connected with הִשְׂכִּיל (comp. Prov. xxii. 11); but it is easier, on account of the collocation, to connect it either with מיד יהוה or with בכתב. Now, as the grammatically (Ps. xl. 8: כָּתוּב עָלָי) admissible connection of the words בִּכְתָב—עָלַי into one notion, "by a writing from the hand of Jehovah given me as a rule" (Berth.), yields a very harsh and obscure sense, and as, moreover, the position of מיד יהוה between בכתב and עלי renders this connection extremely difficult, nothing remains but the connection of מִיַּד יְהוָה עָלַי, "a writing from the hand of Jehovah being or coming upon me," by which is designated a writing springing from divine revelation, an immediate effect of divine inspiration (comp. the known phrase: "the hand of Jehovah came upon me," 2 Kings iii. 15; Ezek. i. 3, iii. 14, etc.). This naturally refers, not to the law of Moses, as the Rabbinical expositors think, but to the proposed building plan, draft, etc., which David refers to divine teaching, in so far as he did not conceive it arbitrarily, but designed it under the influence of the Divine Spirit (which, however, must have been effected in this case not directly by vision, as with Moses on Sinai). Comp. moreover, on the transition into the address without an introductory formula, ch. xxii. 18 f., xxiii. 4 f.—Vers. 20, 21. Closing Admonition and Promise to Solomon.—*Be strong and active;* comp. ver. 10 and ch. xxii. 13.—*For the Lord God, my God, is with thee;* comp. on ver. 9. For the following promise: "He will not fail thee (properly, 'withdraw from thee,' namely, His hand) nor forsake thee," comp. Deut. xxxi. 6, 8; Ps. cxxxviii. 8; Josh. i. 5; Heb. xiii. 5.—*And behold the courses of the priests.* Personal attendance of the priests and Levites, or only of a majority of representatives of their order in the public assembly, can scarcely be inferred from this וְהִנֵּה וגו׳, just as the וְעִמְּךָ, "and with thee," does not necessitate the assumption that the willing craftsmen stood by Solomon, or were assembled around him.—*Every willing man of wisdom for all service,* properly, "with regard to every willing man." The לְ here is not *nota accus.* (as ver. 1, xxvi. 26, xxix. 6), but yet serves to give emphasis to כָּל־נָדִיב (Ew. § 310, *a*), which, though it cannot be translated, is yet not to be erased (against Berth.). For the notion of free-will (נְדִיב לֵב = נָדִיב, 2 Chron. xxix. 31), to designate the higher wisdom and skill of a craftsman, comp. Ex. xxxv. 5, 22, and Latin phrases, as *artes ingenuæ, liberales.* We are to think, moreover, of the same craftsmen as those named, xxii. 15; 2 Chron. ii. 6.—*For all thy matters:* לְכָל־דְּבָרֶיךָ to be explained according to xxvi. 32 (concerns, matters) scarcely: "for all thy words or commands" (as J. H. Mich., Starke, Keil, etc., think).

2. Contributions of the assembled Princes for building the Temple: ch. xxix. 1–9.—*Unto all the congregation,* which consisted, ch. xxviii. 1, merely of the "princes" or more eminent representatives (notables) of the people.—*Solomon, my son, whom alone God hath chosen,* properly a parenthesis: "as the one (אֶחָד) hath God chosen him." For "young and tender," comp. xxii. 5.—*For the palace is not for man.* Only here and ver. 19 stands the later word הַבִּירָה, to denote the temple (with regard to its fort-like size and strength); elsewhere either of the Persian royal castle (Esth. i. 2, 5, ii. 3; Neh. i. 1) or of the castle in the temple at Jerusalem.—Ver. 2. On *a*, comp. xxiii. 15.—*Onyx-stones and set stones.* For שֹׁהַם, onyx (sardonyx, etc.), or perhaps beryl, comp. Gen. ii. 12; Ex. xxviii. 9, 20; Job xxviii. 16; on אַבְנֵי מִלֻּאִים, "stones of settings," Ex. xxv. 7, xxxv. 9, where also onyx-stones, designed for the high priest's ephod and hoshen, are mentioned.—*Rubies and mottled stones, and all kinds of precious stones, and marble stones in abundance.* אַבְנֵי־פוּךְ, properly stones of paint or lead-glance (comp. 2 Kings ix. 35; Isa. liv. 11), perhaps precious stones of very dark glancing colour, of dark purple, as carbuncle or ruby (נֹפֶךְ, perhaps radically connected with פּוּךְ). The אַבְנֵי רִקְמָה, stones of various colours, striped with veins (agate?), as אֶבֶן יְקָרָה, "precious costly stones," in general, אַ׳ שַׁיִשׁ, white marble (the Sept. and Vulg. explain it by an anachronism of Parian marble); comp. the contracted form שַׁיִשׁ, Song v. 15; Esth. i. 6.—Ver. 3. *Over and above all that I have prepared for the holy house,* literally, "upwards of all, out above all." On הֲכִינוֹתִי, without a relative particle connecting it with the foregoing כֹּל, comp. xv. 12.—Ver. 4. *Three thousand talents of gold of the gold of Ophir,* of the finest and best gold; comp. the excursus after 2 Chron. ix. Three thousand talents of gold, reckoned after the holy or Mosaic shekel, would amount to ninety million thalers (about £13,500,000), reckoned after the royal shekel to half as much; and the 7000 talents of silver would amount in the first case to fifteen million thalers (about £2,250,000), in the second case to half that sum. The greatness of this sum shows, at all events, that this includes the whole of David's private property; comp. on xxii. 14 ff.—*To overlay the walls of the houses,* the proper temple buildings (בָּתִּים, as in xxviii. 11), the holy place and the most holy, with the court and the upper chambers, the inner walls of which, 2 Chron. iii. 4–9, were all hung with gold.—Ver. 5. *The gold for golden,* or literally, "for the gold, for the gold," etc.; comp. ver. 2.—*And for all work by the hand of artificers,* for all works to be made by the hand of craftsmen.—*And who is willing* (הִתְנַדֵּב, show oneself willing, as ver. 6; Ezra ii.

68) *to fill his hand this day unto the Lord*, to provide himself with free-will offerings for Him; comp. Ex. xxviii. 41, xxxii. 29, and 2 Chron. xiii. 9. The infinitive מַלְּאוֹת (along with מִלֵּא, 2 Chron. xiii. 9), also Dan. ix. 2; Ex. xxxi. 5.—Ver. 6. *The princes of the houses*, properly, "of the fathers;" הָאָבוֹת for בֵּית הָאָבוֹת; comp. xxiv. 31, xxvii. 1, etc.—*With the rulers of the king's work*, literally, "and with regard to the rulers;" before שָׂרֵי מְלֶאכֶת הַמּ׳ the same superfluous untranslatable לְ as in xxviii. 21. These are "the stewards of all the property and cattle of the king," xxviii. 1, the officers of the royal domains.—Ver. 7. *And gave, for the service of the house of God, of gold five thousand talents.* We must suppose a partial "signing" or guaranteeing of the sums named, not an immediate bare paying down, especially as the bulky contributions in the baser metals, the 18,000 talents of brass and the 100,000 talents of iron, could not possibly be present *in natura.* Even David's gifts of 3000 talents of gold of Ophir and 7000 talents of silver may be regarded as not a proper direct delivery of these large quantities of metals. Moreover, what the princes, according to our passage, contributed was about a half more than that given by David from his private means, namely—1. 5000 talents of gold = 150 million thalers (about £22,500,000), or by the other mode of reckoning, half that sum; 2. 10,000 darics = 75,000 thalers (about £11,250); 3. 10,000 talents of silver = twenty-four million thalers (about £3,600,000); 4. 18,000 talents of brass (copper), and 100,000 talents of iron; 5. Precious stones amounting to an indefinite sum. אֲדַרְכֹּן, with א prosthetic here and Ezra viii. 27, along with דַּרְכְּמוֹן, Ezra ii. 69, Neh. vii. 70 ff., is not a Hebrew designation of the drachma (as Ew. *Gesch.* i. 254 still thinks), but of the daric, a Persian coin, containing 1½ ducats, or 7½ thalers (about 22s. 6d.); comp. Eckhell, *Doctr. numm.* i. vol. iii. p. 551; J. Brandis, *Das Münz-, Maass-, and Gewichtssystem in Vorderasien* (1866), p. 244; see also Introd. § 3, *a*. In darics, the gold coin most current in his time (it is not meant by our author that it existed in David's time), the Chronist states a smaller part of the sum contributed by the princes, and indeed that part which they gave in coined pieces, while he expresses the amount of uncoined gold that was offered in talents.—Ver. 8. *With whom stones were found*, the present possessors of precious stones. Against Bertheau's rendering: "and what was found therewith in precious stones," is the fact that the sing. אִתּוֹ, that is certainly to be taken distributively (comp. Ew. § 319, *a*), cannot possibly refer to the sums or quantities in vers. 6, 7. For the Gershonite Jehiel, comp. xxvi. 21 f., where the name is Jehieli.—Ver. 9. *Was exceedingly glad*, literally, "was glad with a great gladness;" comp. Zech. i. 14.

3. David's Thanksgiving: vers. 10-19.—*Blessed be Thou, Lord God of Israel our father.* Among the partriarchs, as whose well-tried tutelary God and heavenly fountain of blessing Jehovah had now again proved Himself to David (by the operation of so highly joyful an act of faith as the free-will offering of the princes of the people), Israel is here specially set forth, because his life most resembled that of David, especially in this, that the cry, "Lord, I am not worthy of the least of all the mercies," etc. (Gen. xxxii. 10), might and must for him also (see ver. 14) be the fundamental note of his prayer at the close of his fight of faith. At the end of his confession, where the expression is still more solemn, the address is more full: "Lord God of Abraham, Isaac, and Israel, our fathers."—*For ever and ever;* comp. Ps. ciii. 17.—Ver. 11. *Thine, O Lord, is the greatness;* comp. Ps. cxlv. 8; and on "power" (here and ver. 12), Ps. xxi. 14; on "beauty" (here and ver. 13), Ps. xcvi. 6; on "lustre" (נֵצַח, less suitably rendered "victory" by Luther), 1 Sam. xv. 29; on "majesty" (הוֹד, by Luther, against the text: "thanks"), xvi. 27, Ps. xxi. 6. The whole doxology belongs to the apocalyptic in its main figures, as Rev. iv. 11, v. 12, vii. 12, etc.—*Thine, O Lord, is the kingdom, and Thou art exalted as head over all.* מַמְלָכָה, "kingdom, sovereignty," as Ps. xlvii. 8 f.; comp. Matt. vi. 13. מִתְנַשֵּׂא is not the participle, before which אַתָּה, "Thou art," should be supplied (Berth.), but an infinitive noun, "the being exalted;" comp. 2 Kings ii. 21; Ew. § 160, *e*. On "head over all," comp. κεφαλὴν ὑπὲρ πάντα, Eph. i. 22.—Ver. 12. *And the riches and the glory;* the same connection, Prov. iii. 16; comp. also ver. 28; 2 Chron. xvii. 5; 1 Kings iii. 13.—Ver. 13. *And now, our God, we thank Thee*, properly, "now are we thanking and praising Thy name:" the participles express the constancy of the work; comp. xxiii. 5.—*Thy glorious name*, literally, "the name of Thy glory," as Luther here renders, while he has, ver. 3, put "holy house" for "house of holiness."—Ver. 14. *For* (literally, "and for;" וְכִי, as Judg. x. 10) *who am I, and what is my people, that we should be able?* עָצַר כֹּחַ, properly, "to hold or retain strength," then *valere*, be able; comp. 2 Chron. xiii. 20; Dan. x. 8, 16, xi. 6.—*In this way*, as our just completed collection of free-will offerings for the temple (vers. 3-8) has proved. On כָּזֹאת, comp. 2 Chron. xxxii. 15.—Ver. 15. *For we are strangers before Thee, and sojourners;* comp. Ps. xxxix. 13; Heb. xi. 13, xiii. 14. Even in this strong assertion of the vanity and uncertainty of earthly life (on *b*, comp. Job viii. 9; Ps. xc. 9 f., cii. 12; and Jer. xiv. 8) appears, as in the foregoing verse, which recalls Gen. xxxii. 10, an allusion to that which Jacob confessed at the end of his earthly career; comp. Gen. xlvii. 9.—Ver. 16. *All this store.* הָמוֹן, heap of money, wealth, as Eccl. v. 9. For the var. "it" (referring to "the heap") for "her," see Crit. Note.—Ver. 17. *In the integrity of my heart.* יֹשֶׁר לְבָב, as Deut. ix. 5; comp. the foregoing מֵישָׁרִים, "uprightness," Ps. xvii. 2.—*Thy people who are present*, "have found themselves here." On הַ for אֲשֶׁר, comp. xxvi. 28 and ver. 8;

on finding oneself=being present, comp. xxviii. 1; 2 Chron. v. 11.—Ver. 18. *Keep this*, the spirit of willingness, which expresses itself in these gifts. —*Imagination of the thoughts*, as xxviii. 9.—*Stablish their heart* (or "prepare"), as 1 Sam. vii. 3.—Ver. 19. On *a*, comp. ver. 9; on *b* (הַבִּירָה), ver. 1.

4. Close of the public Assembly. Solomon's Elevation to the Throne: vers. 20–25.—*And all the congregation blessed;* בֵּרַךְ with לְ, as ver. 13: הדה, and הלל with לְ. *And they . . . bowed down to the Lord*, they did obeisance before God and the king as His earthly type and representative. For the combination of קדד and השתחוה, denoting now divine, now human, respect, comp. Gen. xxiv. 26, Ex. xii. 27, xxxiv. 8; 1 Kings i. 16, 31; and Ps. xcv. 6, etc.—Ver. 21. *And they killed sacrifices unto the Lord, and offered burnt-offerings.* The same phrases are united, only in inverse order, 1 Sam. vi. 15. זְבָחִים denotes here animal sacrifices in general, but in *b* it signifies, in contrast with the before-mentioned burnt-offerings, peace-offerings (שְׁלָמִים, Ex. xxiv. 5) in connection with the proper joyful feasts.—*On the morrow of that day;* comp. Lev. xxiii. 11; Jonah iv. 7.—Ver. 22. *And they ate and drank.* This describes the joyful feast, as xii. 39; 1 Kings iv. 20; Deut. xii. 7, xvi. 10. —*And the second time made . . . king.* שֵׁנִית, distinct from xxiii. 1, where a first solemn elevation (proclamation) of Solomon to be the successor of his father was reported, with which, however, the ceremony of anointing was not connected. To the present second elevation corresponds that reported 1 Kings i. 32 ff., as the mention there of Zadok as taking part in this solemn act of anointing shows.—*Anointed him unto the Lord* (according to the will of the Lord) *to be ruler*, לְנָגִיד; this is here for the sharper contrast with the following לְכֹהֵן; comp. moreover, xxviii. 4; 1 Kings i. 35.—*And Zadok to be priest.* With this notice, peculiar to the Chronist, began the degradation of the other high priest, Abiathar, of the line of Ithamar, as Solomon formally completed it after his father's death (1 Kings ii. 26 ff.), already in the lifetime of David: it was prepared by Zadok alone being anointed in the presence of the states along with the young king.—Ver. 23. And *Solomon sat on the throne of the Lord as king.* For the anticipatory nature of this notice, comp. on xxiii. 1; for "the throne of the Lord," on xxviii. 5.—*And he prospered; and all Israel obeyed him*, according to the hope of David expressed before, xxii. 13, regarding him. For שָׁמַע אֶל=obeyed, comp. Deut. xxxiv. 9.—Ver. 24. *Also all the sons of King David submitted to Solomon the king*, literally, "gave hand under" (comp. 2 Chron. xxx. 8; Lam. v. 6). We may observe the slight allusion to the soon suppressed attempt of Adonijah (1 Kings i. 5 ff.) which is contained in this statement, quite after the manner of the Chronist (see Principles of History and Ethics, No. 1).—Ver. 25. *Magnified . . . exceedingly;* comp. xxii. 5.—*And bestowed upon him the majesty of the kingdom.* נָתַן עַל, as Ps. viii. 2; הוֹד, as ver. 11.—*Which had not been on any king over Israel before him.* The construction is as partly in Eccl. i. 16, partly in 1 Kings iii. 12. The phrase is somewhat hyperbolical, as there were only two kings of Israel before him (Ish-bosheth our author is wont to ignore, as ver. 27 shows).

5. Close of the History of David: vers. 26–30. —*And the time that he reigned over all Israel*, inclusive of the seven years of his residence in Hebron (which is more exactly fixed, 2 Sam. v. 5, at seven and a half years).—Ver. 28. *In a good old age;* comp. Gen. xv. 15, xxv. 8.—*Full* ("satisfied"; comp. Job xlii. 17) *of days, riches, and glory.* For the combination עֹשֶׁר וְכָבוֹד, see on ver. 12.—Ver. 29. *And the acts . . . first and last.* The author here indicates the simple order which he laid down for his now finished representation of the life of David; see Evangelical and Ethical Reflections, No. 2.—*Behold, they are written in*, properly "on"; comp. ix. 1. For the sources now named, see Introd. § 5, II.—Ver. 30. *With all his reign and his might;* גְּבוּרָתוֹ, here his "display of might," the power shown by him, his brave deeds; comp. 1 Kings xvi. 5.—*And the times that went over him*, the events that befell him. הָעִתִּים, as Job xxiv. 1; Ps. xxxi. 16.—*And over all the kingdoms of the countries*, with which David came into friendly or hostile contact, as Phœnicia, Philistia, Edom, Moab, etc. For the phrase, comp. 2 Chron. xii. 8, xvii. 10, xx. 29.

EVANGELICAL AND ETHICAL REFLECTIONS, APOLOGETIC AND HOMILETIC NOTES ON CH. X.–XXIX.

1. On the historical and practical point of view under which the Chronist regards the brief account of the downfall of Saul and his house, with which he opens his full description of the history of David, he explains himself very clearly in the two closing verses of ch. x. Saul's kingdom must, after a brief existence, make way for that of David, on the simple ground that it was not erected on the foundation of right faith in Jehovah the God of the covenant, and willing submission to Him; that its possessor had not once only, but constantly, cast to the winds that earnest warning voice of the prophet, "Obedience is better than sacrifice," 1 Sam. xv. 22, and neglected even in the last hour to return to such a course, which was alone pleasing to God. Comp. Bengel's appropriate note on those two verses (p. 16 of the "Beiträge zu J. A. Bengel's Schrifterklärung, aus handschriftl. Aufzeichnungen mitgetheilt von Dr. Osk. Wächter," Leipz. 1865): "It is worthy of remark that Saul is not expressly charged, when he died in his sin, with his long hate of David, but rather with the unbelief in which he kept not the word of God, and sought counsel at Endor. David indeed is out of the country a considerable time before Saul's death. . . . . Even at the last Saul might have obtained pardon, if he had earnestly returned to God, and entreated Him. But he lost all."—Comp. also Schlier, "König Saul" (*Bibel*

stunden, Nördlingen 1867), towards the end, and the homiletic notes of Erdmann on 1 Sam. xxxi. (*Bibelwerk*, vi. 337).

2. That our author aimed at no exhaustive treatment of the history of David in its external and internal course—that he rather laboured as partly an excerptor, partly a supplementer, of earlier writers, and so wished to furnish something regarding the history of David contained in the present books of Samuel and Kings, similar in many respects to that which John the Evangelist did for the evangelical history presented by the synoptics,—this he himself indicates in the closing words just considered, when, xxix. 29, 30, he points for that which he may have omitted to the historical works of the prophets Samuel, Nathan, and Gad as his chief sources. But even before he repeatedly indicates his acquaintance with essential elements of the history of David, which, according to his plan, he does not report. Thus, in the notice prefixed as preface or introduction, concerning the downfall of Saul and his house, where he certainly alludes to the incident of the necromancer of Endor, but does not report it (x. 13 f.), and xx. 5, where he names Goliath, but presumes the history of the slaughter by the youthful shepherd David as known; likewise xii. 1, where he mentions the times of the exile and proscription of David under Saul, without entering into the particulars at least of its well-known catastrophes and vicissitudes; xi. 1 and xii. 23, where he likewise points to the rival kingdom of Saul and Abner during the residence of David at Hebron; xx. 1, where the proceedings at Jerusalem during the siege of Rabbath Ammon by Joab are slightly indicated; xxvii. 23, 24, where, by the mention of Ahithophel and Hushai, a similar reference is made to the rebellion of Absalom; and xxix. 24, where the attempt of Adonijah is in like manner touched upon. The omitted parts are, as must have been often manifest, almost always of such a nature as would have served, if brought into the field, to disturb and in some points obscure the lustre of the picture, and throw many a shadow on the otherwise almost uniform light. It is the first growing and youthful but arduously soaring aloft, further, the suffering and persecuted David, not less the despised and derided by all bystanders far and near (but comp. xv. 29); lastly, the deeply guilty and penitent one, whose picture the Chronist avoids to draw, while all the more earnestly he collects all that appears fitted to represent the hero king in his greatness, and the activity of his reign as an uninterrupted chain of splendid theocratic events. To finish a picture that presents David in the meridian height of his glory and mighty achievements is the obvious aim of all that our author adds in the way of supplement on the ground of his sources to the life-picture of the great king as given in the books of Samuel. Such are the whole contents of ch. xii. (the brave men who stood by David even during the reign of Saul, and the number of the warriors out of all the tribes who made him king in Hebron); those of ch. xv. and xvi. (the full delineation of the preparatory, accompanying, and concluding solemnities in the introduction of the ark into its new abode on Zion); finally, those of the closing ch. xxii.-xxix., on the internal history of the kingdom and the preparations for the building of the temple, which coincide only in subordinate points with the much more summary parallel sections of Samuel and 1 Kings, but on the whole exhibit the peculiarity and special tendency of our author in full force, and in so far, notwithstanding their dry statistical character and tedious lists of names and numbers, are of special interest (comp. No. 2). The preference of our author for the exhibition of all the brilliant traits of the history of David, or, if you will, his panegyristic idealizing tendency and method, is shown also in the short remarks of a reflective kind at the close of the several sections, which almost always issue in the exhibition of some brilliant aspect of the reign of David, or of the state of the people and the theocracy under him; for example, passages such as these: "And David became greater and greater, and Jehovah Zebaoth was with him," xi. 9; "Day by day they came to David to help him, until the camp was great, like a camp of God," xii. 22; "His kingdom was lift up on high, because of His people Israel," xiv. 2; "And David's fame went out into all lands; and the Lord brought his fear upon all nations," xiv. 17; "And David reigned over all Israel, and executed judgment and justice for all his people," xviii. 14; "Is not the Lord your God with you, and hath He not given you rest on every side? For He hath given the inhabitants of the land into my hand, and the land is subdued before the Lord and His people," xxii. 18; "But David took not . . . because the Lord had promised to increase as the stars of heaven," xxvii. 23; "And he died in a good old age, full of days, riches, and glory," xxix. 28; "And the Lord magnified Solomon exceedingly in the eyes of all Israel, and bestowed on him the majesty of the kingdom, which had not been on any king over Israel before him," xxix. 25. And the enumerations and arrangements of the names of David's heroes, servants, spiritual and temporal officers (princes), counsellors, etc., subserve the same optimistic and idealizing tendency as presented by the author; and the ever-recurring preference in these enumerations for symbolic numbers, especially for three and thirty (see ch. xii.), seven (the supreme officers of the kingdom and the crown, xviii. 14 ff., and the counsellors of the king, xxvii. 32 ff.), and twelve or twenty-four, which latter numbers appear as the principle regulating the whole spiritual (Levitical-priestly) and temporal hierarchy of officers in the kingdom of David (see especially ch. xxiii.-xxvii.).

3. Next to the selection of material, the arrangement of it, the order followed in the history of David, is characteristic for the author's conception of this brilliant period of the history of salvation before the exile. This order, however, is, as the same closing remark, xxix. 29, to which we owe the above explanation of the choice of material by the author indicates, an extremely simple and elementary one. The author distinguishes "the first and last acts of David;" he divides his material between the two great heads of the earlier and later events of the reign of David (or of the entrance and exit of David) But among the first acts he does not understand David's youth, with his persecutions by Saul, etc. (so that the last acts would embrace the period of his reign, as in the present division of the books of Samuel, the second of which treats of his

reign), but the course of events till shortly before the end of his life, that is, until he took measures for the building of the temple, and the regular transference of the kingdom to his successor, which latter the author regards as the last acts. The point of division separating the last acts from the first is to be sought neither in ch. x. 13 f., for the narrative of the downfall of Saul closing with these verses is merely the preface or introduction to the acts of David; nor in xii. 40 or xiii. 1, for here, where the accounts of the elevation of David to the throne of all Israel, and the close of the seven years' reign at Hebron, come to an end, the author clearly intends no deeper section (against Kamph.). In truth, the transition from the first to the last acts takes place in xxii. 1, where, after representing the glorious external (military and political) course of the forty years' reign of the king, his provisions for transferring as well the sovereignty as the still unsolved problem of the building of the temple to his son Solomon begins to be described—where, accordingly, as it is said in the further course of the narrative, xxiii. 1: "David was old and full of days; and he made his son Solomon king over Israel" (comp. the remarks made, p. 142, on the generalizing import of those words). It is a peculiar trait of the Chronist, distinguishing in a characteristic way his view and method of history from that of the author of the books of Samuel, that he draws a sharp line between the evening of David's life as his ἔσχατα, and the mid-day as his πρῶτα (or between the completion and continuance of his reign), and weaves into the representation of the evening of his life a full retrospect of the whole internal aspect of the royal household under David. The picture thus drawn of the Levitical and priestly, and of the military and civil, government and official hierarchy of the king (xxiii.–xxvii.), forms, together with its frame of reports concerning the collections and preparations of David, and the chiefs of the people for the temple to be built by Solomon (xxii. and xxviii., xxix.), as it were, the legacy of David to his son, the testament of one glorious king to his no less glorious (according to the peculiar Levitical and hierarchical conception of our author indeed, xxix. 25, still more glorious) heir and successor. It is on account of Solomon, the temple-builder, that the author dwells so long on this legacy of his father preparing and stipulating for the building, and that this part of his work rises to the importance of a second half of the history of his father, to an episode in the life of David, comparable with the so-called report of travels by Luke in the third Gospel, or the farewell addresses of our Lord in John xiii.–xvi., bearing in a still higher degree the character of a retrospect and legacy. Beside this very minute representation of the close of David's life, that under the hands of our author, notwithstanding its comparatively brief duration, has assumed the form of an autumn almost equal in length with the preceding summer of life, the spring with its vicissitude of clear sunshine and rough storm is quite cast into the shade; it appears, indeed, by the merely occasional allusions to its incidents which are contained in ch. x.–xii., intentionally reduced to a vanishing point in the development of the whole. Yet, in the section relating to the catastrophe of Saul, ch. x., the author has furnished an independent preface or introduction to the chief object of his representation, and so has given to the whole a threefold arrangement, in which, however, by far the greatest importance belongs extensively and intensively to the second and third parts.

4. The statement of the Chronist has suffered nothing in credibility by this peculiar arrangement and distribution, especially by his dwelling so long on the preparations for building the temple, and the measures taken for transferring the kingdom to Solomon, which are so briefly handled in the introduction to the books of Kings. The solid walls of the old sources appear through the cover corresponding to his individual view and bent, which he has imparted to the building he has erected. This holds as well of the sections on the external government, peculiar to his statement, as of the closing accounts of the king setting his house in order and handing it over to his successor.[1] It appears particularly fitted to awaken confidence in his statement, that no special preference for the wonderful is to be remarked in the sections peculiar to him; that, in fact, some of these sections—for example, xii., xxiii. ff., and xxvii. ff.—report only that which corresponds to the occurrences of every-day life, which might arise in the profane history of any kingdom or people. And even there, where his statement runs parallel with that of the older historical books, scarcely anywhere does any stronger preference appear for the wonderful or extraordinary than in those documents, except, perhaps, his account of the census and the plague, which has certainly a trace of the miraculous more than the older parallel text (xxi. 26). At the most, the suspicion of unhistorical exaggeration might rest on some of the surprisingly high numbers, as they appear in the present text, xii. 23–40, xxii., and xxix. 4 ff., unless partly the obvious possibility of occasional corruption, partly the almost inevitable necessity of the assumption that smaller values than those usually assumed are to be admitted, served very much to diminish the ground which these passages present for critical assaults. Comp. that which is remarked on them in detail (xii. 23 ff., p. 106 f., and xxii. 14, p. 137 f.), and see, moreover, the Apologetic Remarks on ch. xv. 16, p. 119 ff.

5. Homiletic hints for the history of David in rich selection are to be found in Erdmann's elaboration of the books of Samuel (vol. vi. of the

[1] Comp., with regard to the credibility of the statement concerning David's last directions to Solomon, especially the giving of the instructions for the building of the temple, the remark of Bertheau on xxviii. 11–19: "The whole section thus shows that David not only made preparations for building the temple by providing materials, but also gave definite orders for the execution of the work and the making of the vessels to Solomon, and that he proceeded, not according to his own invention and design, but was directed by divine revelation. . . . In the books of Kings, nothing of this occurs; but if we must gather from the accounts of Chronicles, that David not only thought of the temple, but made preparations for it, which could not have consisted in an uncertain collection of materials, we shall not be able to avoid assuming that a communication was made according to which, even in David's time, the plan of the temple was fixed. To execute the building itself was not permitted to David; but he had completed the preparations so far, that Solomon in the fourth year of his reign was able to proceed with the building, and to finish it in the eleventh (1 Kings vi.). The report of David's preparation, which extended to the fixing of the plan for the building, is the historical foundation for the statement in our verses, in which the free handling of the historical material, according to modern views, is as obvious as in the remaining sections of the last two chapters of the first book of Chronicles."

Bibelw.). With respect to the sections peculiar to the Chronist, a small gleaning may here be presented of some noteworthy practical hints from older expositors:—

On ch. xii. 38–40, Starke, after Burmann, remarks: "What is here said of David is a fine figure (type) of the Messiah. . . . He also at first had only a small following; but after He came to His glory, the kingdom of God burst forth mightily, and subjects to Him were collected in all the world. . . . To David come even those of the tribe of Benjamin, the brethren of Saul, the bitter enemy of David; so had Christ disciples from the Jews, even from the Pharisees, His deadly foes; and as we by nature are all His foes, He yet converts us to His love and to faith in Him. . . . At David's anointing was great joy; on all sides was provided store of eating and drinking; even so believers rejoiced at and after Christ's ascension, and because they had all things common." On ch. xvi. 27, comp. the remark (suitable also to the contents of xxiii.-xxvi.) of Bengel, p. 17: "This is so fine in David; he has gone as nigh to the Levites as it was possible for him to do, as if he were one of them; and yet he has invaded no right. How finely devotion and valour are combined! Something quite peculiar has taken place in David's heart." On xxix. 30 he remarks: "How earnest is the dear David become in his old age! How he has come as nigh as possible to the building of the temple!"

2. SOLOMON.—2 CHRON. I.-IX.

a. HIS SOLEMN SACRIFICE AT GIBEON, AND HIS RICHES.—CH. I.

α. The Sacrifice at Gibeon, and the Dream of Solomon: vers. 1–13.

CH. I. 1. And Solomon the son of David was strengthened in his kingdom, and
2 the LORD his God was with him, and magnified him exceedingly. And
Solomon said unto all Israel, to the captains of thousands, and of hundreds,
and to the judges, and to every ruler in all Israel, the chiefs of houses.
3 And Solomon, and all the congregation with him, went to the high place that
was at Gibeon; for there was the tent of meeting of God, which Moses the
4 servant of God had made in the wilderness. But the ark of God had David
brought up from Kiriath-jearim to the place which David had prepared for
5 it: for he had pitched a tent for it at Jerusalem. And the brazen altar, that
Bezaleel the son of Uri, the son of Hur, had made, was there[1] before the
tabernacle of the LORD; and Solomon and the congregation sought him.
6 And Solomon offered there before the LORD, on the brazen altar which
belonged to the tent of meeting; and he offered upon it a thousand burnt-
offerings.
7 In that night did God appear unto Solomon, and said unto him, Ask
8 what I shall give thee. And Solomon said unto God, Thou hast showed
great mercy unto David my father, and hast made me king in his stead.
9 Now, O LORD God, Thy word unto David my father must be true; for Thou
10 hast made me king over a people numerous as the dust of the earth. Give
me now wisdom and knowledge, that I may go out and in before this people;
11 for who can judge this Thy great people. And God said unto Solomon,
Because this was in thy heart, and thou hast not asked riches, treasures, and
glory, nor the life of thine enemies, neither hast thou asked long life; but
hast asked wisdom and knowledge for thyself, that thou mayest judge my
12 people, over whom I have made thee king. Wisdom and knowledge are
given unto thee, and riches and treasures and glory will I give thee, such as
none of the kings that were before thee have had, and none after thee shall
13 have the like. And Solomon came from[2] the high place that was at Gibeon
to Jerusalem, from before the tent of meeting; and he reigned over Israel.[3]

β. Solomon's Power and Wealth: vers. 14–17.

14 And Solomon gathered chariots and riders: and he had a thousand and
four hundred chariots, and twelve thousand riders; and he placed them in
15 the chariot cities, and with the king at Jerusalem. And the king made silver
and gold in Jerusalem as stones; and cedars he made as the sycamores that
16 are in the Shephelah for abundance. And the export of horses for Solomon
was out of Egypt; and the company of the king's merchants fetched a troop

17 for a certain price. And they brought up, and took out of Egypt a chariot
for six hundred silver shekels, and a horse for a hundred and fifty: and
they brought them out for all the kings of the Hittites and the kings of Syria.

[1] So according to the reading שָׁם, which is attested by the Sept., Vulg., some MSS., and most prints while for the almost unmeaning שָׂם (*posuit*, he had set) the majority of MSS. and the Chald. and the Syr. testify.

[2] The Sept., Vulg., Luther, etc., correctly: מֵהַבָּמָה; the לַבָּמָה of the Masoretes, yielding no tolerable sense, appears to have crept into the text by looking back at ver. 3.

[3] The Peschito has "over all Israel;" comp. 1 Kings iv. 1.

EXEGETICAL.

1. Preliminary Remark, and elucidation of ver. 1.—The accounts contained in the foregoing two small sections, to which 1 Kings iii. 4–15 and x. 26–29 are parallel, serve to introduce the report of the building and dedication of the temple, which occupy far the greatest space in the representation given by our author of the history of Solomon (i. 18–vii.). As general superscription is prefixed ver. 1: "And Solomon the son of David was strengthened in his kingdom," properly, "on," or "with, his kingdom," עַל־מַלְכוּתוֹ; comp. וַיִּתְחַזֵּק עַל־יִשְׂרָאֵל, xvii. 1, and xii. 13, xiii. 21, xxi. 4, which parallels likewise show that הִתְחַזֵּק, "be strengthened," does not refer to pretenders to the crown, by setting aside of whom confirmation follows; and hence there is here no concealed allusion to Adonijah (1 Kings ii.).—*And the Lord his God was with him* (comp. 1 Chron. xi. 9), *and magnified him exceedingly*; comp. 1 Chron. xxix. 25, xxii. 5.

2. The Sacrifice at Gibeon: vers. 2–6; comp. 1 Kings iii. 4.—*And Solomon said unto all Israel, to the captains*, etc. This addition of the chiefs of the people and representatives of the kingdom at the sacrifice is not mentioned in the book of Kings; but the matter is understood of itself (comp. the similar cases in the history of David, 1 Chron. xiii. 1 f., xxiii. 2, xxviii. 1).—*The chiefs of houses.* Before רָאשֵׁי, לְ is to be supplied, as the whole phrase is an explanatory apposition to לְכָל־יִשְׂרָאֵל.—Ver. 4. *For there was the tent of meeting of God.* Comp. on 1 Chron. v. 30 ff., xvi. 39 f.—Ver. 4. *But the ark of God had David*, etc.; comp. 1 Chron. xiii. and xv. For the elliptical construction בַּהֵכִין, to (the place) which he prepared for it, where the article in בַּ supplies the place of the relative אֲשֶׁר, comp. 1 Chron. xv. 12, xxvi. 28; also Judg. v. 27; Ruth i. 5.—Ver. 5. *And the brazen altar . . . was there before the tabernacle of the Lord*, that is, the Gibeonite sanctuary was still the legal, as it were the official and historically rightful place for burnt-offerings: comp. 1 Chron. xxi. 29 f., where, on the occasion of the choice of the floor of Ornan on Moriah for a place of burnt-offering, it is shown why David could not go to Gibeon to offer there. On Bezaleel's construction of the brazen (copper) altar of burnt-offering, see Ex. xxxi. 2, xxxvii. 1. On the reading שָׁם, as undoubtedly to be preferred to the Masoretic שָׂם (which arose from an unwarranted reference to Ex. xl. 29), see Crit. Note.—*And Solomon and the congregation sought him*, the Lord, not the altar; comp. דָּרַשׁ אֱלֹהִים, 1 Chron. xxi. 30; 2 Chron. xv. 2. Yet, for the reference of the verb to the altar, may be quoted (Luther: "was wont to seek it"), at all events, Amos v. 5; comp. also 1 Chron. xxi. 28.—Ver. 6. *There before the Lord, on the brazen altar which was at the tent of meeting.* In the Heb., לִפְנֵי יְהוָֹה stands before the relative sentence אֲשֶׁר לְאֹהֶל מוֹעֵד. Because the altar of burnt-offering had its place before the tabernacle (Ex. xl. 6), it is designated as belonging to it; comp. 1 Kings vi. 22.

3. God's Revelation to Solomon: vers. 7–13; comp. 1 Kings iii. 5–15.—*In that night*, that followed the offering. That the manifestation of God to Solomon was effected by a nocturnal vision, seems at least to be indicated here, but is expressly stated in 1 Kings iii. 5, 15.—Ver. 8. *Thou hast showed great mercy unto David my father.* The fuller speech of Solomon in 1 Kings iii. 6–10 appears here (vers. 8–10) much abbreviated.—Ver. 9. *Thy word . . . must be true*, properly, "must be established"; comp. 1 Chron. xvii. 23; 2 Chron. vi. 17; 1 Kings viii. 26.—Ver. 10. *Give me now wisdom and knowledge.* מַדַּע (here with Pattach in the second syllable; elsewhere מַדָּע; also vers. 11, 12) denotes knowledge, insight, and is found, besides the present passage, only in Dan. i. 4, 17 and Eccl. x. 20.—*That I may go out and in before this people*, "may know all that belongs thereto, may worthily govern and defend them" (Starke); the phrase, reminding us of Deut. xxxi. 2, 1 Sam. xviii. 13, 16, 1 Kings iii. 7, denotes the unchecked public activity of the king toward his people.—Ver. 11. *Because this was in thy heart;* comp. 1 Chron. xxii. 7.—*Riches, treasures, and glory.* The same combination appears in Eccl. vi. 2; נְכָסִים, treasures, also in Eccl. v. 18 (with עֹשֶׁר) and Josh. xxii. 8.—Ver. 12. *Wisdom . . . given to thee.* The construction נָתוּן לָךְ, as in Esth. iii. 11 (1 Kings iii. 12, הִנֵּה, with the perf. נָתַתִּי). In the following words, the Lord promises to Solomon riches, treasures, and glory indeed, but not long life, as in 1 Kings iii. 14. Whether this omission is intentional (because Solomon, on account of his subsequent fall, did not attain to old age) appears doubtful in the condensing manner of our author, which shows itself even in this promise of the Lord. On the ethical-eudæmonistic sentence

contained in vers. 11, 12 may be compared the word of Christ in the Sermon on the Mount: "Seek ye first," etc., Matt. v. 32.—Ver. 13. *And Solomon came from the high place.* On the correctness of this reading (מֵהַבָּמָה), see Crit. Note. The following addition: "from the tent of meeting," which appears superfluous after "from the high place," points again to the Gibeonite place of offering, and to the legal validity of the offerings presented there. Of the burnt and peace offerings, with the sacrificial feast, 1 Kings iii. 15, on the return of Solomon to Jerusalem before the ark, our author makes no mention, not because in his view the offering presented at the brazen altar in Gibeon only had legal validity (as Thenius thinks, in defiance of the express statements of our author, 1 Chron. xxi. 18, 26 ff.), but simply because these offerings, as well as the history there following (1 Kings iii. 26–28) of the strife between the two women, and its settlement by the wise judgment of Solomon, appeared to be of no special importance for his plan (chiefly regarding the brilliant, glorious, and magnificent features of Solomon's administration).—*And he reigned over Israel.* These closing words of our verse are introductory to what follows, and would stand more suitably at the head of the following section, vers. 14–17, as they are found, 1 Kings iv. 1, in this more suitable position, and are there enlarged by the addition of כָּל־ before יִשְׂרָאֵל, which the Syr. exhibits here (see Crit. Note).

4. Solomon's Power and Wealth: vers. 14–17.—This short account of that which Solomon had in chariots, riders, and treasures, the Chronist presents as proof of the instant fulfilment of the promise of God to him in this passage, while in 1 Kings x. 26–29 it is found near the close of the reign of Solomon (parallel to the fuller account of a similar nature in 2 Chron. ix. 13 ff.). That accordingly that which is here recorded by our author is adduced a second time, the first time partly abbreviated, partly completed by additions (see ix. 25–28), Thenius (on 1 Kings x. 26 ff.) explains by the assumption of a second occurrence of the section in his sources, and an inadvertent admission of both accounts, the identity of which was discovered too late. More correctly, Berth., Keil, etc., explain that the Chronist used his sources in a free and independent way, and accordingly of purpose admitted the partial repetition of the present account in ch. ix. 25 ff.—*And he placed them in the chariot cities.* Instead of וַיַּנִּיחֵם, "laid them" (so also ix. 25) stands in 1 Kings x. 26 less definitely: וַיַּנְחֵם, "and he brought them"; with regard to the number of the chariots (1400) and riders (12,000), the two texts agree. The "chariot cities" are cities in which the chariots and riders were stationed. They probably lay, partly near rich pasture grounds, partly in the neighbourhood of Egypt, principally in the south of the country; and the conjecture that the Simeonite towns Beth-marchaboth and Hazar-susim (1 Chron. iv. 31) belonged to them (Then., Berth., Kamph.) is on this account the more probable.—Ver. 15. *And the king made silver and gold in Jerusalem as stones.* That the words "and gold" (וְאֶת־הַזָּהָב), which are wanting in the parallels ix. 27 and 1 Kings x. 27, are to be erased, with the Pesch., in our passage also is very improbable; and the Sept. and Vulg. testify for their genuineness in this place. For *b*, comp. on 1 Chron. xxvii. 28.—Ver. 16. *And the export of horses for Solomon*, properly, "which belonged to Solomon."—*The company of the king's merchants fetched a troop for a certain price.* Even so 1 Kings x. 28, only that for the מִקְוֵה there מִקְוֵא is here twice written. For the correct understanding of the passage, see Bähr, *Bibelw.* vol. vii. p. 103.—Ver. 17. *And they brought up, and took out of Egypt;* 1 Kings x. 29: "and there was fetched and brought out" (וַתַּעֲלֶה וַתֵּצֵא instead of our וַיַּעֲלוּ וַיּוֹצִיאוּ), otherwise literally as our passage, except that, perhaps by a corruption of the text, the לְ here wanting before מַלְכֵי אֲרָם is rightly supplied. For the exposition, see also Bähr as above.

b. The Building and the Dedication of the Temple.—Ch. i. 18–vii.

α. Treaty with the Phœnician King, and Preparations for Building: ch. i. 18–ii.

Ch. i. 18. And Solomon determined to build a house for the name of the Lord, and
1 a house for his kingdom. Ch. ii. And Solomon told out seventy thousand
men to bear burdens, and eighty thousand to hew in the mountain, and three
thousand and six hundred to oversee them.
2 And Solomon sent to Huram the king of Tyre, saying, As thou didst
with David my father, and sentest him cedars to build him a house to dwell
3 in, so do also with me. Behold, I build a house to the name of the Lord my
God, to dedicate it to Him, to offer sweet incense before Him, and the shew-
bread continually, and the burnt-offerings for the morning and the evening,
on the Sabbaths and the new moons, and the feasts of the Lord our God:
4 for ever this is ordained for Israel. And the house which I build is great;
5 for our God is greater than all gods. But who is able to build Him a house?
For the heaven, and heaven of heavens, cannot contain Him; and who am I,
6 that I should build Him a house, but to offer incense before Him? And
now send me a wise man to work in gold, and silver, and brass, and iron, and

in purple, and crimson, and blue, and who knoweth to make graven work
with the wise men that are with me in Judah and Jerusalem, whom David
7 my father appointed. And send me cedar-trees, cypresses, and sandal-wood
out of Lebanon; for I know that thy servants can cut timber in Lebanon;
8 and, behold, my servants shall be with thy servants. And shall prepare me
wood in abundance; for the house which I build is to be great and wonderful.
9 And, behold, for the hewers, who fell the trees, I give of wheat as food[1] for
thy servants, twenty thousand cors, and of barley twenty thousand cors, and
of wine twenty thousand baths, and of oil twenty thousand baths.
10 And Huram king of Tyre answered in a letter, and sent to Solomon:
Because the LORD loveth His people, He hath set thee over them as king.
11 And Huram said, Blessed be the LORD God of Israel, that made heaven and
earth, who hath given to David the king a wise son, endued with prudence and
understanding, that may build a house for the LORD, and a house for his king-
12, 13 dom. And now I send a wise man of understanding, Huram my father, son
of a woman of the daughters of Dan; and his father was a Tyrian, who can
work in gold, and silver, in brass, in iron, in stone, and wood, in purple, blue,
and byssus, and crimson, and can do all graving, and devise every device that
is given to him with thy wise men, and the wise men of my lord David thy
14 father. And now the wheat and the barley, the oil and the wine, which
15 my lord spake of, let him send his servants. And we shall fell timber out of
Lebanon according to all thy need, and bring it to thee in floats to the sea of
Joppa, and thou shalt take it up to Jerusalem.
16 And Solomon counted all the men that were strangers in the land of
Israel, after the number which David his father had counted, and they were
found to be a hundred and fifty thousand, and three thousand and six
17 hundred. And he made seventy thousand of them bearers of burdens, and
eighty thousand hewers in the mountain, and three thousand and six hundred
overseers to keep the people at work.

[1] So according to the probable correct reading מַכֹּלֶת (=מַאֲכֹלֶת), as the parallel 1 Kings v. 25 exhibits it for the unmeaning מַכּוֹת ("wheat of beating," "beaten-out wheat"?).

EXEGETICAL.

1. Transition from the Foregoing to the Report of the building of the Temple: ch. i. 18–ii. 1.—*And Solomon determined to build.* So according to the Vulg., Luther, and most of the ancients, while some moderns, as Berth., Kamph., take אמר, with allusion to ch. i. 2, 1 Chron. xxi. 17, in the sense of "command." The context, especially the circumstance that instead of the execution of the building itself only preparations for it follow, favours the older view.—*A house for the name of the Lord* (comp. 1 Kings v. 17), *and a house for his kingdom,* that is, a royal palace for himself, the building of which is not more particularly described (as 1 Kings vii. 1-12), but which is mentioned several times, as ch. ii. 11, vii. 11, viii. 1.—Ch. ii. 1. *And Solomon told out seventy thousand,* etc. This statement, recurring, vers. 16, 17, in another connection, and in a fuller and more definite form, concerning the 70,000 + 80,000 + 3600, in all 153,600, workmen to whom Solomon committed the labours preliminary to the building of the temple, stands here in briefer form, to indicate beforehand the magnitude of the measures undertaken by the king.

2. Solomon's Embassy to Huram of Tyre: vers. 2-9; comp. 1 Kings v. 15-26, which account, agreeing with the present in all essential respects, partly indeed to the letter, is opened with a notice of an embassy sent first by Huram to Solomon (to congratulate him on his accession to the throne), which our author has omitted as not sufficiently important.—*And Solomon sent to Huram king of Tyre.* On the three forms of the name, Huram (Chron.), Hiram (1 Kings v. 15), and Hirom (1 Kings v. 24, 32, vii. 40), of which the last (in Menander in *Joseph. c. Ap.* i. 18, 21: Εἴρωμος; in Herod and Syncell.: Σίρωμος) appears to be the most original, comp. Bähr on 1 Kings v. 15, where, with justice, the doubts of Clericus, Thenius, Ew., Berth., etc., regarding the identity of the present Huram with the like-named contemporary and friend of David, are set aside. Hitzig (*Gesch. des V. Isr.* p. 10; comp. p. 155) gives as the probable time of the reign of Huram or Hirom, 1031-1000 B.C. (?).—*As thou didst with David my father, and sentest him cedars;* comp. 1 Chron. xiv. 1. The consequent to this antecedent is wanting; according to ver. 6 f., it must run thus: "So do also to me, and send me cedars." This construction is like that elsewhere after asseverations and oaths; comp. also Ps. lvi. 7*b* (Ew. §§ 355, 356). Moreover, in the parallel account 1 Kings v. 16 ff., Solomon does not expressly remind Hiram of the aid which he had already given to his father David, but only of this, that David had been prevented by his wars from executing the project of building the

temple. Hence it is clear, from the various differences between the present and the previous form of the letter of Solomon, that it is not an authentic original document that is here given, but the result of free handling of the fundamental thoughts of older sources by the one as well as the other writer. — Ver. 3. *Behold, I build,* literally, "Behold me building," future of state; see Ew. § 306, *d.—To offer sweet incense before Him,* literally, "to perfume," לְהַקְטִיר, with which infinitive (defining the foregoing לְהַקְדִּישׁ more exactly) are zeugmatically connected the other objects named, "shew-bread" and "burnt-offering." For the "sweet incense" and its burning every morning and evening on the altar of incense, comp. Ex. xxv. 6, xxx. 7 f.; for the continual laying of shew-bread (מַעֲרֶכֶת תָּמִיד), Ex. xxv. 30; for the burnt-offering to be made every morning and evening, and on Sabbaths, new moons, and feast days, Num. xxviii. 29 and 1 Chron. xxiii. 31.—*For ever this is ordained for Israel;* comp. the passage already cited, 1 Chron. xxiii. 31, and the לְחֻקַּת עוֹלָם often occurring in the law, for example, Num. xix. 10.—On ver. 4, comp. 1 Chron. xxix. 1, and Ex. xviii. 11, Deut. x. 17.—Ver. 5. *But who is able,* literally, "who will show power;" comp. 1 Chron. xxix. 14. On the following asseveration: "the heaven, and heaven of heavens, cannot contain Him," comp. Solomon's prayer at the dedication of the temple, ch. vi. 18; 1 Kings viii. 27. Obviously we have here a favourite saying of Solomon the theologian and philosopher: that our author has here, of his own will, put this formula in his mouth is improbable.—*And who am I, that I should build Him a house, but to offer,* etc.; that is, not a house for dwelling in, but only for sacrifice and worship (the incense, as symbol of prayer, is here mentioned instead of all offerings), may we build for Jehovah.—Ver. 6. *And now send me a wise man* (skilful, see ver. 12; 1 Chron. xxii. 15; Ex. xxxi. 6) *to work in gold.* That, besides the works in brass and other metals, as they were actually executed by the craftsmen here mentioned, according to ch. iv. 11-16 and 1 Kings vii. 13 ff., skill also in weaving purple, hewing stone, and carving wood is ascribed to them, need not seem strange in Solomon's letter. But it seems surprising that, ver. 13, King Huram also in his reply makes him exercise all these crafts. Yet ancient history knows several instances of universal genius in art; comp. Dædalus, and one Tutilo in St. Gall of the Christian times. On purple (אַרְגְּוָן, later form of ארגמן), comp. Ex. xxv. 4; Dan. v. 7; on crimson (כַּרְמִיל only here, ver. 13, and iii. 14, probably an old Persic word), the תּוֹלַעַת שָׁנִי elsewhere used to denote this fabric; on blue or violet (תְּכֵלֶת), Ex. xxv. 4.—*And who knoweth to make graven work,* literally, "to grave gravings," here of every kind of sculpture in metal or wood (comp. כָּל־פִּתּוּחַ, ver. 13; also 1 Kings vi. 29); elsewhere, specially of graving precious stones, Ex. xxviii. 9, 11, 36, xxxix. 6; Zech. iii. 9.—*With the wise men,* etc.; comp. 1 Chron. xxii. 3, 15, xxviii. 21. In construction, עִם־הַחֲכָמִים goes wit לַעֲשׂוֹת, "to work."—Ver. 7. *And send me . . . sandal-wood out of Lebanon.* If the algum-wood (עֲצֵי־אַלְגּוּמִּים) here named along with cedars and cypresses be actually sandal-wood, which, in the obvious identity of its name with אַלְמֻגִּים, 1 Kings x. 11, can scarcely be doubted, our author, in allowing it to come from Lebanon, involves Solomon in an inaccuracy (at least in expression); for, according to his own later statement (ch. ix. 10; 1 Chron. x. 11), algums belonged rather to the products of Ophir.—Ver. 8. *Prepare me wood in abundance;* the infin. וּלְהָכִין is the continuation of the imperat. שְׁלַח לִי, ver. 7; Keil's attempt to subordinate it to the previous clause is too artificial: "to prepare for me wood in abundance." On *b*, comp. ver. 4.—Ver. 9. *And, behold, for the hewers, who fell the trees.* לַחֹטְבִים (with introductory לְ) is more exactly defined by the added לְכֹרְתֵי הָעֵצִים, and for this reason, that חטב (= the afterwards more usual חצב; comp. vers. 1, 17) appears to our author to need interpretation; comp. besides, for חטב, Deut. xxix. 10; Josh. ix. 21, 23, 27.—*I give wheat as food for thy servants.* For מַכֹּלֶת instead of the defective מַכּוֹת, see Crit. Note.—*Twenty thousand cors.* In this enumeration of the provisions in grain, wine, and oil offered by Solomon, our report seems to be more detailed than the parallel 1 Kings v. 25, which reports only 20,000 cors of wheat for the household of king Hiram, and twenty cors of the finest (beaten) oil for the same, as given by Solomon. But, in truth, the two passages speak of quite different supplies: there of a yearly contribution, which Solomon paid to the Tyrian king during the building at Tyre, but here of the provisions which he sent to the woodcutters placed at his disposal by Huram in Lebanon (so correctly Keil and Bähr on 1 Kings v. 25; otherwise Thenius, Bertheau, etc., who here find statements that are partly contradictory).

3. Huram's Answer: vers. 10-15; comp. 1 Kings v. 21-25.—*Because the Lord loveth His people,* etc. Instead of this compliment (comp. ch. ix. 8; 1 Kings x. 9), in the parallel text 1 Kings v. 22, Hiram begins his letter immediately with the declaration: "I have heard the things thou sentest to me for." On the contrary, an expression of joy concerning Solomon's message as orally given by Hiram precedes the composing and sending of the reply.—Ver. 11. *And Huram said,* namely, as in the foregoing verse; בִּכְתָב, "in writing."—*Blessed be the Lord . . . that made heaven and earth.* Are we to see in this doxology of the Phœnician king, readily following into Solomon's religious thought and phrase (which rises above that in 1 Kings v. 21), the product of a half-poetic fiction, after the manner of a writer after the exile (as Dan. ii. 28, iii. 29 ff., iv. 31 ff.)? It is perhaps more natural to take into

account here partly the courtesies in expression, which friendly sovereigns might and must use, partly the community of speech, and even of religious tradition, which existed between the Phœnicians and Hebrews.—*A wise son endowed with prudence and understanding;* comp. 1 Chron. xii. 32, xxii. 12.—Ver. 12. *Huram my father.* The introductory לְ before the accusative, as ch. v. 26. Luther takes אָבִי for an element of the proper name of the craftsman, who was called Huram-abi (or, ch. iv. 16, Huram-abiv). Most of the ancients as well as moderns take it here, as in ch. iv. 16, as a tropical appellative or name of honour = master, by comparison with Gen. xlv. 8. —Ver. 13. *The son of a woman of the daughters of Dan,* that is, perhaps the city Dan in the tribe of Naphtali; see 1 Kings vii. 14 and the expositors on this passage, especially Thenius and Bähr, whereas certainly Keil (with Berth., Kamph., etc.) defends the more difficult and artificial assumption, that the mother of this craftsman belonged by birth to the tribe of Dan, but by her first husband to that of Naphtali.—*Who can work in gold,* etc. The Phœnician king enhances the praise of his craftsman by recounting a still greater number of crafts than those mentioned by Solomon, ver. 6. Hence the mention of stone and wood (after brass and iron), of byssus (בּוּץ, as 1 Chron. xv. 27), and of "devising every device that is given to him." Comp. for the last phrase, the remarks made, Ex. xxxi. 4, xxxv. 33, on Bezaleel.—On ver. 14, comp. ver. 9; the there expressed offer by Solomon of food for his people Huram expressly accepts.—Ver. 15. *According to all thy need.* צֹרֶךְ, "need," only here in the Old Test. (in Aram. very common); likewise the following רַפְסֹדוֹת, "floats," for which, 1 Kings v. 23, דֹּבְרוֹת.—*To the sea of Joppa,* the sea at Joppa, the port of Jerusalem. Also, with respect to this reply of Huram, and its relation to the often-deviating parallel text 1 Kings v. 21 ff., the above remark (ver. 2) on the two texts of the letter of Solomon applies. Neither text is wholly independent of the other, and neither coincides exactly with a presumed original. Both exhibit certainly a freely imitating or rather extracting (partly also interpolating; see especially the additions made by our author, ver. 13) treatment of the original text; as also Josephus, *Antiq.* viii. 2. 6 f., in his rendering of the pieces, generally agrees with 1 Kings v., but allows himself many peculiar forms of its language. The statements of this historian, that the ἀντίγραφα of the two letters were extant both in the Old Testament and in the public archives of Tyre (*Antiq.* viii. 2. 8), must therefore be received *cum grano salis,* and must refer not so much to the form as to the substance of the documents. Eupolemus, in Euseb. *Præp. evang.* ix. 33, 34, has copied still more freely than Josephus the correspondence between Solomon and Hiram.

4. Expanded Repetition of the Number of Workmen stated in ver. 1: vers. 16, 17.—*And Solomon counted all the men that were strangers in the land of Israel,* all the serfs of Canaanitish descent under the people of Israel; comp. 1 Chron. xxii. 2, to which place there is here express reference (by the following words: "after the number [סְפָר, 'muster,' only here in O. T.] which David his father had counted"). —Ver. 17. The eighty thousand "hewers" (חֹצֵב) in the mountain are chiefly to be regarded as hewers of stone (comp. 1 Chron. xxii. 2), but partly as fellers of timber.—*And three thousand and six hundred overseers* (מְנַצְּחִים; comp. Ezra iii. 8, 9), *to keep the people at work,* "to make them work"; comp. Ex. vi. 5. With the present statements of the number of workmen levied by Solomon agree those contained in 1 Kings v. 27–30, with two points of difference: —1. Of the 30,000 socagers levied out of Israel itself, there first named, that were to cut timbers successively in three parties of 10,000 each, our text says nothing, as the enumeration of our author is perhaps confined intentionally to the גֵּרִים, perhaps, however, through a mistake in quite overlooking the statement in question; 2. instead of 3600 overseers, the author of 1 Kings v. 30 names only 3300; perhaps he had only in view those of lower rank, and not the higher, who, according to 1 Kings ix. 23, amounted in all to 550, namely, 250 Israelites (2 Chron. viii. 10) and 300 strangers. As the Chronist mentions here only the strangers, he enumerates only these 3000 non-Israelite upper overseers, and thus arrives at the total of 3600 מְנַצְּחִים. He was aware also of the existence of 250 Israelite upper overseers, as is clear from ch. viii. 40 of our book.

β. The Building of the Temple, and Making of the Holy Vessels: ch. iii. 1–v. 1.

CH. III. 1. And Solomon began to build the house of the LORD at Jerusalem on
mount Moriah, which was shown to his father David, and which he had pre-
2 pared in the place of David, in the floor of Ornan the Jebusite. And he
began to build in the second month, on the second[1] day in the fourth year of
his reign.
3 And this is the foundation of Solomon, to build the house of God: the
length after the former measure was sixty cubits, and the breadth twenty
4 cubits. And the porch that was before the length, before the breadth of the
house, was twenty cubits, and the height a hundred and twenty[2]; and he
5 overlaid it within with pure gold. And the great house he lined with cypress,
6 and overlaid it with fine gold, and made thereon palms and garlands. And
he garnished the house with precious stones for beauty; and the gold was

7 gold of Parvaim. And he overlaid the house, the beams, the sills, and its
walls and its doors, with gold, and graved cherubim on the walls.
8 And he made the house of the most holy, that its length before the
breadth of the house was twenty cubits, and its width twenty cubits; and
9 overlaid it with fine gold, to six hundred talents. And the weight of the
nails was fifty shekels of gold: and he overlaid the upper rooms with gold.
10 And he made in the house of the most holy two cherubim of sculptured
11 work, and overlaid them with gold. And the wings of the cherubim were
twenty cubits long; the wing of the one was five cubits, touching the wall of
the house, and the other wing five cubits, touching the wing of the other
12 cherub. And the wing of the other cherub was five cubits, touching the wall
of the house, and the other wing five cubits, joining the wing of the first
13 cherub. The wings of these cherubim spread forth twenty cubits; and they
stood on their feet, and their faces to the house.
14 And he made the veil of blue, and purple, and crimson, and byssus, and
raised cherubim thereon.
15 And he made before the house two pillars of thirty and five[3] cubits height;
16 and the capital that was on the top was five cubits. And he made chains in
the ring,[4] and put them on the pillars; and he made a hundred pomegranates,
17 and put them on the chains. And he set up the pillars before the temple,
one on the right and one on the left; and he called the name of the right
pillar Jachin, and the name of the left Boaz.
CH. IV. 1. And he made an altar of brass, twenty cubits its length, and twenty
2 cubits its breadth, and twenty cubits its height. And he made the sea
molten; ten cubits from brim to brim, round about, and five cubits its height;
3 and a line of thirty cubits compassed it about. And figures of oxen[5] were
under it, compassing it round about; ten in a cubit, encircling the sea around:
4 two rows the oxen formed, cast out of its mass. It stood upon twelve oxen,
three looking northward, and three looking westward, and three looking
southward, and three looking eastward; and the sea was set on them above,
5 and all their hinder parts were inwards. And its thickness was a hand-
breadth, and its brim was wrought like the brim of a cup, as a lily blossom,
6 holding in it (many) baths; it contained three thousand.[6] And he made ten
lavers, and put five on the right and five on the left, to wash in them; the
work of the burnt-offering they washed in them; but the sea was for the
7 priests to wash in. And he made ten candlesticks of gold, after their plan,
8 and set them in the temple, five on the right and five on the left. And he
made ten tables, and placed them in the temple, five on the right, and five on
9 the left: and he made basons of gold a hundred. And he made the court of
the priests, and the great court, and doors for the court, and overlaid the
10 door-leaves with brass. And he set the sea on the right side eastward, over
against the south.
11 And Huram made the pots, and the shovels, and the bowls: and Huram[7]
finished the work which he made for King Solomon in the house of God.
12 The two pillars, and the balls, and the capitals on the top of the two pillars,
and the two grates to cover the two balls of the capitals which were on the
13 top of the pillars. And the four hundred pomegranates on the two grates;
two rows of pomegranates on each grate, to cover the two balls of the capitals
14 which were upon the two[8] pillars. And he made[9] stands, and he made lavers
15, 16 upon the stands. One sea, and twelve oxen under it. And the pots, and
the shovels, and the forks,[10] and all their vessels, made Huram his father for
17 King Solomon, for the house of the LORD, of bright brass. In the plain of
Jordan the king cast them, in the clay ground[11] between Succoth and Zere-
18 dathah. And Solomon made all these vessels in great abundance; for the
weight of the brass was not found out.
19 And Solomon made all the vessels that were for the house of God, the
20 golden altar, and the tables with the shew-bread on them. And the candle-
sticks with their lamps, to burn after their rule before the oracle of costly

21 gold. And the flowers, and the lamps, and the snuffers: this was the most
22 perfect gold.[12] And the knives, and the bowls, and the censers, and the
extinguishers of costly gold: and the door of the house, its inner leaves to
the most holy place, and the door leaves of the house for the temple, of gold.
Ch. v. 1. Then was finished all the work that Solomon made for the house of the
Lord: and Solomon brought in the holy gifts of David his father; and the
silver, and the gold, and all the instruments he put among the treasures of
the house of God.

[1] בַּשֵּׁנִי, which the Sept. and Vulg. do not express, appears a gloss brought into the text by the repetition of the foregoing הַשֵּׁנִי.

[2] מֵאָה וְעֶשְׂרִים appears a defective reading, as the Sept. *cod. Al.*, Syr., and Ar. have 20 for 120. Comp. the Exeg. Expl.

[3] According to the parallels 1 Kings vii. 15, 2 Kings xxv. 17, etc., instead of thirty-five (לה) must apparently be read eighteen (יח).

[4] So according to the emendation of Berth.: בָּרָבִיד, instead of the Masoretic בַּדְּבִיר (Sept. ἐν τῷ δαβίρ), which yields no suitable sense.

[5] בְּקָרִים appears a slip of the pen for פְּקָעִים (1 Kings vii. 24), as in *b*, הַבָּקָר for הַפְּקָעִים.

[6] For שְׁלֹשֶׁת אֲלָפִים is to be read, according to 1 Kings vii. 26, אַלְפַּיִם (2000); the שלשת before אלפים seems to have come into the text from the fourfold שלשת in the verse before.

[7] The *Kethib* has here Hiram (חירם), the only time this reading occurs in Chronicles.

[8] For עַל־פְּנֵי read עַל־שְׁנֵי, although פְּנֵי stands also in 1 Kings vii. 42; but see Sept. there.

[9] עָשָׂה seems wrongly written for עֶשֶׂר, as the second time for עֲשָׂרָה. Comp. 1 Kings vii. 43.

[10] מִזְלָגוֹת is perhaps written wrongly for מִזְרָקוֹת, "sprinkling cups," ver. 11. Comp. 1 Kings vii. 44.

[11] For בְּעֲבִי some prints give בַּעֲבִי.

[12] The words הוּא מִכְלוֹת זָהָב are not represented in the Sept.

EXEGETICAL.

Preliminary Remark.—From the description of the building of the temple in 1 Kings vi. and vii., the present account is distinguished—1. By this, that in the introduction more precise statements are made with respect to the plan of the building, but less precise with respect to the time when it began, than there (comp. ch. iii. 1, 2 with 1 Kings vi. 1); 2. By this, that our author describes, in unbroken connection, first (ch. iii. 3–17) the magnitude and arrangement of the edifice itself, then (ch. iv. 1–22) those of its several furnishings in the court and the sanctuary, whereas in 1 Kings vi. and vii. this description meets with two considerable interruptions, inasmuch as—*a.* an account of a divine promise given to the king during the building (ch. vi. 11–13), and—*b.* a description of a palace-building of Solomon, partly concurrent with that of the temple (ch. vii. 1–11), are there inserted; 3. By a somewhat different arrangement of the several objects enumerated and described in 1 Kings; 4. By the greater fulness and circumstantiality of the description, as contained in 1 Kings (for example, with respect to the ten brazen stands, ch. vii. 27–38, which our author, iv. 14, only slightly mentions); and 5. By the here again remarkable excerpting habit of the Chronist. In the following exposition, only that which is peculiar to our author will be fully discussed; but with regard to that which he has in common with 1 Kings, or which he, compared with the more ample details there, only briefly notices, reference will be made to the exposition of Bähr (*Bibelw.* vii. pp. 38–70), which is characterized by solidity and scientific ability.

1. Place and Time of building the Temple: ch. iii. 1, 2.—*And Solomon began . . . on mount Moriah.* Only here is the site of the temple so named; but the designation is no doubt identical with "the land of Moriah" (אֶרֶץ הַמֹּרִיָּה, "land of the appearing of the Lord"), Gen. xxii. 2. The place of the celebrated sacrifice of Abraham was even that floor of Ornan on which David presented his offering, and which he had consequently chosen for the site of the temple, the hill lying north-east of Zion, which is now called "the Haram," after the holy mosque of the Mahommedans standing on it. Comp. Rosen, *Das Haram*, Gotha 1866, and the plan and description in Ph. Wolff's *Jerusalem* (3d edit. 1872), p. 89 ff.—*Which was shown to his father David*, as the future site of the temple; see 1 Chron. xxi. 15 ff. Against this most usual exposition it may certainly be objected (with Keil) that the *Niphal* נִרְאָה elsewhere denotes, not "be shown," but "be seen, appear." Yet the rendering of Keil: "where He (Jehovah) appeared to his father David" (so also the Sept.), has this defect, that the subject Jehovah has to be supplied, and that אֲשֶׁר has to be taken in the sense of אֲשֶׁר שָׁם, as elsewhere only in the phrase בַּמָּקוֹם אֲשֶׁר (Ew. § 331, *c*, 3)—(and) *which he had prepared in the place of David*, which site he (Solomon) had prepared on the place fixed by David. So Berth., Kamph., etc., and in

the main Luther, Starke, and other ancients (for example, Rambach: *quam domum præparavit Salomo in loco Davidis*). On the contrary, the Sept., Vulg., Syr., etc., translate as if במקום stood before אשר הֵכִין, "in the place which David had prepared" (the building of the temple); and Keil, in accordance with his supplying of Jehovah as subject to נִרְאָה, interprets: "who (David) had prepared the house, that is, the building of it, in the place appointed of David." None of these expositions is quite satisfactory; whence it is natural to suppose some corruption of the text.—Ver. 2. *And he began to build in the second month, in the second.* As בַּשֵּׁנִי cannot well (comp. Luther, etc.) signify "on the second day," for this would be expressed by בִּשְׁנַיִם לַחֹדֶשׁ or the like (with the cardinal number), it is strongly to be suspected that the word has come into the text by an error of transcription; comp. Crit. Note. The second month is Ziph, corresponding nearly with our May (comp. 1 Kings vi. 37).—*In the fourth year of his reign*, that is, as Solomon reigned from 1015, about the year 1012 B.C. (comp. Hitzig, *Gesch.* p. 10 f., whose chronological determinations otherwise contain much that is arbitrary; among other things, the assumption that Solomon reigned from 1035 B.C., thus, on the whole, not forty but sixty years).

2. The building of the Temple itself; and first, of the Porch and the Holy Place (or the Front and Middle Room): vers. 3-7.—*And this is the foundation of Solomon;* these are the fundamental proportions which he employed in building. The *inf. Hoph.* הוּסַד is used substantively, as in Ezra iii. 11.—*The length after the former measure*, the Mosaic or holy cubit, that, Ezek. xl. 5, xliii. 13, was a handbreadth longer than the civic cubit of the later time, in and after the exile (comp. on 1 Chron. xxii. 13 f.). Only the length and the width of the temple are here given, not its height, which was, 1 Kings vi. 2, thirty cubits.—Ver. 4. *And the porch, that was before the length*, that extended in front of the oblong house as its entrance,—*before the breadth of the house, was twenty cubits*, was measured in front of the width of the house, twenty cubits. That the breadth or depth of this porch was not twenty cubits, but only ten (1 Kings vi. 3), is not here said, but follows of necessity from the following statements concerning the size of the most holy place compared with that of the holy place, which was twice as long (comp. ver. 3 with ver. 8).—*And the height a hundred and twenty.* A certainly erroneous statement; a front building of 120 cubits height, before a house only thirty cubits high, could not be called אוּלָם, but would have been a מִגְדָּל, "tower" (Keil). Behind the present defective reading is perhaps concealed the statement that the breadth of the porch was ten cubits. Berth. and Kamph. wish to arrange the text after 1 Kings vi. 3: "And the porch, which was before the house, its breadth was ten cubits before it, and the length, which was before the breadth of the house, was twenty cubits." But there are some objections to this emendation; see Keil, p. 235 (Remark 1).—Ver. 5. *And the great house he lined with cypress.* The holy place is called the great house, as forming the chief room of the whole house. "Line," חִפָּה, coinciding essentially with the foregoing צִפָּה, "overlay," stands here twice, first of lining the stone with wood, and then of overlaying or plating this wood with gold.—*Made thereon palms and garlands*, applied to it ornaments of palms and garlands (according to 1 Kings vi. 18, in the form of bas-reliefs cut in the panels of the wall). תִּמֹּרִים = the fem. תִּמֹּרוֹת used in the same sense, 1 Kings vi. 29, 35, figures of palms; this masc. form occurs also Ezek. xli. 28. שַׁרְשְׁרוֹת, properly, chains of gold wire,—see ver. 16 and Ex. xxviii. 14,—but here ornaments wound like a chain on the gilded walls, representing garlands.—Ver. 6. *And he garnished the house with precious stones for beauty;* comp. 1 Chron. xxix. 2, and Bähr on 1 Kings vi. 7.—*And the gold was gold of Parvaim*, from Parvaim, a country, as the etymon of the probable Indian name seems to indicate, situated in the east, but of unknown, and not to be determined, site. On its conjectured identity with Ophir, and the opinions regarding it, see the excursus after ch. viii.—Ver. 7. *And he overlaid the house, the beams*, those of the ceiling, as those next named, the sills that are under the doors. Somewhat more precise than the present statements concerning the internal decorations of the house (the holy place with its porch, which are here in question, as ver. 8 ff. show) are those contained in 1 Kings vi. 18, 29, 30.

3. The Most Holy Place, with its Cherubic Figures and Veil: vers. 8-14.—*And he made the house of the most holy, that its length . . . twenty cubits.* That, besides the length and breadth, the height also was the same, and thus its form was cubic, see 1 Kings vi. 20. Our author does not specially set forth this certainly symbolic circumstance; on the contrary, his love of the ornamental and magnificent leads him to set forth another circumstance omitted in 1 Kings, that the weight of the gold plating for the inner wall of the most holy place was 600 talents.—Ver. 9. *And the weight of the nails*, that served for fastening the gold plate on the wooden lining of the walls. And this statement concerning the weight of the nails being fifty shekels is peculiar to our author, and characteristic of him; as also the following one in *b*, concerning the inner gilding of the upper chambers over the most holy place (comp. 1 Chron. xxviii. 11).—Ver. 10. *Two cherubim of sculptured work*, literally, "a work of imagery." צַעֲצֻעִים, from the Arab. root *zua*, *finxit, formavit*, only here in the O. T.—*Overlaid them with gold*, a remark occurring also 1 Kings vi. 28, but there forming the end of the description of the cherubim.—Vers. 10-12. The description of the size and position of the four outspread wings, each five cubits long, is clumsy and circumstantial, after the Eastern fashion, but at the same time perfectly obvious and clear. The expressions for the mutual contact of the tips of the wings are הִגִּיעַ and (once ver. 12) דָבֵק, properly; cleave, *adhærere.*—Ver. 13. *The wings of these cherubim spread forth twenty cubits*, literally, "were spreading forth (effected

an expansion of) twenty cubits;" comp. on פֹּרְשׂ, 1 Chron. xxviii. 18; 2 Chron. v. 8. Against Berth., who would expel כַּנְפֵי out of the text; see Keil on this passage.—*Stood on their feet, and their faces to the house*, that is, to the holy place, not to one another, as the faces of the cherubs on the mercy-seat (Ex. xxv. 20). That they had in this upright position a height of ten cubits, the author of 1 Kings (vi. 26) affirms in his more exact statement of the proportions. Are we entitled to infer from the statement of our author the human form of the cherubim? This appears at all events very probable; comp. Bähr on 1 Kings vi. 23 ff., and Riehm, "Die Cherubim in der Stiftshütte und im Tempel," *Theol. Stud. und Krit.* 1871, iii. p. 399 ff., where (as in the treatise *De natura et notione symbolica cheruborum*, 1864) this theologian certainly, for the oldest time, conceives the cherubim as theophanic storm-clouds, and represents them in the form of birds, but, for the latter time (and certainly for that of Solomon), affirms a change of this prey-bird form to a winged human form. Similarly H. Schultz, *Alttestamentl. Theol.* i. 337 ff., and Dillmann, Art. "Cherubim" in Schenkel's *Bibel-Lexikon*.—Ver. 14. *And he made the veil of blue, and purple*, etc., thus of the same four materials of which the veil in the tabernacle had been made, and interwoven with the same cherubic figures as it was; see Ex. xxvi. 31. On this פָּרֹכֶת, the inner veil between the holy and the most holy place, the older description of the temple in 1 Kings vi. 21 says nothing.

4. The Two Pillars Jachin and Boaz: vers. 15–17; comp. the much fuller description in 1 Kings vii. 15–22, 41, 42 (also ch. iv. 12 f.).—*And he made before the house* (in the porch) *two pillars of thirty and five cubits height;* in 1 Kings, rather of eighteen cubits; see Crit. Note.—*And the capital that was on the top.* Instead of the הַצֶּפֶת, head-piece (from צפה, cover, overlay), the parallel 1 Kings vii. 16 gives the term כֹּתֶרֶת, "crown, pommel."—Ver. 16. *And he made chains in the ring*, in the girdle-formed network encircling the top of the pillars, that served for the fastening of the pomegranates, and is otherwise called שְׂבָכָה, network, but here רָבִיד, collar (comp. Gen. xli. 42; Ezek. xvi. 11); for רָבִיד is certainly to be read instead of דְּבִיר, which gives no tolerable sense, and has drawn away the old translations to strange explanations (Vulg.: *quasi catenulas in oraculo;* Syr. and Arab.: "chains of fifty cubits length," that is, reaching from the most holy place to the pillars, etc.); comp. the Crit. Note. Moreover, the term רָבִיד seems to be a synonym rather of the שְׂבָכָה, network, mentioned ch. iv. 12, 13, than of the גֻּלּוֹת, "balls, rolls," mentioned in the same place (against Keil).—*Made a hundred pomegranates, and put them on the chains*, perhaps so "that there was an apple on every link of the chain-like ornament" (Berth.). The number 100, which is given also in Jer. lii. 23, determines also merely the one of the two rows of pomegranates which hung on every ring or girdle of the network. That each of these bore 100 apples, and thus the sum total of all the apples on both pillars amounted to 400, is stated ch. iv. 13, in accordance with 1 Kings vii. 42. On ver. 17, especially on the names Jachin and Boaz, see Bähr on 1 Kings vii. 21.

5. The Holy Furniture of the Temple and its Court: ch. iv. 1–10.—Ver. 1. The brazen altar. *And he made an altar of brass*, the altar of burnt-offering. See more particularly concerning its construction, more exactly described in Ezek. xliii. 13–17, and its probably terrace-like appearance, in Keil, *Archæol.* p. 127, with the plan, plate iii. fig. 2. That our verse has no parallel in 1 Kings vi. and vii. is perhaps only accidental, but may arise from this, that there only articles made by Huram (Hiram) are fully described, to which the altar of burnt-offering did not belong. It is, moreover, only incidentally mentioned in 1 Kings, namely, in ch. viii. 22, 64, on occasion of the dedication of the temple, and again in ch. ix. 25.—Vers. 2–5. The Brazen Sea; comp. 1 Kings vii. 23–26 and the expositors thereon.—*A line of thirty cubits compassed it about*, formed the measure of its circumference (the actual existence of such a line is not to be supposed).—Ver. 3. *And figures of oxen were under it*, instead of which 1 Kings vii. 24 has: "and colocynths (or flower buds, according to Bähr) were under the brim of it round about." Our בְּקָרִים therefore appears an error of transcription for פְּקָעִים, as in the second member הַבָּקָר for הַפְּקָעִים.—Ver. 5. *Holding in it* (many) *baths; it contained three thousand.* According to 1 Kings vii. 26, rather only 2000, which number alone suits the size of the vessel as described in ver. 2 (comp. Crit. Note). Moreover, the יָכִיל, "it contained," is by no means disturbing, as Berth. and Kamph. think, who condemn it as a gloss coming into the text from 1 Kings. The pleonastic phrase rather suits the effort of the author to represent the size of the vessel as very great; and the construction is essentially the same as in the following verse.—Ver. 6. The Ten Lavers, with the incidental Statement of the Use of the Brazen Sea.—*And he made ten lavers.* Much more full is 1 Kings vii. 27–38, where the stands bearing these lavers are described with special minuteness.—*To wash in them; the work of the burnt-offering they washed in them*, the flesh of the burnt-offerings to be burned on the altar. On הֵדִיחַ, scour, rinse, as a synonym of רחץ, comp. Josh. iv. 4; Ezek. xl. 38.—Ver. 7. The Golden Candlesticks in the Holy Place. The notice of these is wanting, as well as the following one referring to the ten tables, and the next referring to the two courts, in the parallel text 1 Kings vii. 39, perhaps from a gap in the text. Yet incidental references to these objects are found there; see ch. vi. 36, vii. 12, 48, 49.—*After their plan*, properly, according to their right, כְּמִשְׁפָּטָם, a reference to Ex. xxv. 31 ff.—Ver. 8. *And he made ten tables*, on which to place the ten candlesticks, scarcely for the shew-bread, as seems to follow from ver. 19; see rather on this passage, as on 1 Chron. xxviii. 16 (against Lightfoot), Starke, Bähr, Keil, etc.—*And he made*

basins of gold, bowls or tankards for pouring the libation; comp. Amos vi. 6; scarcely bowls for receiving the blood of the victim (as Berth. thinks).—Ver. 9. *And he made the courts of the priests*, the smaller or inner court (1 Kings vi. 36, vii. 12), or also the upper court, as it is called, Jer. xxxvi. 10, on account of its greater elevation.—*And the great court*, the outer (הָעֲזָרָה connected with חצר); comp. Ezek. xliii. 14 ff., xlv. 19, where it is distinguished as the "lower" or "new" court, from the inner or upper court of the priests. A more precise description of this outer court is wanting as well in 1 Kings vi. and vii., where it is not even mentioned, as in our passage, where only its door leaves overlaid with brass are mentioned.—Ver. 10. Addendum concerning the Position of the Brazen Sea; comp. 1 Kings vii. 39*b*.

6. The Brass Works of Huram: vers. 11–18. The list is opened with the "pots, shovels, and bowls," objects belonging to the furniture of the altar of burnt-offering in the court, that belong properly to the foregoing section. Even so 1 Kings vii. 40, where likewise with וַיְכַל in the middle of the verse we pass to all that was made by Huram.—*The pots, and the shovels, and the bowls.* הַסִּירוֹת (for which 1 Kings vii. 40, defectively: הַכִּירוֹת) are the pots for taking away the ashes; הַיָּעִים, the shovels for removing the ashes from the altar; הַמִּזְרָקוֹת (perhaps to be distinguished from מִזְרָקִים, the sprinkling-bowls or wine tankards in ver. 8*b*), the bowls for receiving and sprinkling the blood.—*And Huram finished the work.* Comp. from this to the end of the section the almost literally agreeing verses 1 Kings vii. 40*b*–47, and Bähr on the passage. For the partial deviations and errors in our text, see Crit. Note.—Ver. 16. *And all their vessels.* Most recent expositors (also Keil) wish to read, after 1 Kings vii. 45: "all these vessels," אֶת כָּל־הַכֵּלִים הָאֵלֶּה, because we cannot think in the "vessels" of the vessels hitherto named. But might not the forms (models) be meant in which the various vessels were cast? The allusion to the foundries of the king in the next verse makes this very probable; but the reading הָאֵלֶּה in 1 Kings vii. 45 appears by no means absolutely settled.—*Made Huram his father.* For אָבִיו, see on ch. ii. 12.—*Of bright brass,* נְחֹשֶׁת מָרוּק, *accus. materiæ;* in 2 Kings the equivalent נְחֹשֶׁת מְמֹרָט stands for this.—Ver. 17. *In the plain of Jordan* (properly, in the circuit of Jordan) *the king cast them, in the clay ground,* properly, "in the densities of the ground," בַּעֲבִי הָאֲדָמָה (or, if the reading בְּעֳבִי is to be preferred, sing.: in the density of the ground; ἐν τῷ πάχει τῆς γῆς, Sept.). According to the older exegesis, the phrase denoted: in the clay ground, *in argillosa terra* (Vulg.). The designation of the hard forms for the casting, which Berth. thinks are mentioned here, should rather be the כָּל־כְּלֵיהֶם of ver. 16.—*Between Succoth and Zeredathah.* In 1 Kings vii. 46 the name of the second place is Zarthan, which is only another form of Zeredathah; comp. Judg. vii. 22.—Ver. 18. *For the weight of the brass was not found out,* or was not determined (Berth.); that is, there was so great a quantity, that, etc. (comp. ch. v. 6).

7. Enumeration of the Golden Vessels of the Sanctuary, with the Close of the whole Account of the Building: ver. 19–ch. v. 1; comp. 1 Kings vii. 48–51, which section also deviates much in its first verses from the present one.—*And the tables with the shew-bread on them.* Originally, perhaps, only an inexact expression (synecdoche), as in 1 Chron. xxviii. 16, this mention of the שֻׁלְחָנוֹת has here certainly the appearance of a multiplicity of tables for the shew-bread. But 1 Kings vii. 48 names quite distinctly only one table.—Ver. 20. *And the candlesticks . . . to burn after their rule* (כַּמִּשְׁפָּט, as ver. 7) *before the oracle*, the "debir," that is, the most holy place. The candlesticks had accordingly their place in the holy place immediately before the veil; and so the altar of incense (comp. Heb. ix. 4).—Ver. 21. *And the flowers, and the lamps.* Comp. Bähr on 1 Kings vii. 49.—*This was the most perfect gold.* מִכְלוֹת זָהָב, properly, "perfections of gold"; the elsewhere not occurring מִכְלוֹת (equivalent to מִכְלָל, Ps. l. 2, or מִכְלוֹל, Ezek. xxiii. 12) appears unintelligible to the Sept., and hence the whole clause is omitted. As it appears superfluous along with the costly gold at the close of the verse before, and is wanting in 1 Kings vii. 49, it awakens critical suspicion.—Ver. 22. *And the knives*, serving perhaps to clean the lamps (with the snuffers), but also for other purposes. Their place among the vessels of the temple is attested also by 2 Kings xii. 14; Jer. lii. 18. For the next named bowls see on ver. 11. The כַּפּוֹת (trays for the incense) and מַחְתּוֹת (extinguishers) are also named 1 Kings vii. 50: on the contrary, the סִפּוֹת (basons) named there first are wanting here.—*And the door of the house.* וּפֶתַח הַבַּיִת appears to be a general collective phrase for the "opening, doorway, outlet of the house;" for it includes two doors, that into the holy place, and that into the holy of holies. The parallel 1 Kings vii. 50: וְהַפֹּתוֹת לְדַלְתוֹת הַבַּיִת, leads to the conjecture that וּפֶתַח is perhaps an error for וּפֹתוֹת, "and the hinges" (in which case also לְדַלְתוֹתָיו must be put for דַּלְתוֹתָיו). Ch. v. 1 agrees almost to the letter with 1 Kings vii. 51. The ו before אֶת־הַכֶּסֶף is best rendered by "namely"; comp. ch. iv. 19; less probable is the rendering: "as well the silver as also the gold" (Keil). For these gifts of David, see the account in 1 Chron. xviii. 10 f.; also 1 Chron. xxvi. 26 f., xxix. 3 ff.

γ. *The Dedication of the Temple:* ch. v. 2–vii. 10.

1. *Removal of the Ark from Zion to the Temple:* ch. v. 2–14.

2 Then Solomon assembled the elders of Israel, and all the heads of the tribes,
the chiefs of the fathers of the sons of Israel, to Jerusalem, to bring up the ark
3 of the covenant of the LORD from the city of David, which is Zion. And all
the men of Israel assembled unto the king in the feast, which was the seventh
4 month. And all the elders of Israel came; and the Levites bore the ark.
5 And they brought up the ark and the tent of meeting, and all the holy vessels
6 that were in the tent; the priests, the Levites,[1] brought them up. And king
Solomon, and all the assembly of Israel that assembled with him before the ark,
sacrificed sheep and oxen, that could not be told or numbered for multitude.
7 And the priests brought the ark of the covenant of the LORD into its place, into
the oracle of the house, the most holy place, under the wings of the cherubim.
8 For the cherubim spread forth their wings over the place of the ark, and the
9 cherubim covered the ark and its staves above. And they made the staves so
long that the ends of the staves were seen from the ark,[2] before the oracle, but
10 they were not seen without: and they were there unto this day. Nothing was in
the ark save the two tables, which Moses put into it at Horeb, where the LORD
11 made [a covenant] with the sons of Israel, when they came out of Egypt. And it
came to pass, when the priests came out of the holy place—for all the priests
12 that were present had sanctified themselves, without observing the courses. And
the Levites, the singers all of them, Asaph, Heman, and Jeduthun, and their
sons and brethren, arrayed in byssus, with cymbals, and psalteries, and harps,
stood at the east of the altar, and with them a hundred and twenty priests
13 sounding with trumpets.[3] And the trumpeters and singers were as one [man] to
sound aloud with one voice to praise and thank the LORD, and when they lifted
up the voice with trumpets, and cymbals, and instruments of song, and with
praising the LORD: For He is good; for His mercy endureth for ever: then the
14 house was filled with the cloud of the house of the LORD. And the priests
could not stand to minister before the cloud; for the glory of the LORD filled the
house of God.

2. *Solomon praises the Lord on his Entrance into the new Temple:* ch. vi. 1–11.

CH. VI. 1. Then said Solomon, The LORD hath said that He would dwell in dark-
2 ness. And I, even I, have built a house of abiding for Thee, and a place for Thy
dwelling for ever.
3 And the king turned his face, and blessed the whole congregation of Israel:
4 and all the congregation of Israel stood. And he said, Blessed be the LORD
God of Israel, who hath spoken with His mouth to David my father, and by His
5 hands hath fulfilled it, saying, From the day that I brought my people out of
the land of Egypt, I chose no city among all the tribes of Israel to build a
house, that my name might be there; and I chose no man to be ruler over my
6 people Israel. And I chose Jerusalem, that my name might be there; and I
7 chose David to be over my people Israel. And it was in the heart of David my
8 father to build a house to the name of the LORD God of Israel. And the LORD
said to David my father, Because it was in thy heart to build a house to my
9 name, thou hast done well that it was in thy heart. But thou shalt not build
the house; but thy son, that cometh forth out of thy loins, he shall build to my
10 name. And the LORD hath established His word that He hath spoken; and I
am risen up instead of David my father, and am set on the throne of Israel, as
the LORD hath spoken; and I have built the house to the name of the LORD God
11 of Israel. And there I have put the ark, wherein is the covenant of the Lord
that He made with the children of Israel.

3. *Solomon's Prayer of Dedication:* ch. vi. 12–42.

12 And he stood before the altar of the LORD, before all the congregation of

13 Israel, and spread forth his hands. For Solomon had made a scaffold of brass,
and set it in the midst of the [outer] court; its length was five cubits, its breadth
five cubits, and its height three cubits; and he stood upon it, and kneeled down
on his knees before all the congregation of Israel, and spread forth his hands
14 towards heaven, And said, LORD God of Israel, there is no God like Thee in
the heaven nor in the earth, who keepest the covenant and the mercy unto Thy
15 servants that walk before Thee with all their heart. Who hast kept with Thy
servant David that which Thou hast spoken to him; and Thou speakest with Thy
16 mouth, and hast fulfilled it with Thy hand, as it is this day. And now, LORD
God of Israel, keep with Thy servant David my father that which Thou hast
spoken to him, saying, There shall not be cut off from thee a man in my sight to
sit upon the throne of Israel, only if thy sons take heed to their way to walk in
17 my law, as thou hast walked before me. And now, LORD God of Israel, let Thy
18 word be verified which Thou hast spoken unto Thy servant David. But will
God in truth dwell with men on the earth? Behold, heaven, and the heaven of
19 heavens, cannot contain Thee; how much less this house which I have built! But
have respect unto the prayer of Thy servant, and to his supplication, O LORD my
God, to hearken unto the cry and the prayer which Thy servant prayeth before
20 Thee. That Thine eyes may be open upon this house day and night, to the
place where Thou hast said that Thou wilt put Thy name; to hearken unto the
21 prayer which Thy servant prayeth in this place. And hearken unto the suppli-
cation of Thy servant and of Thy people Israel, which they shall make in this
place, and hear Thou from Thy dwelling-place, from heaven; yea, hear, and for-
22 give. If a man sin against his neighbours, and he lay on him an oath to make
23 him swear, and he enter into an oath before Thine altar in this house: Then
hear Thou from heaven, and do, and judge Thy servants, to requite the wicked,
and bring his way upon his own head; and to justify the righteous, and give him
24 according to his righteousness. And if Thy people Israel be smitten before the
enemy, because they have sinned against Thee, and shall return and confess Thy
25 name, and pray and entreat before Thee in this house: Then hear Thou from
heaven, and forgive the sin of Thy people Israel, and bring them again unto the
26 land which Thou gavest to them and to their fathers. When the heaven is shut
up, and there is no rain, because they have sinned against Thee, and they pray in
this place, and confess Thy name, and turn from their sin, because Thou dost
27 humble them: Then hear Thou from heaven, and forgive the sin of Thy servants
and of Thy people Israel, because Thou teachest them the good way in which
they should walk, and send rain upon the land which Thou hast given unto Thy
28 people for an inheritance. If there be dearth in the land, if there be pestilence,
blasting, or mildew, locust or waster; if their enemies besiege them in the land
29 of their gates; if there be any plague or sickness. Every prayer, every suppli-
cation that shall be made by any man or by all Thy people Israel, when they
shall know every man his own plague and his own pain, and shall spread his
30 hands to this house: Then hear Thou from heaven, Thy dwelling-place, and
forgive, and render unto every man according to all his ways, as Thou knowest
31 his heart; for Thou alone knowest the heart of the sons of man. That they
may fear Thee to walk in Thy ways, all the days that they live on the ground
32 which Thou gavest to our fathers. And also to the stranger, who is not of Thy
people Israel, but cometh from a far country for sake of Thy great name and
Thy mighty hand, and Thy outstretched arm; if they come and pray towards
33 this house: Then hear Thou[4] from the heaven, from Thy dwelling-place, and do
all that the stranger calleth to Thee for, that all peoples of the earth may know Thy
name, and fear Thee as Thy people Israel, and may know that Thy name is called
34 upon this house which I have built. If Thy people go out to war against their
enemies in the way that Thou shalt send them, and they pray unto Thee toward
this city which Thou hast chosen, and the house which I have built to Thy name:
35 Then hear Thou from the heaven their prayer and their supplication, and main-
36 tain their right. If they sin against Thee, for there is no man that sinneth not,
and Thou be angry with them, and give them up before their enemies, and their

37 captors take them to a far or near land. And they turn their heart in the land
in which they are captive, and turn and pray unto Thee in the land of their
38 captivity, saying, We have sinned, we have been wrong and wicked. And
they return to Thee with all their heart, and with all their soul, in the land of
their captivity, whither they have taken them, and pray toward the land which
Thou gavest to their fathers, and the city which Thou hast chosen, and toward
39 the house which I have built to Thy name: Then hear Thou from the heaven,
from Thy dwelling-place, their prayer and their supplication, and maintain their
40 right, and forgive Thy people who have sinned against Thee. Now, my God,
let Thine eyes now be open, and Thine ears attent unto the prayer of this place.
41 And now arise, O LORD God, unto Thy rest, Thou and the ark of Thy strength:
let Thy priests, O LORD God, be clothed with salvation, and let Thy saints be
42 glad for the good. O LORD God, turn not away the face of Thy anointed; remember the mercies of David Thy servant.

4. *The Divine Confirmation of the Dedication of the Temple:* ch. vii. 1–10.

CH. VII. 1. And when Solomon had ended [his] prayer, the fire came down from
heaven and consumed the burnt-offering and the sacrifices; and the glory of the
2 LORD filled the house. And the priests could not enter the house of the LORD,
3 because the glory of the LORD filled the house of the LORD. And all the sons
of Israel saw the fire come down, and the glory of the LORD upon the house, and
they bowed down their faces to the ground on the pavement, and worshipped and
4 praised the LORD; for He is good; for His mercy endureth for ever. And the
5 king and all the people offered sacrifices before the LORD. And king Solomon
offered a sacrifice of twenty and two thousand oxen, and a hundred and twenty
thousand sheep; and the king and all the people dedicated the house of God.
6 And the priests stood at their posts, and the Levites with instruments of song of
the LORD, which David the king had made, to thank the LORD, that His mercy
endureth for ever, when David praised by their hand; and the priests blew the
7 trumpets[5] before them, and all Israel stood. And Solomon hallowed the middle
of the court that was before the house of the LORD; for there he offered the
burnt-offerings and the fat of the peace-offerings: because the brazen altar which
Solomon had made was not able to receive the burnt-offerings, and the meat-
8 offerings, and the fat. And Solomon kept the feast at that time seven days, and
all Israel with him, a very great congregation, from Hamath to the river of
9 Egypt. And they made on the eighth day a solemn assembly; for they kept the
10 dedication of the altar seven days, and the feast seven days. And in the twenty
and third day of the seventh month he sent away the people to their tents, glad
and merry in heart for the goodness that the LORD had shown to David, and to
Solomon, and to Israel his people.

[1] Before הַלְוִיִּם is to be supplied וְ, according to 1 Kings viii. 4.

[2] מִן־הָאָרוֹן appears to be an error of transcription for מִן־הַקֹּדֶשׁ.

[3] *Kethib:* מְחַצְּצְרִים; *Keri:* מַחְצְרִים; so ver. 13 and ch. vii. 6. Comp. Exeg. Expl. on 1 Chron. xv. 24.

[4] וְאַתָּה, supported by all the witnesses, Bertheau, without reason, changes into אַתָּה (after 1 Kings viii. 43).

[5] *Keri:* מחצרים, as above, ch. v. 12, 13.

EXEGETICAL.

PRELIMINARY REMARK.—The first three sections or acts of this account agree with the parallel 1 Kings viii., mostly to the letter; only a notice referring to the part of the priests, Levites, and singers in the solemnity in vi. 11–13 is peculiar to our author. In the fourth section (vii. 1–10) is found the more considerable deviation, that instead of the blessing pronounced by Solomon on the community of Israel (1 Kings viii. 54–61), the consuming of the offerings by fire from heaven is narrated (vii. 1–3; comp. the similar account in the history of the census and the plague, 1 Chron. xxi. 26 f.).

1. Removal of the Ark from Zion to the Temple: ch. v. 2–14; comp. 1 Kings viii. 1–11 (and thereon, Bähr, *Bibelw.* vii. 72 ff.).—Ver. 3. *In the feast, which was the seventh month.* According to 1 Kings, the statement: "in the month Ethanim," appears to have fallen out before these words, though also הַחֹדֶשׁ might be a mistake for בַּחֹדֶשׁ, "in the seventh month."—

Ver. 5. The supplement of a ו between הכהנים and הלוים (see Crit. Note) seems indispensable; "for even if Levitical priests bore the ark and the holy vessels of the tabernacle into the temple, yet it is certain that the tabernacle itself (its boards, curtains, and coverings) was not conveyed by the priests, but only by the Levites, into the temple to be preserved as sacred relics. The copula ו is perhaps left out only by a copyist, who thought of הכהנים הלוים, Josh. iii. 3; Deut. xvii. 9, 18" (Keil).—Ver. 10. *The two tables which Moses put into it at Horeb*, properly, "gave," נָתַן, as Ex. xl. 20. More clear and full is the parallel text 1 Kings viii. 9: אֲשֶׁר הִנִּיחַ שָׁם, "which he had put there."—Ver. 11. *For all the priests that were present had sanctified themselves.* These words begin the longer parenthesis inserted by the Chronist in the statement, 1 Kings viii. 10, concerning the priests, Levites, and singers, which extends to ver. 13*b*. "That were present," literally, "that were found"; comp. 1 Chron. xxix. 17; Ezra viii. 25.—*Without observing the courses;* that is, on account of the greatness of the solemnity, and the multitude of persons required, the series of exchanging courses of the priests (1 Chron. xxiv.) could not be observed; all the courses must together sanctify themselves and co-operate. For the construction אֵין לִשְׁמוֹר, comp. 1 Chron. xxiii. 26; Ew. § 321, *b*.—Ver. 12. *All of them, Asaph*, etc., properly, "as to all, Asaph," etc.; the introductory לְ, as 1 Chron. v. 25 (see on this passage).—*Sounding with trumpets.* For מַחְצְרִים, see on 1 Chron. xv. 24; comp. also the remarks on the temple musicians and their instruments, 1 Chron. xv. 17–28.—Ver. 13. *And the trumpeters and singers were as one man*, literally, "and it came to pass as one concerning the trumpeters and singers (לְ, as before), that they sounded loud with one voice." For the construction הָיָה לְהַשְׁמִיעַ, comp. Ew. § 237, and on the import of הִשְׁמִיעַ, 1 Chron. xv. 16. The קוֹל אֶחָד, "with one voice," is properly redundant, but is added to the לְהַשְׁמִיעַ to strengthen the notion already lying in אֶחָד, "one" of the *unisono* of the trumpet sound, and the singing of the many voices.—*When they lifted up the voice*, literally, "and as the lifting of the voice"; comp. Ezra iii. 12, ix. 1. The words connect again with ver. 11*a*, and so prepare for the conclusion, which, however, is formed by the last words of the verse: *Then the house was filled with the cloud of the house of the Lord*, the well-known light-cloud (shechinah) dwelling in the tabernacle since the time of Moses, the manifestation of the gracious presence of God in His covenant sanctuary. For ver. 14, comp. 1 Kings viii. 11, and Bähr thereon.

2. Solomon praises the Lord on his Entrance into the new temple: ch. vi. 1–11; agreeing almost literally with 1 Kings viii. 12–21.—We notice some of the never very important deviations of our text.—On ver. 1, comp. Lev. xvi. 1.—Ver. 2. *And I, even I, have built*, etc. Instead of וַאֲנִי בָּנִיתִי, with its emphatic accentuation of the subject, 1 Kings viii. 13 gives בָּנֹה בָנִיתִי, "I have surely built," etc.—Ver. 4. *Blessed be the Lord . . . who hath spoken with His mouth*, etc., a reference to 1 Chron. xi. 2, which promise is here repeated with great fulness, resting indeed on the words of Nathan contained in 1 Chron. xvii. 4–14, to which allusion is made, especially from ver. 8.—Ver. 5. *From the day that I brought my people*, etc. From this to ver. 7, the speech of Solomon, compared with 1 Kings viii. 16 f., appears enlarged, especially by the sentences there wanting, ver. 5*b*: "and I chose no man to be ruler," etc., and ver. 6*a*: "and I chose Jerusalem."—Ver. 11. *And there I have put the ark.* Somewhat otherwise 1 Kings viii. 21: "And I have set there a place for the ark" (מְקוֹם הָאָרוֹן for the simple הארון).

3. Solomon's Prayer of Consecration: vers. 12–42; except the introduction, ver. 13, and the close, vers. 40–42, very closely agreeing with 1 Kings viii. 22–53.—Ver. 13. *For Solomon had made a scaffold of brass.* This whole parenthesis, with the notice concerning the brazen scaffold (properly, "basin," כִּיּוֹר, pot-shaped elevation, platform; comp. Neh. ix. 4) in the court, is wanting in 1 Kings; whether omitted by an old error of the transcriber, as Then. and Berth. think, must remain doubtful.—Ver. 21. *And hear Thou from Thy dwelling-place, from heaven*, for which 1 Kings viii. 30: "hear to Thy dwelling-place, to heaven," perhaps by a mistake in copying.—Ver. 33. *Then hear Thou*, literally, "and Thou hear"; the ו before אַתָּה, introducing the conclusion, is wanting in 1 Kings viii. 43, for which reason Berth. would here also exclude it from the text, contrary to all the MSS.—Vers. 40–42 form a close of the speech of Solomon, deviating greatly from 1 Kings viii. 50–53. Of the allusion there to the deliverance of Israel, as the heritage of the Lord, from the iron furnace of Egypt, and of the promises given by Moses (vers. 51, 53), there is here nothing. On the contrary, the petition there: "Let Thine eyes be open," etc. (ver. 52), is here notably enlarged and strengthened by the important summons: "Now, arise . . . unto Thy rest, Thou and the ark of Thy strength." This summons to the solemn and formal taking possession of the temple, to which the following narrative of the fire coming down on the sacrifice corresponds, is justly declared by Thenius to be original, and defended against the assumption that it is an arbitrary addition made by the Chronist (Berth., etc.); for, in consequence of the absence of this summons to take possession of the sanctuary, the point of the whole prayer is wanting in 1 Kings viii., and the suspicion is raised that there some lines have fallen out at the end. Yet, in respect of form, our author, in his rendering of the close of the prayer, might have rested partly on other old documents, particularly on Ps. cxxxii. 8–10, a passage which coincides almost verbally with vers. 41, 42 (but possibly also the Psalmist might have borrowed from the original edition of Solomon's prayer, correctly retained in our passage), and on Isa. lv. 3, where "the mercies of David" occur, coinciding verbally with our passage (ver. 42*b*), and intended,

indeed, in the same sense (denoting the Lord's merciful dealings with David, not David's pious deeds, as Keil thinks); comp. also Ps. lxxxix. 50.—*And now arise, O Lord God, to Thy rest,* enter now the rest to which the throne of Thy glory has attained. נוּחַ for מְנוּחָה, only elsewhere in Esth. ix. 16–18, and there in the form נוֹחַ; comp. also Num. x. 36: בְּנֻחֹה, as there is here a significant accord with the words of Moses referring to the setting out and resting of the ark in the wilderness.—*And let Thy saints be glad for the good* (בַּטּוֹב, as Job xx. 18; Ps. civ. 28). The parallel Ps. cxxxii. 9 has here more briefly: "and let Thy saints shout for joy" (יְרַנֵּנוּ for יִשְׂמְחוּ בַטּוֹב).—Ver. 42. *Turn not away the face of Thine anointed,* refuse not his prayer; comp. 1 Kings ii. 16. For the "mercies of David," see above.

4. The Divine Confirmation of the Dedication of the Temple: ch. vii. 1–10. The first part of this section, vers. 1–3, is wanting in 1 Kings viii.; the second, except ver. 6, which is there wanting, agrees almost verbally with 1 Kings viii. 62–66. —*And when Solomon . . . the fire came down from heaven.* Both this account of the descent of a miraculous fire from heaven consuming the sacrifice, and that of the filling of the house with the glory of the Lord, along with the adoring worship of the whole community before God wonderfully manifesting Himself, are peculiar to the Chronist. In 1 Kings viii. 54–61, instead of this is found an address of Solomon to the assembly, with the expression of thanks to God for His goodness to Israel, and the petition for the further manifestation of His mercy and grace. The difference, that our author relates something miraculous on which the books of Kings are silent, is similar to that in the history of the census and the pestilence, 1 Chron. xxi. 26. Yet the earlier account of the miraculous filling of the house with the glory of God (v. 11–14) is also found in the author of 1 Kings viii. 10. Thus both narratives agree in attesting a miraculous appearance at the temple dedication; but that of the older writer places this wonder before the prayer of Solomon, without placing a second miracle at the end of this prayer, whereas the Chronist reports a twofold coming of glory of the Lord, the first before the prayer, the second after it, and connected with the consuming of the offering by heavenly fire (or, as it may be supposed, with Keil, consisting in this operation of fire). Arbitrary reduplication of the miracle that had already taken place according to the oldest record and shaping of the supposed second wonder according to the model from the Mosaic time, Lev. ix. 23 f., are charged by modern criticism (Then., Berth., Kamph., etc.) against the Chronist or the younger narrative adopted by him. But it may at least be assumed that the tendency of the Chronist to the history of worship was the occasion of his mentioning the second wonder, whereas the author of the books of Kings, in accordance with his attention to the history of the kingdom, took less interest in this. It was scarcely abhorrence of the miraculous, or preference of the natural and conceivable, on the part of the latter, that led him to avoid the account of the miraculous consuming of the offering; comp. his account of the corresponding wonder in the history of Elijah (1 Kings xviii.), on which our author is silent on other grounds; and see, moreover, Evangelical and Ethical Reflections after ch. ix., No. 3.—*And consumed the burnt-offering and the sacrifices,* the offerings mentioned ch. v. 6, which the king and the people had slain at the entrance of the ark in the temple, and which were slain during the prayer of dedication, but not yet burnt, partly on the altar of burnt-offering, partly on other altars erected specially for them in the inner courts (ver. 7).—Ver. 3. *And all the sons of Israel saw the fire come down.* So also in the original fact of the Mosaic history, Lev. ix. 24.—*And they bowed down . . . on the pavement.* For this pavement (רִצְפָה) or flooring in the court, that we may not certainly conceive to be mosaic work of ornamental variegated stone, as in the Persian citadel at Susa, Esth. i. 6, comp. Ezek. xl. 17, 18.—Vers. 4–10. The solemnities of sacrifice and festival, even to the addition concerning the musical part in ver. 6, are described in exact accordance with 1 Kings viii. 62 ff., even with regard to the number of the victims offered. For these great but not incredibly great numbers (22,000 oxen and 120,000 sheep), comp. partly the remarks on the great feast at Hebron, 1 Chron. xii. 39, partly the notice justly quoted by Berth. from Josephus, *De bello Jud.* vi. 9. 3, according to which, even in the Roman times, within a few hours, 256,500 passover lambs were slain at Jerusalem. These colossal offerings and festivals exceed our conception quite as much as the numbers attesting the magnitude of the present steam or railway trade, or of the modern warfare, transcend the imagination of the ancients.—Ver. 6. *And the priests stood at their posts,* literally, "watches"; comp. ch. viii. 14, xxxv. 2; the Vulg. rightly in substance: *in officiis suis;* to suppose a standing of the priests according to their divisions (Berth.) is unnecessary.—*When David praised by their hand,* that is, executing the song of praise arranged by David, so that he, as it were, praised God by their musical performance. The Vulg. translate in substance correctly, but somewhat freely: *hymnos David canentes per manus suas* (similarly the Sept.). On the whole verse, comp. the similar but somewhat more diffuse notice of the co-operation of the priests and Levites in the solemnity, ch. v. 11–13.—Ver. 7. *And Solomon hallowed the middle of the court,* "the court immediately before the temple forming the middle of the sacred square" (Then.). This whole inner space had Solomon formed as it were into a great altar of sacrifice, on account of the multitude of offerings to be presented. The notice is plainly supplementary, on which account וַיְקַדֵּשׁ (with the ו relat. of mere sequence of thought) may be rendered by the pluperfect.—Ver. 8. *And Solomon kept the feast at that time,* namely, the feast of tabernacles; comp. Lev. xxiii. 36; Num. xxix. 35 ff. On the now following notes of time, and their greater clearness than those of the parallel 1 Kings viii. 65 f., see Bähr on this passage.—Ver. 10. *He sent away the people to their tents,* that is, their homes; comp. 1 Sam. xiii. 2; Ps. lxxviii. 55; and ch. x. 16 (1 Kings xii. 16).—*For the goodness that the Lord had shown to David and to Solomon.* In 1 Kings viii. 66, "and to Solomon" is wanting; but the arbitrary addition of this expression is not therefore to be charged on the Chronist (against Thenius).

δ. *Revelation of the Lord to Solomon on the Completion of the Temple and his House:* ch. vii. 11–22.

CH. VII. 11. And Solomon finished the house of the LORD, and the king's house; and
in all that came into Solomon's heart to do in the house of the LORD, and in his
12 own house, he succeeded. And the LORD appeared to Solomon by night, and
said to him, I have heard thy prayer, and have chosen this place to myself for a
13 house of sacrifice. If I shut up heaven and there be no rain, or if I command
14 the locust to devour the land, or if I send pestilence among my people. And my
people, on whom my name is called, humble themselves, and pray, and seek my
face, and turn from their wicked ways: then will I hear from heaven, and forgive
15 their sin, and heal their land. Now mine eyes shall be open, and mine ears attent
16 to the prayer of this place. And now I have chosen and sanctified this house,
that my name may be there for ever; and mine eyes and my heart shall be there
17 always. And thou, if thou walk before me, as David thy father walked, and do
according to all that I have commanded thee, and observe my statutes and my
18 judgments: Then will I establish the throne of thy kingdom, as I have
covenanted with David thy father, saying, There shall not be cut off from thee
19 a man to rule in Israel. But if ye [and your children][1] turn away, and forsake my
statutes and my commandments, which I have set before you, and go and serve
20 other gods, and worship them: Then will I pluck them out of my land which I
have given them; and this house, which I have sanctified to my name, will I cast
21 out of my sight, and make it a proverb and a byword among all nations. And
this house, which was high,[2] every passer-by shall be astonished at it, and he
22 shall say, Why hath the LORD done this unto this land and to this house? And
they shall answer, Because they forsook the LORD God of their fathers, who
brought them out of the land of Egypt, and laid hold on other gods, and
worshipped them, and served them: therefore hath He brought all this evil upon
them.

[1] וּבְנֵיהֶם seems to have fallen out after אַתֶּם, not merely according to 1 Kings ix. 6, but according to the suffix of the 3d per. in נְתַשְׁתִּים (and also לָהֶם), ver. 20.

[2] For עֶלְיוֹן, which the Vulg. does not give, and the Pesch. and Arab. render by "desolation," עִיִּים (*ruinæ*) appears to have originally stood in the text; thus instead of אֲשֶׁר־הָיָה עֶלְיוֹן there was probably יִהְיֶה עִיִּים, *ruina fiet.* In the parallel text 1 Kings ix. 8, indeed, עֶלְיוֹן stands, and the Sept. renders our passage: καὶ ὁ οἶκος οὗτος ὁ ὑψηλός.

EXEGETICAL.

The parallel text 1 Kings ix. 1–9 agrees in substance, but often not in words, with our section; in particular, the latter contains some farther extensions and explanations of what is there commanded, and a longer independent addition, ver. 12*b*–ver. 16*a*.

Ver. 11*b*.—*And all that came into Solomon's heart.* This is a paraphrase of וְאֵת־כָּל־חֵשֶׁק שְׁלֹ׳, "and all the desire of Solomon"; comp. also for חֵשֶׁק, desire, viii. 6.—Ver. 12. *The Lord appeared to Solomon by night.* The addition: "the second time, as He had appeared to him at Gibeon," 1 Kings ix. 2, is wanting here. On the contrary, 1 Kings ix. wants all that follows from "have chosen this place for myself" to "have chosen and sanctified this house," ver. 16.—Ver. 13. *If I shut up heaven and there be no rain;* comp. vi. 26, 28, where, among other land plagues, the three here mentioned, drought, locust, and pestilence, are named. The twofold הֵן is here equivalent to the אִם, "if," appearing in the third place; comp. Isa. liv. 15; Jer. iii. 1; Job xl. 23; and see our remark on the latter passage.—Ver. 14. *And my people . . . humble themselves.* Comp. vi. 33; Deut. xxviii. 10; Jer. xv. 16; on ver. 15, comp. vi. 40; on ver. 16, comp. vi. 5, 6.—Ver. 17. *And do according to all,* literally, "to do," etc. The וְ before לַעֲשׂוֹת is redundant, and must apparently be erased according to 1 Kings ix.—Ver. 18. *As I have covenanted with David thy father.* כָּרַתִּי without the object בְּרִית appears to be a mistake for דִּבַּרְתִּי; but comp. v. 10.—*There shall not be cut off from thee a man to rule in Israel.* For this in 1 Kings ix. 5 is: . . . "a man on the throne of Israel." Our מושל בישראל seems to be an unintentional variation of the text there, arising from a recollection of Mic. v. 1.—Ver. 19. *But if ye turn away.* For the necessary supplement of וּבְנֵיכֶם, "and your children," comp. Crit. Note.—Ver. 20. *Then will I pluck them;* נָתַשׁ (for the הִכְרִית in 1 Kings ix. 7) in this sense also Deut. xxix. 27; 1 Kings xiv. 15. For the following: "casting out" of God's sight, comp. Deut. ix. 17, Rev. ii. 5; for a "proverb and a byword among all all nations," Deut. xxviii. 37, Jer. xxiv. 9.—Ver. 21. *And this house, which was high.* In favour of the here probably necessary emendation יִהְיֶה עִיִּים, comp., besides the remark in the Crit. Note, Mic. iii. 12; Jer. xxvi. 18; Ps. lxxix. 1. For the following: "every passer-by shall be astonished," comp. Jer. xviii. 16, xix. 8.—*Why hath the Lord done this.* For בַּמָּה 1 Kings has the more usual and intelligible עַל־מָה.

c. The External Glory of Solomon's Kingdom, and his End.—Ch. viii., ix.

α. Solomon's Building, Serfs, Divine Worship, and Navigation: ch. viii.

Ch. viii. 1. And after the course of twenty years, in which Solomon built the house
2 of the Lord, and his own house. The cities which Huram had given to
Solomon, Solomon built, and caused the sons of Israel to dwell in them.
3, 4 And Solomon went to Hamath-zobah, and subdued it. And he built
Tadmor in the wilderness, and all the cities of stores which he had built in
5 Hamath. And he built Beth-horon the upper, and Beth-horon the nether,
6 fenced cities, with walls, gates, and bars. And Baalath, and all the cities of
stores that Solomon had, and all the chariot-cities and cities of the riders,
and all the desire of Solomon which he desired to build in Jerusalem, and in
Lebanon, and in all the land of his dominion.
7 All the people that were left of the Hittites, and the Amorites, and the
8 Perizzites, and the Hivites, and the Jebusites, who were not of Israel. Of
their sons who were left after them in the land, whom the sons of Israel had
9 not consumed, these Solomon levied for serfs unto this day. But of the sons
of Israel[1] Solomon made none to be servants for his work; but they were
soldiers, and captains of his knights,[2] and captains of his chariots and riders.
10 And these were the chiefs of King Solomon's officers,[3] even two hundred and
fifty, that bare rule over the people.
11 And Solomon brought up the daughter of Pharaoh from the city of David
unto the house that he had built for her: for he said, My wife shall not
dwell in the house of David king of Israel; for the places are holy into
which the ark of God hath come.
12 Then Solomon offered burnt-offerings unto the Lord on the altar of the
13 Lord, which he had built before the porch. And by a daily rule, each day
he offered according to the command of Moses, on the sabbaths, and on
the new moons, and on the solemn feasts, three times a year, in the feast of
unleavened bread, and in the feast of weeks, and in the feast of tabernacles.
14 And he appointed, after the order of David his father, the courses of the
priests for their service, and the Levites for their charges, to praise and to
minister before the priests by a daily rule each day, and the porters in their
courses at every gate; for so was the command of David the man of God.
15 And they departed not from the command[4] of the king to the priests and
16 Levites for all things and for the treasures. And all the work of Solomon
was prepared unto the day of the foundation of the house of the Lord, and
until it was finished: the house of the Lord was complete.
17 Then went Solomon to Ezion-geber, and to Eloth, on the sea-side in the
18 land of Edom. And Huram sent him by the hand of his servants, ships and
servants knowing the sea; and they went with Solomon's servants to Ophir,
and fetched thence four hundred and fifty talents of gold, and brought them
to King Solomon.

[1] אֲשֶׁר after וּמִן־בְּנֵי יִשְׂרָאֵל must apparently be erased, as it is wanting in some MSS., and likewise in 1 Kings ix. 22.

[2] For שָׂרֵי שָׁלִישָׁיו is perhaps to be read, as 1 Kings ix., וְשָׂרָיו וְשָׁלִישָׁיו, "and his captains and his knights."

[3] *Kethib:* הַנְּצִיבִים (comp 1 Chron. xviii. 13; 2 Chron. xvii. 2); *Keri:* הַנִּצָּבִים (so 1 Kings ix. 23).

[4] For מִצְוַת some MSS. have מִמִּצְוֹת, though the construction with סוּר by no means requires this change; comp. Ew. § 282, *a.* As little is it necessary, on account of the Sept. and Vulg., which have the plur. (ἐντολάς, *mandatis regis*), to point מִצְוֹת.

EXEGETICAL.

Preliminary Remark.—Here brief notes and aphoristic accounts, mostly referring to the external occasions and events of the reign of Solomon, are put together, as in the parallel 1 Kings ix. 10–28, in such a way that they form as it were a gleaning to the report of the chief work of his reign, the building of the temple. The order is in both places the same: 1. The building or finishing of several cities; 2. The arrangement of the service for these buildings; 3. The report of the dwelling assigned to the daughter of the Egyptian king; 4. Regulations concerning sacrifice; 5. Navigation to Ophir. But the contents of these five paragraphs differ much from one another in the two narratives, especially the first relating to the building of the cities (vers. 1–6; comp. 1 Kings ix. 10–19), where it is clear that we have extracts, not merely differing in the mode of selection from the same sources, and aiding to complete each other, but (with respect to one point at least) actually contradicting one another; see on vers. 1, 2.

1. Solomon's building of Cities: vers. 1–6.—*And after the course of twenty years*, seven years during which the temple was built, and thirteen years during which the royal palace was built, 1 Kings vi. 38, vii. 1. With the same date the statement in 1 Kings ix. 10 opens.—Ver. 2. *The cities which Huram had given to Solomon, Solomon built*, completed and fortified (comp. vers. 4, 5, and 1 Kings ix. 13).—*And caused the sons of Israel to dwell in them*, transplanted Israelites as colonists into them; comp. 2 Kings xvii. 6. 1 Kings ix. 10–13, deviating from the present statement, speaks rather of twenty Israelitish cities not far from Tyre (in "Galil") which Solomon ceded or pledged to the Phœnician king, to indemnify him for the building materials and moneys received from him. These obviously contradictory statements it has been attempted to harmonize in two ways—1. By the assumption that Solomon first ceded the twenty cities to Huram, who, however, because they were in bad condition, or were little worth to him (comp. 1 Kings ix. 12: "and they pleased him not;" and ver. 13: "he called them—contemptuously—the land of Cabul"), restored them to him, whereupon Solomon built them up (Josephus, *Antiq.* viii. 5. 3; Seb. Schmidt, Starke, recently Keil); 2. By the assumption that Solomon gave Huram twenty Israelitish cities, for which the latter gave him twenty Phœnician cities; and the author of 1 Kings speaks exclusively of the former gift, but the Chronist only of the latter (Kimchi and other Rabbis). The former of these two suppositions, for which there is some ground in 1 Kings ix. 12 f., is decidedly preferable. Yet there is much to say for the assumption of modern critics, that our passage contains a remodelling of the old statement in Kings in favour of Solomon; see Bähr on 1 Kings ix.—Ver. 3. *And Solomon went to Hamath-zobah, and subdued it*, "prevailed over it" (חָזַק עַל, as ch. xxvii. 5; Dan. xi. 5). By Hamath-zobah is to be understood, not a city Hamath in the land of Zobah, but rather the land of Hamath not far from Zobah, the Syrian kingdom of Hamath bordering on Zobah; comp. ver. 4, from which it is clear that a district or kingdom, not a city, is meant, as in 1 Chron. xviii. 3, where (in the designation of Hadadezer as "king of Zobah towards Hamath") inversely the situation of Zobah is determined by that of the neighbouring Hamath. For the designation of bordering, or being in the immediate neighbourhood, by the *status constr.*, comp. the connection often occurring in Numbers and Joshua: "the Jordan of Jericho" for "the Jordan by Jericho," Num. xxii. 1, xxvi. 3, 63, xxxi. 12, xxxiii. 48, xxxv. 1, xxxvi. 13, Josh. xiii. 32, etc., and above, 1 Chron. vi. 63 (which see). Moreover, the account of the subjugation of Hamath by Solomon is peculiar to our book. The fact, indeed, is presupposed in 2 Kings xiv. 28, but is not directly mentioned by the author of the books of Kings.—*And he built Tadmor in the wilderness, and all the cities . . . in Hamath*, the latter obviously to protect the borders of this newly-conquered country against the hostile King Rezon of Zobah (and more lately of Damascus); see 1 Kings xi. 23 ff. Tadmor or Palmyra, for only this celebrated old city of the wilderness can be meant by the expressed addition בַּמִּדְבָּר, appears here connected with the kingdom of Hamath, or bordering on it, and made by Solomon to be a border fortress of it. This notice also, so far at least as Tadmor is concerned, is wanting in 1 Kings ix.; for the Tammor named there, among other cities fortified by Solomon, ver. 18 (for which the *Keri* puts תַּדְמֹר), appears rather to be a place in South Palestine, perhaps identical with the Tamar mentioned Ezek. xlvii. 19, xlviii. 28, the Θαμαρά of the Onomasticon of Eusebius, and the present Kurnub; comp. Movers, *Chron.* p. 210; Hitzig, *Gesch.* p. 160; and Bähr on 1 Kings ix. 18. There is no sufficient reason to doubt the truth of the present statement of the Chronist regarding Palmyra; the whole old Oriental tradition (even the Arabic legends in Schultens, *Index geogr. s.v.* תַּדְמֹר) testifies to it.—Ver. 5. *And he built Upper and Nether Beth-horon;* comp. on 1 Chron. vii. 24, and for the second accusative of the object עָרֵי מָצוֹר, "fenced cities," ch. xi. 10, xiv. 6.—Ver. 6. *And Baalath, and all the cities of stores*, cities for the collection of provisions, magazine-cities, as in ver. 4; comp. ch. xvii. 12, xxxii. 28, and Bähr on 1 Kings ix. 19. Moreover, of the places here mentioned, Upper Beth-horon is not named in 1 Kings ix. 15–18, but, on the contrary, the here wanting Hazor, Megiddo, and Gezer (ver. 15).

2. Arrangement of the Serfs: vers. 7–10; comp. 1 Kings ix. 20–23, where, however, as the superscription, ver. 15: "and this is the mode of the levy," shows, a closer connection of this section with the previous statements regarding the buildings (vers. 15–19) subsists, whereas here the section appears to follow the preceding one, without

any connecting link.—Ver. 8. *Of their sons who were left after them in the land.* מִן before בְּנֵיהֶם must apparently be taken as the partitive מִן (some of their sons); but a hyperbaton may also be assumed: מִן־בְּנֵיהֶם אֲשֶׁר for 'אֲשֶׁר מִן־בְּ (Keil). The מִן is by no means to be expunged because it is wanting in 1 Kings ix. 21 (against Berth.).—Ver. 9. *But of the sons of Israel Solomon made none.* On the probable spuriousness of the אֲשֶׁר before לֹא נָתַן, and on the perhaps necessary alteration of the שָׂרֵי שָׁלִישָׁיו, "captains of his knights," into "his captains and his knights," see Crit. Notes.—Ver. 10. *And these were the chiefs of King Solomon's officers.* So according to the *Keri*, coinciding with 1 Kings ix. 23; the *Kethib* שָׂרֵי הַנְּצִיבִים would give the sense: "chiefs of the overseers." The number 250 is confirmed by the Sept. and Vulg. in our passage, whereas the same translators and Josephus, in the parallel 1 Kings ix. 23, present the higher number 550. The explanation of this difference see on ch. ii. 17; in our passage only the Israelitish overseers or taskmasters, in 1 Kings ix. 23 the Canaanitish also, are counted.

3. The Change of the Dwelling-place of the Daughter of Pharaoh: ver. 11.—*The daughter of Pharaoh.* This is most probably the daughter of Psusennes, the last king of the twenty-first (Tanitic) dynasty. In 1 Kings ix. 24 this notice is more easily introduced, as it is preceded by an account of the marriage of Solomon with this daughter of Pharaoh, 1 Kings iii. 1 f., which is wholly wanting in Chronicles.—*For he said, My wife shall not dwell.* This reason for the removal of his wife is not found in 1 Kings ix. 24, yet, by its allusion to the special sanctifying of the house of David by the presence of the ark, it corresponds with the mode of thought characteristic of the Chronist.—*Are holy,* the places into which the ark of the Lord came; הֵמָּה has here in some sort a neuter significance; comp. Ew. § 318, *b.* The statement, 1 Kings ix. 24*b*, that at the time of this transference of the daughter of Pharaoh Solomon built Millo, is wholly wanting in our passage, as not sufficiently important for the tendency of our author.

4. Regulations concerning Sacrifice: vers. 12-16; comp. 1 Kings ix. 25, where the corresponding report appears in a considerably shorter form.—*Then Solomon offered burnt-offerings unto the Lord.* "Then," namely, after the building of the temple was completed, and the dedication finished.—*On the altar of the Lord, which he had built,* on that which had been erected by him in the new sanctuary, no longer on that before the tabernacle in Gibeon, as formerly in the beginning of his reign, ch. iii. 1.—Ver. 13. *And by daily rule each day he offered,* "and in the matter of a day in the day to offer;" the ו before בִּדְבַר is explicative, "namely," and the בְּ before דְּבַר is the so-called בְּ *essentiæ:* "consisting, namely, in the daily, in that which is appointed for every day," according to the law Lev. xxiii. 37. The infinitive לְהַעֲלוֹת stands in the later usage for the *infin. absol.* (Ew. § 280, *d*); comp. for example, 1 Chron. ix. 25, xiii. 4, xv. 2.—*And on the solemn feasts, three times a year,* on the three great festivals, which are then named in order.—Ver. 14. *And he appointed, after the order of David his father, the courses of the priests;* comp. 1 Chron. xxiv. 25, 26, and for the designation of David as "the man of God," Neh. xii. 24.—Ver. 15. *And they departed not from the command of the king.* See the Crit. Note, and comp. for the second member, 1 Chron. xxvi. 20-28.—Ver. 16. *And all the work of Solomon was prepared.* וַתִּכֹּן, as in xxix. 25, xxxv. 10, 16. What is meant here by מְלָאכֶת is shown by the following 'מוּסַד וגו, which may be taken either (with Kamph.) as genitive depending on הַיּוֹם, or (with Berth., Keil, etc.) as apposition to מְלָאכֶת, "unto this day, namely, the founding," etc. In the former case, which appears to us preferable, for the construction with עַד, perhaps Ezra viii. 29 might be compared.—*The house of the Lord was complete,* set up in all its parts, finished as a house of God. The notice, which is found literally the same in 1 Kings ix. 25, is meant to denote, not perhaps the building, but rather the fitting up and arrangement of the temple for divine worship, as brought to final completion. It cannot therefore be regarded (with Berth.) as the subscription to all that precedes from ch. i. 18, but closes only the present paragraph referring to worship, which forms a sort of appendix to the account of the temple building.

5. The Navigation to Ophir: vers. 17, 18.—*Then went Solomon.* Comp. 1 Kings ix. 26, where the reference to this trade with Ophir, otherwise agreeing pretty closely with our passage (26-28), begins with the words: "And Solomon made ships" (ואני עשה instead of the present אז הלך). By "then" our author transfers these nautical undertakings in general to the second half of the reign of Solomon, or the time after the building of the temple and the palace. For Ezion-geber and Eloth on the sea (1 Kings more exactly: "Ezion-geber beside Eloth," and then, "on the shore of the sea"), comp. the expositors on 1 Kings ix.—Ver. 18. *And Huram sent him . . . ships.* It is no more necessary to suppose a transport of ships ready made across the isthmus of Suez than a circumnavigation of Africa. The assumption of a supply of timber for ships, and of mariners, by the Phœnician king, is quite sufficient; and with this (which is defended by Keil, Bähr, etc.) our passage appears to be not contradictory to 1 Kings ix. 27.—*And fetched thence four hundred and fifty talents of gold.* According to 1 Kings ix. 28, the profit amounted only to 420 talents, a difference which may be explained either by assuming a change of the numeral כ into נ, or a fault of memory on the part of one of the two reporters (perhaps a round number chosen by the Chronist). Moreover, it appears to be not a single gain, but the sum total of the gold gained in the repeated voyages to Ophir that is here spoken of; comp. ch. ix. 13.

Appendix.—It is necessary to go somewhat fully into the question of the situation of Ophir, on account of the many scientific memoirs recently published on it, especially in geographical literature and travels (comp. our former brief remarks on Job xxii. 24, and those of Bähr on 1 Kings x. 22).

1. As Ezion-geber on the Red Sea is quite definitely given, both in 2 Chron. viii. 17 f. and 1 Kings ix. 26–28, as the starting-point of the voyages under Solomon to Ophir, and as Jehoshaphat's later attempt to renew this trade, 1 Kings xxii. 49, 2 Chron. xx. 35, was made from the same port, all those conjectures concerning the site of Ophir are to be accounted null that place it anywhere west of Phœnicia and Palestine, whether near the coast of the Mediterranean or any of its bays, or beyond the Mediterranean, in the region of the new world. This includes—*a.* the opinions of Hardt, Calmet, Oldermann, of whom the first sought Ophir in Phœnicia, the second in Armenia, and the third in Iberia; *b.* the different hypotheses referring to certain coasts, islands, or lands of America or Oceanica, as the opinion of Columbus that the Ophir of Solomon was rediscovered in the country of Haiti; that of the Spanish navigator Mendana, under Philip II., who in 1567 designated a group of islands, abounding in gold, and inhabited by cannibals, east of New Guinea, which he took for Ophir by the name of Solomon's Archipelago; that of Arias Montanus, Vatablus, Osiander, P. Fr. Pfeffelius, etc., who identified the gold regions of Peru and Mexico first with Parvaim (ch. iii. 6, Parvaim = Peruaim, double Peru, the two Perus), and then also with Ophir; that of the French engineer Ouffroy de Thoron (in an article in the Genevan journal *Le Globe*, 1869), who thinks that the name Ophir is rather to be found in the Japura, a branch of the Amazon, and in accordance with this, transfers Parvaim and Tarshish (ch. ix. 21) to Brazil; and the partly still more extravagant and uncritical fancies of Abbé Brasseur de Bourbourg, George Brown, in his *Paläorama* (German edit. Erl. 1867), etc. Comp. Ritter, *Erdkunde*, xiv. 353 ff.; *Ausland* 1872, No. 23, p. 532; *Globus*, vol. xvii. p. 382 f., and vol. xxi. p. 244; and Pressel, Art. "Ophir" in Herzog's *Real-Encycl.* x. 656. From the notices of Parvaim (ch. iii. 6) and Tarshish (ch. ix. 21) in our book, not the least hint can be drawn in favour of a western Ophir, or of a western direction of the Ophir trade. For, with regard to Parvaim, the single and quite incidental mention of the gold of Parvaim leaves room for all possible conjectures concerning the import of the name,[1] while yet an eastern situation for this gold country is in itself the most probable (see on ch. iii. 6); and of all the conjectures regarding it, that of Knobel, in which he combines the name with Sepharvaim = Sephar, Gen. x. 30, and places it in the Joktanide South Arabia, or Oman (*Völkertaf.* p. 161), has most in its favour; see No. 5. With regard to the ships of Solomon sailing to Tarshish, as ch. ix. 21 seems to affirm, this rests most probably on a misunderstanding of the phrase: "ships of Tarshish" (see on the passage); and, accordingly, the various hypotheses on the relation of Tarshish to Ophir which have been invented (as that of Michaelis, *Spicileg. geogr. Hebr.* i. 98 ff.): that Hiram's and Solomon's fleets sailed beyond Tarshish, that is, beyond Spain, round Africa, as the Phœnicians did 400 years later under Pharaoh Necho, but in the opposite direction, to Ophir in the East Indies; that of Weston in the *Classic. Journ.* 1821, Sept., p. 17 f., and of Keil in the *Dorpat Contributions*, 1833, ii. 240, and in his earlier *Comm. on the Books of Kings*, 1846, p. 311, according to which the Ophir voyages proceeded from Ezion-geber, and the Tarshish or Spanish voyages from Joppa; that of Seetzen, "Ueber Ophir" in Von Zach's *Monatlicher Korrespondenz*, xix. p. 331 ff., who, in 2 Chron. ix. 21, finds a promontory Tarsis on the Karamanian coast of the Persian Gulf, which is mentioned in the old accounts concerning the Periplus of Nearchus, and endeavours to render probable his removal of Ophir to South Arabia),—are wholly superfluous and groundless.

2. If the eastern situation of Ophir stand, we may take the name first as a general designation of all possible gold-yielding lands east of Palestine, and therefore as an equally indefinite and vague geographical notion with that of Kush in Hebrew antiquity, Scythia among the Greeks, India in the Middle Ages, or Tartary, the Levant, etc., in modern times. But it is against this indefinite and therefore very convenient assumption of Jos. Acosta, Heeren, Hartmann, Tychsen, and Zeune, that, according to all the notices in history of the voyages to Ophir, this must have been a definite country, or, in other words, that the end of this voyage should, no more than Ezion-geber its starting-point, be robbed of its concrete import, and generalized into the indefinite.

3. Among the gold-producing coasts east of Palestine, East India, in particular some province, coast, or island of East India, appears to have a specially high claim to identification with Ophir; for — 1. The name Ophir finds its most convenient meaning in Indian words or local names, whether we combine the form usual in the Sept. Σωφιρά or Σουφίρ (also Σώφηρά, Σωφαρά), as well as the Coptic designation: *Sophir*, for India, with the Sanscr. *Supāra*, "fair coast" (Lassen, *Ind. Alterthumskunde*, i. 107), and with Σουπάρα of Ptolemy = Οὔππαρα in the *Peripl.*, or refer to the pastoral tribe of the Abhira, between the mouths of the Indus and the Gulf of Cambay. 2. Several of the commodities brought to Palestine from Ophir, namely, the peacocks, apes, and the almuggim or sandal-wood (see 2 Chron. ix. 10, 21, and comp. 1 Kings x. 12, 22), are specifically Indian products, that seem to have been brought only thence, and whose export from any non-Indian emporium is scarcely conceivable. 3. The names also of those imports seem capable of a specially easy explanation from the Indian language;

[1] It has been attempted to identify Parvaim with Barbatia, or Parbatia, a town standing, according to Plin. *H. N.* vi. 32, on the Tigris (Castell. *Lex. heptagl.* 3062); to affirm it = Sepharvaim, 2 Kings xvii. 24, on the one hand, and = Siphron, Num. xxxiv. 8, on the other, and accordingly to refer it to the gold-bearing Chrysorrhoas in Syria (*Harenberg, Brem., and Verd. Bibl.* iv. 44); to explain the name as the same with Ophir, and identify the Parvaim-Ophir either with Peru (Arias Mont., etc.; see above) or with Taprobane, now Ceylon (Bochart, *Phaleg*, ii. 27; *Hall. Allg. Welthistorie*, iii. 413; and Starke, *Synops.* on 2 Chron. iii. 6); or lastly, to explain the name from the Indian, and so compare either the Sanscr. *pûrva*, "before, eastern" (Wilford in *Asiat. Researches*, viii. 276; Gesen. *Th.* ii. 1125), or *paru*, "mountain" (Parvaim = δίδυμα ὄρη), as Hitzig on Dan. x. 5, who, however, transfers this double mountain to South Arabia. Comp. also Leyrer's (Art. "Parvaim" in Herzog's *Real.-Encycl.*) reference to the Paryadros range on the gold-bearing Phasis in Colchis, as well as the combination of Knobel preferred in the text.

comp. with קֹפִים, "apes," the Sanscr. *Kapi*, with תֻּכִּיִּים, peacocks, the Sanscr. *Çikhi*, Malabar. *toghei*, with אַלְמֻגִּים or אַלְגֻּמִּים the Sanscr. *valgu* (*valgum*). 4. The length of the voyage, which, according to 2 Chron. ix. 21 (1 Kings x. 22), required so much time, that only once in three years the fleet of Tarshish came and brought gold and other costly wares of Ophir, appears to indicate a country that was at least as far as East India from the northern point of the Red Sea. For these reasons, and partly also on account of some old traditions pointing to India, for instance, in Josephus, *Antiq.* viii. 6. 4, a number of eminent scholars since Bochart (*Phaleg*, ii. 27 ff.), W. Ouseley and Hadr. Reland (*Dissert. miscel.* No. IV., *de Ophir*), of the moderns, especially Lassen (*Ind. Alterthumskunde*), Ritter (*Erdkunde*, xiv. 346–431), and Kiepert (in the *Nationalzeitung* 1872, No. xlvi.), have declared themselves for some coast of India as corresponding to the ancient Ophir.—But several objections may be made to these arguments: To 1. That suitable coincidences of names or accordances with Ophir are presented in East Africa and Arabia as well as in those localities of India (see below); besides, neither the region of Sufara or Supara (near Goa), nor that of Abhira, south-east of the Delta of Indus, is gold-producing, or even specially near any gold district. To 2. That almug-wood, apes, and peacocks, if really exclusive products of India (what may be doubted with regard to the almug-wood from 2 Chron. ii. 7, and cannot be asserted respecting the apes), might very well be brought, not directly from India, but from a port of Arabia, or even East Africa, whither Indian or other ships had carried them. To 3. That the etyma of the names almuggim, kophim, and tukkiim are Indian, as above quoted, is by no means indubitably certain; for in "almuggim," which does not much resemble the Sanscr. *valgu*, the Arabic article *al-* seems rather to be present. That תֻּכִּיִּים is = the Malabar *tôghai* may be doubted on strong philological grounds (see Rödiger in Gesen. *Thes.* p. 1502); and apes might be called קֹפִים, from the Greek κῆπος, κῆβος, which, according to Aristot. *Hist. animal.* ii. 8, Strabo, Plin., etc., designates an Æthiopian species of ape. Moreover, the latest Egyptology has found the latter name (in the form *kap, kaph, kafi*) also on the primeval Egyptian monuments, which renders its Sanscrit origin altogether doubtful (see Dümichen, *Die Flotte einer egyptischen Königin*, 1868; and comp. R. Rösler in the *Ausland*, 1872, p. 648). To 4. That no weight is to be attached to the length of the voyage, when we consider the slow method of the ancients, especially of the ancient sea voyages (comp. *Odyss.* xv. 454 ff.); and this argument might be urged as well in favour of the southern East Africa; even the defenders of the hypotheses implying still farther regions (see No. 1) might avail themselves of it.

4. If from all this the determination of the site of Ophir in East India seems doubtful and precarious, it fares little better with that which has been further urged in favour of the East African coast, especially Sofala, on the channel of Mozambique (about 20° south lat.). Following the steps of the Portuguese travellers of the 16th and 17th centuries, as de Barros, Juan dos Santos, Th. Lopez, Montesquieu, d'Anville, J. Bruce, Robertson in the last century, and recently Quatremère (*Mémoire sur le pays d'Ophir* in the *Mém. de l'Instit. roy.* 1845, tom. xv. ii. p. 350 sq.), Movers (*Die Phönizier*, ii. 3, 58 ff.), the British geographers R. Murchison and J. Crawfurd, and recently the eminent African traveller Karl Mauch, the geographer Petermann partly approving his views (see his *Mittheilungen*, etc., 1872, p. 4, p. 121 ff.), also the director of missions, Wangemann (*Kreuzzeitung* of 30th Jan. 1872), and an anonymous reporter in *Ausland* (1872, No. 10), have endeavoured to render probable the identity of Sofala or some neighbouring South African coast with Ophir. The chief grounds for this view are: 1. To the name Ophir appears to correspond, if not that of Sofala (which seems rather to lead to שְׁפֵלָה, "lowland"), yet that of a mountain Fura or Afura, with ancient, probably Phœnician, ruins, of which the Portuguese were cognisant in the 16th and 17th centuries (see dos Santos, *Æthiopia orientalis*, Evora 1609), and which have been lately rediscovered by K. Mauch, and have been with great probability identified with the Zembabye or Zimbaoe of the Portuguese, the Agysymba of Ptolemy. 2. The wealth of East Africa in gold excels that of East India, especially the East Indian coast; and with regard to the coast of Sofala and the ancient Agysymba or Zimbaoe, its wealth in gold dust and minerals is celebrated by antiquity. The situation of the mountain Fura with the ruins mentioned, dos Santos defines briefly as "in the gold land" (*tracto do ouro*). 3. The wealth also of East Africa in ivory (שֶׁנְהַבִּים, 2 Chron. ix. 21; 1 Kings x. 22) was much greater than that of India; apes also and precious stones the East African emporia could certainly furnish in great abundance. 4. The report of Herodotus iv. 42 concerning the circumnavigation of Africa by Necho, proves that the Phœnicians were wont to extend their voyages from the Red Sea far southward along the east coast of Africa. 5. The ruins lately discovered again by Mauch of the ancient Zimbaoe on the Fura or Afura mountains, with their rough cyclopean stone walls built without mortar, on an average fifteen feet thick and thirty feet high (see the particulars in Mauch's letters to the missionaries Grützner and Merensky in Petermann as quoted, and in a recent letter of Mauch to the African traveller Ed. Mohr, published in the *Weserzeitung*, Dec. 1872), bear a very ancient stamp; the ornaments wrought on them point at least to a time before the Portuguese and the Arabs, and could apparently be derived only from the Phœnicians or Jews, because numerous cedar beams, employed apparently for ceilings, are found in them, and also because one of the two discovered buildings presents, as Mauch asserts, "an imitation of Solomon's temple, a fortress and house of God at the same time" (?). But none of these reasons is decisive; for in regard to—1. The etymology Ophir = Afura, Fura, has about the same precarious value as the combination with the Sanscr. Abhira; Ofir or Ofar (Ofra; see No. 5) of South Arabia has at leas as good a claim to be taken for the biblical Ophir as that region of inner Africa first named by recent writers, which lies, moreover, 200 leagues landward from the coast of Sofala. To 2. Clear traces

that the golden wealth of the region in question was known to the Phœnicians or to the people before the Christian era are still wanting. To 3. Along with ivory, apes, etc., the often quoted classical passages of the Old Testament name also quite distinctly the non-African products, peacocks and (probably) sandal-wood, as imported by the traders of Solomon. To 4. The circumnavigation of Africa under Necho proves nothing for a much earlier period; it is described by Herodotus quite distinctly as something unheard of, quite new and isolated; and from Ptolemy and the old geographers it is evident that the east coast of Africa was known and accessible to the ancients only as far as *Prasum promont.*, the present Cape Delgado, 10–11° south lat., and not farther south. To 5. The existence of the ruins of Zimbaoe before the Portuguese and Arabs, the presence of cedar-wood (?), the supposed partial resemblance to the construction of Solomon's temple, by no means prove its Phœnician or ancient Israelitish origin; to establish this would require much more exact and extensive investigations than those carried on by Mauch in his flying visit of last year (comp. also Petermann as quoted, p. 125).

5. The greatest abundance of probabilities, but certainly nothing more definite or decisive than probabilities, lies with those learned investigators who seek Ophir somewhere in South Arabia, as the Arabian geographers Edrisi and Abulfeda, partly also Bochart, further Niebuhr, Seetzen (in v. Zach as quoted), Volney, Gosselin, Vincent, Rosenmüller, Gesenius, Ewald, Knobel (*Völkertafel*, p. 190 f.), Hitzig (*Gesch. Israels*, p. 156 f.), Bähr, and Keil (on 1 Kings x. 22), the English geographer C. Beke, the French traveller Jos. Halévy, Pressel also (Art. "Ophir" in Herzog as quoted), and Albr. Roscher (*Ptolemäus und die Handelsstrassen in Centralafrika*, Gotha 1857), the latter two with the peculiar modification that they take an island near the coast of South Arabia, perhaps Dahlak in the Red Sea (so especially Roscher), or Socotora (so Pressel), for the proper Ophir, whence Solomon's traders fetched the various products mentioned. If now the latter assumption, which rests on the report by Eupolemus, in Euseb. *Præp. evang.* ix. 30, of an "island Urphe or Uphre" (Οὐφρὴ?), situated in the Erythræan Sea, rich in gold mines, and already found by David, appears very precarious on account of the doubtful character of its voucher, yet the following arguments, that are scarcely to be invalidated, speak for South Arabia in general: 1. In Gen. x. 29 occurs the name Ophir among the Joktanite tribes of South Arabia, and significantly indeed along with another tribe, that likewise bears the name of a gold land, Havilah (Gen. ii. 11). 2. The Arabian geographer Edrisi knew in the present Oman in the south-east of Arabia no less than three places whose names accord with Ophir—are, indeed, essentially like in sound, namely—*a.* Ofar, two days' journey landwards from Sohar, the present Sur; *b.* Afir or Ghafir in El Ahsa; *c.* A Mount Ofir in Bahrein (see Edrisi in *Jaubert*, i. 147, 152 ff.). 3. Many biblical passages attest the great wealth in gold of South Arabia, with special reference to Saba, situated in the south-west, as the account of the queen of Sheba in ch. ix. (1 Kings x.); Ps. lxxii. 15; Isa. lx. 6; Ezek. xxvii. 22; likewise more generally, without special reference to the south-west, several classical authors, as Strabo, xvi. pp. 777, 784; Diodorus, ii. 50, iii. 44, etc. (comp. Bochart, *Phaleg*, ii. 27). 4. The passages of Scripture testify in part that Arabia was rich also in precious stones, especially Isa. lx. and Ezek. xxvii.; and Strabo, as quoted, attests that it produced silver, at least in the country of the Nabatæans. 5. The remaining products named in ch. ix. 10, 21, and 1 Kings x. 12, 22, which might come only from India, or only from Africa, as ivory, apes, peacocks, sandal-wood, must be brought by Arabian and Indian traders to the marts of Arabia Felix, as well to the eastern (Oman, Ophir) as the western (Sheba) part of the south coast, and thence again exchanged into the Phœnician and Hebrew fleets. The high antiquity, reaching far beyond the time of Solomon, of such a trade through South Arabia of Hither Asia, at least with India (therefore also with Africa, especially with Æthiopia and Upper Egypt), is attested in the surest and fullest manner; see Lassen, *Ind. Alterthumskunde*, ii. 593–596; Movers, *Phöniz.* ii. 3, pp. 247, 256. If accordingly we are to seek Ophir with the greatest probability in south-eastern Arabia, the present Oman, there is still much that is obscure in reference to its situation, its mines and metals, its ports, its relation to the neighbouring Sabæa. More exact investigations into the situation of the regions in question, which Moslem fanaticism has almost secluded from Europeans, and for the scientific exploration of which important contributions have been made only in recent times, by v. Wrede, W. Munzinger, Joseph Halévy, and H. v. Maltzan, will alone yield authentic disclosures in this direction. Whether we are warranted in making so sharp a separation of the Ophir of Gen. x. 29 as a country belonging to Arabia, and of that of the books of Kings and Chronicles as a region possibly far removed from Arabia, as the French Vivien de St. Martin declared to be necessary, against Jos. Halévy in a session of the Paris Geographical Society (comp. also F. v. Hellwald in the *Ausland*, 1872, No. 23, p. 536), appears doubtful. It is difficult to produce exegetical grounds for such a separation of the two Ophirs; the juxtaposition of that of Genesis besides a neighbouring Havilah, without doubt also a gold-producing district, appears to favour the opposite conclusion (see above, 1 [and Introd. § 6]).

[To the note at the end of § 6, Introd., may be added the following considerations: 1. It is obvious that the voyage to Ophir, 1 Kings ix. 28, x. 11, 2 Chron. viii. 18, ix. 10, in quest of gold, almug-trees, and precious stones, was distinct from that to Tarshish, 1 Kings x. 22, 2 Chron. ix. 21, for gold, silver, ivory, apes, and peacocks, which was made in three years. 2. It is certain that the former, and most probable that the latter, voyage proceeded from Ezion-geber or Elath on the eastern gulf of the Red Sea, 1 Kings ix. 26, xxii. 48; 2 Chron. viii. 17, xx. 36. In this way the trade of Solomon did not interfere with that of Hiram his ally, which proceeded directly from the seaboard of Phœnicia. 3. Ships going to Tarshish, which was the longer voyage, might visit Ophir by the way, 1 Kings xxii. 48; 2 Chron. xx. 36. As Tarshish was of the line of Javan, and belonged to the west, his country could only be reached from the Red Sea by doubling the Cape of Good Hope. This would account for the three years spent on the voyage. It would also favour the probability that Ophir was to be found on the coast of the Red Sea, either in Arabia or Africa, or both. 4. There are traces in Scripture of the name of a country, especially if it be also the name of the tribe, travelling with the tribe. Thus Asshur, Havilah, Cush, Tarshish, and Ophir may have changed their centre in the course of ages. In particular, Ophir may have had settlements on the east and west of the Red Sea; and Tarshish may have ranged over the south as well as the north of the Straits of Gibraltar. Hence Solomon's traders may have met with Tarshish even on the gold coast of Africa, especially as the coast of this country was particularly inviting to ancient mariners from its slight indentations. As all this is possible, if not probable, we are not warranted in assuming a contradiction, or even an inaccuracy, in the report of the writer of Chronicles.—J. G. M.[1]

β. The Visit of the Queen of Sheba: ch. ix. 1–12.

CH. IX. 1. And the queen of Sheba heard the fame of Solomon, and she came to
prove Solomon with riddles to Jerusalem, with a very great company, and
camels bearing spices, and gold in abundance, and precious stones; and she
2 came to Solomon, and spake to him of all that was in her heart. And Solomon
answered her all her questions, and there was nothing hid from Solomon
3 that he answered her not. And the queen of Sheba saw the wisdom of
4 Solomon, and the house that he had built. And the meat for his table, and
the sitting of his servants, and the attendance of his ministers, and their
apparel, and his cup-bearers, and their apparel, and his ascent[1] by which he
5 went up to the house of the LORD; and there was no more spirit in her. And
she said to the king, True was the word that I heard in my land of thy affairs,
6 and of thy wisdom. And I believed not their words, until I came, and mine
eyes had seen; and, behold, the half of the greatness of thy wisdom was not
7 told me: thou exceedest the fame that I heard. Happy are thy men, and
happy are these thy servants, who stand continually before thee, and hear thy
8 wisdom. Blessed be the LORD thy God, who delighted in thee, to set thee
on His throne as king for the LORD thy God; because thy God loved Israel,
to establish him for ever, and make thee king over them, to do judgment and
righteousness.

9 And she gave the king a hundred and twenty talents of gold, and spices
in great abundance, and precious stones; and there was no such spice as that
10 which the queen of Sheba gave King Solomon. And also the servants of
Huram, and the servants of Solomon, who brought gold from Ophir, brought
11 sandal-wood and precious stones. And the king made of the sandal-wood
walks for the house of God and the king's house, and harps and psalteries for
12 singers: and none such were seen before in the land of Judah. And King
Solomon gave to the queen of Sheba all her desire, whatsoever she asked,
besides that which she had brought unto the king; and she turned, and went
away to her own land, she and her servants.

γ. Solomon's Pomp, Riches, and Glory: vers. 13–28.

13 And the weight of the gold which came to Solomon in one year was six
14 hundred and sixty and six talents of gold. Besides that which chapmen[2] and
merchants brought; and all the kings of Arabia and governors of the country
15 brought gold and silver to Solomon. And King Solomon made two hundred
targets of beaten gold; six hundred [shekels] of beaten gold laid he on one
16 target. And three hundred shields of beaten gold; three hundred [shekels] of
gold laid he on one shield; and the king put them in the house of the forest
17 of Lebanon. And the king made a great throne of ivory, and overlaid it with
18 pure gold. And there were six steps to the throne, and a footstool was
fastened to the throne with gold, and arms on each side of the seat, and two
19 lions stood beside the arms. And twelve lions stood there on the six steps
20 on each side; the like was not made in any kingdom. And all the drinking
vessels of King Solomon were of gold, and all the vessels in the house of the
forest of Lebanon were of precious gold; silver was of no account in the days
21 of Solomon. For the king's ships went to Tarshish with the servants of
Huram: once in three years came the ships of Tarshish, and brought gold
and silver, ivory and apes, and peacocks.

22 And King Solomon was greater in riches and wisdom than all the kings
23 of the earth. And all the kings of the earth sought the face of Solomon, to
24 hear his wisdom, that God had put in his heart. And they brought each his
gift, vessels of silver and of gold, and garments, armour and spices, horses and
25 mules, a rate year by year. And Solomon had four thousand stalls for horses
and chariots, and twelve thousand riders; and he placed them in the chariot-
26 cities, and with the king at Jerusalem. And he was ruling over all kings
from the river unto the land of the Philistines, and to the border of Egypt.
27 And the king made silver in Jerusalem as stones, and he made the cedars as
28 the sycamores that are in the Shephelah for abundance. And they brought
horses to Solomon out of Egypt and out of all lands.

δ. *Close of the History of Solomon:* vers. 29–31.

29 And the rest of the acts of Solomon, first and last, are they not written in
the words of Nathan the prophet, and in the prophecy of Ahijah the Shilonite,
and in the visions of Iddi[3] the seer, concerning Jeroboam the son of Nebat?
30, 31 And Solomon reigned in Jerusalem over all Israel forty years. And Solomon
slept with his fathers, and they buried him in the city of David his father;
and Rehoboam his son reigned in his stead.

[1] וַעֲלִיתוֹ, "and his ascent, his stair," is exhibited by all the Hebrew MSS.; whereas the old translations uniformly read, with the Heb. text, 1 Kings x. 5: וְעֹלָתוֹ, "and his burnt-offerings, which he offered," etc.

[2] On the very divergent variants of the old translations of אַנְשֵׁי הַתָּרִים, see Exeg. Expl.

[3] *Kethib* יֶעְדִּי, *Keri* יֶעְדּוֹ. Doubtless the same prophet is meant who is elsewhere called עִדּוֹ (ch. xii. 15, xiii. 22).

EXEGETICAL.

On account of the mostly verbal agreement of the first two of these three sections with 1 Kings x., and of the last with 1 Kings xi. 41–43, we have only to explain the peculiarities of the present text. For the rest, the expositors of the book of Kings are to be compared.

1. Visit of the Queen of Sheba: vers. 1–12; comp. 1 Kings x. 1–13.—*And the queen of Sheba heard the fame of Solomon.* The difficult addition to "the fame of Solomon" in 1 Kings: "concerning the name of the Lord," is wanting here, whether intentionally or by inadvertence is doubtful.—Ver. 4. *And his ascent by which he went up.* Whether, according to 1 Kings x. 5, וְעֹלָתוֹ וגו׳, "and his burnt-offerings, which he offered," is to be read here also with the old translations (and Josephus, *Antiq.* viii. 6. 5), it is difficult to decide. Bähr takes our reading to be original, and therefore to be restored in 1 Kings.—*And there was no more spirit in her*, she was beside herself; comp. Josh. ii. 11, v. 1.—Ver. 6. *And I believed not their words;* 1 Kings: "I believed not the words."—*The half of the greatness of thy wisdom was not told me.* Slightly different is the phrase in 1 Kings (see Bähr). On מַרְבִּית, "multitude, fulness," comp. 1 Chron. xii. 29; 2 Chron. xxx. 18; Lev. xxv. 37.—Ver. 8. *To set thee on His throne as king for the Lord.* More simply in 1 Kings: "To set thee on the throne of Israel"; as also, in that which immediately follows, the circumstantial "to establish him" (לְהַעֲמִידוֹ) is there wanting, and "for ever" (לְעוֹלָם) is attached as an adverb to "loved."—Ver. 10. *And also the servants of Huram, and the servants of Solomon.* In 1 Kings more briefly: "and also the ships of Hiram." For the then mentioned algum or sandal-wood, see on ch. ii. 7, and the excursus after ch. viii., No. 3.—Ver. 11. *And the king made . . . walks*, not "stairs" (Luther) or "seats" (Thenius, after the Pesch.), but raised walks, pavements, so that these מְסִלּוֹת of our text are essentially the same with the מִסְעָד of 1 Kings (explained by Raschi as רצפה, tesselated pavement).—Ver. 12. *Besides that which she had brought to the king*, besides the gifts in return (equivalents) for that which was presented by her, but more clearly in 1 Kings x. 13. The emendation of Bertheau: אֲשֶׁר הֵבִיא לָהּ for אֲשֶׁר הֵבִיאָה אֶל־, is unnecessary; the rendering of the Vulg.: *et multo plura quam attulerat ad eum*, is inexact and extravagant.

2. Solomon's Riches, Pomp, and Glory: vers. 13–28; comp. 1 Kings x. 14–22.—*Besides that which the chapmen and merchants brought*, literally, "irrespective of the chapmen . . . bringing" (who brought). אַנְשֵׁי הַתָּרִים are properly spies (Num. xiv. 6, xxxiv. 2), here spying, travelling about for trade; this phrase, substantially agreeing with the following סֹחֲרִים (Gen. xxiii. 16), was not understood by the old translators; hence the Vulg. has *legati diversarum gentium* (followed by Berth. and Bähr, 1 Kings x. 15: envoys), the Sept.: πλὴν τῶν ἀνδρῶν τῶν ὑποτεταγμένων; Syr. and Arab.: "besides the tribute of the cities" (הֶעָרִים for הַתָּרִים, and perhaps מִמִּכֶּם for מֵאַנְשֵׁי).—Ver. 16. *Three hundred* (shekels) *of gold laid he on one shield.* For

this 1 Kings x. 17 has "three pounds of gold to one shield," merely a verbal difference, as the mina contains a hundred shekels.—Ver. 18. *And a footstool fastened to the throne with gold.* The participle מְאֻחָזִים, "fastened" (or "enclosed"), refers to the two preceding objects, the steps and the footstool. It is certainly not impossible that originally וְרֹאשׁ עָגֹל לַכִּסֵּה מֵאַחֲרָיו, "and the top of the throne was round from behind," as in 1 Kings x. 19, stood in the text; comp. Thenius and Berth.—Ver. 21. *For the king's ships went to Tarshish.* It is most obvious to regard אֳנִיּוֹת הֹלְכוֹת תַּרְשִׁישׁ as a mistaken paraphrase of the original and usual phrase, found also in 1 Kings x. 22: אֳנִיּוֹת תַּרְשִׁישׁ, "Tarshish-traders" (comp. our East-Indiamen), and thus not find in our passage an actual testimony for voyages of Solomon to Tartessus by the Red Sea (comp. Introd. § 6, No. 5, and the excursus at the end of ch. viii., No. 1). The mistake which is here made by the Chronist standing far away from the events, appears precisely similar to that which occurs in ch. ii. 7 of our book, relative to the algum-trees to be sent from Lebanon, which Solomon desired of Huram (see on this passage). Only if we might understand (with Quatremère, Seetzen, etc.; comp. the excursus on Ophir, No. 1) by Tarshish a place different from Tartessus, or Spain, situated eastward, as the promontory *Tarsis* in the Persian Gulf, which Nearchus doubled with the fleet of Alexander (comp. the supposed Ταρσιάς mentioned by Arrian, *Ind.* 37. 9), may the charge of an error be removed from our author (to which also Petermann seems inclined in his *Geogr. Mittheilungen*, 1872, iv. p. 126). For the other statements of our verse, see the excursus on ch. viii. already quoted.—Ver. 25. *And Solomon had four thousand stalls for horses.* The numerous deviations now following to the close of the section (ver. 28) from 1 Kings x. 26–29, are explained by this, that our author had already introduced, ch. i. 14–17, an account of Solomon's chariots, horses, and horse-trading with Egypt (see on this passage), for which reason in the present place he partly contrasts (especially ver. 28) that which refers to these things, and partly completes it by reports from 1 Kings v. 1, 6; comp. Bähr on these passages.

3. Close of the History of Solomon: vers. 29-31; comp. 1 Kings xi. 41-43, where, however, instead of the three sources named by our author, ver. 29, reference is made merely to the "book of the history of Solomon." For ver. 29 f., see Introd. § 5, II.—Ver. 30. *And Solomon reigned . . . forty years.* Instead of forty years, Hitzig (*Gesch. des V. Isr.* pp. 10 and 161 f.) claims 60 years for the reign of Solomon, because Josephus assigns to the very youthful king, who came to the throne at the age of not more than 20 years (comp. 1 Kings iii. 7), an age of 80 or even 94 years (*Antiq.* viii. 7. 8). But that the reports of Josephus concerning the reign of Solomon are confused and self-contradictory, has been shown by Bengel, *Ordo temp.* p. 95, who has also correctly harmonized the 41 years of Rehoboam when he ascended the throne with the 40 years of the reign of Solomon attested by our passage and 1 Kings xi. 42; comp. Winer, *Realwörterb.*, Art. "Salomo," p. 365.

EVANGELICAL AND ETHICAL REFLECTIONS, APOLOGETIC AND HOMILETIC THOUGHTS, ON CH. I.–IX.

The statement of the Chronist does not differ quite so much from the history of Solomon in 1 Kings 1–11 in its compass and arrangement, as his statement of the history of David from its older parallel in the books of Samuel; in particular, he has not found it necessary in Solomon to go over a previous history of so great weight as that of David in 1 Samuel; and therefore so important insertions and expansions in the inner and religious side of the reign of Solomon were not requisite as in that of David. Yet the form given by him to the history of Solomon's reign deviates from that in 1 Kings, in a way that is characteristic of his theocratic position and pragmatism, in which recurs all that peculiarity which distinguishes his conception and treatment of the history of David.

1. The Levitico-religious element comes out very strong, partly in those brief insertions concerning the co-operation of the priests, Levites, and singers in the festivals, as ch. v. 11–13 (1 Kings viii. 10), viii. 12–16 (1 Kings ix. 25), partly in the fact that our author transfers from the old statement into his own all that serves to signalize the external pomp and glory of Solomon's reign, but not likewise all that relates to his wisdom. Thus we miss in him the narrative of the wise sentence concerning the two contending mothers (1 Kings iii. 16–28), and the description of his wisdom and learning, surpassing all the sons of the east, and all the wise men of Egypt, displaying itself in thousands of proverbs and songs (1 Kings v. 9–14); whereas of that which serves to characterize his great pomp and might, irrespective of the list of his court-officers and twelve princes, 1 Kings iv. 1–20, not only is nothing omitted, but some things appear purposely enhanced by the omission of less favourable trials and circumstances; in particular, the account of the cities received from Huram of Tyre, ch. viii. 1 f. (see on the passage). It is therefore not so much Solomon the incomparably wise as Solomon the incomparably glorious theocratic ruler whose picture he wished to draw. The glory, especially that which displays itself in the rich unfolding of the religious life (comp. Matt. vi. 29), forms the chief immediate object of his representation, not the wisdom, that other quality of the great king set forth as pre-eminently wonderful in the words of Jesus (comp. Matt. xii. 42).

2. That, from the effort to glorify Solomon as much as possible, some facts of his history adverse to this end have been designedly omitted by our author, is evident partly from his proceeding in the same way in the history of David, and partly from the comparison of his narrative with that of the book of Kings. Neither the particulars of Solomon's ascending the throne and beginning his reign, of which those relating to the removal of three evil-doers—Adonijah, Joab, and Shimei—would have cast a less favourable light on his character (see 1 Kings ii.), are related by him, nor is anything mentioned of the evening of his life, disturbed on the one hand by intercourse with idolatrous wives (1 Kings xi. 1–13), and on the other by unfortunate wars and rebellions (by Hadad, Rezon, and Jeroboam). Not

as if the charge of dishonest colouring or violent suppression of the truth could be made against our author on account of those omissions. He betrays, on many occasions, with sufficient clearness, his acquaintance with the omitted facts. As he had alluded (1 Chron. xxix. 24) to the suppression and punishment of the rebellion of Adonijah at the close of his history of David, so he betrays his knowledge of the revolt of Jeroboam in the closing remark of the present section (ix. 29); alludes a little before to the conflicts with Rezon and Hadad (viii. 4; see on the passage); indicates, by the manner in which he mentions the Egyptian king's daughter, his acquaintance with the corrupt influence of foreign wives during Solomon's reign; and afterwards, in the introduction of his history of Rehoboam (x. 3 f.), he does not ignore the account given in the book of Kings of the murmuring of the people dissatisfied with his severity and partial misgovernment. In short, that his reign did not altogether warrant the name Shelomoh (peaceful, prince of peace), that its splendour in a religious and moral respect was tarnished by many dark spots, and hence the heavy judgments (ch. vii. 19–22) that were pronounced by God on him and his descendants began already to take partial effect—all this appears by no means unknown to our author. Already the names of the three prophets whom he quotes, ch. ix., as guarantees for his statement, are a sufficient security that to him was imparted a knowledge of those facts that form, as it were, the dark side of the otherwise so splendid appearance of the wise and glorious prince, in no less fulness than to the author of the book of Kings (who, on his part, does not expressly mention these prophetic vouchers), but that it did not lie in his plan to add certain dark parts to the bright and glowing picture of Solomon's glorious kingdom, the like of which no king over Israel had had (1 Chron. xxix. 25). It may be that, if Solomon's fall into lust and idolatry had been ascertained and credibly reported to him as a transient darkening of his life-path, from which he at length recovered in genuine repentance, he would not have passed in silence over that sad blot on his fame, but would have given to his history such a close as that of Manasseh (xxxiii. 1–20). But he certainly had not found in his sources any more trace than the author of Kings of such closing repentance of the deeply fallen prince.[1] He therefore preferred to cast the mantle of silence over the last times of the prince whom it was now his concern to paint as the ideal of that theocratic glory (δόξα, Matt. vi. 29) long before his time become proverbial among the people.

3. The statement of the Chronist would then only deserve the reproach of historical untrustworthiness, if in an intrinsically incredible direction it departed far from that of the parallel account, and exhibited from beginning to end a greater number of legendary exaggerations of that which is there related into the miraculous. But of such propensity to apocryphal legendary distortion of his materials no trace is to be discovered in our author. The partial deviations in his numbers from those of the older parallel text are by no means to be regarded as exaggerations of smaller proportions there given; they rest often on purely external and accidental corruptions of the text (as, for example, ch. viii. 18, the 450 talents of gold from Ophir, instead of the 420 of the book of Kings; and ch. iii. 4, the 120 cubits height of the porch of the temple), or run out into mere apparent contradictions and misunderstandings (as, for example, with regard to the quantities of provisions for the woodmen, ch. ii. 9, and the number of overseers; see on ch. ii. 17 and viii. 10); and in several decisive cases, where a later exaggerator would have found special occasion for excess, he agrees to the letter with the author of 1 Kings, as in the 22,000 oxen and 120,000 sheep at the dedication of the temple (ch. vii. 5), in the determination of the yearly revenue of Solomon at 666 talents of gold (ch. ix. 13), etc. And elsewhere, that which at first sight looks like an historical exaggeration, reduces itself mostly to misunderstood or, if we will, inadequate expressions of the later historian, who is far removed from the events described, as in the cases mentioned in ch. ii. 7, ix. 21, perhaps also viii. 1, 2. The sole important event of a miraculous character with which the Chronist has enlarged the history of Solomon, compared with that in the book of Kings, is that which he records, ch. vii. 1–3, of the consecration of the sacrifice in the new temple by fire from heaven, a fact which he has handed down in his representation of the history of David, in a passage where the older narrative has nothing of the kind (1 Chron. xxi. 26). Suspicion is excited here partly by the position of the fact after Solomon's long prayer of dedication, whereas the entrance of the glory of the Lord into the new house of God was placed before it (as also in 1 Kings), partly by the complete silence of the older reporter concerning the second miracle, in place of which he introduces an address of Solomon to the assembled people (1 Kings viii. 55–61). But as the separation of the probably single miraculous fact into two acts does not appear inexplicable in the magnitude and strongly evangelical import of the whole scene in question (let us bear in mind also the uncommonly great number of the sacrifices offered on the numerous altars occupying the whole inner court; see on ch. vii. 7), so the silence of the author of 1 Kings concerning a miracle of surpassingly religious (Levitical and priestly) interest cannot be deemed strange or unaccountable, if we properly weigh the prominently theocratic and prophetic interest by which this older writer is influenced; comp. Keil, p. 247: "To communicate this speech of Solomon (1 Kings viii. 55 ff.) to the people quite accords with the plan of the book of Kings, in which the prophetical aspect of the realization of the divine counsel of grace, by the doing and suffering of the kings, prevails; whereas the more minute entering into the history of worship was remote from his plan. The mention of the fire which consumed the sacrifices we should consider warranted in the book of Kings, only if the temple had been thereby consecrated for the abode of the divine gracious presence, or for a sanctuary of the Lord. But the consuming of

[1] See in general, against this hypothesis, which might find support at most in the of itself quite problematical and little probable composition by Solomon of the book Coheleth (and in this view has recently been defended by Bernh. Schäfer in his *Neuen Untersuchungen über das Buch Koheleth*, Freiburg 1870, and by Mart. Stier in *Jahrg.* 1870, part iii. of the *Zeitschrift für luth. Theologie und Kirche*), Hengstenberg, *Gesch. des Reiches Gottes im Alten Bunde*, iii. p. 142, and Bähr in vol. vi. of the *Bibelw.* p. 108 ff.

the victim by divine fire had not this import. Jehovah consecrated the temple for the dwelling-place of His name, for the seat of his gracious presence, only in this way, that in the introduction of the ark into the most holy place He manifested his presence by the cloud filling the sanctuary. The consuming of the sacrifice on the altar by fire from heaven was the confirmatory sign only for this, that He who sat on the mercy-seat in the temple will graciously accept the offerings to be made on the altar of this temple; and, as the people could only approach the Lord before the altar with sacrifice, a confirmation for the people that He from His throne will apply His covenant grace to those who present their offerings before Him; comp. Lev. ix. 23 f. For the plan of the author of Chronicles, namely, to depict exactly the glory of the worship of the past, this divine confirmation of the sacrificial worship, that was to be continually performed in the temple as the only legitimate place of worship, by fire from heaven, was so important a matter, that it could not be omitted, whereas the blessing pronounced by Solomon on the people, as already contained *implicite* in the prayer of consecration, did not seem so important as to be admitted into his work."

4. On Solomon's great wealth, as it is repeatedly described, especially ch. i. 14 ff. and ix. 13 ff., Bengel (on ch. ix. 27) makes the striking remark: "It is strange how soon so much can be accumulated and again vanish away! Men could not endure it if it were always so; they would wander from God, and be distracted by the creatures; as Solomon himself did not long act well. He had the benefit of David as his father; he had gone through tribulation, whereas Solomon entered at once on possession! That is a weighty difference." Comp., with regard to homiletic hints, on the history of Solomon, the copious remarks of Bähr on 1 Kings i. 11 (*Bibelw.* vol. vii.).

3. THE KINGS OF THE KINGDOM OF JUDAH FROM REHOBOAM TO ZEDEKIAH.—CH. X.–XXXVI.

a. REHOBOAM. THE PROPHET SHEMAIAH.—CH. X.–XII.

α. Revolt of the Ten Tribes from the House of David: ch. x. 1–xi. 4.

CH. X. 1. And Rehoboam went to Shechem: for to Shechem was all Israel come to
2 make him king. And when Jeroboam the son of Nebat heard it, and he in
Egypt, whither he had fled from the presence of Solomon the king, then
3 Jeroboam returned out of Egypt. And they sent and called him: and Jero-
4 boam and all Israel came; and they spake to Rehoboam, saying, Thy father
made our yoke grievous: and now ease thou the grievous service of thy father,
5 and his heavy yoke that he put upon us, and we will serve thee. And
he said unto them, Yet three days hence return unto me: and the people
departed.
6 And King Rehoboam took counsel with the elders that stood before
Solomon his father when he was living, saying, How do you advise me to
7 return answer to this people. And they spake unto him, saying, If thou be
kind to this people, and please them, and speak good words to them, they
8 will serve thee all thy days. And he forsook the counsel of the old men
which they gave, and took counsel of the young men that grew up with him,
9 who stood before him. And he said unto them, What do ye advise, that we
may return answer to this people, who have spoken to me, saying, Ease thou
10 the yoke which thy father put upon us? And the young men that grew up
with him spake unto him, saying, Thus shalt thou say unto the people that
spake unto thee, saying, Thy father made our yoke heavy, but do thou ease
our yoke: thus shalt thou say to them, My little finger is thicker than my
11 father's thighs. And now my father laid a heavy yoke upon you, but I will
add to your yoke: my father chastised you with whips, but I will chastise
you with scorpions.
12 And Jeroboam and all the people came to Rehoboam on the third day, as
13 the king had spoken, saying, Come again to me on the third day. And the
king answered them roughly: and King Rehoboam forsook the counsel of
14 the old men. And he spake to them after the counsel of the young men,
saying, My father made your yoke heavy,[1] but I will add thereto: my father
15 chastised you with whips, but I will chastise you with scorpions. And the
king hearkened not to the people; for the cause was of God, that the LORD
might accomplish His word, which He spake by Ahijah of Shiloh to Jeroboam
16 the son of Nebat. And all Israel saw[2] that the king hearkened not unto

them: the people answered the king, saying, What portion have we in David?
We have no inheritance in the son of Jesse; every man to your tents, O
Israel: now look to thy house, David. And all Israel went to his tents.
17 And the children of Israel that dwelt in the cities of Judah, Rehoboam reigned
18 over them. And King Rehoboam sent Hadoram,[3] who was over the socage;
and the sons of Israel stoned him with stones, that he died: and King
19 Rehoboam hastened to get up into his chariot to flee to Jerusalem. And
Israel revolted from the house of David unto this day.
CH. XI. 1. And Rehoboam came to Jerusalem, and assembled the house of Judah
and Benjamin, a hundred and eighty thousand chosen warriors, to fight with
2 Israel, to bring back the kingdom to Rehoboam. And the word of the LORD
3 came to Shemaiah the man of God, saying, Speak unto Rehoboam son of
Solomon, king of Judah, and to all Israel in Judah and Benjamin, saying,
4 Thus saith the LORD, Ye shall not go up, nor fight with your brethren: return
every man to his house; for this thing is come from me: and they hearkened
to the words of the LORD, and returned from going against Jeroboam.

β. Reign of Rehoboam: ch. xi. 5–xii. 16.

5 And Rehoboam dwelt in Jerusalem, and built cities for defence in Judah.
6, 7 And he built Bethlehem, and Etam, and Tekoa. And Beth-zur, and Socho,
8, 9 and Adullam. And Gath, and Mareshah, and Ziph. And Adoraim, and
10 Lachish, and Azekah. And Zorah, and Ajalon, and Hebron, which are in
11 Judah and Benjamin, fenced cities. And he fortified the strongholds, and put
12 captains in them, and stores of food, and oil, and wine. And in every several
city shields and spears, and made them very strong: and he had Judah and
Benjamin.
13 And the priests and the Levites that were in all Israel resorted to him
14 out of all their border. For the Levites left their suburbs, and their posses-
sion, and came to Judah and Jerusalem: for Jeroboam and his sons had cast
15 them off from executing the priest's office unto the LORD. And he ordained
him priests for the high places, and for the he-goats, and for the calves which
16 he made. And after them, out of all the tribes of Israel, such as set their
heart to seek the LORD God of Israel, came to Jerusalem to sacrifice to the
17 LORD God of their fathers. And they strengthened the kingdom of Judah,
and upheld Rehoboam son of Solomon three years; for they walked three
years in the way of David and Solomon.
18 And Rehoboam took him to wife Mahalath, daughter[4] of Jerimoth son of
19 David, and of Abihail[5] daughter of Eliab son of Jesse. And she bare him
20 sons: Jeush, and Shemariah, and Zaham. And after her he took Maachah
daughter of Absalom, and she bare him Abijah, and Attai, and Ziza, and
21 Shelomith. And Rehoboam loved Maachah the daughter of Absalom more
than all his wives and concubines: for he took eighteen wives and sixty[6]
22 concubines; and begat twenty and eight sons, and sixty daughters. And
Rehoboam made Abijah son of Maachah the chief, to be ruler over his
23 brethren: for he thought to make him king. And he dealt wisely, and
distributed of all his sons in all the countries of Judah and Benjamin, unto
all fenced cities; and gave them victual in abundance: and he desired for
them many wives.
CH. XII. 1. And it came to pass, when Rehoboam had established the kingdom, and
strengthened himself, he forsook the law of the LORD, and all Israel with
2 him. And it came to pass in the fifth year of King Rehoboam, that Shishak
king of Egypt came up against Jerusalem, because they had transgressed
3 against the LORD. With twelve hundred chariots, and sixty thousand riders:
and the people were without number that came with him out of Egypt;
4 Lubites, Succites, and Cushites. And he took the fenced cities which per-
5 tained to Judah, and came to Jerusalem. And Shemaiah the prophet came
to Rehoboam, and the princes of Judah that were gathered into Jerusalem

before Shishak, and said unto them, Thus saith the LORD, Ye have forsaken
6 me, and I also have forsaken you in the hand of Shishak. And the princes
of Israel and the king humbled themselves, and said, The Lord is righteous.
7 And when the LORD saw that they humbled themselves, the word of the
LORD came to Shemaiah, saying, They have humbled themselves; I will not
destroy them, but I will soon grant them deliverance; and my wrath shall
8 not be poured out upon Jerusalem by Shishak. But they shall be his
servants: that they may know my service, and the service of the kingdoms
of the lands.

9 And Shishak king of Egypt came up against Jerusalem, and took the
treasures of the house of the LORD, and the treasures of the king's house; he
took the whole; and he took the shields of gold which Solomon had made.
10 And instead of them King Rehoboam made shields of brass, and committed
them into the hand of the captains of the runners, who kept the entrance of
11 the king's house. And when the king entered into the house of the LORD,
the runners came and carried them, and brought them again into the chamber
12 of the runners. And when he humbled himself, the anger of the LORD turned
from him, and he would not destroy him altogether: and in Judah also there
were good things.

13 And King Rehoboam strengthened himself in Jerusalem, and reigned; for
Rehoboam was forty and one years old when he became king, and he reigned
seventeen years in Jerusalem, the city which the LORD had chosen to put His
name there out of all the tribes of Israel: and his mother's name was Naamah
14 the Ammonitess. And he did evil; for he did not direct his heart to seek
the LORD.

15 And the acts of Rehoboam, first and last, are they not written in the
words of Shemaiah the prophet, and of Iddo the seer for the register? and
16 the wars of Rehoboam and Jeroboam were continual. And Rehoboam slept
with his fathers, and was buried in the city of David: and Abijah reigned
in his stead.

[1] For אָבִי הִכְבִּיד, "my father made heavy" (so also 1 Kings xii. 14), the best MSS. and some old prints (1 *Soncin.*, *Complut.*): אָנִי אַכְבִּיד, "I will make heavy" your yoke, and will now add to it. Nordi, Berth., etc., give the latter reading the preference.

[2] רָאוּ is certainly wanting in most MSS., in the old translations (Sept., Vulg., Chald., though not Syr. and Arab.), and in the older polyglots, but can scarcely be spared.

[3] For הֲדֹרָם 1 Kings xii. 18 presents אֲדֹרָם (comp. 2 Sam. xx. 24). So also Sept. *cod. Al.* in our passage, whereas *cod. Vat.* writes Ἀδωνιράμ (comp. 1 Kings iv. 6), probably correct as to the fact; see Exeg. Expl.

[4] With the *Keri*, which alters בֵּן into בַּת, agree several MSS., as well as the Sept. and Vulg. (in the Syr. version the passage vers. 18–23 is altogether wanting).

[5] The ו before אביחיל is certainly wanting in all copies of the Hebrew text, but was read by the Sept., and cannot be dispensed with.

[6] All the MSS. and versions certainly testify to the number sixty; but internal grounds of probability speak for the number, given by Josephus, *Antiq.* viii. 10. 1, of only thirty concubines; comp. the Exeg. Expl.

EXEGETICAL.

PRELIMINARY REMARK.—The Chronist presents only the first section of the history of Rehoboam, relating to the revolt of the ten tribes and the division of the kingdom, in exact, mostly literal, agreement with the account of the books of Kings (comp. ch. x. 1–xi. 4 with 1 Kings xii. 1–24). The proper history of his reign he treats with considerable enlargement, by the addition of several statements, wanting in the parallel text, concerning his building of forts, reception of the priests and Levites from the northern kingdom, and his family affairs (ch. xi. 5–23). He also reports at length the history of the invasion of Shishak, and the subjection of Rehoboam, and records the words spoken by the prophet Shemaiah at the divine command (ch. xii. 1–12; comp. 1 Kings xiv. 25–28). He refers even to the notes of this Shemaiah as his source for this enlarged account (ch. xii. 15).

1. The Revolt of the Ten Tribes: ch. x.; comp. the explanations of Bähr on 1 Kings xii. Here we have only to remark some deviations from the text of Kings.—Ver. 2. *And when Jeroboam . . . and he in Egypt.* 1 Kings: "and he was yet in Egypt" (עוֹדֶנּוּ) our narrator omits, because he had related nothing of Jeroboam's flight from Solomon into Egypt; comp. 1 Kings xi. 26–40).—Ver. 5. *Yet three days* (wait). 1 Kings: "Go (לְכוּ)

yet three days."—Ver. 14. On the reading אַכְבִּיד אֲנִי, deviating from 1 Kings, see the Crit. Note.—Ver. 15. *For the cause was of God*, literally, "for it was a decree (turning) of God." Both נְסִבָּה and its parallel סִבָּה in 1 Kings are ἅπαξ λ.—Ver. 16. *And all Israel saw.* If רָאוּ were to be cast out of the text, according to most ancient testimonies (see Crit. Note), it must be translated: "and all Israel (or 'as to all Israel'), when the king hearkened not unto them, the people answered."—*What portion have we in David?* What have we to do with the house of David? it may take care of itself. See again the fourth line of the strophically-arranged speech.—Ver. 18. On the probable identity of the taskmaster (Luther: "receiver of rents") Adoram, or, as our author writes, Hadoram, with the Adoniram of 1 Kings iv. 6, see Bähr on 1 Kings xii. 18.—Ver. 19. *Unto this day;* comp. 1 Chron. iv. 41, 43, v. 26, and the remarks in the Introd. § 5, I. p. 16.

2. Prevention of the War of Rehoboam with Jeroboam by the Prophet Shemaiah: ch. xi. 1–4. This incident also, that belongs to the history of the revolt of the ten tribes, is recorded by our author in substantial agreement with the author of 1 Kings; comp. 1 Kings xii. 21–24, and Bähr on the passage. Only to 1 Kings xii. 20 (Jeroboam is raised by the ten tribes, in solemn assembly, to the throne of the northern kingdom) no parallel is found in our text, because the Chronist sedulously avoids all particulars concerning the history of the kingdom of Israel.—Ver. 3. *Speak unto Rehoboam . . . and to all Israel in Judah and Benjamin.* Observe the peculiar depth, almost New Testament (reminding us of Gal. vi. 16; Rom. ii. 29, iv. 12) depth of the sense which our author here attaches to the name "Israel." It is otherwise, certainly, ver. 1, and again ver. 16*a*, where he specially designates the northern kingdom by "Israel"; yet in ver. 16 follows immediately after the name Israel, again in that evangelical, deeper, and more universal sense; so ch. xii. 1.—Ver. 4. *For this thing is come from me,* I have decreed the revolt of the disloyal tribes as a punishment for the disobedience of the house of David; comp. ch. x. 15. The there mentioned revelation by Ahijah the prophet of Jeroboam is here confirmed by Shemaiah the prophet of Rehoboam.—*And returned from going against Jeroboam.* For this 1 Kings xii. 24 has: "and turned home, according to the word of the Lord," a deviation arising perhaps from a mere omission in writing. Our text has probably the original; for the twofold mention of the word of Jehovah shortly after one another is somewhat drawling, leading us to suspect a corruption of the text.

3. Building of Forts by Rehoboam: vers. 5–12 (without parallel in Kings).—*And built cities for defence in Judah,* לְמָצוֹר, "for a fort." Judah is here the name, not of the tribe (ver. 10), but of the whole southern kingdom; for a part of the fifteen forts now to be named lay in Benjamin.—Ver. 6. *And he built Bethlehem and Etam.* That Bethlehem was a fort, for which it was fitted by its tolerably high situation on a rocky eminence, we learn only from this passage. On the here mentioned Etam, as different from the more southern one in the tribe of Simeon, see on ch. iv. 32. Tobler (*Dritte Wanderung*, etc., p. 89) has again pointed out our Etam in the Ain Attân, a side glen south-west of Urtâs, or Artâs, the well-known starting-point of Solomon's aqueduct for Jerusalem. For Tekoa, now Tekua, a hill-top covered with ruins, two hours south of Bethlehem, see the Expl. on Josh. xv. 59 and on Amos i. 1.—Ver. 7. For Beth-zur (now Beit-Sur, between Urtâs and Hebron), comp. Fay on Josh. xv. 58; for Socho (now Shuweike, three and a half hours south-west of Jerusalem) and Adullam (perhaps = Dula, six miles east of Beit-jibrin), see the same on Josh. xv. 35.—Ver. 8. *Gath* (comp. 1 Chron. xviii. 1; 1 Kings ii. 39); its situation is not yet exactly ascertained; it is perhaps near Ascalon, where is now found a Wady *el Gat*, north of the ruins of this city (K. Furrer, *Wanderungen*, etc., 1865, p. 133); according to others (for example, C. Schick) = the conical hill *Tel Safieh* in the Shephelah west of Ascalon.—*Mareshah* = the later Marissa (between Hebron and Philistia) and the present Marash, a ruin twenty-four minutes south of Beit-jibrin or Eleutheropolis; comp. Fay on Josh. xv. 44; and for Ziph (on the hills of Judah, one and a quarter hour south-east of Hebron), comp. the same on Josh. xv. 24, 55.—Ver. 9. *Adoraim* = the Idumæan city Ἄδωρα, 1 Macc. xiii. 20, or Δωρά, Josephus, *Antiq.* xiii. 15. 4, now Dura, two and a half hours west of Hebron (Robinson, iii. 209).—*Lachish* = Um Lakish, on the road from Gaza to Hebron; comp. on Josh. x. 3, xv. 39.—*Azekah,* according to 1 Sam. xvii. 1, Josh. x. 10, not far from Socho, but not yet fully ascertained.—Ver. 10. *And Zorah and Ajalon,* both originally (Josh. xix. 41) cities belonging to the tribe of Dan, which afterwards, on the migration of the Danites to North Palestine (Judg. xviii. 1), were probably occupied by the Benjamites, and thenceforth reckoned to the tribe of Benjamin. For the situation of Zorah, see on 1 Chron. ii. 53; for Ajalon (now Jalo), the expositors on Josh. x. 12. These two Benjamite cities are perhaps the most northerly of the fifteen cities fortified by Rehoboam. All the others, including Hebron, which closes the list (formerly Kiriath-arba, now el-Khalil, the ancient patriarchal city), lie south or south-west of Jerusalem, in the middle or south of the tribe of Judah. It follows, perhaps, from this position of the line of forts on the south border of the kingdom of Judah, and thus in the main directed toward Egypt, that Rehoboam began to establish them after the invasion of Shishak (Keil). So far as the arrangement of our section follows a material rather than a chronological principle of division, nothing seems to stand in the way of this assumption; but it can scarcely be reconciled with ch. xii. 4; see on this passage.—Ver. 11. *And he fortified the strongholds,* put them in a good state of defence by nominating captains (נְגִידִים, properly, "princes, leaders"), provisioning them and (ver. 12) arming them properly.—*And he had Judah and Benjamin.* This notice, forming the close of the statement concerning the measures of Rehoboam for the security of his kingdom, leads directly to the following section, which describes the Levitical and priestly followers of Rehoboam as flowing not merely from Judah and Benjamin, but from the whole kingdom.

4. Adhesion of the Levites out of all Israel to the Kingdom of Rehoboam: vers. 13–17—as is to be expected, a notice peculiar to the Chronist, to which, however, the author of 1 Kings affords an indirect confirmation, in so far as he twice refers to the institution of a new non-Levitical priesthood on the part of Jeroboam, 1 Kings xii. 31, xiii. 33 f.—*And the priests and the Levites that were in all Israel resorted to him,* "placed themselves before him to receive his commands, placed themselves at his disposal;" comp. הִתְיַצֵּב in Job i. 6, ii. 1; Zech. vi. 5.—Ver. 14. *For the Levites left their suburbs,* their commons or pasture grounds (מִגְרָשִׁים, as in ch. vi. 40 ff., xiii. 2; Num. xxxv. 2–8).—*For Jeroboam and his sons had cast them off from executing the priest's office.* See the fuller account of the erection of the impure worship of Jehovah with a new non-Levitical priesthood in the kingdom of Jeroboam, 1 Kings xii. 26–31. By the sons of Jeroboam our passage naturally means his successors, none of whom rejected the impure worship which he had introduced. They were also in so far his sons in a spiritual sense, although, with the exception of his immediate successor Nadab, they belonged to other dynasties.—Ver. 15. *And he ordained him priests.* This ויעמד לו וגו' continues the proof begun with the second כִּי in ver. 14.—*For the high places* (in Dan and Bethel, 1 Kings xii.), *and the he-goats,* etc., the idols of the form of he-goats, after the pattern of the Egyptian Pan, to whom, though not Jeroboam himself, yet his later successors, sinking into a still grosser idolatry, offered sacrifice; comp. Lev. xvii. 7, whence the term שְׂעִירִים is taken. The calves named in the third place are the representatives of Jehovah under the form of a calf, as Jeroboam (after the example of Aaron, Ex. xxxii.) had made them, 1 Kings xii. 28, and as they retained their places of worship during the whole period of the northern kingdom in Dan, Bethel, and perhaps elsewhere. According to this state of things, the "calves" should properly have been named before the "he-goats." That the author makes no note of the gradual sinking into grosser idolatry in the development of the northern kingdom, is explained by his theocratic zealous abhorrence of idolatry in general, the various forms and steps of which appear to him all equally bad.—Ver. 16. *And after them . . . such as set their heart,* etc. On נָתַן לֵב, comp. 1 Chron. xxii. 19. What is here related of the emigration of theocratic pious Israelites from the other tribes to Judah and Benjamin is repeated afterwards under Asa (ch. xv. 9) and Hezekiah (xxx. 11). That, moreover, the time during which the reign of Rehoboam gathered and attracted the true worshippers of Jehovah in other tribes amounted only to three years, and afterwards made way for an inclination to foreign and idolatrous customs (on which that accession of pious Israelites from the neighbouring kingdom ceased), is manifest from ver. 17; comp. with ch. xii. 1 ff.

5. Domestic Affairs of Rehoboam: vers. 18–23; again without parallel in the books of Kings, and wanting also in the Syr. version of Chronicles (which arises merely from an oversight).—*Mahalath, daughter of Jerimoth.* The name of the father-in-law of Rehoboam is wanting in the list of the sons of David (1 Chron. iii. 1–8). יְרִימוֹת might possibly be corrupted from יִתְרְעָם, or be a by-form of this name; it is easier to suppose that he was one of the many sons of David by the concubines.—*And of Abihail daughter of Eliab son of Jesse.* As necessary as the supply of the wanting וְ before אֲבִיחַיִל (see Crit. Note) is the taking of this name as the genitive, thus (contrary to the Sept. and Vulg., which rather make her a second wife of Rehoboam) as the name of the mother of Mahalath. For—1. Ver. 19 shows that only one wife of Rehoboam, the mother of the three there named otherwise unknown sons, should be named; 2. Along with the obscure father of Mahalath we expect the name of her mother, who is more celebrated, because she descends from Eliab the brother of David; 3. A daughter of Eliab the eldest brother of David (1 Chron. ii. 13; 1 Sam. xvii. 13) could scarcely have been a wife of Rehoboam the grandson of David; even as granddaughter of Eliab (comp. ver. 20), Abihail suited better in age a son of David than a son and successor of Solomon.—Ver. 20. *And after her he took Maachah daughter of Absalom.* This second wife of Rehoboam is perhaps to be regarded, not strictly as the daughter, but the granddaughter of Absalom, the daughter of Tamar, the only daughter, and perhaps only child, of this unlucky prince; comp. 2 Sam. xiv. 27, xviii. 18, and Josephus, *Antiq.* viii. 10. 1, as well as ch. xiii. 2 of our book.—*And she bare him Abijah.* Only this first-born of Maachah, whose name, moreover, is constantly written Abijam (אֲבִיָּם) in 1 Kings, is more particularly known to us as the successor of Rehoboam; the three younger sons, Attai, Ziza, and Shelomith, do not occur elsewhere.—Ver. 21. *For he took eighteen wives* (נָשָׂא, as in ch. xiii. 21) *and sixty concubines.* On account of the number of daughters immediately after given as sixty, it is not improbable that Josephus, who tells only of thirty concubines, deserves the preference; comp. Crit. Note.—Ver. 22. *To be ruler among his brethren;* to this explanatory apposition to לְרֹאשׁ is added the following כִּי לְהַמְלִיכוֹ, as a further determination of that which the king meant by Abijah's elevation to be chief. On the breviloquence here, comp. Ew. § 351, *c.*—Ver. 23. *And he dealt wisely, and distributed of all his sons in all the countries of Judah and Benjamin;* he showed his prudence as sovereign and as father by appointing his numerous sons as captains in the several forts of his kingdom, employing them usefully, and separating them from one another, to prevent any attempts at rebellion among them.—*And he desired for them many wives,* made many marriages between them and the daughters of the land, both to make them contented and to make firmer connections between his house and the inhabitants of the land. The desiring or asking (שָׁאַל) of wives for his sons became him as their father and natural guardian: the author will scarcely charge him with an immoral, pimp-like gratification of the lusts of his sons.

6. The Invasion of Shishak: ch. xii. 1–12; comp. the briefer narrative of 1 Kings xiv. 25–28. —*And it came to pass, when Rehoboam had established the kingdom, and strengthened himself*, literally, "at the time of the establishing" (כהכין, inf. act. with indefinite subject), and on the strengthening of him or it (כחזקתו, from the *nom. verbale* חזקה, strengthening; comp. xxvi. 16; Dan. xi. 2).—*He forsook the law of the Lord* (by a partial falling into idolatry; comp. 1 Kings xiv. 22 ff.), *and all Israel with him*, all the inhabitants of the southern kingdom, who are here, somewhat to their shame, designated Israelites; comp. ver. 6 and ch. xi. 3.—Ver. 2. *And it came to pass in the fifth year of King Rehoboam*, thus soon but not immediately after his apostasy from the Lord. Concerning Shishak (= Sheshonk, Sesonchis, the first king of the 22d dynasty of Manetho), and the relievo proceeding from him, celebrating the present campaign against the Jews, and victory over Rehoboam, that probably exhibits Rehoboam himself among his captives, see Thenius on 1 Kings xi. 40, and Bähr on 1 Kings xiv. 25.—Ver. 3. *With twelve hundred chariots, and sixty thousand riders.* In 1 Kings these data concerning the strength of the Egyptian army are wanting, though they are by no means incredible. Of the auxiliaries of Shishak, the Lubites (לובים) are certainly those Egyptian Libyans (the *Libyægyptii* of the ancients) who are also named with the Egyptians in ch. xvi. 8, Nah. iii. 9, Dan. xi. 43, and from whom the Lehabim of the Mosaic table of nations are perhaps not different; comp. Knobel on Gen. x. 13. The Succites (סכיים) are, according to the Sept. and Vulg., *troglodytæ*, cave-dwellers, to which the Hebrew etymon seems to point, dwellers in holes of the earth, probably of Ethiopian origin, and inhabiting the mountains of Eastern Egypt. The Cushites are probably inhabitants of Ethiopia proper, that is, Abyssinia, as they are also named, Nah. iii. 9, as allies of Egypt (along with "Put" and "Lubim").—Ver. 4. *And he took the fenced cities which pertained to Judah;* comp. ch. xi. 5 ff. These may not yet have been very strong, or their works proved insufficient against the military force of Egypt; comp. on ch. xi. 10.—Vers. 5–8. The Prophetic Mission of Shemaiah, and the consequent Submission of the Jews and Mitigation of their Punishment,—a section quite wanting in 1 Kings.—*But I will soon grant them deliverance.* כמעט, properly, "for a little," that is, in a short time, soon; comp. Ezra ix. 8 (rightly Berth., Keil, etc., against Kamph., who translates: "a small deliverance").—*And my wrath shall not be poured out upon Jerusalem by Shishak.* No judgment of full extirpation shall overtake the capital; comp. xxxiv. 25.—*That they may know my service and the service of the kings of the lands;* that they may experience what a difference there is between the government of the Lord in the theocracy of Israel, and the so much more oppressive rule of heathen kings.—On vers. 9–11, comp. Bähr's remarks on 1 Kings xiv. 26–28.—Ver. 12. *And when he humbled himself*, literally, "and in his self-humiliation." On the following elliptical phrase: ולא להשחית, "and not to destroy" (did Jehovah's wrath turn itself), comp. the like breviloquence in ch. xi. 12, and the passage there quoted from Ew.—*And in Judah also there were good things.* This was a further motive to the Lord to restrain his wrath, in addition to the first motive, consisting in the repentance of Rehoboam.

7. Close of the History of Rehoboam: vers. 13–16 (comp. 1 Kings xiv. 21, 22, 29–31).—*And King Rehoboam strengthened himself;* comp. ch. i. 1, xiii. 21; concerning the following note of age, which it seems necessary to change into twenty-one years, comp. Bähr on 1 Kings xiv. 21.—*Naamah the Ammonitess*, the daughter of the Ammonite King Nahash (1 Chron. xix. 1), according to a probable note of the Sept. after 1 Kings xii. 24. —Ver. 14. *For he did not direct his heart.* For this phrase, comp. ch. xix. 3, xxx. 19; Ezra vii. 10.—Ver. 15. *Are they not written in the words of Shemaiah the prophet.* On this quotation, and especially on the obscure phrase "for the register" (להתיחש), see Introd. § 5, II.—*And the wars of Rehoboam and Jeroboam*, their smaller dealings and disputes, in which their continued hostile disposition showed itself; see Bähr on 1 Kings xiv. 30.

EVANGELICAL AND MORAL REFLECTIONS ON CH. X.–XII.

1. In the reign of Rehoboam, as the Chronist represents it, is signalized above all the tendency to keep the kingly ideal of David and Solomon pure from the dark stains of untheocratic opinion and destructive apostasy into idolatry. Some time after the beginning of his reign, this corrupt influence comes out distinctly and clearly, accompanied with divine punishments as its evil effect (ch. xii. 1 ff.), though in the first three years Rehoboam and his subjects "walked in the way of David and Solomon" (ch. xi. 17). Yet in the first half of the section, the account of the secession of the ten tribes under Jeroboam, several expressions betray the acquaintance of the author with the fact that corruption had begun already under Solomon. The polygamy and idolatry of this glorious king, and the consequent divine corrections and threatenings of punishment, he had not mentioned in his representation of the history of Solomon (comp. the Evangelical and Ethical Reflections on ch. i.–ix.). But now in Rehoboam there is express reference to that which had been prophesied on account of those errors of Solomon by Ahijah the Shilonite against him, and in favour of Jeroboam (ch. x. 15; comp. 1 Kings xi. 29–39). And this part of our author's narrative indicates that his religious and moral fall had already been productive of many immediate evils in his kingdom, that his government had become latterly quite a misgovernment (comp. 1 Kings xi. 14 ff.), by the mention of the repeated request of the dissatisfied people: "lighten the heavy yoke which thy father laid on us" (ch. x. 4, 9, 10; comp. ver. 15), and by the report of the words of the ten tribes betraying an already deep-seated dissatisfaction with the previous government: "What portion have we in David? We have no inheritance in the son of Jesse" (ver. 16). Thus, according to our author, the ideal time of David and Solomon closes with this, that it

presents at last the germs of a growing and grasping corruption, while that which had to be recorded concerning it is first introduced in the section belonging to Rehoboam, and therefore chiefly in the form of an appendix to the already concluded history of Solomon. Indeed, to our author, the evangelical result of the reign of Solomon is simply that which is brought forward in 1 Kings xi. "Along with a great outgrowth of public prosperity, we observe a gangrene commencing, that gnaws unceasingly, and destroys the religion of the people, the condition of their salvation, and this salvation itself It becomes manifest that the peace, which a merely human ruler can give, bears in itself the germ of decay, that it brings with it temptations, which a lesser anointed of the Lord (like David or Solomon) cannot give the power to withstand. The result of the whole brilliant period is a Kyrie Eleison and an: O that Thou wouldst rend the heavens and come down!" (Hengstenberg, *Gesch. des Reiches Gottes unter dem Alten Bunde*, ii. 2, 146 f.)

2. Thus the Chronist partly only places Rehoboam, with respect to the beginning of his reign, in an unfavourable contrast with the brilliant reign of his father Solomon. In a certain respect (particularly with regard to the tendency to tyrannical cruelty and domineering pride; see ch. x. 10, 14) he puts them on a par, and makes the son only gradually different from the father, by descending a step lower. So with regard to the further course of Rehoboam's reign. At first Rehoboam continues the effort of his father, if not to enlarge, at least to establish the kingdom (comp. ch. xi. 5–12 with i. 14 ff., viii. 1–10, ix. 25–28). But certainly his fortifications are of no avail to ward off the war-storm bursting on the country from Egypt, no more than his defiant threat of a warlike attack could have hindered the dismemberment of the kingdom that still held together under his father (comp. x. 15 ff., xi. 1 ff.). He likewise applied himself during the first three years of his reign to the theocratically pure and correct principles of government which were followed by his father, if not to the last yet during the greater part of his reign, with so much blessing to himself and his people. He thereby makes Jerusalem and the southern kingdom for a time the refuge and gathering-place of the pious worshippers of the Lord of priestly and non-priestly descent from the whole kingdom, and, so to speak, effects the transfer of the tribe of Levi to his sway, so far only as those of them who were scattered among all the tribes can find a settlement in Judah and Benjamin. But this attractive power in the sense of forming and consolidating a theocracy (ch. xi. 13–17) did not last long. After three years, he "forsook the law of the Lord, and all Israel with him" (ch. xii. 1). What Solomon was able to do during at least two-thirds of his reign of forty years, to maintain the "hearing heart" and the true wisdom with which the Lord had endowed him, this Rehoboam was scarcely able to do during a sixth part of his reign of seventeen years. In this also he resembles his father; but he behaves much worse, and seems to surpass him in a bad sense. Hence he has to endure much greater shame and humiliation; for if the Lord had only to threaten Solomon thus: "I will humble the seed of David, but not for ever" (1 Kings xi. 39), this prophetic threat pronounced by Ahijah is now fulfilled in bitter earnest on him and his people (ch. xii. 2 ff.); and what the prophetic interpreter says in behalf of a right understanding of the misfortune that had befallen them (ch. xii. 7, 8) is certainly not altogether comfortless, but at the same time not unconditionally promising. The punishment shall be mild, not of long endurance; but for a time its bitterness shall be required, that they may understand what it is to prefer the rule of a heathen king to the mild sway of God.

3. There is something peculiar in the position which the Chronist gives to the family history of Rehoboam (ch. xi. 18–23). He tells of his eighteen wives and sixty (or, if the number is to be reduced according to Josephus, thirty) concubines with objective candour, without adding a judgment unfavourable to the moral character of the king. While he passes with significant silence over the extravagant polygamy of the latter years of Solomon, to spare the great and wise king, and even thereby indicates the untheocratic and immoral character of an immoderate harem, he seems to find the married life of Rehoboam not more offensive than that of David, of whom he expressly named at least seven lawful wives, and mentioned besides the possession of an indefinite number of concubines, without expressing any disapprobation. The manner also in which Rehoboam procured for his sons many wives from the daughters of the land (ch. xi. 23), he adduces merely as a proof of his prudent dealing, not in the tone of serious blame or moral disapprobation. He places this statement also before the account of his fall into idolatry, without noticing in the way of censure the manifest connection of the two things, the polygamy of himself and his sons, and his giving way to the worship of foreign gods. He almost appears, indeed, as afterwards in the case of Abijah's fourteen wives and thirty-eight children (ch. xiii. 21), to have regarded the taking of many wives and begetting of numerous children as something laudable, serving to multiply and perpetuate the house of David. This manner of thinking is characteristic of the strict theocrats of the later times, that form the transition to the Pharisaic orthodoxy of the New Testament epoch (comp. Introd. § 6). Because the law does not directly forbid polygamy, he readily allows on this point an almost unlimited compliance with the lusts of the flesh, while he censures with strictness the as it were only theocratic error of which the same king becomes guilty by falling into idolatry in the fourth year of his reign, as he had before shown his abhorrence of that still greater idolatrous error of the king and subjects of the northern kingdom in the strongest, indeed almost hyperbolical, terms (ch. xi. 15). We meet here the same rather externally orthodox than morally strict tendency, which our author discovers also in many other points. It is the ethically imperfect and crude, not yet evangelically consecrated and glorified, stage of the legal standpoint of the Old Testament, which is expressed in this lax position of the Chronist with regard to the custom of polygamy. New Testament statements, such as those relating to Moses' regard to the hard-heartedness of the Jews, to the killing power of the letter of the law, to the shadowy and not essential character, to the weakness and impotence of the law (Matt. xix. 8;

2 Cor. iii. 6; Rom. viii. 3; Col. ii. 17; Heb. x. 1, etc.), first receive their full light and deeper meaning by a phenomenon like this (comp. also John i. 17; Gal. ii. 16 ff., iii. 10 ff., iv. 3, 9 ff.).

b. ABIJAH.—CH. XIII.

CH. XIII. 1. In the eighteenth year of King Jeroboam, Abijah became king over
2 Judah. He reigned three years in Jerusalem; and his mother's name was
Michaiah,[1] daughter of Uriel of Gibeah.
3 And there was war between Abijah and Jeroboam. And Abijah began
the war with an army of valiant warriors, four hundred thousand chosen men·
and Jeroboam prepared war against him with eight hundred thousand chosen
4 men, valiant in might. And Abijah arose on Mount Zemaraim, which is in
5 Mount Ephraim, and said, Hear me, Jeroboam and all Israel. Do you not
know that the LORD God of Israel gave the kingdom over Israel to David
6 for ever, to him and to his sons by a covenant of salt? And Jeroboam son
of Nebat, servant of Solomon son of David, arose and rebelled against his
7 master. And vain men, of no account, gathered unto him, and withstood
Rehoboam son of Solomon; and Rehoboam was young and weak of heart,
8 and held not out against them. And now ye are saying that ye will hold
out against the kingdom of the LORD in the hand of the sons of David; and
ye are a great multitude, and with you are golden calves, which Jeroboam
9 made you for gods. Have ye not cast out the priests of the LORD, the sons
of Aaron, and the Levites, and made you priests like the nations of the lands?
whosoever cometh to fill his hand with a young steer and seven rams is a
10 priest to them that are no gods. And we, the LORD is our God, and we have
not forsaken Him; and the priests that minister to the LORD are the sons of
11 Aaron, and the Levites in their business. And they burn unto the LORD
burnt-offerings every morning and every evening, and incense of spices, and
laying of bread on the pure table, and the candlestick of gold and its lamps
to burn every evening: for we keep the charge of the LORD our God; but ye
12 have forsaken Him. And behold, with us, at our head, are God and His
priests, and the clanging trumpets to sound against you: sons of Israel,
fight not against the LORD God of your fathers; for ye shall not prosper.
13 And Jeroboam led round an ambush to come behind them; and they were
14 before Judah, and the ambush was behind them. And Judah turned, and
behold they had the battle before and behind; and they cried unto the LORD,
15 and the priests sounded with the trumpets. And the men of Judah shouted;
and when the men of Judah shouted, God smote Jeroboam and all Israel
16 before Abijah and Judah. And the sons of Israel fled before Judah; and
17 God gave them into their hand. And Abijah and his people smote them with
a great slaughter; and there fell slain of Israel five hundred thousand chosen
18 men. And the sons of Israel were humbled at that time; and the sons of
Judah prevailed, because they trusted in the LORD God of their fathers.
19 And Abijah pursued after Jeroboam, and took cities from him: Bethel and
her daughters, and Jeshanah[2] and her daughters, and Ephron[3] and her
20 daughters. And Jeroboam had no more strength in the days of Abijah; and
21 the LORD smote him, and he died. And Abijah strengthened himself, and
took to him fourteen wives, and begat twenty and two sons and sixteen
22 daughters. And the rest of the acts of Abijah, and his ways, and his words,
23 are written in the commentary of the prophet Iddo. And Abijah slept with
his fathers, and they buried him in the city of David; and Asa his son
reigned in his stead. In his days the land was quiet ten years.

c. ASA. THE PROPHETS AZARIAH SON OF ODED AND HANANI.—CH. XIV.-XVI.

α. Asa's Theocratic Zeal and Care for the Defence of the Kingdom: ch. xiv. 1-7.

CH. XIV. 1. And Asa did that which was good and right in the eyes of the LORD
2 his God. And he took away the altars of the strange gods, and the high

3 places, and brake the pillars, and cut down the Asherim. And commanded
Judah to seek the LORD God of their fathers, and to do the law and the
4 commandment. And he took away out of all the cities of Judah the high
places and the sun-statues: and the kingdom was quiet before him.
5 And he built fenced cities in Judah; for the land had rest, and there was
6 no war with him in those days; for the LORD gave him rest. And he said
to Judah, Let us build these cities, and make about them walls and towers,
gates and bars, and the land is yet before us; because we have sought the
LORD our God, and He hath given us rest around: and they built and pros-
7 pered. And Asa had an army, bearing shield and spear, out of Judah three
hundred thousand, and out of Benjamin, bearing shield and drawing bow,
two hundred and eighty thousand: all these were men of valour.

β. Asa's Victory over Zerah the Ethiopian: vers. 8–14.

8 And Zerah the Ethiopian came out against them with a host of a thousand
9 thousand, and three hundred chariots; and he came to Mareshah. And Asa
went out against him, and they joined battle in the valley of Zephathah at
10 Mareshah. And Asa cried unto the LORD his God, and said, LORD, no one
is nigh Thee to help with the mighty or with no might; help us, O LORD
our God, for we rely on Thee, and in Thy name we go against this multitude:
11 O LORD, Thou art our God; no man may hold out against Thee. And the
LORD smote the Ethiopians before Asa, and before Judah; and the Ethiopians
12 fled. And Asa, and the people that were with him, pursued them unto
Gerar: and the Ethiopians fell, so that there was no recovery; for they were
broken before the LORD, and before His host; and they carried off very great
13 spoil. And they smote all the cities round Gerar; for the terror of the LORD
14 was upon them. And they smote also the tents of cattle, and took sheep in
abundance, and camels, and returned to Jerusalem.

γ. The Prophetic Warning of Azariah Son of Oded: ch. xv. 1–7.

CH. XV. 1, 2. And the Spirit of God came upon Azariah son of Oded. And he
went forth before Asa, and said unto him, Hear ye me, Asa, and all Judah
and Benjamin; the LORD is with you, while ye are with Him; and if ye seek
Him, He will be found of you; and if ye forsake Him, He will forsake you.
3 And many days will be to Israel without the true God, and without a teach-
4 ing priest, and without a law. And he shall return in his trouble unto the
5 LORD God of Israel, and seek Him, and He shall be found of him. And in
those times is no peace for him that goeth out or cometh in, but great vexa-
6 tions on all the inhabitants of the lands. And nation shall be smitten[4] by
7 nation, and city by city; for God hath vexed them with all trouble. But be
ye brave, and let not your hands be slack; for there is a reward for your
labour.

δ. Asa's Reform of Worship, and Renewal of Covenant with the Lord: vers. 8–19.

8 And when Asa heard these words, and the prophecy of Oded[5] the prophet,
he took courage, and put away the abominations out of all the land of Judah
and Benjamin, and out of the cities which he had taken from Mount Ephraim,
and renewed the altar of the LORD, that was before the porch of the LORD.
9 And he gathered all Judah and Benjamin, and the strangers with them, out
of Ephraim and Manasseh, and out of Simeon; for they fell to him out of
Israel in abundance, when they saw that the LORD his God was with him.
10 And they gathered at Jerusalem, in the third month of the fifteenth year of
11 the reign of Asa. And they sacrificed to the LORD in that day, of the spoil
12 they had brought, seven hundred oxen and seven thousand sheep. And they
entered into a covenant to seek the LORD God of their fathers with all their
13 heart, and with all their soul. And whosoever would not seek the LORD God

14 of Israel should be put to death, small or great, man or woman. And they
sware unto the LORD with a loud voice, and with clangour, and with trumpets
15 and cornets. And all Judah was glad at the oath; for they had sworn with
all their heart, and sought Him with their whole desire, and He was found of
16 them: and the LORD gave them rest round about. And also Maachah, the
mother of Asa the king, he removed from being queen, because she had made
an idol for Asherah: and Asa cut down her idol, and crushed it, and burnt
17 it in the brook Kidron. But the high places were not taken away out of
18 Israel; but the heart of Asa was perfect all his days. And he brought the
things which his father and himself had consecrated into the house of God,
19 silver and gold, and vessels. And there was no more war unto the thirty-
fifth year of the reign of Asa.

ε. *The War with Baasha of Israel*: ch. xvi. 1–6.

CH. XVI. 1. In the thirty-sixth year[6] of the reign of Asa, Baasha king of Israel
came up against Judah, and built Ramah, to let no one come out or go in to
2 Asa king of Judah. And Asa brought out silver and gold out of the treasures
of the house of the LORD, and of the king's house, and sent to Benhadad king
3 of Syria, that dwelt at Damascus,[7] saying: A league is between me and thee,
and between my father and thy father: behold, I have sent thee silver and
gold; go, break thy league with Baasha king of Israel, that he may depart
4 from me. And Benhadad hearkened unto King Asa, and sent the captains of
his army against the cities of Israel; and they smote Ijon, and Dan, and Abel-
5 maim, and all the stores of the cities of Naphtali. And when Baasha heard
6 it, he left off building of Ramah, and let his work cease. And Asa the king
took all Judah, and carried away the stones of Ramah, and its timber, with
which Baasha had built, and built therewith Geba and Mizpah.

ζ. *Hanani's Prophetic Warning: Asa's Transgression and End:* vers. 7–14.

7 And at that time came Hanani the seer to Asa king of Judah, and said
unto him, Because thou hast relied on the king of Syria, and hast not relied
on the LORD thy God, therefore is the host of the king of Syria escaped from
8 thy hand. Were not the Ethiopians and the Lubites a huge host, in chariots
and horsemen very many? and when thou didst rely on the LORD, He gave
9 them into thy hand. For the eyes of the LORD run throughout all the earth,
to prove Himself strong for those whose heart relies wholly on Him: thou
10 hast done foolishly in this; for henceforth thou shalt have wars. And Asa
was displeased with the seer, and put him in the prison; for he was in a rage
with him because of this. And Asa oppressed some of the people at that
time.

11 And, behold, the acts of Asa, first and last, behold, they are written in
12 the book of the kings of Judah and Israel. And Asa, in the thirty-ninth
year of his reign, was diseased in his feet, until his disease was very great:
13 and in his disease also he sought not the LORD, but to the physicians. And
Asa slept with his fathers; and he died in the forty-first year of his reign.
14 And they buried him in his own tomb, which he had dug for himself in the
city of David; and they laid him in the bed which was filled with sweet
odours of divers kinds, compounded by art; and they made a very great
burning for him.

[1] On the probable error of the pen here (מִיכָיָהוּ for מַעֲכָה), see Exeg. Expl.

[2] For יְשָׁנָה the Sept. has 'Ἰεσυνά (but Josephus, *Antiq.* viii. 11. 3: 'Ἰσάνας).

[3] For the *Kethib* עֶפְרוֹן, supported by the Sept. and Vulg., the *Keri* is עֶפְרַיִן.

[4] For וְכִתְּתוּ some MSS. read וְכִתְּתוּ; but the *Pual* is required by the context.

[5] Sept. *cod. Vat.:* 'Ἀδὰδ ('Ωδὴδ) τοῦ προφήτου; on the contrary, *c. Al.*, *ed. Ald.*, etc.: 'Ἀζαρίου τοῦ προφήτου. Vulg.: *Azariæ filii Oded prophetæ.* Perhaps the words עֹדֵד הַנָּבִיא should be cancelled as an old gloss. See the Exeg. Expl.

[6] So all the MSS. and versions but the Sept., which has ἐν ἔτει ὀγδόῳ καὶ τριακοστῷ, by a mistake of η for ς, or on the ground of some peculiar chronological reckoning.

[7] Properly, "Darmascus;" see 1 Chron. xviii. 5, 6, and the Crit. Note thereon. For the υἱὸς τοῦ Ἄδερ, given by the Sept. for בן הדד, comp. the Exeg. Expl.

EXEGETICAL.

The histories of both reigns, that of Abijah and that of Asa, are presented here in a very extended form, when compared with the parallel accounts in 1 Kings xv. 1–8, 9–24; and in particular, there are several discourses of a prophetic nature in the history of Abijah, one addressed by this king himself on Mount Zemaraim to Jeroboam and the army of Israel (ch. xiii. 4–12), and in that of Asa, the warnings of the seers Azariah son of Oded and Hanani (ch. xv. 2–7, xvi. 7–10), by the insertion of which the Chronist has considerably enlarged his account. But with respect to the history of war and worship, his representation is a far richer gain from the ancient sources than that preserved in 1 Kings xv.

I. Abijah: ch. xiii.; comp. 1 Kings xv. 1–8. —*In the eighteenth year of King Jeroboam.* This date of the beginning of Abijah's reign is also given in 1 Kings, and also the three years' duration of his reign (he is, moreover, always called אֲבִיָּם; see on ch. xi. 22).—*And his mother's name was Michaiah, daughter of Uriel of Gibeah.* As Abijah's mother is called Maachah, not merely ch. xi. 20 ff., but also 1 Kings xv. 2, the present name מִיכָיָהוּ must be regarded as a mistake for the original מַעֲכָה. Her father, Uriel of Gibeah, is to be regarded as the husband of Tamar the daughter of Absalom, and herself, therefore, as the grand-daughter of the latter; see on ch. xi. 20. From the Maachah, further mentioned ch. xv. 16 (and 1 Kings xv. 13), the mother of Asa, whom he removed from the dignity of a gebirah (mistress, Sultana Walide, queen-mother) for her idolatry, she is scarcely to be considered different; rather is her designation there as mother to be supposed = grandmother, and her continued regency under her grandson Asa is to be explained simply from the brief duration of Abijah's reign, and the probable minority of Asa at his death (comp. Athaliah's attempt to reign instead of her grandson Joash, ch. xxii.). Against the assumption by Thenius and Bertheau of the diversity of the two Maachahs (of whom the mother of Abijah was the daughter of Absalom, but the mother of Asa in reality the one who is here falsely called "a daughter of Uriel of Gibeah"), see Keil, p. 261, Rem.—Ver. 3 ff. Abijah's War with Jeroboam.—*And Abijah began the war with . . . 400,000 chosen men.* Neither this number nor the double number of the warriors of Jeroboam should be taken strictly, as is abundantly clear from the substantial agreement of both numbers with the results of Joab's enumeration under David (800,000 men-at-arms of Israel and 500,000 of Judah; comp. 1 Chron. xxi.). Less probable is the assumption of an error in transcription, resting on a change of the numeral letters, as the cause of these almost incredibly high numbers (Kennicott, *Dissert. Gen.* § 27; J. Pye-Smith, *The Scripture Testimony to the Messiah*, 6th edit. vol. i. p. 29); for to explain the fact in this way, we must assume several such mistakes or corruptions in similar circumstances, which would be very strange. Comp. also on ch. xvii., and Evangelical and Ethical Reflections, No. 3.—Ver. 4. *And Abijah arose on Mount Zemaraim,* obviously a steep cliff or summit lying between the contending armies, from which the king addressed the foe in like manner as Jotham once addressed the Shechemites from Mount Gerizim, Judg. ix. 7. That every single warrior of the host of Israel, numbering several hundred thousands, could have heard his words is not said, and need not be assumed. The situation of Mount Zemaraim is no longer to be ascertained. It was probably in the neighbourhood of Bethel, near which is a town, Josh. xviii. 22, named צְמָרַיִם (Zemaraim), the ruins of which may have been found in el Sumra, between Jerusalem and Jericho, near the valley of the Jordan. At all events, the locality should be sought east of Bethel (Robinson, *Phys. Geogr. of the Holy Land*, p. 38), and this el Sumra may lie too far in a south-easterly direction.—Ver. 5. *Do you not know,* literally, "Is it not to you, concerns it not you, to know?" comp., for example, 1 Chron. xiii. 4.—*That the Lord . . . gave . . . to him and to his sons by a covenant of salt,* by an irrevocable covenant; comp. Lev. ii. 13; Num. xviii. 19. בְּרִית מֶלַח belongs to the whole sentence, as accusative of restriction (therefore: "in the manner of a covenant of salt").—Ver. 7. *And vain men, of no account, gathered unto him,* properly, "sons of worthlessness, children of Belial," a phrase occurring not elsewhere in Chronicles, but again in 1 Kings xxi. 10, 13. On א' רֵקִים, "loose, fickle men," comp. Judg. ix. 4, xi. 3.—*And withstood Rehoboam,* "showed themselves strong against him" (הִתְאַמֵּץ עַל); comp. the (הִתְחַזֵּק לִפְנֵי) resistance afterwards shown on the part of Rehoboam to this opposition.—*Rehoboam was young and weak of heart,* faint-hearted, unstable. The term נַעַר, young, used of Rehoboam when already king, appears not specially to favour the former statement (ch. xii. 13) that he was then forty-one years old, and to require the change of this age into twenty-one years. Moreover, Abijah relates in this his speech the events in the revolt of the ten tribes from Rehoboam in a very inexact way (Rehoboam did not show himself "weak of heart" on that occasion, but rather hard and daring of heart, etc.); for he clearly wishes "to justify his father as far as possible, and roll all the blame of the revolt of the ten tribes on Jeroboam and his worthless followers" (Keil).—Ver. 8. *The kingdom of the Lord in the hand of the sons of David,* the theocratic kingdom founded by David, and hereditary in his house (comp. 1 Chron. xxix. 23 and the like).—Ver. 9. *Have ye not . . . made you priests like the nations of the lands,* not divinely called, but only humanly chosen, priests, like those of heathendom; comp. 1 Kings xii. 31.—*Whosoever cometh to fill his hand,* that is, institute and consecrate himself priest of the new worship; comp.

Ex. xxviii. 41, xxix. 9, xxxii. 29; see 1 Kings xiii. 33. The following words: "with a young steer (literally, with a steer the son of the herd) and seven rams," belong not so much to "fill" as to "cometh" (בּוֹא בְ, as Ps. xl. 8). As according to Ex. xxix. the offerings to be made on the consecration of a priest consisted of a young steer as a sin-offering, a ram as a burnt-offering, and a ram of consecration, and this presented on seven days in succession (thus in all seven steers and fourteen rams), the offering appears here to be imperfectly stated, not on account of an inaccurate report, but because Abijah might know that in fact there had been a considerable deviation from the strict requirements of the law, in order the more speedily to obtain a new priesthood. Indeed, it was a priesthood of non-gods or ungods (comp. Deut. xxxii. 21) which was so founded.—Ver. 10. *And the Levites in their business* ("in the business," במלאכת), performing their office in the legal way; comp. 1 Chron. xxiii. 28 ff.—Ver. 11. *Burn unto the Lord burnt-offerings,* "fumigate, turn into smoke," הִקְטִיר, which is then zeugmatically connected with the laying of the shew-bread and the lighting of the lamps, which are also parts of the priestly office. On these various priestly functions, that are then combined as a "keeping of the charge of the Lord" (Lev. viii. 35), comp. Ex. xxix. 38 ff., xxv. 30 ff., xxvii. 20 ff.; Lev. xxiv. 7 ff.—Ver. 12. *The clanging trumpets to sound* are made prominent, because God had expressly designated them in the law as the pledges on account of which He would remember and help His people in war, Num. x. 9.—Ver. 13 ff. Judah's Victory over the Superior Force of Israel.—*To come behind them;* comp. Josh. viii. 2; Judg. xx. 29 ff.—Ver. 15. *And the men of Judah shouted.* Keil rightly says: "In וַיָּרִיעוּ and בְּהָרִיעַ the loud cry of the warriors and the clanging of the priests with the trumpets are combined, and הָרִיעַ is to be referred neither alone to the war-cry of the combatants assailing the enemy, nor, with Berth. (and Kamph.), to the blowing of the clanging trumpets;" comp. also Judg. vii. 19 ff. (Gideon in the conflict with the Midianites).—Ver. 17. *Smote them with a great slaughter;* for the phrase, see Num. xi. 33; Josh. x. 30. For the number 500,000, which appears inconceivably great as the number of those who fell in the one field at Zemaraim, comp. Evangelical and Ethical Reflections, No. 3.—Ver. 18. *The sons of Israel were humbled* (comp. נכנע in ch. xii. 6 f.), or "weakened" by their enormous loss (comp. Judg. iii. 30, viii. 28; 1 Sam. vii. 13).—Ver. 19. *Bethel and her daughters,* her daughter towns; comp. Neh. xi. 25. Besides this border city of south Israel, well known from Gen. xii. 8, xxviii. 19, xxxv. 15, Josh. vii. 12., etc. (the present Beitin), are named the otherwise unknown Jeshanah (or Jesyna; comp. Crit. Note), and an Ephron, as cities taken by Abijah from the conquered. The last has scarcely anything but the name common with Mount Ephron on the south border of Benjamin (Josh. xv. 9), but should probably be identified with Ophrah near Bethel (Judg. vi. 11), or the town Ephraim situated there, mentioned Josh. xi. 54 (comp. Josephus, *B. J.* iv. 9. 9), especially if we are to read עֶפְרַיִן, with the Masorah; see Crit. Note.—Ver. 20. *And Jeroboam had no more strength;* עָצַר כֹּחַ, as ch. xx. 37; 1 Chron. xxix. 14.—*And the Lord smote him, and he died,* not "snatched him away by a sudden death" (of which nothing is known from 1 Kings), but "smote him, visited him with misfortune (comp. נגף in ver. 15 and ch. xxi. 18) till his death," referring probably to that which is related in 1 Kings xiv. 1–18.—Ver. 21 ff. Family History of Abijah; his End.—*And Abijah strengthened himself* (התחזק, as ch. xii. 13), *and took to him fourteen wives.* Comp. the Evangelical and Ethical Reflections in the previous section, No. 3. Abijah must have had most of these fourteen wives before he ascended the throne, or at least before his war with Jeroboam. That he took them after the war follows only apparently from the position in the narrative, which has no chronologic import.—Ver. 22. *Are written in the commentary of the prophet Iddo.* Comp. on this source of our author, Introd. § 5, II. p. 17.—Ver. 23. *And Asa . . . in his days the land was quiet ten years,* in consequence of the great victory of his father over Jeroboam, and the weakening of the northern kingdom thereby occasioned; comp. ch. xiv. 4, 5, xv. 19.

II. Asa: 1. His Theocratic Zeal and Care for the Defence of the Kingdom: ch. xiv. 1–7; comp. 1 Kings xv. 9–12, 14, 15.—*And Asa did that which was good and right;* comp. ch. xxxi. 20.—Ver. 2. *Took away the altars of the strange gods,* consecrated to strange gods, of the idolatrous foreign countries; comp. Gen. xxxv. 2, 4. That only these, and not also "high places," or illegal places of sacrifice consecrated to Jehovah, were removed by him, is clear from ch. xv. 17.—*And brake the pillars,* the memorial stones erected to Baal (מַצֵּבוֹת); comp. Ex. xxxiv. 13; Judg. iii. 7; 2 Kings iii. 2. Likewise the "Asherim," wooden posts and holy trees consecrated to Astarte; comp. 1 Kings xiv. 23, and Bähr on the passage.—On ver. 3, comp. ch. xv. 12.—Ver. 4. *And he took away . . . the high places and the sun-statues;* חַמָּנִים, the statues before the altars of Baal, consecrated to him as the sun-god; comp. ch. xxxiv. 4; Lev. xxvi. 30; Movers, *Die Phönizier,* i. 343 ff.—*And the kingdom was quiet before him,* that is, under him, under his eye (לְפָנָיו); comp. Num. viii. 22; Ps. lxxii. 5; Prov. iv. 3.—Ver. 5. *Built fenced cities in Judah . . . in those days,* during this quiet of ten years. Comp. Rehoboam's fortifications, ch. xi. 5 ff.—Ver. 6. *Let us build these cities.* What cities? It is not said; but certainly Geba and Mizpah, which were built after the war with Baasha (ch. xvi. 6). Asa assigns as the motive for these buildings: "the land is yet before us," free, open to us, unoccupied by the foe; comp. Gen. xiii. 9.—*And they built and prospered.* Vulg. very free, yet in substance correct; *nullumque in exstruendo impedimentum fuit.*—Ver. 7. *Bearing shield and spear.* The great or long shield (צִנָּה) is here meant, in opposition to the short or round shield (מָגֵן) then mentioned; the same difference as in ch. ix. 15, 16. That the Jews had exclusively only long shields and spears, and the Benjamites only short shields and bows, as armour, need not be assumed; the representation is only relative, summary, and not to be pressed, as also the numbers (300,000 of the Jews and 280,000 of the Benjamites) are obviously only round. They are, moreover, so far as the whole population fit to bear arms is concerned, by no means incredible. With respect to the comparatively high number of 280,000 Benjamites, we are to consider not only their lighter armour (which might be borne by younger and weaker men), but also that Benjamin was an eminently warlike tribe, "a ravening wolf" according to Jacob's prophetic word, Gen. xlix. 27, that must have taken the field with all possible force. Comp. also on 1 Chron. vii. 6–11, and the Evangelical and Ethical Reflections, No. 3.

2. Asa's Victory over Zerah the Ethiopian: vers. 8–14, a section wanting in Kings.—*And Zerah the Ethiopian came out against him.* This Zerah (Sept. Ζαρέ; Vulg. *Zara*) counts with most recent expositors, on account of the similarity of name, as the same with the Egyptian King Osorchon I., successor of Shishak-Sesonchis, and so the second king of the twenty-second or Bubastite Dynasty (comp. Unger, *Manetho*, p. 233; Thenius on 1 Kings xv. 23); whereas Hitzig rather identifies him with the Sabakos of Herodotus (*Gesch. des V. Isr.* p. 165 f.; comp. Herod. ii. 137 ff., 152), but Brugsch takes him for an Ethiopian, not Egyptian, ruler, who, under the reign of Takeloth I. (about 944 B.C.), invaded the south-west of Asia and Egypt as a conqueror. The last assumption certainly agrees best, as well with the Biblical chronology as with the designation of Zerah as a Kushite.—*With a host of* 1,000,000. On this number, as scarcely to be pressed, but rather depending on a rough and ideal estimate, see the Evangelical and Ethical Reflections, No. 3.—*And he came to Mareshah,* mentioned in ch. xi. 9, between Hebron and Ashdod.—Ver. 9. *And Asa went out against him,* literally, "before him"; comp. xv. 2; 1 Chron. xix. 14, xiv. 8.—*In the valley of Zephathah,* scarcely = Tell es Safieh (Robinson, *Pal.* ii. 625), but a place nearer Mareshah, perhaps that described by Robinson, ii. 613.—Ver. 10. *Lord, no one is nigh Thee to help,* no one is able like Thee (literally, "with Thee"; comp. ch. xx. 6; Ps. lxxiii. 25) to help.—*With the mighty, or with no might,* "between the mighty and the impotent" (בֵּין with לְ following, as Gen. i. 13, etc.); the help of God is conceived as imparted either to the mighty or the weak, and therefore as between both. Some conceive the passage otherwise; Vulg., Ramb., S. Schmidt, etc.: *Domine, non est apud te ulla distantia utrum in paucis auxilieris an in pluribus;* Berth., Keil, etc.: "No other than Thou can help in an unequal combat, that is, help the weaker part;" Kamph. (writing conjecturally לְעֵצֶר for לַעְזֹר): "It is impossible that anything could prevail (עָצַר כֹּחַ, as ch. xiii. 20, etc.), whether the mighty or the weak." Substantially correct, though inexact, Luther: "It is no difference with Thee to help among many, or where there is no power."—*In Thy name we go against this multitude,* trusting to Thy help.—*No man may hold out against Thee.* For the omission of כֹּחַ with עָצַר, comp. ch. xx. 37 (1 Chron. xxix. 14; 2 Chron. xiii. 25). On the sentence, comp. (partly at least) Ps. ix. 20*a*.—Ver. 12. *And Asa . . . pursued them unto Gerar,* the old Philistine city, now Khirbet el Gerar, three and a half hours south-east of Gaza.—*And the Ethiopians fell, so that there was no recovery,* not "so that there was none left living" (Berth., Kamph., etc.), but so that they could not rally, *ut eis vivificatio, i.e. copias restaurandi ratio non esset* (J. H. Mich., Keil, etc.). לְאֵין stands for אֵין of the older style, in the sense of "so that not" (comp. Ew. § 315, *c*). מִחְיָה, preservation of life, revival, as Gen. xlv. 5; Ezra ix. 8, 9.—*For they were broken* (נִשְׁבְּרוּ, as Ezek. xxx. 8) *before the Lord, and before His host;* Asa's army is here so called as the instrument of the divine justice against the haughty foe. To think of a host of angels that had contended invisibly on the side of the Jews (Starke and other older writers, with allusion to Gen. xxxii. 2 f.) is without any warrant, as the term מַחֲנֶה, especially in the singular, stands for a single earthly army.—Ver. 13. *And they smote all the cities around Gerar,* probably because, like the Philistines generally, they had made common cause with the Cushites, and joined them against the Jews.—*For the terror of the Lord,* a terror occasioned by the Lord, and therefore the more powerful; comp. xvii. 10, xx. 29; 1 Sam. xi. 7.—Ver. 14. *And they smote also the tents of cattle,* the herds of the nomad tribes in the neighbourhood of Gerar (in the northern regions of the wilderness of Shur and Paran, the old country of the Amalekites).

3. Prophetic Warning of Azariah Son of Oded to Asa returning Home: ch. xv. 1–7 (likewise peculiar to Chronicles).—*Upon Azariah son of Oded.* The names of both father and son occur only here: the identification of Oded with Iddo (ch. ix. 29, xii. 15) is an idle fancy of some ancients.—Ver. 2. *Before Asa,* to meet him; comp. on ch. xiv. 9.—*The Lord is with you, while you are with Him.* Comp. Jas. iv. 8; and with respect to the following sentence, 1 Chron. xxviii. 9; 2 Chron. xii. 5, xxiv. 20; Jer. xxix. 13.—Ver. 3. *And many days will be to Israel without the true God.* The Sept. and Vulg., Luther, Clericus, and most moderns rightly refer these words to the future, and thus conceive them to be a prediction of that which was to happen with respect to the relation of God's people to the Lord,—a prediction of like import with Hos. iii. 4, 5. For this view speaks, on the one hand, the generality of the term "Israel," which appears to be used here in the same ideal sense as in ch. xi. 3, xii. 1, and, on the other hand, the absence of any more precise date in וְיָמִים רַבִּים, by which that which is said is characterized as a general truth holding for all times; but the reference to any definite earlier time, with which, besides, the closing monition in ver. 7 would ill agree, is absolutely excluded. Neither the time of the judges, with its illegal conditions and its closing reformation by Samuel, is described by the prophet (against Vitr. and Ramb.), nor the last decennium of the southern kingdom before the reforms of Asa (as the Syr., Arab., Raschi, Berth., think), nor, finally, the circumstances of the northern king-

dom since Jeroboam (Targ., Tremell., Grotius, etc.). The last opinion is certainly the most arbitrary of all; for what occasion had the prophet to greet the king of the southern kingdom, returning as a conqueror after deliverance from a great danger, with a reflection on the errors and calamities of the northern kingdom? But if we refer the words as a prophecy to the future, no unsuitable limitation must be introduced (as, for example, to the Babylonish exile, of which Kimchi, Mariana, S. Schmidt, have thought). It is the whole future of the people of God, of which the prophet asserts the law: "If ye turn away from God, He will turn away from you." Comp. besides, Evangelical and Ethical Reflections, No. 1. On the "true God," properly, "God of truth," אֱלֹהֵי אֱמֶת, comp. Jer. x. 10 and Isa. lxv. 16 (אֵל׳ אָמֵן). לְלֹא אל׳ א׳, properly, "to not a god of truth"; לְלֹא, not essentially different from לְאֵין, 1 Chron. xxii. 4, 2 Chron. xx. 35, is distinguished from בְּלֹא only as לְ is distinguished from בְּ: the latter expresses the being in a state, the former the falling into it (Keil).—*Without a teaching priest*, without priests to perform the function of teaching (Lev. x. 10; Deut. xxxiii. 10); the special reference to the high priest (Vitr. and others) has no ground in the context. To the defect in teaching priests corresponds the defect in a law; for where there is no מוֹרֶה, there is no תּוֹרָה!—Ver. 5 f. The prophetic address returns after a passing brief promise of salvation (ver. 4*b*) to the description of th lamentable effects of the future apostasy from God.—*N peace for him that goeth out or cometh in*, thus no free, peaceful intercourse; on "going out and in," comp. ch. xvi. 1; Zech. viii. 10; Josh. vi. 1; on the following "great vexations" (מהומות), Deut. xxviii. 20; Amos iii. 9. "All the inhabitants of the lands" are all the inhabitants of the provinces of Israel (or Judah); see ch. xxxiv. 33. The view of the speaker here scarcely extends over the whole inhabited globe (Kamph.), although in the following verse he transcends the boundaries of Judah, and depicts its attraction into the confusion and conflict of the neighbouring nations.—*And nation shall be smitten by nation.* Kamphausen's rendering: "they are pushed nation on nation," is too far-fetched, and by no means required by the meaning of כתת. The Jews had a striking fulfilment of this gloomy foreboding of a *bellum omnium contra omnes* in the times of Nebuchadnezzar; a second in the destruction of Jerusalem by the Romans, with respect to which Christ also makes use of similar prophetic expressions, Luke xxi. 10, 26, and the parallels.—*For God hath vexed them with all trouble;* comp. Judg. iv 15; Zech. xiv. 13.—Ver. 7. *But be ye brave, and let not your hands be slack;* comp. Zeph. iii. 16; Neh. vi. 9; and "the hands becoming slack" as a figure of sinking courage, 2 Sam. iv. 1; Isa. xxxv. 3; Heb. xii. 11. On the closing promise of reward, comp. Jer. xxxi. 16; 1 Cor. iii. 8, xv. 58.

4. Asa's Reform of Worship and Renewal of Covenant with the Lord: vers. 8–19.—*And when Asa heard . . . . this prophecy of Oded the prophet.* The Hebrew text has not וְהַנְּבוּאַת, but וְהַנְּבוּאָה. This circumstance points to a corruption of the passage, as well as the absence of עֲזַרְיָהוּ בֶּן before עֹדֵד, which was to be expected according to ver. 1. As the readings of the Sept. and Vulg. (see Crit. Note) may be only later attempts at emendation, and as the assumption of a double name of Azariah, according to which he was at times called by the name of his father (Starke and other ancients), is certainly as questionable as the transposition of the corresponding names in ver. 1 into "Oded son of Azariah" (Mov.), it appears most advisable to remove the words עֹדֵד הַנָּבִיא from the text as an old gloss (Berth.), or (with Keil) to assume the omission of several words after וְהַנְּבוּאָה (say אֲשֶׁר דִּבֶּר עֲזַרְיָהוּ בֶּן).—*He took courage* (הִתְחַזַּק), according to Azariah's exhortation: "be ye brave," חִזְקוּ.—*Put away the abominations*, properly, "make to pass over (הֶעֱבִיר, as 1 Kings xv. 12) the abominations," the idols; comp. 2 Kings xxiii. 13, 24; Ezek. xxx. 7, 8; Dan. ix. 27.—*Which he had taken from Mount Ephraim*, לכד, as ch. xiii. 19, xvii. 2. According to the former of these passages, it appears that these were the cities that Abijah, Asa's father, had taken. In fact this assumption is necessary, because no war of Asa with the northern kingdom had taken place at this time. A co-operation of Asa as lieutenant or joint-commander with his father in that war seems a questionable assumption, on account of his then very great youth (perhaps his minority; comp. on ch. xiii. 1).—*And renewed the altar of the Lord, that was before the porch of the Lord*, the altar of burnt-offering, that might have been in need of repair sixty years after its erection by Solomon (ch. viii. 12). Yet חִדֵּשׁ, *renovare* (comp. ch. xxiv. 4), might possibly also be taken in the sense of "consecrate again," after the previous defilement by idolatry (Vulg.: *dedicavit;* Berth., Kamph., etc.).—Ver. 9 ff. The Great Festival on the Renewal of the Theocratic Covenant.—*And the strangers with them, out of Ephraim.* That by these strangers are meant not merely the theocratically-disposed immigrants into Judah under Rehoboam (xi. 16), but also a newer addition to them that had come under Asa himself, is expressly asserted in the following words (comp. xxx. 11, 18). The mention of Simeon with Ephraim and Manasseh, and therefore as a district belonging to the northern kingdom, is scarcely to be explained by a migration of many Simeonites to North Palestine (Berth., Kamph.), but rather by th fact that the tribe of Simeon, though in a geographical situation it belonged to the kingdom of Judah, yet in the point of idolatry had made common cause with the northern kingdom by the erection of that impure worship of Jehovah at Beersheba, of which Amos iv. 4, v. 5, viii. 14 speaks along with Bethel and Gilgal (correctly Keil, Net., etc.).—Ver. 10. *In the third month of the fifteenth year of the reign of Asa*, in

the spring of the year 940 B.C.; comp. Hitzig, *Gesch.* p. 197.—Ver. 11. *And they sacrificed . . . of the spoil they had brought*, in the war with the Ethiopians and their allies; for this war, though it broke out in the eleventh year of Asa (ch. xiii. 23, xiv. 8), might have extended even to the present date, and therefore lasted for four years; the statement in ch. xiv. 8–14 admits of this very well.—Ver. 12. *They entered into a covenant*, a new covenant of peace with God; comp. בּוֹא בִּבְרִית, Jer. xxxiv. 10; Neh. x. 30.—Ver. 13. *And whosoever . . . should be put to death*, according to the strict letter of the law, Deut. xvii. 2–6; comp. ch. xiii. 10, 17. Observe the present trace of a far higher age of the book of Deuteronomy than the time of Josiah, where modern criticism places its origin. Comp. Schröder, *Deuteron.* Einl. pp. 25, 32; Kleinert, *Das Deuteron. und der Deutoronomiker*, 1872, especially p. 136 ff.—Ver. 14. *And they sware unto the Lord with a loud voice.* On the musical instruments accompanying this act of the solemn renewal of the covenant, comp. xxiii. 13; Neh. xii. 27 ff.—Vers. 16–18. Comp. Bähr on the almost literally coinciding parallel 1 Kings xv. 13–15.—*And also Maachah, the mother of Asa the king, he removed.* In 1 Kings stands simply אִמּוֹ, "his mother," because there Maachah had been mentioned just before (ver. 10). For the rest, comp. on ch. xiii. 1.—*And Asa cut down her idol, and crushed it, and burnt it.* The "crushing" (comp. Ex. xxxii. 20; 2 Kings xxiii. 15) is mentioned only by the Chronist; in 1 Kings וַיָּדֹק is wanting.—Ver. 17. *Out of Israel* is wanting in 1 Kings. It naturally means the southern kingdom as the legitimate and normal people of Israel; comp. ver. 3.—*But the heart of Asa was perfect*, entirely devoted to the Lord. The עִם יְהוָה expressly added 1 Kings is here omitted, because the שָׁלֵם, as predicate to לֵב, is plain enough of itself (comp. ch. xvi. 9, xix. 9); that is, Asa's exclusive interest in the worship of Jehovah at Jerusalem, not in that (still tolerated) worship on the high places, is distinctly enough expressed.—Ver. 19, introducing the following account of the war.—*And there was no more war unto the thirty-fifth year of the reign of Asa.* The contradiction to 1 Kings xv. 16: "And there was war between Asa and Baasha king of Israel all their days," is in so far only apparent, as מִלְחָמָה there denotes only a state of hostility, here a formal war actually carried on in open field. It is not so easy to explain the difficulty involved in the date: "unto the thirty-fifth year of Asa's reign;" see on xvi. 1.

5. Asa's War with Baasha: ch. xvi. 1–6; comp. 1 Kings xv. 17–23.—*In the thirty-sixth year of the reign of Asa.* As, according to 1 Kings xvi. 8, 10, Baasha died in the twenty-sixth year of Asa's reign, and his successor Elah was killed before two years more had elapsed, and therefore in the twenty-seventh or twenty-eighth year of this king, the misplacing of the war between Asa and Baasha in the thirty-sixth year of the latter involves an error, and a very old one, already noted by the Sept., and provided with an attempt at emendation (see Crit. Note). A mistake of the pen, that, as ch. xv. 19 shows, existed perhaps in the sources of the Chronist, is probably the ground of this error; and 36 appears to have been miswritten for 16 (and in accordance with this, in ch. xv. 19, 35 for 15). From the similarity of the numeral ל (30) to י (10) in the old Hebrew character, this change was very possible; and the circumstance that Asa's reform of worship, ch. xv. 10, took place in the third month of his fifteenth year, agrees on the whole very well with this determination of time; there results an interval of a year or a year and a half between the reform and the new war. The solution preferred by most of the old expositors, that the thirty-sixth year of the kingdom of Asa, that is, the thirty-sixth year from the founding of the kingdom of Judah by Rehoboam, which coincides with the sixteenth year of the reign of Asa, is meant (des Vignoles, Ramb., Starke, Mich., and Hengstenberg, *Gesch. des Reiches Gottes*, iii. 169), is not consistent with the word לְמַלְכוּת, which in this connection always signifies "reign, sovereignty." The attempts made by Movers (*Chron.* p. 255 ff.) and Thenius (on 1 Kings xv.) to explain this surprising mistake are too artificial, and arbitrary (see, on the contrary side, Berth. p. 325). On the following particulars, coinciding almost word for word with 1 Kings xv. 17 ff., comp. Bähr's exposition.—Ver. 2. *And sent to Benhadad.* Instead of the form בֶּן־הֲדַד, presented here and generally in the Old Testament, the Assyrian monuments constantly exhibit this name in the form Binhidri (Schrader, *Die Keilinschriften*, p. 101 f.), thus agreeing with the υἱὸς τοῦ Ἄδερ of the Sept. (= בֶּן־הֲדֵר).—Ver. 4. *And they smote Abel-maim* = Abel-beth-maachah of the parallel text in 1 Kings, as is clear from 2 Sam. xx. 14.—*And all the stores of the cities of Naphtali.* For this 1 Kings has: "And all Cinneroth, with all the land of Naphtali." That the one of the two readings has arisen from the other by misunderstanding or miswriting seems certain; perhaps the כִּנְּרוֹת in 1 Kings is corrupted from מִסְכְּנוֹת (*Gesen.-Dietrich im Lex.*), though our וְאֵת כָּל־מִסְכְּנוֹת עָרֵי נ׳ might possibly also be an explanation of the וְאֵת כָּל־כִּנְּרוֹת עַל אֶרֶץ נ׳, 1 Kings xv., whereby the Chronist might have characterized the high fertility of the district of Cinneroth (or Cinnereth, Josh. xix. 35) by the symbolic expression: "stores (corn-magazines) of the cities of Naphtali" (so Keil).—Ver. 5. *And let his work cease.* Instead of this, 1 Kings xv. 21: "and dwelt in Tirzah." In our וַיַּשְׁבֵּת אֶת־מְלַאכְתּוֹ, scarcely anything else is to be seen but an attempt at interpretation, where the words וַיֵּשֶׁב בְּתִרְצָה had become illegible (Berth., Kamph.); for after the words: "he left off building of Ramah," a second repetition of the thought, that Baasha gave up his undertaking against Judah, was obviously superfluous (against Keil).—Ver. 6. *And built therewith Geba and Mizpah*, the former (Geba of Benjamin in 1 Kings) half an hour north-east,

the latter an hour south-west, of Jerusalem. The historical character of this notice is confirmed by Jer. xli. 9, where a pit made by Asa in Mizpah is mentioned.

6. Hanani's Prophetic Warning: Asa's Transgression and End: vers. 7–14.—*And at that time came Hanani.* This prophet (חֲנָנִי) is otherwise unknown, though he appears to be identical with the father of the prophet Jehu ben Hanani, who about this time announced to Baasha the downfall of his house (1 Kings xvi. 1); comp. xix. 2. That this Hanani was the author of the prophetic sentence (שִׁמְעִי) quoted by Hos. vii. 12, whereby Israel is warned against a league with foreign powers, or more definitely, that the present oracle of Hanani, without naming its author, is quoted in this passage of Hosea, is the quite untenable conjecture of some moderns, for example, Fürst (*Gesch. der bibl. Lit.* ii. 206, 293).—*Therefore is the host of the king of Syria escaped from thy hand*, the occasion has escaped thee of smiting both at once, Baasha of Israel and his presumptive ally the Syrian king. Comp. the rebuke by Elisha of Joash of Israel, for smiting only three times with the arrows instead of five or six times (2 Kings xiii. 15 ff.).—Ver. 8. Confirmatory reference to the victory of Asa over Zerah (xiv. 8 ff.). For the Lubites, comp. on xii. 3 f.—Ver. 9. *For the eyes of the Lord*, etc., literally, for Jehovah, His eyes. On "to prove himself strong for any one," that is, help him mightily, comp. 1 Chron. xi. 10. On "running" about, שׁוֹטֵט בְּ, comp. Jer. v. 1; Zech. iv. 10. Before עִם־לְבָבָם שָׁלֵם אֵלָיו the relative אֲשֶׁר is omitted; comp. 1 Chron. xv. 12.—*For henceforth thou shalt have wars*, entanglements in unhappy worldly transactions, in the dangerous mazes of the policy of the great powers; a prediction of misfortune that was abundantly fulfilled, if not in Asa himself, yet in his successors until the exile.—Ver. 10. *Put him in the prison*, properly, "house of the stocks"; מַהְפֶּכֶת, "turning round," is the well-known instrument of torture for locking round the culprit, in which Jeremiah also and Paul were forced to languish (Jer. xx. 2, xxix. 26; Acts xvi. 24). Comp. the equivalent סַד, Job xiii. 27, xxxiii. 11.—*And Asa oppressed some of the people at that time*, from anger at the deserved censure of the prophet (on the suitableness and importance of this address, see the Evangelical and Ethical Reflections). רָצַץ, properly, "shatter," in *Pi.*: "oppress, misuse," as Job xx. 19.—Vers. 11–14. Asa's End. On ver. 11, comp. Introd. § 5, II.—Ver. 12. *And Asa . . . was diseased in his feet*, probably with gout; the following also: "his disease was very great" (literally, till it reached a great height, עַד לְמַעְלָה), points to severe suffering of this kind.—*And in his disease also he sought not the Lord, but to the physicians.* דָּרַשׁ, first with the accusative of the object אֶת־יהוה, as is usual elsewhere, then with בְּ, by which preposition is elsewhere designated, inquiring or seeking help from God or from idols (1 Chron. x. 14; 1 Sam. xxviii. 7; 2 Kings i. 2 ff.); thus here expressing a superstitious trust in the physicians, and accordingly not opposed to the right of making use of medical aid, especially in cases of sickness; so far from this, that inversely the not seeking of the Lord may be regarded as a not seeking of his priests who were in Israel, analogous to the Egyptian priests, the legitimate physicians (as is done by K. Ad. Menzel in his posthumous work, *Religion und Stadtsidee*, 1872, p. 29).—Ver. 14. Asa's solemn burial is related by the Chronist with surprising detail, probably on account of the heathenish pomp and luxury which it displayed, reminding us of the manner of the Egyptian Pharaohs.—*And they buried him in his own tomb*, literally, "in his own sepulchres;" comp. 2 Kings xxii. 20; Job xxi. 32. This preparation of a burial-place or mausoleum, different from the common tombs of the kings, reminds us of the customs of the Egyptian kings, or at all events (comp. our Remark on Job iii. 14) indicates a haughty inclination to self-apotheosis incompatible with a genuine theocratic disposition; comp. Isa. xxii. 16 ff.—*Laid him in the bed which was filled with sweet odours of divers kinds.* On זְנִים, "kinds," comp. Ps. cxliv. 13, Dan. iii. 5; the term may well serve to describe more precisely the foregoing בְּשָׂמִים, "spices" (Song iv. 10 ff.).—*Compounded by art*, properly, "compounded by compounding of work," by the work of the artificer; comp. Ex. xxx. 25, 35, and 1 Chron. ix. 30. מַעֲשֶׂה is in this connection מַעֲשֵׂה רוֹקֵחַ; the assumption that the latter word is omitted is unnecessary.—*And they made a very great burning for him*, namely, of the sweet-smelling substances of the kind mentioned. Such burnings of incense were always made at the burial of the kings of Judah, as appears from Jer. xxxiv. 5. But what the Chronist notices as culpable is the exaggerated splendour and lavish excess with which the custom was observed in the burial of Asa, as if it were the burial of a Pharaoh of Egypt (comp. Wilkinson, *Manners and Customs*, etc., ii. 385 f.; Uhlemann, *Egypt. Alterthumsk.* ii. 325). Against the assumption of some, as Michaelis (*De combustione et humatione mortuorum apud Hebræos*, in his *Syntagma dissertatt.* i. 225 sqq.), that the body of the king was burned among the spices, see Geier, *De luctu Hebræor.* c. vi., who rightly maintains that such cases as the burning of Saul and his sons were exceptions to the general custom of Hebrew antiquity.

EVANGELICAL AND ETHICAL REFLECTIONS AND APOLOGETIC REMARKS ON CH. XIII.–XVI.

1. To much that is original, and in a theological sense important, in the comparatively full account given by our author of the reigns of Abijah and Asa, belong especially the three speeches which it contains, of which the old parallel text presents neither a brief *résumé* nor even a passing trace. All three are in a high degree characteristic, and point to a primitive tradition, true in all essentials to word and deed as their source. The address of Abijah to the Ephraimites from Mount Zemaraim is strictly an *oratio pro domo*, a defence of a royal representative of the house of David maintaining the good cause of his theocratic inheritance. With no

little skill, and with much diplomatic art as well as downright popular rhetoric; all is put forward that can be said for the legitimate kingdom and worship, and against the usurpation of Jeroboam. There is reference, on the one hand, to the unchangeableness of the covenant with Jehovah (xiii. 5), to the divine origin of the Davidic dynasty (as "a kingdom of the Lord in the hand of the sons of David," ver. 8), to the beauty and established order of the service of God in the central sanctuary at Jerusalem, and to the hereditary legal chartered dignity of the theocratic priesthood (vers. 10–12); and, on the other hand, to the unworthy aims of the revolution party led by Jeroboam (the men of Belial who took advantage of the tender youth, inexperience, and weakness of Rehoboam, ver. 7), to the folly of the worship of the golden calves, the illegal and heathenish character of its priesthood, the hopelessness of a contest with Jehovah, the God of their fathers (vers. 8, 9, 12), in the tone now of fine irony, now of bitter scorn, and now of threatening earnest. The whole, inclusive of the partisan, one-sided, and somewhat distorted reference to the procedure in the separation of the kingdom (ver. 7), appears a masterpiece of political eloquence, the present form of which (taken, no doubt, from the Midrasch of the prophet Iddo quoted in ver. 22) may be ideally conceived; but the chief context and process of thought can scarcely be a pure invention. No less original and characteristic are the two prophetic speeches inserted in the history of Asa's reign. The speech of Azariah son of Oded (ch. xv. 2–7) unfolds at the moment a gloomy picture of the future godlessness of the people forsaking their God more and more, and of the troubles and judgments arising from their unfaithfulness, where the tone of jubilant gladness for the great victory secured, and the announcement of optimistic expectations, would have seemed most natural. Instead of a panegyristic flatterer courting princely favour, a deeply-earnest prophet of woe greets the king returning in triumph, who has certainly words of acknowledgment for that which has been performed by the conquerors, but clothes his praise in the form of an exhibition of necessary connection between devotion to God and the gracious reward of such devotion, and dwells with visible predilection on the times of apostasy, with its tragic consequences, that were coming notwithstanding all the admonitions of the prophets. The speech appears badly enough to suit the festive moment that forms its occasion; but it testifies to the unusually deep glance into the inmost heart of the people which the speaker filled with the terrible earnest of the coming destiny has long taken. And as such testimony, it fails not also of its effect, but rather proves, as the consequent energy of the king in purifying the form of worship shows, a true comfort and strengthening for good (παράκλησις, *confortatio;* comp. הִתְחַזֵּק, Sept. κατίσχυσεν, ver. 8), an impulse at least effectual for a time to return to the path of theocratic truth and righteousness, a model (Hos. iii. 4 f., ix. 3, 4, where there seems to be an allusion to it) and primitive form held in esteem by later prophets of genuine prediction, the fundamental thought of which, as it recurs (*mutatis mutandis*) in the woe-foreboding addresses of an Isaiah to Hezekiah (Isa. xxxix.; 2 Kings xx.), and a Huldah to Josiah (2 Chron. xxxiv. 22 ff.), stands forth not essentially different in the pictures of the future presented in the New Testament (Matt. xxiv. 5 ff.; 2 Thess. ii. 3 ff.; 1 John ii. 18 ff.; Luke xviii. 8, etc.). In severe rebuke of a temporary departure of the king from the path of theological strictness and conscientiousness marked out for him by the prophetic word of Azariah, proceeds the second of the two prophetic speakers, Hanani (ch. xvi. 7–9). With a sharp lecture he treats the king, looking for nothing but praise for his victory over Baasha. That he made not Jehovah but the Syrian heathens his stay, he pronounces not only imprudent but directly "foolish" (ver. 9). His sagacity, not unexercised in political matters, lets him know immediately, under the influence of the illuminating Spirit of God, that the calling in the help of the Syrian power must draw to it the dependence, not merely of the conquered Israelites, but also of the Jews. Wherefore he not only blames the misled prince's weakness of faith and fear of man, and emphatically lays before him, that the eyes of the Lord are only strong for those who serve Him with entire devotion, but hurls upon him a hard נִסְכַּלְתָּ, *stulte egisti* (unduly softened by the Sept. into a weak ἠγνόηκας ἐπὶ τούτῳ). He suffers for this boldness the same punishment which Jeremiah brought upon himself, when he, a no less zealous preacher of the truth that man should not make flesh his arm than Hanani, had spoken hard words against the obstinacy and folly of his contemporaries (Jer. xx. 2; comp. ch. xvii. 5, xix. 15).—Here again is nothing that is not in the highest degree original and powerful, breathing the stern prophetic spirit of Samuel and Nathan. Both speeches may show in their present form the elaborating hand of the Chronist, but in matter they appear with incontestable evidence as documents taken from the prophetic historical sources of the writer, of a time bordering upon and cognate with the spirit of Elijah and Elisha.

2. In a religious and moral respect, the two kings described in our section appear again somewhat better than Rehoboam, who trod in the paths of the degenerate Solomon. In particular, Asa receives due praise for his theocratic zeal, as he busied himself as a reformer of the worship of God, that had been in several ways disfigured by superstition. The Deuteronomic law, which threatens every partaker in such idolatry with death, he not only binds upon the people by an oath (xv. 13 f.), but puts in practice the judicial rigour of this statute even against his own mother (grandmother), as he removes her from her dignity as queen-mother on account of her worship of Astarte, and so makes judgment begin at the royal house itself (ver. 16). Inasmuch as he certainly does not set aside (ver. 17) the worship on the high places, he does not rise to the height of theocratic rigour and purity which was attained in the subsequent reforms of Hezekiah and Josiah. The later time and the end of his reign also were tarnished by bursts of passion and acts of violence towards pious men of God, as the prophet Hanani; and a severe and painful disease is not able to bring him back to the early well-known simplicity of his devotion to Jehovah (ch. xvi. 12; comp. xv. 17). He seeks not the Lord, but betakes himself to the physicians; the impure

juggling method, mingled no doubt with superstition and idolatry, pursued by the medicine men or goetæ of his time, gave him more confidence than the helping hand of the God of truth, with whose witnesses he had also quarrelled. So it fared otherwise with him than with the pious Hezekiah, who without medical aid, by the miraculous help of God obtained through the prophet, was delivered from a dangerous sickness, and had fifteen years added to his life (2 Kings xx.; 2 Chron. xxxii. 24). The word of the wise Sirach was verified in him: "He that sinneth before his Maker shall fall into the hand of the physician" (Sir. xxxviii. 15). Like the woman having the issue of blood, he must become πολλὰ παθὼν ὑπὸ πολλῶν ἰατρῶν, Mark v. 26. In setting forth the impotence of these human helpers exclusively sought by him (comp. Sir. x. 11: μακρὸν ἀῤῥώστημα σκώπτει ἰατρόν[1]), there is no absolute condemnation of medical art or science, but merely a gentle hint of the state of his heart, enslaved to worldly and idolatrous lusts, God-estranged and unbelieving, on account of which might justly be addressed to him the question of the prophet Jeremiah: "Is there no balm in Gilead? Is there no physician there? Why, then, is not the health of the daughter of my people recovered?" Jer. viii. 22; or also that question of Elijah: "Is it not because there is not a God in Israel that ye go to inquire of Baalzebub the god of Ekron?" 2 Kings i. 3. Comp. also, with respect to Asa's religious and moral character, the weighty remark of Bengel (*Beiträge zum Schriftverständniss*, p. 17 f.): "Asa was righteous (xv. 17), and yet he behaved so badly at the last (xvi. 10, 12). How can this be? Answer.—He has not turned to idols all his life long; he has constantly held the Lord to be the right, true, and only God. But it was, as it were, an *atheismus practicus*, that he withdrew his confidence from Him. He thought, Shall I have been pious so long, and yet now receive a reprimand? If he had only received it like David: I have sinned, etc., all would have been right, etc."

3. In an apologetic respect, we have to observe, in conjunction with the remarks made under No. 1, that weighty credentials of an internal kind support the two great wars as the Chronist relates them here, in completion of the very imperfect account in the books of Kings of these episodes in the history of the reigns of Abijah and Asa. That Abijah's conflict with Jeroboam, after the total dissolution of the army of the latter, led to the annexation of the three towns Bethel, Jeshanah, and Ephron to the southern kingdom (ch. xiii. 19), is a notice so definite and concrete, that no scepticism of de Wette and Gramberg, with its assertion of the feigned character of the narrative in question, can be accepted, as, on the other hand, the attempt of Ewald, while admitting a kernel of historical fact, to stamp at least the speech of Abijah on Mount Zemaraim as a free composition of the Chronist, is wrecked on the highly original contents of this speech (see No. 1, and comp. Keil, *Commentar*, p. 264 f., Remarks). The passage 1 Kings xv. 15 also, where the things dedicated by Abijah are mentioned, which his son Asa afterwards brought into the house of the Lord along with his own dedicated gifts, affords an indirect proof that both rulers had gained great victories and taken much spoil from their foes (comp. 2 Chron. xiv. 12 f.), by which must be meant the victory of the former over Jeroboam, and that of the latter over Zerah (comp. Thenius on this passage, and Berth. on Chron. p. 324). The credibility of the account of this last great battle derives support also from what is related at its close of the conquest and spoliation of the cities around Gerar, and the cattle tents of the nomad tribes dwelling south of Palestine, a detail, again, that gives the lie altogether to the suspicion of pure fiction.—Only the very high numbers in the account of the slaughter should be regarded as falling beyond the range of the historically exact. They "are perhaps not to be understood according to the nominal value of the numbers given, but only an expression conceived in figures of the contemporaries of these wars, which imports that the two kings (first Abijah and Jeroboam, then Asa and Zerah) had summoned to the field the whole military strength of their kingdoms" (Keil, p. 265). In the war of Abijah with Jeroboam, this is favoured by the approximative accordance of the numbers 800,000 and 400,000 with results of the census by David, as well as the round ideal sum of 500,000 as the number of those who fell on the side of Israel, a number that perhaps only indicates that Jeroboam had lost more than half his force. In the war with the Ethiopian king, the corresponding assumption is favoured by the round number 1,000,000, as well as by the circumstance that exact accounts, resting on actual numbering, and not on a mere estimate, of the strength of the enemy, were not at the command of the observers and reporters on the Jewish side (comp. above on the passages in question). The necessity of a merely ideal and approximate conception of these numbers is evident, if we compare the statements, resting on actual numbering, of the strength of the men-at-arms in the several tribes in the genealogical summaries (1 Chron. v.-vii.). The smallest of the numbers there named (for example, 44,760, 87,000, 22,034, 20,200, 17,200, 26,000) are round. It is the same with the numbers referring to the warriors from the several tribes at the elevation of David to the throne in 1 Chron. xii.; comp. the remarks on this in p. 120 f.

[1] Ἰατρόν, we believe, in the notorious corruption of the text (see Fritzsche's *Libb. apocr. V. T.* p. 409), with Hitzig (*Der Proph. Daniel*, p. 142), should be read here instead of ἰατρός.

d. JEHOSHAPHAT: THE PROPHETS MICHAH SON OF IMLAH AND JEHU SON OF HANANI.—CH. XVII.-XX.

α. Jehoshaphat's Measures for the External and Internal Defence of his Kingdom: ch. xvii. 1-9.

CH. XVII. 1. And Jehoshaphat his son reigned in his stead, and strengthened himself
2 against Israel. And he placed forces in all the fenced cities of Judah, and
placed garrisons in the land of Judah, and in the cities of Ephraim, which

3 Asa his father had taken. And the LORD was with Jehoshaphat; for he
walked in the former ways of his father David, and sought not unto Baalim.
4 But sought to the LORD God of his father, and walked in His commandments,
5 and not after the doing of Israel. And the LORD stablished the kingdom in
his hand; and all Judah brought presents to Jehoshaphat; and he had riches
6 and honour in abundance. And his heart was lifted up in the ways of the
LORD; and, moreover, he took away the high places and Asherim out of
7 Judah. And in the third year of his reign he sent his princes, Benhail,[1] and
Obadiah, and Zechariah, and Nethaneel, and Michaiah, to teach in the cities
8 of Judah. And with them the Levites, Shemaiah, and Nethaniah, and
Zebadiah, and Asahel, and Shemiramoth,[2] and Jehonathan, and Adonijah,
and Tobijah, and Tob-adonijah, Levites; and with them Elishama and
9 Jehoram, priests. And they taught in Judah, and had with them the book
of the law of the LORD, and went round all the cities of Judah, and taught
among the people.

β. The Effects of these Measures: Jehoshaphat's increasing Power: vers. 10–19.

10 And the fear of the LORD fell upon all the kingdoms of the lands that
11 were around Judah, and they warred not with Jehoshaphat. And some of
the Philistines brought Jehoshaphat presents, and silver in abundance; the
Arabs also brought him flocks, seven thousand and seven hundred rams, and
12 seven thousand and seven hundred he-goats. And Jehoshaphat became ever
greater to the highest degree; and he built in Judah castles and cities with
13 stores. And he had much store in the cities of Judah: and men of war,
14 mighty men of valour, in Jerusalem. And this was the muster of them after
their father-houses: of Judah, the captains of thousands: Adnah the chief,
15 and with him mighty men of valour three hundred thousand. And at his
hand Jehohanan the chief, and with him two hundred and eighty thousand.
16 And at his hand Amasiah son of Zichri, who willingly offered himself unto
17 the LORD; and with him two hundred thousand mighty men of valour. And
of Benjamin: Eliada, a mighty man of valour, and with him, armed with bow
18 and shield, two hundred thousand. And at his hand Jehozabad, and with
19 him a hundred and eighty thousand equipped for the war. These were they
who ministered to the king, besides those whom the king had placed in the
fenced cities in all Judah.

γ. Jehoshaphat's Affinity with Ahab, and the War against Ramoth-gilead: ch. xviii.

CH. XVIII. 1. And Jehoshaphat had riches and honour in abundance, and joined
2 affinity with Ahab. And in the course of years he went down to Ahab
to Samaria: and Ahab killed for him, and the people that were with him,
sheep and oxen in abundance; and he persuaded him to go up with him to
3 Ramoth-gilead. And Ahab king of Israel said unto Jehoshaphat king of
Judah, Wilt thou go with me to Ramoth-gilead? And he said to him, I
am as thou, and my people as thy people; and we will be with thee in the
4 war. And Jehoshaphat said unto the king of Israel, Ask now this day the
5 word of the LORD. And the king of Israel gathered the prophets, four
hundred men, and said unto them, Shall we go to Ramoth-gilead to battle, or
shall I forbear? And they said, Go up; and God will give it into the hand
6 of the king. And Jehoshaphat said, Is there not here a prophet of the LORD
7 besides, that we may ask of him? And the king of Israel said unto
Jehoshaphat, There is yet one man, by whom we may inquire of the LORD;
but I hate him, because he never prophesied good to me, but always evil:
that is Michah son of Imlah: and Jehoshaphat said, Let not the king
say so.

8 And the king of Israel called a chamberlain, and said, Fetch quickly
9 Michah[3] son of Imlah. And the king of Israel, and Jehoshaphat king of
Judah, sat each on his throne, clothed in robes, and they sat in a floor at the

entrance of the gate of Samaria; and all the prophets prophesied before them.
10 And Zedekiah son of Chenaanah made him iron horns, and said, Thus saith
11 the LORD, With these thou shalt push Syria, until they are consumed. And
all the prophets prophesied so, and said, Go up to Ramoth-gilead, and prosper;
and the Lord shall deliver it into the hand of the king.
12 And the messenger that went to call Michah spake to him, saying, Behold,
the words of the prophets are with one mouth good for the king: let now thy
13 word then be as one of them, and speak thou good. And Michah said, As
14 the Lord liveth, what my God saith, that will I speak. And he came to the
king; and the king said unto him, Michah, Shall we go to Ramoth-gilead to
battle, or shall I forbear? And he said, Go ye up, and prosper, and they
15 shall be delivered into your hand. And the king said to him, How many
times shall I adjure thee, that thou speak nothing to me but truth in the
16 name of the LORD? And he said, I saw all Israel scattered upon the moun
tains, as sheep that have no shepherd: and the LORD said, These have no
17 master; let them return every man to his house in peace. And the king of
Israel said to Jehoshaphat, Did I not tell thee that he would not prophesy
good to me, but evil?
18 And he said, Therefore hear ye the word of the LORD; I saw the LORD
sitting upon His throne, and all the host of heaven standing on His right
19 hand and on His left. And the LORD said, Who shall entice Ahab king of
Israel, that he may go up and fall at Ramoth-gilead? And one said[4] this,
20 and another said that. And the spirit came forth, and stood before the LORD,
21 and said, I will entice him: and the LORD said unto him, Wherewith? And
he said, I will go forth, and be a lying spirit in the mouth of all his prophets:
and He said, Thou shalt entice, and shalt also prevail: go forth, and do so.
22 And now, behold, the LORD hath put a lying spirit in the mouth of these thy
23 prophets, and the LORD hath spoken evil against thee. And Zedekiah son of
Chenaanah drew near, and smote Michah on the cheek, and said, Which way
24 went the Spirit of the LORD from me to speak with thee? And Michah said,
Behold, thou shalt see on that day when thou goest from chamber to chamber
25 to hide thyself. And the king of Israel said, Take ye Michah, and carry him
26 back to Amon the governor of the city, and to Joash the king's son. And say
ye, Thus saith the king, Put him in the prison, and let him eat bread of trouble,
27 and water of trouble, until I return in peace. And Michah said, If thou
return at all in peace, the LORD hath not spoken by me: and he said, Hear,
all ye people.
28 And the king of Israel, and Jehoshaphat king of Judah, went up to
29 Ramoth-gilead. And the king of Israel said to Jehoshaphat, Disguised I will
go into the battle; but thou put on thy robes: and the king of Israel dis-
30 guised himself, and they went into the battle. And the king of Syria had
commanded the captains of his chariots, saying, Fight ye not with small or
31 great, but only with the king of Israel. And it came to pass, when the
captains of the chariots saw Jehoshaphat, that they said, This is the king of
Israel; and they compassed about him to fight; and Jehoshaphat cried out,
32 and the LORD helped him, and God turned them away from him. And it
came to pass, when the captains of the chariots saw that it was not the king
33 of Israel, that they turned from after him. And a man drew a bow in his
simplicity, and smote the king of Israel between the joints of the harness:
and he said to the charioteer, Turn thy hand,[5] and carry me out of the host;
34 for I am wounded. And the battle went up in that day, and the king of
Israel was standing in the chariot against Syria until the evening; and he
died at the time of the sun setting.

δ. *Judgment of Jehu the Prophet on the Covenant of Jehoshaphat with Ahab:* ch. xix. 1-3.

CH. XIX. 1. And Jehoshaphat king of Judah returned home in peace to Jerusalem.
2 And Jehu son of Hanani the seer went out to meet him, and said to king
Jehoshaphat, Must we help the wicked, and shouldst thou love them that

3 hate the LORD? and for this is wrath upon thee from the LORD. Yet good
things are found with thee; for thou hast destroyed the Asherim out of the
land, and thou hast directed thy heart to seek God.

ε. *Jehoshaphat's further Reforms of Worship and Law:* vers. 4–11.

4 And Jehoshaphat dwelt at Jerusalem: and he went out again among the
people, from Beersheba to mount Ephraim, and brought them back to the
5 LORD God of their fathers. And he appointed judges in the land, in all the
6 fenced cities of Judah, city by city. And said to the judges: See what ye
do; for ye judge not for man, but for the LORD; and He is with you in judg-
7 ment. And now let the fear of the LORD be upon you; take heed and do
ye; for with the LORD our God is neither iniquity, nor respect of persons,
8 nor taking of gift.—And also in Jerusalem Jehoshaphat appointed of the
Levites and priests, and of the chief of the fathers of Israel, for the judgment
9 of the LORD, and for pleading; and they returned to Jerusalem. And he
commanded them, saying, Thus shall ye do in the fear of the LORD, with
10 truth and a perfect heart. And in[6] every plea that cometh before you of
your brethren that dwell in their cities, between blood and blood, between
law and commandment, statutes and judgments, ye shall advise them, that
they trespass not against the LORD, so that wrath come upon you and your
11 brethren: thus shall ye do, and not trespass.[7] And, behold, Amariah the
chief priest is over you for every matter of the LORD; and Zebadiah son of
Ishmael, the ruler of the house of Judah, for every matter of the king; and
the Levites are officers before you: take courage, and do ye, and the LORD
will be with the good.

ζ. *Jehoshaphat's Victory over the Moabites, Ammonites, and other Nations of the East:* ch. xx. 1–30.

CH. XX. 1. And it came to pass after this, that the sons of Moab and the sons of
Ammon, and with them of the Meunites,[8] came against Jehoshaphat to battle.
2 And they came and told Jehoshaphat, saying, There cometh against thee a
great multitude from beyond the sea, from Syria; and, behold, they are at
3 Hazezon-tamar, that is Engedi. And Jehoshaphat was afraid,[9] and set his
4 face to seek the LORD, and proclaimed a fast over all Judah. And the Jews
assembled to seek the LORD: even from all the cities of Judah came they to seek
5 the LORD. And Jehoshaphat stood in the congregation of Judah and Jeru-
6 salem, in the house of the LORD, before the new court. And said, LORD God
of our fathers, art not Thou God in heaven, and ruler over all the kingdoms of
the nations? and in thy hand are strength and might, and none is with Thee
7 to withstand Thee. Hast not Thou, our God, driven out the inhabitants of
this land before Thy people Israel, and given it to the seed of Abraham Thy
8 friend for ever? And they dwelt therein, and built Thee a sanctuary therein
9 for Thy name, saying: If evil come upon us, sword, judgment, or pestilence
or famine, we shall stand before this house, and before Thee—for Thy name is
in this house—and shall cry unto Thee out of our affliction: then Thou wilt
10 hear and help. And now, behold, the sons of Ammon, and Moab, and mount
Seir, whom thou wouldst not let Israel invade, when they came out of the
11 land of Egypt, but they departed from them, and destroyed them not. And,
behold, they requite us by coming to cast us out of Thy possession which
12 Thou hast given us. Our God, wilt Thou not judge them? for in us is no
might against this great multitude that cometh against us; and we know not
13 what we shall do: but our eyes are upon Thee. And all Judah stood before
the LORD, and their little ones, their wives, and their sons.
14 And upon Jahaziel the son of Zechariah, the son of Benaiah, the son of
Jeiel, the son of Mattaniah, the Levite of the sons of Asaph, came the Spirit
15 of the LORD in the midst of the congregation. And he said, Attend ye, all
Judah, and ye inhabitants of Jerusalem, and thou king Jehoshaphat; Thus

saith the LORD unto you, Be not afraid nor dismayed before this great multi-
16 tude; for the battle is not yours, but God's. To-morrow go ye down against
them: behold, they go up by the hill of Haziz; and ye shall find them at the
17 end of the valley, before the wilderness of Jeruel. Ye shall not have to fight
here: step forth, stand ye, and see the help of the LORD who is with you, O
Judah and Jerusalem: fear ye not, nor be dismayed; to-morrow go out
18 against them, and the LORD will be with you. And Jehoshaphat bowed his
face to the ground; and all Judah and the inhabitants of Jerusalem fell
19 before the LORD, to worship the LORD. And the Levites of the sons of
Kohath, and of the Korhites, stood up to praise the LORD God of Israel with
an exceeding loud voice.

20 And they rose early in the morning, and went forth into the wilderness
of Tekoa; and as they went forth, Jehoshaphat stood up and said, Hear ye
me, Judah and the inhabitants of Jerusalem: Believe in the LORD your God,
and ye shall be established; believe in His prophets, and ye shall prosper.
21 And he advised the people, and appointed men singing unto the LORD, and
praising in holy beauty, when they go out before the armed men, and saying,
22 Give thanks to the LORD; for His mercy endureth for ever. And at the time
when they began with song and praise, the Lord set an ambush against the
sons of Ammon, Moab, and mount Seir, which were come against Judah; and
23 they were smitten. And the sons of Ammon and Moab stood up against the
inhabitants of mount Seir, to cut off and destroy them; and when they had
ended with the inhabitants of Seir, they helped to destroy one another.

24 And Judah came to the watch-tower in the wilderness, and looked to the
multitude; and, behold, they lay as corpses on the earth, and none escaped.
25 And Jehoshaphat and his people came to take their spoil, and they found with
them in abundance, goods and corpses,[10] and costly vessels; and they stripped
off for themselves more than they could carry; and they were three days
26 taking the spoil, for it was great. And on the fourth day they assembled in
the valley of blessing; for there they blessed the LORD: therefore they
27 called the name of the place the valley of blessing unto this day. And they
returned, every man of Judah and Jerusalem, and Jehoshaphat at their head,
to return to Jerusalem with gladness; for the LORD had made them glad over
28 their enemies. And they came to Jerusalem with psalteries, and harps, and
29 trumpets, unto the house of the LORD. And the fear of God was upon all
the kingdoms of the countries when they heard that the LORD fought against
30 the enemies of Israel. And the realm of Jehoshaphat was quiet; for his God
gave him rest round about.

η. *End of the Reign of Jehoshaphat:* vers. 31–37.

31 And Jehoshaphat reigned over Judah: he was thirty and five years old
when he became king, and he reigned twenty and five years in Jerusalem
32 and his mother's name was Azubah, daughter of Shilhi. And he walked in
the way of his father Asa, and departed not from it, so that he did that
33 which was right in the sight of the LORD. Only the high places were not
taken away, and the people had not yet directed their heart to the God of
their fathers.

34 And the rest of the acts of Jehoshaphat, first and last, behold, they are
written in the words of Jehu son of Hanani, which are inserted in the book
of the kings of Israel.

35 And afterwards Jehoshaphat king of Judah allied himself with Ahaziah
36 king of Israel: he was wicked in his doing. And he allied himself with him,
37 to make ships to go to Tarshish: and they made ships in Ezion-geber. And
Eliezer, son of Dodavah[11] of Mareshah, prophesied against Jehoshaphat,
saying, Because thou hast allied thyself with Ahaziah, the LORD hath
broken thy work: and the ships were wrecked, and were not able to go to
Tarshish.

[1] For בֶּן־חַיִל the Sept. (and Syr.) appears to have read בְּנֵי חַיִל; for they translate appellatively, υἱοὺς τῶν δυνάτων. But the word is certainly a proper name; comp. בֶּן־חֶסֶד, 1 Kings iv. 10, and similar names.

[2] The *Kethib* שְׁמִרֵימוֹת is a mere mistake for שְׁמִירָמוֹת, the *Keri*.

[3] *Kethib:* מִיכָהוּ. *Keri:* מִיכָיָהוּ.

[4] The redundant אֹמֵר after וַיֹּאמֶר זֶה is perhaps inserted by a mistake of the transcriber, and therefore, according to 1 Kings xxii. 20, to be erased.

[5] *Kethib:* יָדֶיךָ. *Keri:* יָדְךָ.

[6] וְ before כָּל־רִיב is wanting in the Sept. and Vulg., but if taken explicatively it involves no difficulty.

[7] *Kethib:* תֶאְשְׁמוּ. *Keri:* תֶאְשָׁמוּ.

[8] Instead of מֵהָעַמּוֹנִים is undoubtedly to be read מֵהַמְּעוּנִים, as the ἐκ τῶν Μιναίων of the Sept. shows.

[9] *Kethib:* וַיִּרָא. *Keri:* וַיִּירָא.

[10] Instead of פְּגָרִים, four MSS. in Kennic. and three in de Rossi, likewise some old editions (Complut., Brix., Bomberg. *a.* 1518, 21, Münst.), read בְּגָדִים; so also the Vulg. (*vestes*), and apparently also the Sept., as well as several recent expositors, Dathe, Berth., and Kamph.

[11] For דּוֹדָוָהוּ the Sept. has Δωδία, after which Berth., without sufficient reason, would write דּוֹדִיָּהוּ. Comp. rather such names as Hodaviah, Joshaviah.

EXEGETICAL.

Besides the report in ch. xviii. of the unsuccessful campaign of Jehoshaphat and Ahab against Ramoth-gilead, agreeing almost literally with 1 Kings xxii. 2–35 and the closing section ch. xx. 30–37, which coincides partly in matter and partly in form with 1 Kings xxii. 41–51, the Chronist presents in this enlarged history of the reign of Jehoshaphat only original matter, serving to supplement the books of Kings, and that on the basis of those "words" or records of Jehu ben Hanani, which he himself names as his source in ch. xx. 34.

1. Jehoshaphat's Measures for the Internal and External Defence of the Kingdom: ch. xvii. 1–9.—*Strengthened himself against Israel*, endeavoured to defend and secure himself against attack on the side of Israel (comp. i. 1). This was obviously in the first part of his reign, before he formed affinity with Ahab (xviii. 1), and so long as the recollection of Baasha's attack on his predecessor Asa operated.—Ver. 2. *Placed garrisons in the land;* נְצִיבִים, military posts, as 1 Chron. xi. 16. On *b*, comp. 2 Chron. xv. 8.—Ver. 3. *For he walked in the former ways of his father David*, not in the later ways of David, which were characterized by his crimes regarding Uriah and Bathsheba, by the foolish step of numbering the people, etc.—*Sought not unto Baalim.* לְ here and in the following verse is *nota accusativi*, after the later usage. The Baalim (comp. Judg. ii. 11) comprise all kinds of idolatry, even that finer kind, consisting in the worship of Jehovah under certain animal forms, which is designated in the following verse as the "doing of Israel" that was avoided by Jehoshaphat.—Ver. 5. *And the Lord stablished the kingdom in his hand;* comp. 2 Kings xiv. 5. On the following מִנְחָה, "gift" (= נְדָבוֹת, Ps. cx. 3), comp. ver. 11, where the term denotes the tribute of a subject people. On "riches and honour in abundance," see xviii. 1, also 1 Chron. xxix. 28; 2 Chron. i. 12. —Ver. 6 ff. The Internal Defence of the Kingdom by the Extirpation of Idolatry and the Instruction of the People in the Law.—*And his heart was lifted up in the ways of the Lord*, showed a heightened courage to proceed in a godly walk; גָּבַהּ לֵב here, otherwise than in xxvi. 16, xxxii. 25, etc., not in the bad sense of an ungodly pride, but *sensu bono*. The following "and moreover" (וְעוֹד) points back to ver. 3. For the "high places" and Asherim, comp. on xiv. 2.—Ver. 7. *And in the third year of his reign;* according to Hitzig's not improbable conjecture (*Geschichte*, pp. 9 ff., 198 f.), a jubilee year, and indeed the year 912 B.C. The five princes, nine Levites, and two priests named in the following verse are otherwise unknown.—Ver. 9. *And they taught in Judah*, on the basis of the presently named "book of the law of the Lord," the religious and civil enactments of which, on the occasion of this solemn ecclesiastical visitation of Jehoshaphat (Starke and other ancients), were brought to the recollection and impressed anew on the attention of the Jews. This mention of the book of the law under Jehoshaphat, almost 300 years before Josiah's renewed inculcation and vindication of its authority, is of no small apologetic importance. It shows that, if not the whole Pentateuch in its present form, yet a work already approaching to its present compass, was already extant in the tenth century B.C. (comp. also on xv. 13). And indeed the concrete, detailed, and definite nature of the present notice leaves no doubt of this, that not merely the Chronist living after the exile, but his much older voucher, contemporary with the recorded fact (probably Jehu ben Hanani), bears this testimony to the existence of the Torah at so early a date.

2. The Effects of these Measures: Jehoshaphat's increasing Power: vers. 10–19.—*And the fear of the Lord fell upon all the kingdoms of the lands* (almost literally so, xx. 29; comp. also xiv. 13, xii. 8, etc.). Rightly Rambach observes: *Erat hoc præmium pietatis Josaphati, quod vicini satisque potentes hostes non auderent adversus ipsum hiscere.* On the contrary, Berth. perverts

the theocratic causal nexus set forth clearly enough by the writer, when he remarks on this passage: "Jehoshaphat had time to attend to the instruction of his people, because the neighbouring nations did not then venture to make war on Judah."—Ver. 11. *And some of the Philistines brought.* מִן־פְּלִשְׁתִּים is subject (with partitive מִן).—*And silver in abundance,* literally, "and silver a load"; comp. xx. 25. Falsely the Vulg., which assigns to the term מַשָּׂא, "load," the meaning "tribute" (*vectigal*).—*The Arabs also* (עַרְבִים = עַרְבִיאִים; see xxi. 16, xxii. 1), the Beduin tribes of north-western Arabia, perhaps those whom Asa had subdued by the victory over Zerah (comp. xiv. 14.).—Ver. 12. *And Jehoshaphat became ever greater.* The construction according to Ew. § 280, *b;* עַד־לְמַעְלָה, as in xvi. 12.—*And he built in Judah castles.* בִּירָנִיּוֹת, plur. of בִּירָנִית (= בִּירָה), a Syrian form occurring only here and xxvii. 4. "Cities with stores," as viii. 4.—Ver. 13. *And he had much store.* So rightly Luther, Starke, Keil, Kamph., etc. Of the same signification is מְלָאכָה, Ex. xxii. 7-10. Otherwise (Vulg. *opera magna,* Clericus, Berth., Neteler, etc.): "much labour, great preparations," to which, however, *b* does not suit; comp. also xi. 11.—Ver. 14. *And this was the muster of them,* the result of the muster, or also their "order"; comp. 1 Chron. xxiv. 49.—*Of Judah, the captains of thousands,* leaders, field-marshals. The following statement of the three Jewish divisions of the army under Adnah, Jehohanan, and Amasiah, and of the two divisions of Benjamin under Eliada and Jehozabad (vers. 15-18), is certainly historical, if we only mark the concrete form, bearing the stamp of direct historical truth, of the notice concerning Amasiah: "who willingly offered himself unto the Lord," and also the circumstance that the kind of armour worn by the Benjamites agrees with earlier statements (comp. 1 Chron. viii. 40; 2 Chron. xiv. 7). But the exceedingly high numbers, which give for Judah alone 780,000, for Benjamin 380,000, and thus for both tribes together the total of 1,160,000 warriors, form no inconsiderable difficulty; comp. the Evangelical and Ethical Reflections.—Ver. 19. *These were they who ministered to the king.* אֵלֶּה, "these," refers to the five generals or commanders, not to the thousands of warriors. Likewise the following clause: "whom the king had placed in the fenced cities in all Judah," refers to other officers besides those five, not to other troops besides those already enumerated.

3. Jehoshaphat's Affinity with Ahab: the Campaign against Ramoth-gilead: ch. xviii. Comp. 1 Kings xxii. 2–35, and Bähr on this passage. Here are only the statements peculiar to the Chronist to be expounded.—*And Jehoshaphat . . . joined affinity with Ahab,* in this way, that he gave his son Joram in marriage to Athaliah, daughter of Ahab and Jezebel; see xxi. 6.[1] This affinity, which occasioned the subsequent visit of Jehoshaphat to Ahab, and the participation in his unfortunate campaign, is here clearly mentioned as something mischievous, attended with destructive effects, as the first link of a chain of misfortunes (comp. xix. 2); the וְ before יִתְחַתֵּן has accordingly, as it were, an adversative force, and the verse expresses this thought: "Although Jehoshaphat had riches and honour in abundance, yet he was so foolish as to make affinity with Ahab." Comp. S. Schmidt, *Josaphatus, cetera dives et gloriosus, infelicem adfinitatem cum Achabo, rege Israelitarum, contrahit,* etc. See, for the rest, Evangelical and Ethical Reflections.—Ver. 2. *And in the course of years,* nine years, as the comparison of 1 Kings xxii. 2, 41 with 2 Kings viii. 26 shows; the affinity of Jehoshaphat with Ahab by the marriage of Joram and Athaliah must, according to these passages, have fallen in the eighth, and the death of Ahab, in the campaign against Ramoth, in the seventeenth, year of Jehoshaphat's reign.—*And he persuaded him,* partly by the great banquets and hospitalities which he prepared in his honour (comp. הֵסִית, "entice, tempt," in such places as Judg. i. 14; Job ii. 3; Deut. xi. 7, etc.). In 1 Kings xxii. 3, instead of this persuasive influence on Jehoshaphat, is set forth rather the political motive of Ahab to begin the war against the Syrians in Ramoth-gilead; our author is silent on this, because on principle he does not wish to recount anything of the deeds or enterprises of the northern king.—Ver. 5. *Gathered the prophets, four hundred men.* 1 Kings: "about 400 men," which is the more correct, as the number is obviously a round one. —*Shall we go;* in 1 Kings: "Shall I go," in harmony with the following אִם אֶחְדָּל, "or shall I forbear." Inversely in 1 Kings (ver. 14) both verbs are plural.—Ver. 7. *Prophesied . . . always evil,* literally, all his days (כָּל־יָמָיו), a phrase emphasizing the opposition, which is wanting in 1 Kings.—Ver. 9. *And they sat in a floor.* The וְיוֹשְׁבִים, superfluous on account of the preceding יוֹשְׁבִים, is wanting in 1 Kings.—Ver. 14. *And they shall be delivered into your hand.* Instead of this very definite prediction (which is certainly ironical), the parallel text in 1 Kings has, more indefinitely: "And the Lord shall deliver it into the king's hand."—Ver. 19. See the Crit. Notes.—Ver. 23. *Which way went the Spirit of the Lord from me?* Instead of this circumstantial אֵי זֶה הַדֶּרֶךְ (comp. 1 Kings xiii. 1; 2 Kings iii. 8), 1 Kings xxii. 24 has the simpler and shorter אֵי זֶה.—Ver. 26. *Let him eat bread of trouble, and water of trouble.* Possible is also the translation proposed by Kamph. with reference to Ps. lx. 5: "Let him eat as bread of trouble," etc.—Ver. 30. *And the king of Syria had commanded the captains of his chariots.* In 1 Kings the number of these captains (thirty-two) is also given, by reference

[1] There also concerning Hitzig's hypothesis (founded on 2 Kings viii. 26 and 2 Chron. xxii. 2), that Athaliah was not the daughter, but the sister, of Ahab.

to the earlier war, 1 Kings xx. 24.—Ver. 31. *And the Lord helped him, and God turned them away from him.* This religious reflective remark is wanting in 1 Kings xxii. 32, but is by no means a hindrance to the connection, as Berth. thinks, but rather a very seasonable enunciation of that which, to the writer, necessarily formed the point and force of the whole narrative.—Ver. 34. *And the king of Israel was standing in the chariot.* Instead of the *partic. Hiph.* מַעֲמִיד, "holding himself upright," 1 Kings xxii. 35 has, less distinctly, the *Hoph.* מָעֳמָד, "held upright." The close of the whole narrative, containing accounts of the return of the defeated army, and the more particular circumstances of the death of Ahab (1 Kings xxii. 36-39), is omitted by our author, because it belongs properly to a history of the northern kingdom.

4. The Prophet Jehu's Judgment on the Covenant with Ahab: ch. xix. 1-3.—*And Jehoshaphat . . . returned home in peace to Jerusalem,* so that the prophecy of Michah (xviii. 16) was fulfilled in him.—Ver. 2. *And Jehu the son of Hanani . . . went out to meet him:* the same prophet who, 1 Kings xvi. 1, had acted under Baasha in the northern kingdom; perhaps a son of that Hanani whom Asa in wrath had ordered into prison (xvi. 7 ff.).—*Must we help the wicked, and shouldst thou love them that hate the Lord?* The construction is as in 1 Chron. v. 1, ix. 25 (לְ with the *infin.*). It is to be supposed that the words are spoken in earnest indignation, but they turn with their displeasure rather against the idolatrous tyrant Ahab than against Jehoshaphat, who only for a season walked by his side.—*And for this is wrath upon thee from the Lord;* comp. 1 Chron. xxvii. 24, and with קֶצֶף מִלִּפְנֵי יְהוָה the simpler קֶצֶף יְהוָה, 2 Chron. xxxii. 26. The words point prophetically to the soon after occurring dangerous invasion of the Ammonites, Moabites, and Meunites, and also to the unfortunate sea-voyage from Ezion-geber, ch. xx.—Ver. 3. *Yet good things are found with thee,* things worthy of praise; comp. xii. 12; 1 Kings xiv. 13. For *b* (where the fem. הָאֲשֵׁרוֹת appears instead of the usual plur. masc.), comp. xvii. 4 f., xii. 14.

5. Jehoshaphat's further Reforms of Worship and Law: vers. 4-11.—*And he went out again among the people,* literally, "and he turned and went." Reference is made to the former going out, xvii. 7 ff. The following statement of the south and north boundary of the kingdom of Judah: "from Beersheba to Mount Ephraim," is copied after the similar formula: "from Dan to Beersheba," which refers to the whole land of Israel; comp. Judg. xx. 1; 2 Sam. iii. 10, xvii. 11; 1 Kings v. 5.—*And brought them back to the Lord,* "made them return"; comp. xxiv. 19.—Ver. 5. *City by city,* or "in every city" (לְעִיר וָעִיר; comp. 1 Chron. xxvi. 29), according to the legal precept, Deut. xvi. 18.—Ver. 6. *Not for man, but for the Lord,* in God's name, and according to His holy will, as Θεοῦ διάκονοι, Rom. xiii. 4; comp. also Prov. xvi. 11.—*And he is with you in the judgment,* in the judicial decision, in passing sentence; comp. Deut. xvii. 9, also ch. i. 17; Ex. xxi. 6, xxii. 7, etc. The supplying of יְהוָה as subject to וְעִמָּכֶם is indispensable, as the failure of all attempts to explain it without this supplement, for example, that of the Vulg. (*et quodcunque judicaveritis, in vos redundabit*), shows.—Ver. 7. *And now let the fear of the Lord be upon you* in a preserving way, that ye may beware of judging unjustly. For the phrase, comp. xvii. 10.—*Take heed, and do ye,* do it in a heedful, conscientious way, *cum diligentia cuncta facite* (Vulg.). On the following words, comp. Deut. x. 17, xvi. 19; Ps. lxxxix. 7; Acts x. 34.—Vers. 8-11. The Supreme Tribunal instituted by Jehoshaphat in Jerusalem,—an institution resting on Ex. xviii. 19, 26, Deut. xvii. 8-13; comp. Keil, *Bibl. Archæol.* ii. 250 ff.—*And also in Jerusalem,* not merely in the various fenced cities (ver. 5), where judges of inferior instance were appointed. That besides Levites and priests, laymen, "of the chiefs of the fathers of Israel," tribe-chiefs out of the rest of the people, are named as appointed by Jehoshaphat to be judges, involves no contradiction of 1 Chron. xxiii. 4, xxvi. 29, according to which David had appointed 6000 Levites as "judges and officers" (שֹׁטְרִים); for that these Levites should exclusively administer the law was not there asserted.—*For the judgment of the Lord, and for pleading.* Synonymous with לְמִשְׁפַּט יְהוָה stands, ver. 11, לְכֹל דְּבַר יְהוָה, "for every matter of the Lord"; and synonymous with לָרִיב that passage gives לְכֹל דְּבַר הַמֶּלֶךְ, "for every matter of the king or the state"; so that the sense of the whole is: "for all matters relating to religion or polity." As examples of the former, Berth. well adduces disputes concerning the release of the first-born, dues to the temple, the clean and the unclean, etc.—*And they returned to Jerusalem;* Jehoshaphat and the commission accompanying him returned from their journey through the country and the fenced cities of Judah to Jerusalem; comp. ver. 4. As this statement would have been more suitable before ver. 8, and as any reference of it to others than Jehoshaphat and his companions (for example, to the Levites, priests, and chiefs nominated for the new supreme court, as Rambach, Starke, and others think) is inadmissible, the change proposed by Kamph. of וַיָּשֻׁבוּ into וַיֵּשְׁבוּ, "and they dwelt in Jerusalem" (the supreme judges just nominated), appears not inappropriate.—Ver. 9. *Thus shall ye do,* as is fully stated in ver. 10. On בְּלֵבָב שָׁלֵם, "with undivided heart," comp. xv. 17, xvi. 9; 1 Kings viii. 61.—Ver. 10. *And in every plea.* כָּל־רִיב stands before as *cas. absol.;* the וְ before is explicative; comp. Crit. Note. As "brethren who dwell in their cities" those are designated who bring appeals from the country or the smaller cities of Judah and Benjamin before the supreme court at Jerusalem, and demand its higher decision; comp. Deut. xvii. 8.—*Between blood and blood,* in criminal cases which involve murder and homicide (comp. Ex. xxi. 12 ff.). The fol-

lowing phrase: "between law and commandment, statutes and judgments," applies to a dispute concerning the import or application of certain laws, or a doubt according to what legal enactment the case in point is to be decided (comp. Deut. xvii. 8).—*Ye shall advise them*, by imparting instruction concerning the decisions of the law, admonish (הִזְהִיר, as in Ex. xviii. 20; Eccles. xii. 12), that they may not err by the theoretical or practical abuse of the law, and thereby bring guilt (אָשָׁם) upon the whole people.—Ver. 11. *And, behold, Amariah the chief priest*, scarcely different from the fifth high priest after Zadok, mentioned 1 Chron. v. 37 (see on the passage). The "ruler of the house of Judah," Zebadiah son of Ishmael, is not otherwise known.—*And the Levites are officers before you*, שֹׁטְרִים, as in 1 Chron. xxiii. 4, xxvi. 29.—*The Lord will be with the good;* וִיהִי is here a future, scarcely an optative: "the Lord be with the good." Comp. besides, xx. 17. The good are the judges who discharge their office fitly and well.

6. Jehoshaphat's Victory over the Moabites, Ammonites, and Meunites: ch. xx. 1–30.—*And it came to pass after this*, after the events related in xviii. 19, which fall perhaps six or seven years before the death of Jehoshaphat, and of which the death of Ahab almost certainly falls in the year 897 B.C. A still more exact date for the present war results from the monument of victory of the Moabitish King Mesha, discovered three years ago, which must have been erected very soon after Ahab's death, and shortly before the outbreak of the present war, and therefore about 896 B.C. See Schlottmann, "Der Moabiterkönig Mesa," *Stud. u. Krit.* 1871, p. 587 ff., especially p. 610 ff.; and comp. beneath, Evangelical and Ethical Reflections, No. 4.—*And with them of the Meunites.* מֵהָעַמּוֹנִים can scarcely mean, as many of the ancients, and even Hengst. (*Gesch. d. Reiches Gottes.* ii. 2, 211), think, nations beyond the Ammonites; for even if מִן, according to 1 Sam xx. 22, 37, could have the sense "beyond or remote from," yet vers. 10 and 22 f. point distinctly to a people inhabiting mount Seir. Accordingly we must read, as ἐκ τῶν Μιναίων of the Sept. indicates (comp. 1 Chron. iv. 41), rather מֵהַמְּעוּנִים, and think of the Meunites (Meinites, 1 Chron. iv. 41, *Kethib*) inhabiting the city Maon (מָעוֹן) near Petra as their capital. If in the following verse (with Calmet, Keil, and others) מֵאֱדֹם were read instead of the difficult מֵאֲרָם, every scruple against this assumption (proposed by Hiller, *Onomast.* p. 285, and supported by nearly all the moderns) must vanish. But even without this further emendation, it possesses a high degree of probability; for, according to Josephus, *Antiq.* ix. 1. 2, they were Arabs, and probably inhabitants of Arabia Petræa, who, in alliance with the Ammonites and Moabites, undertook the expedition against Jehoshaphat; and in xxvi. 7 Meunites are named along with Philistines and Arabs as a southern tribe subdued in war by Uzziah.—Ver. 2. *From beyond the sea, from Syria.* For מֵאֲרָם must apparently be read מֵאֱדֹם, "from Edom or Idumæa"; for only this determination of the starting-point agrees with מֵעֵבֶר לַיָּם, "beyond the sea" (the Dead Sea); and the Syr. seems to have read מֵאֱדֹם, while the remaining old versions certainly confirm the Masoretic text. If we adhere to it, "Aram" or Syria must at all events be taken in a very wide sense (=North Arabia); comp. Hengst. as quoted.—*And, behold, they are at Hazezon-tamar, that is Engedi* (comp. Gen. xiv. 7; Josh. xv. 62; Song i. 14; Robinson, *Pal.* ii. 439 f.), where Ain Jidy now lies, at the middle of the west shore of the Dead Sea, about fifteen hours from Jerusalem. The army of the allied foes had, it appears, reached this place through a marsh surrounding the south end of the Dead Sea, or by crossing the south ford of this sea (between the eastern peninsula Lisan and the opposite point of the west shore, not far from the valley Engedi; comp. Hoffmann, *Blicke in die früheste Gesch. des Gelobten Landes*, ii. 26 f.).—Vers. 3–13. Jehoshaphat and the People seek the Help of the Lord.—*And Jehoshaphat . . . set his face*, שׂוּם פָּנִים=נָתַן פָּנִים; comp. Jer. xlii. 15; Dan. ix. 3. On the "proclaiming of a fast over all Judah," comp. Judg. xx. 26; 1 Sam. vii. 6; Joel ii. 15.—Ver. 5. *Before the new court*, the outer or great court (see iv. 9), that might have been built or repaired in Asa's or Jehoshaphat's time, and therefore is here called new. The place before this court, from which Jehoshaphat offered his prayer, was perhaps at the entrance of the inner or priest's court.—Ver. 6. *Lord God of our fathers.* Jehoshaphat thus addresses God, to remind him of his former benefits to his people, to which is then annexed a reference to his absolute omnipotence; comp. Ps. cxv. 3, and on "None is with Thee, to withstand Thee," Ps. xciv. 16; 1 Chron xxix. 12; 2 Chron. xiv. 10, and like passages.—Ver. 7. Comp. Ex. xxiii. 20 ff.; Josh. xxiii. 9, xxiv. 12; also Gen. xiii. 15 f., xv. 18.—Ver. 9. *If evil come upon us, sword, judgment* (שְׁפוֹט only here in this sense), *or pestilence*, etc. The cases enumerated in Solomon's prayer at the dedication of the temple (vi. 22–39) are here summarily recapitulated.—Ver. 10. *The sons of Ammon and Moab . . . whom Thou wouldst not let Israel invade*, from whom our ancestors in the time of Moses and Joshua peacefully withdrew, without attacking them; comp. Num. xx. 14 ff.; Deut. ii. 4, 9, 19, 29; Judg. xi. 17 f.—Ver. 11. *And behold* = "yea, behold."—*Possession which Thou hast given us*, "made us possess," הוֹרִישׁ, as in Judg. xi. 24; Ezra ix. 12.—Ver. 12. *For in us is no might against this great multitude*, "before, in the face of this great multitude"; comp. xiv. 9, etc. For the following expression of confidence: "our eyes are upon Thee," comp. Ps. xxv. 15, cxxiii. 2, cxli. 8. On ver. 13 ("and their little ones"), comp. Jon. iii. 5.—Vers. 14–17. God's Answer by the Prophet Jahaziel.—*And upon Jahaziel . . . the Levite of the sons of Asaph.* The ancestor in the fifth degree of this Jahaziel is said to be Mattaniah, possibly the same son of Asaph who is called, 1 Chron. xxv. 2, 12, Nethaniah (as מ and נ in the formation of *nom.*

propr. are often interchanged). An identity with Mattaniah the son of Heman, 1 Chron. xxv. 4, 16, is not to be thought of.—Ver. 15. *The battle is not yours, but God's;* comp. 1 Sam. xvii. 47; Neh. iv. 14; also Matt. x. 20.—Ver. 16. *Behold, they go up by the hill of Haziz,* perhaps the Wady el Hasasah on the north border of the wilderness of the same name, which stretches from the Dead Sea to Tekoa, and no doubt corresponds to the here-named "wilderness of Jeruel." With this reference to El Hasasah corresponds the rendering of the name הַצִּיץ by 'Ασσεῖς in the Sept., whereas certainly Josephus renders the name by ἀνάβασις λεγομένη ἐξοχῆς (*Antiq.* ix. 1. 2), and thus conceives it as if it were צִיץ (ἐξοχή) with the article; were this view, the necessity of which is by no means established (comp. Ew. *Gesch.* 2d edit. iii. p. 475), confirmed, the hill of Ziz would have to be identified with the steep pass over Ain Jidy (Robinson, ii. 438, 446).—Ver. 17. *Ye shall not have to fight here.* בָּזֹאת, in this conflict with so great a multitude of foes; comp. ver. 15.—Vers. 18, 19. Thanksgiving of Jehoshaphat and the People for the encouraging Promise by the Prophet.—*And the Levites of the sons of Kohath and of the Korhites.* The second וְ before מִן־בְּנֵי הַקָּרְחִים may be only explicative, as the Korhites descended from Kohath, 1 Chron. vi. 18, 22.—Vers. 20–23. The divine promise is fulfilled by an unexpected self-destruction of the foemen.—*And as they went forth, Jehoshaphat stood up,* probably in the gate by which the warriors went forth (the valley or dung-gate, at all events one of those facing the south). On the words: "believe, and ye shall be established," comp. Isa. vii. 9, xxviii. 16; Deut. i. 32.—Ver. 21. *And he advised the people,* busied himself as a sound adviser (יוֹעֵץ), by exhorting to confidence in God; in a similar sense stands יוֹעֵץ אֶל in 2 Kings vi. 8.—*And appointed men singing unto the Lord* (לְ in ליהוה as *nota genitivi*), *and praising in holy beauty:* לְהַדְרַת־קֹ', as otherwise בְּהַדְרַת־קֹ', 1 Chron. xvi. 29; Ps. xxix. 2, cx. 3.—Ver. 22. *And at the time . . . the Lord set an ambush.* מְאָרְבִים signifies *insidiatores, insidiæ* (Vulg.), as in Judg. ix. 25. By these waylayers cannot be meant angels sent by God (Piscat. and other ancients, Ew., Kamph., Berth.—doubtful H. Schultz, *Theol. des A. T.* ii. 322); for such an interference of supernatural powers, good or evil, must have been clearly indicated (as in 2 Kings vi. 17, xix. 35). As little can the מארבים be waylaying Jews, because the Jews, according to vers. 15, 17, 24, were merely spectators of the bloody encounter between their opponents. The waylaying without doubt was done by a part of the confederates themselves, probably some of the Meunites, the inhabitants of mount Seir, who, being eager for booty, had laid the crafty ambush, on whose sudden assault the Ammonites and Moabites must have regarded their Meunite allies as traitors, and thereupon opened the wild game of the self-slaughter of their army. Thus in the main, by comparison with the partly similar event in Judg. vii. 22 ff., J. H. Mich., Cler., Calm., etc., and recently Keil and Hengst. (*Gesch. des R. G.* ii. 2, 213 f.), the latter of whom appears inclined to find in מארבים an allusion to the name Arabs ("the predatory swarms," he thinks, of the tribes of Arabia Petræa and Deserta might have joined the Idumæans), and to lay down a hypothesis similar to that of K. H. Sack (*Theol. Aufsätze,* Gotha 1871), who wishes to make Arabs (עֲרָבִים) also of the ravens (עֹרְבִים) of Elijah, 1 Kings xvii. 6. Comp. also Schlottmann, p. 611, who endeavours to make out the fanaticism of the Ammonites and Moabites, as heathenish polytheistic opponents of the monotheistic Edomites, to be one of the causes of the massacre, but over looks the fact that the Edomites had properly no part in the affair.—Ver. 23. *And when they had ended with the inhabitants of mount Seir,* had completely massacred them in the affray that arose; comp. Dan. xi. 44. On the words: "they helped to destroy one another," comp., for the substantive מַשְׁחִית, xxii. 4; Ezek. v. 16; Dan. x. 8.—Vers. 24–30. The Impression of the Event on the Jews and their Neighbours.—*And Judah came to the watch-tower in the wilderness,* to an elevated point, a rising ground not far from Tekoa, whence the wilderness of Jeruel (ver. 16) might be surveyed.—*And none escaped:* so at least it appeared. The statement is to be understood as ideal, and not strictly real.—Ver. 25. *And they found with them in abundance, goods and corpses, and costly vessels.* Intermediate between רְכוּשׁ, "goods," and כְּלֵי חֲמֻדוֹת, "costly vessels" (comp. Dan. xi. 38), are named "corpses," obviously very surprising. The reading בְּגָדִים, garments, should therefore at once receive the preference; comp. Judg. viii. 25 f.—*And they stripped off for themselves more than they could carry,* literally, "to nothing of carrying"; comp. Num. iv. 24.—Ver. 26. *And on the fourth day they assembled in the valley of blessing.* This "vale of blessing" (Emek-berachah) must be sought near the field of battle. It is evidently the present Wady Bereikut, west of Tekoa, near the road leading from Jerusalem to Hebron, in which pretty broad and open valley the ruins of a place of the name of Bereikut are still preserved (Robinson, *Phys. Geogr.* p. 106); comp. the Caphar Baruka of Jerome in the *Vita S. Paulæ,* with its outlook on the Dead Sea. It is inadmissible, with Thenius and Hitzig (on Joel iv. 2, 12, and *Gesch.* p. 199), to make this valley of blessing the same with the Kidron or the valley of Jehoshaphat. For though Joel iv. 11 f. names the site of the present battle "the valley of Jehoshaphat," it does not follow from this poetico-prophetical designation that he had in view the upper valley of Kidron afterwards so called, which bears this name first in Eusebius, but nowhere in the sacred Scriptures of the Old and New Testament (see Berth. on this passage).—Ver. 27. *For the Lord had made them glad over their enemies;* comp. Ezra vi. 22; Neh. xii. 43.—Ver. 29. *And the fear of God was upon all the kingdoms of the countries* bordering on Judah. On the "fear of God," comp. xvii 10; on the last words, xv. 15, xiv. 4.

7. End of the Reign of Jehoshaphat: vers. 31–37. Comp. 1 Kings xxii. 41–51, a section which there forms the whole account of the reign of Jehoshaphat, but is therefore amplified with some notices that are wanting here—1. With the statement that "Jehoshaphat had peace with the king of Israel," ver. 45 (which appeared superfluous here on account of xviii. 1 ff.); 2. With a passing reference to Jehoshaphat's might and great deeds, ver. 46 (which is wanting here in the corresponding ver. 34, because the most important of these great deeds have been here recorded at length in ch. xvii.–xx.); 3. With a remark on the removal of the rest of the Sodomites out of the land, ver. 47 (which is wanting here, because in the time of Asa, xvi., no notice is taken of these Sodomites who are mentioned in 1 Kings xv. 12); 4. With the notice that Edom had no king, but only a deputy, ver 48 (which is here omitted as unimportant). To these enlargements, as exhibited in the account in 1 Kings compared with our own, are added some partly formal, partly material, deviations, which are set forth in the sequel.—Ver. 33. *The people had not yet directed their heart.* For this 1 Kings xxii. 44 has: "the people offered and burnt incense yet in the high places" (comp. 2 Kings xii. 4, xiv. 4, xv. 4, etc.).—Ver. 34. *The rest of the acts of Jehoshaphat . . . are written in the words of Jehu son of Hanani.* Comp. on this citation, for which in 1 Kings we find merely "the book of the Chronicles of the kings of Judah," Introd. § 5, No. 2.—Ver. 35. *And afterwards Jehoshaphat allied himself with Ahaziah: he* (Ahaziah, not Jehoshaphat, as Berth. thinks) *was wicked in his doing.* This introduction, containing an unfavourable judgment on the covenant with Ahaziah (similar to that pronounced on the affinity with Ahab, xviii. 1), to the narrative of the unfortunate sea-voyage from Ezion-geber, is wanting in 1 Kings. The אַחֲרֵי־כֵן points only in general to the time after the victory over the Ammonites, Moabites, and Meunites. The date of the present undertaking follows more exactly from this, that Ahaziah came to the throne in the seventeenth year of Jehoshaphat, 897 or 896, and reigned two years, that is, till about 894 B.C.—Ver. 36. *To make ships to go to Tarshish.* On the contrary, 1 Kings xxii. 49 has: "Jehoshaphat made ships of Tarshish to go to Ophir for gold." The easiest solution of this difference is the assumption of an error on the part of the Chronist, who made out of the ships of Tarshish ships going to Tarshish; comp. Introd. § 6, p. 25. But if we must rather harmonize the two accounts, we must assume either—*a.* a Tarshish in the direction of Ophir, and thus to the east or south-east, different from the Spanish Tarsis-Tartessus (with Seetzen and others; comp. excursus on ch. viii., No. 1), or *b.* that the confederates had designed both a voyage to Ophir in the east and a voyage to Tarsis in the west, for the latter of which either a circumnavigation of Africa round the Cape of Good Hope or a crossing of Lower Egypt by the canal of Seti (between the *Sin. Heroopolitanus* and the Nile) must have been contemplated.—Ver. 37. *And Eliezer son of Dodavah of Mareshah prophesied,* a prophet only named here and known by the present utterance. On the name Dodavahu, see Crit. Note; for Mareshah, on 1 Chron. xi. 8.—*Were not able to go to Tarshish.* עָצַר, as xiii. 20, xiv. 10, and elsewhere. On the repeated invitation of Ahaziah to Jehoshaphat to prosecute the undertaking, when it failed at first through this mishap and Jehoshaphat's refusal, our author says nothing; otherwise 1 Kings xxii. 50.

EVANGELICAL AND ETHICAL REFLECTIONS, HOMILETIC AND APOLOGETIC OBSERVATIONS, ON CH. XVII.–XX.

1. The history of Jehoshaphat, as our author relates it, certainly exceeds that which is recorded of him in the book of Kings in the richness and multiplicity of its details. But it furnishes no exhaustive or complete picture of that which Jehoshaphat did in war and peace during the twenty-five years of his reign (915–891), as is manifest from this, that the campaign against Mesha of Moab, undertaken in conjunction with Joram of Israel (2 Kings iii.), that fell probably in one of the later years of his reign (at least after the erection of the monument of Mesha, as Schlottmann has shown, *Stud. u. Krit.* 1871, p. 614 ff.), is altogether omitted. But with the completeness, a simple, well-grounded homogeneous form is wanting in the present description. The varied sources used gleam forth throughout; the accounts of war and peace alternate without internal organic connection; the whole by no means bears the character of a narrative produced at a single casting (comp. Berth. p. 350). Yet a certain plan and an overruling simple principle cannot be unobserved in the present sketch. It is obviously the aim of the author to draw in the reign of Jehoshaphat the picture of a government richly blessed of God, and internally, as well as externally, powerful from the good old times of the yet unimpaired theocracy. The fundamental thought which seems to bind the narrative together he expresses in the twice repeated sentence, that "a terror of God came over all the kingdoms of the countries," with which he accompanies first the rule of Jehoshaphat as prince of peace (xvii. 10), and next the great discomfiture of the confederate nations, Moab, Ammon, and Edom (xx. 29). It is the possession of a power far-ruling, spreading on all sides great fear and awe, solid, and resting on purely theocratic sentiment and organic development of the inner powers of the theocratic constitution, not on tyranny and conquest, which our author finds to admire and celebrate in Jehoshaphat. Hence he industriously sets forth, along with his orthodox reform of religion, and his endeavours to raise as high as possible the defensive and military power of the Jewish state (ch. xvii. 2, 14 ff.), that also which was undertaken by him for the upholding of the administration of justice, in particular the institution of a supreme court of judicature at Jerusalem (xix. 8–11). He therefore relates of his military undertakings chiefly those which were either accompanied with decisive consequences, or in which at least God's protective power and gracious help were realized to him on account of his theocratic inclination; thus, of the two wars which, according to 1 Kings xxii. 2 ff., 2 Kings iii. 1 ff., he undertook as confederate of the northern kingdom, the former, that issued more fortunately for him (that against the Syrians in Ramoth-gilead, xviii.), is described at full length, and with all the characteristic traits found in the source common to him and the author of the book

of Kings; whereas he makes no mention of the second, waged along with Joram against Mesha of Moab, probably on account of its less favourable or at least nearly barren issue.[1] Finally, on account of the wish to depict in Jehoshaphat the representative of the Jewish state developed to its full power before the captivity, he expressly places him on a par with David his "father" (forefather); he makes him therefore enjoy the favour and help of Jehovah, because he walked in "the former ways of David," that is, he worshipped God, in the main at least, and irrespective of the worship still tolerated here and there on the high places, in a theocratically pure and lawful way (xvii. 3). With Solomon, of whom Jehoshaphat likewise reminds us as a prince of peace, as a wise and circumspect father of his country, and as an upholder of the administration of justice, he does not compare him, probably because, first, a characteristic element of the reign of Solomon, its great pomp and splendid wealth, appears to have been wanting in the kingdom of Jehoshaphat, and secondly, notwithstanding his endeavours after peace, his reign had taken a far less peaceful course than that of the great Shelomoh (peaceful).

2. Jehoshaphat is the glorious, pious, and mighty David of the southern kingdom: to this result points the whole narrative of our author. From this point of view also will the prodigious numbers be estimated which he gives in describing the disposable forces of Judah and Benjamin under his reign. The there mentioned 780,000 Jews and 380,000 Benjamites can scarcely be accepted as literally true. Their near approach to the numbers resulting from the census taken by David (1 Chron. xxi. 5) seems intended to convey the idea that the kingdom of Judah alone had under Jehoshaphat, the *alter* David, attained a strength which almost matched the power of the twelve still united tribes under the first David (1,100,000 Israelites and 470,000 Jews), that Judah by itself alone had now developed a number and power which surpassed that of the northern tribes at that earlier period. If this be the meaning of those numbers, the less objection needs be made to their surprising magnitude; their ideal character is also plain from the whole connection; and there is as little need to have recourse to the assumption of some error in the transcribing of the numbers or numeral letters, —an expedient, besides, which seems scarcely admissible, on account of the proportionality of the numbers in the several divisions of the troops, as to that of legendary extravagance or arbitrary fiction, whether it be that of the Chronist or of his older voucher (perhaps the prophet Jehu, ch. xx. 34).[2]

3. How far, therefore, the author was from imparting to the here and there ideally-coloured picture which he drew of the great heroic king the form of a panegyric legend or a fabulous eulogium; how true, on the contrary, he remained to his office as a historian,—is shown by the circumstance that here also, as in the case of David, Asa, etc., he adds the shade to the light, and by no means passes over in silence a series of less favourable traits of the administration of Jehoshaphat. Especially his affinity with Ahab, the idolatrous king of Israel, is duly set forth as a fatal deviation from the path of theocratic purity and strictness (comp. Ezra ix. 1 ff., x. 1 ff.; Neh. ix. 2, xiii. 23 ff.) to the slippery ground of international friendship or affinity with idolatrous neighbours (comp. Solomon's Egyptian spouse, viii. 11 f.). On account of this step, and the consequent often going hand in hand with Israel in warlike expeditions, the king had repeatedly to undergo censure by the mouth of God-inspired prophets, first by the stout Jehu ben Hanani, who directly charged him with helping the wicked, and loving them that hate the Lord (xix. 2), afterwards by Eliezer ben Dodavah, who places the failure of the voyage from Ezion-geber under the character of a divine correction for drawing in one yoke with the unbelieving (xx. 37). On the part of two other prophets, indeed, who are introduced in our section, he encounters no such rebuke: Michah son of Imlah treats him when standing out beside Ahab in the favourable light of a relatively theocratic prince, with mild forbearance, and favours him with the promise of a "return in peace" from the defeat and dispersion of the sheep of the house of Israel (xviii. 16); and so what the Levite Jahaziel says, before setting out to the war with the eastern nations, includes nothing but admonitions to take courage, and promises of deliverance by the strong hand of the Lord (xx. 14–17). But certainly the critical situations to which these prophetic words refer are in and of themselves sufficiently serious and menacing: they are crises introduced by the fault of the king, by his inconsiderate entering into ungodly alliances and relations, feeble preludes of that which the unhappy marriage of his son with the daughter of Jezebel should afterwards bring down in heavy judgments on his house and people. On this account, in the dangerous posture of affairs introduced in this way, along with solemn rebuke, comforting encouragement was in place; the certainly guilty king, deserving of punishment, but not in the same degree as the sovereigns of Israel, was yet one with whom, as the rough Jehu acknowledged, "good things were found" (xix. 3). He deserved along with

[1] The passage 2 Kings iii. 27*b* imports in any case an issue of the war with Moab not quite favourable to Joram and Jehoshaphat, even though we understand the expression: "and there was great indignation concerning Israel," only of the displeasure and abhorrence of the human sacrifice offered by the king of Moab, and the consequent retreat from the country of the enemy (as also Bähr on the passage). But the question is, whether Schlottmann (p. 618 f.) is not right in thinking of a divinely sent calamity, such as a plague, by which the united army of Israel and Judah was forced to a speedy retreat under heavy losses. In this case the Chronist would have had so much the more ground for the omission of this record.

[2] Moreover, that which Neteler adduces (p. 212 f.) in support of their numbers in their literal sense deserves attention. 1. The tribe of Simeon at this time belonged to the tribe of Judah (xix. 4?), by which the number of warriors of the latter, amounting to almost 800,000 men, is explained; 2. The Philistines (?) and the Edomites, who were tributary to Judah, may have been compelled to add their contingent to his force; 3. If we reckon the auxiliary troops of Simeon, Philistia, and Edom at 200,000 men, of the remaining 600,000 Jewish troops, on an average, 20,000 men were due to each of the 120 cities which belonged to the tribe (Josh. xv.), which does not seem unnaturally high, as numerous villages belonged to each of these cities; 4. An increase of 130,000 men fit to bear arms since the census of David, in a period of three generations, is nothing wonderful, especially with the accession of many from the other tribes to the southern kingdom, if we consider the extraordinary fertility of the land, the small means of subsistence required in the south, and the industrial productivity of the Jews at that time. A somewhat satisfactory account would thus be furnished with regard to the 780,000 Jewish troops. But how stands it with the 380,000 warriors whom the small rocky and mountainous territory of Benjamin had to produce?

reproving instruction also strengthening encouragement, that he might continue to walk in the ways of his fathers David and Asa (xvii. 3, xx. 32). He was worthy to be aroused to abide in the path of theocratic righteousness, that at least under his rule the inevitable evil effects of that affinity with an idolatrous house might be restrained as far as possible, and the people retained in that moderate state of piety and morality which is indicated (xx. 33) by the sentence: "the people had not yet directed their heart to the God of their fathers." What he himself says and does, also, in conformity with such encouraging and strengthening words of the prophets, bears the stamp of true repentance, humble acknowledgment of his guilt, and firm continuance in the path of righteousness. As the reproof of Jehu appears to have wrought in him the counterpart of that which Asa had once done on the occasion of a similar announcement from Hanani his father (comp. xix. 4 ff.), so his address in the campaign against the eastern nations to the people, or rather in the name of the people to the Lord (xx. 6–11), vies with the following prophetic utterance of Jahaziel in realizing firm confidence in God and triumphant faith. It is, however, a confidence in God resting on the ground of penitent and believing confession of sin which he here expresses; it is a truly penitent and believing resignation to the divine grace working all in all, an essentially evangelical experience of salvation, whence his subsequent admonition to his warriors: "Believe, and ye shall be established" (xx. 20), springs, a monitory and prophetic word, in which he himself becomes a prophet, a prophetic type, and a presumptive prophetic source, from which the greatest of the Old Testament seers for a century and a half afterwards, in all probability, drew their almost literally coinciding words (see on this passage). At all events, the assumption that Isaiah, the seer of Davidic princely blood, consciously rested on this believing word of a royal ancestor, that might have been early celebrated on account of the divine blessing attending it, is a good deal more natural than either the assertion of an only accidental dependence of the similar phrases, or than the easy expedient of a thoughtless hyper-criticism, according to which the Chronist made his royal hero speak after the manner of Isaiah, or use a play of words borrowed from this prophet.

4. It is, before all, the antique, thoroughly fresh, and concrete characteristic, foreign likewise to the tone of mythical legend or arbitrary invention in the sources, as they lie clearly discernible at the ground of our author's narrative, which must be set forth in an apologetic respect, and maintained with all emphasis against such doubts as that above indicated, with respect to the originality of Jehoshaphat's address, xx. 20; or as Gramberg's and Credner's conjecture (expressed on Joel iv. 11), that the whole narrative xx. 1–30 is nothing but a free, half-poetical remodelling of the short statement in 2 Kings iii. 23 f. With regard to the character of our chapter as supported throughout by definite historical traditions and solid sources, Movers and Bertheau have already made striking remarks; comp. the latter, p. 349 ff.: "1. In the accounts of Jehoshaphat's institutions, which were designed to spread the knowledge of the law and secure to his people an orderly administration of justice, the many details and names (among others, that of the high priest Amariah, xix. 11, who was also in other accounts a contemporary of Jehoshaphat) are a sure proof of this, that our historian found exact statements in his sources, if he also elaborated the historical material in his own way. 2. This applies also to the reports of the defensive preparations and the division of the army, xvii. 15–19. 3. In the remarkable narrative of the battle in which the Moabites, Ammonites, and Meunites destroyed one another (xx. 1–30), we discern, indeed, throughout the mode of thought and style peculiar to our author, but we discover also very distinct historical recollections: the localities are exactly described, vers. 16–20; the designation 'new court' is found only in ver. 5 (it must be taken from a source in which the new building was mentioned); the series of the forefathers of Jahaziel, ver. 14, is a proof that he had already drawn the attention of the older writers to him, who were in a position to give an account of his forefathers. This battle of extermination was before the mind of the prophet Joel when he called the place of the divine decision 'the valley of Jehoshaphat' (comp. on xx. 26). . . . The statement in 2 Kings iii. 23 refers to a quite different situation; and as it might have presented the starting-point and the historical ground for the reports in 2 Chron. xx., it is not to be overlooked. 4. Finally, our author must have found reports of the action of the prophets Jehu (xix. 2 f.) and Eliezer (xx. 37), since he tells of the contents of their speeches in their own words. The brief report also in 1 Kings xxii. 41–51 seems to point to the contents of several narratives of Chronicles: 1 Kings xxii. 47 refers to the extirpation of idolatry (2 Chron. xvii. 3–6); 1 Kings xxii. 46 speaks of the military force of Jehoshaphat, of which 2 Chron. xvii. 2, 10–19 treats more fully," and so forth. To the arguments for its authenticity here set forth, mostly taken from the internal value of the sources of our section, with which are to be compared the apologetic discussions of Kleinert (*Das Deuteronomium*, etc., p. 141) respecting the law reform of Jehoshaphat in its relation to Deut. xvii., is to be added a weighty, if only indirect and extra-biblical, testimony—the recently-discovered inscription of Mesha king of Moab, a highly-important monumental document for the history of one of the neighbouring states of the kingdom of Jehoshaphat, which serves to confirm, at least in general, the historical relations as our section represents them, and, especially in a chronological respect, in so far as it proceeds most probably from the time between the campaign described in ch. xviii. and that in ch. xx., fits well into the series of events here described; comp. Schlottmann, as quoted, especially p. 621 ff.

e. Joram: The Letter of the Prophet Elijah.—Ch. xxi.

Ch. xxi. 1. And Jehoshaphat slept with his fathers, and was buried with his fathers in the city of David; and Joram his son reigned in his stead.

2 And he had brethren, sons of Jehoshaphat, Azariah and Jehiel, and
Zechariah and Azariah, and Michael and Shephatiah: all these were sons of
3 Jehoshaphat king of Judah. And their father gave them many gifts of
silver and of gold and of precious things, with fenced cities in Judah; but
4 the kingdom gave he to Joram, because he was the first-born. And Joram
went up to the kingdom of his father, and strengthened himself, and slew all
his brethren with the sword, and also some of the princes of Israel.

5 Joram was thirty and two years old when he became king, and he reigned
6 eight years in Jerusalem. And he walked in the way of the kings of Israel,
as the house of Ahab did; for he had a daughter of Ahab to wife: and he
7 did that which was evil in the eyes of the LORD. And the LORD would not
destroy the house of David, because of the covenant that He had made with
David, and as He had promised to give a light to him and his sons for ever.—
8 In his days Edom revolted from under the hand of Judah, and made them-
9 selves a king. And Joram went over with his princes, and all the chariots
with him; and he rose up by night, and smote Edom, who compassed him,
10 and the captains of the chariots. And Edom revolted from under the hand
of Judah unto this day. Then Libnah revolted at that time from under his
11 hand, because he had forsaken the LORD God of his fathers. He also made
high places in the mountains[1] of Judah, and he debauched the inhabitants of
Jerusalem, and perverted Judah.

12 And there came to him a writing from Elijah the prophet, saying, Thus
saith the LORD God of David thy father, Because thou hast not walked in
the ways of Jehoshaphat thy father, nor in the ways of Asa king of Judah.
13 And didst walk in the way of the kings of Israel, and didst debauch Judah
and the inhabitants of Jerusalem after the whoredom of the house of Ahab;
and hast also slain thy brethren, the house of thy father, who were better
14 than thou. Behold, the LORD will bring a great plague on thy people, and
15 thy sons, and thy wives, and all thy goods. And thou shalt be in great sick-
ness by disease of thy bowels, until thy bowels fall out from the sickness in a
year and a day.

16 And the LORD stirred up against Joram the spirit of the Philistines and
17 the Arabs, that were near the Ethiopians. And they came up into Judah,
and brake into it, and took away all the substance that was found in the
king's house, and his sons, and his wives; and not a son was left him but
18 Jehoahaz, the youngest of his sons. And after all this the LORD smote him
19 in his bowels with an incurable disease. And it came to pass after many
days, namely, about the time of the end of two years, his bowels fell out
with his sickness, and he died with sore pains; and his people made no
20 burning for him, like the burning of his fathers. Thirty and two years old
was he when he became king, and he reigned eight years in Jerusalem; and
he departed without regret;[2] and they buried him in the city of David, but
not in the sepulchres of the kings.

f. AHAZIAH.—CH. XXII. 1-9.

CH. XXII. 1. And the inhabitants of Jerusalem made Ahaziah, his youngest son,
king in his stead; for the troop that came with the Arabs to the camp had
slain all the eldest: and Ahaziah son of Joram king of Judah became king.
2 Forty and two years old was Ahaziah when he became king;[3] and he reigned
one year in Jerusalem: and his mother's name was Athaliah, daughter of
3 Omri. He also walked in the ways of the house of Ahab; for his mother
4 was his counsellor to do wickedly. And he did evil in the eyes of the LORD,
like the house of Ahab; for they were his counsellors after the death of his
5 father, to his destruction. He also walked in their counsel, and went with
Joram son of Ahab king of Israel to war against Hazael king of Syria at
6 Ramoth-gilead: and the Syrians smote Joram. And he returned to be healed
in Jezreel of the wounds[4] which they had given him at Ramah, when he
fought with Hazael king of Syria: and Ahaziah[5] son of Joram king of Judah

7 went down to see Joram son of Ahab at Jezreel; for he was sick. And the
downfall of Ahaziah was from God, in coming to Joram; and when he came,
he went out with Joram against Jehu son of Nimshi, whom the LORD had
8 anointed to cut off the house of Ahab. And it came to pass, when Jehu
executed judgment upon the house of Ahab, he found also the princes of
Judah, and the sons of the brethren [6] of Ahaziah, that ministered to Ahaziah,
9 and slew them. And he sought Ahaziah; and they caught him when he was
hiding in Samaria, and brought him to Jehu, and slew him, and buried him;
for they said, He is the son of Jehoshaphat, who sought the LORD with all
his heart: and the house of Ahaziah had none to retain strength for the
kingdom.

g. Athaliah's Reign and Fall.—Ch. xxii. 10–xxiii.

10 And Athaliah the mother of Ahaziah saw that her son was dead, and she
11 arose and destroyed [7] all the seed of the kingdom of the house of Judah. And
Jehoshabath daughter of the king took Joash the son of Ahaziah, and stole
him from among the king's sons that were slain, and put him and his nurse
in a bed-chamber: and Jehoshabath, daughter of King Joram, wife of
Jehoiada the priest,—for she was Ahaziah's sister,—hid him from the sight of
12 Athaliah: and she slew him not. And he was with them in the house of
God hidden six years; and Athaliah reigned over the land.
Ch. xxiii. 1. And in the seventh year Jehoiada was encouraged, and took the
captains of hundreds, Azariah son of Jeroham, and Ishmael son of Johanan,
and Azariah son of Oded, and Maaseiah son of Adaiah, and Elishaphat son of
2 Zichri, into covenant with him. And they went about in Judah, and gathered
the Levites out of all the cities of Judah, and the chiefs of the fathers of
3 Israel, and they came to Jerusalem. And all the congregation made a cove-
nant in the house of God with the king; and he said unto them, Behold, the
4 king's son shall reign, as the LORD hath spoken of the sons of David. This
is the thing that ye shall do: a third of you, who enter on the sabbath, of
5 the priests and of the Levites, shall be porters at the thresholds. And a
third shall be at the king's house; and a third at the gate Jesod; and all the
6 people shall be in the courts of the house of the LORD. And none shall enter
the house of the LORD, but the priests, and they that minister of the Levites;
they may go in, for they are holy; and all the people shall keep the ward of
7 the LORD. And the Levites shall surround the king, every man with his
weapons in his hand: and whosoever goeth into the house shall be put to
death; and ye shall be with the king, when he goeth in and when he cometh
8 out. And the Levites and all Judah did according to all that Jehoiada the
priest commanded, and took every one his men that went in on the sabbath
with those that came out on the sabbath: for Jehoiada the priest had not dis-
9 missed the courses. And Jehoiada the priest gave to the captains of hundreds
spears and shields and arms, that had been King David's, which were in the
10 house of God. And he set all the people, every man with his weapon in his
hand, from the right to the left side of the house, by the altar and by the
11 house, round about the king. And they brought out the king's son, and gave
unto him the crown and the testimony, and made him king: and Jehoiada
and his sons anointed him, and said, Long live the king.
12 And Athaliah heard the cry of the people running and praising the
13 king, and she came to the people to the house of the LORD. And she
looked, and, behold, the king stood at his place in the entrance, and the
princes and the trumpets by the king; and all the people of the land were
glad, and blew on the trumpets; and the singers with instruments of song,
and the leaders of praise: and Athaliah rent her clothes, and said, Conspiracy,
14 conspiracy! And Jehoiada the priest brought out [8] the captains of hundreds,
the officers of the host, and said unto them, Bring her out from within the
ranges, and whoso followeth her shall be slain with the sword: for the priest
15 had said, Slay her not in the house of the LORD. And they gave her space,

and she went to the entrance of the horse gate[9] by the king's house, and they
slew her there.
16 And Jehoiada made a covenant between himself, and between all the
17 people, and between the king, that they should be the LORD'S people. And
all the people went to the house of Baal, and pulled it down, and brake its
altars and its images; and Matthan the priest of Baal they slew before the
18 altars. And Jehoiada appointed the offices of the house of the LORD by the
hand of the priests, the Levites, whom David had distributed in the house of
the LORD, to offer the burnt-offerings of the LORD, as it is written in the law
19 of Moses, with gladness and with song, in the manner of David. And he set
the porters at the gates of the house of the LORD, that the unclean might not
20 enter. And he took the captains of hundreds, and the nobles, and the rulers
of the people, and all people of the land, and brought down the king from
the house of the LORD: and they went through the high gate into the king's
21 house, and set the king on the royal throne. And all the people of the land
were glad; and the city was quiet, and they had put Athaliah to death by
the sword.

[1] For בֶּהָרֵי, "on the mountains," the Sept. and Vulg. read בְּעָרֵי, "in the cities."

[2] בְּלֹא חֶמְדָּה the Sept. translates οὐκ ἐν ἐπαίνῳ; but the Vulg.: *non recte* (*ambulavitque non recte*). So Luther: "and walked as was not right."

[3] Instead of forty-two, not only the parallel 2 Kings viii. 26, but also the Syr. and Arab. versions (as well as some later MSS. and the Ald. edit. of the Sept.), give "twenty-two years"; but the Vulg., as the Masoretic text and Sept. (Al. and Vat.): εἴκοσιν ἐτῶν.

[4] For כִּי הַמַּכִּים is to be read, with various better MSS., also with the Sept. and 2 Kings viii. 29: מִן הַמַּכִּים. Peculiar is the decision of Neteler (p 325): כִּי is to be retained and rendered by "puncture" (puncture of the wounds).

[5] This is certainly to be read instead of וַעֲזַרְיָהוּ, which seems to be simply an error of the pen.

[6] Instead of "sons of the brethren," בְּנֵי אֲחֵי, the Sept., in accordance with 2 Kings x. 12: ἀδελφούς. But see the Exeg. Expl.

[7] וַתְּדַבֵּר is without doubt, according to 2 Kings xi. 1, to be changed into וַתְּאַבֵּד. (Sept.: ἀπώλεσεν; Vulg.: *interfecit.*)

[8] וַיּוֹצִא is possibly a mistake for וַיְצַו (2 Kings xi. 15), which latter the Syr. and Arab. also read in our passage.

[9] שַׁעַר, besides being superfluous after מְבוֹא, is wanting as well in 2 Kings xi. 16 as in all old versions of our passage, and should be erased.

EXEGETICAL.

Irrespective of the letter of the prophet Elijah (and its accompanying notices concerning the punishment of Joram therein predicted, xxi. 12–19), we are here presented with parallel texts to the accounts of the book of Kings, but certainly parallels to which the special Levitical standpoint of the narrator has often, especially in the description of the fall of Athaliah by the conspiracy conducted by the high priest Jehoiada, imparted a characteristic colouring, involving many deviations from the older text.

1. Joram: *a.* His Beginnings, and his Misgovernment: ch. xxi. 1–11.—*And Jehoshaphat slept with his fathers.* This report of Jehoshaphat's death and burial is carried, according to the usual division of chapters, to the history of Joram, because the first deed of Joram, the general murder of his kindred, is closely connected with the decease of his father, and serves to soil with blood the solemn rites of his funeral (his being "buried with his fathers"), a mode of division corresponding well with the pragmatical turn of the Chronist.—Vers. 2–4. Joram's Sixfold Fratricide.—*Azariah and Jehiel*, etc. It is against the identity, asserted by Jewish expositors, of Jehiel with the Hiel mentioned in 1 Kings xvi. 34, that the latter, who is called a Bethelite (an inhabitant of Bethel), was neither a king's son nor a member of the southern kingdom.—*All these were sons of Jehoshaphat, king of Israel.* On the designation of the southern kingdom by the name of Israel, comp. xii. 1, 6, also ver. 4, xxviii. 19, 27, etc.—Ver. 3. *And their father gave them many gifts.* Comp. what Rehoboam did to his sons, xi. 22 f.—Ver. 4. *And Joram went up;* comp. Ex. i. 8, and on the following phrase, "strengthened himself," ch. i. 1. That the chief motive for the murder of his brothers was their non-concurrence with Joram's and his mother's idolatry, is clear from ver. 13, where they are said to be better than he: this must have applied also to the "princes of Israel" who fell with them as victims in the massacre. Moreover, oriental rulers are wont still in modern times to inaugurate the beginning of their reign with such general murder of their kindred; and Abimelech had already acted the tyrant by the practice of a similar but still more wicked slaughter, Judg. ix. 5.—Vers. 5–11 agree in all essentials with 2 Kings viii. 17–22.—Ver. 6. *For he had a daughter of Ahab to wife.* This quite definite statement excludes the hypothesis of

Hitzig, based upon 2 Kings viii. 26 and 2 Chron. xxii. 2, that Athaliah was rather the sister of Ahab. She is there called Omri's daughter, because the spirit of Omri, the founder of the dynasty, displayed itself most characteristically and powerfully in this his grand-daughter. Grandsons and grand-daughters are not seldom called children of their grandfather, especially if he was celebrated and influential; comp. for example, xi. 20, Maachah the daughter (grand-daughter) of Absalom.—Ver. 7. *And the Lord would not destroy the house of David.* Somewhat different, but coinciding in sense with the present passage, is 2 Kings viii. 19 (see Bähr). In particular, "To give him a light for his sons" (or "in his sons") stands there, for which here: "to give a light to him and his sons." The ו of our author, inserted before לְבָנָיו, appears, moreover, to be neither superfluous nor unsuitable, if it be taken explicatively = "and certainly" (so correctly Keil, against Berth.).—Ver. 8. *In his days Edom revolted from under the hand of Judah,* changed the condition of vassalage to Judah, in which it was held from David to Jehoshaphat (comp. 1 Kings xxii. 48 and above on ch. xx. 35), into that of a fully independent state.—Ver. 9. *And Joram went over with his princes.* עִם שָׂרָיו is possibly corrupted from שֵׂעִירָה, "to Seir" (as should be read 2 Kings viii. 21, instead of צָעִירָה). At the end of the verse are wanting the words there forming the close: "and the people fled to their tents," from which it is evident that the battle was not particularly fortunate for the Jewish king, but simply consisted in cutting his way through the surrounding force.—Ver. 10. *Unto this day,* that is, merely unto the time of the older narrator, used as a source by the Chronist (comp. Introd. § 5, II. p. 19). But this is to be regarded as a writer belonging to the period immediately before the captivity; and therefore it is to be presumed that the re-conquest of the Edomites by Amaziah, xxv. 14 f., was only transient.—*Then Libnah revolted at that time,* probably the present Tell es Safieh (not far from Eleutheropolis, Robinson, *Pal.* ii. 622). The neighbouring Philistines took an essential part in rending it from Joram, in which they were aided also by the Phœnicians (according to Hitzig, *Gesch.* p. 201); comp. Joel iv. 4 f.; Amos i. 9.—*Because he had forsaken the Lord God of his fathers,*—a pragmatic reflection of the Chronist, which is wanting in 2 Kings.—Ver. 11. *He also made high places,* which Asa and Jehoshaphat had removed, xiv. 2 ff., xvii. 6. The following phrase: "debauched," is to be understood of the spiritual whoredom of the worship of Baal; comp. ver. 13. On וַיַּדַּח, "and perverted," comp. Deut. xiii. 6, 11, 14, and Prov. vii. 21.

2. *b.* The Letter of the Prophet Elijah, and the Fulfilment of its Evil Forebodings: vers. 12–19.—*And there came to him a writing from Elijah the prophet, saying* (or "containing," לֵאמֹר). מִכְתָּב is not properly a letter, but a writing, a threatening prophecy in a written form; whether written or at least dictated by Elijah is, from the indefiniteness of the phrase מֵאֵלִיָּהוּ, doubtful; a merely indirect origin from Elijah is obviously reconcilable with this phrase; and as, according to 2 Kings ii. 1 ff., iii. 11, Elijah appears to have been no longer in the land of the living in the reign of Joram (for the inquiry of Jehoshaphat after a prophet during the campaign against Mesha, 2 Kings iii. 11, is answered by pointing, not to Elijah, but only to Elisha, who poured water on the hands of Elijah), it is most natural to suppose the oracle to have been spoken by Elijah against Joram, or rather against Athaliah and her idolatrous house, but first noted down and reduced to its present form by a scholar of Elijah. Comp. Evangelical and Ethical Reflections, No. 2.—Ver. 13. *After the whoredom of the house of Ahab;* comp. on ver. 11.—*And hast also slain thy brethren;* comp. on ver. 4. Even this reference to the murderous deed practised on his not idolatrously disposed brothers, may Elijah have uttered by virtue of his divinely-illuminated prophetic sagacity, at a time when Joram was not yet king, in connection with the other thoughts of the present prediction.—Ver. 14. *Behold, the Lord will bring a great plague,* the devastating invasion of the Philistines and the Arabs, ver. 16 f.—Ver. 15. *Until thy bowels fall out from the sickness in a year and a day,* literally, "days upon days," that is, during many days; comp. שָׁנָה עַל שָׁנָה, Isa. xxix. 1 and Ps. lxi. 7; Judg. xvii. 10. The present determination of time is popular and proverbial, but indefinite. The duration of the malady is given more exactly, ver. 19, in the account of the fulfilment of the oracle.—Ver. 16. *And the Lord stirred up,* in conformity with the prediction communicated. On העיר את רוח, comp. 1 Chron. v. 26. The Arabs that were near the Ethiopians are naturally tribes of Southern Arabia (as the Sabæans, Job i. 15; see on this passage). We know nothing of the causes which lay at the ground of the combination of these tribes with the Philistines to lay waste Judea. Moreover, the Arabs mentioned xxii. 1 are the same as those here designated.—Ver. 17. *And brake into it,* literally, "cleft it," "forced their way into it"; comp. xxxii. 1; 2 Sam. xxiii. 16; 2 Kings xxv. 4.—*And took away all the substance that was found in the king's house.* According to this, Jerusalem must have been conquered by these plundering hordes; yet לְבֵית־הַמֶּלֶךְ may also be rendered "belonging to the king's house" (royal domains), as נִמְצָא לְ certainly signifies something else than נִמְצָא בְ, namely, "possessed by" (comp. Deut. xxi. 17; Josh. xvii. 16), and, besides, the absence of any mention of plundering the temple or its treasures must seem strange, if Jerusalem had been actually taken. We learn, moreover, from the later reference to the occurrence here mentioned, xxii. 1, that only the royal camp was surprised and plundered, not the royal palace in Jerusalem. Comp. Kuhlmey, *Alttestamentl. Studien* (*Zeitschrift für luth. Theologie und Kirche,* 1844, iii. 82 ff.), as well as Keil on this passage.—*And not a son was left him but Jehoahaz.* Not merely capture, but also slaughter, of all the older sons is recorded xxii. 1. The only remaining one is here called Jehoahaz, but there Ahaziah, a name perhaps assumed on ascending the throne;

see on this passage.—Ver. 18. *Smote him* (נְגָפוֹ, corresponding to the נָגַף מַגֵּפָה, ver. 14) *in his bowels with an incurable disease*, literally, a disease with no healing; comp. xx. 21, 25, xxxvi. 16.—Ver. 19. *And it came to pass after many days*, literally, "to days from days," for which is usual the briefer "from days" (מִיָּמִים), Judg. xi. 4, xiv. 8. The next words: "namely, about the time of the end of two years," fix more exactly this somewhat indefinite date. יָמִים stands here, as in ver. 15, in the sense of "year"; the indefinite phrase, denoting properly, "times, periods," receives through the context the same meaning as the Chald. עִדָּן, עִדָּנִין, often in Daniel; for example, Dan. iv. 13, 20, 22, vii. 25; comp. also Vulg. and Syr., which render it directly: "years." Unnecessary and yielding too harsh a sense is Keil's proposal, to take the words צֵאת הַקֵּץ by themselves, and render: "about the time of the end (of his life), about two days (before death)."—*His bowels fell out with his sickness.* עִם, during his painful malady (see the close: "and he died with sore pains"). The disease consisted probably in a very violent dysentery or chronic diarrhœa, whereby the nerve-cuticle of the whole great gut was inflamed, and parts of the mucous tunicle occasionally came off in the form of gut or pipe (resembling a falling out of the bowels); comp. Trusen, *Sitten, Gebräuche und Krankheiten der alten Hebräer*, p. 212, and Friedreich, *Zur Bibel*, p. 270 (where also other literature).—*And his people made no burning for him*, gave him not the honour of a magnificent funeral; comp. xvi. 14. The same is indicated by that which is related in the following verse, that "he departed without regret," בְּלֹא חֶמְדָּה (*sine desiderio, a nemine desideratus*), and that he was not buried in the sepulchres of the kings; comp. xxiv. 25, xxvi. 23. On Luther's and the Vulgate's conception of וַיֵּלֶךְ בְּלֹא חֶמְדָּה, see Crit. Note.

3. Ahaziah's Reign: ch. xxii. 1–9; comp. 2 Kings viii. 26–29, and with regard to the downfall of Ahaziah, ix., x., a copious narrative of the revolution effected by Jehu, of which only a brief abstract (vers. 6–9) is given here, omitting all that refers to the extirpation of the Israelitish branch of the house of Ahab.—*And the inhabitants of Jerusalem made Ahaziah his youngest son king*, the same who was called, xxi. 17, Jehoahaz (in the Sept. *cod. Al.* even as here: Ὀχοζίας). That he was made king by the inhabitants of Jerusalem, indicates that the succession to the throne was disputed, and therefore that a party (the Levites and priests under Jehoiada) was opposed to him, but without prevailing at first against the adherents of Athaliah.—*Had slain all the eldest.* Comp. the remarks on xxi. 17; for this refers to no other fact than that there described.—Ver. 2. *Forty and two years old was Ahaziah;* obviously an erroneous statement, apparently arising from the exchange of the numeral letters כ and מ; twenty-two must certainly be read for forty-two, for Joram was thirty-two years old when he ascended the throne, and reigned in all only eight years: he could not have a son forty-two years old: indeed, as the youngest son of Joram, Ahaziah could not well be over twenty-two years of age, as his father must have begotten him in his eighteenth year, and his elder brothers at a still earlier age, against which assumption no serious objection arises, as it was the well-known custom of the East to marry in early youth, and as a king's son, he will have had no small number of concubines. Only we need not fix the number of his elder brothers at forty-two, to which 2 Kings x. 13 rightly understood does not bind us; see on ver. 8. For the last words: "Athaliah daughter of Omri," comp. on xxi. 6.—Ver. 3. *For his mother was his counsellor to do wickedly*, in her devotion to the idolatry of the house of Ahab; comp. xx. 35, xxi. 6 ff.—Ver. 4. *Like the house of Ahab; for they*, the members of this house. At the close: "to his destruction," as in xx. 23.—Ver. 5. *Walked in their counsel, and went with Joram*, Ps. i. 1; these words are wanting in 2 Kings viii. 28. On Hazael, Benhadad's former general, and then successor, see Bähr on 2 Kings viii. 8 ff.—*And the Syrians smote Joram;* הָרַמִּים, contracted for הָאֲרַמִּים, 2 Kings viii. 28 (as הַסּוּרִים, Eccles. iv. 14, from הָאֲסוּרִים; comp. also Ezek. xx. 30).—Ver. 6. *And he returned to be healed . . . of the wounds.* So it is to be read instead of: "for the wounds," which is unmeaning, and only to be cured by explanatory additions; see Crit. Note.—*And Ahaziah . . .* (see Crit. Note) *went down to see Joram . . . in Jezreel.* This going down was probably from Ramoth, not from Jerusalem; comp. 2 Kings ix. 14 f. (from which, however, nothing very certain on this point is to be inferred).—Ver. 7. *And the downfall of Ahaziah was from God;* "the down-treading" (תְּבוּסָה, occurring only here; comp. מְבוּסָה, Isa. xxii. 5). Instead of "against Jehu," the text has properly: "to Jehu" (אֶל), 2 Kings ix. 21, more definitely "to meet Jehu" (לִקְרַאת); and for "son of Nimshi," Jehu is there (2 Kings ix. 2) more precisely called "son of Jehoshaphat, son of Nimshi." With the history of Jehu's call and anointment by Elijah and Elisha (1 Kings xix. 16; 2 Kings ix. 2 ff.) our author here proves himself to be acquainted, but does not enter into particulars, because the fate of the Jewish royal house was his immediate concern.—Ver. 8. *When Jehu executed judgment;* נִשְׁפַּט, execute judgment,—otherwise with אֵת (Ezek. xvii. 20, xxxviii. 22) or with לְ (Jer. xxv. 31), here with עִם; comp. Joel iv. 2.—*Sons of the brethren of Ahaziah.* As the brethren of Ahaziah named in 2 Kings x. 12 ff. from their great number (42) could only be his brethren in the wider sense (kinsmen, cousins), so the Sept. is wrong in making "brethren" out of these brethren's sons; and it is not less wrong in Bertheau to affirm two different traditions concerning the fact, according to one of which the Jewish princes put to death between Jezreel and Samaria, at Jehu's command, were brothers; according to the other, brothers' sons of Ahaziah; see, on the contrary, Mov. p. 258, Ew. in *Der Isr. Gesch.;* also Bähr, and especially Keil, who sees

no difficulty in the partly very youthful age (between five and eight or nine years) of these princes. — *That ministered to Ahaziah,* were invested with offices in his court, the youngest as pages, as, for example, Daniel and his friends in the court of the Babylonish king, Dan. i. 4 ff. —Ver. 6. *And he sought Ahaziah.* The fuller accounts of the death of Ahaziah in 2 Kings ix. 27, 28 deviate in several respects, in which Ahaziah is mortally wounded, not in Samaria, but in fleeing from Jezreel to Megiddo, and dies at Megiddo. See Bähr on the passage, who rightly rejects Keil's attempt to make up the difference of the two accounts as too artificial.— *And the house of Ahaziah had none to retain strength for the kingdom,* לַעְצֹר כֹּחַ, as in xiii. 20: "to be fit for the kingdom." On the whole sentence, comp. Dan. ix. 26 (וְאֵין לוֹ).

4. Athaliah's Reign of Six Years; Deliverance of Joash: vers. 10–12; comp. 2 Kings xi. 1–3.— *And Athaliah . . . destroyed all the seed.* On the emendation necessary here, according to 2 Kings, see Crit. Note. The "seed of the kingdom of the house of Judah" (the royal seed) embraces naturally the cousins and other remote kinsmen of Ahaziah, the male descendants of Jehoshaphat yet surviving after the catastrophes already mentioned (xxi. 17, xxii. 8).—Ver. 11. *Jehoshabath daughter of the king;* in 2 Kings with name slightly changed: Jehosheba; according to the close of our verse, a sister of Ahaziah, a daughter of Joram, perhaps, by another wife than Athaliah. That Jehoiada the husband of Jehoshabath was perhaps only a priest, not the high priest, see on xxiii. 8.—*That were slain,* or that should have been slain (הַמּוּמָתִים).—Ver. 12. *And he was with them in the house of God hidden.* Thither was he brought from his first hiding-place, the bed-chamber of the royal palace, as soon as the first favourable opportunity presented itself. "With them," with Jehoshabath, her priestly spouse and his nurse (ver. 11). For אִתָּם is, moreover, in 2 Kings xi. 3, the simpler אִתָּהּ, "with her." Comp. for the rest, Bähr on the parallel passage.

5. Athaliah's Fall through the Revolution effected by Jehoiada: ch. xxiii.—According to the parallel in 2 Kings xi. 4–20, Jehoiada employed in his enterprise the royal "runners" or guards, according to our passage, the Levites and priests, without, however, excluding the former (for in ver. 1, five captains of hundreds, that is, of the life-guards, are expressly named), or betraying any design to transform the narrative of the author of Kings into his Levitical sense in an unhistorical way. He stands much more (as is immediately evident from ver. 1) on independent older reports, which he takes in the main from the same sources from which 2 Kings xi. 4–20 is derived; only that he finds these sources richer, and by the addition of still other reports, produces a more complete account of the fact, filling up the parallel in various ways, and even deviating from it in some respects. Here and there his statements are less clear than those of the older texts, and show plainly enough the peculiar colouring of his Levitical standpoint, but without warranting the charge of biassed invention, which de Wette, Thenius, Bertheau, Hitzig (p. 204 ff.), and nearly Movers (p. 307 ff.), here bring against the Chronist. Comp. Bähr on Kings, p. 343, and Keil, pp. 305–310; also Neteler, p. 236 ff. —*In the seventh year Jehoiada . . . took the captains of hundreds,* the centurions of the royal life-guards, as appears from 2 Kings xi. 4 ff. Five of these captains are then named, a guarantee of the well-grounded accuracy of the present narrative. Before the first three of these names stands the introductory לְ (as xvii. 7; 1 Chron. v. 26), and before the last two וְאֵת.—Ver. 2. *And they went about in Judah,* וַיָּסֹבּוּ, as xvii. 9; comp. Song iii. 3; on the following רָאשֵׁי אָבוֹת, "tribe-chiefs," "heads of families," for 'ר' בֵּית א, comp. 1 Chron. viii. 6.—Ver. 3. *And all the congregation made a covenant.* כָּל־הַקָּהָל means, not the whole Israelitish community (Berth.), but according to the context, the congregation of Levites and heads of families appointed by Jehoiada at Jerusalem in the temple. What is related of "the covenant made with the king," the young Joash, is merely completive of the report in 2 Kings xi. 4, not contradictory (against Berth., etc., comp. Bähr on this passage).—*As the Lord hath spoken of the sons of David,* in the oracle of Nathan, 2 Sam. vii. (comp. xxi. 7).— Ver. 4. *A third of you* (properly, "the third part of you," 2 Chron. xxvii. 1) *who enter on the Sabbath, of the priests and of the Levites.* According to this, the first of the three posts is to be occupied by persons "who enter on the Sabbath" (בָּאֵי הַשַּׁבָּת), who are expressly described as belonging to the priests and Levites. In 2 Kings xi. 5 also the first third is so designated, which seems to indicate that there also priests and Levites are regarded as standing under the command of the five captains of hundreds; comp. moreover, the corresponding "coming out on the Sabbath," vers. 7, 9. Keil justly observes (*Apol. Vers.* p. 362 ff., and *Comm.* p. 309 f.), "that the priests and Levites in courses performed the temple service from one Sabbath to another" is known from Luke i. 5; comp. with 1 Chron. xxiv.; whereas nothing is said of such an arrangement on the part of the prætorians, so that by the phrases: entering on the Sabbath (resuming service), and coming out on the Sabbath (retiring from it), we must understand the Levites. If the prætorians (life-guards) were thus intended in 2 Kings xi., this should have been clearly affirmed. From the words spoken of the centurions of the life-guards: "the third part of you," this no more follows than from the fact that in 2 Kings xi. 11 the appointed posts are called הָרָצִים, "the runners, guards." If we assume that for this extraordinary occasion the Levitical attendants were placed under the command of some centurions of the royal guards who were in concert with the high priest, the designation of the men whom they commanded as רָצִים, guards, is fully explained, after these men (on account of the priestly and Levitical elements assigned to them) were described as those "entering and coming out on the Sabbath." Accordingly, if 2 Kings and Chronicles agree in this,

that they presuppose the troops employed by Jehoiada to be composed of Levites, life-guards, and other Jews, they do not essentially differ with regard to the localities which the three divisions of the troops had to occupy. For, according to 2 Kings xi. 5, 6, the first third was to take "the watch of the king's house," the second that at "the gate of Sur," the third that at "the gate behind the runners;" besides, those coming out on the Sabbath were to occupy the temple in two divisions, and so protect the young king (vers. 7, 8). According to our verses, on the contrary, the first third was to be porters at the thresholds, and so (1 Chron. ix. 19, 22) guard the entrance to the temple, the second was to stand (ver. 5) in the house of the king, the third at the gate Jesod, while "all the people" were to fill the court of the house of God. Two of these statements appear quite reconcilable; for the occupying of the king's house is by both texts assigned to a third, and the gate Jesod (foundation-gate) should be the same as the gate סור (the latter is probably miswritten for the former, or it denotes "a gate of retreat," a side gate [?]; comp. Bähr). But with regard to the third, an incurable contradiction appears to exist between the two texts; the "gate behind the runners" must apparently, according to 2 Kings xi. 19, be sought not in the temple but in the royal palace, whereas our author assigns to the corresponding division its post, not here, at one of the palace gates, but at the thresholds of the temple gate. The only possible arrangement would be that proposed as a hint by Keil, that the runners' gate was placed where the passage, mentioned 1 Kings x. 5, 2 Kings xvi. 18, from the palace to the temple was situated, and therefore the division in question was conceived to be guarding at the same time the palace and the temple. It is easier to reconcile that which is said in both passages concerning the employment of the rest of the armed men (in our text, ver. 5: "all the people") to occupy the temple (or in particular its court). Yet here also in the two reporters somewhat diverse conceptions of the event seem to have existed, and in such a way that the author of 2 Kings conceived and represented the whole as a military, the Chronist as a Levitical, measure. Comp. especially in this respect, vers. 6–8.—Ver. 6. *And all the people shall keep the ward of the Lord*, behave in a legal manner, and beware of entering the inner temple chambers, the proper sanctuary. For the phrase, comp. xiii. 11.—Ver. 7. *And the Levites shall surround the king*, not form a dense and close circle around him, but occupy all the entrances to the temple around the chamber of the king.—Ver. 8. *And the Levites and all Judah.* For this 2 Kings has: "and the captains of hundreds." But this is not a real contradiction; in 2 Kings the commanders are named, in our passage the commanded, as the executors of Jehoiada's directions.—*All that Jehoiada the priest commanded.* Neither here nor xxii. 11, nor generally in the accounts of the Chronist, does Jehoiada bear the title of high priest; but even in the book of Kings he is not so called, but either simply Jehoiada, without addition, or "Jehoiada the priest" (2 Kings xi. 15, xii. 3, 8, 10); that he is identical with the הכהן הגדול named 2 Kings xii. 11 is as improbable as that in the parallel 2 Chron. xxiv. 6, 11 (see on the passage) the designation כהן הראש refers to him as high priest. Contrary, therefore, to the usual view, which makes Jehoiada high priest, Neteler appears justly to assume that he was the leading chief of the priesthood (הראש), but not the high priest proper, but that one of his sons was invested with this dignity; with which assumption the absence of Jehoiada's name in the list of the high priests, 1 Chron. v. 30 ff., admirably agrees. That the Azariah named 1 Chron. v. 36, the son of Johanan, who ministered as priest in the house built by Solomon, was the son of our Jehoiada, and thus the high priest acting in his time and under his paternal guidance (2 Kings xii. 11), is a wholly arbitrary conjecture of this learned man, which fails on this account, that, 1 Chron. v. 37, an Amariah is named as son of this Azariah, who can scarcely be different from the high priest Amariah named, ch. xix. 11, as the contemporary of Jehoshaphat.—*For Jehoiada the priest had not dismissed the courses.* המחלקות, the priestly divisions for performing the temple service according to the order made by David, 1 Chron. xxiv.–xxvi. The dismissal (פטר) of these divisions as well as their summoning was the business of the high priest, 1 Chron. xxiv. 6, 19; but Jehoiada may have acted for his son (possibly a minor), just as if he had been high priest himself; comp. as a New Testament parallel, the relation of Annas to his son-in-law Caiaphas, Luke iii. 2; John xviii. 12 ff.—Ver. 9. *And Jehoiada the priest gave . . . spears, and shields, and arms.* שלטים, here probably in the more general sense of weapons, arms, as in Song iv. 4, where, likewise, מגן precedes; yet it might also signify targets (along with shields of another kind); comp. 2 Kings xi. 10 and 2 Sam. viii. 7; Ezek. xxvii. 11. On the captured arms deposited by David as a dedicated gift in the house of God, comp. 1 Chron. xviii. 7 ff. and 2 Chron. ix. 24, xii. 10.—Ver. 10. *Every man with his weapon in his hand.* שלחו, properly, his missile; comp. xxxii. 5; Job xxxiii. 18. The "setting round about the king" is to be understood as the surrounding (ver. 7).—Ver. 11. *And they brought out the king's son.* This account of the crowning of Joash agrees in substance with 2 Kings xi. 12, only that the clapping of the hands as the outward expression of the people's joy is here omitted as unessential.—Ver. 12 ff. Athaliah's Execution, the Renewal of the Covenant, and the Solemn Procession of the King to his Palace,—all this related essentially as in 2 Kings xi. 13–20.—Ver. 13. *And the singers with instruments of song.* This more copious description, corresponding with the favourite manner of the Chronist, of the musical demonstrations of the joyful multitude (comp. 1 Chron. xv. 16, xvi. 42) is wanting in 2 Kings.—Ver. 14. *Brought out;* comp. the Crit. Note.—Ver. 15. *And she went to the entrance of the horse gate.* For this is in 2 Kings: "And she went the way in which the horses entered the king's house." The redundant שער of our passage, beside מבוא, which the old versions do not express, came into the text perhaps by an unsuitable reference to Neh. iii. 28. The horse gate there mentioned, which was a city gate, is not to be thought of here, although Josephus here confuses them.—Ver. 16. *And Jehoiada made a covenant between himself and between all the people.* Instead of "between himself" (בֵּינוֹ) stands in 2 Kings: "between Jehovah," an unimportant difference, for the priest causing the covenant to be made represented Jehovah. That he was the high priest in particular follows no more from this than from ver. 8; comp. on xxiv. 11.—Ver. 17. *And all the people went to the house of Baal.* On the conjectural site of this temple of Baal, comp. Bähr on 2 Kings xi. 18.—Vers. 18, 19 form an enlargement peculiar to our author of the brief statement in 2 Kings: "And the priest appointed officers (offices) over the house of the Lord," wherein, again, the singers and the porters are specially mentioned.—*Whom David had distributed*, had determined to minister before God in certain regularly succeeding divisions; comp. 1 Chron. xxiii. 6, and for the following, Ezra iii. 2, 10. —*And he set the porters at the gates*, properly, "over the gates"; comp. 1 Chron. ix. 23.—*That the unclean might not enter*, literally, "one unclean in respect of anything"; comp. Lev. v. 2, 3; Isa. xxxv. 8.—Ver. 20. *And he took the captains of hundreds, and the nobles* (הָאַדִּירִים, Jer. xiv. 3, Ps. xvi. 3), *and the rulers of the people* (literally, "those ruling among the people"; comp. Isa. xxviii. 14). Instead of this, in 2 Kings: "the captains of hundreds, and the life-guards, and the runners." In the following part also, our author with singular constancy avoids the mention of the runners; for instead of: "and came by the way of the gate of the runners to the king's house" (2 Kings xi. 19), he puts: "and went through the high gate," etc. This high gate appears from xxvii. 3 (comp. also 2 Kings xv. 35) to have been a gate in the temple, not, as probably the runners' gate, in the king's house; but as it might have been situated over against the royal palace (perhaps over the bridge leading from Moriah to Zion), its name involves neither a topographical impossibility nor a contradiction of 2 Kings (comp. Keil on 2 Kings, p. 271).

EVANGELICAL AND ETHICAL REFLECTIONS AND APOLOGETIC REMARKS, ON CH. XXI.–XXIII.

1. The bad seed sown by Jehoshaphat through the unfortunate affinity with the house of Ahab springs up only too soon, and bears corrupt fruit to the royal house and people of Judah. With the malignity of a fury or a demon, Athaliah the daughter of Jezebel proceeds, during the two reigns of her husband Joram and her son Ahaziah that were guided by her, and during the six years of her sole sovereignty, to gloat over the blood of every member of the unfortunate house of David from which the least resistance to her idolatrous course might be apprehended. The all too close connection, no longer, as with Solomon and Hiram, amounting to mere friendship, with the Tyrian princely family, into which Judah, also following the bad example of the house of Omri, had thoughtlessly entered, fearfully avenges itself. The worst Sultanism is transplanted thence into the royal castle on Zion.[1] And as the severe punishment inflicted by Jehu on the house of Omri took place in Jezreel, and swept away at the same time the Jewish king Ahaziah and his male kinsmen in the northern kingdom (884 according to the usual reckoning, 880 according to Hitzig; according to Schrader and Neteler, certainly after 850, as follows from the synchronism of the Assyrian history; see under), the cruel scourge is not yet taken from Judah's back, but continues to lacerate it full six years more. And to all this is added for this kingdom the humiliating and disgraceful circumstance that it is a woman, and even a foreign woman, who usurps the sole sovereignty, and maintains it for those years by the forcible setting aside of the male heir of the house of David. So much the more beneficent appears the manner in which the reform, rendered necessary by this temporary degeneracy of the Jewish royal house and state, was finally executed. No blood-dripping Jehu, spreading terror and amazement around, no tempestuous desolating form of the fanatical zealots in Roman or Herodian times, proves necessary to effect the return from the worship of Baal to that of Jehovah, and the restoration of the theocratic character of the community. The mild, not terrible, but venerable form of a pious priest, closely related by family ties to the royal house of David, accomplishes almost without blood the necessary revolution. The single sacrifice that is needed for this end is the tyrannical and idolatrous stranger who has been the origin of the evil that has broken over the land for the last twenty years. With the slaying, or rather execution, for nothing is said of wild revenge or tumultuary massacre, of her and her Baal-priest Matthan, the judgment on the disturbers of the theocratic order seems to be executed, and peace restored. That our author, by his peculiar mode of elevating the Levitical and priestly element into the factors of the revolution, places in a peculiarly clear light this eminently peaceful course of the same; that he, in harmony, again, with his often otherwise manifested historical tendency, represents the whole in some measure as a revolution carried on with music and song, as a transference, accomplished with ringing notes and flying banners, of the whole people into the camp of the legitimate party (comp. ch. xxiii. 13, 18),—this lends to his representation a peculiar charm, in contrast with the more concise and jejune description, only relating that which is of political or military importance, in the book of Kings. In this narrative, also, the circumstance that the whole people of Judah and Benjamin rises up as one man to shake off the long enough borne and already sufficiently hated foreign yoke by one powerful movement of its neck, stands forth conspicuous in the light of day. It is shown more clearly than in the parallel account of the older history, how slightly the foreign and idolatrous lust had struck its roots into the consciousness and life of the people, and with what comparative rapidity and ease it could be set aside again. A conjecture, to which we must have

[1] Compare the remark of J. H. Michaelis: "Tyrian, Israelitish, Jewish history here coincide. Tyre brought by marriage her then prevalent spirit and misfortune into the Israelitish history. Contemporary with Joram is Pygmalion king of Tyre, who murdered the husband of his sister Dido merely to possess himself of his treasure. Joram likewise after Jehoshaphat's death (2 Chron. xxi.) murdered all his brothers, as it appears, for no other cause (?) but to possess himself of the treasures which their father had bequeathed to them (?)," etc. This latter assumption, though one-sided and exegetically unfounded (comp. on xxi. 4), is yet on the whole very striking.

come on receiving exclusively the narrative of the book of Kings, that a prominent part in the revolution effected by Jehoiada must have been due to the numerically strong Levitical element in the population of the Jewish state,—this conjecture is strikingly confirmed by the Chronist's narrative, with its emphatic marking of the priestly and Levitical character of the catastrophe, and its almost unseemly depreciation of the share of the runners in it (comp. especially on ch. xxiii. 20 f.), without being under the necessity of charging the narrator with any bias in moulding the narrative after his Levitical standpoint. For it would be strange if an event such as this shrewd and bold political stroke of the priest Jehoiada were conducted in so exclusively political and military a way, and with so little participation of the clergy, as appears in 2 Kings.

2. In an apologetic respect, with regard to the account of the fall of Athaliah by means of Jehoiada, we have to refer partly to what has been just observed, and partly to the detail of the exposition. On the contrary, the ill-foreboding writing of Elijah to Joram (ch. xxi. 12–15) needs a more special elucidation in the evangelical and apologetic interest. This remarkable document, the only definite proof of the acquaintance of our author with the existence of the greatest and most powerful prophet of the time of the divided kingdom, presents to the expositor the not unimportant chronological difficulty, that, if actually composed by Elijah, and addressed to Joram as already reigning king of Judah, it necessitates the assumption of an extension of the activity of Elijah far into the twelve years of the reign of the Israelitish Joram (896–884 in the usual reckoning, 857–846 in that of Schrader and Neteler), whereas, according to 2 Kings ii., the taking up of the prophet into heaven seems to have occurred at the latest in the beginning of this reign, thus all events under Jehoshaphat († 890 or 889 in the usual chronology, 850 or 849 in the modern Assyriologic chronology). Various ways have been taken of removing this difficulty. Older Jewish and Roman Catholic expositors (of the latter, for example, Estius, Malvenda, Tirinus, Calmet), and some evangelical moderns (especially Menken, and Dächsel in his *Bibelw.*), make Elijah write after his ascent into paradise, and send it by an angel to Elisha, or a still surviving disciple of the prophet, to forward to Joram. This overstrained supra-naturalistic solution of the problem is equally void of exegetical warrant[1] with the superficial purely natural assumption, that the writer of the letter was not Elijah the Tishbite, but another prophet of the same name (Lightfoot, *Hor. Hebr.* on Luke i. 17), or with the no less arbitrary and text-defying attempt to change the name Elijah (ch. xxi. 12) into that of Elisha (Cleric., Saurin, *Diss.* tom. ii. p. 344). But even the chronological proof of the possibility, that Elijah may have survived the death of Jehoshaphat and the beginning of the reign of the Jewish Joram (890 or 889–884), that he might thus have directed the writing shortly before his departure to the latter king as his contemporary (Seb. Schmid, Lightf. *Op.* t. i. p. 85; Usher, Mai, Burmann, etc., and recently Keil, p. 298, at least tentatively), could only be maintained with difficulty, and only by the assumption of an inaccurate statement on the part of the author of the book of Kings, as the position of that which is related, 2 Kings ii. 1 ff., of the ascension of Elijah is such that it appears to have happened either under the reign of Ahaziah of Israel, the predecessor of Joram, or immediately after his death (896, or eventually 857). There remains after all this only the twofold possibility, that either—1. Elijah wrote the letter some time before his ascension, and left it behind him to one of his disciples, with the charge to hand it to the later King Joram of Judah (Starke, Buddeus, Rambach, etc., and recently Keil, as well as Hengstenberg, *Gesch.* ii. 2, 243), or that, 2. Elijah merely made over by word of mouth the contents of the letter some time before his ascension to one of his disciples, perhaps to Elisha, with the charge to make it known to Joram by a writing composed in his name (Witsius, Gürtler, Hackspan, *Not. philol.* on 2 Chron. xxi.; S. Schmid, *De literis Eliæ ad Joramum*, Argentor. 1717; Wilisch, etc.). The latter assumption, or that of an only ideal authorship of Elijah in relation to the writing, a composition of it ἐν πνεύματι καὶ δυνάμει Ἠλίου (Luke i. 17), but certainly on the ground of an actual prediction of Elijah, has most in its favour. It avoids the inherently improbable supposition, that Elijah wrote with his own hand a letter, which he knew could only be delivered in the course of at least five or six years after his ascension to God (for the writing appears directed to the king, not to the crown prince). On the other hand, it is reconcilable with the indefinite designation of the writing as coming from Elijah (see on ch. xxi. 12), and excludes the suspicion of pseudepigraphic fiction after the manner of so many apocryphal writings of later times, bearing the names of celebrated sages or men of God.[1] It recognises the genuine prophetic content and character of the writing; for it discerns actual prediction, true action of prophetic foresight in it, without overlooking the difference between the author of this prophetic kernel, and the later composer or redactor. Comp. on the possibility or even probability of a divine disclosure being made to Elijah of the future destiny of Joram, the husband of the daughter of Jezebel, as well as of a charge to Elisha to announce afterwards the contents of such a revelation to Joram, on the one hand, Hengstenberg as quoted: "Elijah had (1 Kings xix.) foreseen the elevation of Jehu to the throne of Israel, and the extirpation of the family of Ahab by him; also the accession of

[1] And theological warrant; for as A. Calov. aptly says: *Non triumphantium in cœlis est erudire aut ad pœnitentiam revocare mortales in terra. Habent Mosen et prophetas; si illos non audiant, neque si quis ex mortuis resurrexerit, nedum si quis ex cœlis literas perscripserit, credent* (Luke xvi. 31) Likewise J. J. Rambach on our passage, who declares it inconceivable: *Deum in gratiam impii regis ejusmodi quid fecisse, cujus nullum aliud exemplum extat, immo quod nec necessarium erat, quum plures aliæ essent rationes, quibus Deus voluntatem suam ei manifestare poterat* (Luke xvi. 27, 29). Comp. also the remarks of Keil, p. 298, against Menken.

[1] The Apocrypha of Jewish-Hellenistic literature bearing the name of Elijah belong to a pretty late period, as the *Apocalypsis Eliæ*, from which, according to Origen and the Church-fathers, the quotation in 1 Cor. ii. 9 is to be taken; comp. Fabr. *Cod pseudepigr. V T.* vol. i. p. 1072. Concerning the Elias of the Jewish-Christian fables or legends, comp the reports of Epiphanius. Dorotheus of Tyre, Isidore of Seville, and in the Talmud. There are still Mahommedan or Christian (at least half-Christian) nations in the East, for example in the Caucasus, who worship in Elias (on account of 1 Kings xvii. 1 f.) a kind of rain-god or *Jupiter pluvius* (see *Ausland*, 1872, No. 29. p. 679). What a contrast between this Elijah of the fable and that of Old Testament history, as well, according to 1 and 2 Kings, as our documents preserved in Chronicles!

Hazael, and the heavy misfortune brought by him on the kingdom of Israel. If the future was in this respect disclosed to him, the greatest of all the prophets of the Old Testament, why might not this also have been revealed to him, that Joram, who had already before his decease connected himself with the abominable Athaliah, will, by his grievous sins, bring upon himself the judgment of the Lord?" on the other hand, Keil, p. 299: "To whom God revealed the elevation of Jehu to the throne of Israel, the accession of Hazael, etc., events which took place after the death of Joram of Judah, to whom God already, under Ahab, committed the anointing of Jehu to be king of Israel (1 Kings xix. 16), which, fourteen years after the death of Ahab, Elisha performed by a scholar of the prophet's (2 Kings ix. 1 ff.)—to him the Lord might also in the second year of Ahaziah of Israel, when he announced to this king his death, about seven years before Jehoshaphat's death, reveal the wickedness of his successor Joram, and commit the announcement of the divine punishment. But if Elijah made over the anointing as well of Hazael as of Jehu to his servant Elisha, why might he not also have entrusted to him the handing of the written prediction of woe to Joram?". We find this statement so far completely suitable and convincing, but cannot agree with the two learned men from whom it proceeds in this, that they hold Elijah to be the writer (composer) of the letter in its extant form. We find it much more satisfactory for the establishment of the essential authenticity of the document, if the mediate origin of it from Elijah (the powerful "prophet of deed," who was no man of the pen, and of whose action as a writer nothing is said) is maintained. With this also agree the generally acknowledged contents and tone of the writing, quite irrespective of the personal position of the prophet, which, however, is not on this account to be held (with Berth. and other recent critics) to be an idealizing composition of a later historian; for in that case it would be different only in degree (as a pseudepigraphon within the canon) from the products of the post-canonical literature, above which it seems exalted by its genuine prophetic contents.

h. JOASH: THE PROPHET ZECHARIAH SON OF JEHOIADA.—CH. XXIV.

α. Reign of Joash under the Guidance of Jehoiada: Repair of the Temple: vers. 1–14.

CH. XXIV. 1. Joash was seven years old when he became king; and he reigned forty
2 years in Jerusalem: and his mother's name was Zibiah of Beer-sheba. And
Joash did that which was right in the eyes of the LORD all the days of
3 Jehoiada the priest. And Jehoiada chose for him two wives; and he begat
sons and daughters.
4 And it came to pass after this that it was in the heart of Joash to renew
5 the house of the LORD. And he gathered the priests and the Levites, and
said to them, Go out into the cities of Judah, and gather of all Israel money
to repair the house of your God from year to year, and hasten ye the matter:
6 but the Levites hastened it not. And the king called for Jehoiada the chief,
and said unto him, Why hast thou not required of the Levites to bring in out
of Judah and Jerusalem the tax of Moses the servant of the LORD, and of the
7 congregation of Israel, for the tent of witness? For Athaliah the wicked
doer [and] her sons[1] have broken up the house of God, and bestowed all the
8 consecrated things of the house of the LORD upon Baalim. And the king
commanded, and they made a chest, and set it without at the gate of the
9 house of the LORD. And they proclaimed in Judah and Jerusalem, to bring
in to the LORD the tax of Moses the servant of God upon Israel in the wil-
10 derness. And all the princes and all the people were glad, and they brought
11 and cast into the chest, till it was full. And at the time when the chest was
brought to the survey of the king by the Levites, and when they saw that
there was much money, then went the king's scribe and the officer of the
head priest and emptied the chest, and took it, and carried it to its place
12 again: thus they did day by day, and gathered money in abundance. And
the king and Jehoiada gave it to the work-master of the service of the house
of the LORD, and they hired masons and carpenters to renew the house of the
LORD, and also smiths in iron and brass to repair the house of the LORD.
13 And the workmen wrought, and furtherance was given to the work by their
14 hand: and they set the house of God in its form, and strengthened it. And
when they had finished, they brought before the king and Jehoiada the rest
of the money, and they made of it vessels for the house of the LORD, vessels
for ministering and offering, and cups, and vessels of gold and silver: and
they offered burnt-offerings in the house of the LORD continually all the days
of Jehoiada.

β. Death of Jehoiada: Stoning of his Son, the Prophet Zechariah:
vers. 15–22.

15 And Jehoiada was old and full of days, and he died; he was a hundred
16 and thirty years old when he died. And they buried him in the city of
David with the kings; for he had done good in Israel, and for God and His
17 house. And after the death of Jehoiada came the princes of Judah, and
18 bowed down before the king: then the king hearkened unto them. And
they left the house of the LORD God of their fathers, and served the Asherim
and the idols: and wrath came upon Judah and Jerusalem for this their
19 trespass. And he sent prophets among them, to bring them back to the
20 LORD; and they testified against them, and they did not give ear. And the
Spirit of God clothed Zechariah son of Jehoiada the priest[2]; and he stood up
before the people, and said unto them, Thus saith God, Why transgress ye
the commandments of the LORD, and do not prosper? for ye have forsaken
21 the LORD, and He has forsaken you. And they conspired against him, and
stoned him by command of the king in the court of the house of the LORD.
22 And Joash the king remembered not the kindness which Jehoiada had done
to him, and slew his son: and when he died, he said, The LORD shall see and
require.

γ. Distress of Joash by the Syrians, and his End: vers. 23–27

23 And it came to pass in the course of a year, that the host of Syria came
up against him; and they came to Judah and Jerusalem, and destroyed all
the princes of the people out of the people,[3] and sent all the spoil of them
24 unto the king to Damascus.[4] For the host of Syria came with few men; and
the LORD gave into their hand a very great host, because they had forsaken
the LORD God of their fathers: and they executed judgments upon Joash.
25 And when they went from him, for they left him with many wounds, his
servants conspired against him for the blood of the sons[5] of Jehoiada the
priest, and slew him on his bed, and he died: and they buried him in the
26 city of David, but they buried him not in the sepulchres of the kings. And
these were the conspirators against him: Zabad son of Shimath the Am-
27 monitess, and Jehozabad son of Shimrith the Moabitess. And his sons, and
the greatness[6] of the burden upon him, and the building of the house of God,
behold, they are written in the commentary of the book of the Kings: and
Amaziah his son reigned in his stead.

i. AMAZIAH.—CH. XXV.

α. Duration of his Reign, and its Spirit: vers. 1–4.

CH. XXV. 1. Amaziah became king when twenty and five years old; and he reigned
twenty and nine years in Jerusalem: and his mother's name was Jehoaddan
2 of Jerusalem. And he did that which was right in the eyes of the LORD, but
3 not with undivided heart. And it came to pass, when the kingdom was
established to him, that he slew his servants who smote the king his father.
4 But he put not their sons to death, but as it is written in the law in the book
of Moses, as the LORD commanded, saying, The fathers shall not die for the
sons, nor shall the sons die for the fathers; but every one shall die for his
own sin.

β. The Conquest of the Edomites in the Valley of Salt: vers. 5–13.

5 And Amaziah gathered Judah, and arranged them by father-houses, by
captains of thousands and captains of hundreds, for all Judah and Benjamin:
and he mustered them from twenty years old and upwards, and found them
three hundred thousand choice men, going out to war, holding spear and

6 shield. And he hired out of Israel a hundred thousand mighty men of valour
7 for a hundred talents of silver. And a man of God came to him, saying, O
king, let not the army of Israel go with thee; for the LORD is not with
8 Israel, with all the sons of Ephraim. But go thou; do, be strong for the
battle; [otherwise[7]] God shall make thee fall before the enemy; for with
9 God is power to help and to cast down. And Amaziah said to the man of
God, But what shall we do for the hundred[8] talents which I have given to
the host of Israel? And the man of God said, It rests with the LORD to give
10 thee much more than this. And Amaziah separated them, to wit, the host
that was come to him from Ephraim, to go to their place: and their anger
was greatly kindled against Judah, and they returned to their place in hot
11 anger. And Amaziah took courage, and led forth his people, and went to
12 the valley of Salt, and smote of the sons of Seir ten thousand. And the
sons of Judah took ten thousand alive, and brought them to the top of
the rock, and cast them down from the top of the rock, and all of them
13 were broken in pieces. And the men of the host which Amaziah sent
back from going with him to battle, fell upon the cities of Judah, from
Samaria even to Beth-horon, and smote of them three thousand, and took
much spoil.

γ. Amaziah's Idolatry, War with Joash of Israel, and End: vers. 14–28.

14 And it came to pass, after Amaziah was come from smiting the Edomites,
that he brought the gods of the sons of Seir, and set them up for him as gods,
15 and bowed down before them, and burnt incense to them. And the anger of
the LORD was kindled against Amaziah, and He sent unto him a prophet,
who said to him, Why hast thou sought after the gods of the people, who did
16 not deliver their own people out of thy hand? And it came to pass as he
talked with him, that he said unto him, Have we made thee councillor to the
king? Forbear; why should they smite thee? And the prophet forbare,
and said, I know that God hath resolved to destroy thee, because thou hast
17 done this, and hast not hearkened to my counsel. And Amaziah king of
Judah took counsel, and sent to Joash son of Jehoahaz, son of Jehu king of
18 Israel, saying, Come,[9] let us look one another in the face. And Joash king
of Israel sent to Amaziah king of Judah, saying, The thorn that was in
Lebanon sent to the cedar that was in Lebanon, saying, Give thy daughter to
my son to wife; and a beast of the field that was in Lebanon passed by and
19 trampled on the thorn. Thou sayest, Lo, thou hast smitten Edom; and thy
heart hath lifted thee up to boast: now abide at home; why provokest thou
evil, that thou mayest fall, and Judah with thee?
20 And Amaziah hearkened not; for it was of God that they might be given
21 up, because they sought after the gods of Edom. And Joash king of Israel
went up, and they looked one another in the face, he and Amaziah king of
22 Judah, at Beth-shemesh, which is of Judah. And Judah was smitten before
23 Israel; and they fled every man to his tent. And Joash king of Israel took
Amaziah king of Judah, son of Joash, son of Jehoahaz, at Beth-shemesh, and
brought him to Jerusalem, and brake down the wall of Jerusalem from the
24 gate of Ephraim to the corner gate,[10] four hundred cubits. And all the gold
and the silver, and all the vessels that were found in the house of God with
Obed-edom, and the treasures of the king's house, and the hostages; and he
25 returned to Samaria. And Amaziah son of Joash king of Judah lived after
26 the death of Joash son of Jehoahaz king of Israel fifteen years. And the
rest of the acts of Amaziah, first and last, behold, are they not written in the
27 book of the kings of Judah and Israel? And from the time that Amaziah
turned away from the LORD, they made a conspiracy against him in Jerusalem; and he fled to Lachish: and they sent after him to Lachish, and there
28 put him to death. And they brought him upon horses, and buried him with
his fathers in the city of Judah.[11]

k. Uzziah.—Ch. xxvi

α. His early Theocratic Inclination and Prosperous Reign: vers. 1–15.

Chap. xxvi. 1. And all the people of Judah took Uzziah, when sixteen years old,
2 and made him king instead of his father Amaziah. He built Eloth, and re-
3 stored it to Judah, after the king had slept with his fathers. Sixteen years
old was Uzziah when he became king; and he reigned fifty and two years in
4 Jerusalem: and his mother's name was Jechiliah [12] of Jerusalem. And he
did that which was right in the eyes of the Lord, according to all that
5 Amaziah his father had done. And he continued to seek God in the days of
Zechariah, who understood the visions [13] of God: and so long as he sought
the Lord, God made him prosper.
6 And he went out and fought with the Philistines, and brake down the
wall of Gath, and the wall of Jabneh, and the wall of Ashdod, and built
7 cities about Ashdod and among the Philistines. And God helped him against
the Philistines, and against the Arabs that dwelt in Gur-baal, [14] and against
8 the Meunites. And the Ammonites [15] gave gifts to Uzziah: and his name
9 went even to Egypt; for he became very mighty. And Uzziah built towers
in Jerusalem, at the corner gate and at the valley-gate, and at the corner, and
10 fortified them. And he built towers in the wilderness, and dug many wells;
for he had much cattle in the lowland and in the plain; husbandmen and
vine-dressers in the mountains and in Carmel; for he was a lover of land.
11 And Uzziah had a host of fighting men, that went out to war in troops, by
the number of their muster at the hand of Jeuel [16] the scribe, and Maaseiah
12 the officer, at the hand of Hananiah, one of the captains of the king. The
whole number of the chiefs of the fathers for the mighty men of valour
13 was two thousand and six hundred. And at their hand was an army of three
hundred thousand and seven thousand and five hundred fighting men in full
14 strength, to help the king against the foe. And Uzziah prepared for them,
for the whole army, shields and spears, and helmets and coats of mail, and
15 bows and sling-stones. And at Jerusalem he made engines, the invention of
craftsmen, to be on the towers and battlements, to shoot arrows and great
stones: and his name went forth far abroad; for he was marvellously helped
till he was strong.

β. His Boasting, and Divine Chastisement by Leprosy: his End: vers. 16–23.

16 And when he became strong, his heart was lifted up to do corruptly, and
he transgressed against the Lord his God; and he went into the temple of
17 the Lord to burn incense upon the altar of incense. And Azariah the priest
went in after him, and with him eighty priests of the Lord, men of valour.
18 And they withstood Uzziah the king, and said unto him, It pertaineth not
unto thee, Uzziah, to burn incense unto the Lord, but to the priests, the sons
of Aaron, that are consecrated to burn incense: go out of the sanctuary; for
thou hast transgressed; and it shall not be for thine honour from the Lord
19 God. And Uzziah was wroth, and had a censer in his hand to burn incense:
and while he was wroth with the priests, the leprosy burst forth on his fore-
head before the priests in the house of the Lord from beside the incense-
20 altar. And Azariah the head priest and all the priests looked upon him, and,
behold, he was leprous in his forehead, and they drove him out thence; and
21 even he himself hasted to go out, because the Lord had smitten him. And
Uzziah the king was a leper unto the day of his death, and dwelt in a sick-
house as a leper; for he was cut off from the house of the Lord: and Jotham
his son was over the king's house, judging the people of the land.
22 And the rest of the acts of Uzziah, first and last, Isaiah son of Amos the
23 prophet wrote. And Uzziah slept with his fathers; and they buried him with
his fathers in the burial field of the kings; for they said, He is a leper: and
Jotham his son reigned in his stead.

l. JOTHAM.—CH. XXVII.

CHAP. XXVII. 1. Jotham was twenty and five years old when he became king; and
he reigned sixteen years in Jerusalem: and his mother's name was Jerushah
2 daughter of Zadok. And he did that which was right in the eyes of the
LORD, according to all that his father Uzziah did; only he entered not into
3 the temple of the LORD: and the people did yet corruptly. He built the
high gate of the house of the LORD; and on the wall of Ophel he built
4 much. And he built cities in the mountains of Judah, and in the forests he
5 built castles and towers. And he fought with the king of the sons of Ammon,
and prevailed over them: and the sons of Ammon gave him in that year a
hundred talents of silver, and ten thousand cors of wheat, and ten thousand
of barley: this the sons of Ammon paid him also in the second and third
6 year. And Jotham strengthened himself; for he established his ways before
the LORD his God.
7 And the rest of the acts of Jotham, and all his wars and his ways, lo,
8 they are written in the book of the kings of Israel and Judah. He was
twenty and five years old when he became king; and he reigned sixteen years
9 in Jerusalem. And Jotham slept with his fathers; and they buried him in
the city of David: and Ahaz his son reigned in his stead.

m. AHAZ: THE PROPHET ODED.—CH. XXVIII.

α. *Idolatry of Ahaz: his Defeat by the Syrians and Ephraimites:* vers. 1–8.

CHAP. XXVIII. 1. Ahaz was twenty[17] years old when he became king; and he
reigned sixteen years in Jerusalem: and he did not that which was right in
2 the eyes of the LORD, like David his father. And he walked in the ways of
3 the kings of Israel, and made also molten images for Baalim. And he
burnt incense in the valley of Ben-hinnom, and burnt his sons in the fire,
after the abominations of the nations, whom the LORD had cast out before
4 the sons of Israel. And he sacrificed and burnt incense in the high places,
5 and on the hills, and under every green tree. And the LORD his God gave
him into the hand of the king of Syria; and they smote him, and took from
him a great many captives, and brought them to Damascus:[18] and he was also
given into the hand of the king of Israel, and he inflicted on him a great
6 blow. And Pekah son of Remaliah slew in Judah a hundred and twenty
thousand in one day, all sons of valour, because they had forsaken the LORD
7 God of their fathers. And Zichri, a mighty man of Ephraim, slew Maaseiah
the king's son, and Azrikam, the governor of the house, and Elkanah the
8 vicegerent of the king. And the sons of Israel took captive of their brethren
two hundred thousand, women, sons, and daughters, and stripped them of great
spoil, and brought the spoil to Samaria.

β. *Oded the Prophet procures the Release of the Captives:* vers. 9–15.

9 And a prophet of the LORD was there, of the name of Oded; and he
went out before the host that came to Samaria, and said unto them, Behold,
in the wrath of the LORD God of your fathers against Judah He hath given
them into your hand; and ye slew of them with a rage that reacheth unto
10 heaven. And now ye purpose to subject the sons of Judah and Jerusalem
for bondsmen and bondsmaids to you: are there not even with you yourselves
11 trespasses against the LORD your God? And now hear me, and release the
captives which ye have taken of your brethren; for the hot anger of the LORD
12 is upon you. Then arose men of the chiefs of the sons of Ephraim, Azariah
son of Johanan, Berechiah son of Meshillemoth, and Hezekiah son of Shallum,
13 and Amasa son of Hadlai, against those who came from the war, And said
unto them, Ye shall not bring the captives hither; for with the trespass of

the LORD upon us ye intend to add to our sins and to our trespass: for great
14 is our trespass, and there is hot anger against Israel. And the armed host
left the captives and the spoil before the princes and all the congregation.
15 Then there rose up the men who were expressed by name, and took the
captives, and clothed all that were naked of them from the spoil, and gave
them clothes, and shoes, and food, and drink, and anointed them, and carried
them on asses, all the weary, and brought them to Jericho, the city of palms,
beside their brethren: and they returned to Samaria.

γ. Further Visitations of Ahaz on account of his Idolatry: his End: vers. 16–27.

16 At that time King Ahaz sent unto the kings of Assyria to help him.
17, 18 And again the Edomites came and smote Judah, and took captives. And the
Philistines invaded the cities of the lowland and of the south of Judah, and
took Beth-shemesh, and Ajalon, and Gederoth, and Socho with her daughters,
and Timnah with her daughters, and Gimzo with her daughters: and they
19 dwelt there. For the LORD humbled Judah on account of Ahaz king of
Israel, because he had revolted in Judah, and transgressed greatly against the
20 LORD. And Tilgath-pilneser king of Assyria came against him, and distressed
21 him, and strengthened him not. For Ahaz had plundered the house of the
LORD, and the house of the king and the princes, and given it to the king of
22 Assyria; and it was not a help to him. And in the time of his distress he
23 transgressed yet more against the LORD, this king Ahaz. And sacrificed to
the gods of Damascus that smote him, and said, Because the gods of the kings
of Syria, they help them, I will sacrifice to them, that they may help me: and
24 they were the downfall of him and of all Israel. And Ahaz gathered the
vessels of the house of God, and cut up the vessels of the house of God, and
shut the doors of the house of the LORD; and he made him altars in every
25 corner of Jerusalem. And in every single city of Judah he made high
places to burn incense to other gods, and provoked to anger the LORD God
of his fathers.
26 And the rest of his acts and all his ways, first and last, behold, they are
27 written in the book of the kings of Judah and Israel. And Ahaz slept with
his fathers, and they buried him in the city in Jerusalem: for they brought
him not into the sepulchres of the kings of Israel: and Hezekiah his son
reigned in his stead.

[1] The absent copula before בניה is supplied in the Sept., Vulg., and Luth., and rightly.

[2] The Sept. and Vulg. take הַכֹּהֵן rather as the accus. belonging to Zechariah (τὸν ἱερέα, *sacerdotem*).

[3] The Vulg. and Syr. do not translate מֵעָם; the Sept. (ἐν τῷ λαῷ) appears to have read בָּעָם.

[4] Hebr. דַּרְמֶשֶׂק, as always in Chronicles; comp. 1 Chron. xviii. 5.

[5] For בני יהוידע the Sept. and Vulg. probably read aright בן י׳. The plur. seems a slip of the pen.

[6] So according to the *Kethib* וְרֹב. On the *Keri* יִרֶב, "be multiplied" (the sentence upon him), see Exeg. Expl.

[7] Before יַכְשִׁילְךָ is וְלֹא to be supplied, with almost all recent expositors. See Exeg. Expl.

[8] For לְמֵאוֹת we should certainly read, with the *Keri* (and a considerable number of MSS.): לְמֵאַת.

[9] לְךָ, *Kethib;* the *Keri* is לְכָה. Comp. Exeg. Expl.

[10] שַׁעַר הַפּוֹנֶה, "gate of turning," is undoubtedly an error for שׁ׳ הַפִּנָּה, "corner gate"; comp. xxvi. 9, and especially the parallel 2 Kings xiv. 13.

[11] For בְּעִיר יְהוּדָה the old versions (Sept., Vulg., Syr.) have: "in the city of David."

[12] The *Keri* amends יְכִילְיָה, after 2 Kings xv. 2, into יְכָלְיָה, which is scarcely right.

[13] Instead of בִּרְאוֹת should rather be read, with the Sept. (ἐν φόβῳ κυρίου), Syr., Targ. Raschi, Kimchi, and some Hebrew MSS. of de Rossi: בְּיִרְאַת.

[14] Sept.: ἐπὶ τῆς πέτρας (perhaps thinking of Petra, the capital of Edom).

[15] Sept.: οἱ Μιναῖοι, by mistake (from the preceding τοὺς Μιναίους).

[16] So the *Kethib* (יְעוּאֵל); the *Keri* has יְעִיאֵל (as Ezra viii. 13).

[17] The Sept., Syr., and Arab. have twenty-five, a reading which Houbigant, Dathe, Ewald, Berth., and most moderns prefer. Comp. also J. A. Bengel, in the passage quoted, Introd. § 6, Rem. (p. 28).

[18] Properly "Darmascus"; comp. 1 Chron. xviii. 5, 6; 2 Chron. xvi. 2, xxiv. 23.

EXEGETICAL.

We take together the reports, contained in ch. xxiv.-xxviii., of the five reigns from Joash to Ahaz, partly on account of their general similarity, partly because in 2 Kings xii., xiv.-xvi., we have pretty full and nearly literal parallels to them.

1. Reign of Joash under the Guidance of Jehoiada: Repair of the Temple: ch. xxiv. 1-14.—The parallel account in 2 Kings xii. 1-17 is more detailed in the statement of several circumstances, especially with regard to the repair of the temple, but yet receives many important supplements from the present narrative, which is derived from the same sources, but constructed on different views and principles.—Ver. 2. *All the days of Jehoiada the priest.* Somewhat different in 2 Kings: "during all his days, while Jehoiada instructed him."—Ver. 3. *And Jehoiada chose for him two wives.* וַיִּשָּׂא־לוֹ here obviously expresses this sense, not as in xiii. 21: "took to himself"; for it refers to this, that the young king soon married and begat an heir to the throne.—Vers. 4-14. The Repair of the Temple; comp. Bähr's exposition of 2 Kings xii. 5-17.—*To renew the house of the Lord;* comp. xv. 8, and the synonym "to repair" (properly, "strengthen, make strong again") in ver. 5; 2 Kings xii. 6.—*And hasten ye the matter*, properly, "with respect to the matter." On the relation of the following statement, according to which the Levites hastened not, to the apparently different narrative in 2 Kings, comp. Bähr.—Ver. 6. *And the king called for Jehoiada the chief*, namely, of the priesthood, by which, however, is not necessarily meant the high priest; the phrase כֹּהֵן הָרֹאשׁ, "head-priest, supreme priest," may (as, for example, above xix. 11 of Amariah, or beneath xxvi. 20 of Azariah, under King Uzziah) denote the legal high priest, but has not necessarily this meaning; comp. on xxiii. 8.—*Why hast thou not required of the Levites to bring in*, literally, "asked of the Levites," etc. (comp. Job v. 8; Ps. cxlii. 3)? The "tax" or assessment of Moses (מַשְׂאַת, as ver. 9; comp. Ezek. xx. 40) is that of the sanctuary (heave-offering) imposed, Ex. xxx. 12-16, xxxviii. 25, by Moses, and willingly paid by the community of Israel, of half a shekel a head.—Ver. 7. *For Athaliah . . .* (and) *her sons.* By these "sons" of Athaliah are scarcely meant the priests of Baal (Jerome) or certain bastard sons of the queen (Ewald, *Gesch.* iii. 1, 290), but probably Ahaziah with his brothers and brothers' sons (comp. xxi. 17, xxii. 3 f.), that might have shown their zeal for idolatry at a very early age (comp. Berth., also Hitz. *Gesch.* p. 203).—*Broken up the house of God;* פָּרַץ, as 1 Chron. xiii. 11; Job xxx. 14; Eccles. x. 8.—*All the consecrated things of the house of the Lord;* all the gold and silver vessels, weapons, etc., preserved there as gifts. Of such profanation of the temple treasures by the idolatrous sons of Athaliah, moreover, the Chronist only reports, who here supplements the statements of 2 Kings.—Ver. 10. *Cast into the chest till it was full.* עַד לְכַלֵּה, as xxi. 1 (comp. also עַד כַּלֵּה, 2 Kings xiii. 17, 19); literally, "even to making full," whereby may be meant either the fulness of the number of givers, or even the fulness of the chest that received the gifts. The latter sense, which the Sept and Vulg. express, commends itself most, as ver. 11 shows, and should not therefore have been questioned by Berth., Kamph., etc.—Ver. 11. *And at the time*, etc., literally, "and it came to pass at the time when one brought the chest to the survey of the king," that is, for the royal surveillance or keeping (פְּקֻדָּה, as in xxiii. 18).—*And when they saw that there was much money*, properly, "and on their seeing," etc.—*Thus they did day by day*, literally, "to day by day" (comp. 1 Chron. xii. 22), that is, every day when it was necessary, every time that the chest was full.—Ver. 12. *And the king . . . gave it to the work-master of the service of the house of the Lord.* עֲבֹדַת בֵּית־יְהוָה here, not "service in the house of the Lord," as 1 Chron. xxiii. 24, but labour, repair of the house of the Lord.—*And they hired*, literally, "and they were hiring," continually from day to day; comp. Matt. xx. 1 ff. "Masons and carpenters"; so in 1 Chron. xxii. 14; comp. Ezra iii. 7.—Ver. 13. *And furtherance was given to the work by their hand*, literally, "there went up (was laid, Jer. viii. 22) binding on the work"; on אֲרוּכָה, "binding, healing," comp. Neh. iv. 1; Jer. xxx. 17.—*And they set the house of God in its form;* literally, "on its measure" (Ex. xxx. 32), that is, in the original proportions.—Ver. 14. *And they made of it vessels*, literally, "made it vessels" (into vessels); comp. Ezra i. 7.—*Vessels for ministering and offering*, altar vessels (comp. Num. iv. 12), from which cups (Ex. xxv. 29) and other gold and silver vessels are there distinguished.—*And they offered burnt-offerings . . . all the days of Jehoiada:* as long as he had the direction of the temple worship, it was conducted in a regular and legal way; that it had quite ceased after Jehoiada's death, neither the present phrase nor the subsequent narrative affirms.

2. Death of Jehoiada: Stoning of his Son: the Prophet Zechariah: vers. 15-22. There is no parallel to this section in 2 Kings xii.; but it is of no less importance for the pragmatic understanding of that which is related underneath, ver. 23 ff., concerning the last events in the life of Joash.—*And Jehoiada was old and full of days.* שְׂבַע יָמִים, as otherwise only of the patriarchs Abraham and Isaac, of David (1 Chron. xxiv. 1; comp. xxix. 28), and of Job (xlii. 17), so in general is it used only of five men of God in the Old Testament; comp. Achelis, *Das Zeitalter der Patriarchen*, a contribution to the understanding

of Scripture (Barm. 1871), p. 46. From the following statement of his age as 130 years at his death, it follows that he must have been about 100 years old when he helped his nephew by a successful revolution to the throne (877 B.C. by the common chronology); for the repair of the temple carried on by Joash and him (which he survived for a time, according to ver. 14 of our chapter), fell, according to 2 Kings xii. 7, in the twenty-third year of that king.—Ver. 16. *And they buried him . . . with the kings.* With this honourable distinction bestowed upon him at his death, the directly following record of the slaughter of his like-minded son stands in the same contrast as that presented by Christ, Matt. xxiii. 29 ff., over against the Pharisees.—Ver. 17. *Bowed down before the king*, earnestly entreating; for what? The following words show that it was for permission to worship strange gods along with the Lord. That Joash himself forthwith took part in this worship of idols is not affirmed, but that he bore the full responsibility of it, and afterwards took a direct part in the impiety, is plain from ver. 21 f.; comp. ver. 25.—Ver. 18. *Served the Asherim*, etc.; comp. on ch. xiv. 2. For the flame of wrath (קֶצֶף) which this enkindled, comp. xix. 2, 10, xxix. 8.—Ver. 19. *Testified against them*, by way of warning, pointing to the inevitable consequences of their apostasy; comp. 2 Kings xvii. 13; Ps. l. 7; Neh. ix. 26, 29. Was Joel also among these prophetic monitors? As we may conjecture from his book that his age nearly coincided with the reign of Joash, it is not improbable; comp. Wünsche, *Die Weissagung des Proph. Joel*, Introd. p. 13 ff.; also Keil, *Introd. to the O. T.* p. 322 f.—Ver. 20. *And the Spirit of God clothed Zechariah son of Jehoiada the priest.* On לָבַשׁ, "clothe," comp. 1 Chron. xii. 18. The identity with the Zechariah mentioned by Christ, Matt. xxiii. 35, Luke xi. 51, as slain between the temple and the altar, who is called in the former passage "the son of Barachias," is to be assumed the more certainly, as—1. The place of his death quite agrees there and here (the θυσιαστήριον is the altar of burnt-offering, which stood in the court; comp. ver. 21); 2. An allusion is made in the speech of Christ to our passage before mentioning the martyrdom of Zechariah; see above on ver. 16; and 3. The Barachias named in Matt. xxiii. 35 as the father of Zechariah may have been the son of Jehoiada, and Zechariah his grandson, which is highly probable, from the great age to which Jehoiada attained.—*Stood up before the people*, properly, "above the people" (מֵעַל לְ, as in xiii. 4); the inner court, from which he spoke, and where he was afterwards slain, was higher than the outer, where the people stood.—*And do not prosper*, or: and will be unfortunate, will have no success. The two things are, in a theocratico-prophetical point of view, inseparably connected: the forsaking of the Lord (comp. xii. 5, xv. 2, etc.), and becoming unfortunate; comp. xxvi. 5 (Uzziah).—Ver. 21. *And they conspired against him;* comp. ver. 25; 1 Kings xv. 27, and also ch. xxiii. 13. The true witness of God is slain by stoning, the very penalty which is in the law (Lev. xx. 2, xxiv. 23) imposed on idolaters, to which therefore his murderers were doomed.—Ver. 22. *And Joash . . . remembered not the kindness;* חֶסֶד, as in Mic. vi. 8. Joash appears here designated as the murderer of the son (or grandson) of Jehoiada, certainly not for mere silent connivance at the wicked deed, but for positive and direct participation in it; comp. ver. 21.—*The Lord shall see and require*, or "will see (comp. Ps. lxxxiv. 10) and require" (דרשׁ, here "seek revenge, punish;" comp. Ps. ix. 13; 1 Sam. xx. 16).

3. Distress of Joash by the Syrians, and his End: vers. 23–27. Here again 2 Kings xii. 18–22 affords a parallel, where that which relates to the invasion of the Syrians is narrated more particularly, and their king, Hazael (Haza-ilu of the Assyrian inscriptions), is named as executor of this judgment on Joash.—*And it came to pass in the course of a year*, "in the circuit of a year," the year beginning with the death of the prophet Zechariah.—*That the host of Syria*, as in ver. 24.—*And destroyed all the princes of the people out of the people*, out of the mass of the people (comp. Ps. lxxxix. 20), so that these were spared, but their chiefs, who were the authors of the religious and moral evil (ver. 17 f.), were overtaken by the doom of extermination. On the variants in the old versions with respect to "out of the people," see Crit. Note.—*With few men*, literally, "with smallness of men"; comp. Job viii. 7.—*And they executed judgments upon Joash.* עָשָׂה שְׁפָטִים, as in Ex. xii. 12; Num. xxxiii. 4; Ezek. v. 10, 15; elsewhere with בְּ, here with אֵת (comp. עָשָׂה טוֹב אֵת, 1 Sam. xxiv. 19). The judgment upon Joash refers especially to the mortal wound which he received.—Ver. 25. *For they left him with many wounds.* מַחֲלֻיִים, less suitably translated "diseases" by Luther, occurs only here; but comp. the similar תַּחֲלֻאִים, xxi. 19. With respect to the somewhat surprising "sons of Jehoiada" (instead of son), see Crit. Note.—*And slew him on his bed;* narrated more particularly 2 Kings xii. 21. The burial was not in the tombs of the kings, but in another place, as in the case of Joram; see xxi. 20.—Ver. 26. On the names of the conspirators, of which one is different in 2 Kings xii. (Jozachar for Zabad), see Bähr on this passage.—Ver. 27. *And his sons, and the greatness of the burden upon him*, the greatness of the treasure which he had to send as tribute to Hazael in Syria; comp. 2 Kings xii. 19. So it is perhaps to be explained (with Then. and Kamph.) on the basis of the *Kethib* וְרֹב הַמַּשָּׂא עָלָיו. Possible also is the interpretation adopted by Cleric., Keil, and others: "and the multitude of prophetic oracles concerning him" (comp. ver. 19), though in this case the singular הַמַּשָּׂא is somewhat strange. On the contrary, the reference, attempted by the Vulg., Luther, and others, of the רב המשׂא to the temple tribute (vers. 6, 9) imposed by Joash would require a change into מַשְּׂאַת, and the עָלָיו would not suit this view (for which we should rather expect עַל יִשְׂרָאֵל). The *Keri* יִרֶב gives rise to the sense: "and with

regard to his sons the oracle (that of the dying Zechariah, ver. 22*b*) multiplied itself in them," which is obviously much too obscure, and could scarcely be intended by the Masoretes themselves. The Sept. alters the text quite arbitrarily, καὶ προσῆλθον αὐτῷ οἱ πέντε (חֲמִשָּׁה for הַמַּשָּׂא), and so the Syriac.—*Behold, they are written in the commentary of the book of Kings,* the elaboration of this book; comp. on xiii. 12, and Introd. § 5, ii.

4. Amaziah: *a.* Duration of his Reign, and its Spirit: ch. xxv. 1-4; comp. the essentially parallel verses, 2 Kings xiv. 1-6.—Ver. 2. *And he did . . . but not with undivided heart.* For this is in 2 Kings: "yet not like David his father, he did according to all that his father Joash did." This more particular statement our author avoided, perhaps, on account of the less favourable light in which he had exhibited Joash. The following also: "only the high places were not removed," etc., he omits; perhaps he intended sufficiently to indicate this partial continuance of idolatry by his "not with undivided heart" (comp. xvi. 9).—Ver. 4. *Put not their sons to death,* according to the law, Deut. xxiv. 16; comp. Bähr on 2 Kings xiv. 6.

5. Continuation: *b.* The Conquest of the Edomites in the Valley of Salt: vers. 5-13. Again a section peculiar to the Chronist, for which nothing is found in 2 Kings xiv. 7 but the brief notice that Amaziah smote the Edomites in the valley of Salt, took their city Sela, and gave it the name Joktheel.—*And he mustered them* (comp. Num. i. 3) *and found them* 300,000 *choice men;* thus almost a million less than the force of Judah and Benjamin under Jehoshaphat, ch. xvii., and, if the numbers there are to be considered incorrect, even much less than the sum total of the troops of the south kingdom given in xiv. 7 for the time of Asa. But it is obvious that the number of troops must be shown to be much diminished by defeats sustained during the last reigns and other calamities, and therefore in need of being strengthened by foreign mercenary soldiers, as the following verse clearly proves.—*Going out to war* (comp. 1 Chron. v. 18), *holding spear and shield;* comp. 1 Chron. xiii. 9; Jer. xlvi. 9.—Ver. 7. *With all the sons of Ephraim.* This is a more definite addition to "Israel" (comp. Isa. xvii. 3, xxviii. 1) that appears not unnecessary, because the author often designates the kingdom or people of Judah also as Israel (comp. on xii. 1).—Ver. 8. *But go thou* alone, *do,* or "execute it"; comp. 1 Chron. xxii. 16; Ezra x. 4.—*Be strong for the battle,* (otherwise) *God shall make thee fall before the enemy.* The sense is obvious; "be strong, then will God not let thee fall." Before יַכְשִׁילְךָ is to be supplied וְלֹא, with Ew., Berth., Keil, Kamph., etc.; for the כִּי אִם can neither be taken (with Cleric.) = *sin minus,* nor (with Seb. Schmidt, Ramb., etc.) = *alioquin.* That the text certainly needs emendation is manifest from the arbitrary and diverse interpretations presented by the old translators; for example, the Sept. ὅτι ἐὰν ὑπολάβῃς κατισχῦσαι ἐν τούτοις; Vulg. *quod si vultis in robore exercitus bella consistere;* Luther, "For so thou comest as to show a boldness in fight, God will let thee fall before thy enemies."—*For with God is power to help and to cast down,* literally "present is might in God," etc. For the sentence, comp. 1 Chron. xxix. 12; 2 Chron. xx. 6; also the well-known verse of G. Neumark, "He is the only wonder-man, who now lift up, now cast down can."—Ver. 9. *What shall we do for the* 100 *talents?* In the mouth of a prudent ruler, who counts the cost in all his steps, certainly a very pardonable question, even as the answer given to it is highly worthy of a trustful man of God. גְּדוּד, "troop," that is, a body of mercenaries; comp. xxii. 1; 2 Kings xiii. 20 f.—Ver. 10. *To wit, the host,* etc. לְ before הַגְּדוּד is the defining לְ = namely (comp. ver. 5*a*); the whole is in apposition to the suffix in וַיַּבְדִּילֵם.—*And they returned to their place in hot anger,* literally, "in the glow of anger" (comp. Ex. xi. 8), enraged at the bad usage they had received, and at the prospect of booty being first held out to them and then withdrawn (comp. Acts xvi. 19).—Ver. 11. *And Amaziah took courage.* הִתְחַזֵּק, as in xv. 8; comp. also the חֲזַק of the prophet in ver. 8. On the situation of the valley of Salt (south-east of the Dead Sea), see Bähr on 2 Kings xiv. 7.—Ver. 12. *And brought them to the top of the rock* (לְרֹאשׁ הַסֶּלַע), probably the rock on or at which the Edomite capital Sela lay, so that the rendering "on the top of Sela" (Kamph., etc.) is admissible. The passage in 2 Kings xiv. 7, where the taking of Sela after the victory in the valley of Salt is recorded, and the present one thus complete one another. That the present report of the Chronist is merely derived from a misunderstanding of the text of the old source, somehow become illegible (Then. on 2 Kings xiv. 7), appears an inadmissible assumption on this account, that our writer would not have imputed so frightful and barbarous a proceeding as the throwing of thousands of captive Edomites down a precipice (comp. for the matter of fact, Ps. cxxxvii. 9; Luke iv. 29), on light grounds or on a mere misunderstanding, to a king like Amaziah (comp. on 1 Chron. xviii. 2, xx. 3). Besides, the number 10,000 here, as in the previous verse, is a round number, and not to be pressed in its literal sense.—Ver. 13. *And the men of the host* (literally, "sons of the host," that is, the troops belonging to it) *fell upon the cities of Judah;* comp. for construction, Gen. xxii. 24. This pillaging raid of the mercenaries is to be regarded as simultaneous with the absence of Amaziah in Idumea, and favoured thereby; comp. the similar events in the thirty years' and the seven years' wars; also the invasion of Switzerland by the Armagnacs, and of Elsass under the Emperor Frederic III. (1444), etc.—*From Samaria even to Beth-horon,* that is, with Samaria as starting-point, and Beth-horon (see for its site on 1 Chron. vii. 24) as the termination of their raid, so that all the towns between these two, so far as they belonged to Judah, were exposed to pillage.

6. Close: *c.* Amaziah's Idolatry, War with Joash of Israel, and End: vers. 14-28. The second book of Kings presents no parallel to the statements regarding the desertion of Amaziah to the gods of the conquered Edomites, vers. 14-16. On the contrary, the report of the war with Joash of Israel (vers. 17-24) agrees almost literally with 2 Kings xiv. 8-14, as also the following vers.

25–28 with the closing remarks there, vers. 17–20 —*After Amaziah was come from smiting the Edomites;* comp. 2 Sam. i. 1. The "gods" of the children of Seir are naturally their idols (otherwise פְּסִילִים or שִׁקֻּצִים); and the conquered Edomites are here called children of Seir, not because they were identical with the tribe of Seirites or Meunites (xx. 1, 10, 22) who dwelt with them, but because here, where the peculiarity of their gods as hill-gods came into view (comp. 1 Kings xx. 23), it was very natural to designate them according to the hill-country in which they dwelt.—Ver. 16. *Have we made thee counsellor to the king?* properly, "given"; the plural נְתַנּוּךָ is of communicative import, spoken from the position of the king and his council. With the question: "Why should they smite thee?" comp. the similar one: "Why will ye die, O house of Israel?" (Ezek. xxxiii. 11.)—*I know* (have now observed) *that God hath resolved to destroy thee;* comp. 1 Sam. ii. 25 (Eli); and Ex. vi. 1, x. 1, xi. 1, etc. (Pharaoh).—*Because thou hast done this* (worshipped the gods of Edom), *and hast not hearkened to my counsel.* Thus the prophet declares himself authorized to give counsel to the king, however scornfully the latter may have deprecated this as an assumption on his part.—Ver. 17 ff.; comp. Bähr on 2 Kings xiv. 8 ff.—*Took counsel,* namely, with his counsellors and courtiers; comp. x. 6; 1 Chron. xiii. 1. Luther's rendering is also possible: resolved, came to the decision after counsel taken.—*Come* (לְכָה=לֵךְ, "come on"; comp. Num. xxiii. 13; Judg. xix. 13), *let us look one another in the face,* measure, have a passage at arms with one another.—Ver. 19. *Thou sayest, Lo, thou hast smitten Edom,* or if thou hast smitten. It is, moreover, of the same import if we render (with Luther, Kamph., etc.) "I have smitten."—*And thy heart hath lifted thee up* (or "carried, urged thee;" comp. Ex. xxxv. 21, 26) *to boast,* properly, "to make heavy"; comp. Isa. viii. 23. It is considerably different in 2 Kings xiv. 10; see Bähr on the passage.—Ver. 20. *For it was of God that they should be given up,* literally, "that they might be given into the hand (of the enemy)"; comp. Deut. i. 27; 1 Kings xx. 42, etc.—Ver. 22. *And they fled every man to his tent,* to his house; comp. x. 16; 1 Kings viii. 66.—Ver. 23. *From the gate of Ephraim to the corner gate;* so according to the emendation שַׁעַר הַפִּנָּה for ש' הַפּוֹנֶה, which latter reading gives no rational sense, as the direction in which the gate in question turns itself must have been stated if ש' הַפּוֹנֶה meant the gate turning itself (comp. Ezek. viii. 3).—Ver. 24. *And all the gold,* namely, "he took," a verb (לָקַח) which is to be supplied from 2 Kings xiv. 14.—Vers. 25–28. Comp. Bähr on the parallel 2 Kings xiv. 17–20; and with regard to "the book of the kings of Judah and Israel" (ver. 26), Introd. § 5, ii.—Ver. 28. *In the city of Judah* appears to be an error in copying for "in the city of David," occasioned by the following כָּל־עַם יְהוּדָה (xxvi. 1); comp. Crit. Note. If the Masoretic reading is to be retained, we might be tempted to think of the designation πόλις Ἰούδα, occurring Luke i. 39, which, however, can scarcely be supposed to refer to Jerusalem (see Van Oosterzee on this passage).

7. Uzziah: *a.* His early Theocratic Inclination and Prosperous Reign: ch. xxvi. 1–15; comp. the very brief parallel, 2 Kings xiv. 21, 22, xv. 1, 2, where the present (vers. 6–15) report of the successful wars of Uzziah, his buildings, and his strong military force, is wanting. There, moreover, this king, along with the present name (עֻזִּיָּהוּ, "might of Jehovah"), bears also the name Azariah (עֲזַרְיָה or עֲזַרְיָהוּ, "whom Jehovah helps"). Comp. 2 Kings xiv. 21, xv. 1, 6, 8, 23, 27, where the latter form is used, with 2 Kings xv. 13, 30, 32, 34, where "Uzziah" stands, the form which the Chronist, irrespective of 1 Chron. iii. 12, always uses, and which is also found in the superscriptions of the prophets Hosea, Amos, and Isaiah, as in Isa. vi. 1, vii. 1. The Assyrian cuneate inscriptions (the tablets of Tiglath-pileser; see Schrader, p. 114) present exclusively the form Azariah (Az-ri-ya-hu), whereby the opinion of those who regard this form as the later, or as the result of a mere error of writing, is refuted (so, for example, Gesen.-Dietrich in *Lexicon*). But Hitzig's hypothesis also (*Gesch.* p. 209), that the name Azariah was transformed from that of the high priest contemporary with him (ver. 17) to the king, is refuted by this evidence of Assyrian inscriptions. Much rather the only assumption that remains warranted is: "that the similar names of almost equal import were used simultaneously" (Berth.); as was the case, for example, with Uzziel and Azarel, a descendant of Heman (1 Chron. xxv. 4, 18). Not even the conjecture expressed by Bähr on 2 Kings xiv. 21: "that the name Uzziah appears to have come into more general use after he ascended the throne," will harmonize with the fact that the Assyrian kings know only the name Azariah.—Ver. 2. *He built Eloth.* On the emphatic prefixing of this notice, even before the chronological dates of the following verse, see Bähr on the passage.—Ver. 3. *Reigned fifty-two years in Jerusalem,* 810–759 B.C., according to the usual chronology, though, according to the Assyrian monuments, considerably later (according to Neteler, p. 225 ff., 786–735). On the name of the queen-mother Jechiliah (in 2 Kings Jecholiah, not Jechaliah, as Luther writes), see the Crit. Note.—Ver. 5. *And he continued to seek God,* literally, "and he was to seek God, was out to seek Him"; comp. xxxi. 21; Ezra iii. 12.—*In the days of Zechariah, who understood the visions of God.* Accordingly this Zechariah, who is otherwise unknown (for he cannot be identified with the Zechariah son of Jeberechiah mentioned Isa. viii. 2, as he was at least a generation older), must be considered a prophet, and הַמֵּבִין בִּרְאוֹת הָאֱלֹהִים must be regarded as a chosen periphrasis for הָרֹאֶה, the seer (comp. Dan. i. 17). But as the vision of God cannot be taken as a work of human activity, the reading of the Sept. and other old witnesses (see Crit. Note) commends itself more, which gives the sense "expert in the fear of God," or even "teacher of the fear of God" (comp. Neh. viii. 9). Zechariah remains a prophetic teacher and counsellor of King Uzziah even with this

reading (for his possible priestly character would have been marked by a הַכֹּהֵן); but that he was a "master in divine visions" is not to be read from it; and still less is it to be inferred that he and no other was the author of the oracles of Balaam (as is asserted in an arbitrary way by Fürst, *Gesch. der bibl. Literatur.* ii. pp. 231, 359).—Vers. 6–15. Uzziah's Successful Wars, Building of Cities, etc. (without parallel in 2 Kings).—*And he . . .* fought with the Philistines, to punish their pillaging inroad under Joram (xxi. 16 f.). This punishment must have been inflicted by him in very full measure, probably by the subjection of their whole territory; for the cities said to have been destroyed by him, Gath (see on xi. 8), Jabneh (=Jabneel, Josh. xv. 11, later=Jamnia in the Maccab. and in Josephus), and Ashdod (now Esdud, comp. on Josh. xiii. 3), were at that time the chief places of the Philistines.—Ver. 7. *And God helped him . . . against the Arabs,* who are named also, xvii. 11, with the Philistines. Where Gurbaal was is uncertain; it is by no means to be identified (after the Sept., see Crit. Note) with the Edomite Petra; rather with Gerar (Gen. xx. 1), of which the Targ. thinks. Concerning the Meunites, see on 1 Chron. iv. 41; 2 Chron. xx. 1.—Ver. 8. *And his name went even to Egypt,* literally, "even to the entrance of Egypt." But by the name of Uzziah is scarcely meant merely his fame (Luther), but also his active influence, his power.—*For he became very mighty,* literally, "showed himself mighty (Dan. xi. 7) unto the height" (comp. 1 Chron. xiv. 2, xxix. 25).—Ver. 9. *And Uzziah built towers . . . at the corner gate.* The corner gate (comp. xxv. 23) lay at the north-west end of the city; the valley gate on the west side, where the Jaffa gate is now. On the east, over against these two points belonging to the west side where defence was most needed, is הַמִּקְצוֹעַ, the corner, to be sought—namely, a bend of the eastern wall near the horse gate; comp. Neh. iii. 19, 20, 24, 25. —Ver. 10. *And he built towers in the wilderness,* in the wilderness of Judah, to protect the herds grazing there; comp. 1 Chron. xxvii. 25; Mic. iv. 8; Isa. v. 2; in which latter place mention is made of the digging of a well along with the tower building.—*For he had much cattle in the lowland,* etc., properly, "and in the lowland and in the plain," etc. It appears, therefore, as if three regions were here distinguished—1. The wilderness (of Judah) west of the Dead Sea; 2. The lowlands at the Mediterranean (comp. 1 Chron. xxvii. 28); 3. The plain (הַמִּישׁוֹר), perhaps the plain beyond the Jordan, the territory of the Reubenites, a region specially adapted for grazing, which Uzziah was under the necessity of taking from the Ammonites (ver. 8).—*Husbandmen and vinedressers in the mountains.* Kamph. connects against the accents, "in the plain, husbandmen." He will also explain וּבַכַּרְמֶל neither of the Mount Carmel (Josh. xix. 26; Song vii. 6), nor of Carmel in the south of Judah (1 Sam. xv. 12), but renders "in the fruitful field" (comp. Isa. xxix. 17), for which there is no constraining necessity.—Ver. 11. *And Uzziah had a host of fighting men,* literally, "a host (comp. xiv. 7) maker of war" (comp. ver. 13, xi. 1), that went out to war (comp. 1 Chron. v. 8) in troops (in a marshalled host).—*By the number of their muster at the hand of Jeuel.* בְּיַד, as afterwards, "under the guidance of Hananiah," is expressed by "at the hand" (עַל יַד, as 1 Chron. xxv. 6). The captain Hananiah appears therefore as superintendent, Jeuel and Maaseiah as subordinate executive officers in the business of the muster.—Ver. 13. *And at their hand* (עַל יָדָם, as in the previous verse) *an army of* 307,500 *fighting men.* Thus each of the 2600 father-houses constituted a corps under the command of the bravest among them. The total number of 307,500 warriors agrees in the main with the above statement of the strength of the army under Amaziah, xxv. 5, and presupposes the more certainly an actual numeration for its basis, as it is not a round number.—Ver. 14. *And Uzziah prepared for them;* comp. 1 Chron. xv. 1, xxii. 5. —Ver. 15. *He made engines, the invention of craftsmen,* literally, "devices (חִשְּׁבֹנוֹת, *excogitata*), the device of the deviser" (מַחֲשֶׁבֶת חוֹשֵׁב), skilfully contrived engines of war, as the following words show—a kind of catapults or balisters, for assaulting besieging troops from the walls and towers of defence.—*And his name went forth,* etc.; comp. above, ver. 8.

8. Uzziah: *b.* His Boasting and Divine Punishment by Leprosy; his End: vers. 16–23. Comp. 2 Kings xv. 5–7, where, however, the mere fact of the king's becoming leprous is mentioned, without particularizing the cause, so that in fact the three verses correspond only to our vers. 21–23.—*And when he became strong.* וכחזקתו, as in xii. 1. For the following: "to do corruptly" (השחית), comp. xxvii. 2.—*Went into the temple of the Lord to burn incense,* which, according to Ex. xxx. 7, 27, Num. xviii. 1–7, only priests were to do. Uzziah wished to exercise regal and sacerdotal functions at the same time (as the Egyptian kings, and afterwards the Roman emperors). He fell into the same sin as Saul before him (1 Sam. xiii. 9 f.). It was not the restitution of a formerly legitimate union of regal and sacerdotal power, as it was nominally possessed by David and Solomon (Thenius, Ewald), which was his aim; for only occasionally, and in certain religious solemnities of an extraordinary kind, had those kings exercised several priestly functions, with the permission of the lawful priests (so correctly Bertheau, Keil, etc.).—Ver. 17. *And Azariah the priest.* Whether he was actually high priest is not determined with perfect certainty from his subsequent designation as כֹּהֵן הָרֹאשׁ (as in the case of Jehoiada; see on xxiii. 8); yet it is most probable that the "head priest," who was accompanied with eighty priests, was the actual legitimate holder of high-priestly office. But very improbable is the identity asserted by Keil of this Azariah with the Azariah named in the list of high priests, 1 Chron. v. 36, 37, as the father of Amariah, who belongs certainly to a considerably earlier time (see on this passage). On the predicate "men of valour," בְּנֵי חַיִל, comp. 1 Chron. v. 18.—Ver. 18. *And they withstood Uzziah,* "stood against" him; comp. Dan. xi. 14.—*And it shall not be for thine honour from the Lord God,* that is, thy offering incense serves not, as thou fanciest, to increase

thy honour and glory before God, but rather brings thee shame, because thou thereby showest thyself to be disobedient and apostate.—Ver. 19. *And while he was wroth with the priests, the leprosy burst forth on his forehead*, in punishment of his impious attempt. The punishment is the same that Miriam endured on account of her rebellion against Moses (Num. xii. 10), and with which Elisha's servant Gehazi was visited for his covetousness (2 Kings v. 27). In a physical and pathological sense, also, the malady may have been brought on in all these cases in essentially the same way,—"by a strong physical excitement, which brought the leprosy, already existing as a tendency in the system, suddenly to a visible eruption" (Friedreich, *Zur Bibel*, etc., pp. 223, 230). Wedel (*Exercitationes medico-philologicæ*, ii. 4. 9) quite arbitrarily asserts that Uzziah's malady was not leprosy, but syphilis. Not less arbitrary and contrary to the text is the attempt of K. Ad. Menzel to reduce the whole malady to a bold and sly mystification of the high priest Azariah, who suddenly cried out that he saw the sign of leprosy on the forehead of the king, and by this application of his medical authority so far robbed him of his self-command that he allowed himself to be arrested and put in a place of confinement (*Religion und Staatsidee*, p. 89; comp. on xvi. 13). A special contrast to this crude attempt at a natural explanation by a miracle-rejecting rationalism is presented by the Jewish legend in Josephus, *Antiq.* ix. 10. 4, which makes Uzziah be punished not merely by becoming leprous (supposed to be produced by a sunstroke which fell through the split roof of the temple on his face), but also by a simultaneous violent earthquake, the same which is mentioned Amos i. 1, by which that splitting of the temple roof was effected.—Ver. 21. *And dwelt in a sick-house*, properly, "a house of separation"; see Bähr on 2 Kings xv. 5, where also all that is necessary is remarked on the probable (amounting only to a few years) duration of Uzziah's illness and of Jotham's regency.—Ver. 23. *And they buried him with his fathers in the burial-field of the kings; for they said, He is a leper.* They wished not to defile the proper tombs of the kings by burying his body in them, and therefore buried it in the field adjoining these tombs. In the parallel 2 Kings xv. 7 f. this important detail is wanting.

9. Jotham: ch. xxvii.; comp. 2 Kings xv. 32–38, and Bähr on this passage.—Ver. 2. *Only he entered not into the temple of the Lord;* he abstained from such an impious undertaking as that of his father, xxvi. 16 ff. This remark is wanting in 2 Kings. On the contrary, instead of the rather indefinite: "and the people did yet corruptly" (comp. on xxvi. 16 ff.), we find there the more special statement: "the people still sacrificed and burnt incense on the high places." —Ver. 3. *And on the wall of Ophel he built much;* fortified thus the southern slope of the temple mountain, which is called Ophel (הָעֹפֶל; comp. xxxiii. 14; Neh. iii. 26, 27), and therein continued the fortifications of his father Uzziah, which had applied more to the west and east sides of the city wall. In 2 Kings this is wanting, as also the notice in the following verse of the towns and castles built by Jotham (for בִּירָנִיּוֹת, "castles, forts," see on xvii. 12), while the previous notice regarding the building (anew) of the upper temple gate, the north gate in the inner court of the temple, is also found there.—Ver. 5 *And he fought with the king of the sons of Ammon.* Of this victorious war with the Ammonites, also, nothing is found in 2 Kings. This war, like the buildings, appears to be a continuation of that waged by Uzziah; for, according to xxvi. 8, the Ammonites had also to pay tribute to that king. It was therefore an attempt at revolt, for which they were now punished by Jotham with the imposition of a new and heavier tribute (100 talents of silver, with 10,000 cors of barley and wheat yearly, is pretty well for a not very numerous people).—*This the sons of Ammon paid him also in the second and the third year*, but no longer than during these three years; perhaps on account of the war of Syria and Ephraim with Judah, which took its rise under Jotham, 2 Kings xv. 37, and procured for the Ammonites their former independence.—Ver. 6. *And Jotham strengthened himself*, namely, "in his kingdom"; comp. xiii. 21, and the following: "he established his ways," Prov. xxi. 29.—Ver. 7. *And all his wars.* That these wars of Jotham, of which only one is here mentioned, were uniformly successful is not stated in the text; and therefore the war commenced with Syria and Ephraim, in which Jotham suffered some very severe defeats, may be here included (against Keil). In other respects the closing notices, vers. 7–9, agree essentially with 2 Kings xv. 36, 38.

10. Ahaz: *a.* His Idolatry, and Defeat by the Syrians and Ephraimites: ch. xxviii. 1–8; comp. 2 Kings xvi. 1 ff., where the first four verses, relating to the idolatry of Ahaz, agree tolerably well with vers. 1–4 of our text; while the report of the war given in vers. 5–18 presents considerable deviations from the narrative in our ch., vers. 5 ff., 9, and 16 ff. Comp. on these differences, as well as on the whole report of the war, C. P. Caspari, *Der syrisch-ephraimitische Krieg unter Jotham und Ahas*, Christiania 1849.—*Ahaz was twenty years old.* Thus also 2 Kings xvi. 2; but on account of the age of his son and successor,—Hezekiah being already twenty-five at the death of Ahaz,—it is more probable that the reading of the Sept., Syr., and Arab. is to be preferred, and the age of Ahaz at his accession set down at twenty-five (not, however, at thirty, as Hitzig, *Gesch. Isr.* p. 214, will have it). Moreover, the name Ahaz (אָחָז) is on the Assyrian monuments *Ja-hu-kha-zi*, which is elsewhere = the Hebr. Jehoahaz (יְהוֹאָחָז); see Schrader, pp. 25, 147, 151 ff. This difference "is either to be referred to this, that the later Jews in the Old Testament changed the actual name of the king, namely Jehoahaz, in consequence of his idolatrous propensity, into Ahaz, by the omission of the divine name; or to this, that the Assyrians falsely transferred to Ahaz the like-sounding name of an earlier king (Jehoahaz), as they made Jehu a son instead of a successor of Omri" (Schrader, p. 152). If the first of these two conjectures, according to which Ahaz is a curtailed name, be correct, we may compare the change of such names as Jerubbaal (into Jerubbesheth) or Mephibaal (into Mephibosheth), and also the legend of the mediæval sects, as the Euchites, Bogomiles, etc., that Satan was originally called Satanael, and after

his fall his name was deprived of the last syllable. Comp., moreover, on ver. 21.—Ver. 2 f. *And made also molten images for Baalim;* comp. Ps. cvi. 19; Judg. xvii. 3, etc. Both these words and the following: "and he burnt incense in the valley of Ben-hinnom," are wanting in 2 Kings; but they have there fallen out by an oversight (occasioned by a twofold וְגַם); comp. Bähr on the passage.—*And burned his sons in the fire,* or "made his sons pass through the fire." According to 2 Kings, he performed this barbarous human sacrifice only in the case of one son, which is intrinsically the more probable (comp. 2 Kings iii. 27, xxi. 6); the plur. אֶת־בָּנָיו of our passage is thus, as in xxxiii. 6, merely a rhetorical generalization (Casp., Keil, Bähr, etc.). On vers. 3*b* and 4, comp. Bähr's exposition of the parallel text.—Ver. 5. *The Lord his God gave him into the hand of the king of Syria.* These introductory words of the following report of the war, compared with 2 Kings xvi. 6 ff., demonstrate that our writer proposes to give rather a rhetorically conceived than a strictly historical description of the chastisements inflicted on Ahaz by the Syrians and Ephraimites. Comp. Caspari as quoted, p. 42 ff., and Keil, p. 325 f.: "The facts, which show how Ahaz, notwithstanding the grievous blows which fell on him and Judah, sinned yet more grievously against the Lord his God, are brought out of the historical material into relief, and oratorically represented, so that they display not only the increasing obstinacy of Ahaz, but also, by adducing the conduct of the citizens and warriors of the kingdom of Israel, the depth to which Judah had fallen."—*And they smote him,* literally, "on him," that is, they inflicted a defeat on his army.—*And took from him a great many captives,* "led captive from him a great leading of captives" (שִׁבְיָה, as in ver. 11; Neh. iii. 36).—Ver. 6. *And Pekah, son of Remaliah, slew in Judah* 120,000 *in one day,* that is, in a great battle, with the pursuit and plundering that followed. Against the suspicion cast on this number by de Wette, Gesenius, Winer, and others, as exaggerated, see Caspari, p. 37 ff., who points with justice—1. to the fanaticism of the Israelites and Syrians, who aimed directly at the annihilation of the Jewish power (Isa. vii. 6; 2 Kings xv. 16; comp. also ver. 9); 2. to the military strength of the Jews (307,500), stated shortly before under Uzziah, xxvi. 13, which shows that it was about a third of their force that was put to the sword; 3. to the round number 120,000 (as also the subsequent number of 200,000 captives), showing itself to be the product of a rough estimate, and not an exact enumeration.—Ver. 7. *And Zichri . . . slew Maaseiah the king's son,* probably a royal prince of an older generation, uncle, cousin, or brother of Ahaz, for he himself at this time had scarcely a son of military age. Azrikam also is perhaps to be regarded as a relative of the king, for a "governor of the house" can scarcely designate a president of the temple (according to 1 Chron. ix. 11; 2 Chron. xxxi. 13); rather might it be the title of a higher officer of the royal house or palace.—*And Elkanah the vicegerent of the king,* literally, "the second after the king," his minister (chancellor, vizier).—Ver. 8. *And the sons of Israel took captive of their brethren.* Observe the importance of this reference to the character of the war, as a barbarous strife between brother tribes.

11. Continuation: *b.* Oded the Prophet effects the Release of the Captives: vers. 9-15 (without a parallel in 2 Kings).—*And a prophet of the Lord was there of the name of Oded,* in Samaria, the capital of the northern kingdom. Here, as well as in other places of this kingdom, prophets of the true God appear active till its complete fall (722 B.C.), as in particular the ministry of Hosea teaches, which was likewise exercised on this soil.—*And he went out;* comp. the report, xv. 2, of Azariah son of Oded under Asa.—*In the wrath . . . against Judah.* Not so much your bravery as the judicial sentence of God for the punishment of idolatrous Israel is the cause of the great victory over your adversaries—a victory which you have abused by a frantic slaughter and carnage. On "that reacheth unto heaven," comp. Gen. xviii. 21; Ezra ix. 6.—Ver. 10. *And now ye purpose to subject;* comp. Gen. i. 28; Lev. xxv. 42 ff.—*Are there not even with you yourselves trespasses against the Lord?* look for once at yourselves, whether ye do not perceive there enough of that which inculpates you before God. To this exhortation to repentance is suitably added the warning in ver. 11, to beware of the further abuse of the power given them to execute the divine judgment, and therefore of the unmerciful treatment or even the longer retention of the captives.—Ver. 12 f. Four of the chiefs of Ephraim declare their concurrence with this exhortation and warning of Oded. Their names occur only here, but they present, at all events, a weighty testimony for the concrete historical character and credibility of the present account.—*For with the trespass of the Lord upon us,* that the effect of our heavy guilt with God (ver. 10) may fall upon us, that the heavy punishment of sin may overtake us. אַשְׁמַת יְהוָה is here the effect, the punishment of guilt contracted before God.—Ver. 14. *And the armed host left,* the armed escort who conducted the captives to Samaria. הֶחָלוּץ, as in 1 Chron. xii. 23.—Ver. 15. *The men who were expressed by name,* the notable men mentioned by name in the old records, who specially distinguished themselves at that time by a noble emulation of love and compassion for the poor captives; comp. 1 Chron. xii. 31, xvi. 41; 2 Chron. xxxi. 19. The analogy of these passages forbids us to think only of the four named in ver. 12.—*And clothed all that were naked of them,* literally, "all the nakedness" (*abstr. pro concr.*).—*And anointed them,* because they should return home happy and cheerful.—*And carried them on asses;* to which is appended a limiting and more exactly defining phrase, *all the weary* (or "stumbling," לְכָל־כּוֹשֵׁל). Observe the pictorial reality and epic breadth of the whole description, which exhibits itself even in designating Jericho as the city of palms (comp. Judg. iii. 13), and by the mention of it (as the border town of Judah, whither the captives were first brought; comp. Josh. xviii. 21) accords with the story of the good Samaritan. For, in fact, there is here a grand archetype of the deed of compassion described in this didactic narrative of the Lord, as sure as they were inhabitants of the city and later

country of Samaria, who took so loving an interest in the helpless Jews. The thought that Christ drew directly from this episode of the present war several points of His noble lesson should by no means be absolutely rejected. Comp. Evangelical and Ethical Reflections, No. 3.

12. Close: *c.* Further Visitations of Ahaz on account of his Idolatry; his End: vers. 16–27. Only the part of this section that refers to the relations of Ahaz to the Assyrian world-power (his seeking aid from Tiglath-pileser, his payment of tribute to the same, and his fall occasioned by this slavish submission to the idolatry of Syria and Damascus, vers. 16, 20–25) is reported in 2 Kings xvi. (vers. 7–18), and there, indeed, much more fully than here. On the contrary, there is wanting there a statement of the contemporaneous humiliations of Ahaz by the Edomites and Philistines, as they are here reported, vers. 17–19.—*At that time King Ahaz sent unto the kings of Assyria.* The rather indefinite בָּעֵת הַהִיא admits the assumption that this embassy to Assyria took place immediately after the invasion of Rezin and Pekah (Berth.), as well as that several months or years elapsed between these events (Keil). But according to 2 Kings xvi. 6 ff., the consequence of that first heavy defeat by the Syrians and Ephraimites, the taking of Elath by Rezin (and that which was connected with it, the invasion of the Edomites and Philistines), seems to have been the motive of Ahaz to apply to the Assyrians for aid. The plural "the kings of Assyria" is perhaps not rhetorical, as above, ver. 3, בָּנָיו (Keil), but, as it seems, originally written under the consciousness that the head of the Assyrian government was composed of several factors, namely, the king and the so-called eponymus or archon of the current year; see in particular xxx. 4, where this view seems undeniable; also xxx. 6; and comp. Schrader, *Studien und Kritiken*, 1871, part iv.; *Die Keilschriften*, etc., p. 308 ff.—Ver. 17. *And again the Edomites came*, perhaps made free again by Rezin's expedition against Elath, 2 Kings xvi. 6, from the Jewish yoke, which lay upon them from the time of Amaziah and Uzziah (xxv. 11, xxvi. 2). The tense is to be taken as the pluperfect: "and moreover (וְעוֹד, *et præterea, et insuper*; comp. Isa. i. 5) the Edomites had come"; and so in the two following verses, for they also report something that preceded the fatal treaty with Tiglath-pileser, and served to bring it about.—Ver. 18. *And the Philistines invaded.* Of the places conquered by them, Beth-shemesh (1 Chron. vi. 44), Ajalon (1 Chron. vi. 54), and Socho (2 Chron. xi. 7) have occurred already in our book. For Gederoth (in the Shephelah), comp. Josh. xv. 41; for Timnah, now Tibneh, Josh. xv. 10; for Gimzo, now Jimsu, a large village between Lydda and Beth-horon, Robins. *Palest.* iii. 271 The mention of daughter cities (literally, "daughters") along with the chief places, as in xiii. 9.—Ver. 19. *For the Lord humbled Judah on account of Ahaz king of Israel.* Ahaz is perhaps ironically so named; for the title "King of Israel" can scarcely be an honourable designation in him, as in Rehoboam (xii. 6) or Jehoshaphat (xxi. 2), or as in his forefathers in general, ver. 27. It contains, perhaps, an allusion to the contrast between his idolatrous reign and the mind and walk of the true "Israel of God" (comp. Gal. vi. 16, Caspari, Keil, etc.). —*Because he had revolted in Judah.* So is כִּי הִפְרִיעַ with בְּ following certainly to be taken, not as Kamph. and others think: "because he made Judah refractory"; comp. rather Ex. v. 4, which speaks also against the rendering of the Vulg.: *eo quod nudasset eum auxilio*, and of Luther (that he made Judah naked).—Ver. 20. *And Tiglath-pilneser.* Concerning this form, as corresponding not so well to the Assyrian as the Tiglath-pileser of the other Old Testament sources, see on 1 Chron. v. 6; for the conjectural identity of Pul with Tiglath-pileser, see on 1 Chron. v. 26. —*And distressed him, and strengthened him not.* This is the only rendering agreeable to the context, according to which, חִזְּקוֹ here, contrary to its usual intransitive meaning, expresses the active sense of strengthening (*confortare, roborare*). See for justification of this rendering against Luther, Then., Bertheau, etc. (who take חזק according to xxvii. 5, Jer. xx. 7, etc. = "overcome"): "he oppressed and besieged him, but subdued him not," in particular Keil on this passage; rightly also Neteler and Kamph.—Ver. 21. *For Ahaz had plundered the house of the Lord.* This was at the time that he sent the embassy with its cry for help to the mighty Assyrian king (ver. 16), for with empty hands he need not approach him (comp. also 2 Kings xvi. 7, 8). חלק here is not "divide" (Luther), but "plunder, *spoliare*" (Vulg.); comp. חֵלֶק, booty, share of spoil (Num. xxxi. 36; Job xvii. 5). The strong expression corresponds to the rhetorical tone of the narrator; thereby the certainly historical statement shows that the treasures of the king's house, as well as those of the "princes" (the high officers of the palace, or perhaps also the princes of the royal house; comp. on ver. 7), must have contributed, that the gift (שֹׁחַד, see 2 Kings xvi. 8) sent with the ambassadors might be worthy of acceptance. That Ahaz paid tribute to Tiglath-pileser is attested, besides our passage and the report in 2 Kings xvi. 7–9 (comp. also Isa. xxxvi. 5, where Rabshakeh charges Hezekiah with revolt from Assyria), also by the Assyrian monuments. In line 61 of an inscription composed in the last year of Tiglath-pileser's reign (ii. R. 67), it is said that this king received tribute (*madatu*) from "Mittini of Askalon, Ahaz (Jehoahaz—Ja-hu-kha-zi) of Judah, Kozmalak of Edom." That here Ahaz is spoken of as a tributary of the great king, and not Uzziah (as H. Rawlinson thought on account of the surprising form of the name), is shown by the naming of the rulers of Philistia and Edom, who in Uzziah's time would scarcely have been co-ordinated with the Jewish king, the naming of whom along with Ahaz is quite consistent with the contents of the verses of our chapter. Comp. Schrader, p. 151 ff.—Ver. 22. *And in the time of his distress*, a date of like indefiniteness and pliability with בָּעֵת הַהִיא in ver. 16. That the revolt of Ahaz to the gods of the Syrians thus took place after the distresses which the Edomites, Philistines, and Syrians prepared for him, cannot be definitely concluded from this passage; rather it seems to follow from

ver. 23 that he had already, during the war with Rezin, begun to testify his respect for the gods of his foe and his country. There is therefore no proper contradiction between our passage and 2 Kings xvi. 10 ff.; only that there is given a more concrete and definite report concerning this turning of Ahaz to the Syrian gods than in our section, which also, again, bears an eminently rhetorical and pathetic character, as indeed all that is related from ver. 5 onwards.—Ver. 24. *And Ahaz . . . cut up the vessels of the house of God,* that is, as is stated more precisely in 2 Kings xvi. 17, he broke out the sides of the bases, removed the lavers from them, transferred the sea from the brazen oxen to a stone pavement, etc.—*And shut the doors of the house of the Lord,* that is, according to xxix. 3, 7, the doors not of the court, but of the temple itself, or the porch before the holy and most holy places. Accordingly, the shutting of these doors signified that he suspended the worship of God in the holy and in the most holy place, while he left the altar of burnt-offering in the court; with which 2 Kings xvi. 15 f. agrees, although there the erection of a separate altar of burnt-offering, built after the model of Damascus of Syria, beside the brazen altar of Solomon, is reported (see Bähr on the passage).—*And made him altars in every corner of Jerusalem.* Among these altars is included the new altar of burnt-offering in the court, 2 Kings xvi. 10-16, built at the command of Ahaz by the priest Uriah after the pattern of the idol-altar at Damascus. The כָּל in בְּכָל־פִּנָּה is not to be pressed, nor, for example: "under every tree," in ver. 4, nor the phrase: "in every single city of Judah," in the following verse.—Ver. 25. *And provoked to anger the Lord* (כעס, *hiph.*, as in Deut. xxxii. 16; 1 Kings xiv. 9).—Vers. 26, 27; comp. the briefer closing notice in 2 Kings xvi. 19, 20.—*And they buried him in the city in Jerusalem;* thus not: "in the city of David," as is usually said, and further not: "in the sepulchres of the kings of Israel" (see on ver. 19), but apart from the proper tombs of the kings—perhaps in the field mentioned in xxvi. 23, where the leprous Uzziah was buried. 2 Kings xvi. 20 reports nothing of such an exception that was made with respect to the grave of Ahaz.

EVANGELICAL AND ETHICAL REFLECTIONS AND HOMILETIC HINTS ON CH. XXIV.-XXVIII.

1. A period of fully a century and a half (877-727 in the usual chronology) is occupied by the five reigns here combined, comprising a reign of forty, of nearly thirty, and of fifty-two years. But none of them yields any permanent gain for the development of Judah into the normal form of a truly theocratic condition, as the deep corruption exhibited under the last, an instance of decided misrule, shows. When the Canaanitish idolatry, naturalized by Athaliah, after a short predominance, was again expelled, as an element utterly foreign to the Davidic house and the Jewish people, five reigns regularly following in legitimate succession, of which perhaps none was begun otherwise than under favourable auspices, and with joyful hopes on the side of the theocratic party, furnish before the end of 150 years the sad result of a decided relapse into that idolatry. For the less insidiously evil and murderous than merely weak policy of Ahaz in every instance must be regarded as such a relapse, though it might not be the Tyrian-Canaanitish idolatry of Athaliah to which he chiefly yielded, but the Damascene-Syrian superstition of his adversary Rezin, and though, further, the outward form and show of the legitimate worship was perhaps better observed under him than under the priest-opposing daughter of Omri. On the whole, it is manifest that under Ahaz the corruption of religion and morals had gnawed more deeply than at that time, and struck firmer roots into the consciousness and customs of the people. It is now, at least, quite contrary to the state of things then, directly a priest, perhaps the high priest (Uriah, 2 Kings xvi. 10 ff.), who readily enters into the king's idolatrous intentions, and lends a hand to desecrate the sanctuary of Jehovah with foreign modes of worship, elaborated after heathen models; a characteristic which the Chronist perhaps only neglected expressly to mark, because it disgusted and annoyed him to report anything so unreasonable and abominable as this treason of a priest of the Lord. And as the priest, so the people does not now, at the beck of a true witness, as then of Jehoiada, rise up as one man to put an end to the foreign hateful thing at one blow, but presents so little resistance to the seductions to spiritual and corporeal adultery proceeding from the court, that it remains, during a reign of almost sixteen years, on the path of Baal-worship, and establishes not only idolatrous altars in every corner of Jerusalem, but also high places for burning incense to strange gods "in every single city of Judah" (comp. xxviii. 24, 25), without standing up in righteous indignation against such a course, or even earnestly seeking a return to theocratic obedience. That it could come to this a century and a half after the events under Athaliah, tells not of a gradual progress to a better state of things, but rather of a slow but irresistible sinking into worse and worse—of a constant ripening of the people for that fearful judgment of God which now fell on the kindred people of Ephraim immediately after the death of Ahaz at the end of these 150 years, and with respect to which for Judah, with all the energy of many attempts at reform (especially under Hezekiah and Josiah), nothing beyond a postponement, a delay of less than 150 years more was secured.

2. None of the four comparatively theocratic reigns before Ahaz had been able to check the descent of the people with uneasy certainty and constancy on this downward path to final corruption; for none possessed the reverence for God and law, untainted by heathenish abominations, which characterized the rule of an Asa or Jehoshaphat. For Joash maintained a decidedly theocratic demeanour only so long as his paternal friend, instructor, and counsellor Jehoiada governed him, or so long as those two symbols given him (xxiii. 11) at his accession—the crown as the sign of power, and the law as the sign of theocratic wisdom—exercised their united influence over him;[1] after whose death he permits, at

[1] Comp. Luther's marginal note on this passage: "Finely are both the crown and the book presented to the king, that he might be not only mighty, but also wise, or (as we may say) know God's word and right. Thus, even now, we make kings with a sword and book."

the request of the worldly-minded "princes of Judah" (representatives of the higher nobility, to whom the "priestly power" might long since have well been an abomination), the entrance again of idolatry, and causes the faithful witness of the truth, warning them of the evil consequences of such a course, the son of his instructor Jehoiada (and therefore his near relative), to be slain in the court of the temple. Whereupon also the threatened judgment of God, accomplished by a desolating raid of the Syrian Hazael, suddenly enters, and in a very short time brings about the end—and that a terrible end—of the unfaithful king. This reign resembles in more than one respect the history of such rulers of the Middle Ages or of modern times as the German emperors Otto III. and Henry IV., or in many respects Louis XIV. of France, who enjoyed the guardianship of excellent regents of the spiritual order at the beginning of their career, but afterwards failed to beware of the evil consequences of their passing over to a false independence. Not much better or happier was the reign of Amaziah, whose early measures, as the sparing of the children of the murderers who conspired against Joash (xxv. 4; comp. Deut. xxiv. 16) shows, were entirely accordant with the precepts of the law; but who afterwards, in consequence of a successful war with Edom, which seems to have made the conqueror presumptuous, degenerated into heathenish practices, offered the tribute of worship to the gods of the conquered Edomites (naturally without meaning to abolish the legitimate worship of Jehovah, proceeding on some sort of theoretical and practical mingling of the two modes of worshipping God), and added to this the further folly of a supercilious provocation of the powerful Joash of Israel to war. A severe humiliation by this foe, as a reward for this haughty bearing (conjoined with which are here, again, scornful neglect and rough treatment of one of the prophets of Jehovah, ver. 16), here also failed to delay the issue; and the end of the king, effected by a band of traitors and conspirators, ver. 27, was as violent as that of his father. With respect to external politics as well as military and economic (financial) consolidation of their power, the two following reigns appear to have been more fortunate. The vigorous Uzziah, reigning more than a half century, restores in many respects once more the glorious days of a Jehoshaphat, especially with regard to the maintenance of his sway over the southern tribes, and the great advance of the defensive power and financial capability of the country. But when the true spiritual adviser whom he long followed, the prophet Zechariah, was separated from him, he also exhibited haughtiness, daring arrogance, and false independence in spiritual things. And if his people were not involved in the judgment incurred by this guilt, yet his transgression brought on himself a heavy and shameful fall, for which there was no recovery on this side the grave. He dies as one "smitten of God" (Isa. liii. 4; comp. Job ii. 7, vi. 4 f., xvi. 12 ff.) in a sick-house, and does not even in death partake of the honour due to a king of the line of David, and also a powerful and celebrated prince (xxvi. 28). To his son Jotham, reigning a much shorter time, but in a like spirit and with like external fortune, a humiliation of the same kind is certainly spared; for "he entered not into the temple of the Lord," ventured on no such daring stretch of his authority as Uzziah in his attempt to burn incense. And how far he was thereby from being without guilt, or free from inward participation in such offences, is shown by the reckless audacity with which his on and successor, during his whole reign (of equal length with that of his father), ventured to addict himself to the demoralizing idolatry of the neighbouring nations, and to procure for it unlimited entrance among his people. Of the father of such a son we can form no very favourable opinion, even if the scanty notices of our author announce little or nothing positively unfavourable concerning him.

3. The penal judgment of God for such continued yielding to the seducing and corrupting influence of heathenism, as it was decreed against Judah, soon after the corruption had broken forth in all its grossness, in the so-called war with Syria and Ephraim, appears, according to the representation of the Chronist, to have been terribly great and severe. More than 100,000 fighting men fall as the sacrifice of a single battle-field, and almost double that number of women, children, and other prisoners of war are dragged away as slaves, and owe their instant unconditional release to the compassion of their kinsmen, the victorious Ephraimites, evoked by a bold and vehement prophetic admonition; so that in this case the Jews were put to shame by the more righteous and pious conduct of the citizens of the neighbouring kingdom (which, however, took place on the very eve of their religious and political ruin). But the spiritual blessing which should have sprung from so heavy and deeply humiliating a visitation was gone. No trace of the return of the heart to the true God and to His law comes to light in the subsequent accounts concerning the acts and events of the reign of Ahaz. And the calamities added to that great defeat, the invasions of the Edomites and Philistines, as well as the distress from the Assyrian king, whose alliance naturally soon proved to be an oppressive sovereignty, produce, instead of repentance toward God, only increasing submission to the idols. As slave-children with venal servility kiss the rod with which they are chastised, so Ahaz thinks he must present more demonstrations of respect to the gods of his victorious foes, in proportion as they prepare for him heavier humiliations. And no one among the people brings him back from such folly; the voice of no prophet, though they press as strongly and closely upon his ear as that of an Isaiah (Isa. vii.–x.), is able to check the criminal course into which he has gone with his princes, his counsellors, and his strong party among the people. First under his son Hezekiah, repentance and amendment, the path to which was already prepared in many hearts by the previous afflictions, come to light; and that unusually severe judgment of God finally proves to be a wholesome corrective measure, the effect of which is to save, create new life, and purify; comp. Hezekiah's own reflections on it, xxix. 9,—a passage which, at the same time, deserves to be taken into account as a supplementary testimony to the greatness of the loss suffered by the people from the defeats in question.

4. In the representation of the author of the

books of Kings, this pragmatic connection of the defeats of Ahaz, especially that inflicted on him by the Syrians and Ephraimites, with his sins and his sinking into ever worse impenitence and idolatry, is less sharply and clearly exhibited than in the strong, rhetorically-coloured, and generally animated and impassioned style adopted by our author. But its substantial credibility can suffer no damage from this, that it here and there presents other points of view, and in part connects the events otherwise. As the reports of the Chronist, giving great prominence to the Levitical element in the revolution conducted by Jehoiada, as well as in the contributions for the temple and its repair under Joash, in contrast with those of the books of Kings, do not deserve to be cast in the shade and disparaged; or as that which our author more specially relates concerning Uzziah's transgression and punishment from his Levitical point of view is not to be suspected in comparison with the allusive brevity of the older parallel account; even so we have no right to hesitate with regard to that which is peculiar to him in the description of the Syro-Ephraimitish war. The roundness, resting rather on an estimate than an exact enumeration, of the high numbers in xxviii. 6–8 is the only thing that is to be conceded to the judgment of the opponent calling in question the strict historical accuracy of his narrative (see above on this passage). All other details of this description clearly rest on good historical ground; neither the names of the persons that fell, ver. 7, in the great engagement with Pekah among the king's relatives and nearest circle, nor those of the nobles of Ephraim who supported by their vote the admonition of Oded to release the Jewish captives (ver. 12), look like mere invention. The invention of such names, in order to invest an account, legendary in itself, with the appearance of historical truth, would, in fact, be an inconceivable monstrosity, a *unicum* in the history of literary fictions. But they both hold and support each other, the undeniable historical reality of these names, and the credibility of the facts with which they are connected and environed. The entrance also of the prophet Oded, and the words spoken by him, are accredited by the reacting power of these concrete names. What is done to the Jewish captives by those four chiefs of Ephraim seems purely inconceivable without a vehement admonition, such as that spoken by Oded according to vers. 9–11. Caspari therefore declares it to be the "highest levity" (against Gesenius, in his *Commentary on Isaiah*, p. 269, and other impugners of the historical truth of this prophetic utterance) to hold the report in vers. 9–11 to be unworthy of credit, and yet to regard the contents of ver. 12 ff. as historical. And in the same relation of supplement and of correspondence to 2 Kings stands in general all that our author reports different from the statements there concerning Ahaz and the steps taken by him for the furtherance of idolatry. As the remarks made by him, vers. 17–19, concerning the invasions of the Edomites and Philistines, agree excellently with 2 Kings xvi. 6, so between that which he relates, vers. 23–25, regarding the idolatrous profanation of the temple and its vessels and 2 Kings xvi. 10–16 there is no contradiction whatever, but merely a relation of supplement and confirmation. On the whole, it would seem superfluous, indeed almost paltry, after Caspari's emphatic and pertinent argument in favour of the essential harmony of the two reports of the war, to enter further into subtle critical disquisitions or wide apologetic investigations regarding their apparent or even real points of difference.

n. HEZEKIAH: THE PROPHET ISAIAH.—CH. XXIX.–XXXII.

α. Hezekiah's Beginnings; the Cleansing and Consecration of the Temple: ch. xxix.

CHAP. XXIX. 1. Hezekiah became king when he was twenty and five years old, and
he reigned twenty and nine years in Jerusalem; and his mother's name was
2 Abijah, daughter of Zechariah. And he did that which was right in the eyes
of the LORD, according to all that David his father had done.
3 He, in the first year of his reign, in the first month, opened the doors of
4 the house of the LORD, and renewed them. And he brought in the priests
5 and Levites, and assembled them in the broad way of the east, And said
unto them, Hear me, ye Levites; now sanctify yourselves and sanctify the
house of the LORD God of your fathers, and remove the filthiness out of the
6 holy place. For our fathers have transgressed and done that which was evil
in the eyes of the LORD our God, and have forsaken Him, and have turned
7 their face from the dwelling of the LORD, and shown the back. They have
also shut the doors of the porch, and put out the lamps, and have not burned
incense nor offered burnt-offering in the holy place unto the God of Israel.
8 And the displeasure of the LORD was against Judah and Jerusalem, and He
delivered them to horror,[1] to astonishment, and to hissing, as ye see with
9 your eyes. And lo, our fathers have fallen by the sword, and our sons and
10 our daughters and our wives are in captivity for this. Now it is in my
heart to make a covenant with the LORD God of Israel, that the hotness of
11 His anger may turn away from us. My sons, now delay not; for the LORD
hath chosen you to stand before Him to serve Him, and to be His ministers
and incense-burners.

12 Then the Levites arose, Mahath son of Amasai, and Joel son of Azariah,
of the sons of the Kohathites; and of the sons of Merari, Kish son of Abdi,
and Azariah son of Jehalelel;[2] and of the Gershonites, Joah son of Zimmah,
13 and Eden son of Joah. And of the sons of Elizaphan, Shimri and Jeuel;[3]
14 and of the sons of Asaph, Zechariah and Mattaniah. And of the sons of
Heman, Jehuel[4] and Shimi; and of the sons of Jeduthun, Shemaiah and
15 Uzziel. And they gathered their brethren, and sanctified themselves, and
came at the command of the king, by the words of the LORD, to cleanse the
16 house of the LORD. And the priests went into the interior of the house of
the LORD to cleanse, and brought out all the uncleanness that they found in
the temple of the LORD into the court of the house of the LORD; and the
17 Levites took it to carry it out abroad into the brook Kidron. And they
began on the first of the first month to sanctify, and on the eighth day of the
month they came to the porch of the LORD; and they sanctified the house of
the LORD eight days, and in the sixteenth day of the first month they made
18 an end. And they went in to Hezekiah the king, and said, We have cleansed
all the house of the LORD, and the altar of burnt-offering and all its vessels,
19 and the table of shew-bread and all its vessels. And all the vessels which
King Ahaz in his reign cast away in his infidelity we have prepared and
sanctified, and behold, they are before the altar of the LORD.

20 And Hezekiah the king rose early and gathered the rulers of the city,
21 and went up to the house of the LORD. And they brought seven bullocks,
and seven rams, and seven lambs, and seven he-goats for a sin-offering for the
kingdom, and for the sanctuary, and for Judah, and he bade the sons of
22 Aaron the priests to offer them on the altar of the LORD. And they killed
the cattle, and the priests received the blood and sprinkled it on the altar;
and they killed the rams, and they sprinkled the blood upon the altar; and
23 they killed the lambs, and they sprinkled the blood upon the altar. And
they brought the he-goats of the sin-offering before the king and the congre-
24 gation, and they laid their hands upon them. And the priests killed them,
and offered their blood for sin upon the altar, to atone for all Israel; for the
25 king had ordered the burnt-offering and the sin-offering for all Israel. And
he set the Levites in the house of the LORD, with cymbals, with psalteries,
and with harps, by the command of David, and Gad the king's seer, and
Nathan the prophet; for by the LORD was the commandment by His pro-
26 phets. And the Levites stood with the instruments of David, and the priests
27 with the trumpets. And Hezekiah said to offer the burnt-offering on the
altar; and when the burnt-offering began, the song of the LORD began also
28 with the trumpets,[5] and after the instruments of David king of Israel. And
all the congregation worshipped, and the song was sung, and the trumpets
29 sounded;[6] the whole until the burnt-offering was ended. And when they
made an end of offering, the king and all that were with him bowed down
30 and worshipped. And Hezekiah the king and the princes said to the Levites
to praise the LORD with the words of David and Asaph the seer; and they
praised with gladness, and bowed down and worshipped.

31 And Hezekiah answered and said, Now ye have filled your hand unto the
LORD, draw nigh and bring sacrifices and thank-offerings into the house of
the LORD: and the congregation brought sacrifices and thank-offerings, and
32 every one that was willing of heart, burnt-offerings. And the number of the
burnt-offerings, which the congregation brought, was seventy bullocks, a
hundred rams, two hundred lambs; all these for a burnt-offering to the
33 LORD. And the consecrated things were six hundred oxen and three thou-
34 sand sheep. Only the priests were too few, and they could not flay all the
burnt-offerings, and their brethren the Levites assisted them till the work
was ended, and till the priests had sanctified themselves; for the Levites
35 were more upright of heart to sanctify themselves than the priests. And
also the burnt-offering was in abundance, with the fat of the peace-offerings,
and the libations for the burnt-offering: and the service of the house of the

36 LORD was established. And Hezekiah and all the people were glad that
God had prepared the people; for the thing was done suddenly.

β. The Passover: ch. xxx.

CH. XXX. 1. And Hezekiah sent to all Israel and Judah, and wrote letters also to
Ephraim and Manasseh, to come to the house of the LORD at Jerusalem, to
2 keep the passover unto the LORD God of Israel. And the king took counsel
with his princes, and all the congregation in Jerusalem, to keep the passover
3 in the second month. For they could not keep it at that time, because the
priests had not sanctified themselves sufficiently, nor had the people gathered
4, 5 to Jerusalem. And the thing pleased the king and all the people. And they
settled the thing, to issue a proclamation in all Israel, from Beer-sheba even
to Dan, to come to keep the passover unto the LORD God of Israel at Jeru-
6 salem; for they had not kept it with a multitude as it was written. And the
posts went with the letters from the hand of the king and his princes through
all Israel and Judah, and at the command of the king, saying, Ye sons of
Israel, return unto the LORD God of Abraham, Isaac, and Israel, and He will
return to the escaped remaining to you from the hand of the kings of Assyria.
7 And be not ye like your fathers and your brethren, who revolted against the
LORD God of their fathers, and He gave them up to desolation, as ye see.
8 Now be not stiff-necked like your fathers; yield yourselves to the LORD, and
go into His sanctuary, which He hath sanctified for ever, and serve the LORD
9 your God, that the hotness of His anger may turn from you. For if ye return
to the LORD, your brethren and your children shall find compassion before
their captors, and they shall return to this land; for the LORD your God is
gracious and merciful, and He will not turn His face from you if ye return
to Him.

10 And the posts passed from city to city in the land of Ephraim and Ma-
11 nasseh and unto Zebulun; and they scoffed at them and mocked them. But
some men of Asher and Manasseh and Zebulun humbled themselves, and
12 came to Jerusalem. Also the hand of God was upon Judah to give them
one heart to do the command of the king and the princes, by the word of the
LORD.

13 And much people assembled at Jerusalem to keep the feast of unleavened
14 bread in the second month, a very great congregation. And they arose and
took away the altars that were in Jerusalem; and all the altars for incense
15 they took away, and cast into the brook Kidron. And they killed the pass-
over on the fourteenth of the second month: and the priests and the Levites
were ashamed, and sanctified themselves, and brought burnt-offerings into the
16 house of the LORD. And they stood in their place after their rule, according
to the law of Moses the man of God, the priests sprinkling the blood from
17 the hand of the Levites. For there were many in the congregation that were
not sanctified; and the Levites took charge of the killing of the passovers for
18 all that were unclean, to sanctify them unto the LORD. For a multitude of
the people, many from Ephraim and Manasseh, Issachar and Zebulun, had
not cleansed themselves, yet they ate the passover not as it was written: for
19 Hezekiah prayed for them, saying, The good LORD pardon[7] every one That
hath prepared his heart to seek God, the LORD God of his fathers, though
20 not in the cleanness of the sanctuary. And the LORD heard Hezekiah, and
21 healed the people. And the sons of Israel that were in Jerusalem kept the
feast of unleavened bread seven days with great gladness; and the Levites
and the priests were praising the LORD day by day, with instruments of
22 might to the LORD. And Hezekiah spake to the heart of all the Levites who
had good understanding of the LORD: and they ate[8] the feast seven days,
offering sacrifices of peace, and confessing to the LORD God of their fathers.

23 And the whole congregation resolved to keep other seven days with glad-
24 ness. For Hezekiah king of Judah gave to the congregation a thousand
bullocks and seven thousand sheep; and the princes gave to the congregation

a thousand bullocks and ten thousand sheep: and a great many priests sanc-
25 tified themselves. And all the congregation of Judah, and the priests and
Levites, and all the congregation that came out of Israel, and the strangers
26 that came from the land of Israel, and that dwelt in Judah, were glad. And
there was great gladness in Jerusalem; for since the days of Solomon son of
27 David king of Israel was not the like in Jerusalem. And the priests [and] the
Levites[9] arose and blessed the people: and their voice was heard, and their
prayer came up to His holy dwelling, to heaven.[10]

γ. Further Religious Reforms of Hezekiah: ch. xxxi.

CH. XXXI. 1. And when all this was finished, all Israel that were present went out
to the cities of Judah, and brake the statues, and cut down the asherim, and
pulled down the high places and the altars out of all Judah and Benjamin,
and in Ephraim and Manasseh, completely: and all the sons of Israel returned,
every man to his possession, unto their cities.

2 And Hezekiah appointed the courses of the priests and the Levites after
their courses, every man according to his service, of the priests and the
Levites for burnt-offering and peace-offering, to minister, and to thank, and to
3 praise in the gates of the camp of the LORD. And the king's portion of his
property for burnt-offerings, for the burnt-offerings of the morning and of the
evening, and the burnt-offerings for the sabbaths, and the new moons, and
4 the set feasts, as it is written in the law of the LORD. And he said to the
people, the inhabitants of Jerusalem, to give the portion of the priests and
5 the Levites, that they might be stedfast in the law of the LORD. And when
the word came forth, the sons of Israel brought abundantly the first-fruits of
corn, must, and oil, and honey, and all the increase of the field; and the tithe
6 of all they brought in abundance. And the sons of Israel and Judah that
dwelt in the cities of Judah, they also brought the tithe of oxen and sheep,
and the tithe of holy things[11] consecrated unto the LORD their God, and laid
7 them in heaps. In the third month they began to lay down the heaps, and
8 in the seventh month they finished them. And Hezekiah and the princes
came and saw the heaps, and they blessed the LORD and His people Israel.
9, 10 And Hezekiah inquired of the priests and Levites concerning the heaps. And
Azariah the chief priest, of the house of Zadok, answered him and said, Since
they began to bring the offerings into the house of the LORD, we have eaten
and been satisfied, and left in abundance; for the LORD hath blessed His
11 people, and this great store is left. And Hezekiah said to prepare chambers
12 in the house of the LORD, and they prepared them. And they brought in
the offerings and the tithe and the consecrated things faithfully; and over
13 them Conaniah[12] the Levite was ruler, and Shimi was second. And Jehiel,
and Azaziah, and Nahath, and Asahel, and Jerimoth, and Jozabad, and Eliel,
and Ismachiah, and Mahath, and Benaiah were overseers under Conaniah[12]
and his brother Shimi, by the appointment of Hezekiah the king, and Azariah
14 the ruler of the house of God. And Kore, son of Jimnah the Levite, the
porter toward the east, was over the freewill-offerings of God, to distribute
15 the offering of the LORD, and the most holy things. And by him stood Eden,
and Minjamin, and Jeshua, and Shemaiah, Amariah, and Shechaniah in the
cities of the priests, with truth to give to their brethren, in the courses, to the
16 great as to the small. Beside their register of males from three years old
and upward, to every one that entereth into the house of the LORD, for the
17 rate of each day, for their service in their charges by their courses. And the
register of the priests by their father-houses; and the Levites from twenty
18 years old and upward, in their charges by their courses. And to the register
of all their little ones, their wives, sons, and daughters, for all the congrega-
tion; for in their faithfulness they sanctified themselves in the holy thing.
19 And for the sons of Aaron the priests, in the fields of the suburbs of their
cities, in every city [were appointed] men who were expressed by name, to give
portions to every male among the priests, and to all the register of the Levites.

20 And Hezekiah did thus in all Judah, and did that which was good and right
21 and true before the LORD his God. And in every work which he began in
the service of the house of God, and in the law and the commandment to seek
his God, with all his heart he did, and prospered.

δ. *Expedition of Sennacherib against Jerusalem, and averting of the threatened Danger by Divine Help:* ch. xxxii. 1–23.

CH. XXXII. 1. After these events, and this faithfulness, Sennacherib king of Assyria
came and entered into Judah, and besieged the fenced cities, and thought
2 to break into them for himself. And Hezekiah saw that Sennacherib was
3 come, and his face was for war against Jerusalem. And he took counsel with
his princes and his mighty men to stop the waters of the fountains, which
4 were without the city; and they helped him. And much people was gathered,
and they stopped all the fountains, and the brook that flowed through the
land,[13] saying, Why should the kings of Assyria come and find much water?
5 And he strengthened himself, and built up all the wall that was broken, and
raised it to the towers,[14] and another wall without, and strengthened Millo in
6 the city of David, and made weapons in abundance, and shields. And he set
captains of war over the people, and gathered them to him in the broad
7 way at the gate of the city, and spake to their heart, saying, Be brave and
strong, fear not nor be dismayed for the king of Assyria, nor for all the
8 multitude that is with him; for with us is more than with him. With him
is an arm of flesh; and with us is the LORD our God, to help us, and to fight
our battles: and the people relied upon the words of Hezekiah king of
Judah.
9 After this Sennacherib king of Assyria sent his servants to Jerusalem, and
he himself stood against Lachish, and all his power with him, against
Hezekiah king of Judah, and against all Judah that was at Jerusalem, saying,
10 Thus saith Sennacherib king of Assyria, Whereon do ye trust, and why sit
11 ye in restraint in Jerusalem? Doth not Hezekiah mislead you to deliver you
to die by hunger and thirst, saying, The LORD our God shall deliver us from
12 the hand of the king of Assyria? Hath not this Hezekiah removed his high
places and his altars, and said to Judah and to Jerusalem, saying, Before one
13 altar shall ye worship, and burn incense upon it? Know ye not what I and
my fathers have done to all the peoples of the lands? Have the gods of the
nations of the lands been at all able to deliver their lands from my hand?
14 Who was there among all the gods of these nations, that my fathers extirpated,
that could deliver his people out of my hand, that your God should be able to
15 deliver you from my hand? And now let not Hezekiah deceive you nor
seduce you in this way, neither believe him; for no god of any nation or
kingdom was able to deliver his people from my hand, nor the hand of my
16 fathers; much more your God shall not deliver you from my hand. And his
servants spake yet more against the LORD, and against Hezekiah His servant.
17 And he wrote a letter to rail on the LORD God of Israel, and to speak against
Him, saying, Like the gods of the nations of the lands who have not delivered
their people from my hand, so shall not the God of Hezekiah deliver His
18 people from my hand. And they cried with a loud voice, in the Jewish
tongue, to the people of Jerusalem that were on the wall, to affright them
19 and trouble them, that they might take the city. And they spake to the
God of Jerusalem as against the gods of the peoples of the earth, the work of
men's hands.
20 And for this Hezekiah the king, and Isaiah son of Amoz the prophet,
21 prayed and cried to heaven. And the LORD sent an angel, and cut off every
valiant hero and leader and captain in the camp of the king of Assyria: and
he returned with shame of face to his own land; and he came into the house
of his god, and they that came out of his own bowels[15] there slew him with
22 the sword. And the LORD saved Hezekiah, and the inhabitants of Jerusalem,

from the hand of Sennacherib king of Assyria, and from the hand of all,[16] and
23 defended them around. And many brought a gift to the LORD at Jerusalem,
and jewels to Hezekiah king of Judah; and he was exalted in the eyes of all
nations thereafter.

ε. Sickness, Remaining Years, and End of Hezekiah: vers. 24–33.

24 In those days Hezekiah was sick unto death, and he prayed unto the
25 LORD: and He spake unto him, and gave him a sign. And Hezekiah repaid
not according to the benefit done to him; for his heart became proud, and
26 there was indignation against him, and against Judah and Jerusalem. And
Hezekiah humbled himself for the pride of his heart, he and the inhabitants
of Jerusalem; and the indignation of the LORD came not upon them in the
days of Hezekiah.
27 And Hezekiah had very much riches and glory; and he made himself
treasuries for silver, and gold, and precious stones, and spices, and shields, and
28 all articles of desire. And storehouses for the increase of corn, and must, and
29 oil; and stalls for all kinds of cattle, and flocks for the folds.[17] And he
made him cities, and possession of flocks and herds in abundance; for God
30 had given him very much substance. And this Hezekiah stopped the upper
outflow of the water of Gihon, and led it[18] straight down to the west of the
31 city of David: and Hezekiah prospered in all his work. And so in the case
of the ambassadors of the princes of Babel, who sent to him to inquire of the
wonder that was done in the land, God left him, to try him, to know all that
was in his heart.
32 And the rest of the acts of Hezekiah, and his kindness, behold, they are
written in the vision of Isaiah the prophet, son of Amoz, in the book of the
33 kings of Judah and Israel. And Hezekiah slept with his fathers, and they
buried him in the height of the sepulchres of the sons of David; and all
Judah and the inhabitants of Jerusalem gave him glory in his death: and
Manasseh his son became king in his stead.

[1] *Kethib:* זַוָעָה (as in Jer. xv. 4, etc.); *Keri:* זַעֲוָה (as, for example, in Deut. xxviii. 25).

[2] For the name יְהַלֶּלְאֵל the Sept., *c. Al.*, gives Ἰαλλήλ; *c. Vat.*, Ἰλαλεήλ; Vulg., *Jalaleel.*

[3] *Kethib:* "Jeuel"; *Keri:* "Jeiel"; comp. 1 Chron. ix. 35, and elsewhere.

[4] *Kethib:* "Jehuel"; *Keri:* "Jehiel." The latter form in xxxi. 13 is the *Kethib.*

[5] The Sept. does not express the וְ before עַל־יְדֵי. The Vulg. and Syr. appear to have read it, but render very freely.

[6] *Kethib:* מחצצרים; *Keri:* מחצרים; as in 1 Chron. xv. 24; 2 Chron. v. 12, vii. 6, xiii. 14.

[7] The Sept., Vulg., and apparently the Syr., though it translates rather freely, give up here the Masoretic division of the verse, and join יְכַפֵּר בְּעַד immediately with the following verse. So also R. Kimchi, and after him most of the moderns.

[8] For וַיֹּאכְלוּ, "and they ate," the Sept. appears to have read וַיְכַלּוּ (καὶ συνετέλεσαν).

[9] The וְ before הַלְוִיִּם in some MSS., and in the old versions (Sept., Vulg., Syr.), seems a gloss from ver. 25. Comp. for the asyndeton: "the priests, the Levites," for example, xxiii. 18.

[10] For לשמים some MSS. and old prints have השמים (accus. of direction).

[11] For מַעְשֵׂר קָדָשִׁים the Sept. (ἐπιδέκατα αἰγῶν καὶ ἡγίασαν) seems to have read וְעֵז וְהִקְדִּישׁוּ, and so named "goats" also along with oxen and sheep.

[12] For כּוֹנַנְיָהוּ the *Kethib* has twice (vers. 12, 13) כָּנַנְיָהוּ (so also Luther).

[13] Instead of בְּתוֹךְ־הָאָרֶץ the Sept. has read בְּתוֹךְ־הָעִיר; but the Masoretic reading is to be preferred on real grounds; comp. ver. 30; 2 Kings xx. 20; Sir. xlviii. 17.

[14] For וַיַּעַל עַל־מִגְדָּלוֹת (words which the Sept. leaves untranslated), from the *et exstruxit turres desuper* of the Vulg. וַיַּעַל עָלֶיהָ מִגְדָּלוֹת seems to have originally stood in the text (Ew., Keil, Kamph., etc.).

[15] The *Kethib* מיציאו is miswritten for מִיְּצִיאֵי (contracted from מִן and יְצִיאֵי, constr. pl. of יָצִיא), a form like מִילִידֵי, 1 Chron. xx. 4

[16] Some MSS. place אֹיְבָיו after מִיַּד־כֹּל, a supplement which, unnecessary in itself, is not confirmed by the Sept. or Vulg.

[17] The Sept. (*καὶ μάνδρας εἰς τὰ ποίμνια*) appears to have had another reading; perhaps also the Vulg. (*caulasque pecorum*); comp. Luther's translation: "and folds for the sheep."

[18] *Kethib:* וַיְיַשְּׁרֵם (Pi.); *Keri:* וַיְשָּׁרֵם (Pi. contracted).

EXEGETICAL.

PRELIMINARY REMARK.—While the military and political side of the reign of Hezekiah, its relation to the Assyrian monarchy, its threatened annihilation by the invasion of Sennacherib, with the divine deliverance from this catastrophe, the later sickness and recovery of the king, and his proceedings with the ambassadors of Babylon,—while all this is much more fully narrated in the books of Kings (2 Kings xviii. 8–xx. 9), and in the parallel records of the book of Isaiah, than here, our author, on the contrary, treats much more fully and clearly of the reformation of worship by Hezekiah at the beginning of his reign, his cleansing and reconsecration of the temple, his grand and general celebration of the passover, in which many north Israelites participated, and his other measures for the order and purification of religious life. To the sections concerning this inner religious and theocratic side of the reign of Hezekiah, ch. xxix.–xxxi., correspond in 2 Kings merely the seven introductory verses of ch. xviii., so that almost the whole contents of those three chapters are peculiar to the Chronist.

1. Hezekiah's Beginnings: the Cleansing and Consecration of the Temple: ch. xxix.—*Hezekiah became king.* יְחִזְקִיָּהוּ, the fullest form of this name, signifies "whom Jehovah strengthens," as the somewhat shortened חִזְקִיָּהוּ, Isa. xxxvii. 1 ff., or חִזְקִיָּה, 2 Kings xviii. 1 ff., means "strength of Jehovah." The Assyrian monuments present the form *Ha-za-ki-ya-hu,* corresponding to that of Isaiah; see Schrader, p. 168 ff. Moreover, vers. 1, 2 agree almost throughout with 2 Kings xviii. 1–3. For the chronology see Evangelical and Ethical Reflections, No. 3.—Vers. 3–19. The Cleansing of the Temple.—*He in the first year of his reign, in the first month,* that is, in Nisan, the first month of the ecclesiastical year, not (as Caspari thinks, *Beiträge zur Einleitung in das Buch Jesaia,* p. 111) in the first month of the reign of Hezekiah. How long, that is, how many months, he had reigned when he in the first month of the new year began his measures of reform, remains uncertain; the assumption of Von Gumpach (*Die Zeitrechn. der Babylonier und Assyrer,* p. 99) and Bertheau, that Hezekiah's reign began with the first month (Tisri) of the previous year, appears a bare conjecture in face of the indefiniteness of the statement in our text.—*And renewed them,* repaired them—a renovating process which is more exactly described in 2 Kings xviii. 16 as an overlaying with gold plate.—Ver. 4. *And assembled them in the broad way of the east,* not, perhaps, in the inner court (Bertheau, Kamph.), but in an open area outside the whole temple building, on the south-east or east; comp. Ezra x. 9, Neh. viii. 1, 3, 16.—Ver. 5. *Now sanctify yourselves,* an indispensable prerequisite for a worthy and effectual performance of the business of cleansing the temple; comp. ver. 15 and Ex. xix. 10. On נִדָּה, filthiness, as a designation of idolatry, comp. Lam. i. 17; Ezra ix. 11; and the synonym טֻמְאָה in ver. 16.—Ver. 6. *For our fathers have transgressed*—Ahaz and his contemporaries, for the statement in ver. 7 suits these only. On "to turn the back" (properly "give"), comp. Neh. ix. 29.—Ver. 7. *They have also shut the doors of the porch,* and thus of the whole temple, for only through the porch was there access to the holy and most holy place; comp. xxviii. 24, where also the new altar of burnt-offering erected by Ahaz in the court after the heathenish model is mentioned, which the Chronist, according to our passage ("nor offered burnt-offering"), regarded by no means as a lawful place of worship.—Ver. 8. *And the displeasure of the Lord,* etc.; comp. xix. 2, 10, xxiv. 18, xxxii. 25; and for the following strong terms: "horror, astonishment, and hissing," Deut. xxviii. 25; Jer. xix. 8, xxiv. 9, xxv. 9; Lam. ii. 15; and also ch. xxx. 7. For ver. 9 comp. the Evangelical and Ethical Reflections on the verse before, No. 3.—Ver. 10. *Now it is in my heart;* comp. vi. 7, ix. 1; 1 Chron. xxii. 7, xxviii. 2.—Ver. 11. *My sons,* familiar, persuasive address, as in Prov. i. 8, etc.—*Now delay not,* literally, "withdraw yourselves not" (תִּשָּׁלוּ, Niph. of שָׁלָה; comp. Job xxvii. 8). On *b,* comp. xxvi. 18; 1 Chron. xxiii. 13; Deut. x. 8.—Ver. 12. *Then the Levites arose.* Of the following fourteen names, Joah son of Zimmah, and Kish son of Abdi, occur already in the Levitical genealogy, 1 Chron. vi. 5 f., 29; Mahath, Eden, and Jehiel recur in xxxi. 13–15.—Ver. 13. *And of the sons of Elizaphan, Shimri.* That of this family two Levites are expressly mentioned, is explained by the high repute which Elizaphan or Elzaphan, son of Uzziel, son of Kohath (Ex. vi. 18), enjoyed as prince of the house of Kohath in the time of Moses (Num. iii. 30). Hence their co-ordination here, on the one hand, with the three Levitical head families, and on the other with the three singing families of Asaph, Heman, and Jeduthun.—Ver. 15. *And they gathered their brethren,* the remaining Levites present in Jerusalem.—*At the command of the king by the words of the Lord;* comp. xxx. 12; 1 Chron. xxv. 5. The king's command was founded on the divine prescription of the law.—Ver. 16. *And the priests . . . brought out all the uncleanness . . . into the court,* all the sacrificial vessels employed in idolatry, perhaps also the remains of the idolatrous offerings, and the like. For טֻמְאָה, see on ver. 5; for the brook Kidron, comp. xv. 16, xxx. 14.—Ver. 17. *They began on the first of the first month.* On the first eight days of the month they employed themselves in the cleansing of the court, the eight following in that of the temple itself, so that they had finished on the sixteenth.—Ver. 19. *And all the vessels which King Ahaz . . . cast away;* comp. xi. 14. These are the brazen altar of burnt-offering, the brazen sea, and the lavers on the stands; see

2 Kings xvi. 14, 17. For הֵכִנוּ, abbreviated form of הֲכִינוֹנוּ (1 Chron. xxix. 16), see Ew. § 196, b.—*And behold, they are before the altar of the Lord,* the altar of burnt-offering.—Vers. 20–30. The Sacrifices at the Reconsecration of the Temple. —Ver. 21. *And they brought seven bullocks.* The seven bullocks, rams, and lambs were, as the sequel shows, to serve as a burnt-offering, the seven he-goats, ver. 23, as a sin-offering; comp. Ezra viii. 35.—Ver. 22. *And the priests received the blood,* "took it," as in ver. 16.—Ver. 23. *Laid their hands upon them,* "leaned their hands upon them," comp. Lev. i. 4, from which it moreover follows that this laying on of hands took place also in the burnt-offerings. Perhaps it is specially mentioned only in the case of the sin-offering, because the circumstance that the king and the congregation (naturally its representatives, the princes) directly laid their hands on the sin-offering clearly exhibited the relation of the expiatory act to the whole of Israel; comp. the following verse.—Ver. 24. *And the priests . . . offered their blood for sin upon the altar,* literally, "made their blood to atone"; חִטֵּא, as in Lev. iv. 30, 34, ix. 15. The whole of Israel is not merely the southern kingdom (Judah and Benjamin), but, as xxx. 5 ff. shows, the whole of the twelve tribes; Hezekiah's great expiatory act was intended to affect even the Ephraimites. —Ver. 25. *And he set the Levites . . . with cymbals*; comp. 1 Chron. xv. 16, and with respect to the command of David, ch. viii. 14. For Gad and Nathan as counsellors and assistants of David in his arrangement of the temple service, comp. 1 Chron. xxi., xxix. 29.—*By His prophets,* "by the hand of His prophets," is an explanatory apposition to בְּיַד יְהוָה, and denotes that the divine commandment is accomplished by the instrumentality of the prophets.—Ver. 26. *With the instruments of David,* with the instruments introduced into the divine service by David; comp. 1 Chron. xxiii. 5 and xv. 16.—Ver. 27. *And when the burnt-offering began, the song of the Lord began,* that is, the praise of the Lord by singing with musical accompaniment; comp. 1 Chron. xvi. 42, xxv. 7.—*And after the instruments of David,* literally, at the hands of the instruments of David; comp. 1 Chron. vi. 16, xxv. 2, 3, 6; 2 Chron. xxiii. 18. The instruments of David appear, accordingly, as governing and leading the whole musical performance, according to a view of the relation between singing and music somewhat different from the modern.—Ver. 28. *And the song was sung,* properly, "was singing, sounded." The sense of the whole verse is obvious: during the whole time of the offering the praising musical performance continued. Accordingly ver. 30 also must be understood not as if the Levites had struck up a song of praise on the close of the offering at the command of the king, but in the sense of a supplementary notice of this, that they were Davidic and Asaphic songs, which the Levitical singers performed during the solemnity. Asaph is here called a seer (חֹזֶה), as elsewhere also Heman (1 Chron. xxv. 5) and Jeduthun (2 Chron. xxxv. 15).—*And they praised with gladness,* "even unto gladness," as in 1 Chron. xv. 16.—Vers. 31–36. The Presenting of Sacrifices, Thank-Offerings, and Free-Will Offerings, as the Closing Act of the Consecration.—*Now ye have filled your hand unto the Lord,* "have consecrated yourselves to His service"; comp. xiii. 9; Ex. xxviii. 41, xxxii. 29, etc. The words appear addressed only to the priests; but as the following sentence: "Draw nigh and bring sacrifices and thank-offerings," etc., according to ver. 32 ff., applies to the whole community, this is to be considered as included with the priests, and participating in their office. Our passage belongs, therefore, to the Old Testament testimonies for the universality of the priestly dignity in the kingdom of God, like Ex. xix. 6; Hos. iv. 6; Isa. lxi. 6.—*Sacrifices and thank-offerings,* that is, perhaps, "sacrifices even thank-offerings," or "sacrifices as thank-offerings"; for, according to Lev. vii. 11, 16, the thank-offerings (תּוֹדוֹת) appear as a special class of sacrifices (זְבָחִים or זִבְחֵי שְׁלָמִים), along with vows and free-will offerings.—Ver. 33. *And the consecrated things,* הַקֳּדָשִׁים, the holy things; here the animals presented as thank-offerings. This is clear not only from ver. 32, but also from such passages as xxxv. 13; Neh. x. 34.—Ver. 34. *Only the priests were too few, and they could not flay all the burnt-offerings.* "In private burnt-offerings the flaying of the animal was the business of the worshipper, Lev. i. 6; but in those presented on festivals in the name of the community, it was the business of the priests, in which, because it had no specially priestly character, the Levites might help" (Keil).—On חִזֵּק, "strengthen," here "assist," comp. xxviii. 20; Ezra vi. 22.—*For the Levites were more upright of heart to sanctify themselves than the priests,* who, perhaps because they were nearer the court, were more deeply involved in the idolatrous movement under Ahaz. יִשְׁרֵי לֵב, properly, *rectiores animo,* better inclined, under a more righteous impulse.—Ver. 35. *And also the burnt-offering was in abundance,* the voluntary burnt-offerings, ver. 31 f. (70 oxen, 100 rams, 200 lambs in number), which were added to the proper sacrifice of consecration; and hence the burden of labour on the priests was very great. For the fat pieces next mentioned, comp. Lev. iii. 3–5; for the libations as an accompaniment of the burnt-offering, Num. xv. 1–16.—*And the service of the house of the Lord was established,* prepared, arranged; comp. ver. 36, xxxv. 10, 16. The "service" (עֲבֹדָה) is the regular sacrificial worship in the temple, not its cleansing and consecration, as Berth. thinks.—Ver. 36. *Were glad that God had,* etc.; עַל אֲשֶׁר הֵכִין = עַל הַהֵכִין; comp. 1 Chron. xxvi. 28. This refers not, perhaps, to the willingness of the people, which God effected by His grace (Ramb., Berth.), but the cleansing of the temple and restoration of the true theocratic worship, which was accomplished by the willing part taken by the people.—*For the thing was done suddenly,* with unexpected readiness; comp. ver. 3.

2. The Passover: ch. xxx.—Vers. 1–12. Preparations for it.—*And wrote letters also to Ephraim and Manasseh,* to those belonging to the northern

kingdom, who are here named by their chief tribes; comp. vers. 5, 10.—Ver. 2. *And the king took counsel* (comp. xxv. 17) . . . *to keep the passover in the second month.* Such an after-celebration of the passover is permitted by the law, Num. ix. 6-13, to those who, from Levitical defilement, or being on a journey, were prevented from celebrating it at the right time, on the 14th Nisan. On this decision of the law Hezekiah here rests in transferring the whole celebration from the first to the second month, because, as is expressly stated, ver. 3, those two cases of hindrance (impurity of the priests, and distance of the greater part of the people from Jerusalem) were actually involved. Peculiar, yet destitute of sufficient ground, is the assumption of Hitzig (*Gesch.* p. 219), that the law in Num. ix. 6 ff. was first occasioned by Hezekiah's after-celebration of the passover, even as almost all the laws of the fourth book of Moses originated in the times of Hezekiah.—Ver. 3. *Because the priests had not sanctified themselves sufficiently.* לְמַדַּי, compounded of לְ, מָה, and דַּי, signifies properly, "to that which was enough," *ad sufficientiam*, and, in connection with לֹא, expresses here the thought that a sufficient number of sanctified Levitically clean priests could not be ready in the month of Nisan to celebrate the passover at that time (בָּעֵת הַהִיא); comp. xxix. 34. Observe, moreover, how clearly the contents of this verse, as well as the following, point to this, that the celebration of the passover, of which it treats, was to take place, and did take place, in the next month, after the consecration of the temple, and therefore in the first year of Hezekiah's reign. Comp. at the close of this chapter.—Ver. 5. *And they settled the thing*, resolved upon it; comp. xxxiii. 8; Neh. x. 33. For the proverbial form: "from Beer-sheba even to Dan," to designate the whole territory of Israel, comp. Judg. xx. 1; 1 Sam. iii. 20; 2 Sam. iii. 10, etc.; see above on xix. 4.—*For they had not kept it with a multitude;* so is לֹא לָרֹב most probably to be taken. The celebration should take place with a numerous concourse of people; comp. ver. 13; Ezra iii. 4. The explanation followed by Kimchi, then by Luther, and recently by de Wette: "For not for a long time," is verbally inadmissible (comp. for לָרֹב, in the sense of "in multitude, numerous," also ver. 24). A statement also follows in ver. 26 of the length of time during which the passover had not been celebrated by great numbers.—Ver. 6. *And the posts went*, the royal couriers (whether belonging directly to the king's guards is, notwithstanding xxiii. 1 ff., uncertain); comp. Esth. iii. 13, 15, viii. 14.—*Remaining to you from the hand of the kings of Assyria*, of Tiglath-pileser and his viceroys (archons, eponyms); see on xxviii. 16. Pul (whether different from Tiglath-pileser, comp. on 1 Chron. v. 26) cannot be here intended, because he led no Israelites captive; see 2 Kings xv. 19. Neither can Shalmaneser be meant, as he came to the throne almost at the same time with Hezekiah, and his invasion took place in the sixth year of this king, while that which is here recorded belongs to the first year; see under ver. 27.—Ver. 8. *Now be not stiffnecked like your fathers*, since the time of Jeroboam. On "making the neck stiff" = being stiffnecked, comp. 2 Kings xvii. 14; Neh. ix. 16 f.; on "giving the hand," for yielding oneself, vowing allegiance to, 2 Kings x. 15; Ezra x. 19; Ezek. xvii. 18 (as also 1 Chron. xxix. 24, Lam. v. 6, "submit to"); for the close of the verse, xxix. 10.—*Your brethren and your children shall find compassion before*, literally, "shall be for compassion before your captors;" comp. Neh. i. 11.—Ver. 10. *And unto Zebulun;* thus not quite to the extreme north border (not literally even to Dan, ver. 5). Observe the concrete historical character of this notice, by no means favouring the suspicion of a pure fiction of these reports on the part of our author. The messengers also might very easily reach Zebulun (and the southern Asher, ver. 11) in the interval between the 16th Nisan (xxix. 17) and the 14th of the following month; they could scarcely have travelled to the more northern Naphtali, next to Dan (Laish), and North Asher. But these most northern parts of the country had been quite wasted and depopulated by Tiglath-pileser; see 2 Kings xv. 29. That which is here stated (vers. 10, 11) agrees still less with the hypothesis of Caspari and Keil, that all that is related in our chapter happened in the time after the fall of Samaria (see under ver. 27), as the artificial attempts at adaptation by Keil show.—Ver. 12. *Also the hand of God was upon Judah to give them one heart.* The phrase: יַד הָאֱלֹהִים הָיְתָה בְּ, here *sensu bono* of the blessed effect of the divine power (comp. Ezra viii. 22), otherwise usually in the sense of judicial punishment (Ex. ix. 3; Deut. ii. 15, etc.).—*By the word of the Lord;* comp. xxix. 15.—Vers. 13-22. The Festival itself.—*Took away the altars;* those erected by Ahaz for idolatrous burnt-offerings and incense; comp. xxviii. 24.—Ver. 15. *And the priests and the Levites were ashamed;* a clause referring to ver. 3, which points by way of supplement to this, that the present full participation of the Levitical spirituality, in contrast with the former deficiency (especially with regard to the priests, xxix. 34), was owing to the feeling of shame meanwhile awakened in the whole order on account of their former participation in idolatry.—Ver. 16. *And they stood in their place.* עֹמֶד, "place, stand," as xxxv. 10; Dan. viii. 17, 18.—*After their rule;* comp. 1 Chron. vi. 17.—*The priests sprinkling the blood from the hand of the Levites*, that is, the Levites handed them the blood to sprinkle on the altar. That the Levites here did this, whereas this handing of the blood was the part of the several worshipping householders (xxxv. 6; Ezra vi. 20), is explained, ver. 17, by pointing out that only the Levites were as yet all properly cleansed, and not the remaining multitude (רַבַּת here, and ver. 18, a neuter substantive before the preposition, and not an adverb, as in Ps. cxx. 6).—Ver. 18. *Many from Ephraim and Manasseh, Issachar and Zebulun.* The Chronist reports this not from "an excess of national feeling," as if he wished to represent the whole northern kingdom as subjected to the Jewish king Hezekiah (H. Schultz, *Theologie des Alten T.* ii. 309), but simply because some of the tribes of the northern kingdom, then governed by Hosea, and already on the verge of total ruin, had sent representatives to the passover of Hezekiah, to signify that the feeling of national guilt was awakened in them in all its strength. That in ver. 11 the tribes of Asher, Manasseh, and Zebulun, but here Ephraim, Manasseh, Issachar, and Zebulun, are named as "humbled" (returning penitent to the theocratic centre of worship), appears to rest on definite historical grounds, the nature of which we cannot now determine.—*Yet they ate the passover not as it was written*, as Levitically unclean, and thus contrary to the precept, Num. ix. 6; comp. Josephus, *de B. Jud.* vi. 9. 3, and under ver. 26.—*The good Lord pardon.* With these closing words of ver. 18 (יהוה הטוב יכפר בעד) are to be immediately connected, notwithstanding the Masoretic division of the verses, the initial words of ver. 19: "Every one that hath prepared his heart to seek God." בְּעַד stands thus before the relative sentence, ver. 19 [rather before כָּל־], without אֲשֶׁר (as אל, 1 Chron. xv. 12). On כִּפֵּר, in the sense of forgiving, comp. Ps. lxv. 4; Lev. xvi. 6, 11.—*Though not in the cleanness of the sanctuary*, though they did not strictly comply with the legal prescriptions concerning the purity to be observed in approaching the sanctuary. A remarkable mildness and almost evangelical freedom of view are expressed in these words.—Ver. 20. *And healed the people*, forgave their guilt, healed them in an ethical respect; comp. Ps. xli. 5; Hos. xiv. 5; Jer. iii. 22. The healing of disease or of death, that was to be apprehended as punishment for their guilt (Lev. xv. 31), is scarcely intended (against Berth. and Kamph.).—Ver. 21. *And the sons of Israel that were in Jerusalem*, "were found"; comp. xxix. 29, xxxi. 1.—*With instruments of might to the Lord*, instruments by which they ascribed might to the Lord, glorified His might (comp. Ps. xxix. 1), therefore with instruments for praising the might of the Lord. Interesting, but not quite certain, is the interpretation of Kamphausen, who takes בִּכְלֵי עֹז by itself in the sense: "with instruments of might," that is, with loud sound.—Ver. 22. *And Hezekiah spake to the heart of all the Levites*, spake hearty, loving, encouraging words to them.—*Who had good understanding of the Lord*, of the service of the Lord.—*And they ate the feast seven days.* We are scarcely to read with the Sept. (see Crit. Note): "And they completed the feast;" for the reading: "eat the feast," appears simply modelled after the known: "eat the passover," as the following: "offering sacrifices of peace," clearly shows (comp. also Ps. cxviii. 27). Moreover, the collective worshippers, not merely the Levites and priests, are the subject.—*And confessing to the Lord God of their fathers*, namely, with praise and thanksgiving—not, perhaps, with penitent confession of their guilt, as some of the ancients thought. הַתּוֹדָה is quite the ἐξομολογεῖσθαι of the Hellenistic Greek (and so of the Sept. in our passage).—Vers. 23–27. The Feast of Seven Days after the Passover.—*Resolved to keep* ("make") *other seven days with gladness.* שִׂמְחָה, adverbial accusative for בְּשִׂמְחָה.—Ver. 24. *For Hezekiah . . . gave to the congregation* (properly, heaved, gave as a heave-offering; comp. xxxv. 7) *a thousand bullocks*, etc.; that is, the king and princes had contributed victims so liberally for the passover, that they had not consumed the whole during the seven days of the feast, but had still provision for so long an after-feast.—*And a great many priests sanctified themselves;* the extraordinary abundance of offerings could thus be overtaken; comp. ver. 3, xxix. 34.—Ver. 25. *And the strangers that came from the land of Israel, and that dwelt in Judah.* These strangers (גֵּרִים) from Israel and Judah are here, as certainly as they were distinct from "the congregation that came out of Israel" (= Ephraim), that is, from the Ephraimites mentioned vers. 11, 18, actually "strangers," that is, proselytes. It is otherwise in xv. 9, where those dwelling as strangers among the Jews, from Ephraim and Manasseh and Simeon, are simply the Israelites that have migrated thence.—Ver. 26. *For since the days of Solomon . . . was not the like in Jerusalem*, no so fair and sublime a festival celebrated by so great a multitude. But the point of comparison is perhaps not any passover under Solomon, but rather the feast of the consecration of the temple under this king (vii. 1–10). This resembles the passover of Hezekiah in this respect, that, with the feast of tabernacles following, it lasted also fourteen days. Because this only is intended, and not any passover of Solomon, there is no contradiction between our passage, or in general between that which is depicted in our chapter and xxxv. 18, and 2 Kings xxiii. 22. If in the latter passage it is said of Josiah's passover: "There was not holden such a passover from the days of the Judges," this remark refers, in the first place, to the purity and legitimacy of the feast; and in this respect the present celebration by Hezekiah was defective, just as our author has expressly acknowledged.—Ver. 27. *And the priests* (and) *the Levites arose;* comp. Crit. Note. That the benediction of the priests was heard, and actually penetrated to His (God's) dwelling in the heaven, our historian might conclude with sufficient certainty, from the further gladness and elevation of heart which he had to recount in the two following chapters of Hezekiah's reign (in its inner as well as outer aspect).

On the date of Hezekiah's passover, first Keil (*Komment. zu den Büchern der Könige*, 1845, p. 515 f.), then Caspari (*Beiträge zur Einleitung in das Buch Jesaiä*, p. 109 ff.), and again Keil (*Komment. zur Chron.* p. 343 ff.), laid down the opinion that it was held not in the first year of his reign, in the next month after the cleansing of the temple, but considerably later, namely, after the destruction of the kingdom of the ten tribes, in his sixth year. Against this assumption, and for the usual view, according to which the Chronist in our chapter means to report something immediately following the feast of the consecration described in ch. xxix., speak—1. The ו *consec.* in וַיִּשְׁלַח at the beginning of ver. 1; 2. The statement in ver. 3, that "the priests had not sanctified themselves sufficiently," which clearly refers to xxix. 34, and does not at all permit the interposition of a period of six years between the two chapters; 3. The naming of the second month in ver. 2, which is certainly to be understood from xxix. 3, 17 (the "first month," that is, Nisan, in the first year of his reign), and therefore to be referred to the first year of Hezekiah. To these in themselves decisive grounds, which Keil vainly endeavours in a long discussion to invalidate, are to be added, as further cogent arguments—4. The circumstance that our author, if he had actually meant to represent the passover as instituted after the fall of Samaria and the destruction of the northern kingdom, and even with reference to the condition and necessity of the population occasioned by this catastrophe, must have expressly said so, as such an important motive for including the Ephraimites as partakers in the feast could not have been passed over in silence; 5. The circumstance that the manner in which these northern guests and their seats are mentioned in vers. 6, 10 f. and 18 suits only the time after the invasion of Tiglath-pileser, not that after the fall of Samaria (see on these passages, especially ver. 11); 6. The circumstance that the description given in vers. 10-12 of the preparations for the festival, compared with the opening of the description of the feast itself in ver. 13, makes only a short duration of these preparations probable; 7. And lastly, the circumstance that the appearance of a not inconsiderable number of communicants from the northern kingdom agrees very well with that which is attested in 2 Kings xvii. 2 of the comparatively pious and theocratic character of Hosea, the last king of Ephraim, and, on the contrary, can scarcely be reconciled with the report there, ver. 24 ff., given concerning the moral and religious condition of the population left in the northern kingdom after the defeat of Hosea and the fall of Samaria. The usual assumption, which makes the temple consecration and the passover to take place in immediate succession in the first year of Hezekiah, appears from all this to be most agreeable to the text, and alone truly corresponding with the historical relations that have to be taken into account.

3. Further Religious Reforms of Hezekiah: ch. xxxi.—On ver. 1, comp. 2 Kings xviii. 4, where, however, on the one hand, the destruction of the images and altars also in Ephraim and Manasseh is not mentioned; on the other hand, the breaking of the figure of the brazen serpent (Nehushtan) is narrated, which our report does not expressly mention.—*All Israel that were present;* comp. xxx. 21. For the statues (monuments) and asherim, comp. on xiv. 2.—*And in Ephraim and Manasseh completely.* With reference to Ephraim and Manasseh, that is, the northern kingdom (comp. xxx. 10), this "completely" (עַד לְכַלֵּה) is naturally to be understood *cum grano salis*, and not to be pressed as a strictly literal statement. The report that in Manasseh and Ephraim also the places of idolatrous worship were removed, could scarcely, on account of 2 Kings xvii. 24 ff., be brought into harmony with the assumption of Keil that these facts are to be placed after 722 B.C.—Ver. 2. *And Hezekiah appointed . . . after their courses*, according to the classification originating with David; comp. 1 Chron. xxiv.; 2 Chron. viii. 14.—*Every man according to his service*, properly, "at the mouth of his service"; comp. Num. vii. 5, 7.—*In the gates of the camp of the Lord*, in the temple as well as in the court of the priests; comp. 1 Chron. ix. 18 ff.—Ver. 3. *And the king's portion of his property for burnt-offerings*, that is, the king furnished what he had to contribute to the burnt-offering in victims out of his possession (which is described underneath, xxxii. 27 ff., as very great). Comp. the prescriptions of the law that here come into account, Num. xxviii. 3 ff., xxix. 1 ff.—Ver. 4. *And he said to the people . . . to give the portion of the priests and Levites*, namely, the firstlings and tithes of the increase of the cattle and the field; see Ex. xxiii. 19; Num. xviii. 12, 21 ff.; Lev. xxvii. 30-33. The motive, "that they might be stedfast in the law of the Lord," expresses the thought, that in order to fulfil their official duties they must be able to live free and untrammelled by earthly cares; comp. Neh. xiii. 10 ff.; 1 Cor. ix. 4 ff.; 2 Thess. iii. 9; 1 Tim. v. 17 f.—Ver. 5. *And when the word came forth*, properly, "spread forth"; comp. Job i. 10. The "sons of Israel" there mentioned are first only the inhabitants of Jerusalem, as ver. 6 shows, for there first is mention made of the remaining "sons of Israel" (immigrants from the northern kingdom) and "sons of Judah."—Ver. 6. *And the tithe of holy things consecrated unto the Lord their God.* If in Num. xviii. 8 ff. not tithe (מַעֲשֵׂר) but heave-offerings (תְּרוּמוֹת) of all consecrated things, that is, of all the consecrated gifts of the Israelites, are said to fall to the Levites, this difference from our statement is only apparent, not warranting any emendation of the text after the reading of the Sept. (ἐπιδέκατα αἰγῶν, καὶ, etc.; see Crit. Note). This is merely a diversity of the phrase; what is called, Num. xviii., "terumoth," is here designated tithe, because the terumoth were in like manner "a remnant of that which was consecrated to the Lord, as the tithe was a remnant of all the cattle and field produce" (rightly Keil, against Berth. and Kamph.).—Ver. 7. *In the third month they began to lay down*, or found; to form the heaps by gathering together the gifts in grain. The third month, in which Pentecost falls, is the time of the finished harvest, as the seventh month (with the feast of tabernacles) is that of the finished fruit and wine harvest. For the form לְיסּוֹד, with dag. in ס, see Ew. § 245 *a*.—Vers. 9-19. The Application and Preservation of the Collected Gifts.—*Inquired . . . concerning the heaps*, he inquired how it came that so great a quantity of gifts was accumulated. Only to this meaning of his question does the following answer of the high priest correspond, especially the closing sentence of it.—Ver. 10. *And Azariah the chief priest.* Whether this be the same as the Azariah occurring, xxvi. 17, in the history of Uzziah, forty years before, is at least very uncertain.—*And this great store is left*, literally, "and that which is left (forms) this great store." Perhaps וְנוֹתָר simply is to be read instead of וְהַנּוֹתָר (Kamph.).—Ver. 11. *And Hezekiah said to prepare in the house of the Lord*, perhaps not new store-rooms (לְשָׁכוֹת, as 1 Chron. ix. 26), but only a portion of those already built by Solomon (1 Kings vi. 5) for the reception of the stores (הָכִין, as 1 Kings vi. 19).—Ver. 12. *And they brought in the offerings*, the first-fruits, ver. 5. On the word "faithfully," conscientiously, comp. xix. 9.—*And over them*, over the first-

fruits, tithe, and consecrated things. For the name Conanjahu, comp. the Crit. Note; for the term "second" (next after him), מִשְׁנֶה, see 1 Chron. v. 12; 2 Kings xxv. 18.—Ver. 13. *And Jehiel, and Azaziah, and Nahath.* Two of these names, Jehiel and Nahath, occurred also in xxix. 12, 14; whether they refer to the same persons is doubtful.—*Overseers under Conaniah,* literally, "at the hand of Conaniah."—*By the appointment of Hezekiah,* or by his order. The Azariah, "ruler of the house of God," named along with the king is the high priest named ver. 10 (comp. 1 Chron. ix. 11).—Ver. 14. *And Kore . . . the porter toward the east;* comp. 1 Chron. ix. 18. It was his part to distribute "the offering of the Lord," the portion of the peace-offering belonging to the Lord, and by him transferred to the priests (Lev. vii. 14, 32, x. 14 f.), "and the most holy things," the part of the sin and trespass offerings to be eaten by the priests in the temple (Lev. vi. 10, 22, vii. 6).—Ver. 15. *And by him* (properly, "at his hand," ver. 13), under him, under his oversight.—*With truth* (comp. ver. 12). This the Vulg. perhaps rightly connects with the following words: "conscientiously to give," though against the accents. The object of this "giving" is that share of firstlings, tithes, and consecrated things which the Levites dwelling in the priestly cities were entitled by law to receive.—Ver. 16. *Beside the register of males,* with the exception of the registered males from three years old and upwards who have "entered into the house of the Lord," that is, are consecrated to the temple service in Jerusalem, and are therefore otherwise provided for (exempted from the provision in the priestly cities when they were at home); comp., for example, Samuel, etc.—*For the rate of each day;* לִדְבַר־יוֹם בְּיוֹמוֹ, as viii. 13 f.; Neh. xi. 23. —Ver. 17 is, like ver. 16, a parenthesis, referring to the registers of the priests and Levites.—*And the register of the priests.* וְאֵת, according to Ew. § 277, *d;* comp. Neh. ix. 34. On the twentieth year of the Levites, at the beginning of their official functions, comp. 1 Chron. xxiii. 24, 27.—Ver. 18 is connected with ver. 15, after the two parentheses vers. 16 and 17. With the dative there, לַאֲחֵיהֶם, corresponds the וּלְהִתְיַחֵשׂ, which likewise depends on לָתֵת, "to give to their brethren," *and to the register of all their little ones for all the congregation.* This לְכָל־קָהָל applies to the whole community of the Levites, including wives and children, not merely to the priestly order (as S. Schmidt, Ramb., Kamph. intend).—*For in their faithfulness they sanctified themselves in the holy thing,* בֶּאֱמוּנָתָם, as 1 Chron. ix. 22. The "sanctifying themselves" (הִתְקַדֵּשׁ) refers to the disinterested and righteous distribution of the "holy thing," that is, the offerings which they were entitled to receive.—Ver. 19. *And for the sons of Aaron . . . in the fields of the suburbs of their cities;* comp. Deut. xxv. 34; Num. xxxv. 5.—*Were appointed men who were expressed by name,* men of repute; comp. xxviii. 15; 1 Chron. xii. 31. These officers, according to what follows, had the charge of the Levitical and priestly families occupying the land around the priestly cities, as those mentioned in ver. 15 had the charge of the priests and Levites in these cities.—Vers. 20, 21. Close of the Report of Hezekiah's Reforms in Worship.—*And did that which was good and right* (comp. xiv. 1) *and true before the Lord;* הָאֱמֶת, as in xxxii. 1; Zech. viii. 19.—*And in every work which he began . . . to seek his God,* or also, "seeking his God," while he sought Him; comp. xxvi. 5; Ezra vi. 21.

4. Sennacherib's Expedition against Jerusalem, and End: ch. xxxii. 1–23. Comp. the full parallel account in 2 Kings xviii. 13–xix. 37, and in Isa. xxxvi., xxxvii., to which the present narrative, notwithstanding its parenetic, rhetorical brevity, makes some not unimportant additions. With the three parallel delineations is to be compared the full Assyriologic commentary of Schrader, pp. 168–212.—*After these events and this faithfulness, Sennacherib,* etc., properly, "Sancherib" (Sept.: Σενναχηρείμ in Chronicles, Σενναχηρίβ in 2 Kings and Isaiah), the *Sin-ahi-irib* or *Sin-ahi-ir-ba* ("Sin," the moon-god, "gives the brothers much") of the Assyrian inscriptions; according to the Assyrian canon of sovereigns, the son, reigning 705–681 B.C., and successor of Sargon, the successor of Shalmaneser and conqueror of Samaria; comp. Evangelical and Ethical Reflections, No. 3.—*And thought to break into them for himself,* to take them; comp. xxi. 17.—Ver. 2. *And his face was for war against Jerusalem;* comp. xx. 3; Luke ix. 53.—Ver. 3. *Took counsel . . . to stop the waters of the fountains,* not to close them up wholly, but to cover them over (Luther, cover), and draw away their waters by subterranean channels.—Ver. 4. *And they stopped . . . and the brook that flowed through the land,* the Gihon, the brook of the valley of Ben-hinnom; comp. ver. 30; 2 Kings xx. 20.—*Why should the kings of Assyria . . . find much water?* On the phrase, comp. Isa. v. 4; for the plural "kings," above on xxviii. 16.—Ver. 5. *And he strengthened himself* (וַיִּתְחַזֵּק), as xv. 8, xxiii. 1. —*And built up all the wall that was broken;* comp. Neh. iv. 1; Prov. xxv. 28.—*And raised it to the towers,* or, raised its towers, according to the probably original reading; see Crit. Note. The Masoretic text gives the quite unsuitable meaning, "and rose upon the towers," or, "and brought to the towers" (the wall? or the war engines?). —*And another wall without,* he built or repaired. This refers to the wall enclosing the lower city, or Acra, which already existed, according to Isa. xxii. 11, the repair of which is here noticed. For Millo, comp. on 1 Chron. xi. 8; for the weapons made to defend these fortifications,—arrows, missiles, and shields,—comp. xxiii. 10, xxvi. 14.—Ver. 6. *And gathered them to him in the broad way at the gate of the city;* whether on the same open area at the gate as that mentioned xxix. 4, toward the east, must, from the indefiniteness of the expression, remain uncertain; comp. also Neh. viii. 1, 16.—*And spake to their heart;* comp. xxx. 22.—Ver. 7. *For with us is more than with him;* comp. 2 Kings vi. 16 and the following verse, which gives the particulars how there is "more" (רַב, not "a greater," as Luther translates) with Hezekiah and the Israelites than with the enemy. On "an arm of flesh" as a designation of human impotence and apparent power

comp. Isa. xxxi. 3, Jer. xvii. 5, Ps. lvi. 5; on "to fight our battles," 1 Sam. viii. 20, xviii. 17.—Vers. 9-19. Sennacherib's Advance to Jerusalem. Comp. the more ample account, 2 Kings xviii. 17-36.—*And he himself stood against Lachish;* comp. xxv. 27.—*And all his power with him,* literally, "all his sovereignty" (מֶמְשַׁלְתּוֹ); comp. Isa. xxxiv. 1.—Ver. 10. *Whereon do ye trust?* literally, "whereon are ye trusting and sitting in restraint?" (distress; comp. Deut. xxviii. 53 ff.; 2 Kings xxiv. 10, xxv. 2; Ezek. iv. 7).—Ver. 11. *Doth not Hezekiah mislead you?* literally, "is not Hezekiah misleading you (מַסִּית, as 2 Kings xviii. 32), to deliver you to die by hunger?" etc. —On ver. 12, comp. 2 Kings xviii. 22; on vers. 13-15, comp. 2 Kings xviii. 35, Isa. xxxvi. 20, xxxvii. 11-13.—Ver. 16. *And his servants spake yet more,* the servants already, ver. 9, mentioned, whose Assyrian titles (Tartan, Rabsaris, and Rabshakeh, 2 Kings xviii. 17; on which comp. Schrader's illustrations, p. 198 ff.) our author thinks fit not to adduce, as he omits the whole contents of their blasphemous speeches.—Ver. 17. *And he wrote a letter.* This was, according to 2 Kings xix. 14, at a later period, after Rabshakeh had reported to him the obstinate resistance of the Jewish people; whereas the speech here reported in ver. 18 of the servants of Sennacherib in the Jewish tongue is there (in 2 Kings) addressed to the Jews at the same time with the first negotiation. Our author has apparently traced the course of things in a real rather than a chronological order, because his aim was to exhibit an impressive advance in the steps (first a speech of the servants in the Assyrian tongue, then a letter of Sennacherib to Hezekiah, and lastly a demand to surrender in the Jewish tongue), from the same rhetorical motive that led him also before, on the occasion of the war with Syria and Ephraim, xxviii. 16 ff., to co-ordinate the facts not so much in a temporal as in a real sequence.—Vers. 20-23. Hezekiah's and Isaiah's Prayer, and the Divine Help; comp. 2 Kings xix. 14-35 ff.; Isa. xxxvii. 15-19.—*And for this,* עַל־זֹאת, on account of this railing on the God of Israel, which they must have heard.—Ver. 21. *And the Lord sent an angel;* comp. 2 Kings xix. 35 ff., and Bähr on this passage. The "valiant heroes" destroyed by the angel are the common soldiers (comp. xvii. 14), along with whom are then specially named the "leaders and captains" (officers and generals). On "with shame of face," comp. Ezra ix. 7, Ps. xliv. 16; on "they that came out of his own bowels"=sons, comp. Gen. xv. 4, xxv. 23, 2 Sam. vii. 12, xvi. 11; and see the Crit. Note.—Ver. 22. *And defended them around,* literally, "led them around," וַיְנַהֲלֵם (for which Berth. and Kamph., because the word is omitted in the Syr. and Arab., think ought to be read וַיָּנַח לָהֶם, "and gave them rest around"); comp. נִהַל, in the sense of protecting, Ps. xxxi. 4; Isa. xlix. 10, li. 18, etc.—Ver. 23. *And many brought a gift to the Lord;* comp. xvii. 11, xxvi. 8; 2 Kings xx. 12. Among the "many" seem to be reckoned, as the following clause shows, members of the neighbouring nations, who had been delivered by the helpful interposition of the God of the Jews from the same calamity of war and danger of ruin.

5. Sickness, Remaining Reign, and End of Hezekiah: vers. 24-33.—*In those days Hezekiah was sick.* Considerably fuller in 2 Kings xx. 1-11 and Isa. xxxviii.—Ver. 25. *And Hezekiah repaid not according to the benefit done to him,* literally, "according to the benefit in him"; comp. Ps. cxvi. 12.—*For his heart became proud,* literally, "lifted itself up"; comp. xxvi. 16. Wherein the proud uplifting consisted, namely, in the boastful exhibition of his treasures to the ambassadors of Babylon (2 Kings xx. 12 ff.), is not here said, but is briefly indicated in ver. 31; neither is the manner in which "indignation came upon him" (comp. xix. 10; 1 Chron. xxvii. 24), namely, by a prophetic warning and announcement of punishment (Isa. xxxix. 5-7; 2 Kings xx. 16 ff.), more particularly defined. The mode of narrative in our section is generally that of the epitome. On ver. 26 comp. Isa. xxxix. 8; 2 Kings xx. 19. —Vers. 27-31. Hezekiah's Riches, and Building of Cities and Water-courses.—*And Hezekiah had very much riches;* comp. 2 Kings xx. 13, and the earlier accounts in the reigns of David (1 Chron. xxix. 28), Solomon (2 Chron. i. 12 ff.), and Jehoshaphat (xviii. 1). Besides the metals themselves, are mentioned also among his treasures spices (as Dan. xi. 8) and "shields," that is, costly gilded weapons and the like (comp. Isa. xxxix. 2).—Ver. 28. *And storehouses for the increase of corn.* מִסְכְּנוֹת (*p. transpos. lit.* for מִכְנְסוֹת, from כנס, heap up), magazines; comp. Ex. i. 11; 1 Kings ix. 19; 2 Chron. viii. 4.—*And stalls for all kinds of cattle,* literally, "for all cattle and cattle." אֻרָוֹת, "stalls," properly, "racks;" comp. the only orthographically different אֻרְיוֹת, ix. 25, and at the close of our verse, אוֹרוֹת, which seems to mean folds. But perhaps the last clause is corrupt, and instead of "flocks for the folds," rather (with the Sept. and Luther) an inversion of the terms is to be assumed; see Crit. Note.—Ver. 29. *And he made him cities,* עָרִים, perhaps watchtowers for the keepers of the cattle; comp. on xxvi. 10 and 2 Kings xvii. 9.—*And possession of flocks and herds in abundance;* comp. Job i. 3; for רְכוּשׁ, possession, xxxi. 3.—Ver. 30. *This Hezekiah stopped;* see on vers. 3, 4.—*And led it straight down to the west of the city of David,* led it, the water of the brook Gihon, flowing by the city on the east, by a subterranean channel westward into the city.—Ver. 31. *And so in the case of the ambassadors of the princes of Babel.* Instead of וְכֵן (that cannot be rendered, with Luther and others, in an adversative sense by "but" or "though") we expect וְלֹא or רַק לֹא, "only not." But the author does not intend to represent the interview with the ambassadors of Babylon as an exception to the otherwise prosperous career of the king, but rather as a confirmation of that which is said in this respect; and especially as Hezekiah was not punished for the perversity of his conduct at that time, but only humbled, and for himself, at least, spared the deserved judgment of God (comp. ver. 26). The plural "princes of Babel," instead of the sing., which, according to 2 Kings xx. 12 ff., we might expect, is perhaps

to be interpreted as the term kings in xxviii. 16, xxx. 6, xxxii. 4. On the king Merodach-baladan, and on the chronology of this event, see Evangelical and Ethical Reflections, No. 3.—Vers. 32, 33. Close of the History of Hezekiah.—*And his kindness,* literally, "kindnesses" (חֲסָדִים, otherwise than vi. 42); comp. rather Neh. xiii. 14 (against Keil).—Ver. 33. *And they buried him in the height* (or also "the ascent"; comp. xx. 16) *of the sepulchres of the sons of David,* that is, in a place higher than the previous tombs of the kings, as in these, perhaps, there was no longer sufficient space.—*And gave him glory,* namely, by the burning of spices and the like, as at the death of Asa (xvi. 14; comp. xxi. 19).

EVANGELICAL AND ETHICAL REFLECTIONS AND APOLOGETIC REMARKS (ESPECIALLY WITH REGARD TO CHRONOLOGY) ON CH. XXIX.–XXXII.

1. The relation of our author concerning the history of Hezekiah includes in itself two unequal parts of tolerably heterogeneous materials,—a detailed report of the reforms in worship with which the king began his reign (xxix.-xxxi.), and an excerpted and compressed description of the chief warlike events and other public acts and occurrences of his reign (xxxii.). This plan, combining the supplementing with the excerpting process, clearly shows that it is Hezekiah the reformer of worship, and not the warlike prince and pious ruler, that he intends first and chiefly to depict. As a reformer of worship, Hezekiah deserves indeed to be held up along with Josiah, among all the kings from Solomon to the exile. The thoroughgoing spirit, strong faith, and energy displayed in his measures leaves all that had been formerly undertaken by Asa and Jehoshaphat far behind; and even the later Josiah, notwithstanding the character of stricter legality which his measures bore, cannot compare with him, inasmuch as the reforming activity of Hezekiah prepared the way for his own, and thus he stood, as it were, on the shoulders of Hezekiah, and had to look up to what was accomplished by the latter as his model. Between those less efficient and less decided predecessors and this successor, more zealous indeed, but less favoured by fortune, and aiming at no perpetuity of his labours, Hezekiah stands as the greatest hero of faith, as the purest evangelical character among the Jewish kings of the Old Testament. His work forms, by virtue of his powerful, ruthlessly stringent opposition to idolatry, and his honourable zeal for the law, coupled with sincere devotedness of heart to God, a striking typical parallel to that of the evangelical princes in the age of the Reformation,—John the Constant, Philip the Magnanimous, Edward VI., Gustavus Vasa, etc.; while his predecessors, Asa, Jehoshaphat, and Joash, correspond merely to the better disposed kings and emperors of the Middle Ages maintaining a certain independence towards Rome (as Frederic Barbarossa, Louis IX. of France, etc.); but in Josiah is presented the type of such *epigoni* of the more potent manifestations of the Reformation period as Ernest the Pious of Saxe Gotha, Frederic IV. of Denmark, etc. So far as such parallels between Israelitish and Christian history are allowable,—but that they should be instituted with great precaution and the most careful avoidance of the imminent danger of arbitrary trifling, is shown by very many warning examples, especially in the region of the Roman Catholic theological literature of recent times,[1]—it is natural to set beside the great reformatory activity of King Hezekiah the contemporary movement of a powerful reform and revival of the whole religious and moral life by such heroes of prophecy as Isaiah, Micah (and as probably an older Zechariah, author of Zech. ix.-xi.), and to suppose the one conditioned and supplemented by the other,—his action as the renovator of the religious life and the external theocratic order and discipline, and the endeavour of these prophetic men after the purification of the religious consciousness and the quickening of the moral conscience of their people. For certainly his religious reform would not have been practicable without the co-operation of this contemporaneous life-reform by his prophetic friends and counsellors; and we can as little separate the royal reformer Hezekiah from the royal seer, as those princes of the Reformation age from the Reformers Luther, Melanchthon, Bugenhagen, Calvin, etc.[2] Indeed, the circle of those wise men around Hezekiah, to whom, according to Prov. xxv. 1, was due the then completed collection of the old Solomonic proverbial literature, and in reference to whom Hezekiah himself has been called the Pisistratus of the Israelitish literature (Delitzsch, *Kommentar über den Psalter*, ii. 377), we may well assert to be a moment of the typical parallelism, and regard the work of these men as a type of the humanists contemporary with the Reformers, and often lending them support.

2. That in our author these manifestations, contemporaneous with Hezekiah, and co-operating with him, the importance of which certainly should not be undervalued, retire into the background, and that he mentions the prophet Isaiah only once in passing (xxxii. 20), and those wise "men of Hezekiah" not at all, corresponds exactly with his character as a historian abiding always by the priestly and Levitical point of view. The credibility of his narrative cannot be disputed on account of this onesidedness. A great number of highly definite and concrete statements in the chapters peculiar to him attest the character of their contents as well founded, and free from any suspicion of fiction. Thus the names of the fourteen Levites in xxix. 12–14

[1] We refer especially to the writings of Phil. Krementz (present Bishop of Braunsberg),—*The Old Testament as the Type of the New* (Coblenz, 1863); *Israel the Type of the Church, attempt to elucidate the history of Christianity by the typical history of Israel* (Mainz, 1865); *The Gospel in the Book of Genesis, or the Life of Jesus typified by the History of the Patriarchs Abraham, Isaac, Jacob, and Joseph* (Coblenz, 1867); *The Life of Jesus the Prophecy of the History of His Church* (Freiburg, 1869): likewise to such works as that of the barefooted Carmelite Carl St. Aloysius, *The History of Man, a Divine Work of Creation on the Region of the Moral World* (Würzburg, 1861), and so forth. A useful counterpart to the extravagances of these works, with their parallelistic trifling, is pointed out by W. J. Thiersch: *Genesis, according to its Moral and Prophetical Import* (Frankfurt a M. 1869).

[2] Compare the remarks of Rudelbach on the typical relation of the Old Testament prophets to the Reformers in several of his writings; for example, in *Reformation, Lutherthum, und Union*; in his biography of Savonarola (p. 283 ff.); in the treatise, *Die Grundtwig'sche Theorie und die Lutherische Kirche* (in the *Zeitschrift für die gesammte lutherische Theologie*, 1857, i. p. 12). To this should be added the far and wide custom since the Reformation itself (for example, in Zwinglius in his letter *ad Zasium*, in Melanchthon, etc.) of drawing parallels between Luther and such prophets of the first rank as Elijah, Isaiah, etc. Comp. also Ewald, *Geschichte des Volkes Israel*, iii. 1, pp. 321, 341.

rest as undoubtedly on historical tradition as those of the others in xxxi. 12–15. And as little as these names can be invented, will that which is related, xxx. 1 ff., 10 f., 18 ff., and xxxi. 1, concerning the participation of inhabitants of the kingdom of the ten tribes in Hezekiah's religious acts and reforms bear a fictitious character. The authenticity of these statements is liable to no manner of doubt, view them chronologically as we will—whether we refer them, with Keil and Caspari (see on xxx. 27), to events that happened after 722 B.C., or, with the majority of expositors, assign them a place in the first years of Hezekiah's reign. The excerpt also from 2 Kings xviii.–xx. and Isa. xxxvi.–xxxix., which he presents in ch. xxxii., proves, by its essential agreement with these fuller parallels, the conscientiousness and reliableness of the procedure of our author. Where he presents smaller supplements to the reports there,—as, for example, in his accounts of the fortifications and measures of defence by Hezekiah in ver. 5 (comp. ver. 30),—these supplements bear in themselves their warrant as actual and trustworthy. And where he, in accordance with his rather real than chronological grouping of events, makes alterations in the order of the facts to be related, as in vers. 16–18 (comp. also vers. 24–31), there never results a representation strictly contrary to history. We are to note, moreover, the circumstance, significant of his theocratic idealizing tendency, and recalling analogous omissions in the history of the reigns of David, Solomon, and Jehoshaphat, that he passes over various incidents less favourable to the character of Hezekiah as a specially fortunate and illustrious ruler; for example, the facts that Sennacherib not only besieged but took many Jewish cities (comp. xxxii. 1 with 2 Kings xviii. 13); that Hezekiah was compelled to pay a large tribute to the same sovereign, and for this purpose to take off the gold plating of the temple doors (2 Kings xviii. 16); that he rent his clothes and put on sackcloth (2 Kings xix. 1), etc., and, on the whole, reports only that which proves his glorious and happy government. His representation of the work of Hezekiah has thus received a peculiarly optimistic colouring, beside which that of the other fuller report looks almost like pessimism. But even the sharpest critic would scarcely be able to show that the Chronistic narrative, notwithstanding its idealistic onesidedness, involves any misstatement of facts or distortion of history.

3. An important and difficult inquiry, that, however, concerns the narrative of our book equally with the older parallel text, is involved in the synchronism of the history of Hezekiah in the sacred Scripture and in the contemporary Assyrian monuments. While the most important event of this history in a temporal or spiritual respect, the fall of Samaria or the destruction of the northern kingdom by Shalmaneser and Sargon (namely, by Shalmaneser [Salmanu-âser, "God Salman is good"] as beginner, and by Sargon [Sarrukin, "mighty the king"] as finisher of the besieging and destroying work),[1] according to the unanimous testimony of both sources, is to be placed in the year 722 (or 721) B.C., with regard to the next more important event, the invasion of Sennacherib (ch. xxxii. 1–23, and the parallel), a difference is exhibited of not less than thirteen years between the statements of the Assyrian monuments and those of sacred Scripture. For those assign this expedition to the year 701, full twenty years after the accession of Sargon and the fall of Samaria; whereas the Bible (2 Kings xviii. 13; Isa. xxxvi. 1) places it in the 14th year of Hezekiah, only eight or nine years after the fall of Samaria, which took place in the sixth year of this king, 714 B.C. A reconciliation of these very diverse dates seems at present impossible; and as there is a great number of Assyrian inscriptions which agree in assigning the great Egypto-Palestinian expedition of Sennacherib to the fourth year of his reign (that is, as he must have reigned 705–681, to the year 701), it seems necessary to abandon the biblical date as incorrect, and to substitute for the 14th the 27th or 28th year of Hezekiah as the date of the event. A further chronological difference appears to open between the Bible and the inscriptions with regard to the embassy of the Babylonian king Merodach-baladan to Hezekiah (2 Kings xx. 12 ff.; Isa. xxxix. 1 ff.). If we hold this Merodach-baladan (Assyro-Babylonian, *Marduk-habal-iddina*, "Merodach bestowed the son"; see Schrader, p. 213) to be identical with the Μαρδοκέμπαδος of the Ptolemaic canon, the fifth king of Babylon according to this document, the whole transaction in question must, as the synchronism of the Assyrian inscriptions and of this canon determines the years 721–710 as the period of this monarch's reign, be placed a number of years before the invasion of Sennacherib, on the presumption that this fell in 701. And even if we take, not that Mardokempad (or Marduk-habal-iddina), but a later sovereign of the same name reigning only a short time (six months), mentioned by Berosus (or Alexander Polyhistor) in Eusebius, *Chron. Armen.* i. p. 19, edit. Mai, for the Merodach-baladan of Holy Scripture, as is done by Winer, Knobel, Hitzig, and recently by Schrader (p. 213 ff.), yet the reign even of this second Merodach falls before 701, namely, according to the canon of Ptolemy, in the year 704 or 703. The transposition of the reports in question seems therefore unavoidable. The statement in Isa. xxxix. (and 2 Kings xx. 12 ff.) concerning Hezekiah's display of his treasures before the ambassadors of Babylon must apparently be placed, with Oppert ("Die biblische Chronologie, festgestellt nach den assyrischen Keilinschriften," in the *Zeitschrift der Deutschen Morgenl. Gesellschaft*, 1869, p. 137 ff.), Delitzsch (*Komment. zu Jes.* 2d edit. 1869), Diestel (on Knobel's *Isaiah*, 4th edit.), and Schrader (*Keilinschriften*, p. 218), before the account in Isa. xxxvi. f. (2 Kings xviii. f.) of the expedition of Sennacherib, say about ten years, or (with Schrader) at least two or three years; and the full treasure-chambers which Hezekiah shows to the ambassadors must be regarded as those which Sennacherib had not yet emptied (2 Kings xviii. 13 ff.), not (with Keil, Knobel, Thenius, Bähr, Neteler, and others) as replenished from the booty left on the part of the hastily retreating army of Sennacherib, nor even as remaining sufficiently full notwithstanding the contribution imposed

[1] This relation of the Shalmaneser of 2 Kings to the Sargon of Isa. xx., Oppert and Schrader (*Stud. und Krit.* 1870, p. 527 ff.; 1871, p. 679 ff.) have now finally established, against the identity or only nominal diversity of these two governors asserted by many (M. v. Niebuhr Dunker, Sayce, Riehm, etc.). Comp. also Diestel, in Knobel's *Isaiah*, 4th edit. p. 169.

by the Assyrians.—The question, whether we are warranted or necessitated by the diverging dates of the monuments of profane history to assume so important chronological inaccuracies or perversions in the biblical sources, that is, in the here substantially agreeing reports of the second book of Kings, the book of Isaiah, and Chronicles, should scarcely be decided so hastily and unceremoniously in favour of the former testimonies, as has been done by Schrader (p. 292 ff.), in accordance with Diestel (pp. 169, 325), Rohling (in the *Literar. Handweiser für das Kathol. Deutschland*, 1872, No. 124), and others. With regard, also, to the wide differences between the Assyrian and biblical chronology before the reign of Hezekiah, which amount,[1] in the estimate of Assyriologists, sometimes to forty or fifty years, the greatest possible precaution and reserve is to be recommended in drawing conclusions unfavourable to the authority of Holy Scripture. For if not in the way proposed by Oppert (according to which a break in the list of Assyrian eponyms for nearly fifty years would have to be assumed, and the great difference for this early period derived therefrom; which, however, Schrader, in the *Zeitschrift der Deutschen Morgenl. Gesellschaft*, vol. xxv. p. 449 ff., declares to be inadmissible[2]), yet in some other way, sooner or later, a greater approximation of the divergent testimonies might easily be accomplished, and so the difference of the dates at least considerably reduced—just as the chronological deviations of the Egyptian monuments from the biblical statements were formerly held by many Egyptologists to be more considerable than is now generally the case, after a more thorough and extensive investigation of the existing sources. Neteler has made an attempt, in several respects untenable and precipitate, to reconcile the divergences on both sides in the parts of his *Commentary on Chronicles* that refer to chronology (pp. 195 ff., 224 ff., 263 ff.), in which he brings down the reigns of the Israelitish and Jewish kings from the division of the kingdom (which he dates at 933 instead of 975 B.C.) to Zedekiah by several decennia (from Josiah at least by several years), and accordingly makes Jehu reign 846–819, Uzziah 786–735, Ahaz 720–705, Hezekiah 706–678 (from 692 with his son Manasseh as co-regent), Josiah 637–607. That this attempt, as well on the biblical side—here chiefly by arbitrary assuming of various co-regencies, as of Amaziah with his father Joash, of Uzziah with Amaziah, of Hezekiah with Ahaz, and of Manasseh with Hezekiah—as on the Assyriologic, rests on several untenable presuppositions (in the latter respect, for example, on the long-since refuted opinion of the identity of Sargon with Shalmaneser), needs no further demonstration. Comp. Schrader's critical counter remark in his review of Neteler's commentary in the *Literarischen Centralblatt* of the year 1872. As little can we certainly regard the onesided chronology of Schrader, founded on the Assyrian documents, as absolutely satisfactory, especially as it involves not a few uncertainties, and often rests on documents not yet fully interpreted.[3]

o. MANASSEH AND AMON.—CH. XXXIII.

α. Manasseh: vers. 1–20.

CH. XXXIII. 1. Manasseh was twelve years old when he became king, and he reigned
2 fifty and five years in Jerusalem. And he did that which was evil in the
eyes of the LORD, like the abominations of the nations whom the LORD had
3 cast out before the sons of Israel. And he built again the high places which
Hezekiah his father had pulled down, and reared up altars for Baalim, and
4 made asheroth, and worshipped all the host of heaven, and served them. And
he built altars in the house of the LORD, although the LORD had said, In
5 Jerusalem shall my name be for ever. And he built altars to all the host of

[1] Comp. the juxtaposition of some of the biblical with the corresponding Assyrian dates, as they are presented by Schrader, p. 299:—

	Assyrian Monuments.	Bible.
Ahab, . . .	854 (battle at Karkar)	918–896 (reign of Ahab)
Jehu, . . .	842 (payment of tribute)	884–857 („ Jehu)
Uzziah, . .	745–739 (at war with Tiglath-pileser)	809–759 („ Uzziah)
Menahem, .	738 (payment of tribute)	771–761 („ Menahem)
Pekah, . .	734 (conquered by Tiglath-pileser)	758–738 („ Pekah)
Hosea, . .	728 (last year in which Aus'ih paid tribute t Tiglath-pileser)	729–723 („ Hosea)
Fall of Samaria,	722	722 (fall of Samaria)
Hezekiah, . .	701 (expedition of Sennacherib)	714 (expedition of Sennacherib)
Manasseh, . .	681–673 (payment of tribute)	696–642 (reign of Manasseh).

After differing at first about forty or fifty years, then about twenty or thirty, the Assyrian chronology merges into the biblical in Hosea; in the fall of Samaria the two reckonings coincide; and so mainly in the reign of Manasseh; but with regard to the expedition of Sennacherib, a deviation of full thirteen years again takes place.

[2] Comp. also *Die Keilinschriften und das Alte Testament*, p. 300 f.: "By this (granted that such an assumption [as the break of the list of eponyms for forty-seven years] were admissible) the difference between the Bible and the monuments would be expunged so far as the times of Ahab and Jehu are concerned: but Jehu would have paid his tribute, which, according to Oppert's calculation, must have been presented in the year 888, four years before his accession to the throne, 884. But in the time of Azariah and Menahem the omission of the forty-seven years would produce a still greater gap; at the most, twenty or thirty years would have to be cast off, etc. . . . And besides, . . . this whole notion of a break in the list of eponyms is untenable, and, irrespective of its internal improbability, is simply wrecked on the parallel lists of reigns and the rotation of officers, extending over from the one reign to the other, which is thereby preserved to us.

[3] Comp., as the most recent attempt at a critical chronology of this period, the treatise of H. Brand: *Die Königsreihen von Juda und Israel nach den bibl. Berichten und den Keilinschriften*, Leipzig 1873.

6 heaven in the two courts of the house of the LORD. And he caused his sons
to pass through the fire in the valley of Ben-hinnom; and he practised sorcery,
and divination, and enchantment, and appointed conjurors and soothsayers:
7 he wrought much evil in the eyes of the LORD to provoke Him. And he set
the carving of the image which he had made in the house of God, of which
God had said to David and to Solomon his son, In this house, and in Jeru-
salem, which I have chosen out of all the tribes of Israel, will I put my name
8 for ever. And I will no more remove the foot of Israel from the soil which I
have appointed for your fathers,[1] if only they will hold on to do all that I
have commanded them, in all the law and the statutes and the judgments
9 given by Moses. And Manasseh led astray Judah and the inhabitants of
Jerusalem, to do more evil than the nations whom the LORD had destroyed
10 before the sons of Israel. And the LORD spake to Manasseh, and to his
people; but they did not attend.

11 And the LORD brought upon them the captains of the host of the king of
Assyria, and they took Manasseh in fetters, and bound him with chains, and
12 carried him to Babel. And when he was in affliction, he besought the grace
of the LORD his God, and humbled himself greatly before the God of his
13 fathers, And prayed unto Him; and He was entreated of him, and heard
his supplication, and brought him again to Jerusalem into his kingdom: and
14 Manasseh knew that the LORD He is God. And after this he built the outer
wall of the city of David, to the west of Gihon, in the valley, and at the
entrance of the fish gate, and encompassed Ophel, and made it very high, and
15 put captains of war in all the fenced cities of Judah. And he took away the
strange gods and the image out of the house of the LORD, and all the altars
that he had built in the mount of the house of the LORD, and in Jerusalem,
16 and cast them out of the city. And he built[2] the altar of the LORD, and
offered on it sacrifices of peace and thanksgiving, and commanded Judah to
17 serve the LORD God of Israel. But the people still sacrificed in the high
places, but only to the LORD their God.

18 And the rest of the acts of Manasseh, and his prayer unto his God, and
the words of the seers that spake to him in the name of the LORD God of
19 Israel, behold, they are written in the history of the kings of Israel. And his
prayer, and his being heard, and all his sin, and his apostasy, and the places
in which he built high places, and set up asherim and carved images, before
20 he was humbled, behold, they are written in the history of Hozai.[3] And
Manasseh slept with his fathers, and they buried him in his own house: and
Amon his son reigned in his stead.

6. Amon: vers. 21–25.

21 Amon was twenty and two years old when he became king, and he reigned
22 two years in Jerusalem. And he did that which was evil in the eyes of the
LORD, as Manasseh his father had done; and Amon sacrificed unto all the
23 carved images which Manasseh his father had made, and served them. And
he humbled not himself before the LORD, as Manasseh his father humbled
24 himself; for he, Amon, multiplied trespass. And his servants conspired against
25 him, and slew him in his own house. And the people of the land smote all
the conspirators against King Amon: and the people of the land made Josiah
his son king in his stead.

[1] For לַאֲבוֹתֵיכֶם the Sept., Vulg., Syr., etc., read לַאֲבוֹתָם, which is preferred by many moderns since Luther (Berth., Kamph., etc.).

[2] וַיִּבֶן is the *Kethib* in most MSS. and editions; some MSS. and many old editions, however, give וַיִּכֶן as the *Kethib* and ויבן as the *Keri*. At all events, וַיִּכֶן appears to be the original reading, for which also the Vulg. (*restauravit*) and Syr. testify.

[3] For חוֹזָי the Sept. read הַחֹזִים ("words of the seers," as in ver. 18); comp. Introd. § 5, ii.

EXEGETICAL.

The idolatrous proceedings in the beginning of Manasseh's reign are depicted by our author, vers. 1–10, mostly in verbal agreement with 2 Kings xxi. 1-10. Instead of the summary report there following (vers. 11–16) of the threatening words of the prophets addressed to him, he appends the narrative of Manasseh's removal to Babel, his repentance and conversion, vers. 11–17, for which the book of Kings has no parallel. The closing notices of Manasseh's reign (vers. 18-20), and that which relates to Amon (vers. 21–25), are again in close agreement with 2 Kings xxi. 1 ff., 19 ff.

1. Idolatrous Proceedings at the Beginning of Manasseh's Reign: vers. 1-10; comp. Bähr on the parallel.—*Manasseh was twelve years old.* For the occurrence of this king's name (in the form of *Minasi*) on the Assyrian inscriptions, see Evangelical and Ethical Reflections, No. 2.—*And he reigned fifty-five years in Jerusalem*, 696–641 B.C. (according to the usual chronology, which can scarcely be disputed). Against the length of the reign of Manasseh, as our report states it in harmony with 2 Kings, Scheuchzer (*Phul und Nabonassar*, Zürich 1850) and v. Gumpach (*Die Zeitrechnung der Assyrer und Babylonier*, 1852, p. 98 ff.) have raised objections, and attempted to reduce it to thirty-five years. Bertheau (*Komment.* p. 406) concurs with them in this; and Neteler endeavours to confine at least the independent reign of Manasseh approximately to the same narrow measure, as he makes him reign fourteen years (say 692–678) in common with Hezekiah, and then forty or forty-one years (678–638) alone. On the contrary, Schrader (pp. 225 ff., 238 ff.) shows that no reduction whatever of the fifty-five years is requisite, as the Assyrian monuments bear no testimony against a reign of more than half a century for this king.—Ver. 3. *And reared up altars for Baalim.* In 2 Kings stands the sing.: "for Baal"; as also in the following words: "made an asherah." The phrase of the Chronist appears here to be rhetorically generalizing and climactic; comp., moreover, xiv. 2, xxviii. 2, xxxi. 1.—Ver. 6. *And he caused his sons to pass through the fire.* According to 2 Kings, this happened only to one son (בְּנוֹ for בָּנָיו), precisely the same difference as above in Ahaz (xxviii. 3; comp. 2 Kings xvi. 3); see on xxviii. 3. The Chronist alone states that this horrid human sacrifice took place in the valley of Ben-hinnom; in 2 Kings this note is wanting.—*And he practised sorcery and divination*, etc., "bewitched with an evil eye (עוֹנֵן connected with עַיִן), and divined (נִחֵשׁ, properly, watched serpents), and muttered" (כִּשֵּׁף, whispered charms; comp. Deut. xviii. 10). The third of these phrases is wanting in 2 Kings; whereas the following words: "appointed conjurors and soothsayers" (literally, "made a conjuror and a wizard"), agree again verbally with that text.—Ver. 7. *And he set the carving of the image . . . in the house of God.* In 2 Kings, "the carving (פֶּסֶל, as here, 'carved image,' as distinguished from מַסֵּכָה, 'molten image,' xxviii. 2; comp. xxxiv. 3) of the asherah." The term סֶמֶל, "idol, image," arising perhaps from Deut. iv. 16, appears here and ver. 15, as in Ezek. viii. 3, to be a contemptuous and abhorrent designation of the asherah.—*Will I put my name for ever;* לְעֵילוֹם only here for לְעוֹלָם.—Ver. 8. *Which I have appointed for your fathers*, "fixed," as in xxx. 5. Instead of "your," perhaps "their" is the original reading; see Crit. Note.—Ver. 10. *And the Lord spake to Manasseh*, by the mouth of His prophets, whose speech in the parallel text, 2 Kings xxi. 11–16, is also given in a summary form; whereas our author omits these words (words of the seer, ver. 18), though not without adding a reference to them (see under ver. 18), as contained in the "history of the kings of Israel."

2. Manasseh's Captivity and Conversion: vers 11–17.—*The Lord brought upon them.* According to the Assyrian monuments, this took place about 647, under King Assurbanipal, the Sardanapalus of the Greek historians.—*Took Manasseh in fetters*, scarcely in nets or hooks (חוֹחַ synonymous with חַח, 2 Kings xix. 28; Ezek. xix. 4; comp. also Job xl. 26), as if Manasseh were to be represented as an untamed wild beast, Ps. xxxii. 9 (Keil). Rather is חֹחִים to be taken simply as a synonym of the following נְחֻשְׁתַּיִם, "brass fetters, double fetters" (comp. Judg. xvi. 21; 2 Sam. iii. 34; and also 2 Chron. xxxvi. 6), as it is taken in this sense by the Sept. (δέσμοις), Vulg. (*catenis*), and several Rabbins. There is as little reason to think of a place, Hohim, where he was taken captive (Then.), as of a thorn hedge, into which (comp. 1 Sam. xiii. 6) he had rushed through fear (Starke and other ancients), or even of a tropical meaning of the phrase, according to which בַּחֹחִים should be: "with deceit, not in open conflict" (Cellarius, *Disput. de Captivitate Babylonica*, and others). For the question of the credibility of a carrying away of Manasseh in chains, and that to Babel, comp. the Evangelical and Ethical Reflections, No. 3.—Ver. 12. *And when he was in affliction* (comp. xxviii. 22) *he besought the grace of the Lord*, literally, "stroked or smoothed" the face of the Lord; comp. Ex. xxxii. 11; 1 Sam. xiii. 11; 1 Kings xiii. 6; Dan. ix. 13. The contents of this penitent prayer of the captive king were handed down to the Chronist by those old sources which he quotes ver. 18 f., namely, the "history of the kings of Israel," and the "history (words) of Hozai." The "prayer of Manasses" in the Old Testament Apocrypha is scarcely identical with this older record, which lay before our author; it appears to have been composed originally in Greek, is wanting in many older manuscripts of the Sept., and is first communicated from the *Constit. Apostolicæ*, ii. 22 (2d or 3d century), on which account the Council of Trent excluded it from the canon of the Romish Church. Yet recently, Jul. Fürst (*Geschichte der bibl. Literatur*, ii. 399 ff.) has defended the document as genuine (after the ancients; see J. A. Fabricius, *Bibliotheca Græca*, ed. Harles, iii. 732 ff.).—Ver. 13. *And He was entreated of him.* The Apocryphal accounts in the Targ. on our passage, in the *Const. Ap.* p. 9, in Johannes Damascen. Ἱερὰ παραλλ. ii. 15, in Anastasius on

Ps. vi., etc., contain all kinds of wonders concerning the way in which God delivered the penitent Manasseh (by sudden melting or sudden breaking of his chains, etc.). Comp. O. F. Fritzsche, in the *Kurzgefassten exegetischen Handbuche zu den Apokryphen des Alten Bundes*, i. p. 158, and Ew. *Geschichte*, iii. 1, p. 378.—Ver. 14. *And after this he built the outer wall*, perhaps that on which Hezekiah had already built (xxxii. 5); בָּנָה stands, therefore, as often, for finishing a building (elevating). The absence of the article from חוֹמָה, however, cannot constrain us at once (with Berth. and others) to translate "an outer wall," as, on the other hand, the emendation proposed by Arnold (Art. "Zion," in Herzog's *Realencycl.* xviii. 634), הַחוֹמָה הַחִיצוֹנָה, is scarcely necessary.—*Of the city of David* (literally, "to the city") *to the west of Gihon in the valley*, that is, in that valley between the city of David (Zion) and the lower city (Akra), which in its south-eastern outlet was afterwards (in Josephus, etc.) the cheesemakers' valley, or the valley Tyropæon. These words first assign the direction of the wall towards the west, and the following words: "at the entrance of the fish gate," denote, again, the direction towards the east; for the fish gate lay, according to Neh. iii. 3, near the north-east corner of the lower city and the tower Hananeel.—*And encompassed Ophel*, with that outer wall which he carried from the fish gate and the north-east corner on to the south, and then round Ophel (see xxvii. 3). So, no doubt correctly, Berth. and Kamph.; for against the assumption of Arnold (in p. 9) and Keil, that a special wall is here intended, distinct from the former, to enclose Ophel, is the following statement: וַיַּגְבִּיהֶהָ מְאֹד, "and made it very high," which clearly refers to the former wall.—*And put captains of war;* comp. xvii. 2, xxxii. 6.—Ver. 15. *Took away the strange gods;* comp. vers. 3-7. On the closing words: "and cast them out of the city," xxix. 16 and xxx. 14 are to be compared. Moreover, according to 2 Kings xxiii. 6, 12, this removal of the idols, and their altars, appears not to have been complete; for, according to these verses, much of this sort still remained for Josiah to remove (comp. also ver. 17), which constrains us to assign either an incomplete, or at least a transitory and by no means permanent character to the reform of worship by Manasseh.—Ver. 16. *And he built the altar of the Lord*, the altar of burnt-offering, of which, moreover, it is not to be assumed from this remark that Manasseh had before removed it from the temple court (as Ew. *Geschichte*, iii. 1. 367, holds). The building, at all events, is to be regarded as a repairing (comp. xxiv. 4 ff.; 1 Kings v. 32); even if וַיָּכֶן were the original reading (see Crit. Note), the same sense of repairing would result.

3. Manasseh's End; Amon: vers. 18-25.—For vers. 18, 19, see above on vers. 10, 13; and with regard to the history (words) of Hozai, Introd. § 5, ii. p. 20 (also Crit. Note on this passage).—Ver. 20. *And they buried him in his own house;* more exactly, 2 Kings xxi. 18: "in the garden of his house, in the garden of Uzza." This garden of Uzza the Englishman Lewin believes he has found in the so-called Sakra, on the east side of the Haram. He affirms that there also the Maccabean King Alexander was buried, on which account the burying-place in question occurs in Josephus, *de B. Jud.*, under the name of the grave of King Alexander (comp. *Athenæum*, 1871, March, pp. 278, 309).—Ver. 21 ff.; comp. 2 Kings xxi. 19-26, and Bähr on this passage. The concise report of our passage says nothing of Amon's mother (as also, ver. 1, the mention of Manasseh's mother is wanting), and at the close contains nothing of the burial of the king nor of the sources employed, but, on the contrary, appears enlarged by a parallel drawn between him and Manasseh, according to which he did not humble himself as his father had done (ver. 23).

EVANGELICAL AND ETHICAL REFLECTIONS, HOMILETICAL AND APOLOGETIC REMARKS, ON CH. XXXIII.

1. The evangelical import of the captivity and conversion of Manasseh consists mainly in this, that it is a pregnant type of the conversion of the ungodly by means of divine chastisement,—a significant confirmation and impressive exhibition of that truth, preached by all the prophets and men of God of the Old Testament, that God the Lord is found only of those who seek Him, that His call to repentance comes to no sinner too late (the *nusquam conversio sera* of Jerome, *Comm. in Ezech.* xviii. 21; *Ep.* 16 *ad Damasum*, c. 1; *Ep.* 39 *ad Paulam*, 1; *Ep.* 42, 107, 147, etc.), that He "killeth and maketh alive, bringeth down to Sheol and bringeth up" (1 Sam. ii. 6; comp. Ps. xxx. 4, lxxxvi. 13, cxvi. 3), that always again His comforting "return" sounds anew in the ear of the penitent sinner (comp. Joel ii. 12; Ezek. xxxiii. 11). As a deeply impressive illustration and verification of the text: "Call upon me in the day of trouble; I will deliver thee, and thou shalt glorify me," Ps. l. 15, from the history of the Old Testament, the event forms at the same time a very significant parallel to the New Testament parable of the prodigal son (Luke xv.), as well as to those similar exemplifications of the evangelical process in the appropriation of salvation (as the woman that was a sinner, Zacchæus, the robber, etc.), of which that evangelist, who stands in the same relation, as supplementer to the other evangelists, as the Chronist to the older historians of the Old Testament, possesses an exceedingly precious treasure.

2. To this general evangelical importance of our history is to be added its special prefigurative relation to the judgment of the Babylonish captivity, which took place half a century after it. What was announced once in the reign of Hezekiah by the fearfully earnest warning of the destruction of the northern kingdom, and then also by the direct message of Isaiah addressed to the king, as the final doom of the Jewish people persisting in the way of unfaithfulness to God (Isa. xxxvi. 6 f.; 2 Kings xx. 17 f.), this appears to be here realized by the transportation of Manasseh to Babel already in literal truth and full extent. Through the grace of the Lord, moved by the entreaty of the penitent Manasseh, the worst and most terrible calamity—a long exile, with its dissolving and unsettling consequences for the whole state—is at once averted; and as once to Hezekiah, for his personal life and reign during fifteen years, so

now to his son is granted a prolongation of nearly fifty years for the existence of the whole kingdom. Manasseh's lot thus stands intermediate between that which Hezekiah and that which the last kings—Jehoiakim, Jehoiachin, and Zedekiah—experience, as the reform of the religious life attempted by him after his return from Babel, but unsatisfactory and by no means permanent, falls in the middle between the reforms of Hezekiah and Josiah, with whose thorough energy and decision it certainly cannot be remotely compared.

3. From the absence of a parallel to our report in 2 Kings xxi., the hypercriticism of our century has sought to refer to the region of unhistorical legend either the whole history of Manasseh (de Wette, Gramberg, Graf, Nöldecke; comp. Introd. § 5, p. 22, and § 7, p. 29), or at least that of his conversion and the reform of worship consequent upon it; comp. what is asserted in the latter respect by Movers (*Chron.* p. 328 ff.), Ewald (*Gesch.* iii. 1. 366 ff.), Berth. (*Chron.* p. 408), and Hitzig (*Gesch.* p. 230 f.). The mythifying of the whole history, and therefore of the account of the capture and deportation of Manasseh to Babel, appears in the present state of historical investigation to be a glaring anachronism. This has been also perceived by Hitzig, who, after he had declared (*Begriff der Kritik*, etc. p. 180 f.) the captivity of Manasseh to be an invention derived from the prophecy of Isa. xxxix. 6, has recently (*Gesch.* as quoted) acknowledged the historical validity of this fact; whereas Graf has in his last work (*Die geschichtlichen Bücher des Alten Test.* 1866, p. 174) adhered to his former (*Studien und Krit.* 1859, iii.) absolutely sceptical treatment of the whole narrative. In the face of the most recent Assyriologic investigations of Rawlinson, Oppert, Schrader, etc., a further persistence in such a position could only be regarded as an inveterate unscientific obstinacy. The assumption, indeed, which was at first thought to be confirmed by the Assyrian monuments, namely, that it was Esarhaddon who, on the occasion of his campaign against Phœnicia, about 677, took Manasseh captive and carried him to Babel (an assumption with which the report of Abydenus in Eusebius, *Chron.* i. p. 54, concerning a conquest of "Lower Syria" by Axerdis, that is, Esarhaddon, may very well combine), would scarcely be reconcilable with the most recent state of these investigations. The capture and Babylonish exile of Manasseh cannot be transferred to so early a time as the third or fourth year of Esarhaddon, who, according to Ptolemy and the inscriptions, reigned 681–668. For even if an inscription of this Assyrian king, in a list enumerating twenty-two names of tributary Syrian ("Chattite," Hittite) kings, distinctly mentions a *Minasi sar Yahudi*, and thus, at all events, testifies that Manasseh belonged to the vassal-princes of that great king (comp. Schrader, pp. 227, 238), yet the same evidence reverts to a considerably younger inscription, wherein Asurbanipal (Sardanapalus), Esarhaddon's successor, in a list of tributary Syro-Phœnician princes, along with the kings of Tyre, Edom, Moab, Gaza, Ascalon, Ekron, Gebal, Arvad, enumerates also between Tyre and Edom a *sar Yahudi*, "king of Judah," who again, as is clear from the names of his contemporary neighbouring princes, can be no other than Manasseh. Accordingly his deportation, together with the attempt at revolt which no doubt occasioned it, may very well have taken place under this later sovereign; and that it did so is rendered highly probable by several circumstances, particularly this, that so long as Esarhaddon reigns we hear nothing, but under his successor Asurbanipal very much, of the disquiet and revolt of the vassals in Hither Asia against the Assyrian power. Hence the deportation of Manasseh by the Assyrian troops to Babel, and his short stay in captivity there, are to be placed under Asurbanipal about the year 648, when the Babylonish viceroy, *Sammughes* or *Samul-sumukin*, headed the western vassal-princes in an insurrection against the sovereign residing at Nineveh, and thereby occasioned a victorious expedition of the Assyrian army against them. The combination, keeping in view that point of time at the beginning of Esarhaddon's reign, which has been adopted by Bertheau, Keil, and Neteler, after J. Cappellus, Ussher, des Vignoles, Prideaux, Calmet, Rambach, J. H. and J. D. Michaelis, and recently Ewald, Duncker (*Gesch. des Alterthums*, i. 697 ff., ii. 592, 3d ed.), Reinke (*Beiträge zur Erklärung des A. T.* viii. p. 127 f.), Hitzig (*Gesch.* as quoted), Thenius (on 2 Kings xxi.), must accordingly be corrected; see the searching and cogent proof by Schrader in the often quoted work (p. 238 ff.), with which also the not essentially different combination of J. Fürst (*Gesch. der bibl. Literatur*, ii. pp. 340, 372 f.) is to be compared, although the king Sarak there named as captor of Manasseh, as Schrader has proved, p. 233, is a later sovereign, different from Asurbanipal, the Asur-idil-ili of the inscriptions.[1] And with regard to Babylon as the place of deportation, and to the mode of removal with chains and iron fetters, Schrader has produced the most satisfactory explanations and confirmatory parallels from the Assyrian monuments; since, with regard to the latter point, he shows from an inscription of Asurbanipal that even King Necho I. (*Ni-ik-ku-u*) suffered a "binding of the hands and feet with iron bands and chains when he was carried captive to Nineveh about this time,"[2] and referring to this fact justly remarks: "But what might thus befall the king of Egypt might certainly as well be inflicted on a Jewish prince" (p. 243). The final judgment of this distinguished Assyriologist concerning our fact runs thus: "There is nothing to cast suspicion on the notice of the Chronist, and his report is sufficiently intelligible from the state of things about 647 B.C."

4. But even with respect to the history of Manasseh's conversion and his subsequent reforms, the report of our author in vers. 13–17 contains nothing to justify the suspicion of the above-named critics (with whom also Schrader in the

[1] With respect also to the date (645 or a subsequent year), as well as some other circumstances, the combination of Fürst deviates from that of Schrader; among other things in this, that Fürst endeavours to prove historically a league of Manasseh, after his return from Babylon, with Psammetichus of Egypt (?), and so forth.

[2] The words of the inscription, which are remarkable as parallel to ver. 11 of this chapter, run thus: "The Sarludari (and) Necho they seized, then bound with iron bands and iron chains the hands and feet." There also mention is made of a subsequent kindness to the captive Egyptian king in Nineveh and his return in company with royal "officers and governors" to Egypt. It was thus by no means an unheard of or extraordinary thing that befell Manasseh at this time; only in the manner of the divine decree and the restoration lies the difference.

main accords, so far as he assumes the legendary as well as the historical in the report). For—1. In close connection with this history is communicated, ver. 14, a notice of the buildings and fortifications of Manasseh that resembles anything but a mere invention or fable, and the separation of which from the surrounding accounts, as if it only were historical and they were fabulous embellishment, is impossible (as the highly unfortunate attempt of Graf, as quoted, p. 174, proves). 2. The report also, ver. 16, of the restoration of the altar of the Lord by Manasseh, is much too historically definite and concrete to be fairly taken for the product of a biassed imagination or a fabulous rumour. 3. The removal, noticed ver. 15, of the strange gods, of the idol, that is, the figure of the asherah (2 Kings xxi. 7) and of the idol-altar, must by no means be thought necessarily connected with the complete annihilation of these monuments of idolatry, as if there were here a contradiction of 2 Kings xxiii. 6, 12; rather the complete destroying, crushing, and reducing to powder there mentioned, which Josiah thought it necessary to inflict on these monuments, directly suggest the thought that Manasseh neglected that which was important, and proceeded with too much mildness and forbearance (towards the priests of this idolatrous worship). Even the phraseology employed is against the assumption that the Chronist reports anything contradictory of those passages of the second book of Kings; for our author knows very well how to distinguish between הֵסִיר, "remove" (or even הִשְׁלִיךְ, "cast out," ver. 15), and שִׁבַּר, הֵדַק, כָּרַת, and similar words, denoting the annihilation of the images or altars, according to such passages as xv. 16, xxxi. 1, xxxiv. 4 (comp. Keil, p. 365). 4. To the assumption that neither Manasseh's reform of worship was truly thorough and radical, nor his conversion solid and permanent, there is not the least objection; on the contrary, ver. 17 speaks expressly against the conception that he had swept away the monuments of idolatry as thoroughly as his father Hezekiah had done, or his grandson Josiah afterwards did; and the remainder of his reign and life, after his return from Babel (647–642 or 641), amounting perhaps to five years, left him quite time enough to relapse a second time partially or wholly into the idolatrous and immoral course of his earlier days. 5. If, accordingly, as is not merely possible, but probable, his return to the worship of the Lord was not a permanent change, but merely an episode in the long series of acts and events in his reign, it will be the less surprising if, in the judgment as well of the men of his day as of posterity regarding this sovereign, a division arose, so that only here and there express mention is made of the temporary repentance and better theocratic disposition wrought in him by the calamity of his exile; while he was otherwise, and perhaps usually, without any reference to this circumstance, reckoned among the sovereigns who were to be rejected from the theocratic standpoint. That accounts have been preserved to us in the canon by representatives of both of these views—that besides the present report, relatively favourable to Manasseh, the decidedly unfavourable account of the book of Kings, that uses the phrase "sins of Manasseh" several times (2 Kings xxiv. 3, xxiii. 26; comp. Jer. xv. 4) almost as a proverb, has come down to us,—this can by no means be called more wonderful than, for example, the existence of two relations, a more idealizing and a more realistic (duly emphasizing the dark along with the light), concerning the transactions in the reign of a David, a Solomon, a Jehoshaphat, or than the very dimly coloured picture of the religious and moral conduct of the northern kingdom, as the indications of our author, obviously betraying a certain aversion and rooted antipathy, exhibit it, compared with the far more favourable delineations of the books of Kings. In abatement of that which the opponents have specially to allege from the last-quoted passages against the credibility of the account of Manasseh's reforms, comp. also especially Keil, p. 366. If this be the case with the conversion of Manasseh, the passages 2 Kings xxiv. 3, xxiii. 26, Jer. xv. 4, where it is said that the Lord removed Judah out of His sight on account of the sins of Manasseh, lose all significance for the opposite view. Manasseh is here presented as the man who by his ungodliness rendered the doom of Judah and Jerusalem inevitable, because he so corrupted Judah by his sins that he could no longer turn truly to the Lord, but fell back ever more into the sins of Manasseh. In like manner it is said, 2 Kings xvii. 21, 22, of the ten tribes, that the Lord cast them off because they walked in all the sins of Jeroboam, and departe not from them.

p. JOSIAH: THE PROPHETESS HULDAH.—CH. XXXIV., XXXV.

α. Josiah's Beginnings; the Extirpation of Idolatry: ch. xxxiv. 1–7.

CH. XXXIV. 1. Josiah was eight years old when he became king, and he reigned
2 thirty-one years in Jerusalem. And he did that which was right in the eyes
of the LORD, and walked in the ways of David his father, and declined not to
3 the right hand nor to the left. And in the eighth year of his reign, while he
was yet a youth, he began to seek after the God of David his father; and in
the twelfth year he began to purge Judah and Jerusalem of the high places,
4 and the asherim, and the carved images, and the molten images. And they
pulled down before him the altars of Baalim; and the sun-statues which were
above them he hewed down; and the asherim, and the carved images,
and the molten images, he broke and pounded, and strewed upon the
5 graves of them that had sacrificed to them. And the bones of the priests he
6 burned upon their altars,[1] and he purged Judah and Jerusalem. And in the

cities of Manasseh, and Ephraim, and Simeon, even unto Naphtali, in their
7 ruins[2] around. And he pulled down the altars and the asherim, and he cut
down the carved images to pound them, and hewed down all the sun-statues
in all the land of Israel; and he returned to Jerusalem.

β. The Purging of the Temple and the Recovery of the Book of the Law: vers. 8–21.

8 And in the eighteenth year of his reign, when he purged the land and the
house, he sent Shaphan son of Azaliah, and Maaseiah the governor of the
city, and Joah son of Joahaz the chancellor, to repair the house of the LORD
9 his God. And they came to Hilkiah the high priest, and delivered the money
that was brought into the house of God, which the Levites that kept the
thresholds had gathered from the hand of Manasseh and Ephraim, and from
all the remnant of Israel, and from all Judah and Benjamin, and the inhabit-
10 ants[3] of Jerusalem. And they put it into the hand of the work-masters who
were appointed over the house of the LORD; and the work-masters who
worked in the house of the LORD gave it to restore and repair the house.
11 And they gave it to the carpenters and masons, to buy hewn stones and
timber for girders and for joists of the houses, which the kings of Judah had
12 destroyed. And the men wrought faithfully at the work, and over them
were appointed Jahath and Obadiah the Levites of the sons of Merari, and
Zechariah and Meshullam of the sons of the Kohathites, to oversee; and the
13 Levites, all that had skill in instruments of song. And over the carriers, and
14 overseeing all that were doing the work in any manner of service. And
when they took out the money that was brought into the house of the LORD,
15 Hilkiah the priest found the book of the law of the LORD by Moses. And
Hilkiah answered and said to Shaphan the scribe, I have found the book of
the law in the house of the LORD: and Hilkiah gave the book to Shaphan.
16 And Shaphan brought the book to the king, and returned to the king a
17 report, saying, All that was committed to thy servants, they do. And they
have poured out the money that was found in the house of the LORD, and
18 given it into the hands of the overseers and of the workmen. And Shaphan
the scribe told the king, saying, Hilkiah the priest hath given me a book:
19 and Shaphan read in it before the king. And when the king heard the
20 words of the law, then he rent his clothes. And the king commanded Hil-
kiah, and Ahikam son of Shaphan, and Abdon[4] son of Micah, and Shaphan
21 the scribe, and Asaiah the servant of the king, saying: Go, inquire of the
LORD for me, and for them that are left in Israel and in Judah, concerning the
words of the book that is found; for great is the wrath of the LORD that
is poured out upon us, because our fathers have not kept the word of the
LORD, to do after all that is written in this book.

γ. Consultation of Huldah the Prophetess, and Solemn Reading of the Law in the Temple vers. 22–33.

22 And Hilkiah and those who were appointed[5] by the king went to Huldah
the prophetess, the wife of Shallum son of Tokehath, son of Hasrah, keeper
of the wardrobe; and she dwelt in Jerusalem in the second (quarter); and
23 they spake to her to this effect. And she said to them, Thus saith the LORD
24 God of Israel, Say ye to the man who sent you to me, Thus saith the LORD,
Behold, I will bring evil upon this place, and upon its inhabitants, all the
curses that are written in the book which they have read before the king of
25 Judah: Because they have forsaken me, and have made burnings[6] to other
gods, to provoke me to anger with all the works of their hands; and my
26 wrath is poured out on this place, and will not be quenched. And to the
king of Judah, who sent you to inquire of the LORD, thus shall ye say:
Thus saith the LORD God of Israel of the words which thou hast heard.
27 Because thy heart was tender, and thou didst bow down before God, when
thou heardest His words against this place and its inhabitants, and thou didst
bow down before me and didst rend thy garments and weep before me, so

28 have I also heard thee, saith the LORD. Behold, I will gather thee to thy
fathers, and thou shalt be gathered to thy grave in peace, and thine eyes
shall not see all the evil that I will bring upon this place and upon its inha-
29 bitants: and they brought the king word again. And the king sent and
30 gathered all the elders of Judah and Jerusalem. And the king went up into
the house of the LORD, and all the men of Judah, and the inhabitants of Jeru-
salem, and the priests and the Levites, and all the people, great and small; and
one read in their ears all the words of the book of the covenant that was found
31 in the house of the LORD. And the king stood in his place, and made the
covenant before the LORD, to walk after the LORD, and to keep His command-
ments and testimonies and statutes with all his heart and with all his soul,
32 to perform the words of the covenant which are written in this book. And
he caused all that were found in Jerusalem and Benjamin to stand to it; and
the inhabitants of Jerusalem did according to the covenant of God, the God
33 of their fathers. And Josiah took away all the abominations out of all the
countries of the sons of Israel, and bound all that were found in Israel to
serve the LORD their God: all his days they departed not from the LORD God
of their fathers.

δ. *The Passover:* ch. xxxv. 1–19.

CH. XXXV. 1. And Josiah kept a passover unto the LORD in Jerusalem; and they
2 killed the passover on the fourteenth of the first month. And he set the
priests in their charges, and strengthened them for the service of the LORD.
3 And he said unto the Levites, who taught all Israel,[7] who were consecrated
to the LORD, Put the holy ark into the house which Solomon son of David,
the king of Israel, built; it shall not be a burden on your shoulders: now
4 serve ye the LORD your God, and His people Israel. And make you ready[8]
in your father-houses by your courses, after the writing of David king of
5 Israel, and after the description of Solomon his son. And stand ye in the
sanctuary after the divisions of the father-houses of your brethren, the sons
6 of the people, and a part of a father-house of the Levites [for each]. And kill
the passover, and sanctify you, and prepare your brethren, to do according to
7 the word of the LORD by Moses. And Josiah dealt to the sons of the people
sheep, lambs, and kids, all for paschal offerings, for all that were found, to the
number of thirty thousand, and three thousand bullocks: these were of the
8 property of the king. And his princes presented a free gift to the people, to
the priests, and to the Levites: Hilkiah, and Zechariah, and Jehiel, rulers of
the house of God, gave unto the priests for the passover-offerings two thousand
9 and six hundred [sheep], and three hundred oxen. And Conaniah, and Shemaiah,
and Nethaneel, his brethren, and Hashabiah, and Jeiel, and Jozabad, chiefs of
the Levites, presented to the Levites for passover-offerings five thousand [sheep],
10 and oxen five hundred. And the service was prepared, and the priests stood
in their place, and the Levites in their courses, at the command of the king.
11 And they killed the passover, and the priests sprinkled [the blood] from their
12 hand, and the Levites flayed. And they removed the burnt-offering to give
them to the divisions of the father-houses of the sons of the people, to offer
unto the LORD, as it is written in the book of Moses; and so with the oxen.
13 And they roasted the passover with fire, according to the ordinance; and the
holy things they sod in pots and kettles and pans, and brought them quickly
14 to all the sons of the people. And afterwards they made ready for themselves
and for the priests: because the priests the sons of Aaron were engaged in
offering the burnt-offering and the fat until night; and the Levites prepared
15 for themselves and for the priests the sons of Aaron. And the singers
the sons of Asaph were in their place, according to the command of
David, and Asaph, and Heman, and Jeduthun the king's seer; and the porters
were at every gate: it was not necessary for them to depart from their service,
16 for their brethren the Levites prepared for them. And all the service of the
LORD was prepared that day, to keep the passover, and to offer burnt-offerings

17 on the altar of the LORD, at the command of King Josiah. And the sons of
Israel that were present kept the passover at that time, and the feast of
18 unleavened bread seven days. And there was no passover like that kept in
Israel from the days of Samuel the prophet; nor did all the kings of Israel
keep such a passover as Josiah kept, and the priests, and the Levites, and all
19 Judah and Israel that were present, and the inhabitants of Jerusalem. In
the eighteenth year of the reign of Josiah was this passover kept.

ε. *Josiah's Battle with Necho of Egypt, and End:* vers. 20–27.

20 After all this, when Josiah had prepared the house, Necho king of Egypt
came up to fight at Carchemish, on the Euphrates; and Josiah went out against
21 him. And he sent ambassadors to him, saying, What have I to do with thee,
O king of Judah? I am not against thee this day, but against the house of
my war;[9] and God hath commanded me to make haste: withdraw thee from
22 God, who is with me, that He destroy thee not. And Josiah turned not his
face from him, but disguised himself,[10] to fight with him, and hearkened not
unto the words of Necho from the mouth of God, and he came to fight in the
23 valley of Megiddo. And the archers shot at King Josiah: and the king said
24 to his servants, Remove me, for I am sorely wounded. And his servants
removed him from the chariot, and put him on his second chariot; and
brought him to Jerusalem, and he died, and was buried in the sepulchres of
25 his fathers: and all Judah and Jerusalem mourned for Josiah. And Jeremiah
lamented for Josiah; and all the songsters and songstresses spake of Josiah
in their laments unto this day, and they made them an ordinance for Israel:
and, behold, they are written in the Lamentations.
26 And the rest of the acts of Josiah, and his kindness, as it is written in the
27 law of the LORD, And his deeds, first and last, behold, they are written in the
book of the kings of Israel and Judah.

q. JEHOAHAZ, JEHOIAKIM, JEHOIACHIN, ZEDEKIAH: CLOSE.—CH. XXXVI.

α. *Jehoahaz:* vers. 1–4.

CH. XXXVI. 1. And the people of the land took Jehoahaz the son of Josiah, and
2 made him king instead of his father in Jerusalem. Jehoahaz was twenty and
three years old when he became king; and he reigned three months in
3 Jerusalem. And the king of Egypt put him down[11] in Jerusalem, and fined
4 the land a hundred talents of silver and a talent of gold. And the king of
Egypt made Eliakim his brother king over Judah and Jerusalem, and turned
his name to Jehoiakim: and Necho took Jehoahaz his brother and carried
him to Egypt.

β. *Jehoiakim:* vers. 5–8.

5 Jehoiakim was twenty and five years old when he became king; and he
reigned eleven years in Jerusalem; and he did that which was evil in the
6 eyes of the LORD God. Against him came up Nebuchadnezzar king of Babel,
7 and bound him in fetters, to carry him to Babel.[12] And Nebuchadnezzar
brought of the vessels of the house of the LORD to Babel, and put them in
8 his palace at Babel. And the rest of the acts of Jehoiakim, and his abominations which he did, and that which was found against him, behold, they are
written in the book of the kings of Israel and Judah: and Jehoiachin his son
reigned in his stead.

γ. *Jehoiachin:* vers. 9, 10.

9 Jehoiachin was eight years[13] old when he became king; and he reigned
three months and ten days in Jerusalem: and he did that which was evil in
10 the eyes of the LORD. And at the turn of the year, King Nebuchadnezzar
sent and brought him to Babel, with the goodly vessels of the house of the
LORD; and he made Zedekiah his brother king over Judah and Jerusalem.

δ. *Zedekiah:* vers. 11–21.

11 Zedekiah was twenty-one years old when he became king, and he reigned
12 eleven years in Jerusalem. And he did that which was evil in the eyes of
the LORD his God; he humbled himself not before Jeremiah the prophet, from
13 the mouth of the LORD. And he also rebelled against King Nebuchadnezzar,
who made him swear by God: and he stiffened his neck, and hardened his
14 heart from turning unto the LORD God of Israel. Also all the chiefs of the
priests and the people transgressed very much, after all the abominations of
the heathen; and polluted the house of the LORD, which He had hallowed in
15 Jerusalem. And the LORD God of their fathers sent to them by His messengers,
rising early, and sending; because He had compassion on His people and His
16 dwelling-place. And they mocked the messengers of God, and despised His
words, and scoffed at His prophets, until the wrath of the LORD rose against
17 His people, till there was no healing. And He brought up against them the
king of the Chaldees, and slew their young men with the sword in the house
of their sanctuary, and He spared neither young man nor maiden, the old nor
18 the grey-headed; the whole He gave into his hand. And all the vessels of
the house of God, great and small, and the treasures of the house of the LORD,
and the treasures of the king and his princes; the whole he brought to Babel.
19 And they burned the house of God, and pulled down the wall of Jerusalem,
and burned all its palaces with fire, and destroyed all its goodly vessels.
20 And he carried away those that remained from the sword to Babel; and they
became servants to him and his sons until the reign of the kingdom of Persia:
21 To fulfil the word of the LORD by the mouth of Jeremiah, until the land had
enjoyed her sabbaths: all the days of the desolation she rested to fulfil seventy
years.

ε. *Close: the Return from Captivity under Cyrus:* vers. 22, 23.

22 And in the first year of Cyrus king of Persia, that the word of the LORD,
by the mouth of Jeremiah, might be fulfilled, the LORD stirred up the spirit
of Cyrus king of Persia, and he made proclamation in all his kingdom, and
23 also in writing, saying, Thus saith Cyrus king of Persia, All the kingdoms
of the earth hath the LORD God of heaven given me; and He hath charged
me to build Him a house at Jerusalem: whoso is among you of all His
people? The LORD[14] his God be with him, and let him go up.

[1] מִזְבְּחוֹתִים is probably an error of transcription for מִזְבְּחוֹתָם

[2] Instead of the *Keri* בְּחַרְבֹתֵיהֶם, that appears formed after Ezek. xxvi. 9, or Neh. iv. 7, but yields no suitable sense, we should point בְּחָרְבֹתֵיהֶם, *in ruinis eorum* (comp. Ps. cix. 10). The *Kethib:* בָּחַר בָּתֵּיהֶם, "he chose (examined, searched) their houses," is scarcely warranted by the usage of speech.

[3] The *Kethib* וַיִּשְׁבִּי is undoubtedly to be preferred to the *Keri* וַיָּשׁבוּ, "and they returned."

[4] For עַבְדּוֹן the Syr. presents עַכְבּוֹר, which seems to be the original reading according to 2 Kings xxii. 12.

[5] For אֲשֶׁר הַמֶּלֶךְ is to be read, according to the Sept.: ואׄ אמר המׄ, "and whom the king had commanded.

[6] *Kethib* וַיְקַטְּרוּ, "have burned offerings"; *Piel*, as 2 Kings xxii. 17: "have burned incense."

[7] *Kethib* המבונים, perhaps only a slip of the pen for הַמְּבִינִים (*Keri*), "the teaching, instructing"; some MSS. give this directly as the *Kethib;* some have המכינים, which is perhaps only another way of miswriting the original המבינים.

[8] The *Kethib* הִכּוֹנוּ (*imp. Niph.* "make you ready") is undoubtedly to be preferred to the *Keri* הָכִינוּ, "prepare ye" (comp. ver. 6).

[9] The difficult phrase אֶל־בֵּית מִלְחַמְתִּי is not translated by the Sept.; the Vulg. gives the very free rendering: *sed contra aliam pugno domum.* The original text is perhaps still to be discovered from 3 Esdras i. 25: ἐπὶ γὰρ τοῦ Εὐφράτου ὁ πόλεμός μού ἐστι, namely, אֶל־פְּרָת מִלְחַמְתִּי (comp. also Josephus, *Antiq.* x. 5. 1). So at least O. F. Fritzsche (on 3 Esdras), Berth., and Kamph.

[10] Instead of הִתְחַפֵּשׂ, "disfigured, unrobed himself," the Sept. read (ἐκραταιώθη) הִתְחַזֵּק (comp. xxv. 11); the Vulg. (*præparavit*) and 3 Esdras (ἐπεχείρει) appear only to have run into the indefinite.

[11] Instead of וַיְסִירֵהוּ, "and removed, put him down," the Sept. read (ἔδησεν) וַיַּאַסְרֵהוּ, agreeing with 2 Kings xxiii. 33. But the Vulg., Syr., and 3 Esdras confirm the Masoretic reading. The last (3 Esdras i. 33) seems to have read וַיְסִירֵהוּ מִמְּלֹךְ, with a supplement which Berth., Kamp., and others pronounce necessary before בירושלם.

[12] The Sept., Vulg., and 3 Esdras change לְהוֹלִיכוֹ into the past וַיּוֹלִיכֵהוּ; comp. Exeg Expl.

[13] שְׁמוֹנֶה, though the Sept. and Vulg. give the number 8, is certainly an error of the pen for שמנה עשרה; comp 2 Kings xxiv. 8, also some Hebr. manuscripts, the Syr. and Arab. in our passage.

[14] For יְהוָה the parallels Ezra i. 3 and 3 Esdras ii. 5 present יְהִי, which is perhaps the original form.

EXEGETICAL.

Preliminary Remark.—Whereas in 2 Kings xxii. and xxiii. the several moments of the reforming action of Josiah are so combined that they appear all conditioned and determined by the repair of the temple, and the discovery in it of the book of the law, the Chronist separates the several acts or steps of his reforming activity more exactly, and indeed chronologically, as he makes the work of the king begin with the eighth year of his reign, the commencement of his more energetic proceedings to fall in the twelfth, and its end in the eighteenth (comp. on xxxiv. 3). In other respects the two accounts agree substantially, though the Chronist has related the cleansing of Judah and Jerusalem from idolatry (xxxiv. 3–7) with great brevity, and, on the contrary, the great passover (xxxv. 1–19) so much the more fully; whereas the author of 2 Kings, in accordance with his less careful attention to the history of the Levitical worship, has reversed this method, and treated of the passover quite briefly. Both historians relate the closing catastrophe of the history of Josiah at nearly the same length and in much the same manner, though the Chronist gives vent to the pragmatic reflective connection of this tragic end with the previous transactions of his reign (2 Kings xxiii. 25 f.). He proceeds, lastly, quite in the form of an epitome in his statements concerning the four last reigns, in ch. xxxvi., to which the author of the books of Kings devotes a great deal of space.

1. Josiah's Beginnings; the Eradication of Idolatry: ch. xxxiv. 1–7.—Vers. 1, 2 agree with 2 Kings xxii. 1, 2, especially with regard to the eulogy applied to Josiah (alone of all kings), that he "declined not to the right hand nor to the left"; only the mention of his mother (Jedidah, daughter of Adaiah) is wanting in our passage.—Ver. 3. *And in the eighth year of his reign*, when he was sixteen years old. The "seeking after God," as xxii. 19 and elsewhere. On the relation of the present chronological statements, especially that referring to the twelfth year of Josiah's reign as the date of the beginning of the abolition of idolatry, in 2 Kings xxii. 3 ff. and ver. 33 of our chapter, see Bähr's full discussion (*Bibelw.* vii. 453 f.). This agrees with the conclusion of almost all recent expositors in this, that neither the Chronist nor the author of 2 Kings proceeds exactly in chronological order, in so far as the latter compresses the whole measures of the purification of worship and extirpation of idolatry into the eighteenth year of his reign; but the former (according to vers. 4–7, which are to be taken partly as proleptic) attaches to that which was put in operation in the twelfth year part of that which was only carried into effect in the eighteenth year, as he himself indicates at the close of the chapter (ver. 33).—Ver. 4. *And they pulled down before him the altars of Baalim, and the sun-statues . . . he hewed down;* comp. xxxiii. 3, xxxi. 1; and for the sun-statues especially, xiv. 4; and for that which follows, xv. 16.—*And strewed* (the dust of the ground images) *upon the graves of them that had sacrificed to them*, literally, "upon the graves that sacrificed to them." In 2 Kings xxiii. 6, perhaps more exactly the ashes of the great asherim merely are designated as strewn upon the graves of the idolaters.—Ver. 5. *And the bones of the priests he burned*: for the particulars, see 2 Kings xxiii. 13, 14 16–20.—Ver. 6. *And in the cities of Manasseh, and Ephraim, and Simeon, and unto Naphtali,* that is, in all the land, from the most southern to the most northern part of the tribes. That the regions belonging to the northern kingdom (among which here, as in xv. 9, Simeon also is named as a tribe addicted to idolatry) were at that time wasted by the invasion of Shalmaneser and Sargon, is indicated by the addition: "in their ruins around." For the exclusive admissibility of this reading (בְּחַרְבֹתֵיהֶם), see Crit. Note. Moreover, the present account (with the parallel statement in 2 Kings xxiii. 19 f.), according to which the kingdom of Josiah included again in some measure all the twelve tribes, is certainly to be estimated in the same way as the statement in xxx. 18, according to which, even in the beginning of Hezekiah's reign, before the northern kingdom had fallen, a partial annexation of its inhabitants to the southern kingdom in respect of worship had taken place. Here also it is only the introduction of the remnant of the inhabitants of the north into the work of the purification of worship that is spoken of, not the exercise of a formal sovereignty over their country. What Neteler says, p. 261, of a supposed "reunion of the country of Israel with the kingdom of Judah" under Manasseh, and of an inheritance of this collective Israelitish kingdom, restored to its original compass, on the part of Josiah son of Manasseh, is devoid of all definite hold in the text as well of the books of Kings as of Chronicles.—Ver. 7. *Pulled down the altars;* here first is the chief sentence to the (in the form of an absolute sentence, ver. 6) premised determination of the scene of the king's action.—*And the asherim;* לְהֵדַק is a perfect-like (retaining the vowel of the perfect) infinitive with לְ, on which see Ewald, § 238, *d.*—*And he returned to Jerusalem*, from his campaign against the idols, which had carried him into the former region of Ephraim

and Simeon. In 2 Kings xxiii. 20 also is this notice found, but there certainly in reference to the eighteenth year of Josiah. A chronological contradiction of the two accounts, however, can scarcely be found in this circumstance; comp. Bähr on the passage.

2. The Purging of the Temple and Recovery of the Book of the Law: vers. 8–21. Comp. 2 Kings xxii. 3–13, and Bähr on the passage.—*In the eighteenth year . . . when he purged.* לְטַהֵר is neither "after the purging, after he had purged" (Luther, de Wette, etc.), nor "in order to purge" (Berth., Kamph.), but a note of time and circumstance "in the purging" (Keil, Net.); comp. Jer. xlvi. 13. In the naming of Shaphan, his designation as scribe or royal secretary (2 Kings xxii. 3) has perhaps fallen out of the text of our account by a mere oversight, for the two other officers named by the Chronist (reporting more exactly than 2 Kings) are introduced by the addition of their titles. For "repair (literally, 'strengthen') the house of the Lord," see on xxiv. 5, and also on ver. 9 of the present report concerning the repair of the temple under Joash (xxiv. 11–13); see, moreover, the Crit. Note on ver. 9.—Ver. 10. *Put it into the hand of the work-masters*, etc. וַיִּתְּנוּ is a resuming of the same verb in the foregoing verse, but connected with עַל־יַד, "into the hand," by which the sense of "handing" is reached. For the plur. עֹשֵׂה הַמְּלָאכָה (for עֹשֵׂי ה'), comp. 1 Chron. xxiii. 24. —*The work-masters . . . gave it*, etc.; so according to the received text; but if, as 2 Kings xxii. 5 seems to show, a לְ has fallen out before עֹשֵׂי, it should be rendered: "they gave it to the work-masters" (or labourers). The latter reading appears the more suitable, though it cannot be affirmed that it is the original one.—Ver. 11. *And timber for girders and for joists of the houses*, literally, "to joist the houses"; comp. Neh. iii. 3, 6. This means, naturally, not any houses of the city, but the buildings of the temple.—*Which the kings of Judah had destroyed*, let go to ruin; a like exaggeration of phrase as in the case of Athaliah, xxiv. 7.—Ver. 12. *And the men wrought faithfully at the work*, literally, "were working." For באמונה, "truly, conscientiously," see on xxxi. 12.—*To oversee* the building; comp. לְנַצֵּחַ in essentially the same meaning, Ezra iii. 8.—*And the Levites, all that had skill in instruments of song;* comp. 1 Chron. xv. 16, xxv. 7; Dan. i 17. These closing words of ver. 12 are to be connected with ver. 13*a*, so that the repeated וְ is = "as well as." This is simpler and less violent than the proposal of Bertheau, accepted by Kamph., to erase the first וְ of ver. 13, and annex the words "over the carriers" to ver. 12. On ver. 14, comp. 2 Kings xxii. 8.—*The book of the law of the Lord by Moses*, that is, the Mosaic law (comp. for the phrase, xxxiii. 8). The whole Torah at all events is meant, not merely Deuteronomy, as the modern critical school (last of all, Hitzig, *Gesch.* p. 236) think; and not merely the groups of laws contained in the three middle books of the Pentateuch (according to Bertheau's hypothesis, *Beiträge zur israelit. Gesch.* p. 375). Decisive grounds against these modern hypotheses, especially so far as they endeavour to connect the assertion of an origin from Manasseh or even Josiah with our passage, see in Kleinert, *Das Deuteronomium und der Deuteronomiker*, 1871, and in Klostermann, "Das Lied Mosis und das Deuteronomium," *Theol. Stud. und Krit.* 1871, ii.; 1872, ii. and iii. Comp. also Stähelin, *Einleit. ins A. T.* (1862) p. 242 ff.; J. Fürst, *Gesch. der bibl. Literat.* i. 351 ff.; and Bähr on 2 Kings xxii. 7.—Ver. 16. *And Shaphan brought the book to the king.* Somewhat different in the parallel 2 Kings xxii. 9, where at first it is only related: "and Shaphan the scribe came to the king," and where, therefore, no עוֹד, "yet," stands in the following: "and brought the king word." The structure of the words in the Chronist appears in every respect the younger, although none of its deviations is of any essential importance; comp. Keil on this passage.—Ver. 17. *Given it into the hands;* comp. on ver. 10 at the beginning.—Ver. 20. *And Ahikam son of Shaphan*, the father of Gedaliah and protector of Jeremiah; see Jer. xxvi. 24, xl. 5. For the probable originality of the reading "Achbor" for "Abdon," see the Crit. Note. The Achbor of this passage appears the same who is so named Jer. xxvi. 22, xxxvi. 12. —Ver 21. *And for them that are left in Israel*, literally, "for that which is left"; a significant phrase, like the parallel 2 Kings xxii. 13: "for the people and for all Judah." The expression "that is poured out" (נִתְּכָה) stands for the essentially synonymous "that is kindled" (נִצְּתָה) of the parallel.

3. Consultation of Huldah, and Solemn Reading of the Law in the Temple: vers. 22–33. Comp. 2 Kings xxii. 14–20, xxiii. 1–3, and Bähr on this passage.—*Went to Huldah . . . the wife of Shallum.* The forefathers of this husband of Huldah are called in 2 Kings, not Tokehath and Hasrah, but Tikvah and Harhas.[1] Which of these (nowhere else occurring) names are original cannot now be decided. For "the second" quarter or district of the lower city, see Bähr.—*And they spake to her to this effect*, namely, as Josiah had said to them; this כָּזֹאת, which reminds us of xxxii. 15, is wanting in 2 Kings.—Ver. 24. *All the curses*, etc.; in 2 Kings less strong: "all the words."—Ver. 25. *And my wrath is poured out on this place.* As in ver. 21, here again stands the verb נתך instead of נצת, the one usual in the parallel (2 Kings xxii. 17), which latter, moreover, the Sept. expresses also in our passage, perhaps because it appears to suit better the following words: "and will not be quenched." —Ver. 27. *Because thy heart was tender . . . when thou heardest his words.* In the original text the construction is somewhat different, namely, "the words which thou hast heard" (ver. 26 for example), "because thereby thy heart was made tender, and thou didst bow down before God, when thou heardest," etc. The words הַדְּבָרִים אֲשֶׁר שָׁמַעְתָּ, absolutely prefixed, can scarcely be translated. In 2 Kings xxii. 19, moreover, the words "against this place" are rendered still

[1] Not Harham, as Luther and after him also Bähr (changing the ס into ם) write.

more distinct by the addition wanting here: "that they should become a desolation and a curse."—Ver. 28. *And they brought the king word again;* comp. ver. 16.—Ver. 32. *Caused all . . . to stand to it,* namely, to the covenant. In 2 Kings xxiii. 3, instead of וַיַּעֲמֵד stands rather the *Kal* וַיַּעֲמֹד, joined with בַּבְּרִית, "and all the people stood to the covenant."—Ver. 33. *And Josiah took away all the abominations.* For the relation of this statement, that reverts to vers. 3–7 in the way of recapitulation, to 2 Kings xxiii. 4–20, see above, Preliminary Remark, and on ver. 3. By "all the countries of the sons of Israel" are here meant the territories of the former kingdom of the ten tribes, as distinguished from Jerusalem and Benjamin, ver. 32 (that is, Jerusalem, Judah, and Benjamin). Comp. above, ver. 6, also 2 Kings xxiii. 15, 19, where in particular Bethel and the cities of Samaria are mentioned as places of the former Israel that were subjected to the great purging process of Josiah.—*And bound all . . . to serve* (וַיַּעֲבֵד לַעֲבֹד), "caused to serve," bound to the service of the Lord.—*All his days they departed not from the Lord.* This theocratic behaviour of the people during the whole reign of Josiah can, at all events, have only been external, without true conversion of heart, and therefore without real constancy; see Evangelical and Ethical Reflections, No. 1.

4. The Passover: ch. xxxv. 1–19. Comp. 2 Kings xxiii. 21, 23; as also the tolerably close Greek version of our section in 3 Esdras i. 1–21 (in Tischendorf's edit. of the Sept. the first book of Esdras).—*And they killed the passover on the fourteenth day of the first month;* thus, though Hitzig (*Gesch.* p. 235) doubts it without any ground, at the time prescribed by law, otherwise than in the passover of Hezekiah, xxx. 2 ff. The year of this solemnity is (ver. 9; see on this verse) the eighteenth of Josiah's reign, and therefore 623 (or 622) B.C.—Ver. 2. *And he set the priests in their charges* (watches; comp. vii. 6, viii. 14), in their functions; comp. 1 Chron. xxiii. 32.—*And strengthened them for the service of the Lord,* by comforting, encouraging exhortation, as also by instructions in their legal functions; comp. Neh. ii. 18, where חִזֵּק stands in the same sense, and xxix. 5.—Ver. 3. *Who taught all Israel.* Comp. הֵבִין in Neh. viii. 7, 9, also the synonymous למד above, xvii. 8, 9. For the following designation of the Levites as "consecrated to the Lord," that is, alone entitled to enter His sanctuary and conduct His holy service, comp. xxiii. 6.—*Put the holy ark into the house.* These words are somewhat surprising, and admit of various interpretations, as a parallel yielding a more definite explanation is wanting. But although not הָשִׁיבוּ, "bring back," but תְּנוּ, "give place," is the verb used, yet the assumption of a previous removal of the ark from its place in the holy of holies appears to present itself with constraining necessity, even if we think (with many ancients, as well as Berth. and Kamph.) of Manasseh or Amon as the author of this temporary transference of the ark; in which case, however, it would be very surprising that nothing should be expressly stated in the reign of these godless kings concerning so profane a violation; or if (with Starke and others) we consider Josiah's repair of the temple to be the occasion of the temporary removal of the ark from its place, which is undoubtedly the simplest and best supposition. Quite arbitrary is the hypothesis of some ancients, that the ark was, in the days of the idolatrous kings, sometimes carried round the country as a means of strengthening the faith of the people, and Josiah now forbids this custom in the present words (see v. Mosheim in Calmet's *Bibl. Untersuchungen,* vi. 226 ff.); and equally so the Rabbinical conceit, that Josiah here gives orders to remove the ark from its place in the holy of holies to a subterranean chamber, to place it in safety from the impending destruction of the temple. But even the rendering: "Leave the holy ark in the house, leave it in the temple, to which it properly belongs" (Keil, after the ancients), is arbitrary; and so is Neteler's attempted emendation, which, against the grammar, would change the imperat. תְּנוּ into the perf. תָּנוּ (from תנן = נתן, "give"), and translate accordingly: "And he said to the Levites, Those who taught all Israel, who were consecrated to the Lord, have put the ark of the sanctuary into the house," etc. Were such an explanation of the passage possible, how surprising that it is first discovered in the 19th century!—*It shall not be a burden on your shoulders;* comp. Num. iv. 15, vii. 9. The sense of these words can only be: ye have to minister to the ark of the Lord not as a moveable sanctuary, to be carried laboriously on the shoulders, through the wilderness or from city to city, but as the throne of God standing in the centre of the temple; the times of the toilsome and perilous (comp. 1 Chron. xiii. 9) transport of the ark are over; an easier ministry before this sanctuary, but not the less conscientiously to be discharged, now lies upon you. If we take the words thus (with Keil, Kamph., etc.), there seems to be no necessity for Bertheau's assumption that the Levites at the passover had carried round the ark on their shoulders in an inconsiderate way, and Josiah therefore instructed them that this function of carrying was no longer binding on them with regard to the ark of the covenant.—Ver. 4. *And make you ready* (see Crit. Note) . . . *after the writing of David,* properly, "in the writing," etc. (בְּ, as in xxix. 25). There were then writings or notes (מִכְתָּב, as in xxxvi. 22, 1 Chron. xxviii. 19) of David and Solomon, in which these kings had established as law their prescriptions for the ministry of priests and Levites in the sanctuary, from which also our author had directly or indirectly drawn his former communications on this subject (1 Chron. xxiii.–xxvi.); comp. Introd. § 5, for example, and the preliminary remark in explanation of 1 Chron. xxiii.–xxvi.—Ver. 5. *And a part of a father-house of the Levites* (*for each*); so that to every division (פְּלֻגָּה, as Ezra vi. 18) of the non-Levitical father-houses may correspond a part of a Levitical father-house (comp. 1 Chron. xxiv. 6). In this way it is not necessary to erase וְ before חֲלֻקַּת in the sense of "and indeed," or "namely" (against Berth.).—Ver. 6. *Kill the passover and sanctify you,* namely, by washing, before ye hand to the priests the blood to sprinkle

on the altar; comp. xxx. 16 f.—Vers. 7-9. The King and his Princes bestow Victims.—*And Josiah dealt to the sons of the people;* הֵרִים, bestow as a heave-offering, as in xxx. 24, Ezra viii. 25.—*To the number of* 30,000 head of small cattle, and 3000 bullocks,—the latter, as appears from ver. 13, for slaying and consuming as peace-offerings. All this was from the king's domains; comp. xxxi. 3, xxxii. 29.—Ver. 8. *And his princes presented a free gift;* so is לִנְדָבָה to be taken here (comp. the corresponding לַפְּסָחִים for passover-offerings in the verse before), not as an adverb, "willingly," as Berth. thinks. How many the princes gave as free gifts is not here mentioned (it is otherwise in xxx. 24); for the three "rulers of the house of God" named in *b* as in ver. 9, and six chiefs of the Levites, are certainly as different from "the princes of the king" as the spiritual office-bearers in any kingdom are from the temporal. Moreover, of the three princes of the house of God, Zechariah, named next after the high priest Hilkiah, appears to be his nearest subordinate or deputy (כֹּהֵן מִשְׁנֶה, 2 Kings xxv. 18); but the third, Jehiel, seems to be the head of the line of Ithamar (comp. Ezra viii. 2, and Berth. on this passage). Of the six chiefs of the Levites named in ver. 9, three—Conaniah, Shemaiah, and Jozabad—have the same names with those named in xxxi. 12-15 on the occasion of the reform of Hezekiah, but are scarcely the same persons.—Ver. 10 ff. depicts the preparation of the passover and the sacrificial feast connected with it.—*And the service was prepared* (or arranged, Luther), comp. ver. 16, xxix. 35; for the following, also xxx. 16 f.—Ver. 12. *And they removed the burnt-offering;* הֵסִיר is here to separate the parts of the victim that were to be burned on the altar; comp. Lev. iii. 9 f., iv. 31. These parts are here called הָעֹלָה, because, as the law of the peace-offering, Lev. iii. 6-16 (especially vers. 11 and 16), directs, they were wholly burned as the burnt-offering, and, moreover, on the flesh of the evening sacrifice. A special burnt-offering is not to be thought of, because such were not prescribed on the evening of the 14th Nisan for the passover; the only offerings to be presented thereon were the paschal lambs.—*To give them to the divisions;* "them," namely, the separated pieces, to be burned as burnt-offerings.—*And so with the oxen;* they also (those special gifts in oxen mentioned vers. 7-9, 3800 head in all) were presented not as burnt-offerings or holocausts to be wholly burned, but as peace-offerings, to be eaten as a joyful festival in part, that is, after taking away the fat that was to be burned.—Ver. 13. *And they roasted the passover with fire, according to the ordinance;* see Ex. xii. 8, 9. The "holy things" (הַקֳּדָשִׁים) are the slain oxen (see xxix. 33). If it is further said of these, that their flesh, after being sodden in pots, etc., is to be brought "quickly" to the sons of the people, that is, the non-Levitical partakers in the feast, it does not follow that this was done on the first evening of the feast, the 14th Nisan, and thus that all that was provided, passover lambs and peace-offerings, was consumed on the very first evening (as Berth. and apparently also Kamph. think). On the contrary, Keil justly remarks: "Such a junction or rather mingling of the feast prepared of the roasted lambs with the eating of the boiled beef would have been so rude an offence against the legal prescriptions concerning the passover, that we shall not ascribe it either to King Josiah and the priests, or even to the author of Chronicles, as the latter expressly remarks that they proceeded in the festival according to the prescription of the law of Moses, and according to the ordinance." Accordingly, that which is here and in the two following verses recorded concerning the preparation of the offering and the feast refers not merely to the opening evening, but to the whole seven days of unleavened bread.—Ver. 14. *And afterwards,* when the laity were provided for.—*Because the priests . . . (were engaged) in offering the burnt-offering and the fat until night,* and thus could not cook and prepare for themselves, the Levites must do this for them. Burnt-offering and fat appear to denote one and the same thing, and so to form a hendiadyoin; or also the conjunctive ו between the two phrases appears to be explicative (Keil).—Ver. 15. *And the singers . . . were in their place* (comp. 1 Chron. xxiii. 28, xxv. 1, 6). What is here recorded concerning the co-operation of the singers and the porters in the solemnity clearly refers, as the comprehensive character of the scene shows, not merely to one, but to all the seven days of the feast. The phrase "that day," at the beginning of ver. 16, does not oppose this view, but reverts to the 14th Nisan as the fundamental day of the festival; comp. the sing. יוֹם in Gen. ii. 4 and in ver. 17, which shows most directly and clearly the correctness of our interpretation.—Ver. 18. *And there was no passover like that kept . . . from the days of Samuel.* This does not contradict xxx. 26, for there the point of comparison is the magnificence and numerous participation in the solemnity; here, on the contrary, its theocratic purity and legitimacy. Comp. above on that passage, as well as Bähr on the parallel 2 Kings xxiii. 22. On "all Judah and Israel that were present," that is, so far as they were present, comp. xxxiv. 33.—Ver. 19. *In the eighteenth year of the reign of Josiah was this passover kept;* thus in the same year in which, according to xxxiv. 8, the full execution and conclusion of Josiah's reform of worship took place (comp. on ver. 1). There is no proper chronological difficulty in this date, which is also found in 2 Kings xxiii. 23; for the 18th year which is here spoken of is a reign and calendar year (Bähr), and if dated from the autumn, from that time till the legal term of the paschal feast, about the middle of Nisan (in the spring of the following calendar year), all that is related in xxxiv. 8-33 may take place. And all the more because not a little that referred to the cleansing and repair of the temple might have been already prepared in the previous years of Josiah's reign (from the 12th, xxxiv. 3).

5. Josiah's Battle with Necho of Egypt, and End: vers. 20-27. Comp. 2 Kings xxiii. 25-30.—*After all this . . . Necho, king of Egypt, came up;* not the Necho I. (*Ni-ik-ku-u sar Mi'-im-piu S'a-ai,* "king of Memphis and Sais," on an inscription of Asurbanipal) mentioned xxxiii. 11, who had reigned before 664, but the successor of

Psammetichus, Necho II., who reigned till about 605. The Assyrian (or rather Babylonian) king who is attacked by Necho in the present campaign is probably Asur-idil-ili, the Sarak of Abydenus and Syncellus (see Schrader, p. 231 ff.), or even, if Nineveh was already fallen, Nabopolassar (see Then., Berth., Bähr, etc.), but by no means Sardanapalus (v. Gumpach, *Zeitrechnung der Babyl. und Assyr.* p. 146), who was much earlier. For Carchemish = Circesium, on the Euphrates, comp. the expositors on Isa. x. 9; Jer. xlvi. 2.[1]—Ver. 21. *What have I to do with thee?* properly, "what is there to me and thee?" comp. Judg. xi. 12; 2 Sam. x. 9; John ii. 4.—*I am not against thee this day,* "I am come up" (עָלִיתִי), my attack is not on thee; after עָלֶיךָ the suffix of the second pers. is rendered emphatic by an added אַתָּה, which would be expressed in English by "even thee."—*But against the house of my war.* These words must, if original, be interpreted like the phrase: "man of wars of Tou," 1 Chron. xviii. 10, or the similar form in 2 Sam. viii. 10, and would thus denote the hereditary foe of the Egyptian king. But it seems more natural to amend, as in 3 Esdras i., according to the Crit. Note.—*And God hath commanded me to make haste.* By this God, to whose command he was obedient, Necho means not any Egyptian deity, as the Targ. as well as some recent expositors (appealing to Herodotus, ii. 158) think, but, according to ver. 22, the true supreme God, the acknowledgment of whom in the mouth of Necho cannot surprise us more than xxxvi. 23 in the edict of Cyrus. The older expositors assume a special divine command (*sive per somnium, sive per prophetam aliquem ad ipsum a Judæa missum*) without sufficient necessity; what Necho had recognised as agreeable to the will of his Egyptian deity, that he transfers at once to a supposed indication of the will of Jehovah. —Ver. 22. *But disguised himself to fight with him;* he gave up his true character, the part of the peaceful, which he was bound to play, and engaged against the will of God in combat with Necho. Perhaps, however (with Berth., Kamph.), the reading of the Sept.: "but made himself strong for battle" (comp. xxv. 11), is to be preferred. A literal disguise, such as that of Ahab, xviii. 29, should in no case be thought of (against Starke and other ancients, also Neteler). For the well-founded opinion of our author, that the battle of Josiah with Necho was a contravention of the divine will, see Evangelical and Ethical Reflections, No. 1. For the valley of Megiddo, see on 2 Kings xxiii. 29 f.—Ver. 24. *And his servants . . . put him in his second chariot,* perhaps a more commodious one, which he had with him besides the war chariot. Not so exact 2 Kings xxiii. 30.—Ver. 25. *And Jeremiah lamented for Josiah.* This lamentation of Jeremiah was certainly included in the collection of lamentations (קִינוֹת) on Josiah mentioned immediately after at the end of the verse, but is no longer found in the present Lamentations of Jeremiah, which must be regarded as a later collection than that here named. Perhaps the passages in Jer. xxii. 10, 18, and Zech. xii. 11 contain allusions to the older laments in memory of Josiah that are here intended; comp. Nägelsbach on Jeremiah, and Köhler on Zechariah. — Ver. 26. *And his kindness;* חֲסָדִים, as in xxxii. 32 of Hezekiah, but more exactly defined in our passage by the addition: "as it is written in the law of the Lord," corresponding to the characteristic peculiarity of Josiah, as a prince living and reigning in the strictest sense according to law.

6. Jehoahaz: ch. xxxvi. 1–4. Comp. 2 Kings xxiii. 30–35.—*And the people of the land took Jehoahaz;* the same mode of elevation to the throne as in Josiah, xxxiii. 25, and Uzziah, xxvi. 1. In the present case, the will of the people took effect in a usurping way, as the younger brother (Jehoahaz, or properly Shallum; see 1 Chron. iii. 15, and comp. remarks on this passage) was preferred to the older Jehoiakim, perhaps because they had learned to fear the latter on account of the tyrannical spirit early manifested by him (comp. on ver. 8).—Ver. 3. *Put him down.* For the here probably necessary supplement of מִמְּלֹךְ after וַיְסִירֵהוּ, see Crit. Note. On the terms 100 talents of silver and a talent of gold, which are also found in 2 Kings xxiii., see Bähr on this passage.

7. Jehoiakim: vers. 5–8. Comp. 2 Kings xxiii. 36–xxiv. 7.—*Jehoiakim was twenty and five years old when he became king,* and so two years older than his brother Shallum-Jehoahaz.—*Against him came up Nebuchadnezzar;* according to the Assyrio-Babylonian monuments, *Nabiuv-kudurriusur* (comp. the Hebrew form נְבוּכַדְרֶאצּוֹר, Jer. xlix. 28 and Ezra ii. 1, *Kethib;* likewise Ναβοκοδρόσορος in Alex. Polyhistor, Megasthenes, and Abydenus). The name (according to Schrader, p. 235) is compounded of the idol name *Nabiuv* or *Nabu,* the subst. *Kudur,* "crown" (κίδαρις), and the imperat. *usur* or *nasar,* "protect," and means: "Nebo, guard the crown" (not Nebo guards the crown, as Keil states our passage and at Dan. i. 1).—*And bound him in fetters,* as befell Manasseh, and as the Assyrio-Babylonish sovereigns were wont to do to all captive princes; comp. on xxxiii. 11.—*To carry him to Babel.* That this carrying to Babel was only intended, not executed, almost all recent expositors justly assume; comp. besides Movers (*Chron.* p. 333), Bertheau, Keil, Neteler on our passage, also Bähr on 2 Kings xxiv. 1 ff., Nägelsbach on Jer. xxii. 17 ff., as well as my remarks on Dan. i. 2. If the Sept., which presents a text often deviating from the Masoretic text, and amplified with many additions, makes out of "to carry him" (לְהוֹלִיכוֹ) an actual "and carried him" (καὶ ἀνήγαγεν αὐτὸν εἰς Βαβυλῶνα), and also 3 Esdras and the Vulg. translate accordingly (*et vinctum catenis duxit Babylonem*), this has its ground in the erroneous assumption derived mainly from a onesided view of Dan. i. 2, as if already the misfortune of being carried to Babel had befallen Jehoiakim, which, according to the sequel, first overtook his son Jehoiachin, whereas he himself, according to the express statement of ver. 5, reigned eleven years at Jerusalem (the last of these eleven years, natur-

[1] Recently G. Maspero (*De Carchemis oppidi situ et historia antiquissima, Lut. Par.* 1872) has attempted to identify Carchemish with the town Mabug = Βαμβύκη or Hierapolis, north-east of Aleppo, following the lead of Ephraem on 2 Kings xxiii. 30.

ally, as the vassal of Nebuchadnezzar). On the date of this first invasion of Nebuchadnezzar, according to Dan. i. 1 "in the third year of Jehoiakim," about 606 or 605 B.C., comp. our remarks in the Introd. to the book of Daniel, § 8 (*Bibelw.* xvii. 28, 30 ff.). On ver. 7, comp. Dan. i. 2; Ezra i. 7.—Ver. 8. *And his abominations which he did;* not certainly a mere designation of the idolatry of Jehoiakim (as Berth. thinks, who understands עָשָׂה תוֹעֵבוֹת of the making of idols), but also of his other evil deeds—for example, his shedding of innocent blood, 2 Kings xxiv. 4. The next phrase: "and that which was found against him," is a still more general and comprehensive expression for these evil deeds; comp. xix. 3.

8. Jehoiachin: vers. 9, 10. Comp. the fuller account, 2 Kings xxiv. 8–17.—*Jehoiachin was eight years old.* That the number eight here is, at all events, a miswriting for eighteen, see in Crit. Note. Not merely in 2 Kings xxiv. 8 is Jehoiachin designated as a youth of eighteen years at his accession, but Ezek. xix. 5–9 makes him appear at least as old, since he is depicted as a young lion, who practised man-stealing, oppressed widows, and laid waste cities, abominations which a boy of eight years could not have committed. Against Bertheau's opinion, that it follows from 2 Kings xxiv. 12, 15, Jer. xxii. 26, where Jehoiachin's mother is mentioned along with him, that he was still in his minority, and thus the present statement of the Chronist that he is only eight years old is correct, is the joint mention of the queen-mother in the account of the accession of a new king which is usual in the books of Kings, and occurs, for example, also in Jehoahaz (2 Kings xxiii. 31), Jehoiakim (xxiii. 36), and Zedekiah (xxiv. 18). For the name Jehoiachin, and its relation to the kindred form Jechoniah or Coniah, comp. on 1 Chron. iii. 16.—Ver. 10. *And at the turn of the year,* in the spring, when men are wont to open the campaign (comp. 2 Sam. xi. 1; 1 Kings xx. 22).—*And brought him to Babel* ("caused him to come") *with the goodly vessels,* etc. In the mention of these "goodly vessels" (as in xxxii. 27) there is an advance in comparison with "some of the vessels," as in ver. 7. The spoliation under Jechoniah (598 B.C.) was more thorough than under Jehoiakim.—*And he made Zedekiah his brother king over Judah and Jerusalem.* That this designation of Zedekiah, the last king before the exile, as the brother of Jehoiachin is inexact, and, according to 2 Kings xxiv. 17, to be explained by father's brother (uncle, דּוֹד), or even directly changed into this term, is shown by the full list of Josiah's four sons already communicated by the Chronist, 1 Chron. iii. 15 f. Comp. on this passage, especially on 1 Chron. iii. 16, where also mention is made of Mattaniah, the name borne by Zedekiah before he ascended the throne.

9. Zedekiah: vers. 11–21. Comp. 2 Kings xxiv. 18–xxv. 21, also Jer. lii. and 3 Esdras i. 44–55.—*Zedekiah was twenty-one years old.* The younger Zedekiah, brother of Jehoiachin, and nephew of Mattaniah Zedekiah (see 1 Chron. iii. 16), could not have been so old at the time when Jehoiachin, being eighteen years old, was deposed. The eleven years of Zedekiah's reign extend from 598 to 587.—Ver. 12. *Humbled himself not before Jeremiah the prophet from the mouth of the Lord,* who spoke from the mouth of God; comp. xxxv. 22; Jer. xxiii. 16. Of these prophetic warnings and threatenings addressed by Jeremiah to Zedekiah, Jer. xxi. 4 ff. especially comes into account; comp. also Jer. xxxvii. 2 ff. —Ver. 13. *And he also rebelled against king Nebuchadnezzar.* This revolt is also censured by the prophet Ezekiel (Ezek. xvii. 13 ff.) as a grievous transgression. — *And he stiffened his neck* (showed himself stiff-necked; comp. 2 Kings xvii. 14; Jer. xix. 15, etc.) *and hardened his heart,* "made his heart firm." Comp. Deut. ii. 30, where God is said to harden and make stiff-necked; which does not, however, warrant the conclusion that he must also here be the subject of וַיְקַשׁ, as Bertheau thinks; comp., on the contrary, Deut. xv. 7.—Ver. 14. *Also all the chiefs of the priests and the people transgressed very much;* comp. Ezek. viii. 6 ff., where priests and people are described as sunk in base idolatry under the last kings, Jehoiakim, Jehoiachin, and Zedekiah, while prominence is expressly given to the "elders of the people" (ver. 11) and the priests (ver. 16) as the chief participators in these abominations. Neither there nor here would a reference of the accusation concerning idolatrous abominations to an earlier time than that of the last kings, namely, to that of Manasseh and Amon, be justified (against Berth.). From the circumstance that in the prophetic discourses of Jeremiah such complaints of idolatry are less vehement under Zedekiah, no inference can be drawn against this view. The phrase: "chiefs of the priests," denotes here, as in Ezra x. 5, the presidents of the twenty-four classes, together with the high priests, and therefore the same whom Ezekiel has in view in the twenty-five men in the temple; comp. Hitzig, *Gesch.* p. 238.—Ver. 15. *Sent to them by his messengers, rising early and sending,* constantly and earnestly; הַשְׁכֵּם וְשָׁלוֹחַ, as in Jer. xxvi. 5, xxix. 19, xxxv. 14 f.—*Because He had compassion on His people,* exercised forbearance toward them, did not wish to deliver them over instantly to condign punishment.—Ver. 16. *And they mocked,* literally, "were mocking." מַלְעִיבִים (also occurring in Syriac in the sense of *subsannantes*) is ἅπ. λεγ., of like import with מַלְעִגִים, xxx. 10. Also the following מִתַּעְתְּעִים (*Hithp.* of תעע), "ape, befool," occurs only here; the equivalent *pilel,* see in Gen. xxvii. 12. On the contents of the present accusation, comp. especially Ezek. xxxiii 22. If, then, at first only Ezekiel, the prophet of the exiles, is named as mocked by the people, yet it cannot be doubted that mocking and reproach were often cast upon the other prophets, especially Jeremiah, whose bold exhortations to repentance had to encounter so much opposition on the part of the ungodly population under the last kings before the exile. There is, therefore, in the plural "messengers of God" and "prophets" no exaggeration, though there may be some rhetorical generalization in the expression.—*Till there was no healing,* till the threatening judgment could no longer be averted. Comp. on the phrase, xxi. 18, xxx. 20; Prov. vi. 15.—Ver. 17. *And slew their young men with the sword.* To וַיַּהֲרֹג, "slew," or "caused to slay," also is God the subject, as to

the foregoing and following verbs. To bring in Nebuchadnezzar here as the subject is to import an unnecessary harshness of construction (against Keil, Neteler). The temple, where the young men were slain, is designated the "house of the sanctuary," because they had profaned it by their idolatry; comp. ver. 14*b*. The Sept. (τοῦ ἁγιάσματος αὐτοῦ) unnecessarily changes בֵּית מִקְדָּשָׁם into בּ' מִקְדָּשׁוֹ (vii. 20).—*The whole He gave into his hand;* comp. Jer. xxvii. 6, xxxii. 3, 4. The neutral הַכֹּל, notwithstanding that persons only are previously named, is used, in view of the vessels and treasures about to be mentioned in the following verse; yet it may be rendered "them all."—Ver. 19. *And they burned;* comp. Jer. xxxix. 8; 2 Kings xxv. 9.—*And destroyed all its goodly vessels* (comp. Isa. lxiv. 10, also ver. 10), literally, "to destroy"; comp. לְהַשְׁחִית in xii. 12.—Ver. 20. *And he carried away those that remained from the sword,* literally, "the remnant from the sword." The following words: "and they became servants to him and his sons," coincide with the prophecy, Jer. xxvii. 7.—Ver. 21. *To fulfil;* לְמַלֹּאת, as in 1 Chron. xxix. 5; Dan. ix. 2. The oracle here quoted stands in Jer. xxv. 11 f. (comp. Jer. xxix. 10), where, however, only the seventy years' duration of the Babylonish bondage is predicted; but nothing is said of a representation of these seventy years as an expiation or requital for the neglect of the sabbath years. This symbolizing of the seventy years' duration of the exile predicted by Jeremiah, contained in the words: "until the land enjoyed her sabbaths," is taken from the passage Lev. xxvi. 35, where such an expiation of neglected sabbath-year solemnities by an equally long time of desolation was announced to the people; and the added remark: "all the days of the desolation she rested" (kept a sabbath), is taken word for word from this passage of Leviticus. That there were exactly seventy neglected sabbath-years, and therefore a period of 490 years on account of which the seventy years of exile (with the beginning of the Persian monarchy as *terminus ad quem*, see ver. 20) were decreed, our author scarcely assumes. The *terminus a quo* of his reckoning of the neglected sabbath-years need not be sought exactly 490 years before the beginning of the exile (606 or 605), in the time of the last judges, Eli and Samuel; and we can scarcely suppose the whole period of the kingdom down to the exile to have been marked by the neglect of the sabbath-years, since under such theocratic sovereigns as David, Solomon, and Hezekiah, the observation of the precept in question was scarcely omitted. The whole statement is only approximate (like that in xxxv. 18 regarding the passover of Josiah, and its relation to the preceding one); it is in no way fitted to be the basis of any calculations, whether of the number of sabbath-years neglected till the exile, or of the point from which these acts of neglect date.

10. Close; The Return from the Captivity under Cyrus: vers. 22, 23. Comp. Ezra i. 1–3 (also 3 Esdras ii. 1–5); and on the coincidence of the beginning of Ezra with the close of Chronicles, Introd. §§ 2 and 3.—*And in the first year of Cyrus,* in the first year of his sovereignty over the former Babylonian-Assyrian monarchy, immediately after the taking of Babylon. For the name Cyrus (כּוֹרֶשׁ, Pers. *Quurus*), see the expositions on Ezra i. 1 and Isa. xliv. 28.—*That the word of the Lord . . . might be fulfilled;* לִכְלוֹת (from כלה, *perfici*, xxix. 34) thus = לְמַלְּאוֹת of the verse before, as the same prediction of Jeremiah is spoken of there as here.—*And he made proclamation,* literally, "let go a cry"; comp. xxx. 5.—Ver. 23. *All the kingdoms of the earth hath the Lord God of heaven given me.* In the same way as Necho, xxxv. 21, Cyrus knows and confesses himself the instrument or the "anointed" (Isa. xlv. 1) of the most high, living, and only true God, but designates Him not by the common name "God," like the former, but at once as Jehovah, the name of the God of the Jews, whose existence and identity with his own supreme god he at once acknowledges, and therefore as the "God of heaven," by the title which his supreme god, Ahuramazda, was wont to receive at the heads of all the royal edicts of the Persian sovereign. Comp. Evangelical and Ethical Reflections, No. 3.—*Whoso is among you all of his people, the Lord his God* (be) *with him.* That here probably יְהִי is to be read instead of יְהוָֹה, see in Crit. Note. On the abrupt termination of the narrative after these words of the royal edict, see Introd. as quoted above.

EVANGELICAL AND ETHICAL REFLECTIONS AND HOMILETIC HINTS ON CH. XXXIV.–XXXVI.

1. The last mighty outburst of the theocratic spirit under Josiah, which brought in at the same time the last flourishing epoch of the Jewish kingdom and people, is depicted by our author with comparative fulness in one respect, namely, as regards the great passover after the purging of the temple, which accords with his Levitical leanings, with much greater fulness than by the author of the books of Kings. If he not only celebrates the theocratic purity, exactitude, and legitimacy of this festival, as one the like of which had not been held during the whole period of the kings (from the days of Samuel the prophet, xxxv. 18), but praises the pious deeds of Josiah as it is written in the law of the Lord, xxxv. 26, designates the single case in which he renounced his character as a prince of peace, walking strictly according to law, as a disguising of himself, as being untrue to himself (xxxv. 22), and in the very opening of his description gives him a commendation which was given to no other king, namely, that he walked in the ways of David his father, and declined not to the right hand nor to the left (xxxiv. 2), nothing of all this appears to be exaggerated; on the contrary, the whole extremely favourable picture of the prince is correctly conceived and faithfully rendered from the standpoint of our author. In the second book of Kings, while no specially Levitical leaning affects the pragmatism of the narrator, the praise of his walking in the footsteps of David, without declining to the right or left, is set forth with equal prominence; and a special aspect of his theocratic disposition and demeanour, his zeal in the extirpation of idolatry, is there described still more minutely and commended with more fulness (2 Kings xxiii. 4–20) than in the account before us, which compresses that which

is here referred to, as already sufficiently known, into a brief sketch of a few verses. But as there, so here, it is manifest, amid the glory of his theocratic success, that his strenuous efforts were unsatisfactory, and insufficient to effect a permanent recovery, a true regeneration of the people of God. That, notwithstanding the sincerity of his conversion, "the Lord turned not from the great hotness of His anger which was kindled against Judah because of the provocations of Manasseh," but rather the divine sentence of extirpation against the kingdom of Judah remained unrevoked (2 Kings xxiii. 26 f.),—this our author certainly does not say in the express words of the older parallel text; indeed he appears, according to xxxiv. 33, to add to the testimony for the sincerity of the king's conversion the assurance of the reality of the conversion of the people, when he writes: "All his days they departed not from the Lord God of their fathers." But even this "all his days" contains a fatal limitation of the praise here bestowed on the endeavours of Josiah; and the lamentable state of idolatrous degeneracy which betrayed itself immediately under his sons (xxxvi. 5 ff.), and which was the fault no less of the maladministration of these last kings than of the apostasy of the chiefs of the priests and the people (xxxvi. 14), sufficiently shows that the adherence of Judah to the law of the Lord during the period from the reform of Josiah to his death was by no means sincere or truly genuine, but rather the complaints uttered in the last days of the kingdom by Jeremiah, of the unfaithfulness, the inner apostasy, and immorality, uncleanness, corruption indeed, of the people (Jer. xi., xiii., xxv., etc.), were fully justified. The insufficiency of mere reforms of the theocratic worship, healing only the surface, not the deep seat of the wound, and accordingly, as all that could serve the king as the standard for his reforming action lay in the ordinances of worship, the inadequacy of the law to the production of true life, that ἀδύνατον τοῦ νόμου (Rom. viii. 3), that impotence of the law to secure true freedom, true righteousness, and assured hope of the heavenly inheritance (Gal. iii. 4; Rom. vii.),—all this came out with astonishing clearness in the history of the reform of Josiah, which was pursued with so much zeal and sudden success, and yet yielded so transient a result. The king hears the words of the law discovered in the temple; the curses which it pronounces on the infidelity of the apostates pierce through his heart; he rends his garments, weeps, and bows down in deep, sincere sorrow before God. He succeeds also in inspiring the rulers of the people, if not with the same spirit of sincere repentance, yet with the fiery zeal that turns to the monuments and instruments of idolatry, and repeats the deeds of an Elijah. And what does he effect by all this? The stern message of Huldah announces this to him: for himself, and for the duration of his reign, he shall enjoy the blessings of walking with God; in peace he shall be gathered to his fathers' sepulchres; his eyes shall not see all the misfortune which the Lord is determined to bring upon his kingdom and city; for His wrath is now once for all poured out on this place, and nothing is now able to quench it (xxxiv. 23-28). It is impossible more thoroughly and powerfully to exemplify and exhibit what is the curse which the law works (Gal. iii. 13) than by these words of Huldah, of which it can scarcely be said whether they are more an exhortation to repentance or a promise of mercy (comp. the in many ways similar address of Azariah ben Oded to King Asa, xv. 1-7). And not even the salvation and blessing which they promise the king on account of his personal piety —that he shall depart in peace to his fathers—is fulfilled in a perfectly satisfactory way. Josiah departs before he has seen all the misfortune that the Lord has threatened to send, but as a brand plucked from the fire! Not in a painless way is he brought home to his fathers, but through conflict, war, and bloodshed, as he himself had willed. The only infidelity of which he made himself guilty in an otherwise irreproachable walk is avenged by a certainly only temporal (slaying only the body, not the soul), but yet terribly sharp and severe punishment; and even thereby is the series of judgments which bring on the end of the Jewish state and kingdom immediately introduced.

2. Josiah's defeat and tragic decease is the beginning of the end. As a fair but rapidly-overspreading evening glow after a dull, rainy day indicates the approaching nightfall, so his reform of worship, as the last powerful movement of the theocratic spirit, almost immediately precedes the sinking of the people of God into the murky night of political annihilation and protracted subjugation. It goes rapidly down, after its better administration of the people and the kingdom had once risen to a certain height; and, like that better emperor of the house of Palæologus shortly before the fall of the Byzantine Empire, or like the reign of Louis XVI. as the forerunner of the terror of the French Revolution, had delayed for a short time the execution of the sentence of extirpation, already ripened into an inevitable decree under the last preceding kings. The Chronist indicates this rapid riding of the dead that came on after the decease of Josiah, this entrance of the galloping consumption into the long since internally rotten and putrid state of Judah, by the extreme brevity with which he despatches the last four reigns. In a way more summary still than the author of the books of Kings, who likewise does not dwell very long on them, he depicts the ungodly practice of the first three successors of Josiah, to none of whom he devotes more than four verses, and for none of whom he has any word of praise or acknowledgment—not even for Jehoahaz, with respect to whom he does not indeed employ the formula used of the following two, in harmony with 2 Kings, "and he did that which was evil before the Lord" (comp., on the contrary, 2 Kings xxiii. 32), but simply on account of his epitomizing habit, as he hastens to the end, not because he cherished any better opinion of him. On Zedekiah he dwells somewhat longer; but not to report more fully the public acts of this unfortunate last of the Davidic kings, nor to depict the terrible catastrophe of wasting and destruction forming the close of his reign with the same fulness as in 2 Kings xxv. or Jer. lii., but only to exhibit the ungodliness and perversity, carried out to the end, of the course of both king and people, in a pragmatic, reflective way, as the cause of the inevitable judgment (see vers. 13-16), and to display the contrast between this course and the incessant but always ineffectual cries of admonition and warning coming from the prophet Jeremiah (vers. 12, 21). His report of

the fall of Jerusalem and the beginning of the Babylonish captivity (vers. 17–20) is, compared with the fuller accounts of the parallels, in fact, as compendious as possible, but by its very conciseness and brevity produces only the deeper and more powerful impression.

3. The conclusion of his historical account, xxxvi. 22, 23, is also characteristic for the standpoint and method of our author. While the author of the books of Kings (2 Kings xxv. 27–30) closes with a notice of the release of the captive king Jehoiachin in the middle of the exile, by the grace of the Babylonian king Evilmerodach, and thus, in correspondence with his paramount interest in the personal fate of the king, reports a mere prelude of the final release of Judah from the exile, and not the very release itself, our work closes with a notice, though brief, of the cessation of servitude in a foreign land by the gracious edict of Cyrus. In this characteristic trait is exhibited the historian who bears on his priestly heart the fortune of the whole people, not merely of the royal house. As he had set forth immediately before the divinely decreed and prophetically attested necessity of a servitude of seventy years, to compensate for the past neglect of seventy sabbath-years, so he cannot but point, at the close of his work, to the final fulfilment of this prediction. The internal organic connection of this closing notice, by which the fair perspective opens into a new and more fruitful beginning of the history of the covenant people after the exile, with that which was recorded immediately before concerning the last kings before the exile and their downfall, is as clear as day, and precludes any such opinion as that the contents of vers. 22, 23 stood originally only at the beginning of Ezra, and was afterwards added at the close of our work by a later hand (comp. Introd. § 3, p. 7). But these closing verses betray their originality and integral connection with the whole preceding work not only by the manifest reference to predictions of Jeremiah and Moses quoted in ver. 21, but also by this, that they add to that earlier testimony from the mouth of Necho to the fate of Israel-Judah as divinely decreed and carried on (xxxv. 21) by the counsels of the supreme living God, the God of heaven (xxxvi. 22), a second such testimony on the part of a holder of the heathen world-power; as if it were intended to prove to superfluity that God's judicially strict but also gracious rule over His deeply guilty and corrupt people might be known in its reality, and according to its salutary effect on the people, even on the part of the heathen executors of His judgments. Necho and Cyrus appearing as witnesses of the divine truth, as involuntary and more or less unconscious heathen prophetic announcers of the severity and the goodness of God in reference to the destiny of His people, as prophetic dispensers of blessing to Israel,—as Balaam formerly,—the one as a foe, but the other as a friend and protector, yea, as the type of its future Messiah (comp. Isa. xlv. 1);—in this light the close of our history presents the relations of the heathen world-powers to the people of God when entering the period of its development after the exile. His representation in this respect corresponds with the mode of thought of the prophets before the exile, especially Jeremiah, to whom the world-power external to Israel had ceased to appear as something absolutely opposed to God, so that they frequently warn their people against foolish opposition to it, and inculcate willing submission to its authority (comp. *Bibelw.* xv. p. x. ff., and especially E. Vilmar, "Der Prophet Jeremia," in the monthly journal *Bew. des Glaubens*, Bd. v. 1869, p. 19 ff.); and on the other hand, with the view of the world taken by the prophetic men of God of and after the exile, as Daniel, Zechariah, etc., in accordance with which the dependence of the destiny of Israel on such of the world-powers as were occasional executors of the judicial and beneficent providence of God is presupposed as a thing understood of itself, a certain mission-call of Israel in reference to the heathen nations around is preached, and the continuance of this state to the entrance of the Messianic era is announced (comp. *Bibelw.* Bd. xvii. pp. 3 f., 37 f., 41; also Hengstenb. *Gesch. des Reiches Gottes*, ii. 2, p. 277 ff.). It is of no small consequence that the Old Testament Chronicles, the most comprehensive historical work of sacred literature, closes with such universalistic views of Israel's call of salvation to all nations, and of the future union of all in faith in Jehovah as the one and only true God. Its end thus turns to its beginning. Setting out from the first Adam, the author concludes his work with the consoling expectation of the future and not far distant, but rather, in the reconstruction of the theocracy promoted by the edict of Cyrus, already guaranteed and necessarily involved restitution of the blessed kingdom of the second Adam, the Redeemer of the world.

THE END.